PERSONALITY
An Introduction to Theory and Research

THE DORSEY SERIES IN PSYCHOLOGY

EDITOR HOWARD F. HUNT *Columbia University*

BARNETTE (ed.) *Readings in Psychological Tests and Measurements* rev. ed.

BENNIS, SCHEIN, STEELE, & BERLEW (eds.) *Interpersonal Dynamics: Essays and Readings on Human Interaction* rev. ed.

COURTS *Psychological Statistics: An Introduction*

DENNY & RATNER *Comparative Psychology: Research in Animal Behavior* rev. ed.

DESLAURIERS & CARLSON *Your Child Is Asleep: Early Infantile Autism*

DEUTSCH & DEUTSCH *Physiological Psychology*

FISKE & MADDI *Functions of Varied Experience*

FITZGERALD & MCKINNEY *Developmental Psychology: Studies in Human Development*

FLEISHMAN (ed.) *Studies in Personnel and Industrial Psychology* rev. ed.

FREEDMAN (ed.) *The Neuropsychology of Spatially Oriented Behavior*

HAMMER & KAPLAN *The Practice of Psychotherapy with Children*

HENDRY *Conditioned Reinforcement*

KLEINMUNTZ *Personality Measurement: An Introduction*

KOLSTOE *Introduction to Statistics for the Behavioral Sciences*

LIEBERT & SPIEGLER *Personality: An Introduction to Theory and Research*

MADDI *Personality Theories: A Comparative Analysis*

MARKEL *Psycholinguistics: An Introduction to the Study of Speech and Personality*

ROZEBOOM *Foundations of the Theory of Prediction*

VON FIEANDT *The World of Perception*

PERSONALITY

An Introduction to Theory and Research

ROBERT M. LIEBERT
Senior Investigator, Fels Research Institute
and
Associate Professor, Antioch College

MICHAEL D. SPIEGLER
Assistant Professor, University of Texas

1970
THE DORSEY PRESS, Homewood, Illinois
Irwin-Dorsey Limited, Georgetown, Ontario

First Printing, May, 1970

Library of Congress Catalog Card No. 76–118190

PRINTED IN THE UNITED STATES OF AMERICA

To Diane and Shelly

Preface

Like most ventures of its type, this volume grew out of the authors' classroom teaching. When we began, we had taught undergraduate courses in personality and had developed goals for ourselves and our students. Since these goals directly guided our efforts as textbook writers, it is fitting to make them public. We believe that an introductory course in personality should have four purposes: (*a*) to introduce the undergraduate psychology major to important theoretical and research issues in the field, (*b*) to provide the student who will *not* take further psychology courses with interesting and accurate information about the application of psychology to important human concerns, (*c*) to present selected examples of research which typify both good scientific methodology and the investigation of meaningful problems, and (*d*) to prepare and interest the student in more advanced courses in personality and psychopathology. All that follows was directed by these aspirations.

In another vein, the foremost guideline for this book has been our belief that rigorous science, sophisticated theory, and clarity of presentation need not be antagonistic goals for the scientist or the teacher. It is, of course, all too easy to find florid jargon and abstruse formulations in the literature of psychology, but it is our opinion that such writing arises more often from muddled thinking than from truly incisive theory and research. Thus we have tried to present our subject matter in clear and understandable language, without doing injustice to the material or its readers. Although the book is written with undergraduates in mind, we hope that the interested housewife will find it readable and that graduate students may use it for review.

As the title and format of this book suggest, we believe that the psychology of personality is best viewed as a true marriage of theory and research and that an occasional weekend flirtation is not sufficient. We have therefore tried to illustrate the permanence and inevitability of the union by showing that, for any psychological account of the nature of man, there exists a mutually dependent relationship between theory construction and data collection. Similarly, we have attempted to stress the relatively enduring principles and strategies employed by personality theorists and researchers, and to do so through both "classical" and contemporary examples.

Personality courses are among the most popular offerings of a psychology department, but they are often disappointing to the student who wants information which bears on his own life. To serve this need (which we feel *is* a legitimate one), we have tried to illustrate concepts and principles through examples which might "hit home" to the contemporary college student. We have also introduced a feature which may capitalize on, and perhaps help to stimulate, the college student's intellectual skepticism. Periodically, the reader is invited to perform small, easily implemented demonstrations or experiments, so that he may personally examine the validity of various propositions discussed in the text. These "personalized demonstrations," all of which have met with success in our own personality classes, are designed to illustrate both theory and research methodology.

In preparing this volume we received invaluable help from many colleagues and students, not all of whom can be named here. Special thanks are due to Eileen Kelly, Larry W. Morris, Hans H. Strupp, and Sallie Webber for reading and criticizing various chapters; to George Williams for helping to draft part of one of the chapters; to the students in Psychology 211 at Vanderbilt University during the summer of 1968, who endured the inconvenience and frustration of using an evolving, dittoed textbook and gave us valuable feedback on the first written form of the manuscript; to Lyndia Crotteau and Carol Lyons, both for their untiring secretarial skills and for abiding the pressures to which we subjected them; to Carol Ann and Luis Fernandez for organizing our reference material; to Sharon Swenson for completely shouldering the job of securing permission to quote materials and reproduce illustrations and data; and to Betty Scott, whose expertise and patience helped beyond measure to see the book through its final stages. The facilities and cooperation available at Vanderbilt University (where the book was drafted) and Fels Research Institute were unstinting, greatly facilitating the manuscript's production.

Our greatest debt, however, is to our wives for their personal support through the many moments when we hassled with the manuscript and with each other, and for their understanding when our work left little time for them. That we have dedicated this book to them acknowledges our debt, but cannot pay it.

Yellow Springs, Ohio
Palo Alto, California
April, 1970

ROBERT M. LIEBERT
MICHAEL D. SPIEGLER

Contents

chapter 1 **STRATEGIES FOR THE STUDY OF PERSONALITY** 1

Scope of the Study of Personality, 2
Defining Personality, 3
The Role of Theory, 6
The Strategic Importance of Research, 9
Demonstration 1–1: An Illustration of Erroneous Impressions, 9
References, 11

chapter 2 **METHODS OF PERSONALITY RESEARCH** . . 13

The Experimental Method, 13
The Correlational Method, 19
The Case Study Method, 27
References, 33

chapter 3 **THE INTRAPSYCHIC APPROACH: PSYCHOANALYTIC PERSONALITY THEORY** . . . 35

Subjective Phenomena and Their Assessment, 36
Major Characteristics of Psychoanalytic Theory, 39
Instincts and Libido, 41
Psychosexual Development, 42
The Structure of Personality, 51
Anxiety, 57
Conflict and the Mechanisms of Defense, 58
Humor and the Unconscious, 63
References, 66

chapter 4 **THE INTRAPSYCHIC APPROACH: APPLICATION OF PRINCIPLES** 68

Symbolism and Dreams, 68
Recent Dream Research, 72

Psychoanalytic Psychotherapy, 79
"An Analysis of a Phobia in a Five-Year Old Boy," 83
Projective Techniques, 87
References, 93

chapter 5 TRAIT AND TYPE APPROACHES: THEORETICAL ALTERNATIVES 95

Historical Antecedents, 95
Traits and Types: The Problem of Definition, 97
Constitutional Theories, 98
The Genetic Approach to Personality, 110
Allport's Trait Theory, 114
References, 125

chapter 6 TRAIT AND TYPE APPROACHES: FACTOR ANALYSIS AND METHODS OF ASSESSMENT 126

Multivariate Research and Factor Analysis, 126
Self-Report Personality Inventories, 141
References, 162

chapter 7 COGNITIVE APPROACHES TO PERSONALITY 165

Kelly's Psychology of Personal Constructs, 166
Demonstration 7–1: The Role Construct Repertory Test, 182
Festinger's Theory of Cognitive Dissonance, 194
References, 211

chapter 8 MOTIVATIONAL THEORIES: NEEDS. . . . 214

Murray's Personology, 214
The Achievement Motive, 231
References, 242

chapter 9 MOTIVATIONAL THEORIES: SELF-ACTUALIZATION 243

The Basic Underpinnings of Roger's Theory, 243
Demonstration 9–1: The Q-Sort, 248
Client-Centered Psychotherapy, 261
Demonstration 9–2: Perceiving from Another's Internal Frame of Reference, 265
The Fully Functioning Person: Self-Actualization, 268
References, 273

chapter 10 LEARNING APPROACHES TO PERSONALITY: CLASSICAL CONDITIONING AND DRIVE REDUCTION 274

Historical Antecedents: Pavlov and Watson, 274
Classical Conditioning and Complex Behavior, 282
The Concept of Drive Reduction, 294
References, 306

chapter 11 LEARNING APPROACHES TO PERSONALITY: OPERANT CONDITIONING 309

Thorndike's Law of Effect, 309
Skinner's Operant Conditioning Approach, 310
Demonstration 11–1: The Observation and Recording of Operant Behavior, 316
Demonstration 11–2: Operant Conditioning of Human Behavior, 335
Recent Applications of Operant Conditioning, 341
References, 352

chapter 12 LEARNING APPROACHES TO PERSONALITY: OBSERVATIONAL LEARNING 355

Observational Learning: The Problem of Definition, 356
Miller and Dollard's Theory of Imitation, 357
The Acquisition-Performance Distinction of Bandura and Walters, 363
The Pervasive Role of Imitation, 369
Applied Uses of Modeling, 391
Postscript, 404
References, 405

AUTHOR INDEX 411

SUBJECT INDEX 417

chapter 1

Strategies for the Study of Personality

This book offers a general introduction to the study of personality and deals with the issues involved in developing a theory of human behavior. So many personality theories have been advanced by psychologists, philosophers, theologians, and social commentators of other disciplines that it would be impossible to discuss all of these positions in detail. Moreover, even if complete coverage were possible, a mere catalog of viewpoints would probably not be the best way to introduce the scientific study of human behavior. Therefore, instead of detailing an exhaustive list of theories, we shall stress the major *strategies* which psychologists have followed in developing conceptualizations of human behavior. For each strategy we shall describe several representative theories and detail the manner in which the strategy has guided empirical research. In our examination we will attempt to give a general picture of the diversity of available positions, the points they emphasize, the nature of the evidence they consider, and the assumptions they make. In this way we hope to illustrate both the rational and the empirical bases which underlie major theoretical positions and, at the same time, summarize existing knowledge about the causes of human behavior.

To proceed systematically, the study of personality, like all scientific endeavors, requires a strategy. Moreover, all of the approaches to personality that we shall discuss can be examined in terms of their explicit or implicit strategies, and to understand and evaluate them, we must be familiar with their strategic components. Thus, we shall first consider the elements involved in a strategy for studying personality.

Strategy, as we shall use it here, refers to a plan for directing and evaluating a large-scale exploration. A strategy for the study of personality thus includes: (1) a statement of one's domain of interest, (2) a statement of one's initial *assumptions* (i.e., those points which will be taken for granted or presumed to be true), (3) a delineation of the special terms or constructs which will be employed, and definitions of these, (4) an indication of the type of evidence which will be considered, (5) formulation of *hypotheses* (testable relationships between variables of interest), (6) rules for evaluating hypotheses, and (7) procedures for integrating accumulated information into a formal statement or *theory*. A strategy, then, might be said to be a plan for integrating theory and research and includes both.

SCOPE OF THE STUDY OF PERSONALITY

Interest in understanding ourselves and our fellow men has compelling justification. To begin with, it is natural for us to be curious about our own behavior, what determines our personalities, and "how we got that way." Furthermore, our daily lives are filled with concerns that relate to the assessment and prediction of personality. Virtually all social interaction requires that we evaluate, and try to predict the behavior of, other persons with whom we must deal. For example, on the basis of a relatively short interaction, college students must attempt to determine whether a newly made acquaintance will make a suitable date, whether rushees will fit into a fraternity or sorority, or whether a given professor will be sympathetic to handing in a paper late because a neighbor's dog made a meal of the first draft.

A number of distinctions have been erected by psychologists who are concerned with human behavior. Interest in interpersonal relations, attitude change, and the influence of major social forces has typically fallen in the domain of *social psychology*. *Developmental* or *genetic psychology* places emphasis on the historical antecedents of a person's behavior and is concerned with maturational and social influences as human beings advance from infancy through childhood and adolescence to adulthood and old age. When someone's behavior is markedly different from the usual norms of his society, and especially when these differences may jeopardize himself or others, then the phenomena are of particular interest to workers in the field of *abnormal psychology*, including the theoretical and experimental work of *psychopathology* and the applied work of *clinical psychology*. Applied fields such as *human engineering*, *industrial psychology*, *personnel psychology*, *educational psychology*, and *school psychology* are concerned with specific human enterprises. Additionally, *experimental psychology* may involve the study of single aspects of the organism, such as physiology, sensation and perception, learning, motivation, and emotion.

Because of these distinctions, the term *personality psychology* has typically been reserved for the study of "normal" behavior in all its aspects, particularly when the single individual rather than a larger social unit is the primary object of interest. In this book, however, we shall freely cross these traditional boundaries in order to present the largest possible framework for the understanding of human behavior. It should be noted that we are not breaking precedent in this regard, for such widely known theorists as Sigmund Freud, Carl Rogers, and B. F. Skinner have all regularly crossed these same boundaries in an effort to develop an adequate picture of man and his behavior.

DEFINING PERSONALITY

Thus far we have spoken of *personality* without specifically defining the term. This is because there are numerous extant definitions, and one's theoretical orientation or "model of man" has implications for a definition. For example, a deterministic, biologically oriented model of man necessarily leads to a definition that stresses heredity as an important determinant of personality. On the other hand, if one views man as an adaptive being whose behavior is primarily controlled by situational variables, the definition that emerges might stress such things as socialization, imitation, and learning.

It is not necessary for the beginning student of personality to start with *a* definition. In fact, a complete definition of personality is actually a statement of a theory of personality. That is, in order to fully understand what a particular theorist means by the term *personality,* it is necessary to examine his theory. For example, conspicuously missing from the small sample of definitions presented below is the name of Sigmund Freud. Since for Freud personality is synonymous with the *psyche* (mind), his theory of personality (see Chapter 3) is a theory of psychology in general. Freud theorized that personality was made up of the *id, ego,* and *superego,* three structures of the psyche, and that it is their interaction which determines behavior. Much of Freud's personality theory deals with these three structures and their interrelationship and, therefore, Freud's definition of personality *is* his theory of personality.

Many personality psychologists have, however, given concise, condensed definitions of personality, usually acknowledging that they are incomplete. The following are examples of such definitions (Sanford, 1963):

Allport: Personality is the dynamic organization within the individual of those psychophysical systems that determine his unique adjustments to his environment (pp. 494–95).

Newcomb: . . . personality . . . is known only as we observe individual behavior. (I am using the term "personality," by the way, in the inclusive sense of referring to the individual's organization of predispositions to behavior.) What I want to suggest is that the *kind* of behavior from which we can learn most about personality is role behavior. By observing John Doe in such capacities as husband, host, employee, and employer, we can discover those kinds of order and regularity in his behavior which are the goal of the student of personality (p. 496).

Eysenck: Personality is the more or less stable and enduring organization of a person's character, temperament, intellect and physique, which determines his unique adjustment to his environment (p. 496).

Bronfenbrenner: A conception of personality as a system of relatively enduring dispositions to experience, discriminate, or manipulate actual or perceived aspects of the individual's environment (including himself) (p. 497).

Sullivan: . . . the relatively enduring pattern of recurrent interpersonal situations which characterize a human life (p. 497).

Cattell: Personality is that which permits a prediction of what a person will do in a given situation. . . . Personality is . . . concerned with *all* the behavior of the individual, both overt and under the skin (p. 496).

Hilgard: . . . the sum total of individual characteristics and ways of behaving which in their organization or patterning describe an individual's unique adjustment to his environment (p. 497).

Even from this brief sample, the following kinds of strategic issues with respect to definition become apparent. First, we must decide, in defining personality and developing a theoretical description of it, whether our area of interest will be limited to "external effect" or whether we can talk about "internal structure." It is obvious that our direct knowledge of others is limited to what we can see of their behavior, and we can never directly know what is "inside" a person. We may say that Tom is happy in order to provide a summary label for his smiles, jovial conversation, or his invitation to take us all out for a beer, but we are speaking of his external behavior and not necessarily of any private, internal state that he is experiencing. Psychologists who subscribe to the *behavioristic* view (which holds that our primary concern should be with observable responses rather than presumed internal states [see Chapter 10]) argue that the scientific study of personality can be no more than an examination of observable responses. Other psychologists have argued that personality must refer to some internal structure. Tom, who *appears* happy, may in fact be miserable inside; a prim and proper girl may be seething with sexuality; and, in general, a man's behavior may not reflect his "real" personality. Although this orientation has a good deal of intuitive appeal, there are a number of logical problems associated with it. We shall return to them in Chapter 3.

Second, we must ask whether we can talk about personality in terms of enduring characteristics or *traits*. We are accustomed in our daily language to saying such things as "John is quiet" or "Sharon is irresponsible." We seem to be talking as if these were properties of the individual rather like the color of his eyes, which are always apparent and virtually unchangeable. Clearly, however, such statements are not likely to be true without exception. John may be very outspoken about his hobby, stamp collecting, and Sharon may be very careful in keeping the sorority's records despite the fact that she has not gotten a single class assignment in on time in the past three years. Thus, both a definition of personality and a theory of personality must account for the similarities as well as the inconsistencies in a given person's behavior across situations and across time. Some theories of personality have minimized the importance of situational differences in human behavior, while others have argued that these situational differences are not sources of spurious "error" but rather are the primary data for understanding the behavior of others.

Third, whereas all personality psychologists would agree that each individual's personality, however it is defined, is unique, there is controversy over the implications of this fact for the study of personality. If no individual is exactly like any other, does this imply that personality should be studied by making exhaustive investigations of single individuals with the goal of understanding their behavior completely? Such research would lead to laws about the behavior of a specific person. Supposedly, however, science deals with general laws, implying that personality should be studied by investigating specific aspects of personality in a wide variety of persons with the aim of formulating laws of behavior which hold for people in general. This controversy is between the *idiographic* and the *nomothetic* approaches (respectively), and we shall have occasion to discuss both points of view in this book.

Finally, in developing a perspective of personality we must decide whether it is proper to describe our goal as solely *prediction* and *control* of behavior or whether an additional goal, usually called *understanding*, is necessary for an adequate theory of personality. Whereas prediction and control are easily defined and specified, the meaning of "understanding" is elusive and ambiguous. By understanding we usually mean comprehension of the processes involved in a phenomenon, but the level of comprehension which is sufficient for a person to say "I understand" varies from individual to individual. Understanding is thus a highly subjective matter.

An additional problem arises from the fact that many theories of personality, including almost all of those that examine personality in terms of hypothesized inner structures, provide us with an extensive vocabulary of names for various needs and drives, mechanisms, levels, complexes, stages, character types, and so on. Consider the statement: "He behaves that way because he is an *introvert*." Such naming may seem to provide both explanation and understanding. However, some critics have argued that such "explanations" are easy to come by but virtually worthless. B. F. Skinner (1953), the prominent behaviorist, has noted:

When we say that a man eats *because* he is hungry, smokes a great deal *because* he has the tobacco habit, fights *because* of the instinct of pugnacity, behaves brilliantly *because* of his intelligence, or plays the piano well *because* of his musical ability, we seem to be referring to causes. But on analysis these phrases prove to be merely redundant descriptions (p. 31).

These and other issues concerning the definition and domain of personality will be considered throughout this book.

Before leaving the problem of the definition of our subject matter, several rather obvious but nevertheless important points should also be noted. First, the term *personality*, as we shall use it in this book, and as it is used by all personality psychologists, does not imply any *evaluation* of a person's character, social graces, or abilities. When the layman speaks of Larry as having a "great personality" he may be referring to his pleasant disposition, his generosity, or his concern for the welfare of others, but this evaluative use of the word is generally outside the realm of the scientific study of personality.

Second, although the terms *personality* and *behavior* are often used interchangeably, there is an essential difference. *Personality* is an abstraction or hypothesized construction derived from *behavior*, which is directly observable (Mischel, 1968). As we have mentioned previously, all we can ever "really" know about human personality is that which we observe directly. From these observations the psychologist typically develops various *hypothetical constructs* to describe and explain the lawfulness of human behavior. Although we may speak of personality and personality theories as if they actually existed, their only existence is in the minds of men. This is true not only of theories of personality and other theories in psychology but also of much theorizing in the so-called natural sciences such as physics, chemistry, and astronomy.

THE ROLE OF THEORY

It is often because of a lack of theory that problems go unresearched or unresolved. It is extremely difficult to investigate a phenomenon unless one has at least some tentative ideas about its nature, its relationship with other phenomena, and so on. Consider the undergraduate psychology student in an independent study course who was interested in the effect of popular music on teen-agers. He spent the entire semester trying to design a workable experiment to investigate the problem and never did succeed. Among other things, he failed to delimit his area of study and made no attempt at formulating hypotheses about the relationship of various aspects of popular music to other measurable events. In other words, he did not begin with a theory! While it is probably true that the student was justifiably reluctant to formulate a complete theory concerning the effects of popular music on teen-agers because he felt that he lacked sufficient training or knowledge to do so (a feeling that he shared with many scientists), he should have at least formulated a tentative plan for approaching the problem. The student would then have been able to perform some experiment to test his neophyte hypotheses.

What, more generally, is the role of theory? A theory in psychology, or any other science, must first organize and condense already existing facts and information, and in this capacity it plays mainly a descriptive role. A given phenomenon can be described in many ways. Condensation of any event will require assumptions, and the theory which makes the least number of assumptions, all other things being equal, is usually considered the "best" theory.[1]

A theory should not only describe past events but it should also predict future ones. Thus, a second purpose of theory is to provide a basis for prediction of events and outcomes that have not yet been investigated. This purpose clearly implies that a theory must be *testable* and capable of being refuted or *falsified.* Not only must the theory make specific predictions but it must also translate its assumptions and predictions into *empirical hypotheses* that can actually be tested. It has often been noted that theories fail to survive as much because they are untestable as because they are disconfirmed. Alternatively, theories that are poorly formulated or based on an inadequate strategy may be improperly tested and thus be "self-fulfilling." George A. Kelly (1955), whose Theory of Personal Constructs we shall discuss in a later chapter, illustrates the way in which an implicit theoretical construct about others may be "confirmed" in a rather redundant fashion:

> A man construes his neighbor's behavior as hostile. By that he means that his neighbor, given the proper opportunity, will do him harm. He tries out his construction of his neighbor's attitude by throwing rocks at his neighbor's dog. His neighbor responds with an angry rebuke. The man may then believe that he has validated his construction of his neighbor as a hostile person.
>
> The man's construction of his neighbor as a hostile person may appear to be "validated" by another kind of fallacy. The man reasons, "If my neighbor is hostile, he will be eager to know when I get into trouble, when I am ill, or when I am in any way vulnerable. I will watch to see if this isn't so." The next morning the man meets his neighbor and is greeted with the conventional, "How are you?" Sure enough, the neighbor is doing just what was predicted of a hostile person (pp. 12–13).

It is probably true that the layman usually has an *implicit* theory and definition of personality which he uses in everyday interpersonal relations. Individual implicit personality theories differ from the theories we shall discuss in this book in several important respects. First, the theories

---

[1] This assertion, which is itself an assumption, is often referred to as the "Law of Parsimony."

we shall examine in later chapters are formalized and set down in terms that can be communicated to others. It is not that we cannot formalize or communicate our own personal theories of human behavior to others; it is just that we generally do not do so. Second, formalized theories are based on observations of many different people. Although we may meet different individuals in our daily lives, we usually do not make an explicit effort to observe their behavior, its antecedents and consequences, and its generality. Furthermore, most personal theories are based more on the observation of ourselves than on observation of other persons. Finally, formalized personality theories, once formulated, are then tested repeatedly in research and often aspire to meet relatively rigorous standards of experimental methodology and control. Implicit personality theories are not subjected to such testing.

There is much philosophical debate concerning that nature of "proving" or "disproving" a theory, and in order to avoid getting into the fray of a yet raging conflict, we will simply make several conservative statements in this regard. First, *a theory*, like an hypothesis, *is never proved or disproved* by empirical evidence. The most that research can do is to find support for a theory, while the absence of such findings does not usually refute the theory.[2] Thus, with each new substantiating piece of evidence the psychologist gains more confidence in the theory. If after a number of experimental tests a theory failed to receive support, the psychologist would be forced to turn to a new theory or begin revisions on the existing one. In this case, for all practical purposes the theory would have been refuted. However, strictly speaking, it would not have been proven false.

In practice, it should be noted, supportive evidence or positive results seem to carry more weight with the scientist than do nonsupportive evidence or negative results. If one were to make a tally sheet of the positive and negative findings of research relevant to a particular theory, it would be necessary to have substantially more negative results than positive results (perhaps in a ratio of 50 or even 100 to 1) for a scientist to feel that his theory was no longer (or perhaps never was) useful. It is a fact of science that theories, once adopted, die slowly.

We have been speaking of the importance of research in testing a theory, but it should be kept in mind that whole theories are never tested by experimentation. Rather, an hypothesis, or set of hypotheses, relevant to a specific aspect of the theory is investigated. Because of this, the proponents of a theory must restrict their research conclusions to what has actually been shown by relevant experimentation. This is of enormous strategic importance, since it is often tempting, when a piece of

---

[2] A theory can be decisively disconfirmed if some empirical consequence that is *absolutely* necessary for the theory turns out not to occur. However, psychological theories are rarely this determinate and "tight."

research has been conducted within a particular theoretical perspective, to interpret the results as providing more general support for the theory than can actually be reasonably concluded from the data available.

For example, many personality psychologists have attempted to find the basic elements of personality structure by asking persons to rate close friends on a variety of descriptive scales. Using a statistical technique for summarizing data called *factor analysis* (see Chapter 6), investigators then looked for common elements or *factors* of description. It was regularly found that the same five factors emerged in many different studies. They were extroversion, agreeableness, conscientiousness, emotional stability, and culture (Mischel, 1968). This line of research was based on the general theory that persons do in fact possess a limited number of stable personality characteristics or traits.

Do these highly consistent results confirm the general theoretical position? A sophisticated analysis by Passini and Norman (1966) revealed that they may not. The previous studies all assumed that one person's description of another was determined primarily by the actual characteristics (personality) of the person being rated. Passini and Norman created a situation in which ratings of others could not be based on extensive knowledge of them because the raters were asked to describe complete strangers! Nonetheless, the same pattern of five factors emerged. Thus, while the *results* of the earlier studies were not challenged, the original *interpretation* was forced to give way to the simpler one that the structure found revealed the pervasive character of the *labels* we use to describe all persons rather than about the way people really are.

THE STRATEGIC IMPORTANCE OF RESEARCH

In the chapters that follow, we have sought to emphasize the research basis for each of the major theoretical positions. Occasionally the beginning student of personality feels that research is unnecessary to support the more "obvious" arguments of a theory or position. Often, however, the seemingly obvious does not hold up under careful examination. The following demonstration[3] can serve to illustrate the manner in which impressions may appear very powerful but, like cotton candy, often prove to have very little substance.

DEMONSTRATION 1–1: AN ILLUSTRATION OF ERRONEOUS IMPRESSIONS

Most of us have had the experience of reading horoscopes in the newspapers and may well have commented that it is difficult to imagine any-

[3] This book contains a number of demonstrations in which you can actually participate and which will allow you to illustrate for yourself both the principles and the problems associated with the study of personality.

one being "taken in" by these overly general descriptions and predictions. It is possible, however, that a more sophisticated version of the same kind of generalized descriptions can be extremely effective and even lead persons to believe that they have an entirely unique description of themselves. Using this experimental hypothesis, Ulrich, Stachnik, and Stainton (1963) asked the students in educational psychology classes to take two personality tests. A week later the students were given a written interpretation of their tests scores, which appeared to represent the careful efforts of the professor. As a second part of the study, other students were given instructions in administering the same two personality tests to a friend. For both phases of the study the people whose personalities were "being interpreted" were asked to rate the accuracy of the "interpretation" (on a scale ranging from excellent to very poor) and to make any additional comments about the "interpretation" which they felt were important.

Despite the individualized appearance of the personality description, all persons were given exactly the same "interpretation" (though the order of the statements varied) and, in fact, no actual interpretations were made of the tests. The description read:

> You have a strong need for other people to like you and for them to admire you. You have a tendency to be critical of yourself. You have a great deal of unused capacity which you have not turned to your advantage. While you have some personality weaknesses, you are generally able to compensate for them. Your sexual adjustment has presented some problems for you. Disciplined and controlled on the outside, you tend to be worrisome and insecure inside. At times you have serious doubts as to whether you have made the right decision or done the right thing. You prefer a certain amount of change and variety and become dissatisfied when hemmed in by restrictions and limitations. You pride yourself as being an independent thinker and do not accept others' opinions without satisfactory proof. You have found it unwise to be too frank in revealing yourself to others. At times you are extroverted, affable, sociable, while at other times you are introverted, weary, and reserved. Some of your aspirations tend to be pretty unrealistic (Ulrich *et al.,* 1963, p. 832).

When the students who had been administered the personality tests by the professor rated the "interpretations," virtually all rated them as good or excellent. In the second phase of the study, approximately 75 percent of the people who had been tested by the admittedly inexperienced students also rated the assessment of themselves as good or excellent. Furthermore, the comments that subjects made clearly indicated an acceptance of these interpretations as accurate and individualized descriptions of their own personalities. One student who had been given his tests and interpretation by the professor said: "On the nose! Very good. I wish you had said more, but what you did mention was all true without a doubt. I wish you could go further into this personality sometime." Another subject who had been given the tests and interpretation by a student commented: "I believe this interpretation fits me individually, as there are too many facets which fit me too well to be a generalization" (Ulrich *et al.,* 1963, p. 833).

The outcome of this experiment serves to illustrate the ease with which statements made under the aegis of psychology and personality testing can be very influential even when they have little real substance. In an unpublished study, the present authors have tried a similar experiment in their personality classes using as a personality test ink blots of the kind found on page 90. Even with such a loosely structured test, we find that the examinees show overwhelming acceptance of a statement such as the one quoted from Ulrich and his associates.

To replicate this experiment for yourself, tell a friend that you are learning how to use personality tests in class and have him make three different drawings for you. First ask your friend to draw a picture of himself, then another picture of himself but this time as he would like to look, and finally a picture of a member of the opposite sex. (The Draw-a-Person test is a projective test which uses this technique to assess personality; we shall have more to say about projective tests in a later chapter.) Then, in your own handwriting, copy the interpretation above and about a week later offer this assessment to your friend. After he has had an opportunity to read it, ask him to rate the interpretation (excellent, good, average, poor, or very poor) and give you some feedback as to how well you are doing as a "psychological examiner." After this part of your experiment is completed, it is important that you reveal to your friend the real nature of the experiment. Complete explanation of the experimental deception, often called "debriefing," may evoke further comments of interest and also remove any possibility that permanent misconceptions about psychological testing will result from participation.

The foregoing demonstration suggests the importance of doing research before making statements about personality. In the next chapter, we shall consider the three major methods of personality research.

REFERENCES

Kelly, G. A. *The psychology of personal constructs.* New York: Norton, 1955.

Mischel, W. *Personality and assessment.* New York: Wiley, 1968.

Passini, F. T., and Norman, W. T. A universal conception of personality structure? *Journal of Personality and Social Psychology,* 1966, 4, 44–49.

Sanford, N. Personality: Its place in psychology. In S. Koch (Ed.), *Psychology: A study of a science.* Study II, Vol. 5. *The process areas, the person, and some applied fields: Their place in psychology and science.* New York: McGraw-Hill, 1963. Pp. 488–592.

Skinner, B. F. *Science and human behavior.* New York: Macmillan, 1953.

Ulrich, R. E., Stachnik, T. J., and Stainton, N. R. Student acceptance of generalized personality interpretations. *Psychological Reports,* 1963, **13,** 831–34.*

---

* Quoted material reprinted with permission of authors and publisher.

chapter 2

Methods of Personality Research

In the previous chapter, we considered the nature of personality and the importance of integrating facts or *data* into a comprehensive theory. The present chapter introduces the methods which have been used to systematically gather information about personality and examines the strengths and weaknesses of each. While an understanding of method must precede our examination of formal theories, we have attempted to include numerous examples in our discussion so as to provide context and substance for the various methods as they are described and evaluated.

Three major research methods have been used to study personality—the *experimental, correlational,* and *case study* methods. These methods all have one essential element in common—they all involve *observation* of one sort or another. The differences lie in the manner in which the observations are made and in the way the data from the observations are analyzed. We shall briefly examine these research approaches so that the reader may be in a better position to critically examine the personality research described in the remainder of the text.

THE EXPERIMENTAL METHOD

The most valuable procedure used in personality research is the experimental method. To understand its components, we shall consider a recently reported study in which the investigators were interested in persons' feelings of responsibility during an emergency (Darley and

Latané, 1968). As with many research problems, this study was instigated by a provocative social event, which Darley and Latané describe in the following way:

> Several years ago, a young woman was stabbed to death in the middle of a street in a residential section of New York City. Although such murders are not entirely routine, the incident received little public attention until several weeks later when the New York *Times* disclosed another side of the case: at least 38 witnesses had observed the attack—and none had even attempted to intervene. Although the attacker took more than half an hour to kill Kitty Genevese, not one of the 38 people who watched from the safety of their own apartments came out to assist her. Not one even lifted the telephone to call the police (1968, p. 377).

The surprising lack of intervention by any of the observers in this case appears to be inconsistent with all of the humanitarian and cooperative norms which our society attempts to foster. The incident itself may provoke several alternative explanations or *hypotheses* to account for the fact that no assistance was rendered to the victim. For example, it is possible that, contrary to our common beliefs, persons are simply not willing to assist others whom they do not know, even in an obvious emergency. But this is a very general hypothesis, and the events described above did not happen in a vacuum. Perhaps, then, some identifiable characteristics of the situation mitigated persons' willingness to come to the aid of the victim. She might have been helped if "things had been different." Different in what way? At this point the investigators must formulate, in fairly precise terms, some specific characteristics of the situation which might have reduced the willingness of others to provide assistance and feel responsibility. The following were suggested:

> In certain circumstances the norms favoring intervention may be weakened. . . . One of these circumstances may be the presence of other onlookers. For example . . . each observer, by seeing lights and figures in other apartment house windows, knew that others were also watching. However, there was no way to tell how the other observers were reacting. These two facts provide several reasons why any individual may have delayed or failed to help. The responsibility for helping was diffused among the observers; there was also a diffusion of any potential blame for not taking action; and finally, it was possible that somebody, unperceived, had already initiated helping action (p. 377).

These possibilities may now be seen to converge upon a single, testable *experimental hypothesis,* namely that "the more bystanders to an emergency, the less likely, or the more slowly, any one bystander will intervene to provide aid" (p. 378). At this point the hypothesis is still untested. It is no more than an idea or possibility, but the idea is now well formulated as a general proposition and can be tested in a new, *controlled situation. Control* in psychological research has three different meanings: control over the behavior of the subject under study (what he is allowed to do), control of the behavior that is observed and recorded, and control over the influences of the environment or circumstances present in the situation.

The controlled situation must meet all of the logical demands of the proposition but exclude other factors which have not been hypothesized to be relevant. What are the demands in the present example? First, a situation must be created in which subjects can be made to perceive a true emergency as occurring in their presence. Second, it must be possible for each subject to be aware of the number of other "bystanders" present. Third, subjects must be unable to get information about the reactions or behavior of the other bystanders. Finally, precise measurement of the *variables of interest* (speed and frequency of reaction to the seeming "emergency") must be possible.

To meet these requirements, college students were told, in the Darley and Latané experiment, that they were going to participate in a discussion of personal problems dealing with college life. When a subject arrived for the experiment, he was taken to a small room, instructed to put on headphones with an attached microphone, and told to listen for instructions. By means of the headphones, the experimenter explained how the "discussion" was to be run. Subjects were told that the purpose of their being placed in individual rooms was to preserve anonymity (actually other persons were simulated by tape-recorded statements) and that, in order to foster more open discussion, the experimenter would not listen to the discussion while it was in progress. Finally, each person was to speak for two minutes, in turn, during which time only his microphone was turned on. Thus, only one person at a time could be heard.

The first person to speak, the "victim" to be, mentioned in the course of his comments that he was subject to seizures similar to epilepsy. After the subject spoke (always last), it was the victim's turn again. Following several brief, calm, and coherent comments, the victim began to stutter and his words became increasingly incoherent as he verbally feigned a seizure.

Each subject was placed in the situation just described, but the number of other people the subject believed were in the discussion varied. In one condition, subjects heard only the victim's voice (two-person group); in a second condition, subjects listened to one other voice besides the victim's (three-person group); subjects in a third condition heard four other voices in the discussion besides the victim's (six-person group). Thus, the *independent variable,* the condition or stimulus which the experimenter manipulated or had under his control, was the number of persons which subjects thought to be part of the discussion.

A *dependent variable* is that part of a subject's behavior which changes as the independent variable changes. The name "dependent variable" comes from the fact that it *depends* on, or is controlled by, the conditions set up or selected by the experimenter. In our example, the dependent variables were the *speed* and *frequency* of reaction to the "emergency." Speed of reporting the emergency was defined as the time elapsed from the beginning of the victim's seizure until the subject left his room to summon aid. The frequency of reaction was simply the proportion of subjects in each group who summoned aid within six minutes after the emergency began.

An *experimental hypothesis* involves a statement about the effect of manipulating the independent variable upon the dependent variable. Accordingly, it was hypothesized in the experiment that the more people who witness an emergency (the independent variable), the less likely and the more slowly (the dependent variables) will any one witness intercede in the victim's behalf. If the three groups of subjects differed (on the dependent variables) from each other in the predicted direction (i.e., the most aid coming from subjects in the two-person group and the least from the six-person group), the experimenters would then want to be in a position to say that the difference was due to the independent variable and only to the independent variable. If, for example, the two-person group had a higher percentage of "civic-minded" subjects than either of the other groups, the greater aid given by these persons might be due to a *difference in the characteristics of the sample* of subjects rather than to the number of people in the discussion group. Or, if the six-person group heard a less convincing seizure by the victim, this might account for their reluctance to help him. To eliminate or minimize the possibility of such alternate explanations being as viable as the experimental hypothesis, every effort was made to equate the groups with respect to characteristics of the subjects and the treatments they received.

Before an experiment begins, the experimenter attempts to assign subjects to groups or conditions in such a way that the people in each group do not differ on any *relevant* variables. To equate subjects on *all* variables is an impossible task, since in the last analysis each person is different from every other person. But in any given experiment, certain characteristics of the subjects are particularly important because they have a high probability of affecting the dependent variables. There are two common procedures that are used to equate groups of subjects. The first involves *matching* people on relevant variables. In the simple case of two groups, persons would be matched in equivalent pairs, and then one member of each pair would be assigned, at random, to each of the groups. If age and sex were likely to affect subjects' performance in an experiment (for example, a study involving physical strength and stamina), each pair of subjects would be made up of people of the same sex and age. The same procedure generalizes to studies which employ more than two groups.

Often it is difficult to identify relevant subject characteristics on which people can be matched or, because of a limited sample of subjects, matching is impossible. In either case, if people are *randomly* assigned to groups (i.e., each person has an equal chance of being assigned to each group), the differences among groups with respect to subject composition tend to be minimized. Such randomization is the most common procedure for assigning subjects to experimental groups, and, in fact, it has become standard practice among psychologists to assume that subjects were randomly placed in groups unless stated to the contrary.

Once the groups have been made as similar as possible, it is necessary for all subjects to receive exactly the same treatment except for the independent variable or variables. Thus, the only difference between the three groups in our example was the number of people perceived to be part of the discussion. To ensure the same treatment for all groups, standard procedures were employed. For example, by using tape-recorded simulation of other discussants, all subjects were exposed to identical voices.

The major results of Darley and Latané's experiment are shown in Table 2–1. From this table it can be seen that the experimental hypothesis was confirmed for both dependent variables. The two-person group had the highest percentage of subjects responding to the emergency and the fastest average reaction time, while the six-person group had the lowest percentage of subjects responding and the slowest average reaction time.

TABLE 2–1

Effects of Group Size on Likelihood and Speed of Response (after Darley and Latané, 1968)

Group Size	*Number of Subjects*	*Percent Responding by End of Seizure*	*Mean Time in Seconds*
2 (subject, and victim)	13	85	52
3 (subject, victim, and 1 other)	26	62	93
6 (subject, victim, and 4 others)	13	31	166

In considering these data, it is important to keep in mind that *on the average* people who were supposedly alone with the victim were more helpful than people who thought four other persons were also witnessing the victim's plight. When experimentation is done with groups of subjects, the average (that is, the *mean*) performances of the groups are compared. Thus, there may have been subjects in the two-person condition who took longer to respond to the emergency than some of the subjects in the six-person condition. But, when the average performances of the subjects in each treatment condition were examined, the two-person group was considerably more helpful than the six-person group.

Without going into great detail, a few comments should be made concerning statistical tests for differences.[1] In reporting the results of research, the phrase *significant difference* between treatment groups is often used. When employed in this context, the word *significant* does not refer to importance (i.e., social significance). A statistically significant difference is one that has a low probability of occurring by chance alone and thus reflects a difference which could be reliably expected in other samples, that is, a "real" difference. If all relevant variables other than the independent variables are controlled for (by holding them constant for all groups, for example), then the experimenter can conclude that the difference is a function of the independent variables which he has manipulated.

A variety of statistical tests are used to assess *statistical significance* at a given level of probability. Traditionally in psychological research, a difference is considered statistically significant and therefore admissible as evidence if the odds are 5 in 100 or less that the difference is not a chance finding. This level of significance is called the .05 level (commonly written "$p < .05$" and read "probability less than 5 percent"). Generally, the greater the likelihood that a difference is not due to chance alone, the more confidence an experimenter places in his results.[2]

For practical purposes, small differences are often meaningless. For example, it would be difficult to think of a group of persons who on the average summon aid a second faster than another group as being more concerned with helping in an emergency. Optimally, manipulating independent variables will lead to both statistically significant and practically meaningful differences among experimental conditions, as was the case in Darley and Latané's study. The difference between 52 and 166 seconds certainly could mean the difference between the victim's living or dying in a real emergency.

Laymen sometimes criticize psychological research because it frequently deals with questions more in terms of "science for science's sake" than of relevancy to man's daily living and his problems. The subject

---

[1] For more detailed discussion of statistical significance as well as other statistical concepts touched upon in this chapter, the reader should see Wallis and Roberts (1956) for a highly readable account and such introductory statistics texts as Edwards (1958), Hays (1963), McCall (1970), and Smith (1962).

[2] Some caution must be employed in taking this rule to its extremes, for when very large samples of subjects are employed (for example, several hundred or more), extremely small differences *can* be statistically significant. The question still remains whether such a difference is *important*.

matter may seem too abstract to be relevant to everyday human behavior. Or, the research problem may appear important to the man on the street, but the method of investigation may seem wholly artificial and therefore devoid of meaning for him. Darley and Latané's study of bystander intervention is certainly immune to the former criticism but not to the latter. Why does interest in the behavior of witnesses to crime and brutality lead to investigating the reactions of college students to the verbal anguish of another person heard over headphones? Can we generalize from this laboratory setting to the streets of our large urban centers? Would it not be better to observe bystander behavior in an actual incident like the one which prompted the experiment? It is true that something is lost when an investigation of human behavior moves into less authentic circumstances. In controlled laboratory experimentation, we actually gain less total information about the problem at hand, but we gain more reliable information about a specific aspect of the problem.

While experimental research can sometimes be used for exploratory purposes, initial research seeking a broad spectrum of information often involves the correlational method, to which we now turn our attention.

THE CORRELATIONAL METHOD

Correlation, as the name implies, deals with the co- or joint relationship between two or more variables. The method answers research questions put in the form of: "Do variable *X* and variable *Y* go together or vary together?" Questions of relationship are frequently asked in psychology. Is the type of mental illness related to one's socioeconomic status? Is there a relationship between late toilet training and compulsiveness in adulthood? Is the frequency of dating behavior related to marital success and happiness? The correlational method is characterized by the fact that all subjects are observed under identical conditions. Thus, rather than manipulating variables, the measurements (observations) are of already existing characteristics of the subjects.

It is easy to mistakenly label some research studies as experimental when they are actually correlational in nature. To illustrate this point, consider the following simple hypothetical example. A psychologist comes into a class and administers two tests to the students—one is a measure of creativity and the other is a measure of anxiety. For each subject he now has both a creativity and an anxiety score. Note that all subjects are treated exactly alike. Each is given the same two tests, in the same room, at the same time, and so on. Note also that the experimenter makes no attempt to influence creativity or anxiety; he is merely measuring these variables as they occur. In analyzing the data, which might look like that presented in Table 2–2a, the researcher deals with the pair

that how closely two variables are related depends only on the absolute size of the correlation coefficient. Thus, a correlation coefficient of +.60 and −.60 are equivalent with respect to the extent to which one variable can be anticipated from the other.

Because correlation coefficients range in absolute value between 0 and 1.00, it is tempting to view them as percentages (i.e., when multiplied by 100) and thereby assume that a correlation of .50 is twice as large as one of .25. This is an error. The appropriate rule of thumb is to compare *squared* correlation coefficients as an estimate of the percentage of variance that the two variables have in common. Thus, in a sense, a correlation of .71 is approximately twice as large as a correlation of .50—i.e., $(.71)^2 = .50$ and $(.50)^2 = .25$.

It is often convenient and enlightening to plot correlations graphically as a *scatter diagram.* Figure 2–1 presents several such scatter diagrams. The horizontal axis represents the values of one variable while the vertical axis represents the values of the other. Each point corresponds to the scores of one subject on the two variables. Notice that in the case of perfect positive or perfect negative correlation, all the points fall in a straight line. Thus, by knowing a person's score on one of the variables (it makes no difference which one), we can perfectly predict the score on the other variable. Where there is perfect correlation, either positive or negative, the plot shows no "scatter" (i.e., deviation from the perfect line of correlation). In the case of a moderately large correlation, there is some scatter about the line of perfect correlation, but the scores tend to fall within an ellipse. Finally, where there is virtually no correlation, there is much scatter of the scores, and the shape of the scatter tends to look like a circle.

Correlational research does not always employ the correlation coefficient. The method of correlation is a research method and not a statistical procedure. As long as each subject is treated in the same way and measurements are made of already existing characteristics of the subjects, we are dealing in correlational research. The correlation coefficient has been discussed in some detail because of its frequent use and because it illustrates the underlying principles of correlation.

Correlational research can be viewed as compromising the control provided by experimentation for an economical means of making a broad inspection of a problem. By substituting measurement of already existing characteristics of the subject for manipulation, the correlational strategy often permits much of the naturalness of the situation to remain. As we have seen, lack of control has its drawbacks, but among its strong points is that an absence of control may bring the investigation closer to "real life" than the controlled experiment can.

Behavior is almost always *multiply determined* (i.e., caused by a number of variables operating at the same time and in conjunction with

FIGURE 2–1

Scatter Diagrams Showing Various Degrees of Relationship

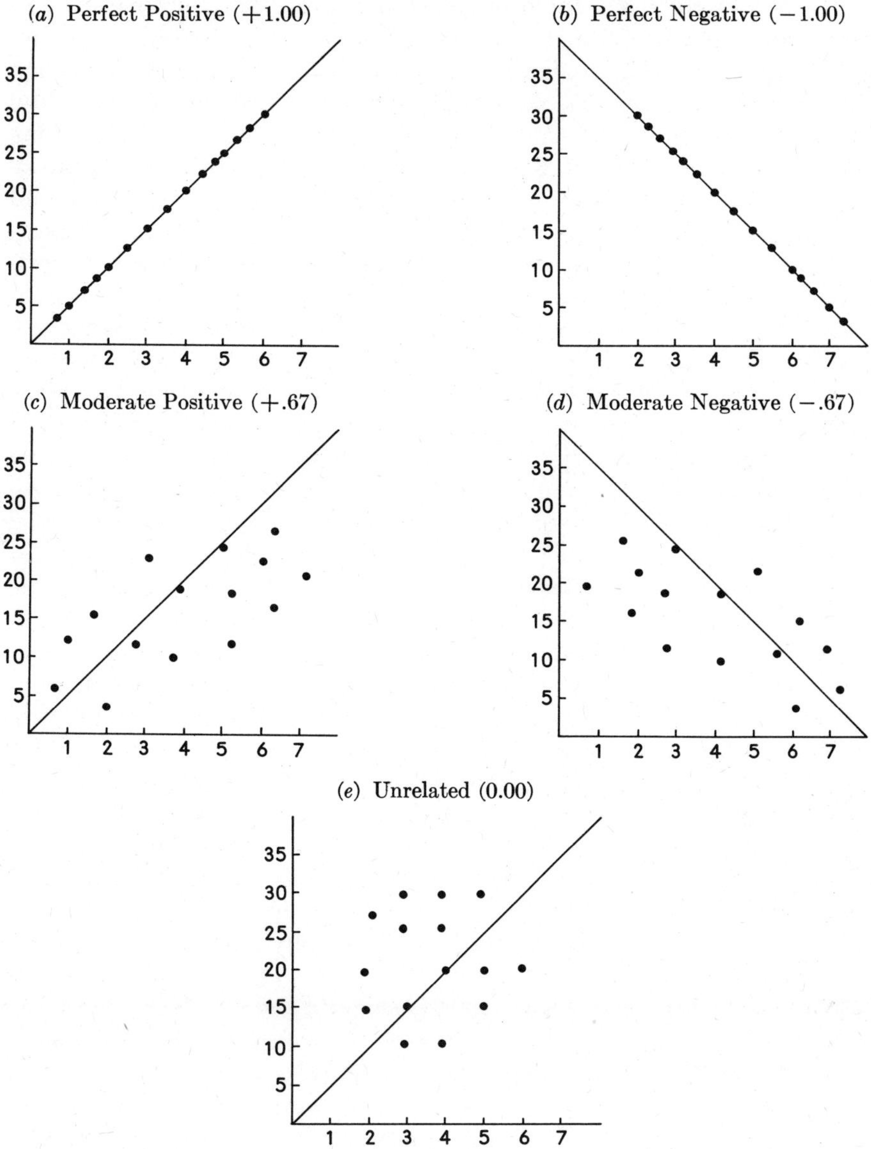

one another), and the correlational design can easily take this "fact of nature" into account by studying the relationship of many variables with one another. Although experimentation can also deal with multideterminants by manipulating more than one independent variable at a time, it is rare in practice for a single experiment to employ more than three independent variables, and many experiments have only one.

Generally, there are three reasons that correlation is used instead of experimentation. First, there are a number of variables which do not lend themselves to manipulation by the experimenter without becoming highly artificial. (Organismic variables such as sex, age, birth order, and so on, are completely unmanipulable.) In the study of childrearing practices, for example, it is virtually impossible to place rigid controls over lengthy and complex situations such as the home environment and the relationship of parents and children. Similarly, psychological investigations of death, suicide, and mourning have necessarily been correlational in nature, since these variables cannot be controlled by the experimenter. Furthermore, sometimes it is questionable whether an experimental manipulation will work, whereas the "natural manipulation" of the variables is certain to have an effect on the subject. This is another case where the correlational method may be favorably compared with the experimental approach. For example, the 1964 U.S. Surgeon General's report dealing with the relationship between cigarette smoking and lung cancer was an event which provided a credible statement of the health hazards of tobacco which could not have easily been simulated in the laboratory. After the report appeared, it was possible to relate giving up cigarettes to familiarity with the evidence—a unique opportunity to study attitude change under conditions of intense personal involvement.

Second, there are situations where direct manipulation is possible but unethical, as in the case where a subject would have to suffer severe pain or physical injury.

Third, psychologists use a correlational method instead of an experimental one when it is initially more economical to do so. Rather than creating a particular condition in his subjects, the investigator may find that much time, money, and effort can be saved if measurements can first be taken of subjects who are already in that condition. Thus, a psychologist interested in the relationship between anxiety and test performance might administer questionnaires during a class examination to tap the already present state of anxiety in the subjects and then correlate these scores with the grade on the examination. This approach is to be distinguished from creating different levels of anxiety in subjects by telling some of them, for example, that the results on the test will have an important influence on their being accepted into graduate school and telling others that the results will be kept confidential.

Whether a correlational approach is truly efficient in the long run will depend on the price paid for the lack of adequate controls. Perhaps the most useful aspect of correlational research is as a preliminary step to controlled experimentation. Pilot studies which are correlational in nature can serve to direct the investigator toward behavior which may have been previously ignored or overlooked and suggest hypotheses which can then be tested in experimental settings. Tentative hypotheses about certain relationships can also be subjected to correlational study before experimentation is undertaken. Then, if the hypothesized relationships hold, the researcher will feel more confident in conducting extensive experimentation which is capable of leading to information about cause and effect.

Sometimes a researcher has the opportunity to see how relationships investigated under highly controlled experimental conditions apply to real-life situations. The massive power failure which encompassed much of the eastern seaboard of the United States on November 9–10, 1965, offered a rare opportunity for a field investigation of an in-process crisis. One group of alert psychologists capitalized on this "natural manipulation" to test their laboratory findings concerning individual differences in anxiety and affiliation in relation to birth order (Zucker, Manosevitz, and Lanyon, 1968). The blackout occurred in New York City at about 5:30 P.M. at the height of the transportation rush hour. The result was that thousands of people on their way home from work were forced to spend the night in public places. In the early morning hours, Zucker and his colleagues asked persons in a large bus terminal and a hotel lobby, both of which were illuminated by emergency power, to complete a questionnaire concerning demographic information such as age, education, birth order, and so on, and their feelings about being stranded for the night. The subjects were asked to rate their preference for being alone or with other people, on a five-point scale, and to assess their anxiety by responding to the following question, also on a five-point scale: "How nervous or uneasy did you feel during this experience (i.e., the blackout experience over the course of the evening)?" Besides the self-reported retrospective measure of affiliative preference obtained on the questionnaire, the investigators noted, before approaching a subject, whether he was talking to or standing with someone else, and this information became a dichotomous index of actual gregariousness (i.e., affiliative or nonaffiliative) at the time of the data collection.

Previous research had shown that firstborns tend to be more anxious than later borns when they are placed in an anxiety-arousing situation, and Zucker and his associates found some further evidence for this relationship. Additionally, the results of numerous laboratory studies had found that firstborns express a greater preference to be with other people than to be alone when exposed to stress-inducing conditions. This hypothesis received support in the actual crisis situation for women only.

The major drawback of correlational research is that the investigator has very little control over relevant variables. Since the researcher does not manipulate or control the variables under study, cause and effect relationships cannot be investigated easily using the correlational research method. A substantial correlation between two variables means that each can be predicted from the other but does not tell us whether either is the cause of the other. All we are entitled to say is that the two vary together. There is, for example, a high positive correlation between the number of churches in a city and the number of crimes committed in that city; the more churches a city has, the more crimes are committed in that city. Does this mean that religion fosters crime? Certainly not. That crime fosters religion? Unlikely. The correlation is due to a third variable —population—which leads to an increase in both churches and crime. Or consider the high positive correlation between the number of drownings and the consumption of ice cream. Here the third causitive factor is temperature. The warmer the weather, the more people that are swimming (and the more people that drown) and the more ice cream that is sold and eaten. The fact that we cannot infer causation from correlation does not mean that a cause and effect relationship does not exist. It merely means that we need to have more information to speak of causation.

To summarize, when a substantial correlation between variable *X* and variable *Y* is found, one of three possibilities exists with regard to cause and effect. *X* may cause *Y*. *Y* may cause *X*. Or *Z*, a third variable, may be responsible for both *X* and *Y*. In the case of the correlation of certain variables, at least one of the three possibilities may be manifestly absurd. If a high correlation between sex and intelligence is found, the possibility that intelligence causes sex can be immediately dismissed for obvious reasons. The alternatives are then narrowed to two. An individual's sex may determine his intelligence. Or, parents may treat children differently with respect to the educational advantages given them as a function of their sex. In this latter case, sex is only an indirect causative factor, and differential familial treatment would be the direct cause of variations in intelligence. Also, whenever one variable precedes another in time, the latter cannot lead to the former. Thus, depending on the nature of the variables under study, some information concerning causation may be gleaned from correlational research.

There are instances, however, where it is not necessary to know if one of the measured variables is causing another or if an "outside" variable is responsible. One such case is in applied areas of psychology in which prediction of a criterion is all that is required. For example, a college admissions committee needs information to predict success in college. Typically there is a high positive correlation between grades in high school and scores on entrance examinations and academic achievement in college. Thus, the committee can do its job effectively without reference to causes.

In brief, the correlational method permits the investigator to economically obtain information about relationships, but not causal relationships, regarding a large number of individuals or variables or both and may be easily applied to "real-life" data. The final research method which we shall discuss also focuses directly on life situations but studies a single individual.

THE CASE STUDY METHOD

A familiar and quite commonplace method of studying personality is the biography. When a detailed account of a single individual is used in personality research, in a hospital by physicians, or in a community service agency by a social worker, it is typically called a *case history* or *case study*. Although the case study is the least systematic and least controlled research method and is mainly descriptive in nature, it does have a place in the scientific study of personality.

There are numerous examples of case studies being used *didactically* as examples of prototypical behavior. For example, in an attempt to illustrate the classification of abnormal behavior the following short case history was used as an example of an obsessive-compulsive reaction, which is characterized by the presence of persistent, disturbing thoughts and the urge to repeatedly perform stereotyped acts.

Michael R., a twenty-three-year-old single man, applied for treatment to a psychiatric clinic in a medium-sized midwestern town. He was living alone in a small apartment in that town.

Michael was the older of two children born to a rather vitriolic couple. His father was an ex-college athlete and part-time alcoholic, whose only interest in his children was the thought of developing their athletic ability. His mother was a violent-tempered woman who frequently flew into tantrums, which usually were initiated by the father's alcoholic disorderliness. Harsh physical punishment was not at all uncommon, and Michael had the occasional experience of being thrown bodily out of the house and being locked out a whole night, even for minor misdemeanors. His younger sister was an accomplished athlete, while Michael was clumsy, uncoordinated, and eventually, uninterested. This situation provoked jealousy and hostility in Michael, and prohibited a warm relationship with his sister, who was the father's favorite. Although of very superior intelligence, Michael had a great deal of difficulty in school, generally because of disciplinary matters. He preferred sketching and painting to any of the formal courses offered, and persisted despite the taunts of his family and schoolmates. Michael chose to attend the nearby state university, which offered a fine program in art education. He graduated from that school, but was very dissatisfied with his progress, and felt that he had not learned anything. He then took a job as an elevator operator, forsaking any attempt to find employment which would utilize his artistic ability.

Throughout his life, Michael had an intense fear of stinging insects such as wasps and hornets. If he passed a man on the street who appeared to have an athletic physique, he would be beset with the fear that the man would attack him. He also had a fear of heat and fire, and this fear was accompanied by the persistent thought that he would step on discarded lighted matches or cigarettes. He was extremely neat and orderly in all his affairs, carrying this to the point where everything had to be "lined up" neatly. He realized that these concerns were unreal and irrational, but nevertheless they persisted. He was always dissatisfied with his social relationships, feeling that others ridiculed, belittled, and disliked him. He did little or no dating, and never had a genuinely warm friendship with anyone.

When applying for treatment, Michael entered the room with a list of the things which bothered him, and he proceeded to read this list to the interviewer. The list was divided into four subcategories, namely, "anxiety, sexual thoughts, anger, and miscellaneous." It was felt that Michael was in need of therapy, and might possibly benefit from it, although many potential difficulties were recognized in his rigid attitudes. However, because he was making plans to move back to his home town soon thereafter, Michael was advised to seek treatment in the latter community (Zax and Stricker, 1963, pp. 169–70).

Such a use of the case study helps to bring the student out of the realm of abstract conceptions and into the realm of concete examples. A danger in this technique is that it may lead to the false conclusion that all cases of a particular genre are exactly the same. This problem can be somewhat circumvented when more than one case history is presented and the commonalities among them as well as the idiosyncrasies of each are pointed out.

In a similar vein, case studies can be extremely useful in *illustrating procedures*, such as methods of psychotherapy, where it is often insufficient to merely learn the principles involved. One must also be able to see how the principles are applied. Ayllon (1965) illustrates the management of "some behavioral problems associated with eating in chronic schizophrenic patients" in the following case study:

Anne was a near mute catatonic who for the last 16 years would not eat unless a nurse led her to the dining room, gave her a tray, silverware, and food, and seated her at the table, then urged her to eat and occasionally spoonfed her.

A 14 day baseline of Anne's behavior associated with meals was obtained. Not once during this period did she go to the dining room on her own, nor did she help herself to food. This information suggested that her difficulty in both these behaviors was being maintained by the attention she received from the nurses as a function of this difficulty. The nurses were instructed not to take the patient to the dining room but to help her as much as before once she entered the dining room.

During the 21st week of this program, it was decided to shape her behavior in the dining room so that the patient would go through the cafeteria line completely on her own, without the nurse's assistance (for four weeks previous to shaping, no records were taken once she had entered the dining room). The nurses were instructed not to help the patient in the dining room, but to reinforce her by dropping some candy on her tray, only after she had picked up a tray, silverware, and one edible item (p. 74).

Case studies have also been used to present data concerning an *unusual case*. Probably the most famous of these is "A Case of Multiple Personality" (Thigpen and Cleckley, 1954) in which a 25-year-old married woman, "Eve White," displayed three very distinct personalities. Eve White had been seen in psychotherapy for several months because of severe headaches and blackouts. Her therapist described her as a "retiring and gently conventional figure." One day during an interview,

As if seized by a sudden pain she put both hands to her head. After a tense moment of silence, her hands dropped. There was a quick, reckless smile and, in a bright voice that sparkled, she said, "Hi there, Doc!" The demure and constrained posture of Eve White had melted into buoyant repose. . . . This new and apparently carefree girl spoke casually of Eve White and her problems, always using *she* or *her* in every reference, always respecting the strict bounds of a separate identity. When asked her own name she immediately replied, "Oh, I'm Eve Black" (p. 137).

Following this startling discovery, Eve was observed over a period of 14 months in a series of interviews amounting to approximately 100 hours. (During this time, still a third personality emerged.) This case study is valuable because it is one of only a few detailed accounts of a rare phenomenon, a true multiple personality.

Recently, fictional case studies of abnormal behavior (particularly in children) have become very popular. The writer, most often a psychiatrist or clinical psychologist, draws upon the case histories of a number of individuals and his experience in treating them. Good examples include *Jordi, Lisa and David, One Little Boy,* and *I Never Promised You a Rose Garden.*

Case studies are sometimes used to test hypotheses and have been said to confirm theories. The justification of such use is questionable. Freud used case histories extensively to support psychoanalytic theory, and in fact they were the only evidence he presented for his hypotheses. His case studies, including that of Little Hans, to be discussed in a later chapter, all suffer from the critical flaw of being open to many interpretations. Thus, while Freud used these studies as evidence for his hypotheses, others can (and have) explained the same observations from an entirely different theoretical viewpoint. For this reason, and others which will be mentioned shortly, case studies are poor substitutes for controlled experimentation when one's purpose is to muster support for a theory.

On the other hand, case studies can sometimes be helpful in *disconfirming* the implications of a theory. When a theory purports to be universally true (i.e., in all cases), case studies can provide *negative instances* of the theory. A single negative instance, an example that is covered by the domain of the theory yet does not conform to the theory, is sufficient to reject the notion of universality. Freud conceived of the "Oedipus complex" (discussed in detail in Chapter 3) as a universal phenomenon, and accordingly the anthropological studies which demonstrated that there are cultures in which young boys do not exhibit the Oedipus complex have been viewed by some as casting serious doubt on Freud's original hypothesis. Of course, a somewhat modified position may still be tenable.

When theories do admit to the possibility of exceptions or nonapplicable instances, negative instances in the form of case studies can still serve to cast some suspicion on the usefulness of the theory in explaining the phenomenon in question. Often such a case study is accompanied by an alternative explanation which seems more plausible in the light of the new evidence which the case study has brought to light. As striking as the negative instance seems to be and as convincing as the new explanation appears, they can only be viewed as partial, indeed very tentative, evidence against an existing theory. There is no substitute for controlled experimentation for deciding among alternative theories. However, the case study which is a negative instance can alert scientists to the possibility that an extant theory may need reevaluation.

As a method of personality research, the case study has several advantages. First, it is an excellent method for examining the personality of a single individual in great detail. For example, in a clinical setting, where the focus of interest is on one and only one person, the case study is found to be most useful. However, most research psychologists studying personality are more interested in people in general than one person in particular. Thus, for personality research, the case study can only be considered an adjunct technique for data collection.

A second advantage of the case study, intimately related to the first, is that it allows an individual's idiosyncrasies, complexities, and contradictions to be examined. However general the laws of human behavior are, each man is very much a unique individual. As mentioned previously, sometimes it is of interest to focus upon a particular person rather than persons in general. Occasionally, a psychologist primarily interested in making statements about man's behavior in general will use a large number of case histories, and in this situation the inconsistencies which appear may be of special significance.

It is ironic that the most glaring deficit of the case study method can be its most redeeming quality. Here we are speaking of the *lack of control* which usually characterizes case studies. By allowing things to vary as they will, the case study has a greater potential for revealing new and perhaps serendipitous findings. This is especially true with regard to control over the dependent measures. If the dependent measures are specified in advance and only those measures are collected, the experimenter may miss some vital observations which are not measured. Suppose we are interested in studying the reactions of a college student to failing an examination. We will place no restrictions (control) over the subject's behavior or the environmental influences but will decide ahead of time that we will measure his reaction to failing the test by means of questionnaires and physiological indices of anger and worry. We may very well find some important information concerning the relationship between failing a test and these emotions. But suppose the student showed not only heightened anger and worry but also increased feelings of love and joy. This is somewhat of an unexpected finding, but if indices of these "positive" emotions were not included as dependent measures, we would never have known about it. In fact, it often is the case that unexpected data become even more significant than the anticipated data and subsequently become the subject of further investigation. As Skinner's (1956) first informal principle of scientific methodology states: "When you run onto something interesting, drop everything else and study it" (p. 223).

Usually the case study method does not specify the observations to be made but rather attempts to record as much of the entire situation as possible. (In this regard, modern techniques such as video tape recording make such a goal more realistic.) The advantage of placing no restrictions on the measures to be taken is sometimes outweighed by the problem of sorting through the data and making sense out of them. Anyone who has sat down for an evening of editing reels of home movies has some idea of what a problem this could turn out to be.

Let us return to our example of the student and his reactions to failing an examination. It would be necessary to observe him, unobtrusively, during all his examinations. Furthermore, unless he were an especially poor student, we might have to observe him over a very long period of time while we waited for him to flunk an examination. He might fool us and go through four years of college without once failing a test. In that case we would congratulate him, of course, but where would our research be? We would have lost a tremendous expenditure in time and effort. The absurdity of such a plan of action is not difficult to see.

To circumvent the problem of being in the right place at the right time, the psychologist typically waits for the critical event to happen and at some later time collects his observations. These observations are in the form of detailed *retrospective* reports by the subject and any other people who happened to observe him. The problem with such *post hoc* data collection is that the observers (the subject and others) tend to forget what has happened and, perhaps even more important, lose the feelings that accompanied the original critical situation. Additionally, observers not only forget details but their "stories" also tend to change with the passage of time. Things are now seen in a different perspective, especially when the incident under study has been somewhat stressful for the subject. Memories are mixed with present thoughts and feelings in a process similar to that which occurs when someone tries to reconstruct a dream after he has awakened. Thus, unless the data for the case study are gathered at the time the crucial incident occurs, the accuracy of the case material is open to question. The case of Eve White, mentioned previously, is one example of a nonretrospective case study. Once it was decided that she was to be the subject of an extensive investigation, the data were systematically collected at each interview.

Still another advantage of the case study method should have become apparent in the foregoing discussion. The case study typically deals with a person in his natural environment as opposed to an artificial laboratory setting. Since ultimately theories of personality are intended to explain the behavior of persons in "real-life" situations, it is apparent that case studies have compelling *external validity*. That is, they directly examine the phenomena in which we are ultimately interested.

The case study can be recommended as a method for personality research for at least one additional reason. We have pointed out that it can include among its data the richness and complexity of personality. Although such data may not be specific enough to be used in *support* of a theory, they often are the source of hypotheses about man's behavior. These hypotheses, once formulated on the basis of the case history material, can then be tested by a more controlled and rigorous research method.

Most of the disadvantages of the case study method have already been mentioned in passing. To recapitulate, the technique is usually retrospective, and thus its reliability is questionable. The data it yields are unique in that they generally come from a single individual and therefore it is difficult to generalize to other people. Another disadvantage is the fact that case histories are open to a variety of interpretations, since there are no definite guidelines for deciding among two or more seemingly tenable hypotheses which account for the same data. Finally, the data from case studies are qualitative rather than quantitative. Without going into a detailed explanation of why measurement is essential to psychology or any science, it should simply be noted that quantification leads to finer, more precise descriptions of behavior. Thus, the case study is lacking an essential characteristic of science.

Whether the disadvantages of the case study method outweigh its advantages for studying personality depends upon the purpose of the investigation. It is reasonable to think of the case study method as a preliminary and adjunct technique rather than as a viable research method in itself.

Single-Subject Design. In the foregoing discussion, we have observed that the case study method is typically identified with the detailed examination of a single case, whereas other research methods focus upon the behavior of many persons. It is possible, however, to use a carefully controlled experimental method with a single individual. This instance, often called the *single-subject design,* systematically examines the influence of one or more controlled variables upon a specified aspect of behavior in a controlled environment. The single-subject design has been used extensively by researchers who have adopted the operant approach put forth by B. F. Skinner (Chapter 11).

Baer (1968) and his associates at the University of Kansas report a single-subject *experiment* in which the influence of teachers' attention upon the crying tantrums of a four-year-old boy is examined. It was initially observed that the boy had an average of eight crying episodes per morning in the nursery school setting and that the teachers paid attention to him whenever these tantrums occurred. These first observations constitute the *base line* for the experiment. In the second phase of the experiment, the child's teachers withdrew all attention from this undesirable behavior. The withdrawal is characterized as follows:

> If previously she has been attending at times to an undesirable behavior, now she ignores it—perfectly. She is not punitive, nor is she offended. She simply becomes selectively deaf and blind—anesthetic, if necessary—to that particular behavior of the child. If she is attending to him when he performs it, she finds she must attend to some other business at that instant (p. 4).

During a 10-day period in which the crying was ignored, the boy's rate was reduced to virtually no crying. Next, and this is perhaps the most critical aspect of the single-subject design, the teachers were asked to resume their attention to crying episodes (*the reversal phase*). The crying episodes completely "recovered" (i.e., the rate returned to that found in the base-line period) within three days. Finally, the teachers again removed their attention, whereupon the inappropriate crying dropped out permanently.

It should be apparent from this example that the single-subject design can be used as a well-controlled experiment. Rather than recording the complexity of the individual case, the single-subject design is used to demonstrate a principle of behavior through the systematic treatment of a single individual under controlled conditions.

REFERENCES

Ayllon, T. Some behavioral problems associated with eating in chronic schizophrenic patients. In L. P. Ullmann and L. Krasner (Eds.), *Case studies in behavior modification.* New York: Holt, Rinehart & Winston, 1965. Pp. 73–77.

Baer, D. M. Some remedial uses of the reinforcement contingency. In J. M. Shlien (Ed.), *Research in psychotherapy*. Vol. III. Washington, D.C.: American Psychological Association, 1968. Pp. 3–20.

Darley, J. M., and Latané, B. Bystander intervention in emergencies: Diffusion of responsibility. *Journal of Personality and Social Psychology*, 1968, **8**, 377–83.

Edwards, A. L. *Statistical analysis*. (Rev. ed.) New York: Holt, Rinehart & Winston, 1958.

Hays, W. L. *Statistics for psychologists*. New York: Holt, Rinehart & Winston, 1963.

McCall, R. B. *Fundamental statistical concepts*. New York: Harcourt, Brace & World, 1970.

Skinner, B. F. A case history in scientific method. *American Psychologist*, 1956, **11**, 221–33.

Smith, G. M. *A simplified guide to statistics for psychology and education*. (3d ed.) New York: Holt, Rinehart & Winston, 1962.

Smoking and health: Report of the advisory committee to the Surgeon General of the Public Health Service. Washington, D.C.: U.S. Department of Health, Education, and Welfare, Public Health Service, 1964.

Thigpen, C. H., and Cleckley, H. A case of multiple personality. *Journal of Abnormal and Social Psychology*, 1954, **49**, 135–51.

Wallis, W. A., and Roberts, H. V. *Statistics: A new approach*. New York: Free Press, 1956.

Zax, M., and Stricker, G. *Patterns of psychopathology*. New York: Macmillan, 1963.

Zucker, R. A., Manosevitz, M., and Lanyon, R. I. Birth order, anxiety, and affiliation during a crisis. *Journal of Personality and Social Psychology*, 1968, **8**, 354–59.

chapter 3

The Intrapsychic Approach: Psychoanalytic Personality Theory

All theory and research in personality appears to share the common goal of conceptualizing human behavior in a way that will facilitate prediction and anticipate those events which produce change. All views of personality must ultimately make an appeal to what they can *do;* theories with no pragmatic ("real-life") value are likely to be discarded rather than disproven. In this chapter, we shall discuss an approach to personality which, in various forms, has guided diverse applied activities, from personnel selection to treatment of psychological disorders, for most of the present century.

Historically, one of the most appealing and seemingly natural ways to conceptualize our own behavior and the behavior of other men has been to try to determine the *intention* of each act. Intention is a critical notion in all sorts of personal relations. Jean Piaget, a famous Swiss psychologist, has found that children as young as seven may acknowledge that a small amount of purposeful damage is "naughtier" than substantial damage that occurs through ignorance or oversight. Our legal system places great emphasis on the degree to which harmful acts are premeditated. For example, the law prescribes incarceration for as little as one year for killing another man if intent cannot be shown. It is common for people to state the intended purposes of their own behavior as a matter of course and to be interested in determining the motives of other men.

Whereas *what* we do is available to anyone who chooses to look and see, *why* we do something presumably can be answered only by examining our past histories and our present psychological states. However, answers to both of these questions are often entirely unavailable to the observer and, if required, must be found out by indirect means.

Thus, an interest develops in determining those events which take place "inside" the other person. The determination of such subjective phenomena has usually been called a search for *intrapsychic* factors. This chapter will discuss the intrapsychic perspective of personality, examining some of the major research methods and findings which have been advanced from this viewpoint. Our discussion will begin with the logical and strategic problems involved in studying subjective phenomena, such as an individual's private motives or feelings, which we as observers can be aware of only indirectly.

SUBJECTIVE PHENOMENA AND THEIR ASSESSMENT

Inclusion of subjective phenomena in any analysis of personality introduces a number of problems. These phenomena must be identifiable to theorists and other observers before they can be considered as determinative in behavior. Thus, the first problem is to objectify, at least in part, the private experiences of other men. Then, it is necessary to establish some evidence that the observable indices of subjective phenomena and intrapsychic events which have been selected bear some relationship to the phenomena of interest. Suppose, for example, we chose a facial frown as an index of the internal state of "unhappiness." We would then have to decide how close the presumed relationship between frowning and unhappiness was. Are frowning persons always unhappy? Do unhappy persons always frown? Under what circumstances would we say a frowning person is *not* unhappy? Can a person who is always smiling and laughing still be experiencing unhappiness? These questions are vital ones in the development of a theory, and, additionally, they parallel similar questions which are raised in our daily lives when we try to understand the motives and feelings of others.

Next, if we are to deal with the individual's private experiences, we must decide the degree to which he himself is aware of them. Can a person be ignorant of his own motives and be unaware or mistaken about his own feelings about other persons, places, or events? It is now commonplace, for example, to speculate that an individual who expresses an excessive degree of certainty about his own abilities, like the roaring lion, is expressing not self-confidence but self-doubt. Are there grounds for such assumptions? How often do they hold? What is the value and what are the limitations of looking at other men (and ourselves) in this light? These and other questions must be raised and answered by both theory and research which hope to examine intrapsychic events.

Two general roads appear to be open to finding information relevant to an individual's private experiences—direct and indirect assessment. The first strategy that might be employed is to directly ask him about his feelings, attitudes, beliefs, and privately felt stresses. The problem inherent in this strategy is that we may not be able to "trust" his reports. Even from a commonsense point of view it is apparent that there are many circumstances in which an individual will distort both his feelings and his own stated recollection of his behavior to make them more compatible with the perceived social demands. For example, social psychological studies have found that after an election which is narrowly won by one candidate, an overwhelming majority of voters will claim that they voted for the winner. It is improbable that these citizens have really "forgotten" how their ballots were cast. Rather, it seems likely that they are deliberately modifying their statements so as to be in the "winner's circle." As we shall come to see, the possible operation of such distorting psychological processes has been extensively formalized in intrapsychic theories. But, even apart from such formalization, our everyday experiences suggest that there are many circumstances in which we should not place heavy reliance on an individual's report of those events of which he alone has direct knowledge.

Despite these problems, both laymen and psychologists often accept persons' verbalizations concerning their own inner states, feelings, phantasies, and other private information without qualification. Direct self-reports are useful in many circumstances both conceptually and as real predictors of behavior. As Dement (1965) has noted: "We accept . . . these concepts without qualification because long experience has shown over and over that they *do* correlate with observable events in the real world. Their function is to bridge the gap between sensory input and motor output; to help order the intervening processes that govern human behavior" (p. 142). For example, a wide variety of external stimulation, ranging from pinpricks to burning torches to sharp blows will lead most adults to say "ouch." We observe quickly that we can predict many of the events that a person has not yet experienced which will lead him to report pain. The assumption that the individual *really is* experiencing an intense internal feeling proves, in this example, to be highly serviceable. Objective evidence that the individual is in fact experiencing internal sensations with particular characteristics cannot be provided; on the other hand, such rigorous proof appears hardly necessary in view of the obvious utility of assuming that his feelings are real.

In numerous other situations, however, there is excellent reason to conclude that self-reports about private experiences are less useful and in fact may be quite misleading. In virtually all circumstances where accurate representation of one's feelings might lead to negative consequences, psychological research and common experience alike suggest that the individual's statements about himself may provide no reliable information. Moreover, self-descriptions of internal experience are of necessity mediated by language, and it is often necessary to understand the connotative use of the individual's language and verbal expression before his descriptions can have much value. Mischel (1968), for example, points to the statement of a psychiatric patient who said, "I'd be in better shape if I were a mustard cutter" (p. 238). He goes on to note:

> A literal interpretation of these complaints would be entirely misleading. In the first instance, for example, the person who talked about his being in "better shape" had no discernible weight problems and his reference to "mustard cutting" had little to do with food. Rather, these descriptions, like most human statements, are abstractions about behavior that cannot be grasped intelligently without pinning them to relevant referents (pp. 238–39).

Thus, a second strategy is often used by workers interested in identifying intrapsychic phenomena. This strategy assumes that we must use *indirect* methods in order to identify an individual's subjective phenomena. Indirect methods are assumed to be necessary because either (1) we cannot trust the individual's report because of various considerations which might lead him to be inaccurate or (2) we have reason to assume that the individual himself cannot accurately verbalize and directly state what his own motives and internal conditions are.

Indirect methods of assessment may take the form of paper-and-pencil tests, "projective tests," free associations and dreams, or may become part of an interview. The common characteristic which identifies the method is the effort to obtain information about private experience without stating (and presumably without revealing) the specific purpose of the inquiry.

* * *

Sigmund Freud, a Viennese physician who was born in 1856 and died in 1939, developed the first systematic intrapsychic theory of personality and called his position *psychoanalysis.* Over the years personality psychologists who have been in fundamental agreement with Freud's approach to personality (i.e., an intrapsychic strategy) have made a number of revisions and additions to his theory. In keeping with the basic plan of this book, which is to present major strategies used in the study of personality and illustrate the strategies with detailed accounts of representative theories, we shall primarily discuss Freud's psychoanalytic theory. As our discussion proceeds, it will become increasingly clear that

Freud's is a *biological* viewpoint, stressing innate, universal determinants of personality and behavior. While it is true that Freud did address himself to many social and cultural phenomena (for example, socialization, parent-child relationships, interpersonal relationships, and so on), he nonetheless felt that these phenomena were the result of human personality rather than the reverse. It is on this point that many of the so-called *neo-Freudians* or *neoanalysts* took major exception to *traditional* (Freudian) psychoanalysis. When discrepancies between traditional and neoanalytic viewpoints are important, they will be mentioned. Unless otherwise stated, we shall be discussing Freud's theory of personality in the present chapter.

MAJOR CHARACTERISTICS OF PSYCHOANALYTIC THEORY

Before examining psychoanalytic personality theory in detail, it will be helpful to briefly sketch an overview of the major characteristics of Freud's position.

First, psychoanalytic theory is a *deterministic* point of view. Freud held that all behavior is determined or caused by some force within us and therefore all behavior has meaning. One of Freud's earliest and most widely cited clinical observations was the finding that even the simplest occurrences of human behavior can be traced to complicated psychological factors of which the individual may be totally unaware. Perhaps the best known of these occurrences are the so-called "Freudian slips" made in speech, writing, and reading. The error presumably reveals something of the person's "inner" thoughts or feelings or "real" intent. Examples in which the unconscious thoughts are obvious include substituting "playbody" for "playboy" and "Fraud" for "Freud." In regard to omissions in writing, Freud (1951)[1] interestingly noted:

> Even the Bible did not escape misprints. Thus we have the "Wicked Bible," so called from the fact that the negative was left out of the seventh commandment. This authorized edition of the Bible was published in London in 1631, and it is said that the printer had to pay a fine of two thousand pounds for the omission (p. 63).

Among the clearest examples of the thoroughgoing determinism which Freud (1963) used are those related to "accidental" forgetting and losing of objects:

> If anyone forgets a proper name which is familiar to him normally or if, in spite of all his efforts, he finds it difficult to keep it in mind, it is plausible to suppose that he has something against the person who bears the name so that he prefers not to think of him (p. 52).

[1] The dates refer to the actual references used and thus do not always correspond to the original publication of the work.

> We lose an object if we have quarreled with the person who gave it to us and do not want to be reminded of him; or if we no longer like the object itself and want to have an excuse for getting another and better one instead. The same intention directed against an object can also play a part, of course, in cases of dropping, breaking, or destroying things (p. 54).
>
> Here is the best example, perhaps, of such an occasion. A youngish man told me the following story: "Some years ago there were misunderstandings between me and my wife. I found her too cold, and although I willingly recognized her excellent qualities we lived together without any tender feelings. One day, returning from a walk, she gave me a book she had bought because she thought it would interest me. I thanked her for this mark of 'attention,' promised to read the book and put it on one side. After that I could never find it again. Months passed by, in which I occasionally remembered the lost book and made vain attempts to find it. About six months later my dear mother, who was not living with us, fell ill. My wife left home to nurse her mother-in-law. The patient's condition became serious and gave my wife an opportunity of showing the best side of herself. One evening I returned home full of enthusiasm and gratitude for what my wife had accomplished. I walked up to my desk, and without any definite intention but with a kind of somnambulistic certainty opened one of the drawers. On the very top I found the long-lost book I had mislaid" (p. 55).

Freud noted that he could "multiply this collection of examples indefinitely," and he used incidents like these as an indirect assessment technique to understand facets of an individual's personality that would otherwise be unavailable to anyone else.

A second major characteristic of psychoanalytic theory is that it is a *dynamic* point of view. Like many other personality theorists, Freud felt that it was essential for a comprehensive understanding of personality to have a statement of the source of motivation for human actions. Freud postulated that this source of motivation was a unitary power source or energy source which can be found within the individual, and he labeled this source the *libido* (psychic energy).

Third, psychoanalytic theory can be usefully conceived of as a *developmental* point of view. Freud felt that human development follows a more or less set course from birth, and he divided development into a series of stages which all persons must pass through. Freud's theory is also developmental in the sense that it stresses the importance, indeed the dominance, of early development as a determinant of an individual's adult personality.

Finally, psychoanalysis is *structural* in nature. Freud postulated that there are three basic structures or aspects of one's personality—the *id, ego,* and *superego*—and that it is the dynamic interaction or conflict between these structures which determines behavior. Further, psychoanalysis is based on a structural point of view in that it posits levels of awareness or consciousness at which persons function—*conscious, preconscious,* and *unconscious.*

INSTINCTS AND LIBIDO

Instincts are inborn predispositions to behave in characteristic ways, and they are said to possess differing amounts of energy. The quantity of energy which a particular instinct represents at some specific point in time is its *drive.* Drive is an important notion because in real life the objects which will satisfy an instinct are sometimes blocked by social or physical barriers. The more "driving power" available to the instinct, the greater the barriers which it can overcome.

Psychoanalytic theory divides human instincts into two basic classes.[2] The first class deals with the basic physical needs of existence, including breathing, hunger and thirst, and the excretory functions. Objects or circumstances to satisfy these instincts are usually available in direct form, and their satisfaction is typically simple and straightforward, allowing relatively little drive or tension to become attached to them. However, an instinct such as hunger can become abnormally strong under unusual circumstances. For example, the Donner party, a group emigrating to California in the 19th century, was caught by severe snowstorms while crossing the High Sierras near what is today the Nevada-California state line. When starvation was imminent, the social contract binding the group broke down, and they are reputed to have engaged in cannibalism before being completely wiped out.

The second group of instincts are those related to sexual urges. *Libido* or *psychic energy* is the energy of the sexual instincts. In this context, "sex" refers to almost all pleasurable actions and thoughts, including, but not exclusively, erotic activity. Psychic energy is the energy for all mental activity (e.g., for thinking, perceiving, imaging, remembering, problem solving, and so on) and is somewhat analogous to, though not the same as, physical energy.

Libido is conceptualized as potentially building up in pressure or thrust in very much the same way as water might develop tremendous pressure in a series of pipes when no external valve is open. With regard to the water pipe analogy, we know that if there is an increase in pressure and there is no outlet for this pressure, the pipe will burst.

[2] Freud proposed another distinction among the instincts which, while not widely accepted by his followers, has some historical interest. He suggested that in addition to the instincts of life (*Eros*) there was in all men a death instinct (*Thanatos*). Thanatos was said to be present from birth and was generally described as the tendency of all life to strive to return to its inorganic form. By positing the death instinct, Freud hoped to account for self-destructive acts such as suicide, in which Thanatos is turned inward, and war and other forms of aggression, in which case Thanatos is presumably turned outward.

Further, it will burst at its weakest point. Psychoanalytic theory argues that increase in the pressure or tension of psychic energy is a natural consequence of an intrapsychic conflict. Reduction of this tension is necessary for an individual's functioning, and it also produces a highly pleasurable experience, since tension is experienced as unpleasant or painful. Tension reduction, which assumes a prominent place in psychoanalytic theorizing, is formally called the *pleasure principle.* If the individual's psychic energy does not have an opportunity to discharge in normal or socially acceptable ways, then pressure will increase and finally, as with the analogy of the water pipe, will burst out violently at the weakest point in the personality.

Freud's psychic energy system is a *closed* system. That is, each person may be thought of as possessing a fixed quantity of libido at any given time as a reservoir or source of all of his sexual expression and mental activity. This characteristic of a limited amount of psychic energy has a number of important consequences which all involve the basic notion that when libido is consumed for one purpose it cannot simultaneously be used for another. Thus, for example, the young man who is constantly thinking of his fianceè, has difficulty doing very much else (for example, reading an assignment in his personality textbook).

Freud contended that man's basic motivation is sexual in nature—man is a *hedonic* (pleasure-seeking) being. As we shall see shortly, societies place obstacles in the way of living completely or even predominantly in terms of satisfying one's pleasure-seeking instincts. In capsule form, then, Freud's theory of personality deals with the manner in which man handles his sexual needs in relation to a society which usually prevents direct expression of these needs. Each individual's personality is a function of his particular compromise between his sexual instincts and the society's restraints on them.

PSYCHOSEXUAL DEVELOPMENT

Psychoanalytic thinking places a great premium on the importance of early experience and suggests that many of the early social and personal experiences of the child become the prototypes or models for later feelings and behavior.

While Freud's interest in the facts of the intrauterine environment and the birth process was relatively moderate, several of his followers assigned a very critical role to these aspects in the development of personality. One psychoanalytic theorist, Fodor (1949), even asserted that the violence of parental sexual intercourse during pregnancy may have a traumatic effect which can be traced throughout the child's later life and revealed through his dreams.

Otto Rank (1929), whose name is most often associated with the concept of the *birth trauma* (although historically Freud's recognition of it came first), argued that the initial biological separation from his mother, which the child experiences at birth, becomes the prototype for all later anxiety. Biological separation becomes a representation in later life for loss and separation. Rank suggested that every enjoyable act and every pleasure which the individual experiences is oriented toward regaining the pleasure of the intrauterine environment. Thus, for example, sexual intercourse for the male represents a return to the mother's womb.

Freud himself suggested that before birth the child is in fact leading a relatively calm, peaceful, and undisturbed existence. In a warm, safe environment, he sleeps, exercises, and evacuates when he pleases. After birth this "ideal" existence changes radically. His needs and desires are to a large degree now under the control of others (for example, his parents), and immediate satisfaction and tension reduction is rarely, if ever, possible as it was during the previous nine months. Further, at the time of birth, the child has not yet developed mechanisms of defense (which will be discussed in a later section) with which to cope with the immediate pressures (anxiety) that face him.

Stages of Psychosexual Development

Freud divided human development into a series of universal stages which persons pass through from infancy to adulthood. The stages are delimited by the primary *erogenous zone* (an area of the body which is particularly sensitive to erotic stimulation) at the time. That is to say, at any particular time in the developmental sequence, one body area—the mouth, the anus, or the genital region—seems to supercede other areas as a source of pleasure. Thus, the stages of development are called *psychosexual* to indicate that the development is actually of the sexual instinct as it moves through the erogenous zones.

Each psychosexual stage has a particular *conflict* which must be resolved before the individual can pass on to the next stage. That is, at each stage the individual's libido is invested in behavior involving the erogenous zone which is predominant at the time. However, since each individual has a fixed amount of libido, the libido must be freed (i.e., the conflict must be resolved) from the primary erogenous zone of the stage it is presently in so that it can be reinvested in the primary erogenous zone of the next stage. Freud used an analogy of military troops on the march to explain this rather complicated process. As the troops march, they are met by opposition (conflict). If they are highly successful in winning the battle (resolving the conflict), virtually all of the troops (libido) will move on to the next battle (stage). The greater the difficulty in winning the battle, the more troops will be left behind on the battlefield and the fewer troops will be able to move on to the next confrontation.

In psychosexual development there are two basic reasons for an individual having difficulty leaving a stage and going on to the next one. Either the person's needs relevant to the psychosexual stage have not been met (frustration) or his needs have been so well satisfied that he is reluctant to leave the stage (overindulgence). Frustration or overindulgence (or a combination of the two) result in *fixation* at a psychosexual stage. Fixation involves leaving a portion of libido permanently invested in a stage of development which has been past and is analogous to the dead troops left behind in battle. Inevitably, some libido is fixated at each psychosexual stage. When the proportion of libido fixated at an earlier stage of development is small, only vestiges of earlier modes of obtaining satisfaction are seen in later behavior. However, when a substantial proportion of libido is fixated at an earlier stage, the individual's personality may become dominated by modes of obtaining satisfaction or tension reduction which were used in the earlier stage.

Oral Stage. During the first year of life, the child's mouth is the most prominent source of both his tension reduction (for example, eating) and pleasurable sensations (for example, sucking). The child is said to be in the *oral stage* of development since the libido is centered around the oral cavity.

More generally, the young child during this stage of his life is characterized by the psychological states of *dependence* and *incorporation.* We observe that he is psychologically immature, must be taken care of by others, and has his primary contact with the world through "taking things in" (through his mouth) and "spitting things out." Strupp (1967) broadens Freud's basic notions concerning the oral stage when he says that "the focal point of the child's personality organization at this period is not necessarily the mouth per se but *the total constellation of immaturity, dependency, the wish to be mothered, the pleasure of being held, the enjoyment of human closeness and warmth*" (p. 23).

These early experiences, attitudes, and aspects of social interaction are the prototypes for all future social behavior. Individuals who are fixated at the oral stage are likely to hold an optimistic view of the world, to develop dependent relationships in adulthood, to be unusually friendly and generous, and expect the world, in turn, to "mother them." It is particularly important to note that this type of theorizing, which is central to psychoanalytic thinking, lays the groundwork for explaining whole patterns of behavior in terms of early events and sets the tone for catagorizing adults into character types.

Some neo-Freudians have divided the oral stage into two phases. Thus far in our discussion we have only described the first phase, *oral eroti-*

cism, which is characterized by the pleasure of sucking and oral incorporation. The second phase, *oral sadism,* commences with the eruption of teeth. Biting and chewing now become part of the potential behavioral repertoire of the child, and the developing individual is able to behave aggressively and destructively. A person fixated at this phase of the oral stage is likely to be pessimistic, cynical, and aggressive in later life.

The oral stage ends when the child is weaned, and weaning thus becomes the crucial *conflict* of the oral stage. The more difficult it is for the child to leave his mother's breast (or his bottle) and its accompanying sucking pleasure, the greater will be the proportion of libido left at the oral stage.

Anal Stage. With the weaning of the child, the libido shifts from the oral region to the area of the anus. Pleasure is obtained at first from expelling feces and later from retaining them. This is not to say that the child did not derive similar pleasure during the oral stage. However, during the second and third years of life, anal pleasure predominates just as oral pleasure predominated during the first year of life. Up until the anal stage, relatively few demands are made on the child. During the second year of life, however, parents in most Western cultures begin to make demands on their offspring, particularly with respect to bowel and bladder control. Thus, the conflict in the anal stage is one between the demands of the id, which seeks pleasure from defecation, and the constraints of the society, which require that the child develop self-control with respect to excretion.

If the child is able to easily accede to his parents' toilet training demands, he will develop the basis for successful self-control. However, the child may have difficulty in developing sphincter control and thus meeting the increasing demands of his parents. Two fundamental strategies for coping with the frustrations of toilet training are open to the child. The child may attempt to "counterattack" by defecating at moments which are particularly inappropriate or inconvenient for his parents (for example, immediately *after* being taken off the "potty"). If the child discovers that this is a successful means of social control, he may come to employ the same type of strategy for handling frustration in general. It is interesting to note, for example, that in our culture verbal statements of extreme anger and hostility are often expressed in colloquial terms which make reference to the anal function. Excessive use of such hostile or inappropriate outbursts in later life characterizes a person who would be labeled an *anal aggressive character.*

Alternatively, the child may adopt the strategy of meeting his parents' demands by complete retention of his feces. This in itself is pleasureable (i.e., gentle pressure against the intestinal walls), and, in addition, it may prove to be a powerful way of manipulating his parents (for example, through parents' increased concern over the child's failure to have a bowel movement). If the strategy is successful, it may set the stage for similar behavior patterns in later life. Thus, persons who are stingy, hoarding, and stubborn are often termed *anal retentive characters.*

Phallic Stage. During the fourth and fifth years of life, the libido is centered in the genital region. Children at this age are frequently observed examining their genitalia, masturbating, and otherwise getting pleasure from their primary sexual apparatus. Furthermore, in our culture, verbal expressions of curiosity and interest regarding birth and sex are often heard at about this age. The conflict in the phallic stage is the last and the most crucial one with which the young child must cope. The conflict involves the child's unconscious wish to possess the opposite-sexed parent and at the same time to do away with the same-sexed parent. Freud called this situation the *Oedipus complex.* The name is derived from the Greek myth[3] in which Oedipus unknowingly kills his father and marries his mother. The Oedipus complex operates somewhat differently for males and females, and so we shall consider the sexes separately.

The little boy's first love object is his mother. As the libido centers in the genital zone, his love for his mother becomes erotically tinged (i.e., incestuous). However, the boy's father stands in the way of his sexual desires for his mother, and thus the father becomes his rival or enemy. Concomitant with his antagonism for and wish to eliminate his father, the boy fears that his father will retaliate. The little boy's casual observations that women lack penises suggests to him that his father's revenge will be extracted in the form of castration. This threat of castration, which is called *castration anxiety,* forces the boy to give up his wish to possess his mother. The resolution of the Oedipal conflict is said to occur when the boy *represses* (puts out of consciousness) his incestuous desires for his mother and identifies with his father. The latter process is called *defensive identification* and follows from the boy's reasoning thusly: "I cannot directly possess my mother, for fear of being castrated by my father. I can, however, possess her *vicariously* [through another's experience]. That is, I can get some of the joy of possessing my mother *by becoming like my father.*" The boy thus resolves his conflict by incorporating his father's behaviors, attitudes, and values, thereby simultaneously eliminating his castration anxiety, possessing his mother vicariously, and assimilating those behaviors necessary for appropriate sex-role behavior.

The Oedipus complex for the little girl, sometimes called the *Electra complex,*[4] is considerably more complicated and less clear than it is for

[3] The myth has been popularized by Sophocles' tragedy, *Oedipus Rex.*

[4] In Greek mythology, Electra persuaded her brother to murder their mother and their mother's lover, who together had killed their father.

the young boy.[5] The little girl's first object of love is also her mother. However, during the phallic stage, when her libido is centered in the genital zone, the little girl is likely to discover that while her father and other males (such as a brother) have penises, she and her mother (and other women) do not. She reasons that she must have had a penis at one time, and she blames her mother for her apparent castration. This, along with other disappointments in her mother (for example, those revolving around conflicts in earlier psychosexual stages), leads to some loss of love for her mother and subsequent increased love for her father. Her love for her father, which is erotically tinged, is coupled with envy because he has a penis. *Penis envy* is, in some sense, the counterpart of castration anxiety. However, unlike castration anxiety, which motivates the little boy to renounce his incestuous desires, penis envy carries with it no threat of retaliation by the mother, since the ultimate punishment, castration, has no meaning for the girl. It is not clear exactly how the feminine Oedipal conflict is resolved, although Freud does state that its solution comes about later in life and that it is never fully resolved. It is obvious that even though the mother does not hold the threat of castration over her daughter's head, she would express considerable displeasure over incestuous relations between her husband and daughter. Presumably the impracticality of fulfilling her Oedipal wish causes the girl to *repress* (put out of consciousness) her desires for her father and identify with her mother (i.e., *defensive identification*).

We have presented the general "formula" for the Oedipus complex, and it should be kept in mind that the exact pattern it takes for each individual is a function of his prephallic stage history and the specific familial circumstances during his phallic stage. Freud considered the resolution of the Oedipal conflict to be crucial, since he postulated that all neuroses were due to an incomplete (unsuccessful) solution.

Freud's ideas concerning infantile sexuality and especially the Oedipus complex are no doubt among the most difficult to comprehend or accept. This was true more than half a century ago when Freud introduced his revolutionary theory, as it probably is today for students being introduced to these notions for the first time. It is easy for us to accept the conflicts of the oral and anal stages; though we may not recollect being weaned and toilet trained, there is good evidence in our present behavior that we were. Not only is it not clear to us that we once had incestuous desires toward our opposite-sexed parent, but the very idea is completely contrary to our present morality. Freud's answer to such allegations was simply that we cannot remember nor accept our own Oedipus complex because we have long since repressed the ideas (as part of our resolution of the last conflict in our psychosexual development).

[5] It might be noted that, in general, Freud had more difficulty theorizing about women than about men.

Latency Period. Following the resolution of the Oedipus complex, at about the age of five, children of both sexes pass into a period known as *latency*. Latency is *not* a stage of psychosexual development, since during this period, which lasts from the end of the phallic period to the onset of puberty, the libido is said to become dormant with respect to the sexual instincts. The libido is channeled into activities such as school, interpersonal relations with children of the same age, hobbies, and so on. Freud said little about this period of life, although other psychoanalytic writers have placed considerable emphasis on it.

Genital Stage. The final stage of psychosexual development begins at puberty when the young adolescent starts to mature sexually and lasts through adulthood until the onset of senility, at which time the individual tends to regress to pregenital behavior (i.e., of the oral, anal, or phallic stage). The libido is again focused in the genital area but is directed toward heterosexual (rather than autoerotic) pleasure. An individual who has reached the genital stage without having left large amounts of libido fixated at one of the three pregenital stages will be able to lead a "normal" life, free of neurosis, and enjoy a genuine heterosexual relationship.

Although all psychoanalytic theories of personality place a heavy emphasis on the importance of early periods of development for later life, neo-Freudians have tended to de-emphasize the biological and sexual determinants of behavior and to focus upon social development. In order to illustrate how development can be conceived of with greater stress on social factors (from a psychoanalytic framework), we shall briefly outline the developmental sequence proposed by one prominent neo-Freudian, Erik Erikson. While Erikson does not discount biological and psychosexual influences on the developing individual, he emphasizes the influence of the individual's society and culture.

Erikson's "Eight Ages of Man"

Erikson has outlined eight stages of *psychosocial* development, each of which represents an *encounter* with the environment. Each stage is designated by a conflict between two alternative ways of handling the encounter, one adaptive and the other maladaptive. In a sense, all of the eight conflicts are present at birth, although they come to the fore at different periods of life. Thus, at a particular time they must be resolved (i.e., by adopting the adaptive alternative) for the individual to be fully prepared for the conflict which predominates next. A diagram of the stages, plotted against periods of physical and/or psychosexual development, is presented in Table 3–1. Each row of the table delineates a conflict at its particular time of ascendance. The purpose of the blank boxes is to emphasize the interaction among the stages of psychosocial

TABLE 3–1

Erikson's Diagram of the Eight Stages of Psychosocial Development

VIII	MATURITY								EGO INTEGRITY vs. DESPAIR
VII	ADULTHOOD							GENERATIVITY vs. STAGNATION	
VI	YOUNG ADULTHOOD						INTIMACY vs. ISOLATION		
V	PUBERTY AND ADOLESCENCE					IDENTITY vs. ROLE CONFUSION			
IV	LATENCY				INDUSTRY vs. INFERIORITY				
III	LOCOMOTOR-GENITAL			INITIATIVE vs. GUILT					
II	MUSCULAR-ANAL		AUTONOMY vs. SHAME, DOUBT						
I	ORAL SENSORY	BASIC TRUST vs. MISTRUST							
		1	2	3	4	5	6	7	8

Source: Erikson, 1963.

development. The blank squares appearing to the left of the square containing the name of the conflict represent the influence of stages which have passed (i.e., of conflicts no longer predominant), while the blank squares to the right represent the influence of later forms of conflicts which have not yet come to the fore.

Basic Trust vs. Mistrust. Initially, according to Erikson, the infant must develop sufficient trust to let his mother, the provider of his food and comfort, out of his sight without anxiety, apprehension, or rage. Such trust involves not only confidence in the predictability of the mother's behavior but also requires trusting oneself. This conflict occurs during the period of life which Freud referred to as the oral stage of psychosexual development.

Autonomy vs. Shame and Doubt. Next, the individual must develop a sense of autonomy. This sense is originally developed through bladder and bowel control and parallels the anal stage of traditional psychoanalytic theory. If the child fails to meet his parents' expectations in this regard, shame or doubt may result. The shame of being unable to demonstrate the self-control demanded by parents may become the basis for later difficulties, just as the experience of attaining adequate self-control in childhood may lead to feelings of autonomy in later life. Erikson (1963) suggests:

This stage, therefore, becomes decisive for the ratio of love and hate, cooperation and willfulness, freedom of self-expression and its suppression. From a sense of self-control without loss of self-esteem comes a lasting sense of good will and pride; from a sense of loss of self-control and of foreign overcontrol comes a lasting propensity for doubt and shame (p. 254).

Initiative vs. Guilt. Initiative vs. guilt is the last conflict experienced by the preschool child and thus occurs during the period Freud designated as the phallic stage. During this time, the child must learn to appropriately control his feelings of rivalry for his mother's attention and develop a sense of moral responsibility. At this stage, the child initially indulges in phantasies of grandeur, but in actuality he may feel meek and dominated. To overcome these latter feelings he must learn to take role-appropriate initiative by finding pleasurable accomplishment in socially and culturally approved activities, such as creative play or caring for younger siblings.

Industry vs. Inferiority. The conflict between industry and inferiority begins with school life or, in primitive societies, with the onset of formal socialization. The child at this time must apply himself to his lessons, begin to feel some sense of competence relative to his peers, and face his own limitations if he is to emerge as a healthy individual. Note that these important developments occur during the time when, from Freud's point of view, the child is in a period of latency.

Identity vs. Role Diffusion. With the advent of puberty the individual must begin to develop some sense of identity for himself. *Identity,* as used by Erikson, refers to the confidence that others see us as we see ourselves. Of particular importance for identity formation is the selection of an occupation or career, although other factors may be involved. If an identity is not formed, *role confusion,* which is often characterized by an inability to select a career or further educational goals and overidentification with popular heroes or cliques, may occur. Role confusion can be overcome through interaction with peers or elders who are informed about various professional or occupational opportunities (if this is the locus of the conflict) or who accept the adolescent's perception of himself.

Intimacy vs. Isolation. By young adulthood the individual is expected to be ready for true intimacy. He must develop cooperative social and occupational relationships with others and select a mate. If he cannot develop such relationships, he will be, and feel, isolated. This is the period which Freud referred to as the genital stage, and Erikson (1963) notes that when Freud was asked what a healthy person should be able to do well he curtly answered: "*'Lieben und Arbeiten'* (to love and to work)" (p. 265). Erikson feels this formula cannot be improved on.

Generativity vs. Stagnation. A mature man, however, must do more than establish intimacy with others. He "needs to be needed" and to assist the younger members of society. *Generativity* is concern with guiding the next generation, and if it is not accomplished, the individual may feel stagnated and personally impoverished.

Ego Integrity vs. Despair. If all of the preceding conflicts are not suitably handled, despair may result in later life. Disgusted with himself and correctly realizing that it is too late to start another life, the individual lives his last years in a state of incurable remorse. In contrast, to become psychosocially adjusted and have a lasting sense of integrity, the person must develop each of the adaptive qualities we have discussed. Erikson (1963) emphasizes that all men, regardless of their culture, can achieve such adjustment: ". . . a wise Indian, a true gentleman, and a mature peasant share and recognize in one another the final stage of integrity" (p. 269).

THE STRUCTURE OF PERSONALITY

Levels of Consciousness

Psychoanalysis divides the mind into three sections with respect to consciousness or awareness. The *conscious* part of the mind includes all that we are immediately aware of at a given point in time. Freud's conception of the conscious is very close to our everyday use of the term, with the possible exception that he held that only a very small proportion of our thoughts, images, memories, and so on, were contained in consciousness. Thus, the mind, like an iceberg, is nine-tenths below the surface.

The *preconscious* includes cognitions which are not conscious but can be brought into consciousness with little or no difficulty. For example, as you read these words you are trying to think about the material being presented. However, unless a test on this information is imminent (and perhaps even then), you could easily begin to think of an upcoming vacation or next week's date. These thoughts were in your preconscious.

Finally, we come to the area of the mind which plays the most important role in psychoanalytic theory, the *unconscious*.[6] Freud contended that most of our behavior is directed by forces (instincts, wishes, desires, and so on) of which we are totally unaware (that is, they are out of consciousness). In contrast to preconscious thoughts, unconscious ones enter consciousness only in disguised or symbolic form.

---

[6] The term *subconscious* is not part of formal psychoanalytic nomenclature, though presumably in its common usage it refers to everything that is below consciousness (i.e., the preconscious and unconscious).

In Freud's early theorizing, the concept of the unconscious played a major role. Later (around 1920) Freud revised his theory somewhat to include three basic structures—id, ego, and superego. The functions which were formerly relegated to the unconscious were now primarily taken over by the id. Basically, the relationship of the earlier and later constructs is that "all of the id is unconscious, but not all of the unconscious is id." The relationship of the personality structures to the levels of awareness is illustrated in Figure 3–1.

FIGURE 3–1

The Relationship of the Personality Structures to the Levels of Awareness

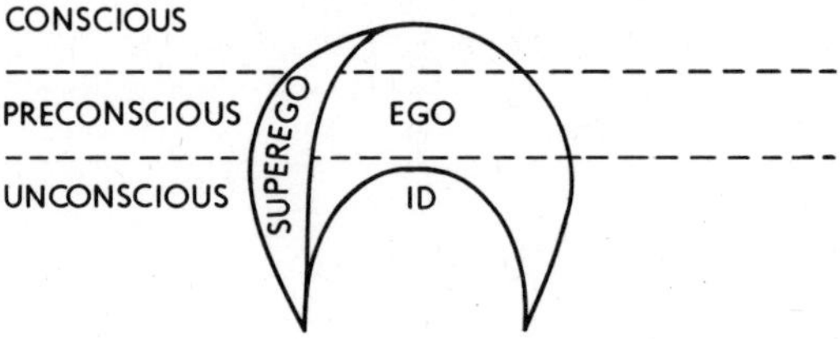

Source: Adapted from Wolman, 1968.

Three Structures of Personality

Id. The *id*[7] is said to be the original system of personality. It contains everything psychological that is present at birth. The id is a reservoir for all instincts and derives its power directly from bodily needs and processes. As bodily needs such as hunger and thirst build up, they must be satisfied, and the resulting increase in tension must be discharged. When the id alone governs this discharge, no *delay of gratification* is possible. The id cannot tolerate increases in energy and presses for immediate satisfaction. In other words, the id is governed by the *pleasure principle,* which we have already had occasion to mention.

The id employs two basic techniques for obtaining tension reduction —*reflex action* and *primary process.* The primitive id is a reflex apparatus which reacts automatically and immediately to various internal and external irritants to the body, thereby promptly removing the tension or distress which the irritant provides. Reflex action may be observed in such inborn mechanisms as sneezing, blinking, and coughing.

Since the id cannot tolerate any delay of gratification or of tension reduction, we would expect that very young children would "cry" for care as soon as an appetite or need appears which they cannot satisfy.

[7] Literally the "it," since Freud used the German word *es* in his original description.

(Infants are, of course, quite capable of satisfying some of their needs, such as the need to urinate.) This appears to be exactly what happens. Thus, when an individual's drive requires some object from the outside world, such as food or water, unless the object is immediately available, the id's *primary process* will form a memory image of the required object. For example, when the infant is hungry, the primary process will produce an image of food. This hallucinatory experience is called *wish fulfillment,* and remnants of it can be seen in adulthood as, for example, when a thirsty traveler imagines he sees water.

The primary process is a crude mechanism in that it is not able to differentiate between the actual required object which will satisfy a need and a memory image of the object (for example, between food and an image of food). Thus, although the id may be temporarily satisfied with a memory image, the primary process does nothing to actually reduce tension. Obviously, we cannot eat nor long survive on images of food. If the infant's needs were met immediately (as they were prior to birth), no problem would arise with the primary process. But inevitably there must be delay of gratification (a mother, for example, cannot be available constantly to nurse or feed her baby), and the infant must learn to tolerate the delay. The capacity to tolerate delay of gratification begins with the infant's growing "realization" that there is an external world (something which is "not me") which has to be taken into account and considered apart from, but interrelated with, the infant himself. This comes about with the development of the second structure of the personality, the *ego.*

Ego. The *ego* develops out of the id, which is to say that it "borrows" some of the id's psychic energy for its own functions. In contrast to the pleasure principle of the id, the ego is governed by the *reality principle* and has as its aim postponing the discharge of energy until an appropriate situation or object in the real world is discovered or produced. The ego does not attempt to thwart the pleasure seeking of the id, but rather it temporarily suspends pleasure for the sake of reality. Whereas the purpose of the primary process is to indicate what object or situation is necessary to satisfy a particular need, the role of the *secondary process* is to create a strategy for actually obtaining the satisfaction. The ego, then, is characterized by realistic thinking or problem solving and is the seat of intellectual processes. Daydreaming is an example of a secondary process which illustrates the reality-bound nature of the ego. Although we enjoy the pleasurable phantasy of a daydream, we do not mistake the phantasy for reality as we do in a nocturnal dream, which is a primary process.

For a person to function as an individual as well as a member of his society, he must learn not only to deal with the direct constraints of physical reality but also to adhere to social norms and prohibitions.

Further, he must conform to society's "laws" in the absence of external monitors (i.e., when there is no realistic fear of apprehension, punishment, or failure). Beginning around the third or fourth year of life, children start to judge and evaluate their own behavior independently of immediate threat or reward. Freud postulated that such self-control is maintained by the third personality structure, the *superego*.

Superego. The *superego* is the internal representative of the values of one's parents and society. It strives for the *ideal* rather than the real. Regardless of the utility of behavior, the superego will judge whether or not an individual's actions are *right,* whether they are in accord with the moral values of society.

The superego has been divided by many psychoanalytic writers into two substructures. The *ego ideal* represents the idealized behavior patterns of the individual in terms of the demands of society. Like one's parents, the ego ideal is said to reward the individual for acceptable action in the moral sphere. The *conscience,* on the other hand, is that part of the superego which punishes the individual through feelings of guilt for engaging in actions or even thoughts which society does not sanction.

How does the superego relate to the other structures of personality? The role of the superego in the life of the adult can be described by the following three points: (1) it inhibits, rather than just postpones as the ego does, the impulses of the id, particularly those of a sexual or aggressive nature; (2) it persuades the ego to attend to moralistic rather than realistic goals and presumably accounts for various types of self-sacrifice and altruistic behavior; (3) it directs the individual toward striving for perfection.

The presence of the id in personality is explained through instincts and bodily needs, and the ego develops because of the requirements of dealing with reality. These are plausible explanations and, presuming the structures, they require little elaboration. The explanation of the superego, because of the remarkable social function which it must serve, is considerably more complex.

Prior to Freud's treatment of the subject, internal restraints on one's actions of the kind we call "ethical" or "moral" were presumed to come from a "still, small voice" which had been provided by God (Brown, 1965). Freud argued that moral conscience is not born with man, and in fact, that quite the reverse is true. The neonate has no concern for the welfare of others and is interested only in his own immediate satisfactions. Moral concerns must somehow be acquired after birth.

Psychoanalytic theory discusses the development of the superego in terms of the child's "taking in" the values of his parents at about the fourth and fifth years of life. This process of "taking in" parental values, which is intimately linked to the Oedipal conflict, is explained in terms of four related concepts—*internalization, incorporation, introjection,* and *identification.* Although these four terms are sometimes used synonymously or interchangeably in psychoanalytic writings, important and interesting theoretical distinctions can be made among them. Internalization is the most general of the terms and will therefore be discussed first.

INTERNALIZATION. Children cannot discriminate between the values and beliefs of the external world and those to which they personally adhere (i.e., those in an "inner world"). Further, despite earlier theological suggestions to the contrary, it is now quite clear that humans are not born with innate values or attitudes, and it is unlikely that they develop them without some training by society. From birth onward the child is continually exposed to the values of the external world, and later these come to be adopted as his own. For example, "Daddy says it is wrong to steal" will become "It is wrong to steal." This transition, implying in the second instance that the child holds the value as his own, is the cornerstone of socialization. In psychoanalytic theory the process through which these representations of the environment become a part of the individual is given the general name *internalization.* By this definition, internalization includes virtually all imitation of others and lays the groundwork for what Rapaport (1951) called "socially shared thinking." For example, a man invited to a dinner party would know that a coat and tie was called for, and this reflects internalization of a socially shared standard.

INCORPORATION. Whereas internalization is the process of making expressions of the external world part of the individual's own reference scheme, the term *incorporation* refers to the *mechanism* whereby such internalization comes about. The term is derived from the psychoanalytic description of the oral stage of development. It will be recalled that pleasure during this period derives from stimulation of the lips and the oral cavity. The act of eating for example, is actually *incorporating* food from the outside world into the body. The child must learn to take food into his mouth, and this behavior becomes the prototype for taking in values and norms. Thus, incorporation is a general mode of responding and may be considered the primary mechanism of internalization.

INTROJECTION. When the ego or superego provide partial or complete barriers for an id impulse, *introjection* is said to have taken place. Used as a noun, "introjections" refer to those internalized prohibitions or restrictions which operate as barriers for suppressing or otherwise redirecting the asocial psychic energy of the id. Thus, the suppression of behaviors which are inconsistent with reality or those which are socially reprehensible but which lead to immediate gratification for the performer (such as theft, dishonesty in business, and so on) is introduced and maintained in the individual's personality through the process of introjection.

IDENTIFICATION. The psychoanalytic literature reveals that the term *identification* has been used in at least three different ways. First, identification refers to a perceptual process whereby the individual comes to match as well as distinguish his mental images from objects or events in the real (external) world.

Second, *defensive identification* refers to *sex typing* (becoming like the same-sexed parent) as a solution to the Oedipus complex. Third, *anaclitic identification* involves the child's coming to value his parents because of the love, warmth, and comfort which they provide for him. Because his parents act so as to satisfy most of the child's basic needs (although usually not as immediately as the id demands), the child becomes highly dependent upon them. The child comes to produce representational images of his parents and their behavior, and these images become psychologically satisfying to the child. Thus, the pleasurable experience felt by being in actual contact with his parents may now also be felt by being in contact (i.e., thinking about) with internal representational images of them. The rewarding experiences of this contact can become self-generating if the child matches his image to reality by *making himself similar to his parents,* a process which is called *anaclitic identification.* Anaclitic identification is basic to the formation of the superego, since when a child identifies himself with his parents he also identifies himself with their standards and ideals.

The Relationships among the Structures of Personality. To briefly summarize the development of the structures of the personality, recall that at birth only the id exists. Later, in response to the demands of reality, the ego develops out of the id. Finally, the superego develops as an outgrowth of the ego and serves as the societal or moral representative in the personality. When all three structures have been formed, the psychic energy which once belonged solely to the id is divided among the id, ego, and superego. The fixed amount of libido fluctuates among the three structures. As depicted in Figure 3–2, the ego serves as a mediator among the three basic forces acting upon an individual—the demands of the id, the requirements of reality (of the external environment), and the limitations imposed by the superego. It is therefore the task of the ego to see that instinctual needs are met in a realistic and, at the same time, socially approved, manner. The arbitration between forces acting within and upon the personality requires the expenditure of psychic energy. The more successful the ego is at minimizing intrapsychic conflicts, the more energy will be "left over" for the higher mental functions of the ego (for example, creativity).

Before leaving our discussion of the personality structures, it must be made clear that the id, ego, and superego are *hypothetical constructs.* They are "convenient fictions" created by Freud in an effort to under-

FIGURE 3–2

The Ego as the Mediator of Personality

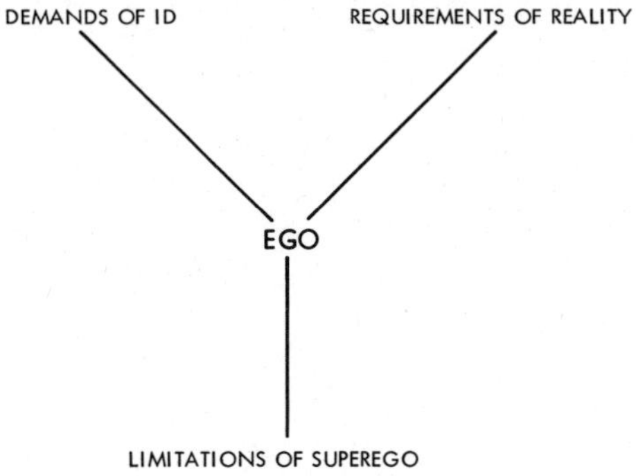

stand and explain the complexities of human personality. Although they are sometimes spoken of as if they were real entities which could be identified in the brain or even as if they were little men inside our heads (as when we say, "the id demands"), they are merely ways of designating different processes or functions of personality.

ANXIETY

In 1923, Sigmund Freud published a little book called *The Problem of Anxiety*. In it he asserted that anxiety was "the fundamental phenomenon and the central problem of neurosis." Reviewers have often noted that his concept of the development of anxiety is not clearly formulated (for example, Levitt, 1967). Despite both ambiguities and shifts in terminology that may be found throughout Freud's writings on this subject, a summary statement of the psychoanalytic concept of anxiety is both desirable and necessary to obtain an overall picture of psychoanalytic theory.

As we have mentioned previously, the prototype for all anxiety experienced in later life begins at birth. The individual leaves the shelter of the intrauterine environment and suddenly finds that his needs are not immediately satisfied in this new world. "A diffuse tension arises which is a consequence of the infant's vague awareness that his id needs may be frustrated because he is helpless to satisfy them by himself. He perceives dimly that he cannot survive without the attention of his mother" (Levitt, 1967, p. 21). This is the experience of *primary anxiety*. It is present until the individual begins to form an ego and mechanisms of defense.

Freud went on to identify three types of anxiety appearing in later life which are distinguished on the basis of the circumstances which provoke them. *Objective anxiety* refers to the fear and anticipation of danger provoked by a threatening object or situation in the external world. Feelings of apprehension for wild animals, military combat duty, and exposure to infectious diseases are often realistic, adaptive responses to one's environment. They have reasonable objective criteria, subside when the danger subsides, and realistically guide our behavior. Neurotic and moral anxiety, however, do not find their basis in reality and have been called the troublemakers with respect to psychological well-being (Levitt, 1967).

Neurotic anxiety begins with an id-ego conflict. The young child soon learns that some of his id-inspired demands can lead to punishment from parents or other social agents. The prospective clash between impulse and realistic constraints produces a danger signal, the experience of anxiety. This anxiety is at first conscious, but the ego soon takes control of untoward impulses and they are "driven underground" (repressed) and remain present only as an unconscious threat. Id impulses experienced unconsciously, although barred from action by the ego, persist in creating the experience of danger known as neurotic anxiety.

Moral anxiety, on the other hand, is generated by an id-superego conflict. When untoward id impulses begin to press for action (or are even experienced in conscious thought), the superego threatens with the punishing experience of *shame* or *guilt.* However, since the impulse itself is unconscious, the individual finds no conscious conflict which he can objectively handle, but instead finds the unpleasant experience of moral anxiety. Reduction of objective anxiety can be accomplished by sensible action in the face of danger, but neurotic and moral anxiety must be warded off by the ego defense mechanisms.

CONFLICT AND THE MECHANISMS OF DEFENSE

The production of satisfactory modifications or disguises for unacceptable impulses might be considered to be the very substance of what is *intrapsychic* about intrapsychic theories. Increases in psychic energy, emanating from the id, produce tension and press for tension reduction. This reduction is accomplished by attaching the energy to potential sources of gratification, a process called *cathexis.*[8] Broadly speaking, energy can be invested in external objects ("object cathexis") or in the self ("ego cathexis"). Emotional attachments to people, including parents, lovers, and enemies, to one's work, to ideals, and so on, exemplify the former. Varieties of self-love, which are sometimes extreme, characterize the latter. Barriers to particular cathexes and struggles for the

[8] *Cathexis* is both a verb and a noun, both process and object of the process. As a noun, the plural is *cathexes.*

investment of psychic energy are the hallmarks of intrapsychic conflict. What are the nature of these barriers? In most psychoanalytic writings they are described as energized opposing forces to immediate tension reduction and are called *countercathexes.* It is, however, difficult to reconcile the presence of such counteracting energy with the assertion that all energy emanates from the id. Where does the power to oppose id impulses come from? The best effort to resolve this inconsistency suggests that energy from the id is somehow "trapped" during the formation of the ego and superego. Blum (1953) has summarized it this way:

> As nearly as it is possible to figure out, the following seems to be the prevailing orthodox opinion: both the ego and superego in the course of their formation acquire amounts of energy which are specifically at their disposal. . . . In case of conflict . . . the ego calls its reserves to active combat duty to fight off the invading id impulses. This is the notion of countercathexis . . . (p. 103).

Conflict, as used above, can be defined as any situation in which the direction and discharge of energy demanded by one of the structures of personality is at odds with the requirements of one or both of the other structures. All the possibilities for conflict, along with an example of each, is presented in Table 3–2.

In principle, conflicts may be resolved by complete elimination of an impulse, the redirection of energy from its original objects, or by a

TABLE 3–2

Possible Conflicts of the Personality Structures and an Example of Each

Conflict	*Example*
ID vs. EGO	The choice between getting a small immediate reward and a larger reward which requires some period of waiting (i.e., *delay of gratification*).
ID vs. SUPEREGO	Deciding, when you are overpaid or undercharged whether to return the difference.
EGO vs. SUPEREGO	Choosing between acting in a realistic way (e.g., telling a "white lie") and adhering to a potentially costly or unrealistic standard (e.g., always telling the truth).
ID and EGO vs. SUPEREGO	Deciding whether to retaliate against the attack of a weak opponent or to "turn the other cheek."
ID and SUPEREGO vs. EGO	The decision faced by devout Roman Catholics as to the use of contraceptive devices.
EGO and SUPEREGO vs. ID	Choosing whether to "act on the impulse" to steal something you want and cannot afford. The ego would presumably be increasingly involved in such a conflict as the probability of being apprehended increases.

victory for the original impulse in undiluted form. In psychoanalytic theory, it is assumed that the first alternative can never occur. An impulse can be banished from conscious awareness but not from the total personality. The battle, then, is between redirection and unbridled expression of energy. The possible strategies of redirection receive considerable attention in psychoanalytic theory because they are said to give rise to and explain the final behavior which the layman sees as the personality of the individual. Since the strategies have the common feature of defending the individual from unreasonable or undesirable thoughts which lead to anxiety, they are called *defense mechanisms.*

Common Ego Defense Mechanisms

Although it is helpful for didactic purposes to distinguish among specific ego defense mechanisms, people rarely defend against anxiety with a single mechanism. An individual's characteristic modes of defense are typically a combination of different defense mechanisms. Furthermore, as will become apparent in the following examples, there is considerable overlap in the way the defense mechanisms operate to protect the ego from overwhelming anxiety.

Sublimation. Many instinctual impulses may be altered so as to be channeled to completely acceptable, and even admired, social behaviors. Depriving an impulse of its primitive character while at the same time allowing it some expression is the defining characteristic of *sublimation.* Psychoanalysts consider that many common human activities which are pursued vigorously reflect the sublimation of id impulses. The surgeon and the soldier, for example, may both be regarded as having found a socially acceptable outlet for sadistic impulses in their professional activities. Sublimation is the only truly *successful* defense mechanism, since it succeeds in permanently redirecting undesirable impulses. All other defense mechanisms are to some degree unsuccessful in that a continual warding-off of the disagreeable impulse is required.

Repression. *Repression* is the process whereby an undesirable impulse is actively and totally excluded from consciousness. As a solution of conflict it is characterized by a continual war to contain primitive desire. Psychoanalytic theory acknowledges that repression may occur in "healthy" individuals but, unlike sublimation, it exacts a severe price.

> Many impulses in the healthy personality are thus permanently banned from awareness, but at the expense of being excluded from the development of the total personality. It is as if the ego had slammed the door against a dimly perceived threatening intruder, but once the door has been shut, the ego will never know whether the intruder was indeed as threatening as he was believed to be, or, whether it is worth spending energy in keeping him out. . . . Once this energy is used for repressive purposes, it cannot be used as "free" energy in the task of adaptation (Strupp, 1967, p. 51).

In Freud's early writing, "repression" was used as a general term and considered to be synonymous with "ego defense." Thus, many of the remaining defense mechanisms may be construed as operating in the service of repression.

Reaction Formation. An important manifestation of repressing an impulse is said to be the active and vigorous pursuit of its antithesis. Persons who "really" desire one thing may often on the surface seem to desire its opposite. It is often difficult to tell whether a given bit of behavior is an undisguised manifestation of an impulse or a manifestation of the opposite of the apparent impulse. A single observation of a person's behavior is never sufficient to ascertain which is the case. However, if enough is known about the person to be sure that a particular behavior is in direct opposition to his more usual pattern of behavior, then it may be reasonable to entertain the hypothesis that *reaction formation* is responsible. But there is the possibility that the person's usual pattern of behavior is itself a reaction formation, and if this is the case, indirect assessment techniques are necessary to support the hypothesis that reaction formation has taken place.

An important hallmark of reaction formation is the persistence or excess of the behavior in question (i.e., "going overboard"), as Shakespeare (in *Hamlet*), who antedated Freud and the term reaction formation by more than 300 years, observed: "The lady doth protest too much. . . ." The apparently puritanical female, particularly one who responds with numerous gasps in the face of sexual advances, may be construed as the very person who is most seething with underlying desire and sexuality. Similarly, an individual's avowed love for a sibling or spouse may sometimes be interpreted as profound but disguised hate.

Undoing. *Undoing* is a defense mechanism which has been described as going one step beyond reaction formation (Blum, 1953). It is closely tied to the clinical syndrome of "compulsive behavior." Thus, an individual who has committed or has even thought of committing some act which is deviant according to prevailing ethics or morality may continually act out some retributive or "cleansing" behavior. Recall that both Lady MacBeth and Pontius Pilate washed their hands dramatically, as if to free themselves from the respective executions in which they were involved.

Projection. The legitimacy of a desire or a thought often depends on the condition of the outside world. For example, it is readily acknowledged by most people in our culture that it is wrong to cheat an honest man, but at least somewhat less reprehensible to swindle someone who was planning to swindle you. It follows that one way to assuage untoward impulses is to reconstrue the outer world so as to make our actions more acceptable. The defense mechanism of *projection* involves attributing our own unacceptable and disturbing impulses or strivings to someone or something other than ourselves. It has often been observed that, under stress, we tend to see in others precisely those characteristics which we abhor in ourselves. Thus, a student who cheats on examinations may attribute the "high curve" (and his own low grade) to the prevalence of cheating by others. Projection has been viewed by many psychoanalysts as a universal defense mechanism. It has provided the basis for personality assessment through various *projective techniques.* Finally, it should be noted that scapegoating is a form of projection.

Displacement. Whereas projection involves the attribution of an impulse to another person, *displacement* involves the shifting of an impulse from an unacceptable and threatening object in the environment to a more acceptable and less threatening object. A common example of displacement is that of the husband who is bawled out by his boss and rather than express his hostility toward him, which is obviously a threatening and unadaptive strategy, he redirects his anger toward his wife or children at home. As we shall see in a later section dealing with Freud's case of Little Hans, displacement is the primary mechanism involved in phobias. According to the psychoanalytic viewpoint, the phobia or irrational fear originates with a realistic or unrealistic fear of some object or person which cannot be easily avoided. In order to reduce the intense anxiety which repeated contact with the feared object induces, the individual displaces his fear to another object which he can easily avoid and which is symbolically related to the originally feared object.

Regression. One frequently used method of coping with frustration and anxiety is to escape to a mode of living that is more satisfying and pleasant. *Regression* involves such a retreat to an earlier period of development, which, for adults, is a pregenital psychosexual stage. Common examples of regression include sleeping, dreaming, smoking, fingernail biting, talking baby talk, getting drunk, overeating, breaking the law, losing one's temper, and so on. Hall (1955) interestingly notes that "some of these regressions are so commonplace that they are taken to be signs of maturity" (p. 96).

Rationalization. After performing an unacceptable act or thinking a threatening thought, people frequently alleviate the anxiety or guilt which ensues by finding a "perfectly reasonable" (rational) excuse for their behavior. *Rationalization,* as this defensive strategy is called, is often used as a mechanism for maintaining self-esteem. Thus, for example, when a young woman is "stood up" by her date, she may tell herself and her friends that she "really" didn't want to go out with the fellow. Such a rationalization has been colloquially labeled "sour grapes" after the fable of the fox who was unable to reach some grapes and thus concluded that they were sour.

Denial. Still another way to handle painful experiences and thoughts is to deny their existence. Sometimes a person will refuse to believe that a loved one has died and will continue to behave as if he were still alive.

A more common form of *denial* which most of us engage in from time to time involves phantasy or play. People may find temporary relief from reality by daydreaming about how things would be if some unpleasant circumstance had not occurred. Children deny their inferiority through play, as when a young boy assumes the role of a strict father while playing "house."

HUMOR AND THE UNCONSCIOUS

Laughter and humor are a pervasive part of human existence. Virtually all people enjoy laughing at a joke, funny story, or humorous incident. A good sense of humor is considered socially desirable, and we tend to look with suspicion on those people who do not laugh at our witticisms. In fact, there is a commonly held notion that laughter is a necessity for psychological well-being. Yet for all its pervasiveness in our daily lives, little scientific study has been made of humor. It is certainly legitimate to ask such questions as what makes a joke funny and why some people seem to laugh more than others. Although a number of philosophers have commented on the nature of humor in their writings (Thomas Hobbes and Immanuel Kant, for example), the first, and perhaps the only, comprehensive theory of humor was developed by Freud.

Simply stated, Freud's theory says that humor[9] serves the function of vicariously gratifying a forbidden impulse or wish. Freud's observation that more humor is concerned with sex or aggression than with anything else is probably no less true today than when he made the observation. The pleasure gained from humor arises from a sudden reduction of inner tension or anxiety. The anxiety is due to the intrapsychic conflicts concerning the expression of a strong drive or impulse. The id, governed by the pleasure principle alone, demands expression of the impulse, while the superego, the guardian of cultural taboos, fights to inhibit the expression of the impulse. Thus, for a joke to appear funny, it must first arouse some tension or anxiety and then relieve this tension. Consider the following joke. *Standing on a golf course green, one golfer is vigorously choking another to death. A third party arrives on the scene and casually says to the aggressor, "Excuse me, bud. Your grip's all wrong."* In the first part of the joke, the scene is set simply as an act of aggression which, because direct expression of aggression is frowned upon in our culture, leads to some amount of anxiety. What follows, the punch line, is funny

[9] Freud made a distinction between tendentious humor, which serves some aggressive or sexual purpose, and nontendentious (innocent) humor, which involves the pleasure from the mental activity of the joke technique (for example, puns, incongruities, and the like). In this section, we shall be speaking only of humor in the former sense.

because the theme is no longer aggression, but rather an unanticipated somewhat casual and *unrelated* remark. The change of content serves to reduce the tension. In Freud's words: ". . . *this yield of pleasure corresponds to the psychical expenditure that is saved*" (1960, p. 118).

Similar to the defense mechanism of sublimation in which unconscious and culturally taboo impulses are given an outlet in socially acceptable endeavors (for example, conventionalized outlets for aggression such as prizefights, football games, tennis matches, and other competitive sports), humor, according to the psychoanalytic writers, helps "normal" men control their primitive impulses.

> . . . wit is a product of civilization. It is a bypath for emotional outlet. Jokes that are particularly desirable are those dealing mainly with sex control or with other oppressions put on us by civilization [most particularly control of aggression]. If you can crack a joke of this type and thus give vent to some of your repressed feelings, you and your audience obtain a good, vicarious outlet. It is for this very reason that we can look upon jokes as disguised expressions of something that is very deep and fundamental but which must be held in check by civilization (Brill, 1955, p. 140).

Working primarily from Freud's notions of humor, a limited amount of experimentation has been conducted on the psychology of humor. We shall examine several recent studies.

If, as Freud suggested, inhibitions of impulses play a major role in the enjoyment of aggressive humor, then the following two hypotheses should hold: "(1) a heightening of inhibitions surrounding expression of aggressive impulses should result in decreased ability to enjoy aggressive humor; (2) this effect should be more pronounced the stronger and the more blatant the aggressive content of the humorous material" (Singer, Gollob, and Levine, 1966, p. 2). To test these notions, Singer and his associates first asked male undergraduates to rate five etchings by Goya. Half the subjects looked at brutal and sadistic scenes from the Spanish artist's *Disaster of War* series with the purpose of heightening their inhibitions against such wanton cruelty (inhibition condition). The other half of the subjects viewed five benign social scenes (control condition). Immediately following this phase of the experiment, the students were asked to rate a series of 12 cartoons for funniness and amount of aggression portrayed. Four of the cartoons concerned highly aggressive interpersonal incidents (for example, "A woman sits reclining in a chair. Beside her is a rifle aimed at the door with a string running from door to trigger. She says, 'It's not locked, honey!' "). Four other cartoons dealt with mild interpersonal aggression (for example, "A service station attendant is shown wiping the oil dipstick on his customer's tie as he comments, 'Oil's pretty dirty.' "). The remaining four cartoons had little or no aggressive content (for example, "A group of people and a zoo keeper are grinning widely in front of the hyena cage. The zoo keeper comments, 'Contagious, isn't it?' ").

As predicted, the subjects in the inhibition condition rated the mildly aggressive cartoons as slightly less funny and the highly aggressive cartoons as considerably less funny than the subjects in the control condition. Furthermore, the investigators made a partial check of the effectiveness of their inhibition-inducing manipulation by having subjects describe how they felt during the initial phase of the experiment (this was done after the experiment was concluded). It was found that significantly more inhibition than control subjects said they had felt "revulsion," "disgust," or "depression" while viewing the Goya works. Thus, when inhibition is operationally defined by these emotional reactions, the experimental hypotheses receive support. That is, persons do find aggressive humor less funny when their inhibitions concerning the expression of aggression are heightened. Furthermore, when these inhibitions are sensitized, the more aggressive the content of the humor, the less funny it will seem.

In the case of aggressive or sexual humor, Freud contended that in order for it to be considered funny rather than revolting or disgusting it must somehow distract the person so that he is not fully aware of the unacceptable impulses involved. Otherwise, the anxiety induced by the joke would be too great, and the ego defense mechanisms would be mobilized to mitigate the tension to the point where relief from it would not give rise to the pleasurable experience of humor.

It is no doubt a common occurrence for people to laugh at a joke and then, after some time has passed, find it distasteful rather than humorous when they think about the more unacceptable aspects of it. The so-called "sick jokes" which involve human cruelty or ridicule usually lead to such an experience (as, Son: "Why is mommy so pale?" Father: "Shut up and keep digging."). Gollob and Levine (1967) put these notions to an experimental test by having female subjects rate the funniness of cartoons (very similar to the ones employed by Singer *et al.*, 1966) both before and after they had their attention drawn to the aggressive content by asking them to explain the joke. The results of this study showed that whereas high-aggressive cartoons were judged to be highest in funniness initially, after the subjects were asked to explain them (10 days later), they were rated less funny than either low-aggressive or nonsense cartoons.

Freud's idea that humor involves an emotional release has more recently been couched in terms of the concept of physiological arousal. Humorous situations contain elements which make for heightened arousal (autonomic activation), while other elements serve to reduce the level of arousal. Thus, it follows that the greater a person's arousal before relief, the greater will be the funniness of the humor. In an ingenious experiment, Shurcliff (1968) tested this hypothesis. Using anxiety as an index of arousal, Shurcliff divided his subjects into three experimental groups corresponding to the degree of anxiety experimentally induced. Subjects were brought individually to the laboratory, ostensibly to assess their reaction to small animals. Three cages were visible to the subject but were arranged in such a fashion that only the occupants of the first two cages, white laboratory rats, could be seen. Subjects in the low-anxiety group were told that their task would be to pick up the rat in the third cage and hold it for five seconds. The experimenter emphasized that the rat was docile and that the subject should have no difficulty. For the moderate-anxiety condition, the subjects were shown two slides which supposedly contained blood samples from the rats in the first two cages. It was explained to the subject that he would have to obtain a blood sample from the third rat. He was instructed in how to do this and told that the task was easier than it appeared. Finally, the subjects in the high-anxiety condition also were told that they would have to draw blood from the third rat, but they were shown bottles containing "blood" from the first two rats and instructed in the procedure for taking a large quantity of blood with a hypodermic needle. These subjects were cautioned about the difficulty of the task and were told that the rat might bite them.

At the start of the task, the subjects in each condition reached into the third cage and, much to their surprise and relief, discovered a toy rat! They were then asked to rate the humor of the situation as well as their anxiety prior to seeing the toy rat (as a check on the effectiveness of the experimental manipulation of inducing different levels of anxiety). As predicted, the higher the subject's anxiety prior to seeing the "rat" they were to handle, the funnier they found the situation.

These studies, which attempt to validate Freud's theory of humor, are particularly significant because they represent one of the few aspects of psychoanalytic theory that has been operationally defined and put to a relatively rigorous test in laboratory experimentation. Furthermore, at present, there seem to be no viable alternative explanations which do a substantially better job of explaining the empirical results of these investigations.

REFERENCES

Blum, G. S. *Psychoanalytic theories of personality*. New York: McGraw-Hill, 1953.

Brill, A. A. *Lectures on psychoanalytic psychiatry*. New York: Vintage Books, 1955.

Brown, R. *Social psychology*. New York: Free Press, 1965.

Dement, W. C. An essay on dreams: The role of physiology in understanding their nature. In *New directions in psychology,* Vol. II. New York: Holt, Rinehart & Winston, 1965. Pp. 135–257.*

Erikson, E. H. *Childhood and society.* New York: Norton, 1963.

Fodor, N. *The search for the beloved.* New York: Hermitage, 1949.

Freud, S. *The interpretation of dreams.* J. Strachey (Trans. and Ed.). New York: Science Editions, 1961.

Freud, S. *Introductory lectures on psycho-analysis.* Vol. 15. *The standard edition of the complete psychological works of Sigmund Freud.* J. Strachey (Trans. and Ed.). London: Hogarth Press, 1963.

Freud, S. *Jokes and their relation to the unconscious.* Vol. 8. *The standard edition of the complete psychological works of Sigmund Freud.* J. Strachey (Trans. and Ed.). New York: Norton, 1960.

Freud, S. *Psychopathology of everyday life.* A. A. Brill (Trans.). New York: New American Library, 1951.

Gollob, H. F., and Levine, J. Distraction as a factor in the enjoyment of aggressive humor. *Journal of Personality and Social Psychology,* 1967, **5**, 368–72.

Hall, C. S. *A primer of Freudian psychology.* New York: New American Library, 1955.

Levitt, E. E. *The psychology of anxiety.* New York: Bobbs-Merrill, 1967.†

Mischel, W. *Personality and assessment.* New York: Wiley, 1968.

Rank, O. *The trauma of birth.* New York: Harcourt, Brace, 1929.

Rapaport, D. (Ed. and Trans.) *Organization and pathology of thought: Selected sources.* New York: Columbia University Press, 1951.

Shurcliff, A. Judged humor, arousal, and the relief theory. *Journal of Personality and Social Psychology,* 1968, **8**, 360–63.

Singer, D. L., Gollob, H., and Levine, J. Inhibitions and the enjoyment of aggressive humor: An experimental investigation. Paper presented at the meeting of the Eastern Psychological Association, New York, 1966.

Strupp, H. H. *An introduction to Freud and modern psychoanalysis.* Woodbury, N.Y.: Barron's Educational Series, 1967.

Wolman, B. B. *The unconscious mind: The meaning of Freudian psychology.* Englewood Cliffs, N.J.: Prentice-Hall, 1968.

chapter 4

The Intrapsychic Approach: Application of Principles

Having explored the major hypotheses and arguments of psychoanalytic theory, we now return to the major question of all conceptualizations of personality and ask how human behavior can be assessed, predicted, and modified within the framework of Freud's position. Our answer begins with the interpretation of dreams.

SYMBOLISM AND DREAMS

Freud assumed that human behavior is made complex by conflicts among the structures of personality. It follows that to understand any one man's personality we must reveal the particular conflicts which he is experiencing and uncover the mechanisms through which their resolution is being accomplished or attempted. Almost by definition, these conflicts are not going to be available to the individual's conscious awareness, and therefore we cannot simply ask him to describe the "wars" that are going on within.

Psychoanalytic theory argues that we can begin to unravel the personality through examining the disguised forms of conflict which make their way to the conscious surface of personality. This task may be partially accomplished through the exploration of symbolism and dreams. The argument is based on the supposition that, whereas conflicts and hidden desires are prevented direct expression by the defense mechanisms, "leaks" can occur in indirect or symbolic forms of expression. Dreams were seen by Freud as a fertile ground for discovering symbolic representations of conflict, and he considered the disguised impulses and desires to be found in them sources to be carefully analyzed.

Among the characteristics of dreams which Freud noted, two are particularly important. First, dreams typically reveal conflicts in a condensed form. *Condensation* is a technical term in psychoanalytic theory referring to the hypothesis that the expressions of a dream are highly compressed forms of the conflicts which they represent. Second, and closely related to the principle of condensation, is Freud's supposition that dreams are *overdetermined.* The characters and events in a dream rarely have a single meaning. Rather, they are the result of interactions of many psychological sources.

In his *Interpretation of Dreams* (1961), Freud recognized four sources of dreams which can operate *simultaneously:* (1) external sensory stimulation, (2) internal sensory excitation, (3) internal organic somatic stimulation, and (4) psychic sources of stimulation.

Freud (1961) made the following observation concerning *external sensory stimulation:*

> By unintentional movements during our sleep we may uncover some part of our body and expose it to sensations of chill, or by a change in posture we may ourselves bring about sensations of pressure or contact. We may be stung by a gnat, or some small mishap during the night may impinge upon several of our senses at once. Attentive observers have collected a whole series of dreams in which there has been such a far-reaching correspondence between a stimulus noticed on waking and a portion of the dream that it has been possible to identify the stimulus as the source of the dream (p. 23).

Such instances, as in the case where a ringing noise appears in our dream and we subsequently awaken to the ringing of our alarm clock, are familiar to us all. Freud makes it clear that identification of these events in no way precludes the possibility that the dream was also generated by other causes.

Internal sensory excitations, as described by Freud (1961), are only subtly different from external ones:

> . . . scarcely a single visual dream occurs without the participation of material provided by intraocular [within the eye] retinal excitation. This applies especially to dreams occurring soon after falling asleep in a dark room, while the source of stimulus for dreams occurring in the morning shortly before waking is the objective light which penetrates the eyes in a room that is growing light. The changing, perpetually shifting character of the excitation . . . corresponds precisely to the constantly moving succession of images shown us by our dreams (p. 33).

Internal organic somatic stimuli are said to play their greatest role when the internal organs are aroused (either chronically or acutely) beyond their usual level. Thus, Freud (1961) notes:

In the case of digestive disorders dreams contain ideas connected with enjoyment of food or disgust . . . the influence of sexual excitement on dreams can be adequately appreciated by everyone from his own experience and provides the theory that dreams are instigated by organic stimuli with its most powerful support (p. 35).

And what of *psychic sources of stimulation*, those which are of greatest interest to the theory? Two intrapsychic processes may give rise to dreams: (1) the desire to fulfill a wish which is not permitted direct expression and (2) the expression of dissatisfactions, apprehensions, and

TABLE 4–1

Some Common Symbols and Their Meaning in Psychoanalytic Dream Analysis

Symbol	*Meaning*
Emperor and empress (king and queen)	Parents
Elongated objects (sticks, tree trunks, umbrellas)	Penis
Boxes, cases, and chests	Uterus
Rooms*	Women
Steps, ladders, and staircases	Sexual intercourse
Playing with a little child	Masturbation
Water, bathing	Birth
Decapitation	Castration

* Freud (1961) notes: "In this connection interest in whether the room is open or locked is easily intelligible" (p. 354).

fears of which the individual is unaware in waking life. These intrapsychic sources of stimulation cannot manifest themselves directly and are therefore either symbolized or intertwined with the other three dream sources. The interpretation of symbolic dream material is acknowledged to be difficult work, but it is presumably made somewhat easier by the fact that some symbols are *universal* and therefore have a common meaning for all dreamers and dreams. Table 4–1 presents some of the universal symbols which are said to frequently appear in dreams.[1]

An Example of Dream Interpretation

To understand the manner in which dreams are interpreted, an example of a short dream cited by Freud (1961) will serve us well. The

[1] For Freud, symbols had almost exclusively a sexual meaning. However, other psychoanalytic theorists such as Carl Jung, an early disciple of Freud who later broke with him, have given a broader interpretation to symbolism.

dreamer, a patient of Freud's, was a woman who, we are told, was still quite young but had been married for a number of years. She had recently received news that a friend of hers, Elise L., a person of about her own age, had just recently become engaged to marry. Shortly thereafter she had the following dream:

> *She was at the theatre with her husband. One side of the stalls* [theater boxes] *was completely empty. Her husband told her that Elise L. and her fiancé had wanted to go too, but had only been able to get bad seats—three for 1 florin 50 kreuzers—and of course they could not take those. She thought it would really not have done any harm if they had* (p. 415).

Freud begins his discussion of this rather brief dream by analyzing the symbolic meaning of the monetary units. He notes first of all that this particular symbol has as a partial determinant an unimportant event of the previous day. The dreamer had learned that her sister-in-law had recently been given a gift of 150 florins (exactly 100 times the amount dreamt of) and had further hastened to spend this gift on jewelry. Freud also directs our attention to the fact that *three* tickets are mentioned in the dream, whereas Elise L. and her fiancé would, of course, only have required two tickets for themselves. Examination of previous statements made by the dreamer revealed a connection: ". . . her newly-engaged friend was the same number of months—*three*—her junior" (p. 415).

Attention is then given to the statement that one side of the stalls was entirely empty. Recently, when the patient had wished to attend a play, she rushed out to purchase tickets days ahead of time and, in doing so, incurred an extra booking fee. When the patient and her husband arrived at the theater, they in fact found that one half of the house was almost entirely empty. This bit of information, according to Freud, raises two important points. First, it accounts in part for the appearance of the fact of "empty stalls" in the dream. Additionally, and perhaps more important in terms of intrapsychic theory, there is the meaning of the empty stalls vis-à-vis the underlying meaning of the dream. In the patient's actual life, her experience with the theater tickets could clearly lead to the conclusion that she was excessively hasty about running out to buy tickets and thus had to pay an additional, unnecessary price. Freud assumes that the same *meaning* may be hidden with respect to her feelings about her own marriage and that, in symbolic form, they are revealed by the dream. Thus, the following final interpretation of the meaning of the dream for the patient is offered:

> "It was *absurd* to marry so early. There was *no need for me to be in such a hurry.* I see from Elise L.'s example that I should have got a husband in the end. Indeed, I should have got one *a hundred times* better" (a *treasure*) "if I had only *waited*" (in antithesis to her sister-in-law's *hurry*). "My money" (or dowry) "could have bought *three* men just as good" (p. 416).

Psychoanalytic theorists including Freud have tended to disparage the often used distinction between clinical practice and research. Thus, they consider the interpretation of dreams (of the kind presented above) to be valuable both as a clinical technique for the assessment of a patient's conflicts and as a method of research, the results of which may be used to support their theoretical position. While the analysis of dreams is both intriguing and penetrating, many personality psychologists have argued that such analyses are highly *inferential* and have thus eschewed the study of dreams as a legitimate scientific enterprise. Recently, however, William Dement and his associates have provided some powerful demonstrations that dreams and other phenomena associated with sleep may be brought under objective scientific scrutiny. Further, the evidence which these experimenters have gathered strongly suggests that value is to be found in Freud's general hypothesis that dreams are important psychological phenomena.

RECENT DREAM RESEARCH

Perhaps the major reason that systematic laboratory research of dreams was slow in developing is that these phenomena appeared to be entirely private events in which the only person who could serve as direct observer was the dreamer himself. Thus, "Although we may tell each other our dreams at every opportunity, there is no certainty that we are all talking about the same thing" (Dement, 1965, p. 138). It therefore appears possible to argue that dream research could not be subjected to proper scientific scrutiny unless the dream itself could be made to appear objectively, as on a television screen, while the dreamer was asleep.

Such television screens are not likely to become available in the near future, but some remarkable techniques for objectively studying dreams and other sleep-related phenomena have been developed. Perhaps the two most important of these are the continuous recording of brain wave patterns from sleeping subjects and the parallel recording of eye movements. Brain waves are recorded by means of an *electroencephalogram* (EEG), which is a tracing, plotted against time, of the frequency and potential (voltage) of electrical currents emitted by the brain (see Figure 4–1). The frequency of the electrical currents from the brain is measured horizontally on the EEG, so that the closer together the tracings, the greater is the frequency. The electrical potential is measured vertically on the EEG, so that the greater the amplitude or height of the tracings, the greater is the electrical potential. EEG recordings are made by placing electrodes directly on the scalp, a procedure which is painless, noninjurious to the subject, and does not appear to disturb sleep.

Eye movements have been measured during sleep in several ways, including taping the eyelids open, lifting the eyelids with fine threads, and placing small electrodes around the orbits of the eyes and measuring the differences in electrical potential produced by displacement of the eyeballs (Dement, 1965). Because of its minimal disturbance and highly precise measurement, the last technique mentioned is now the most favored. Figure 4–2 shows a subject wearing both brain-wave and eye-movement electrodes. Research with these measuring instruments has

FIGURE 4–1

Sample EEG Patterns for the Waking State and the Four Stages of Sleep

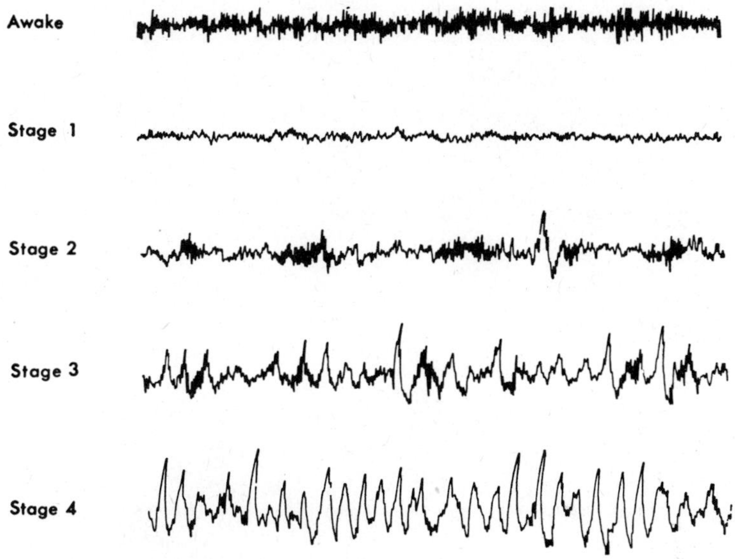

Source: Dement, 1965.

provided information which has proven to be of great value in understanding dreams.

EEG Patterns and Stages of Sleep

Prior to the systematic investigation of sleep, it was commonly thought that sleep was a more or less uniform state of the organism varying, if at all, only in its "depth." EEG research has revealed, however, four easily recognized stages of sleep which are distinguishable from waking patterns and from each other. Stages of EEG in the sleep cycle have been observed across species, and in humans they can be observed from birth to old age. A specimen EEG recording appears in Figure 4–1. The awake state is characterized by continuous fluctuations of 8 to 13 cycles per second. This pattern is often called the *Alpha Rhythm.* As Figure 4–1 shows, Stages 2, 3, and 4 are all characterized by bursts of waxing and waning waves which last about one to two seconds and have been called *sleep spindles.* Stage 1, as seen in the figure, is characterized by an absence of sleep spindles and has less Alpha Rhythm than found in the waking state. Not surprisingly, the original formula-

FIGURE 4–2

A Sleeping Subject with EEG and Eye Movement Electrodes

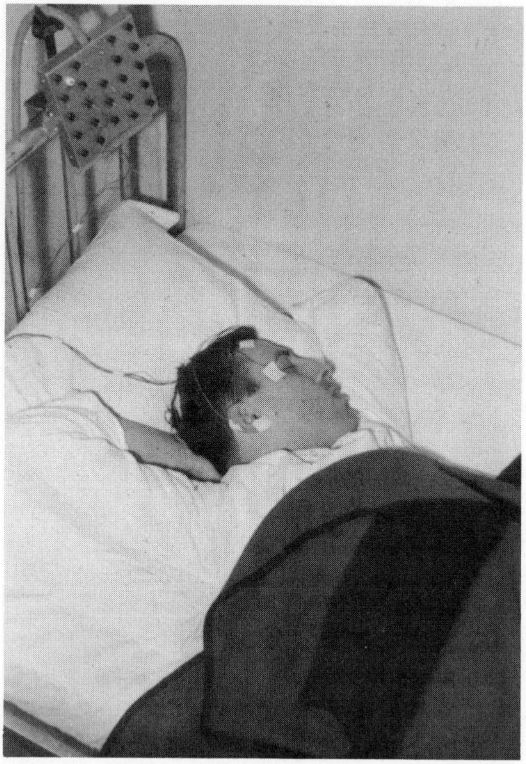

Courtesy of Dr. William Dement.

tion of this data was that the development of high-amplitude, low-frequency waves, which increase from Stage 1 to Stage 4, are correlated with a reduction in nervous activity and responsivity. In other words, it was hypothesized that Stage 1 is "light sleep" while Stage 4 is "deep sleep." However, as we shall see presently, this formulation requires some modification because of the unique characteristics of Stage 1. Thus, although the brief period of Stage 1 at the beginning of sleep may be considered "light sleep," the intervals of Stage 1 at the end of the sleep cycle do not fit onto a depth-of-sleep continuum with Stages 2, 3, and 4 because of the unique concomitant variables associated with this latter phase of Stage 1 sleep (for example, maximal relaxation and dreaming).

Eye Movements and the Stages of Sleep

Sleeping persons are not totally quiescent. Apart from a variety of gross body movements and the EEG changes which we have just discussed, they can be observed to make periodic eye movements underneath their closed lids. Further, one investigator (Rechtschaffen) reports that sleeping subjects (as determined by EEG) whose eyes were taped open can give "the uncanny appearance of being wide awake and looking about" (Dement, 1965, p. 151). During Stage 1 sleep, bursts of *rapid eye movements* (REM's) can be observed, and these have been called *rapid eye movement periods* (REMP's). Rapid eye movements appear to be characterized in the following ways: (1) they appear *only* during Stage 1 sleep; (2) they are very similar to the movements involved in visual perception while awake; (3) REM sleep is associated with greater muscular relaxation than found at any other time during the sleep cycle; and (4) REM sleep is not associated with gross body movements (interestingly, snoring does not occur during REM sleep).

Having reviewed some of the recently accumulated data relating sleep to physiological indices, it is appropriate to ask in what way do these advances lead to a greater comprehension of sleep and dreaming as psychological phenomena? It is to this question that we shall next turn our attention.

Sleep and Dreaming

In 1953, Aserinsky and Kleitman reported a major body of findings on REM sleep, much of which has been summarized in the previous section. They awakened their subjects from sleep a total of 50 times, 27 times when REM's were occurring and 23 times when they were not. Upon being awakened, subjects were asked if they had just been dreaming. When aroused from REM sleep, subjects answered affirmatively more than 70 percent of the time. In contrast, when awakened while REM's were *not* occurring, subjects reported that they were dreaming less than 18 percent of the time. This finding was a major breakthrough. In Dement's (1965) words, it was "the first time that a statistically significant correlation between an objectively measurable sleep variable and dream recall had ever been achieved" (p. 170). It was, however, only the beginning, and three major questions remained. Did dreaming, the subjective experience, actually occur during the period of rapid eye movement? Does dreaming occur *only* during rapid eye movement sleep? And finally, could this finding lead to a greater understanding of the role of dreaming for other human functions? Investigators interested in these questions now had a scientific foothold for pursuing them.

The first question has been approached in terms of two ingenious hypotheses. First, it was reasoned that if dreams actually occur during REM sleep, then the subjective duration of the dream should be proportional to the duration of rapid eye movement observed prior to awakening the subject. Dement's (1965) results were very positive:

> In one series of trials, subjects were awakened either 5 minutes or 15 minutes after the onset of REMs and were asked to choose the correct interval on the basis of whatever dream material they recalled. A correct choice was made in 92 of 111 instances. In another series, high correlation coefficients were obtained between the number of words in the dream narratives and the number of minutes of REMP preceding the awakenings. Finally, using the method of introducing an external subawakening stimulus into the ongoing dream . . . a precise amount of dream content could be delimited and later compared to the actual duration of the corresponding segment of REMP. When the delimited portion of the dream story was acted out, the time required was almost exactly the same as the duration of the objective record . . . (p. 172).

Second, and perhaps even more impressive, are the data confirming the hypothesis that the specific kind and direction of eye movement should be related to the reported content of the dream. In other words, does the dreamer scan his dream images in the same way that he would visually scan similar events in a waking state? Dement and Wolpert (1958) found that this was indeed the case. Their study showed that frequent individual movements during a REMP were associated with reports of active dreams (for example, running or fighting) while REMP's with sparser individual movements were followed by reports of less active dreams (for example, staring at a distant object).

The evidence suggests that dreams do in fact occur during REM sleep. Nonetheless, the possibility remains that dreams also occur at other times and that they are merely retained or recalled better during REMP's than at other times. Some dream recall has been reported for *nonrapid eye movement* (NREM) sleep, and therefore perhaps dreaming can occur during these periods as well. Nevertheless, some interesting data favor the conclusion that dreaming occurs only during REM sleep. The research strategy employed was to record a REMP but to hold off awakening the subject until the REM was terminated. If dreaming occurs only during REM sleep, it should be reported with decreasing frequency as the time between REM termination and awakening increases. If, on the other hand, some dreaming occurs in the absence of REM's, dream recall from an NREM period should not be related to the proximity of a REM period. But a clear relationship was obtained.

Dement and Kleitman (1957) reported 29 percent dream recall when subjects, *awakened during NREM*, were awakened within eight minutes after termination of a REMP. In contrast, awakenings following a REMP by more than eight minutes produced dream recall only 4 percent of the time. "The interpretation of these results was that dreaming . . . occurred only during REM sleep, and that occasional instances of NREM recall occurred when the memory of the dream persisted long enough to be recalled . . . after it had actually ended" (Dement, 1965, p. 189).

The practical value of these hypotheses and findings for the study of dreaming is apparent. The total amount of dreaming that a subject experiences can be measured objectively by recording eye movements and brain waves, stimuli can be introduced in an effort to modify dreams, and a person can be deprived of dreaming (by awakening him at the onset of every REMP) without his being deprived of sleep. If dreaming serves an important psychological function, examination of this last possibility should be particularly revealing.

The Consequences of Dream Deprivation

Fisher and Dement undertook a major research effort to determine the importance of dreaming in humans. Dement (1965) has described their initial procedures succinctly:

> Each time subjects began to dream, as indicated by the appearance of REMs and Stage 1 EEG patterns, they were awakened, kept awake for a few minutes, and then allowed to go back to sleep. This procedure was continued throughout the entire night. . . . Subjects slept in the laboratory without disturbance for several nights to evaluate their average nightly sleep time and average nightly dream time. They were then "dream deprived" by the above technique for two to five *consecutive* nights, and immediately following this, they were again allowed to sleep without disturbance for an additional number of "recovery" nights (p. 239).

The consequences of this procedure were striking. All of the subjects showed an increase in number of REMP's. To suppress dreaming, they had to be awakened progressively more often as deprivation time increased. Further, during the "recovery" nights, frequency of dreaming went up sharply. For some subjects, it was more than 50 percent higher than it had been during the original base line. In Dement's (1965) words: "It was as if the dreaming that had been lost was being made up —that an increased tendency to dream had been built up during the period of suppression" (pp. 239–40). And there were other consequences.

Recall that psychoanalytic theory posits the functions of dreaming to be the discharge of repressed impulses and the intrapsychic realization of unrealizable wishes. Presumably, then, consequences of dream deprivation should be found in the waking state. Such was the case. The investigators reported that all of their subjects showed some "abnormalities," including anxiety, irritability, fatigue, and loss of concentration; six of the male subjects developed ravenous appetites. Perhaps, however, these results are merely generated by interference with sleep and did not reflect the dream deprivation per se. Fisher and Dement were aware of this possibility and controlled for it:

> Each subject . . . underwent an additional series of awakenings which exactly duplicated the dream deprivation series, except that the awakenings fell outside of rapid eye movement periods. Each time an eye movement period started, it was allowed to continue without interruption. In this situation, the subjects were equally disturbed and lost an equal amount of sleep . . . (Dement, 1965, p. 240).

No increase in dreaming or other psychological disturbance was found for these controlled awakenings. Thus, it appears legitimate to conclude from these data that behavioral "abnormalities" observed when subjects were awakened during REMP's were due to dream deprivation.

In Dement's research with humans, it was decided to follow each deprivation period with a period of recovery, and the results clearly supported the desirability of this procedure. It is reasonable to hypothesize that long-term deprivation would have devastating effects on behavior, but obviously experimental research with humans cannot be ethically conducted in this regard. One investigator, Jouvet (1962; cited in Dement, 1965), has reported some relevant analogs with laboratory animals. He destroyed a small area of the brain[2] of cats, which led to complete cessation of REM sleep but left the animals normal in all other respects. Their behavior showed remarkable changes, including fixed staring, continuous foot movements, and perpetual agitation. Some animals, possibly because the lesion was incomplete, showed a recovery of REM sleep, which was soon followed by disappearance of their "abnormal" behavior. If REM sleep did not reappear, the cats died in a state said to resemble acute manic delirium. These data strongly suggest the importance of dreaming for psychological well-being.

There appears to be little question that dreaming, an intrapsychic event, is an important phenomenon that can be objectively examined and related to overt behavior. However, it should be noted that at least one effort to replicate Dement's findings, using a sophisticated design in which some subjects were deprived of NREM sleep before their REM deprivation, failed to obtain statistically significant results (Foulkes, Pivik, Ahrens, and Swanson, 1968). Foulkes *et al.* present an interesting list of methodological problems associated with REM deprivation re-

---

[2] An area in the pons known as the brain stem *nucleus pontis caudalis.*

search, some of which involve subjects' sophistication. For example, although the ostensible purpose of the experiment was to relate various aspects of sleep to body temperature (of which regular measures were taken), many subjects asked: "Is this going to be a dream deprivation experiment?" and one subject, after being deprived of NREM sleep, commented, "If you do this often enough, a fellow could learn how not to dream" (p. 412).

Perhaps further research will reveal more precisely the degree to which sleep and dreaming serve the functions attributed to them by psychoanalytic theory, and also clarify the role of subjects' expectancies in some of the outcomes reported thus far. Even at the present time, however, it is clear that psychoanalytic theory has provided the major impetus for an exciting line of research.

PSYCHOANALYTIC PSYCHOTHERAPY

The observations which led Freud to the elaborate theory of personality we have examined were made in the context of his clinical practice. Freud was educated as a physician specializing in neurology. In the latter half of the 19th century, the science of neurology was making little progress in treating mental disorders. One of the exceptions to this general state of affairs was the work of Jean Charcot in Paris, with whom Freud studied for about a year. Charcot used hypnosis in his treatment of hysterics. In hysteria, more commonly called *conversion reaction* today, the patient suffers from seemingly physical ailments, such as a paralyzed limb or a defective sense organ, for which no physical cause can be found. Charcot hypnotized his hysteric patients and then directly ordered them (hypnotic suggestion) to renounce their symptoms. The orders were generally effective as long as the patient remained in the hypnotic state. However, upon awakening, the hysterical symptoms almost inevitably returned. This peculiar and intriguing combination of success and failure seemed extremely important to Freud, and he was eager to find procedures which would make the hypnotic cure both more enduring and more understandable.

Shortly after returning from his studies with Charcot, Freud opened his private practice in Vienna and became associated with Josef Breuer, a prominent Viennese physician who also practiced hypnosis though in a slightly different way. Rather than directly willing his hysteric patients' symptoms away, Breuer asked his hypnotized patients to *recall* and then *relive* the traumatic experiences which had caused the hysteria. The patient's reenactment of the trauma which produced his neurosis was accompanied by a great emotional release in the form of tears and words and seemingly led to cure. Unlike Charcot's findings, these changes persisted after the patient awakened. Breuer hypothesized that it was the recollection of the events and the resulting discharge of dammed-up emotions (later to be called libido by Freud) which led to the alleviation of the symptoms and the cure of the neurosis. Indeed, the name given this treatment was *catharsis,* which is the Greek word for purification.

Freud initially treated his patients, who were almost exclusively hysterics, by hypnosis. He rejected Charcot's method of direct influence in favor of Breuer's more indirect "hypnocatharsis." But Freud was not always successful in hypnotizing his patients and soon substituted the technique of asking nonhypnotized patients to concentrate on recalling past events that were associated with their illnesses. He found that, given sufficient freedom, patients wandered in their thoughts and recollections and that this led to a superior understanding of the patient's unconscious processes. Freud called this technique *free association,* and it became the cornerstone of psychoanalysis.[3]

In free association, the patient is told to renounce his conscious censorship and say whatever comes to mind without regard to social convention, logic and order, seeming importance or triviality, and despite feelings of embarrassment or shame. These instructions have sometimes been called the *fundamental rule* of psychoanalysis. To facilitate free association, Freud had his patients recline on a couch while he sat behind and out of view of the patient. Such a position, reminiscent of sleep, was thought to bring a person closer to unconscious primary processes and to stimulate phantasy and memory. With the therapist out of view, the patient is not constantly reminded of his presence, and free association is thereby made easier. This physical setup also gives the therapist more freedom, since he does not have to be aware of his own facial expressions, movements, and reactions.

The term *psychotherapy* has come to be thought of as synonymous with a "talking cure," although with new psychotherapeutic techniques, such as the so-called *behavior therapies* (see Chapters 10–12), this equation is becoming an overgeneralization. But almost a century ago, when Freud began to practice psychoanalysis, verbal psychotherapy was virtually unknown. Even more startling was the revolutionary change in the patient-therapist relationship which took place in the treatment of psychological disturbances. Hitherto the patient had played only a passive role in his cure, while the physician had actively treated him. Freud's new therapeutic procedures reversed these roles. Now it became the patient's job to work (to free-associate and reenact important childhood experiences) and the therapist's task to act as a compassionate but neutral observer who occasionally made significant interpretations about the origin and nature of the patient's intrapsychic conflicts. Many of

---

[3] The term *psychoanalysis* has been used thus far as the name of Freud's personality theory. Here the term refers to psychoanalytic psychotherapy. In this latter sense, *psychoanalysis* and *psychoanalyst* (one who performs psychoanalysis) are often abbreviated as *analysis* and *analyst,* respectively.

Freud's contemporaries reacted in astonishment to this new psychotherapy, and remarked indignantly that Freud *listened* to his patients! But, perhaps because Freud's treatment was often successful, psychoanalytic psychotherapy caught on fast. In fact, many of both Freud's followers and his detractors urged him to write more on treatment techniques and less on his theory of the mind.

Freud viewed all mental illness as a manifestation of repressed conflicts and dammed-up libido which is seeking expression. However, because of the traumatic or culturally taboo nature of these conflicts, they cannot come to the surface (i.e., become conscious). Thus, Freud reasoned that the goal of psychotherapy must be to bring wishes, thoughts, and emotions which have long since been repressed out of awareness (i.e., in childhood) into the conscious part of the mind. Free association is the initial step in penetrating the unconscious, but free association is not sufficient in and of itself. Unconscious material comes to the conscious surface only in disguised fashion or symbolic form during free association (as it does in dreams). It is thus the task of the analyst (therapist) to translate the symbolism and interpret this unconscious material for the patient. Besides the patient's free associations, interpretations are made of dreams, symptoms, behavior in and out of therapy, the patient's relation to the analyst, past experiences, and so on. The analyst's interpretations help to reconstruct childhood experiences which led to the conflict producing the neurosis.

In Freud's own words, this process:

> . . . resembles to a great extent an archaeologist's excavation of some dwelling-place that has been destroyed and buried. . . . The two processes are in fact identical, except that the analyst works under better conditions and has more material at his command to assist him, since what he is dealing with is not something destroyed, but something that is still alive. . . . But just as the archaeologist builds up the walls of the building from the foundations that have remained standing, determines the number and position of the columns from the depressions in the floor and reconstructs the mural decorations and paintings from the remains found in the debris, so does the analyst proceed when he draws his inferences from the fragments of memories, from the associations and from the behavior of the subject of analysis (cited in Wolman, 1968, pp. 168–69, from S. Freud, Construction in psychoanalysis. In *The standard edition of the complete psychological works of Sigmund Freud.* Vol. 23. London: Hogarth Press and the Institute for Psycho-analysis, 1962. Pp. 257–69).

From the analyst's interpretations the patient gains insight into the nature and origin of his neurosis. Insight is not a mere intellectual understanding of his personality and its inner conflicts and drives. Rather it is an *experiencing* of parts of the personality which have become unconscious. As the neo-Freudian Frieda Fromm-Reichmann put it:

The aim of psychoanalytic therapy is to bring these rejected drives and wishes, together with the patient's individual and environmental moral standards, which are the instruments for his rejections, into consciousness and in this way place them at his free disposal. In doing this the conscious self becomes strengthened, since it is no longer involved in the continuous job of repressing mental content from his own awareness. The patient can then decide independently which desires he wants to accept and which he wishes to reject, his personality no longer being warped or dominated by uncontrollable drives and moral standards. This process permits growth and maturation (cited in Munroe, 1955, p. 520).

Early in his treatment of neurotics, Freud observed that his patients often resisted being cured. *Resistance,* as Freud came to call these impediments to successful treatment, can be both conscious and unconscious. In the former case, the patient is aware that he is somehow impeding his progress in analysis. For example, a patient who does not want to talk about a dream or thoughts which are passing through his mind is consciously resisting. In unconscious resistance, the patient is not aware that he is "fighting" the treatment. For example, the ego defense mechanisms may keep unconscious material from coming out in free association, or the patient may forget to come to a therapy session (unconsciously motivated forgetting). Unconscious resistance is more difficult to overcome than its conscious counterpart, but at the same time it is more significant, since it is another manifestation of the patient's unconscious strivings.

Perhaps the most important of all forms of unconscious resistance is that of *transference.* Transference refers to all the feelings that the patient experiences toward the analyst which are *distorted displacements* from significant figures in the patient's past. For example, the patient may act as if the analyst were his father or mother. Transference can be both positive (involving feelings of love, respect, or admiration) and negative (involving emotions such as hatred, jealousy, and disgust). Freud viewed transference rather narrowly in that he considered all transference to be a reliving of the patient's Oedipus complex. This viewpoint is consonant with Freud's conception that all neurosis has its origin in an unsuccessful resolution of the Oedipus complex. Thus, Freud maintained that psychotics and patients with so-called *character disorders* (long-standing maladaptive patterns of living) were not amenable to psychoanalytic treatment. These people were presumed to be fixated at prephallic stages of psychosexual development, which meant that much of their psychic energy had been invested or fixated in earlier conflicts and was therefore not available for transference. But as early as 1920 many psychoanalysts other than Freud began to broaden the definition of transference to include the reenactment of feelings to significant adults which occurred in any stage of development. The view that psychotics and persons manifesting other nonneurotic disorders could form a transference relationship with the analyst led a number of psychotherapists to begin treating such patients by psychoanalysis (for example, Sullivan with schizophrenics and Reich with character disorders).

Transference is an impediment to psychoanalysis because it is an inappropriate reaction. The analyst is not really the patient's father. At the same time, the inappropriateness of the patient's feelings makes transference an excellent illustration for the patient of his significant earlier experiences and their importance to him. An integral aspect of psychoanalysis is the interpretation of instances of transference. Relative to other interpretations which the patient is asked to accept (emotionally as well as intellectually) and about which he is expected to gain insight into his past, interpretations of the patient's feelings toward the analyst are easily seen as inappropriate in the therapy situation (i.e., the analyst gives the patient no provocation to either love or hate him) but pertinent in another situation (i.e., some significant relationship in the patient's childhood). Thus, transference is both a form of resistance and a road to the unconscious.

Although in traditional psychoanalysis the analyst's role is one of a neutral observer, occasionally he may inadvertently become emotionally involved with his patient during a therapy session. This is most likely to occur when a transference reaction is in progress. For example, because of the analyst's own childhood experiences and conflicts, he might be particularly vulnerable to feelings of flattery in response to a female patient's sexual desires for him or to feelings of anger in response to a male patient's hostility toward him. Freud called such transference of the analyst's past experiences to the therapy situation *countertransference*. Just as the patient must be made aware of the fact that some of his feelings toward the therapist are displaced from an earlier time and from a different person, so too the therapist must understand the nature of his countertransference. In the case of the patient's transference, it is the analyst who interprets the significance of the feelings for the patient. The analyst must also make similar interpretations for himself with regard to countertransference, and in order to do this successfully, he must be aware of his own childhood conflicts, unconscious desires and thoughts, personality weaknesses, defense mechanisms, and so on. This is one of the major reasons that an essential part of a psychoanalyst's training is his own psychoanalysis.

"AN ANALYSIS OF A PHOBIA IN A FIVE-YEAR OLD BOY"

The major research method of psychoanalytic theory has been the case history. Freud spent almost 12 hours per day for most of his professional life seeing patients, and he used their case histories as both the source of hypotheses for building his theory and as evidence to support the theory that emerged. It is therefore appropriate, in order to indicate the nature of psychoanalytic evidence, to describe in some detail one such case history. "The Analysis of a Phobia in a Five-year Old Boy" (Freud, 1957) is an unusual case in that Freud saw the boy, Hans, only once. Nonetheless, he relied heavily on this case, and others have widely acclaimed it as a cornerstone of evidence for psychoanalytic theory. Glover (1956) has noted:

> In its time the analysis of Little Hans was a remarkable achievement and the story of the analysis constitutes one of the most valued records in psycho-analytical archives. Our concepts of phobia-formation, of the positive Oedipus complex, of ambivalence, castration anxiety, and repression, to mention but a few, were greatly reinforced and amplified as the result of this analysis (p. 76).

The case material which forms the basis for the analysis was collected by Little Hans's father, a close friend and intellectual disciple of Freud's who kept detailed records of his son's development and regularly reported to Freud concerning the boy's problems and difficulties through the first four years of his life.

The first observation of importance for the case was made when Hans was three. At this time, he began to show considerable interest in his penis, which he referred to as his "widdler." This interest naturally led to tactile examination of the organ, and one day, when he was about three and a half, his mother found him engaged in what was presumably autoerotic play. She threatened him thusly: " 'If you do that, I shall send for Dr. A. to cut off your widdler. And then what will you widdle with' " (Freud, 1957, pp. 7–8). Hans also developed an interest in the widdlers of other people and of animals. He was particularly interested in seeing his mother undressed so that he could inspect her widdler.

When Hans was three and a half, his baby sister, Hanna, was born, a significant event which Freud (1957) described as "The most important influence upon the course of Hans' psychosexual development" (p. 113). Two major reactions are recorded in conjunction with this event. First, Hans expressed overt hostility toward the new arrival. Part of the hostility, however, was soon suppressed and disguised by symbolism. Freud notes: "From that time forward fear that yet another baby might arrive found a place among his conscious thoughts . . . his hostility, already suppressed, was represented by a special . . . fear of the bath" (p. 114). It will be recalled that *bath* symbolizes birth (Table 4–1).

Hans soon developed a network of related irrational fears or *phobias* which reflected the intrapsychic conflict which he was now experiencing. First, while in the street, he was "seized with an attack of anxiety," but no object was initially identified with the anxiety. It had, presumably, grown from the periods of depression in which he was separated from his mother, as when Hanna was born, but its character had become changed. "It soon became evident that his anxiety was no longer reconvertible into longing; he was afraid even when his mother went with him" (p. 114). Moreover, a more specific fear soon emerged from the more generalized longing and anxiety. Thus, "in the meantime indications appeared of what it was to which his libido (now changed to anxiety) had become attached. He gave expression to the quite specific fear that a white horse would bite him" (pp. 114–15).

Further, we learn that the onset of the problem was not as sudden as it initially appeared. In fact, it was immediately antedated by a dream to which Freud ascribes considerable importance, and which occurred a few days before the first attack of anxiety. In the dream Hans's mother had gone away. Freud comments:

> This dream alone points to the presence of a repressive process of ominous intensity. We cannot explain it, as we can so many other anxiety-dreams, by supposing that the child had in his dream felt anxiety arising from the somatic cause and had made use of the anxiety for the purpose of fulfilling an unconscious wish which would otherwise have been deeply repressed. We must regard it rather as a genuine punishment and repression dream, and, moreover, as a dream which failed in its function, since the child woke from his sleep in a state of anxiety. We can easily reconstruct what actually occurred in the unconscious. The child dreamt of exchanging endearments with his mother and of sleeping with her; but all the pleasure was transformed into anxiety, and all the ideational content into its opposite (p. 118).

Shortly after these incidents, Hans's father began, under Freud's direction, the first bit of therapy. Hans was told by his parents that his anxiety was a consequence of masturbation, and he was advised to break the habit. Further, he was encouraged to explore his memory and subsequently disclosed an incident of the previous summer which appeared related to his now profound fear of horses. He recalled hearing a father admonish his daughter: " 'Don't put your finger to the horse; if you do, it'll bite you' " (p. 119). We are instructed by Freud to observe the similarity between this expression and the earlier warning which Hans himself had received from his mother regarding masturbation.

The analysis undertaken by Hans's father was judged to be meeting with some success in overcoming the boy's presumed fear of castration. Several incidents soon occurred which were interpreted as a symbolic expression of his appetite for his mother. Hans developed a phantasy or waking daydream in which there were two giraffes and one was heard to cry out because Hans had taken away the other. In the second phantasy incident, Hans imagined himself forcing into "a forbidden space," and in the third he was smashing a train window. Freud notes:

Some kind of vague notion was struggling in the child's mind of something that he might do with his mother by means of which his taking possession of her would be consummated; for this elusive thought he found certain pictorial representations, which had in common the qualities of being violent and forbidden, and the content of which strikes us as fitting in most remarkably well with the hidden truth. We can say only that they were symbolic phantasies of intercourse. . . . (pp. 122–23).

Hans was at this point informed by his father that he was really afraid of his father rather than of horses, and that this fear existed because he, Hans, simultaneously harbored jealousy of his father and hostile wishes against him. Hans was told that the similarity between his father and the horses might be noted. Freud observes: "The black on the horses' mouths and the things in front of their eyes (the moustaches and eyeglasses which are the privileges of a grown-up man), seemed . . . to have been directly transposed from his father to the horses" (p. 123). After this phase of the analysis, carts, furniture vans, horses that looked big and heavy or moved quickly or *fell down* all became fear-provoking objects or incidents to Hans. Soon a new recollection from the past appeared, and a resultant therapeutic effort was made. Hans recalled:

He went for a walk with his mother, and saw a bus-horse fall down and kick about with its feet. . . . He was terrified, and thought the horse was dead; and from that time on he thought that all horses would fall down. His father pointed out to him that when he saw the horse fall down he must have thought of him, his father, and have wished that he might fall down in the same way and be dead . . . a little while later he played a game consisting of biting his father, and so showed that he accepted the theory. . . . From that time forward his behavior to his father was unconstrained and fearless, and in fact a trifle overbearing (p. 125).

However, the fear of horses did not go away, and a new intrapsychic preoccupation appeared. Hans became concerned about defecation, and developed a "lumf" complex. Explanation of these thoughts was said to be found in "an analogy between a heavily loaded cart and a body loaded with faeces, between the way in which a cart drives out through a gateway and the way in which faeces leave the body, and so on" (p. 127). That the lumf complex was in fact related to procreation was corroborated, Freud argues, by another, newer phantasy. Hans imagined that a plumber unscrewed the bath in which he was sitting and then, with "his big borer," the plumber stuck Hans in the stomach. Soon Hans was afraid of bathing in the big tub in his home, and at the same time confessed the wish that his mother might drop Hanna in the bath while bathing her. His own fear of bathing was said to be a fear of retribution.

How can a fear of heavily laden carts, a preoccupation with lumf, and falling horses be related to one another and interpreted? Freud was prepared to suggest the following:

. . . little Hanna was a lumf herself—that all babies were lumfs and were born like lumfs. We can now recognize that all furniture vans and drays and buses were only storkbox carts, and were only of interest to Hans as being symbolic representations of pregnancy; and that when a heavy or heavily loaded horse fell down he can have seen in it only one thing—a childbirth, a delivery. Thus, the falling horse was not only his dying father but also his mother in childbirth (p. 128).

Freud reports several additional phantasies, similar to and supportive of those mentioned already, and finally two concluding phantasies with which both the case and the therapy end. In one of them, Hans imagined that the plumber gave him a new and bigger widdler than he had previously possessed. Freud describes this as "a triumphant, wishful phantasy, and with it he overcame his fear of castration" (p. 131). The last phantasy clearly acknowledged Hans's Oedipal desire. He dreamt of marrying his mother and having many children by her. Instead of patricide, this phantasy "promotes" Hans's father to marriage with his grandmother. And thus, Freud says, "With this phantasy both the illness and the analysis came to an appropriate end" (p. 132).

PROJECTIVE TECHNIQUES

The intrapsychic approach to personality places a heavy emphasis on unconscious factors in the determination of behavior. Since the individual is (by definition) not directly aware of these factors, indirect methods of assessment are necessary to uncover the unconscious determinants of behavior. We have already discussed analysis of slips of the tongue and "accidental" mistakes, interpretation of dreams, and free association as means of getting a glimpse into a person's unconscious. In this section, we shall turn our attention to the use of *projective techniques* in assessing unconscious motives and feelings. While their major application is in clinical settings, projective techniques are also used in personality research (for example, Murray's Thematic Apperception Test, which will be discussed in Chapter 8).

The Nature of Projective Techniques

All projective techniques are based on the assumption, which can be called the "projective hypothesis," that when an individual is forced to impose meaning or order on an ambiguous stimulus or situation, his response will be a projection or reflection of his feelings, attitudes, desires, urges, and so on (compare the earlier discussion on projection as a mechanism of defense, pages 61–62).

There are a variety of existing projective techniques with a wide range of stimulus materials and responses required of the subject. Some projective techniques require that the subject make *associations* to stimuli such as ink blots or words. Some involve the *construction* of stories about pictures which are open to a variety of interpretations (for example, the Thematic Apperception Test). Other projective techniques require the subject to *complete* sentences (such as "I often feel . . .") or stories. In still other projective techniques, the subject must *express* himself through drawings (for example, the Draw-a-Person Test) or by acting out a loosely specified role (as in psychodrama). Finally, there are projective techniques in which the subject *chooses* between a variety of stimuli indicating those he likes best and least (for example, in the SzondiTest the stimuli are photographs of psychiatric patients with different diagnoses) or *orders* stimuli (as in the Picture Arrangement Test).

Although there is considerable variety in the type of stimuli presented to the subject and the type of response required of him, all projective techniques have several important characteristics in common. The stimulus material, be it an ink blot, a picture, or the first part of a sentence, is relatively unstructured and ambiguous, which means that the subject is forced to impose some order or structure of his own. The subject is usually not told the purpose of the test, nor is he usually aware of how his responses will be scored or interpreted. The subject is told that there are no "right" or "wrong" answers. Each response is considered to reveal a true and significant aspect of the individual. Finally, the scoring and interpretation of projective methods of personality assessment are generally lengthy and relatively subjective procedures.

It should be noted that we have in our discussion thus far referred to projective *techniques* rather than projective *tests*. Although some projective techniques may appear quite similar to assessment procedures which are commonly called tests (sentence completion techniques, for example, are reminiscent of "fill-in-the-blank" items used in school examinations), others are substantially different from the usual variety of tests. Additionally, and of more significance, most projective techniques do not meet the generally agreed upon psychometric standards of a test (for example, they are not standardized; see Anastasi, 1968).

In keeping with the purpose of this book (i.e., to provide the reader with a basic grasp of the strategies which have been used to conceptualize personality), we shall illustrate the general nature of projective techniques with a discussion of the most widely used projective procedure, the Rorschach Ink Blots.

The Rorschach Ink Blots

Although the use of ink blots to learn something about an individual (for example, his imaginativeness) was not a new idea when Hermann Rorschach, a Swiss psychiatrist, began his experiments in the early part of the 20th century, Rorschach was the first to make a systematic attempt to assess personality by the use of a standard set of blots. His efforts began with experiments on a variety of geometric forms in different colors. Later Rorschach shifted his interest to less structured ink blots. The results of his work were first published in his 1921 monograph entitled *Psychodiagnostik,* which was subtitled "Methodology and results of a perceptual-diagnostic experiment (interpretation of accidental forms)." Regrettably, Rorschach died the year after the publication of his monograph, and it was left to others to elaborate on the basic procedures he had outlined.

Description of the Ink Blots. The Rorschach Ink Blot technique (usually called simply the "Rorschach") consists of 10 nearly symmetrical ink blots, 5 of which have some color and 5 of which are in black and white. The blots are printed and centered on pieces of white cardboard slightly less than 7 inches by 10 inches in size. Figure 4–3 (page 90) presents ink blots similar to the kind used in the Rorschach. The blots were originally made by spilling ink on a piece of paper and then folding the paper in half.

Administration. The Rorschach is usually administered individually, although there has been some experimentation with group forms (for example, Harrower and Steiner, 1944; Hire, 1950). The administration of the ink blots is typically divided into two basic phases. In the *performance proper,* the examiner merely tells the subject that he is going to be shown a number of ink blots and his task will be to tell what he sees in each of them. Sometimes it is necessary for the examiner to explain the task further (he may add, "People see different things in the ink blots, and I want to know what you see"), but in order to keep the task unstructured, the examiner tries to say as little as possible. During the performance proper, the examiner merely records *what* the subject tells him he sees in each blot. Additionally, a record is kept of the subject's reaction time (the time from the presentation of the card to the subject until his first response), the total time taken to respond to each blot, and the position in which the card is held while the subject is making each response. If the subject asks whether he may turn the card, how many responses he should make for each blot, or similar questions, the examiner tries to respond in such a way so as to leave the decision to the subject.

When the subject has finished responding to all 10 ink blots, the second phase of the administration, the *inquiry,* begins. Starting with the first card again, the examiner reminds the subject of each of his responses and inquires *where* on the blot he saw what he did and *how* he saw each response (i.e., what about the ink blot made it look like it did).[4]

---

[4] Two additional phases are occasionally employed after the inquiry if the examiner feels that he does not have sufficient information about the subject's reactions

FIGURE 4–3

A Set of Ink Blots Similar to Those Employed by Rorschach

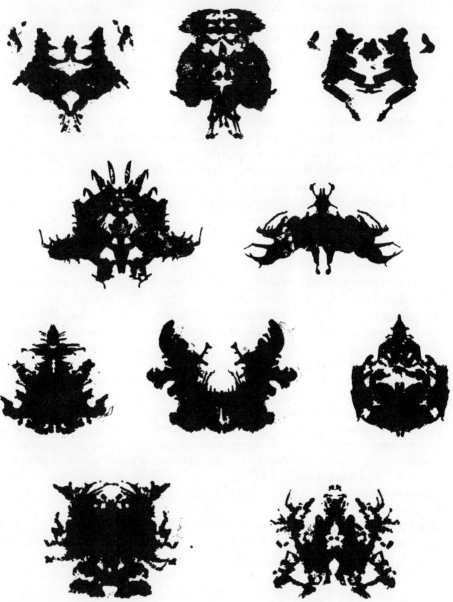

Source: Kleinmuntz, 1967

The scoring and interpretation of Rorschach responses is an involved and detailed procedure, and a number of different systems for scoring and interpretation have been devised. We shall illustrate the general nature of these procedures by briefly examining the characteristics for which responses are scored and some examples of interpretations based on the Klopfer and Davidson (1962) system.

Scoring. Each response is scored for five major characteristics: location, determinant, popularity-originality, content, and form level. *Location* refers to where on the card the concept was seen. There are five main categories of location: (1) *whole* (the entire blot is used for the concept), (2) *large usual detail* (which is easily marked off from the rest of the blot), (3) *small usual detail* (which is easily marked off from the rest of the blot), (4) *unusual detail* (an area of the blot, large or small, that is generally not employed by subjects), and (5) *white space* (a reversal of figure and ground).

The *determinant* of a response deals with the qualities of the blot that lead to the formation of the concept. The four major categories of determinants are: (1) *form* (shape—as, "the outline looks like a bear"), (2) *movement* (the concept involves physical movement—as, "a flying butterfly"), (3) *shading* (use of lighter and darker areas to suggest such physical features as texture and depth—as, "the bearskin looks thick and furry"), and (4) *color* (for example, "red roses").

Popularity-originality refers to the frequency with which particular responses are given by subjects. A response is scored as *popular* when it occurs very frequently (Klopfer and Davidson designate only 10 responses as popular responses) and *original* when it occurs very infrequently (i.e., a response given by no more than 1 percent of subjects). Many responses are neither popular nor original and thus are not scored for this characteristic.

Content is scored in terms of the subject matter of the concept. The usual scoring categories include: *human figures* ("two men playing drums"), *anatomy* ("an X-ray of a man's chest"), *sex* ("a woman's breast"), *animals* ("a bear"), *geography* ("a map of Florida"), and *man-made objects* ("a large boot").

Finally, each response is given a *form-level* rating (ranging from a

---

to the ink blots. In the *analogy* phase, the examiner asks whether an aspect of the blot that applied to one response also applies to another (for example, "Here the shape of the blot made it look like something to you; does the shape of this blot also help you see something?"). The *testing-the-limits* phase is introduced only when the subject has given very few responses and fails to make any reaction to certain significant and obvious stimuli in the blots. Here the examiner specifically introduces a concept and asks the subject whether he can see it in the blot. Because the fundamental unstructured situation is changed in the testing-the-limits phase, responses obtained by this procedure are generally not scored, though the examiner may gain impressionistic information which is helpful in understanding the subject.

low of -2.0 to a high of $+5.0$), which is an indication of how accurately the concept is seen and how closely the concept fits the blot.

Interpretation. While scoring the Rorschach is a detailed procedure, interpretation is even more complex. Most often the responses are subjected to a *formal analysis* in which the way a response was arrived at is examined.[5] It is neither possible nor appropriate to provide a detailed explanation of the interpretation of Rorschach responses here. However, in an effort to give the reader the flavor of Rorschach interpretation, we shall present a few examples of the kinds of inferences made. It is important to keep in mind that a given response or set of responses is always viewed in terms of both general norms and the other responses made by the subject. Further, the interpretations are actually hypotheses, and their validity or usefuless varies with the purpose of assessment and the individual case in question.

The location of responses is said to reflect the subject's intellectual approach to the ink blots in particular and to stimuli in his life in general. Whole responses indicate the subject's ability to organize material, integrate details, and deal with abstract and theoretical conceptions. The use of details in the blots indicates an interest in specific and concrete concepts, while an emphasis on small details may reflect a compulsive need to be exact and accurate.

The determinants of responses are hypothesized to be concerned with emotional aspects of personality. The use of form is said to signify the subject's degree of emotional control; a large proportion of responses determined by form may indicate an ability to deal with situations without becoming emotionally involved. Shading is related to the need for affection and close ties with others, while color as a determinant reflects the subject's responsivity to stimuli in the external environment (especially other people).

The use of many popular responses (eight or more) may indicate a need to see things as other people do, and, in contrast, a small number of popular responses may reveal an inability to conceptualize things as others do. Original responses (more than three) of good form level are characteristic of superior intellect and originality.

The variety of content which a subject uses in his responses is an index of his breadth of interests. Additionally, the variety of concepts employed may be an index of intelligence; the more varied the content categories employed, the more intelligent the person is.

Form level is said to be an indication of intellectual capacity and

---

[5] Occasionally, Rorschach responses are interpreted by a *content analysis,* which examines the types of concepts seen in the blots, or a *sequence analysis,* which examines, card by card and response by response, the subject's behavior while responding to the blots in an effort to test certain hypotheses that present themselves to the examiner during the administration.

functioning. Thus, poor form level reflects a low intellectual level as well as a loss of contact with reality.

Present Status of the Rorschach. Despite the fact that the Rorschach is the most widely used projective technique, empirical studies of its validity have yielded largely negative results (see, for example, Anastasi, 1968). Nonetheless, since most clinicians use the technique in conjunction with many other sources of information, proponents of the Rorschach still claim that no disconfirmation of its worth in guiding their individual clinical judgments has been presented. Thus, Anastasi (1968) claims that the value of projective techniques ". . . is proportional to the skill of the clinician and hence cannot be assessed independently of the individual clinician using them" (p. 518).

REFERENCES

Anastasi, A. *Psychological testing.* (3d ed.) New York: Macmillan, 1968.

Aserinsky, E., and Kleitman, N. Regularly occurring periods of eye motility, and concomitant phenomena during sleep. *Science,* 1953, **118,** 273–74.

Dement, W. C. An essay on dreams: The role of physiology in understanding their nature. In *New directions in psychology,* Vol. II. New York: Holt, Rinehart & Winston, 1965. Pp. 135–257.*

Dement, W. C., and Kleitman, N. The relation of the eye movements during sleep to dream activity: An objective method for the study of dreaming. *Journal of Experimental Psychology,* 1957, **53,** 339–46.

Dement, W. C., and Wolpert, E. The relation of eye movements, body motility, and external stimuli to dream content. *Journal of Experimental Psychology,* 1958, **55,** 543–53.

Foulkes, D., Pivik, T., Ahrens, J. B., and Swanson, E. M. Effects of "dream deprivation" on dream content: An attempted cross-night replication. *Journal of Abnormal Psychology,* 1968, **73,** 403–15.

Freud, S. *The analysis of a phobia in a five-year old boy.* Vol. 10. *The standard edition of the complete psychological works of Sigmund Freud.* J. Strachey (Trans. and Ed.). London: Hogarth Press, 1957.

Freud, S. Construction in psychoanalysis. Vol. 23. *The standard edition of the complete psychological works of Sigmund Freud.* London: Hogarth Press and the Institute for Psycho-analysis, 1962. Pp. 257–69.

Freud, S. *The interpretation of dreams.* J. Strachey (Trans. and Ed.). New York: Science Editions, 1961.

Glover, E. *On the early development of mind.* New York: Hillary, 1956.

Harrower, M. R., and Steiner, M. E. *Large-scale Rorschach techniques.* Springfield, Ill.: Charles C Thomas, 1944.

* Quoted material by Frank Barron et al. Copyrighted © 1965 by Holt, Rinehart and Winston, Inc. Reprinted by permission of Holt, Rinehart and Winston, Inc.

Hire, A. W. A group administration of the Rorschach: Method and results. *Journal of Consulting Psychology,* 1950, **14,** 496–99.

Jouvet, M. Recherches sur les structures nerveuses et les mechanismes responsables de differentes phases du sommeil physiologique. *Archives Italiennes de Biologie,* 1962, **100,** 125–206.

Kleinmuntz, B. *Personality measurement: An introduction.* Homewood, Ill.: Dorsey Press, 1967.

Klopfer, B., and Davidson, H. H. *The Rorschach technique: An introductory manual.* New York: Harcourt, Brace & World, 1962.

Munroe, R. L. *Schools of psychoanalytic thought.* New York: Dryden Press, 1955.

Wolman, B. B. *The unconscious mind: The meaning of Freudian psychology.* Englewood Cliffs, N.J.: Prentice-Hall, 1968.

chapter 5

Trait and Type Approaches: Theoretical Alternatives

Type theories of personality are among the first to be found in recorded history. These early conceptualizations of behavior assumed, as do their modern counterparts, that there are enduring, stable personality differences *which reside within the person* and that a determination of these is the best means of predicting human behavior. The purpose of the next two chapters is to explore these positions.

HISTORICAL ANTECEDENTS

While we are not merely interested in the curious relics of history, modern trait and type theories, perhaps more than other approaches, owe some of their thinking to the ideas of past centuries. It is therefore instructive to examine these ideas before turning to the strategies which are found in contemporary theory and research.

Ancient type theories assumed that men could be divided into a relatively small number of types, according to their personalities, and that by knowing a man's type one could predict with reasonable accuracy the way in which he would behave in a variety of circumstances. The ancient Hebrews used this perspective of man to conduct what may have been the first formal effort at personality assessment. In the following quotation from the Old Testament, it is apparent that this perspective was dichotomous, with the goal of describing only two types of men, those who could be ferocious fighters and those who lacked this quality.

> And the Lord said unto Gideon, The people that are with thee are too many for me to give the Midianites into their hands. . . . Now therefore go to, proclaim in the ears of the people, saying, Whosoever is fearful and afraid, let him return and depart early from Mount Gilead. And there returned of the people twenty and two thousand; and there remained ten thousand.
>
> And the Lord said unto Gideon, The people are yet too many; bring them down unto the water, and I will try them for thee there. . . . So he brought down the people unto the water: and the Lord said unto Gideon, Every one that lappeth of the water with his tongue, as a dog lappeth, him shalt thou set by himself; likewise every one that boweth down upon his knees to drink. And the number of them that lapped, putting their hand to their mouth, were three hundred men: but all the rest of the people bowed down upon their knees to drink water. And the Lord said unto Gideon, By the three hundred men that lapped will I save you, and deliver the Midianites into thine hand: and let all the other people go every man unto his place (*Judges,* 7:2–7).

A second ancient type theory, the *theory of the four temperaments,* is closely akin to several contemporary theories and to a goodly number of the layman's conceptions of personality. The position has as its basis the Greek hypothesis that the physical universe can be described in terms of four basic elements: air, earth, fire, and water. Hippocrates, often called the "father of medicine," extended this argument to man himself, by suggesting that the body is composed of four corresponding "humors": blood, black bile, yellow bile, and phlegm. Galen later postulated that an excess of any of these humors led to a characteristic temperament or "personality type": sanguine (hopeful), melancholic (sad), choleric (hot-tempered), or phlegmatic (apathetic). Although this ancient psychophysiological theory of personality is no longer taken seriously, the four temperaments have survived to this day as part of our language.

Conspicuous even to the ancients, however, was the fact that there are clearly more than four types of people. Thus, extensive catalogs of types emerged. The notion of identifying types of men continued, with only minor changes, as the popular conception of personality for thousands of years. Among the most striking of the modifications that did appear was the hypothesis that one could guess a man's behavior and personality from his physical appearance. In William Shakespeare's play, *Julius Caesar,* for example, Caesar advises Marcus Antonius:

> Let me have men about me that are fat;
> Sleek-headed men, and such as sleep o' nights:
> Yond Cassius has a lean and hungry look;
> He thinks too much: such men are dangerous.
>
> (Act I, Scene II)

The belief advanced in the foregoing quotation is in fact still rather popular today; many persons believe that they can identify a "criminal type" by his physical appearance, while they often ascribe innocence to persons of placid complexion and manner.

Most historical views of human behavior were really no more than suggestions and ideas for understanding man. However, with the advent of more sophisticated scientific perspectives, it became apparent that these suggestions and loose hypotheses would have to give way to more formal statements of man's nature and to interlocking conceptualizations that might properly be called theories.

TRAITS AND TYPES: THE PROBLEM OF DEFINITION

In contemporary writing, both popular and scientific, the terms *trait* and *type* have come to be used in several different ways. It is important that we examine these uses so that we may clarify the manner in which our discussion will be restricted.

First, *type* and *trait* are often used as summary labels for observed differences in behavior. To say of a friend "At parties he is usually the shy type" is merely to conveniently summarize our observations. In the same vein, Guilford (1959) defined a trait as "*any distinguishable, relatively enduring way in which one individual varies from others*" (p. 6). Used in this way, the terms have no necessary theoretical implications and serve merely to facilitate communication.

Second, traits and types have been considered by many personality psychologists to be real entities, actually residing within persons. They are, in other words, bona fide characteristics of the individual, like the color of his eyes (which is unquestionably a biological trait in the Mendelian sense), which can and must be discovered. Gordon Allport (1966) described this strategy as *heuristic realism* and noted the implication that "the person who confronts us possesses inside his skin generalized action tendencies (or traits) and that it is our job scientifically to discover what they are" (p. 3). Yet another, and perhaps more important, implication lies in this strategy; namely, a person's traits are now assumed to *cause* his behavior. Thus, it would become legitimate to say that the individual behaves aggressively at least in part because he has an aggressive disposition or trait or is an aggressive type.

Our primary interest will be in those theories which approach traits and types in this last way, looking for enduring characteristics of the person which determine his behavior. Intrapsychic theories have invoked some of these same assumptions but, as Mischel (1968) has pointed out, they differ from trait approaches in that they do not assume additivity:

> Much of the research on traits, especially the work of psychometricians [psychologists who specialize in techniques of measuring personality], has been guided by a cumulative quantitative measurement model. In such a cumu-

> lative model trait indicators are related *additively* to the inferred underlying disposition. . . . For example, the more submissive behavior the person displays, as by endorsing more submissive content on an inventory, the stronger the underlying trait of submissiveness. In contrast, psychodynamic theory posits highly *indirect,* nonadditive relations between behavior and hypothesized underlying states. Thus submissive behavior may be interpreted as a sign of underlying aggression, or of passivity-hostility conflicts, or of resistance disguising some other threatening characterological problems (p. 6).

In most earlier theories and some contemporary ones, traits and types have been linked to observable physical characteristics of the individual, and sometimes to presumed corresponding constitutional differences. We shall begin our discussion with an examination of *constitutional theories* of personality.

CONSTITUTIONAL THEORIES

The Logic of the Constitutional Approach

The basic argument underlying the constitutional approach to personality is that *there are differences in the physical constitution of individuals and that often these differences cause differences in behavior.* It is apparent that the assertion, if viable, has far-reaching consequences for both predicting and understanding individual differences in personality. We shall first discuss some basic tenets of the argument and then turn to the theory and research which is related to it.

The logic of the constitutional position was concisely set forth by Williams (1967) in an essay on "The Biological Approach to the Study of Personality." His argument consists of five main points.

The first point is that *interspecies* (comparison of one species to another) biological differences exist and that the fact of these differences suggests *intraspecies* (within the species) differences.

> It is beyond dispute, of course, that dogs, cats, rats, and monkeys, for example, show species differences with respect to their patterns of conditionability. Stimuli which are highly effective for one species may be of negligible importance for another. If hereditary factors make for inter-species differences, it is entirely reasonable to suppose that intra-species differences exist for the same reason (p. 22).

Second, Williams observes that intraspecies differences have regularly been found in experimental work with animals. Experimental psychology, particularly the pioneering work of Ivan Pavlov, has placed great emphasis on conditioning. Williams argues, however, that a major aspect of Pavlov's findings is the pervasive suggestion of constitutional differences among his dogs, an aspect of his research rarely cited by learning theorists.

What was not quoted by the behavioristic school were correlative findings by Pavlov which are highly pertinent. Pavlov found as a result of extensive study of many dogs that they often exhibit innate tendencies to react differently to the same stimulus. He recognized in his dogs four basic types: (1) excitable, (2) inhibitory, (3) equilibrated, and (4) active, as well as intermediate types (p. 21).

Third, Williams cites an impressive battery of evidence that humans show intraspecies differences in their biological and hereditary makeup. For example:

. . . normal stomachs vary greatly in shape and about six-fold in size. . . . Arising from the aortic arch are two, three, four, and sometimes five and six branch arteries . . . each person exhibits a distinct breathing pattern as shown in the spirograms of different individuals under comparable conditions. . . . The morphology of the pituitary glands which produce eight different hormones is so variable, when different healthy persons are compared, as to allow for several fold differences in the production of individual hormones . . . the male sex glands vary in weight from 10 to 45 grams in so-called "normal" males . . . (p. 23).

Fourth, behavioral indices of these physiological differences also exist and frequently show up in basic research with humans involving the ability to discriminate stimuli.

Investigations involving "cold spots," "warm spots," and "pain spots" on the skin indicate that each individual exhibits a distinctive pattern of each. In a relatively recent study of pain spots in twenty-one healthy young adults, a high degree of variation was observed. . . . One young man "A" showed seven percent of the area tested to be "highly sensitive," while in another, "B," the right hand showed one hundred percent "highly sensitive" areas. On A's hand, forty-nine percent of the area registered "no pain" under standard pain producing test conditions. On B's hand, however, there was no area which registered "no pain" (pp. 23–24).

Williams' summary point calls for a greater integration of this pattern of findings and reasoning into psychological research.

It seems indefensible to assume that people are built in separate compartments, one anatomical, one physiological, one biochemical, one psychological, and that these compartments are unrelated or only distantly related to each other. Each human possesses and exhibits unity. Certainly anatomy is basic to physiology and biochemistry, and it may be logically presumed that it is also basic to psychology (pp. 22–23).

The constitutional theories, which we shall examine next, are in agreement with this conclusion and have endeavored to support it with theoretical structure and research evidence.

Kretschmer's Position

In 1921, Ernst Kretschmer, a German psychiatrist, published a volume entitled *Physique and Character.*[1] In it were to be found the rudiments of the first modern constitutional theory of personality. Kretschmer's position, like Freud's before him, was instigated by observations made in the clinical practice of psychiatry. The two major categories of *psychosis* (severe psychological disturbance in which the individual is no longer able to function in society) recognized in Kretschmer's day were *schizophrenia* and *manic-depressive psychosis.* The former diagnosis was ascribed to individuals who showed a loss of emotional behavior and reactions, while the latter category included persons characterized by extreme elation (mania) or extreme depression or sometimes a cyclic movement from one to the other.

Kretschmer felt that he had observed a regular relationship between assigned psychiatric diagnosis and the physique of his patients. He set out to demonstrate this relationship by creating a limited number of categories of physique and then relating these categories to psychiatric diagnosis. Kretschmer also asserted that "normal" personality was related to physique, but apparently collected no systematic data to support his contention. We shall therefore limit ourselves to his research findings with psychotics.

Types of Physique. In order to determine types of physique, Kretschmer and his associates began by developing a "constitutional inventory" consisting of more than 70 items. To illustrate the degree of detail in which they were interested, a portion of the inventory dealing with skin blood vessels is reproduced in Table 5–1. The data themselves were collected in a thoughtful and systematic manner.

> We noticed, and immediately filled in point for point, the foregoing list, the patient standing naked before us in bright daylight, and we ruled a red line under whichever member of the groups of descriptions fitted the case. According to the pronouncedness of the characteristic whether it was strong or weak, we drew a single or a double line, so that we saved the time which a written description would have required, and obtained a diagram that provides a perfectly intelligible survey, which conveyed to us at a glance, later on, with no trouble at all, not only the general impression, but each detail of physique, and thus we could make a comparison between every single point in different diagrams in a second (1926, p. 9).

Examinations of this type were carried out on approximately 400 psychiatric patients. The data seemed to reveal three basic physiques:

---

[1] The English translation by W. J. H. Sprott (1926) has been used.

TABLE 5–1

A Portion of Kretschmer's "Constitutional Inventory" Dealing with Blood Vessels

Skin blood vessels:		clearly visible in face	dimly visible on hands and feet	invisible on body
Head:	bluish	dark-red	medium	pale
Hands:	bluish	dark-red	medium	pale
Feet:	bluish	dark-red	medium	pale
Hands and feet:		damp	medium	dry
Body:		damp	medium	dry
Hands and feet:		warm	medium	cold
Body:		warm	medium	cold

Source: Adapted from Kretschmer, 1926.

asthenic, athletic, and *pyknic* and a small number of anomalous patterns grouped together as *dysplastic.* The asthenic type appeared to be:

. . . a lean narrowly-built man, who looks taller than he is, with narrow shoulders . . . thin muscles and delicately boned hands; a long, narrow, flat chest, on which we can count the ribs . . . thin stomach, devoid of fat . . . the way the weight of the body lags behind the length . . . stands out clearly (1926, p. 21).

In contrast, the following is a "rough impression" of the athletic type.

A middle-sized to tall man, with particularly wide projecting shoulders, a superb chest, a firm stomach, and a trunk which tapers in its lower region . . . the solid long head is carried upright on a free neck . . . the over-developed musculature stands out through only a thin sheath of fat (1926, pp. 24–25).

The pyknic male bears little resemblance to either of these two. He is a man of:

. . . middle height, rounded figure, a soft broad face . . . the magnificent fat paunch protrudes from the deep vaulted chest which broadens out toward the lower part of the body. . . . It seems then as if the whole mass of the shoulders were slipping downwards and inwards over the swelling chest; and the head also plays a part in this static displacement: it sinks forward between the shoulders . . . the neck no longer seems, as is the case with other types, a slim round column, which carries the chin . . . the point of the chin is directly joined with the upper forehead (1926, p. 29).

Less uniformity is to be found among the dysplastics, who are primarily distinguished by the unusualness of their appearance. Kretschmer noted that:

. . . we describe as dysplastic types a high degree of profile angularity, asthenic emaciation, or athletic sturdiness . . . such forms of growth . . . vary

FIGURE 5–1

The Four Body Types

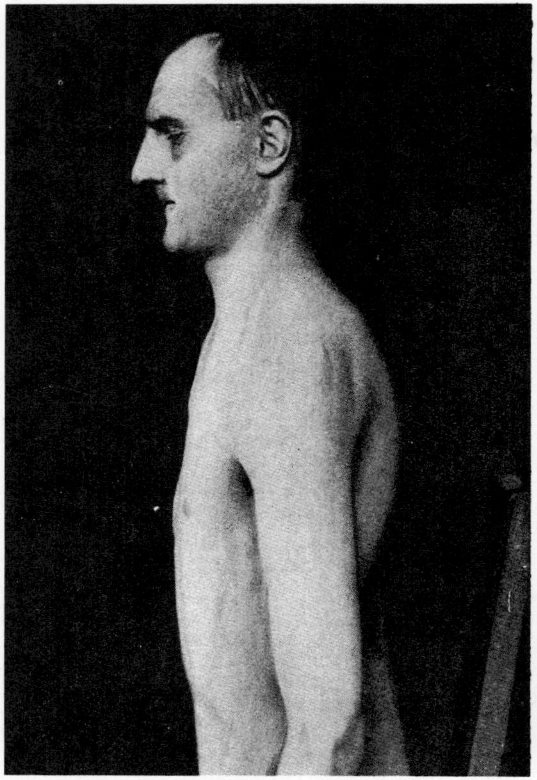

Asthenic

Athletic

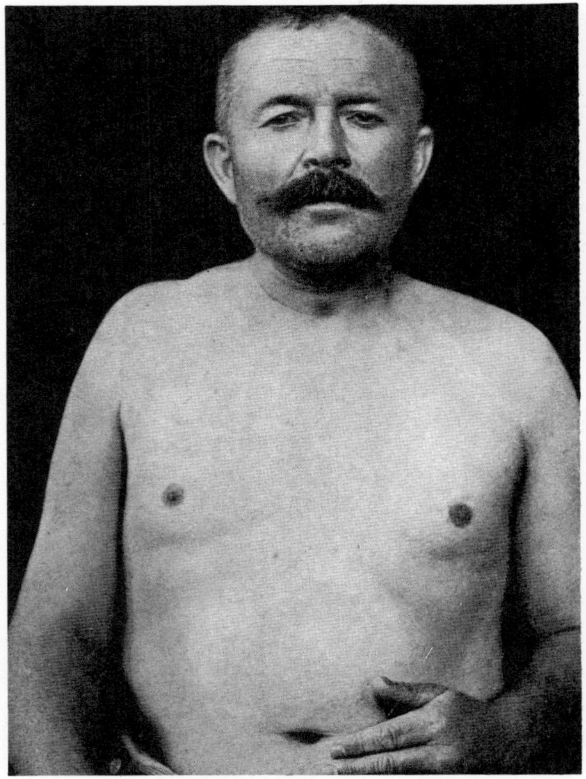

Pyknic

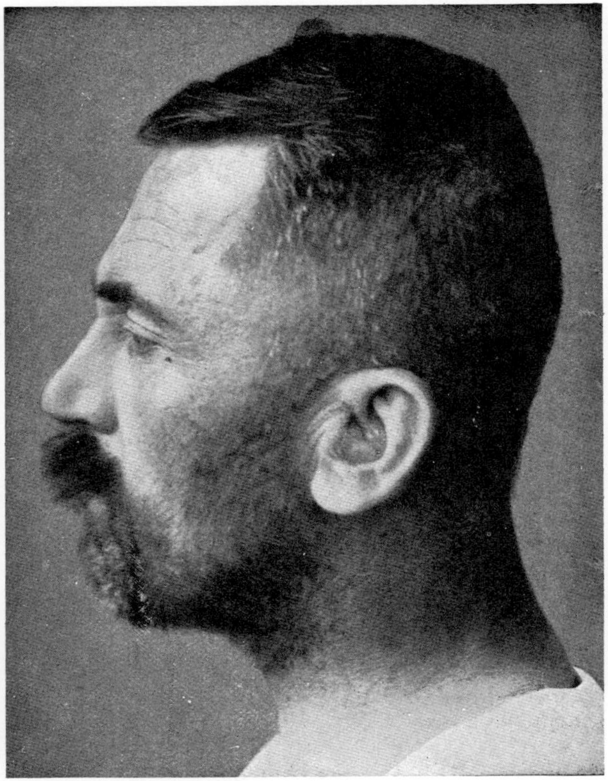

Dysplastic

Source: Kretschmer, 1926.

very markedly from the average and commonest form of the type in question . . . not only the extremes, but also the majority of cases fall well outside the typical form; they even impress the laity as rare, surprising, and ugly (1926, p. 65).

Figure 5–1 is a reproduction of Kretschmer's examples of the foregoing types (pages 102–03).

Physique and Psychiatric Diagnosis. The remaining problem for Kretschmer and his associates was to relate these body types to the psychiatric diagnosis of the patients. The data revealed a clear pattern. Persons of the asthenic, athletic, and dysplastic body type were more likely to be schizophrenic than manic-depressive. For persons of pyknic build, on the other hand, manic-depressive psychosis was the more probable diagnosis. Some of the data reported by Kretschmer are summarized in Table 5–2.

TABLE 5–2

The Relationship of Physique and Psychiatric Diagnosis (based on 243 patients)

	Schizophrenic	*Manic-Depressive*	*Total*
Asthenic and athletic	91.2%	8.8%	100.0%
Dysplastic	100.0	0.0	100.0
Pyknic	6.5	93.5	100.0

Source: Adapted from Kretschmer, 1926.

Kretschmer believed that this striking evidence for a relationship between physique and personality would be paralleled by reliable relationships with "normal" (nonhospitalized) persons, but it remained for William Sheldon to collect the data.

Sheldon's Constitutional Theory

In his 1942 book entitled *The Varieties of Temperament,* Sheldon set forth both the argument and the data to support a comprehensive psychology of constitutional differences that would be applicable through the full range of "normal" as well as "abnormal" persons. Sheldon regarded his task as: (1) the development of an adequate classification of physique—the structural or *static* aspect of humans; (2) the development of an adequate classification of temperament—the functional or *dynamic* aspect of humans; and (3) the empirical quest for an enduring, reliable relationship between the static and the dynamic views of man. Sheldon (1942) introduced his three goals as follows:

> . . . physique and temperament are clearly two aspects of the same thing, and we are not surprised if we are led to expect that the dynamics of an individual should be related to the static picture he presents. It is the old notion that structure must somehow determine function. In the face of this expectation it is rather astonishing that in the past so little relation has been discovered between the shape of man and the way he behaves . . . there are dynamic and static variables which correlate sufficiently highly to reaffirm our faith in the possibility of a useful science of constitutional differences (pp. 4–5).

To see how Sheldon attacked the problem, we shall first examine his search for primary components of morphology (physique), then his search for the components of temperament, and finally his endeavors to relate these two aspects of man. As the description of Sheldon's investigations proceeds, it will become apparent that although the scope of his theory and research is greater than that of Kretschmer, the basic strategy is the same.

The Primary Components of Physique. Sheldon and his associates, following the lead of Kretschmer and his co-workers, studied body types by simultaneously examining many physiques to search for regularities. A large number of persons were photographed, under standard conditions, from the front, side, and rear. When the 4,000 photographs from their first study were examined, Sheldon and his colleagues found that, even to the unaided eye, a certain orderliness was apparent. But refining this impression into systematic evidence for distinguishable components of physique required a rigorous procedure. Thus, two formal criteria were introduced.

> (1) Could the entire collection of photographs be arranged in an ascending (or descending) progression of strength in the characteristic under consideration, with agreement between experimenters working independently? (2) In the case of a suspected new component of structural variation, is it, upon examination of the photographs, found to be impossible to define this apparently new component in terms of mixtures, regular or dysplastic, of the other components already accepted? (1942, p. 6).

Employing these criteria, three primary components of body structure were identified and named *endomorphy*, *mesomorphy*, and *ectomorphy*. The names were new, and the statement of their continuity introduced a cautious flavor, but they were remarkably like the body types found by Kretschmer. In the endomorph the digestive system predominates; the individuals are usually fat and are said to "float high in the water," and the musculature is underdeveloped. Mesomorphs tend to be "hard, firm, upright, and relatively strong and tough." A mesomorph's skin is thick, his blood vessels are large, and his appearance is overwhelmingly one of sturdiness. Finally, ectomorphs are characterized by "fragility, linearity, flatness of the chest, and delicacy throughout the body." In Sheldon's scheme, however, persons are not merely "typed" as one or another. Rather, on the basis of many measurements, a person is *somatotyped* by the assignment of three numbers, each ranging from 1 to 7, which represent the strength of each of the components of body structure. This procedure is used because:

> As these components occur in nature they are single, continuous variables. The designation of the somatotype merely serves the purpose of bracketing a physique within defined boundaries . . . but the somatotype provides the basis for a morphological taxonomy that is both comprehensive and statistically manipulable (Sheldon, 1942, p. 7).

In somatotyping, the first numeral refers to endomorphy, the second to mesomorphy, and the last to the ectomorphic component. Thus, a muscular, powerful man might approach the somatotype 1–7–1, while an average individual with respect to physique might be somatotyped 4–4–4.

The Primary Components of Temperament. Temperament, according to Sheldon, refers to the dynamic aspects of a man, which may run a long gamut from complex bodily movements to the expression of specific beliefs and attitudes. However, between the extremes, Sheldon argued there is a level of functioning "where basic patterns of motivation manifest themselves." The problem is to produce an operational (as opposed to a conceptual) definition of temperament and to empirically identify its components. Kretschmer's prior work provided no assistance in this regard, for he had *assumed* the validity of psychiatric diagnoses (schizophrenia and manic-depressive psychoses) as distinguishable personality syndromes.

Sheldon began his search for the primary components of temperament with a list of 650 "alleged traits." The list was derived from many sources, including the personal observations and speculations of the investigators. Inspection of the list revealed, however, that many of the trait names were redundant in terms of the ideas which they represented. A list of 50 traits sufficed to encompass the essential content of the original 650. Armed with this list, Sheldon proceeded to rate his first sample of subjects (33 male graduate students and young instructors) for a full academic year. The ratings were based on interviews, observations while engaging in their ordinary daily activities, and repeated social interactions with the investigators. As with the data on physique, inspection revealed a consistent pattern. Some traits appeared regularly to be related to each other but unrelated to the remaining characteristics in the list. Sheldon (1942) wrote:

. . . we soon found that three groups of traits showed positive intercorrelation among themselves, *and negative correlation with all or nearly all of the other traits.* At this time this was not particularly what we wanted to find, for the writer then entertained a hypothesis that probably at least four primary components existed . . . (p. 14).

The Scale of Temperament that emerged from this first correlational study was modified through eight additional studies by looking for additional consistent traits, not yet in the list, which seemed to characterize persons who fell near one of the polar extremes of the previous scale. Finally, using a sample of 100 male subjects, a list of 60 traits was selected, 20 for each of the components which had come to be named *viscerotonia, somatotonia,* and *cerebrotonia.* The nature of these components can be seen in the short form of the scale, having 10 traits for each component, which is reproduced in Table 5–3.

TABLE 5–3

A Short Form of Sheldon's Scale of Temperament

I *Viscerotonia*	*II* *Somatotonia*	*III* *Cerebrotonia*
Relaxation in posture and movement	Assertiveness of posture and movement	Restraint in posture and movement, tightness
Love of physical comfort	Love of physical adventure	Overly fast reactions
Slow reaction	The energetic characteristic	Love of privacy
Love of polite ceremony	Need for and enjoyment of exercise	Mental overintensity, hyperattentionality, apprehensiveness
Sociophilia	Love of risk and chance	Secretiveness of feeling, emotional restraint
Evenness of emotional flow	Bold directness of manner	Self-conscious motility of the eyes and face
Tolerance	Physical courage for combat	Sociophobia
Complacency	Competitive aggressiveness	Inhibited social address
The untempered characteristic	The unrestrained voice	Vocal restraint, and general restraint of noise
Smooth, easy communication of feeling, extraversion of viscerotonia	Overmaturity of appearance	Youthful intentness of manner and appearance

Source: Adapted from Sheldon, 1942.

The scale itself appears disarmingly straightforward, but its recommended use is extremely demanding. Users were admonished to observe the subject closely for at least a year in many situations, to conduct at least 20 interviews, to take a complete medical and personal history, and to scrutinize "such special clinical matters as the individual case may indicate." Sheldon felt that the scale was useless for self-rating and that it could be successfully used for rating others only when highly trained examiners employed it for extended periods of time.

The Relationship between Physique and Temperament. Once adequate taxonomies of both physique and temperament had been developed, the most crucial step, the demonstration of a consistent relationship between the two aspects of man, remained. Two hundred white males were selected as subjects and were somatotyped. Over a five-year period, these subjects were rated on Sheldon's Scale of Temperament following the rigorous standards previously outlined. The results of this study were striking. Each of the three body types was *positively related to one and only one* of the temperamental components and *negatively related to the others.* This finding is powerful evidence for the constitutional position, since it demonstrates that "human structure and human behavior are . . . far from unrelated." The reader may want to attempt to guess which class of temperament (viscerotonia, somatotonia, and cerebrotonia) went with each of the three classes of physique (endomorphy, mesomorphy, and ectomorphy) before examining Table 5–4, which summarizes Sheldon's findings.

TABLE 5–4

The Correlations Sheldon Found among the Primary Components of Physique and Temperament Using 200 Male Subjects

	Endo-morphy	Viscero-tonia	Meso-morphy	Somato-tonia	Ecto-morphy	Cerebro-tonia
Endomorphy	+1.00	+ .79	− .29	− .29	− .41	− .32
Viscerotonia		+1.00	− .23	− .34	− .40	− .37
Mesomorphy			+1.00	+ .82	− .63	− .58
Somatotonia				+1.00	− .53	− .62
Ectomorphy					+1.00	+ .83
Cerebrotonia						+1.00

Source: Adapted from Sheldon, 1942.

Table 5–4 is a *correlation matrix* which gives the correlation of each of the body types and temperaments with every other. Only the top half of the matrix is needed, since the lower half is merely a mirror image of the top half. The diagonal of the matrix contains correlation coefficients of +1.00, which indicates that each variable is perfectly correlated (positively) with itself. Looking at the first row of the matrix, we see that endomorphy is positively related to viscerotonia (+.79) and negatively related to somatotonia (−.29) and cerebrotonia (−.32), the other two classes of temperament. Thus, endomorphy is positively related to one and only one of the components of temperament. Furthermore, still looking in the first row of the matrix, we see that endomorphy is negatively related to both mesomorphy (−.29) and ectomorphy (−.41), which lends support to the notion that the three basic physiques are relatively independent. Similarly, an examination of the correlations between viscerotonia and somatotonia (−.34) and viscerotonia and cerebrotonia (−.37) substantiates the relative independence of the three basic temperaments. The relationship which held for endomorphy and viscerotonia (i.e., high positive) also held for mesomorphy and somatotonia (+.82) and for ectomorphy and cerebrotonia (+.83).

While Table 5–4 is a concise presentation of Sheldon's findings, it does not fully capture his perspective toward the individual cases. Each of the 200 cases is described in some detail in the original report. For example, the single case of 1–1–7 in the sample is described as:

. . . a weak, inconspicuous youth who has succeeded in making an acceptable integration in the face of what must be regarded as a poor constitutional endowment. He is inoffensive, quiet, defenseless . . . somewhat below average in mental endowment. He has no special gifts of a productive or creative nature, although he is said to possess unusually sensitive appreciation of art. He has a fairly strong endowment of sexuality, which has been expressed mainly in excessive masturbation . . . since he has little access to women, he cleaves to men. He is what might perhaps be called an "intellectual homosexual," but he is not a true homosexual. His masturbational imagery is entirely feminine. . . . He will never offend anyone, and he thus offers one of the essential requisites for success in many endeavors (Sheldon, 1942, p. 290).

The sample also contained two individuals with the 4–6–1 physique. These men completely lacked ectomorphic characteristics, were near the top on mesomorphy, and had some endomorphic endowment. Sheldon's description of them is made more interesting because of the way in which he reconciles what are at first blush quite different characters.

Two examples of this rare, extremely massive and powerful physique; both are Jewish and both are graduates of medical school. One is a successful psychoanalyst, the other an institutionalized manic-depressive. . . . [The first] achieved a successful integration in the face of a difficult pattern of temperament. . . . At times he was almost manic, showing extreme aggression. . . . At times he suffered severe depression of spirits. . . . His psychoanalysis started when he was a senior medical student. As it progressed, he became much better integrated, showed the traditional symptoms of the "conversion experience," and during the succeeding years he has been a happy and excessively vigorous person. . . . He is now a passionate proselyter to psychoanalysis as the true pattern for universal salvation, and he himself is doing well as a young analyst. It can hardly be doubted that psychoanalysis has in this case filled, at least temporarily, a religious need. . . . [The other] showed an early history remarkably similar to the last, except that there was a weaker viscerotonia. . . . During the early periods of depression, he kept more to himself and did not pour out his grief so easily. He went into a frank manic-depressive psychosis at age 30, and a year later has shown little sign of improvement (Sheldon, 1942, pp. 355–56).

The constitutional approach to personality, as reflected in the work of Kretschmer and Sheldon, has as its primary interest the identification of a relationship (i.e., correlation) between physiological and psychological endowment. No necessary causal relationship is implied by these correlational data (see Chapter 2). Some personality researchers, however, have specifically avowed genetic causation in personality. The investigations and particular theories which this outlook has generated have focused mostly upon abnormal behavior, with a particular interest in demonstrating a genetic etiology for schizophrenia.

THE GENETIC APPROACH TO PERSONALITY

The Logic of Genetic Research: Twin Study Method[2]

Out of every 85 births, one is a multiple birth producing two children.[3] Approximately two thirds of all twins are, however, "fraternal," or, technically, *dizygotic,* meaning that they developed from separate ova and sperm. Fraternal twins thus share only a birthday with their "womb-mates" and are otherwise no more alike genetically than siblings born separately. The small remaining group, the "identical" or *monozygotic* twins, consists of twins who have developed from the same ovum and sperm and are consequently unequivocally alike. Identical twins have held a fascination for many, both in and out of science, not only because of their statistical rarity but also because of their tremendous potential for learning the extent to which hereditary factors influence behavior.

Twin research in personality involves the following assumptions. First, identical twins are genetically alike, whereas fraternal twins are not. Second, the social and environmental experiences of twins, reared together, are alike.[4] Therefore, greater similarity on measures of personal-

---

[2] Two other methods of genetic research have been customarily employed. The *pedigree* or *family history method* traces the occurrence of a personality trait over generations of families. The *contingency method of statistical prediction,* of which the twin study method is a special case, compares the incidence of a trait in blood relatives with various degrees of consanguinity (for example, parents, grandparents, cousins, and so on) and in the general (nonconsanguineous) population.

[3] To the extent that new "birth control" drugs can influence the probability of multiple births, these odds may be only approximate today.

[4] It is rare that this assumption is met not only because no two individuals can have truly identical environments but more importantly because identical twins may be more likely to receive similar treatment than fraternal twins. For example, identical twins are often provided with matched clothing, similar haircuts, and so on.

ity between identical twins, when compared with fraternal twins, is a consequence of genetic contribution. Given this reasoning, the research strategy is one of selecting a good dependent measure of personality and determining the degree of *concordance* (similarity) among many pairs of twins who are both identical and fraternal. The largest body of work to date which has followed this strategy has involved the search for etiology in schizophrenia, and the relevant theory and research has been spearheaded by a German psychiatrist, Franz Kallmann. Many reviewers have considered the data reported by Kallmann to provide unequivocal evidence of a major genetic component in schizophrenia (Jackson, 1960).[5]

Kallmann's Data

Kallmann examined large samples of persons diagnosed as schizophrenic and determined the percentage who had twins also diagnosed schizophrenic. The results of several of his studies are presented in Table 5–5. Since in all three samples the proportion of persons diagnosed schizophrenic is overwhelmingly higher when the twin also diagnosed schizophrenic is monozygotic, it is easy to see why many have found in Kallmann's data compelling evidence for a genetic etiology of schizophrenia.

TABLE 5–5

Percentage of Persons Diagnosed Schizophrenic Given a Twin Also Diagnosed Schizophrenic Reported by Kallmann

		1946	*1950*	*1954*
Dizygotic	Same sex	17.7		
	Opposite sex	11.5		
	Combined	14.7	14.5	12.5
Monozygotic	Not separated	91.5		
	Separated	77.6		
	Combined	85.8	86.2	86.2

Source: Adapted from Jackson, 1960.

Despite the powerful correlational data, Kallmann's work has a number of important failings. Jackson (1960) has correctly observed that inferring genetic causation of schizophrenia from work such as Kallmann's involves two assumptions:

(1) that individuals have been exposed to stress or psychogenic trauma similar to that experienced by schizophrenics without developing schizophre-

[5] Jackson, who provides a summary of the reviews, does not himself agree with this conclusion.

nia; (2) that many cases exist of identical twins who have been reared from infancy or early childhood in separate and distinct environments and yet both have developed schizophrenia (p. 38).

The first point, Jackson observes, presumes that we know which psychological conditions ("psychogenic traumas") are conducive to schizophrenia. While there are numerous and *divergent* speculations on this point (based on correlational or case history data), there is neither agreement nor compelling evidence which speaks to the issue.

With respect to the second assumption, present circumstances are even less favorable.

> . . . let it be said here regarding twins who are alleged to have been reared apart and who both developed schizophrenia that an exhaustive search of American and European literature of the past forty years has uncovered only two such cases (Jackson, 1960, p. 40).

The last point requires some amplification when it is juxtaposed with the "separated" category in Table 5–5. Jackson notes that Kallmann's term *separated* refers "only to *separation five years prior to the psychosis*" and points out that:

> Because his age group ranged from 15 to 44 years, and because his average age of subjects is stated to be 33 years . . . it is obvious that the twins were not apart during their formative years. Indeed, most remained together well past the usual age for marriage; and even this late in life separation resulted in a significant decrease in concordance for schizophrenia (p. 40).

It appears, then, that Kallmann's data do not allow for an unequivocal separation of the effects of heredity and environment. However, taking Kallmann's data together with more recent studies, the suggestion that there is *some* genetic component to schizophrenia is still fairly compelling (Mowrer, 1969). The next genetic personality research which we shall examine is not subject to such sharp criticism.

The Heritability of Normal Personality: Gottesman's Demonstration

We have noted that most genetic personality research has focused upon abnormal behavior patterns and that this research has been plagued by a number of methodological flaws. However, one recent study has focused upon genetic determinants of normal personality and, moreover, has been far more sensitive to methodological problems than its predecessors. The investigation was reported by Gottesman (1963) in a monograph entitled "Heritability of Personality: A Demonstration."

Gottesman began by enumerating *all* of the same-sexed twins enrolled in public high schools in the Minneapolis–Saint Paul area, thereby drawing his twin sample from a population of over 31,000 children.

Voluntary cooperation of more than half of the twin pairs in this sample was then secured. Gottesman legitimately noted that his sample "compares favorably in size with the majority of twin studies reported in the psychological literature. In representativeness, it is superior to the majority" (p. 4).

The next problem was to determine with high certainty which of the pairs were monozygotic (MZ) and which dizygotic (DZ). Most previous researchers had failed to fully appreciate the importance of Gottesman's observation:

> If twins differ in sex or any other known inherited characteristic they cannot be MZ twins. However, if the characteristics are alike, the possibility remains that the twins are DZ. Given a number of simply inherited and widely distributed traits, it is possible to state the probability of monozygosity or dizygosity for a given pair of twins. It is to be noted, however, that all such diagnoses of monozygosity, no matter how many characteristics are identical, will always be statements of probability; that is, the probability of sharing the given number of traits in common (p. 5).

With this strategy in mind, Gottesman used the combined criteria of blood typing on nine blood groups, fingerprint ridge count, height and weight, and judgments by geneticists, psychologists, and artists. The probability of a chance likeness on all of these characteristics, given that the twins were actually dizygotic, is about 1 in 200. Thus, Gottesman's procedure engendered high certainty that he had successfully distinguished between monozygotic and dizygotic pairs. Furthermore, the 68 pairs were found, by this assessment procedure, to consist of 34 monozygotic pairs and 34 dizygotic pairs, precisely the estimate which would be made from prior knowledge of twin frequencies.[6]

Gottesman's Assessment of Personality. The personality measures Gottesman used in his study were derived from three paper-and-pencil tests. The first was the Minnesota Multiphasic Personality Inventory (MMPI), which consists of 550 statements about one's self which must be answered true or false. The MMPI is typically scored for 10 clinical scales, each representating a personality trait (for example, depression, social introversion-extroversion, and so on). The second test used was Cattell's High School Personality Questionnaire (HSPQ), which was specifically developed for use with persons between the ages of 12 and 17. Its 280 forced-choice items form 14 scales (also representing personality traits), which are said to "cover all the major dimensions involved in any comprehensive view of individual differences in personality"

---

[6] Of the total population of twins, one third would be monozygotic and two thirds dizygotic. However, among the latter, *half* would be opposite sexed. Thus, an equal number of monozygotic twins (who are, by definition same sexed) and same-sexed dizygotic twins would be expected.

(Gottesman, 1963, p. 7). Finally, subjects' IQ scores were available.

Of the 24 scales on the two personality tests, 6 (5 from the MMPI and 1 from the HSPQ) were found to be more closely related for monozygotic than for dizygotic twins. Paradoxically, on the HSPQ, four of the scales which showed a zero correlation for the monozygotic twins were significantly related for the dizygotic twins. The remaining scales did not differentiate between monozygotic and dizygotic pairs. IQ scores were more closely related for monozygotic than for dizygotic pairs.

Overall, Gottesman's results seem to suggest *some* hereditary component on *some* measures of personality. That is, when important methodological considerations are taken into account, there is some evidence for a relationship between heredity and personality. However, the evidence, which requires a good deal of cautious qualification, has revealed some inexplicable peculiarities (Why, for example, should fraternal twins be *more* alike than identical twins on 4 of the 24 personality dimensions?) and clearly demands further research.

Although we have focused thus far upon constitutional and genetic type and trait positions, these are not the only approaches to the study of types and traits. The monumental trait theory of Gordon Allport, which we shall consider next, pays little attention to genetic and constitutional variables.

ALLPORT'S TRAIT THEORY

As noted earlier in this chapter, Allport took a trait position whose fundamental assumption is that personality *exists* (heuristic realism) and that the psychologist's job is to find and describe it within the person. In 1966, Allport somewhat retrospectively examined the position which he first put forth in 1931. Recognizing the difficulties it involved, he asserted that the job of finding out "what the other fellow is really like" should not be shunned because of these considerations.

> The incredible complexity of the structure we seek to understand is enough to discourage the realist, and to tempt him to play some form of positivistic gamesmanship. He is tempted to settle for such elusive formulations as: "If we knew enough about the situation we wouldn't need the concept of personality"; or, "One's personality is merely the way other people see one"; or, "There is no structure in personality but only varying degrees of consistency in the environment." Yet the truly persistent realist prefers not to abandon his commitment to find out what the other fellow is really like (Allport, 1966, p. 3).

Where does the task of finding out what a person is really like begin? According to Allport (1960), personality must reside in a "psychophysical matrix" which is literally within the person.

> Human personality has a locus—within the skin. To be sure, its imagination and memory range far and wide, but these acts are well grounded in a

psychophysical matrix of some order. On another plane of existence, personality may be freed from its space-time bondage, but on the plane where the psychologist dwells, it must be viewed as an organic unity accessible to study through its acts, its verbal report and even its reflex and physiological functioning (p. 20).

But looking within the skin is not enough of a guideline. We must further decide what units to employ. What are the specific structures for which we search? Allport's answer is that we are looking for traits. His original statement of the characteristics of traits and the assumptions he makes about them appeared in 1931. They were relisted (and still judged to be defensible) in 1966. His eight assertions were:

1. *Traits have more than nominal existence.*
2. *Traits are more generalized than habits.* Brushing one's teeth, Allport notes, may well be a habit but is not properly called a trait (although an underlying trait—for example, cleanliness—might account for it).
3. *Traits are* (at least) *determinative in behavior.* Traits direct action and are not mere structural artifacts. Nor do they, as the intrapsychic structures posited by Freud, require energizing from somewhere else.
4. *Traits may be established empirically.* Allport was steeped in the tradition of experimental psychology and acknowledged unequivocally that theorists must finally defer to their data.
5. *Traits are only relatively independent of other traits.* Allport suggested that the following example was illustrative of this assertion:

In one study, expansion correlated with extroversion to the extent of +.39; ascendance with conservatism, +.22; humor with insight, +.83; and so on. This overlap may be due to several factors, the most obvious being the tendency of the organism to react in an integrated fashion: when concrete acts are observed or tested, they reflect not only the trait under examination but also, and simultaneously, other traits. . . . It seems safer, therefore, to predict that traits can never be completely isolated for study, since they never show more than relative independence of one another (Allport, 1960, p. 133).

6. *Traits are not synonymous with moral or social judgments.*
7. *Traits may be viewed either in the light of the personality which contains them, or in the light of their distribution in the population.*
8. *Acts, and even habits, that are inconsistent with a trait are not proof of the nonexistence of the trait.*

The Dimensions of Traits: Pervasiveness within a Personality

Allport has proposed that an individual's traits may be classified in terms of the degree to which they pervade his personality. He specifically distinguished among three levels of traits, although he acknowledged that "these three graduations are arbitrary and are phrased mainly for convenience of discourse" (1961, p. 365).

The most pervasive traits are referred to as *cardinal dispositions.* A cardinal disposition dominates the individual's entire existence. It cannot remain hidden and often makes its possessor famous. The proper names of historical and fictitious characters which become trait adjectives in our language, such as *quixotic, machiavellian,* and *lesbian,* suggest what is meant by a cardinal disposition, as do the use of the names themselves (for example, "He is a real Beau Brummel."). According to Allport, few persons have cardinal dispositions.

Central dispositions refer to the relatively small number of traits which tend to be highly characteristic of the individual. They might be thought of as those characteristics which one would enumerate when writing a detailed letter of recommendation. Given this sort of definition and the further suggestion that all persons can be characterized by central dispositions, a vital question becomes: "How many central dispositions does the average person have?"

Addressing himself to this question, Allport (1961) asked 93 students "'to think of some one individual of your own sex whom you know well'" and "'to describe him or her by writing words, phrases, or sentences that express fairly well what seem to you to be the essential characteristics of this person'" (p. 366). Most students listed between 3 and 10 essential characteristics. The average number was 7.2.

Secondary dispositions are those characteristics of the individual which operate only in limited settings. Preferences for particular kinds of food, fairly specific attitudes, and other "peripheral" or situationally determined characteristics of the person would be placed in this category.

The Dimensions of Traits: Comparison with Other Personalities

Allport also argued that traits may be viewed either as characteristics which allow us to compare one person with another (as we might compare body weights) or as unique characteristics of the individual which need not invite, or even permit, comparison with others. Trait comparisons across people involve the assumption of *common traits* and have often been referred to as part of the psychology of "individual differences."

Life situations continually require us to compare people. Businessmen must choose between prospective candidates for a secretarial position; colleges must identify the best applicants for higher education; and in most situations where the job or role is fixed, someone is required to identify the personality or person who "fits." While most of us make such rough and approximate comparisons between persons daily, the researcher committed to a theory of common traits must formalize both his criteria for identifying a common trait and his procedures for measuring it.

This task is exemplified in a study by Allport and Allport (1928) in which the investigators were interested in finding a common dimension or trait which they labeled *ascendance-submission.* The first step was to develop a *scale* or test which *operationalizes* the dimension of interest. The scale which they developed asked individuals to respond to a variety of situations in which the alternatives for action could be characterized as either dominating another or being dominated oneself. For example:

> Someone tries to push ahead of you in line. You have been waiting for some time, and can't wait much longer. Suppose the intruder is of the same sex as yourself, do you usually:
>
> Remonstrate with the intruder _______
> "Look daggers" at the intruder or make clearly audible comments to your neighbor _______
> Decide not to wait, and go away _______
> Do nothing _______
>
> (Allport, 1961, p. 338)

How does one score the responses? Allport (1961) points out:

> A mere guess would be of little value. Actually, an empirical scoring procedure was devised. In a large group of men and women (the test has separate forms for each), seven friends were asked to rate the subjects on the trait in question. The group was then divided into quarters, depending on whether their average ratings were high, low, or moderate on ascendance and submission. . . . If an answer were nearly twice as common among submissive people, it was scored minus. . . . The diagnostic power of each reply was thus determined empirically. In some cases there was no differential frequency between subjects rated ascendant and those rated submissive. In such cases the scoring value is 0 (pp. 426–27).

In our example, "remonstrate with the intruder" is a moderately ascendant response and is scored +2, " 'look daggers' at the intruder . . ." and "do nothing" are moderately submissive responses and are scored −2, and "decide not to wait, and go way" is an even more submissive response and is scored −3. The scoring system reveals a shrewdness of method, but it does not supply any evidental value, since for Allport the proof of the trait's existence lies in its *reliability.* The reliability of a measure (test) refers to its consistency or repeatability and is customarily expressed as a correlation coefficient. If a test has high *test-retest reliability* (consistency between administrations), when the same test (or an equivalent form) is given to the same persons at a later time, each person should place about the same on the scale on both occasions. Here the correlation is between test administrations. If a test has high *internal reliability,* all or most of the items in the test tend to be measuring the same thing, and thus the correlation is between items or groups of items. Trait theory requires that an individual who is ascendant in one situation (i.e., on one item) should also tend to be so in other situations. Allport has reported that the test for ascendance-submission has a test-retest reliability of +.78 and an internal reliability of +.85, thereby indicating a moderately high degree of reliability for the trait in question.

Common traits, according to Allport, when scaled for the population at large, often prove to have a *normal distribution.* That is, the scores of a large sample, when plotted on a graph, appear to produce a continuous bell-shaped curve, with the majority of cases piling up as average scores in the middle and the number of high and low scorers tapering off as one looks at the more extreme positions. Many physical characteristics (for example, height and weight) are normally distributed (i.e., when plotted they form a normal curve), and human intelligence is thought to be distributed normally. Allport's test for ascendance-submission appears to be normally distributed, as seen in Figure 5–2.

FIGURE 5–2

The Distribution of Scores from a Test Measuring Ascendance-Submission

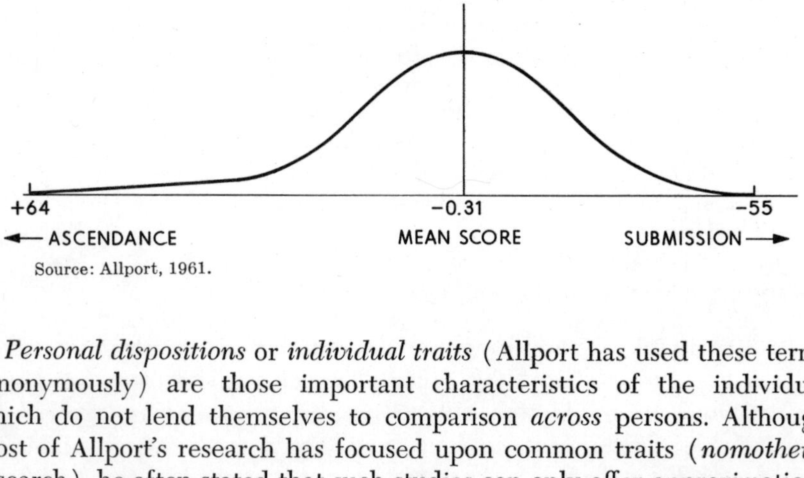

Source: Allport, 1961.

Personal dispositions or *individual traits* (Allport has used these terms synonymously) are those important characteristics of the individual which do not lend themselves to comparison *across* persons. Although most of Allport's research has focused upon common traits (*nomothetic* research), he often stated that such studies can only offer approximations of what persons are really like—that is, we must ultimately study the individual *idiographically* (without comparison to others). He insisted that "the key-qualities which we seek must . . . be *personal,* not universal" adding that:

. . . I am not repudiating the use of nomothetic factors, nor of test-scales, ratings and dimensions. More of my own research and writing has been devoted to this type of approach to personality than to any other. The resulting "common traits," I find, have utility for *comparative* purposes, for approximations to the modes of adjustment that similarly constituted individuals in similarly constituted societies can be expected to acquire. . . . What I argue is that . . . we must acknowledge the roughness and inadequacy of our universal dimensions. Thereby shall we enhance our own ability to understand, predict and control. By learning to handle the individuality of motives and the uniqueness of personality, we shall become better scientists, not worse (1960, p. 148).

This task is accomplished, according to Allport (1966), by searching "for the natural cleavages that mark an individual life" (p. 7), a procedure illustrated in his *Letters from Jenny* (1965). This case study was based on the personal letters of Jenny Gove Masterson, which:

. . . tell the story of a mother-son relationship and trace the course of a life beset by frustration and defeat. . . . Between the ages of fifty-eight and seventy she wrote a series of 301 letters to two young friends, a married couple living and teaching in an eastern college town. The tie of friendship extended back to the time when the husband . . . had been the roommate of Jenny's son . . . at college, about ten years before the beginning of the correspondence. . . . The correspondence begins in earnest in March, 1926, and continues without interruption for eleven and a half years, until Jenny's death in October, 1937 (Allport, 1965, p. v).

The letters were evaluated by 36 judges, who read them in sequence and assigned a total of 198 descriptive adjectives to Jenny based on their overall impression of her personality. Many of the adjectives were synonymous, and when they were combined, eight central traits emerged. Since there was little information about Jenny other than what is contained in her letters, the accuracy of this impressionistic (commonsense) analysis (i.e., its external validity) could not be assessed. However, it was possible to compare the impressionistic description with one derived from a more systematic method of analysis. The procedure involved a determination of the frequency with which various key or "tag" words in the letters were used in conjunction with one another. The resulting data were factor-analyzed (see Chapter 6) yielding seven traits. When the traits derived from the two divergent methods (one impressionistic and the other statistical) are compared, there are differences in terminology, but a marked similarity of description is nevertheless apparent, as can be seen in Table 5–6 (page 120).

Allport interprets the similarity of the two analyses as evidence for the validity of the conclusions about Jenny's personality and at the same time construes the disparities found as confirming the utility of the idiographic approach:

. . . the judges, it seems, gain much from the running style of the letters. Since the style is constant it would not appear in a factorial analysis. . . . The

TABLE 5–6

Evaluation of Jenny's Personality from Her Letters Based on Impressionistic and Factor-Analytic Assessment

Commonsense Traits	*Factorial Traits*
Quarrelsome-suspicious Aggressive	Aggression
Self-centered (possessive)	Possessiveness
Sentimental	Need for affiliation Need for family acceptance
Independent-autonomous	Need for autonomy
Esthetic-artistic	Sentience
Self-centered (self-pitying)	Martyrdom
(No parallel)	Sexuality
Dramatic-intense	("Overstate")

Source: Adapted from Allport, 1966.

common-sense traits *cynical-morbid* and *dramatic-intense* are judgements of a pervading expressive style in Jenny's personality and seem to be missed by factoring procedure (1966, p. 8).

But is not the assignment of a list of traits to Jenny a mere variation on the dimensional or comparative approach? According to Allport, the answer is no. The idiographic approach is not necessarily characterized by an absence of either labels or statistics. It is characterized by the positive quality of letting the behavior of the person under study, rather than an existing battery of tests, measuring instruments, or types, dictate the description which will emerge.

Integration of Personality: The Proprium

Allport's fifth characteristic of traits asserts that they are only relatively independent of one another. Since traits interact, it is reasonable to suppose some sort of executive function not unlike Freud's use of the term *ego*. Indeed, the terms *ego* and *self* often appear in Allport's writing as labels for the unifying force in personality. These labels have, according to Allport (1961), referred to at least seven different aspects of "selfhood." They are listed in the order of their probable occurrence in the growing child.

1. A sense of the bodily self, as when the child begins to distinguish between his fingers and the objects which they hold.
2. A sense of continuing self-identity, developed as the child begins to

understand that *he* is the continuing referent for his own name.
3. A sense of pride or self-esteem, reflected in the young child's delighted "I beat you" (as, for example, when he wins a competitive game).
4. A recognition of extensions of self in one's possessions (for example, "This is *my* bike").
5. A self-image ("I am naughty").
6. A sense of self as a problem solver, with a rational capacity which can be imposed upon problems.
7. Finally, the individual develops some defining objective(s) which become "the cement holding a life together . . . its 'directedness' or 'intentionality.' "

Allport (1961) argued that these seven aspects of selfhood can be united, asserting that they are all "states of self-relevance that we *feel* . . . involved in matters of importance to the organized emotional life of the individual" (p. 127). He further observed that the name used to unite these feelings cannot be *ego* or *self,* because these terms have already been spoken for, and have in fact been used differently by different theorists. Allport suggests the term *proprium* to unite the seven aspects of selfhood. Allport argues that the concept is important for several reasons. First, the subjective or felt side of ourselves is something we all know about, hence it would be foolish for psychologists to ignore it (as some have) merely because it is a difficult notion to study. Second, there is some evidence that a man's performance in a variety of tasks can be significantly influenced by the degree of self-involvement. Third, acknowledging the existence of a proprium opens up lines of research such as the determination of which *propriate feelings* (feelings of self) are most pervasive, gnawing, or uncomfortable.

In one study, for example, college students were asked to state the type of inferiority feelings they had (if any) and whether they felt persistent feelings of inferiority about themselves. The results of the study; which appear in Table 5–7, suggest an interesting hierarchy of

TABLE 5–7

Inferiority in College Students

	Percentage Reporting Persistent Inferiority Feelings	
Type of Inferiority Feeling	*Men (243)*	*Women (120)*
Physical	39	50
Social	52	57
Intellectual	29	61
Moral	16	15
None at all	12	10

Source: Allport, 1961.

importance. Also, it appears that men have fewer feelings of inferiority than women. Allport suggests that this latter finding occurs because we are still living in a "man's world" in which the emancipation of women is not yet complete.

The Transformation of Motives: Functional Autonomy

Allport acknowledges that the personality must be dynamic and that individuals must somehow be impelled to action. However, unlike Freud, Allport holds that motivation is to be found within the structures of personality (traits) rather than as an orthogonal force. Further, motivation for Allport is contemporaneous, meaning that it can be understood in the present rather than as the distorted dregs and monsters of previous needs and strivings. To these ends, Allport formulated a general law of motivation called the principle of *functional autonomy* which he defined as "*any acquired system of motivation in which the tensions involved are not of the same kind as the antecedent tensions from which the acquired system developed*" (1961, p. 229). The nature of functional autonomy is illustrated in the following example:

Joe, let us say, is the son of a famous politician. As a young lad he imitates everything his father does, even perhaps giving "speeches." Years pass and the father dies. Joe is now middle-aged and is deeply absorbed in politics. He runs for office, perhaps the selfsame job his father held. What, then, motivates Joe today? Is it his earlier fixation? . . . The chances . . . are that his interest in politics has outgrown its roots in "father identification." There is historical continuity but no longer any functional continuity. Politics is now his dominant passion; it is his style of life; it is a large part of Joe's personality. The original seed has been discarded (Allport, 1961, pp. 228–29).

Allport has distinguished between two levels or forms of functional autonomy, *perseverative* and *propriate*. Perseverative motives refer to biologically derived rhythms, patterns of physical movement, and habits which once were adaptive but no longer serve a useful purpose. Though perseverative motives are present in all persons as well as in infrahuman species, they are not essential to the fundamental organization of the personality. Allport (1961) introduces five lines of evidence to support the existence of these motives.

First, he finds supportive evidence from infrahuman behavior as the burrowing of molluscs "whose habits of burrowing in the sand and reappearing depend on the movements of the tide, will, when removed from the beach to the laboratory, continue the same rhythm without the tide" (p. 230). Addiction, as to tobacco and alcohol in humans, provides a second line of evidence. "Circular mechanisms" such as a child's self-perpetuating babbling provide a third. Fourth, humans can often be observed perseverating on tasks of no extrinsic meaning, as when one tries unsuccessfully to remember the name of a third-grade teacher and is then consumed with the task until the name can be retrieved from memory. Finally, our adherence to familiar and routine patterns of behavior as reflected in our desire to dine at a set hour each day and in feelings of homesickness suggests the presence of perseverative functional autonomy.

In contrast to the "lower-level" perseverative motives, *propriate strivings* or motives refer to acquired interests, values, and attitudes. As their name implies, propriate strivings are intimately tied to the organization of the personality (i.e., to the proprium) and in a large measure account for the individual's overall style of life. Propriate strivings thus play a major role in determining one's behavior. In our earlier example dealing with the son of a famous politician becoming a politician himself, the son was motivated by propriate, rather than perseverative, functional autonomy. Allport (1961) makes three basic observations which support his concept of propriate motivation.

First, Allport (1961) observes that there are many occasions in which ability turns to interest.

> Now the original reason for learning a skill may not be interest at all. For example, a student who first undertakes a field of study in college because it is required, because it pleases his parents, or because it comes at a convenient hour may find himself absorbed in the topic, perhaps for life. The original motives may be entirely lost. What was a means to an end becomes an end itself (pp. 235–36).

Second, Allport notes that acquired interests and values often have selective power. One study has shown, for example, that people with an aesthetic interest will read more articles pertaining to art than will less aesthetic people (Engstrom and Power, 1959). Finally, Allport asserts that a person's self-image becomes a major organizing factor in his life. He says:

> I am speaking here of the highest levels of organization in personality. Most theories of personality (especially those postulating "unchanging energies") overlook the motivational power of higher-level formations. . . . The more important instance of functional autonomy is found in the complex propriate organization that determines the "total posture" of a mature life system.
>
> A prominent ingredient of this master dynamism is the sense of responsibility one takes for one's life. The way one defines one's role and duties in life determines much of one's daily conduct (Allport, 1961, p. 237).

What evidence of the presence of such organizing principles exists? Some interesting work on religious orientation by Allport and his colleagues is relevant.

The problem is this. Studies of church attenders have found them to show more ethnic prejudice, on the average, than nonattenders. This finding is apparently contradictory to Christian teachings. Perhaps the controlling factor, Allport argued, is an orientation orthogonal to church attendance. Thus, it was "tentatively assumed that two contrasting but measurable forms of religious orientation exist" (Allport, 1966, pp. 5–6). An *extrinsic* orientation represents "an instrumental value serving the motives of comfort, security, or social status" (p. 6) rather than true devotion. In contrast, an *intrinsic* orientation holds that faith is "a supreme value in its own right" (p. 6).

A scale was devised to assess a person's predominant orientation toward religion. Two of the items from the scale follow. Agreement with the first statement is indicative of an extrinsic orientation, while agreement with the second is indicative of an intrinsic orientation.

What religion offers me most is comfort when sorrow and misfortune strike.

My religious beliefs are what really lie behind my whole approach to life.

The utility of Allport's distinction between intrinsic and extrinsic orientation was determined by correlating religious orientation with various scales of ethnic prejudice. As can be seen in Table 5–8, in each case an extrinsic orientation is positively related to prejudice (extrinsic orientation tends to be associated with prejudice), while an intrinsic orientation is negatively related to prejudice (intrinsic orientation tends to be associated with an absence of prejudice).

This research, like most of Allport's work, is interesting because of the nature of the topic which it addresses. The method, however, is not a direct outgrowth of Allport's trait approach. In the case of the research

TABLE 5–8

The Relationship between Religious Orientation among Church Attenders and Various Forms of Ethnic Prejudice

Denominational sample	*Religious Orientation*	*Type of Prejudice*	*Correlation*
Unitarian (N = 50)*	Extrinsic	Anti-Catholic	+.56
	Intrinsic	Anti-Catholic	−.36
	Extrinsic	Anti-Mexican	+.54
	Intrinsic	Anti-Mexican	−.42
Catholic (N = 66)	Extrinsic	Anti-Negro	+.36
	Intrinsic	Anti-Negro	−.49
Nazarene (N = 39)	Extrinsic	Anti-Negro	+.41
	Intrinsic	Anti-Negro	−.44
Mixed† (N = 207)	Extrinsic	Anti-Semitic	+.65

* Indicates number of subjects in sample.
† From Wilson (1960).
Source: Allport, 1966.

just discussed, the presence of a single "organizing principle" was supported but the results are not interpretable only by Allport's theory. One research method, factor analysis, has grown directly out of the general assumptions of a trait strategy, and it is this method to which we shall turn our attention in the next chapter.

REFERENCES

Allport, G. W. *Letters from Jenny.* New York: Harcourt, Brace & World, 1965.

Allport, G. W. *Pattern and growth in personality.* New York: Holt, Rinehart & Winston, 1961.*

Allport, G. W. *Personality and social encounter: Selected essays.* Boston: Beacon Press, 1960.

Allport, G. W. Traits revisited. *American Psychologist,* 1966, **21,** 1–10.

Allport, G. W., and Allport, F. H. *The A–S reaction study.* Boston: Houghton Mifflin, 1928.

Engstrom, W. C., and Power, M. E. A revision of the study of values for use in magazine readership research. *Journal of Applied Psychology,* 1959, **43,** 74–78.

Gottesman, I. I. Heritability of personality. *Psychological Monographs,* 1963, **77,** 1–21.

Guilford, J. P. *Personality.* New York: McGraw-Hill, 1959.

Jackson, D. *The etiology of schizophrenia.* New York: Basic Books, 1960.

Kretschmer, E. *Physique and character: An investigation of the nature of constitution and of the theory of temperament.* W. J. H. Sprott (Trans.). New York: Harcourt, 1926.

Mischel, W. *Personality and assessment.* New York: Wiley, 1968.

Mowrer, O. H. The behavioral vs. disease model of psychopathology—Do we need new patterns of training and treatment? Paper presented at the Third Annual Meeting of the Association for the Advancement of Behavior Therapy, Washington, D.C., September 1–2, 1969.

Sheldon, W. H. *The varieties of temperament: A psychology of constitutional differences.* New York: Harper, 1942.

Williams, R. J. The biological approach to the study of personality. In T. Millon (Ed.), *Theories of psychopathology.* Philadelphia: Saunders, 1967. Pp. 19–31.

chapter 6

Trait and Type Approaches: Factor Analysis and Methods of Assessment

In the previous chapter we discussed the basic underpinnings of trait and type approaches and considered several alternative theories. The present chapter is primarily concerned with some of the methods which have been devised for trait research and assessment.

MULTIVARIATE RESEARCH AND FACTOR ANALYSIS

The Logic of Factor Analysis

Raymond B. Cattell, a prominent trait theorist, has quipped that "the trouble with measuring traits is that there are too many of them!" (1965, p. 55). Cattell (1965) was referring to the procedure, central to most trait research, "to fancy some particular trait . . . and to concentrate on its relations to all kinds of things" (p. 55). This procedure, Cattell argues, has many disadvantages, the most salient being that trait researchers cannot compare or integrate their findings with one another, nor agree on what is a referent for such commonly researched traits as "anxiety." If a common method were employed, which allowed for interrelating the various findings of trait research and the simultaneous examination of many traits, this problem would be solved. A statistical technique with these properties is available and has come to be called *factor analysis.* In this section, we shall examine the basic assumptions and principles of factor analysis and consider some research which has been based on this technique.

Cattell and most other researchers who have used factor-analytic techniques believe that there are natural, unitary structures in personality which underlie the various trait names and behaviors which have traditionally been examined. Freud, it will be recalled, assumed the existence of three structures in all persons, while Allport assumed that each individual had a unique (trait) structure. Cattell (1965), in contrast to both, believes that there is a common structure across personalities which must be determined *empirically,* in the same way that the elements of the physical universe were discovered.

> The problem which baffled psychologists for many years was to find a method which would tease out these functionally unitary influences in the chaotic jungle of human behavior. But let us ask how, in the literal tropical jungle, the hunter decides whether the dark blobs which he sees are two or three rotting logs or a single alligator? He watches for movement. *If they move together*—come and disappear together—*he infers a single structure.* Just so, as John Stuart Mill pointed out in his philosophy of science, the scientist should look for "concomitant variation" in seeking unitary concepts (p. 56, italics added).

In the jungle of human behavior, however, perfect covariation is rarely to be found. Psychological variables do not seem to *always* go together. We may get a fleeting glimpse of some strong covariations but never the perfect data generated by Cattell's alligator. The correlational method, discussed in Chapter 2, allows for the evaluation of degrees of relationship which are not perfect, and it is the statistical correlation coefficient which is at the heart of factor-analytic procedures. However, factor analysis uses not one or two correlations, but instead examines the entire *array of intercorrelations* among the variables of interest. Although factor analysis was first developed in 1904 by Charles Spearman, a British psychologist and statistician, its recent popularity is a result of the availability of high-speed computers, without which much of the current work using the technique would be virtually impossible.

Consider the hypothetical *correlation matrix* which appears in Table 6–1. It contains the correlations of each of seven measures with every other measure. What this matrix tells us is that there is a high positive relationship between *a* and *b*(+.7), *a* and *c*(+.8), *a* and *d*(+.8), *b* and *c*(+.9), *b* and *d*(+.7), *c* and *d*(+.8), *e* and *f*(+.8), *e* and *g*(+.7), *f* and *g*(+.7), and virtually no systematic relationship (i.e., correlation coefficients in the vicinity of 0) between *a* and *e*(−.1), *a* and *f*(.0), *a* and *g*(.0), *b* and *e* (+.1), *b* and *f*(+.1), *b* and *g*(.0), *c* and *e*(−.1), *c*

TABLE 6–1

Hypothetical Correlation Matrix

Measure	*a*	*b*	*c*	*d*	*e*	*f*	*g*
a	+1.0	+ .7	+ .8	+ .8	− .1	.0	.0
b		+1.0	+ .9	+ .7	+ .1	+ .1	.0
c			+1.0	+ .8	− .1	− .1	− .1
d				+1.0	.0	− .1	.0
e					+1.0	+ .8	+ .7
f						+1.0	+ .7
g							+1.0

and *f*(−.1), *c* and g(−.1), *d* and *e* (.0), *d* and *f*(−.1), *d* and g(.0).

Despite the rather clear-cut nature of our hypothetical correlation matrix and the relatively small number of variables included (it is not uncommon for 100 or more variables to be correlated with each other in factor-analytic studies), the complexities and sheer time needed to summarize and interpret the data contained in the matrix should be apparent from the enumeration of results just presented. One of the major functions of factor analysis is to reduce large sets of data (most often in the form of correlation matrices) to manageable units. By means of complex mathematical formulas, the data are reduced to the smallest number of relatively homogeneous (and usually independent) dimensions, called *factors,* which accounts for the relationships (correlations) among the variables. While further explication of factor-analytic procedures is beyond the scope of this book (and is not necessary for an understanding of the theory and research based on factor analysis which we shall discuss), the following discussion of the hypothetical correlation matrix in Table 6–1 should give the reader a feeling for the basic strategy which underlies the analysis.

Inspection of the matrix reveals that among the seven measures (*a* through *g*) there is a distinct pattern to be found. Specifically *a, b, c,* and *d* seem to "go together." They are highly correlated with one another but show little or no relationship (i.e., near 0) to the other three measures. Similarly, *e, f,* and *g,* are highly related to one another but not to the other measures. Thus, two units or *factors* emerge from the seven measures. These might be labeled sterilely (for example, factor *X* and factor *Y*), or the investigator could inspect the several related measures for their common qualities and provide a more meaningful name than *X* or *Y* for the two factors. However, the naming itself would be a *subjective judgment* and not a logical consequence of the statistical procedures involved.

To make our example more concrete, suppose the measures were aptitude tests for academic fields where $a =$ English, $b =$ fine arts, $c =$ history, $d =$ French, $e =$ mathematics, $f =$ physics, and $g =$ engineering. Factor X would then consist of English, fine arts, history, and French, and factor Y would consist of mathematics, physics, and enneering. In this case, the naming of the factors would be easy, though in practice naming factors is rarely so clear-cut.

A number of personality psychologists have turned to factor analysis as a strategy for directing their research and theorizing. We shall discuss two of the more prominent theorists, Cattell and H. J. Eysenck.

Cattell and the Multivariate "Experiment"

Cattell (1965) proposes that there should be three broad sources of data about personality, which he labels *L*-data, *Q*-data, and *T*-data. *L*-data refer to that information which can be gathered from the life record of the individual and are usually taken from ratings by observers as to the frequency and intensity of occurrence of specific kinds of behavior. *Q*-data consist of information gathered from questionnaires and interviews. The common feature of *Q*-data is that the individual answers direct questions about himself, based on his own observations and introspection (for example, "Do you have trouble making and keeping friends?"). Data gathered from so-called *objective tests* are referred to as *T*-data. Teachers and educators might well be tempted to call questionnaire and essay data (i.e., *Q*-data) "objective," whenever these are scored in some standardized way so as to lead two or more examiners to exactly the same conclusion. However, Cattell argues that these procedures are often not objective in another sense, since the individual may "give himself airs" or otherwise attempt to fabricate or distort his responses. Elaborate checks might be devised to assuage these possibilities, but they are no more than locking the barn door after the horse is stolen. Thus, Cattell (1965) defines an objective test as one in which "the subject is placed in a miniature situation and simply acts . . . [and] *does not know on what aspect of his behavior he is really being evaluated*" (p. 104).

Cattell argues that these three sources of data can and must be integrated to capture the full complexity of human personality. Traditionally, psychologists have looked at only one slice at a time and their experiments, Cattell asserts, have been *univariate;* that is, experiments which vary one (independent) variable and examine one (dependent) variable. In contrast, the *multivariate* approach has the advantage that "with sufficient analytical subtlety we can tease out the connexions from the behavior of the man in his actual life situation—without the false situation of controlling and manipulating" (1965, p. 20). (Cattell calls such research multivariate experiments but, by the more usual definition [see Chapter 2] they are not really *experiments* at all, for the very reason that they eschew manipulation and control.)

We shall now examine Cattell's assertion that:

> . . . the development of beautiful and complex mathematico-statistical methods like factor analysis has enabled us to take natural data, much as the clinician has long done—except that normals are now included—and to find laws and build sound theories about the structure and functioning of personality (1965, p. 23).

Three Dimensions (Traits) of Personality Derived from L- and Q-Data. Cattell describes some research in which several hundred young men and women were rated by people who knew them well on 50 different "trait elements" (the elements from which the traits are factor-analytically derived). A sample of 10 of these trait elements appears in Table 6–2.

TABLE 6–2

Ten (of 50) Trait Elements on Which Young Men and Women Were Rated

1. *Adaptable:* flexible; accepts changes of plan easily; satisfied with compromises; is not upset, surprised, baffled, or irritated if things are different from what he expected.	vs.	*Rigid:* insists that things be done the way he has always done them; does not adapt his habits and ways of thinking to those of the group; nonplussed if his routine is upset.
2. *Emotional:* excitable; cries a lot (children), laughs a lot, shows affection, anger, all emotions, to excess.	vs.	*Calm:* stable, shows few signs of emotional excitement of any kind; remains calm, even underreacts, in dispute, danger, social hilarity, etc.
3. *Conscientious:* honest; knows what is right and generally does it, even if no one is watching him; does not tell lies or attempt to deceive others; respects others' property.	vs.	*Unconscientious:* somewhat unscrupulous; not too careful about standards of right and wrong where personal desires are concerned; tells lies and is given to little deceits; does not respect others' property.
4. *Conventional:* conforms to accepted standards, ways of acting, thinking, dressing, etc.; does the "proper" thing; seems distressed if he finds he is being different.	vs.	*Unconventional, eccentric:* acts differently from others: not concerned about wearing the same clothes or doing the same things as others; has somewhat eccentric interests, attitudes, and ways of behaving; goes his own rather peculiar way.

TABLE 6–2 *Continued*

5. *Prone to jealousy:* begrudges the achievement of others; upset when others get attention, and demands more for himself; resentful when attention is given to others.	vs.	*Not jealous:* likes people even if they do better than he does; is not upset when others get attention, but joins in praise.
6. *Considerate, polite:* deferential to needs of others; consider others' feelings; allows them before him in line, gives them the biggest share, etc.	vs.	*Inconsiderate, rude:* insolent, defiant, and "saucy" to elders (in children); ignores feelings of others; gives impression that he goes out of his way to be rude.
7. *Quitting:* gives up before he has thoroughly finished a job; slipshod; works in fits and starts; easily distracted, led away from main purposes by stray impulses or external difficulties.	vs.	*Determined, persevering:* sees a job through in spite of difficulties or temptations; strong-willed; painstaking and thorough; sticks at anything until he achieves his goal.
8. *Tender:* governed by sentiment; intuitive, empathetic, sympathetic; sensitive to the feelings of others; cannot do things if they offend his feelings.	vs.	*Tough, hard:* governed by fact and necessity rather than sentiment; unsympathetic; does not mind upsetting others if that is what has to be done.
9. *Self-effacing:* blames himself (or nobody) if things go wrong; reluctant to take credit for achievements; does not seem to think of himself as very important or worthwhile.	vs.	*Egotistical:* blames others whenever there is conflict or things go wrong; often brags; quick to take credit when things go right; has a very good opinion of himself.
10. *Languid, fatigued, slow:* lacks vigour; vague and slow in speech; dawdles, is slow in getting things done.	vs.	*Energetic, alert, active:* quick, forceful, active, decisive, full of pep, vigorous, spirited.

Source: Cattell, 1965.

When a set of correlations among the ratings on the 50 trait elements is subjected to a factor analysis, Cattell finds that a number of factors, perhaps as many as 20, emerge.[1] To determine the relative importance of these factors, they are placed in a hierarchy in terms of the degree (expressed as a proportion) to which a factor "explains" or "accounts for" (technically, the *variance accounted for*) all the trait elements (variables) as a group. Then letters of the alphabet are simply assigned to the factors, with the letter *A* assigned to the factor accounting for the most variance, *B* to the next most important, and so on. Cattell (1965) suggests that this procedure permits one to look at the obtained patterns of results "without prejudice from earlier clinical notions or traditional

[1] The number of factors which adequately summarize a given set of data depends upon the nature of the data and the specific mathematical procedures (type of factor analysis) employed. Thus, with a particular set of data, the total number of factors extracted could vary slightly with different factor-analytic procedures.

popular terms" and notes as an aside that "the investigators of vitamins did just the same, in a parallel situation, where the entities could be identified in terms of their *effects* before truly interpretative chemical labels could be attached to them" (p. 65).

Let us consider the three most important factors (i.e., *A, B,* and *C*) which Cattell found. As part of the factor analysis, the ratings on each of the 50 trait elements, on which the subjects were rated, were correlated with each of the factors which had been found. The resulting correlations are technically called *factor loadings.* The elements which *loaded* (correlated) most highly both in a positive and in a negative direction (recall that the magnitude of a correlation is independent of its sign) are listed in Table 6–3.

TABLE 6–3

Elements (Ratings) Which Load on Source Trait *A:* Affectothymia-vs.-Sizothymia

A + (*Positively Loaded*)		*A* − (*Negatively Loaded*)
Good-natured, easygoing	vs.	Critical, grasping
Cooperative	vs.	Obstructive
Attentive to people	vs.	Cool, aloof
Softhearted	vs.	Hard, precise
Trustful	vs.	Suspicious
Adaptable	vs.	Rigid

Source: Cattell, 1965.

Cattell then inspected information of the type found in Table 6–3, in search of a meaningful name for the factor. He observed that the general characteristics of *A* were similar to the grosser characteristics that Emil Kraepelin[2] had used to distinguish between schizophrenia and the so-called cyclic psychoses. The latter group included manic-depressive psychosis, which we have seen to contrast with schizophrenia in Kretschmer's work. This observation suggested that terms reflecting the parallel might be used—namely, *cyclothymia* and *schizothymia.* However, the dimension (trait) name finally selected was "affectothymia vs. sizothymia." Cattell's (1965) reasons are interesting:

. . . since the tests . . . are likely to be recorded for schoolchildren and discussed with parents, it has seemed best to avoid misunderstandings by using finally the new title for it now adopted, namely *sizothymia,* instead of schizothymia, for *sizo,* deriving from the same root as "size" in painting, means "flat" and refers to what psychiatrists call the "flatness of affect," i.e., the absence of lively and vibrant emotion. . . . It is this coldness and aloofness which, more than anything else, characterizes the *normal A* (minus), i.e., the sizothyme. . . . It will also recommend itself to the psychologist to refer to the

[2] Kraepelin was a German psychiatrist who is largely credited with the traditional (and currently used) scheme of psychiatric classification.

cyclothyme, when normal, as an affectothyme, because the primary characteristic is affect or emotion, not merely the cyclical ups and down of elation and depression which occur in the abnormal, cyclically insane person (pp. 66–67).

Cattell argues that factor *A* (as well as *B* and *C*) is a *source trait,* indicating that it is an underlying variable which is a source or determinant of overt behavior. Cattell (1950) feels that source traits are important because they "promise to be the real structural influences underlying personality" (p. 27). However, not all traits are source traits, since "sometimes things go together by reason of overlap of several influences" (1965, p. 67). More common is the case where a factor emerges because of the combined action of several apparently discrete influences. Such factors, which are clusters of overt variables that tend to go together, are referred to as *surface traits.* For example:

. . . among men in the street there is a correlation cluster or surface trait among such things as large vocabulary, some understanding of mathematics, of history, etc. We recognize that a person high on this *surface trait* is likely (*a*) to have had a longer education, (*b*) to be naturally more intelligent, and (*c*) to have a studious temperament. Here three distinct factors of personality and personal history combine to give a single pattern (1965, pp. 67–68).

In this example, natural intelligence (*b*) and studious temperament (*c*) are presumed to be source traits.

Let us return to our discussion of factor *A,* affectothymia-sizothymia. If it is a source trait, we would expect that the same pattern of results that emerged from the *L*-data (i.e., the ratings on the 50 trait elements) should appear in *Q*-data. That is, if a trait is really an underlying dimension of personality, it should be reflected in all measures of personality. Sample questionnaire responses which load highly on factor *A* are given in Table 6–4 (page 134).

Considering the information which is summarized in Table 6–4 and referring back to the earlier ratings, Cattell (1965) concludes: "The warm sociability at one pole, and the aloofness and unconcern with people at the other are as evident here as in the observers' ratings" (p. 71).

With respect to the ratings on the 50 trait elements, Cattell (1965) concludes that the second largest source trait, factor *B,* ". . . looks like nothing less than general intelligence, and correlates well with actual test results" (p. 72).

Concerning the third largest source trait, factor *C,* he notes that:

The essence of *C* factor appears to be an inability to control one's emotions and impulses, especially by finding for them some satisfactory realistic expression. Looked at from the opposite or positive pole, it sharpens and gives scientific substance to the psychoanalytic concept of "ego strength," which it [factor *C*] has come to be called (1965, pp. 73–74).

TABLE 6–4

Factor A in Questionnaire Responses

1. I would rather work as:	
a) An engineer	*b*) *A social science teacher*
2. I could stand being a hermit?	
a) True	*b*) *False*
3. I am careful to turn up when someone expects me	
a) *True*	*b*) False
4. I would prefer to marry someone who is:	
a) A thoughtful companion	*b*) *Effective in a social group*
5. I would prefer to read a book on:	
a) *National social service*	*b*) New scientific weapons
6. I trust strangers:	
a) Sometimes	*b*) *Practically always*

Note: A person who selects all of the italicized answers has a highly affectothyme temperament, whereas selection of all the nonitalicized responses would indicate sizothymia. Most people, presumably, would fall between these extremes.
Source: Cattell, 1965.

To illustrate the nature of the source trait "ego-strength" exemplary *L*- and *Q*-data are presented in Table 6–5.

Apparent from the sample of Cattell's research which we have discussed is the fact that Cattell has used factor analysis in a highly

TABLE 6–5

L- and *Q*-Data for Source Trait *C*

Behavior Ratings which Load on C

C+ (Positively loaded)	*C*− (Negatively loaded)
Mature	*vs.* Unable to tolerate frustration
Steady, persistent	*vs.* Changeable
Emotionally calm	*vs.* Impulsively emotional
Realistic about problems	*vs.* Evasive, avoids necessary decisions
Absence of neurotic fatigue	*vs.* Neurotically fatigued (with no real effort)

Factor C Questionnaire Responses

Do you find it difficult to take no for an answer even when what you want to do is obviously impossible?	
(*a*) yes	(*b*) *no*
If you had your life to live over again, would you	
(*a*) *want it to be essentially the same*	(*b*) plan it very differently?
Do you often have really disturbing dreams?	
(*a*) yes	(*b*) *no*
Do your moods sometimes make you seem unreasonable even to yourself?	
(*a*) yes	(*b*) *no*
Do you feel tired when you've done nothing to justify it?	
(*a*) *rarely*	(*b*) often
Can you change old habits, without relapse, when you decide to?	
(*a*) *yes*	(*b*) no

Note: A person who selects all of the italicized answers has high ego-strength, whereas selection of all the nonitalicized responses would indicate low ego-strength.
Source: Adapted from Cattell, 1965.

exploratory way. Moreover, he has both innovated trait names and claimed new support for the constructs of other theories (for example, "ego-strength"). Prominent among factor analysts who have employed the method in the service of a somewhat different strategy (although still within the framework of a general trait approach) we find H. J. Eysenck, whose position we shall consider next.

Eysenck's Position

Hans Jergen Eysenck is, like Raymond Cattell, one of the foremost personality theorists to rely heavily on factor-analytic procedures. He has argued that a theory of personality must be based on empirically supported dimensions of personality and has sharply criticized those theories which are overloaded with subtle, undefined, and unsupported structures. One must, however, take some definition or conceptualization on a priori grounds, and Eysenck (1948) speaks of personality as:

> . . . the sum-total of the actual or potential behavior-patterns . . . determined by heredity and environment, it originates and develops through the fundamental interaction of . . . the cognitive sector (intelligence), the conative sector (character), the affective sector (temperament), and the somatic sector (constitution) (p. 25).

Given this position, which formally avows interest in both constitutional and environmental determinants of personality, one must empirically search for major dimensions of personality. Whereas Eysenck has admired Cattell's willingness to "prospect" for a lengthy list of traits, Eysenck himself has chosen to search for a small number of basic personality *types*. Traits, the components of the more general types, have not been sought in most of his factor-analytic studies.

Eysenck's first major search for types of personality was conducted during World War II. Using a multitude of ratings and classifications of a total of approximately 10,000 subjects, factor-analytic procedures led Eysenck to the identification of two major dimensions (factors) of personality: *introversion-extraversion*[3] and *neuroticism.* (Later work suggested the addition of a third dimension, *psychoticism.*)

Factor naming, as we have previously noted, is a subjective procedure divorced from the statistical operations themselves, a point which is well illustrated in the case of Eysenck's introversion-extraversion factor. The major evidence for this dimension came from a study of neurotic soldiers, among whom two groups of symptoms were found which formed the poles of the introversion-extraversion dimension. The "introverts" tended to show anxiety, depression, obsessional tendencies, apathy, irritability,

---

[3] Note that Eysenck's term is *extra*version and not *extro*version.

and autonomic dysfunctions, while the "extraverts" were likely to show hypochondriasis (imaginary illnesses), sex anomalies, poor work histories, and low intelligence. The labeling is contrary to many prevalent definitions of introversion and extroversion. For example, the label is not intended to connote a dimension of "sociability," though social forwardness is the very dimension which leads the layman to describe someone as an extrovert. In fact, Eysenck suggests that an extravert, according to his system, could be "emotional, shy and reserved."

Neuroticism, as referred to in Eysenck's system, refers to the polar opposite of stability. In his book *The Scientific Study of Personality* (1952), Eysenck devotes an entire chapter to the operational definition of neuroticism. Eysenck turns to numerous sources of data to discriminate neurotics from normals, including psychiatric diagnoses, paper-and-pencil tests, behavioral tests of such things as suggestibility and manual dexterity, and constitutional differences. We shall examine a few of these sources. Not surprisingly, ratings show neurotics to be distinguishable from normals on such items as emotional instability, dependence, apprehensiveness, and so on.

The Maudsley Medical Questionnaire[4] is one of the instruments which Eysenck has often used in his personality research. Ten of its 40 items are presented in Table 6–6; neurotics show a higher percentage of endorsement on these items than normals.

TABLE 6–6

Examples of Items on the Maudsley Medical Questionnaire
(neurotics answer "yes" to more items than normals)

Do you find it difficult to get into conversation with strangers?	Yes	No
Do you worry too long over humiliating experiences?	Yes	No
Are your feelings easily hurt?	Yes	No
Do ideas run through your head so that you cannot sleep?	Yes	No
Do you sometimes feel happy, sometimes depressed, without any apparent reason?	Yes	No
Do you daydream a lot?	Yes	No
Do you sweat a great deal without exercise?	Yes	No
Do you often feel disgruntled?	Yes	No
Do you often feel self-conscious in the presence of superiors?	Yes	No
Are you troubled with feelings of inferiority?	Yes	No

Source: Eysenck, 1952.

A second paper-and-pencil measure to distinguish between neurotics and normals, self-reported preferences, is illustrated by an interesting study which compared the food aversions of the two groups (Gough, 1946). The findings of this study, which appear in Table 6–7, clearly reveal that neurotics have considerably more distaste for food than

[4] Eysenck is Director of Psychology at the Maudsley Hospital, London, England.

TABLE 6–7

Aversion of Neurotics and Normals for 20 Foods

Food	*Percentage of Neurotics Disliking*	*Percentage of Normals Disliking*
Tea	29.1	9.0
Grapefruit juice	38.0	4.3
Bean soup	34.2	5.5
Potato soup	45.6	5.1
Salmon	31.6	8.7
Beefsteak	1.3	.0
Veal chops	20.3	2.4
Chicken	8.9	1.2
Fried eggs	16.4	1.2
Cottage cheese	51.9	14.6
Swiss cheese	36.7	8.7
Lima beans (broad beans)	24.0	6.7
Cabbage	35.4	12.2
Corn	12.7	1.6
Mushrooms	53.2	25.2
Radishes	26.6	9.8
Tomatoes	11.4	2.4
Cantaloupe	13.9	3.5
Cherries	13.9	.0
Pears	8.9	0.8

Source: Adapted from Eysenck, 1952.

normals, and incidently provide information about the relative preferences of both groups.

A third measure used by Eysenck, Hull's body sway test of motor suggestibility, also clearly distinguishes between neurotics and normals, not only as dichotomous classes, but also on a continuum from normal to severely neurotic. The subject is merely asked to stand with his eyes closed and his hands at his sides. With his feet together, the subject listens to the following (recorded) instructions: "You are falling, you are falling forward, you are falling forward all the time. You are falling, you are falling, you are falling now . . ." (Eysenck, 1952, p. 106). A thread attached to the subject's clothing runs to a mechanical pointer which indicates on a scale the amount of body sway forwards and backwards. The data, presented graphically in Figure 6–1 (page 138), clearly indicate that motor suggestibility increases with increasing neuroticism for both males and females.

The foregoing investigations of Eysenck and his associates illustrate the strategy he has employed with respect to basic research. Eysenck has argued that his approach may also be fruitfully employed in dealing with practical social problems. We shall consider an example of the application of the dimensional approach to a real-life problem, the employability of "mental defectives."

In considering 104 males who were institutionalized in Britain be-

FIGURE 6–1

Average Suggestibility of Normals and Neurotics Showing Increase Suggestibility as "Neuroticism" Increases

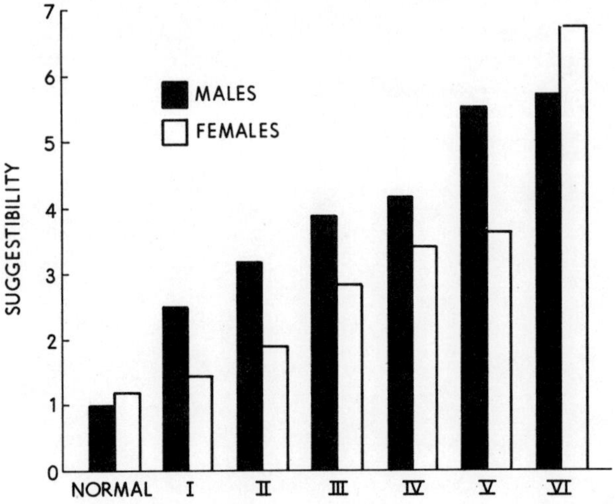

Source: After Eysenck, 1952.

cause they had been "certified" as mental defectives, Eysenck (1952) reports that:

> . . . the average level of ability of this group is represented by an I.Q. level of about 75. Thus the average score of this group is well above what one would normally have expected to be the maximum score [for persons called defective]. Indeed, scores as high as I.Q. 120 and above were recorded by isolated individuals . . . (p. 246).

While there are many possible interpretations of these surprising findings, Eysenck suggests they may be explained in terms of his neuroticism dimension.

> . . . we must consider the possibility that certification is carried out on the basis, not merely of intellectual defect, but of a combination of mental defect and neuroticism. The child that is merely dull, with an I.Q. of 60 or 65, may easily escape certification; the child that is less dull, but is also suffering from emotional instability, is far more likely to be found an unbearable nuisance by Society, and to be certified a mental defective. . . . High emotional stability could then counterbalance a low I.Q., while low stability would offset even a moderately high I.Q. (1952, p. 247).

On the basis of this reasoning, Eysenck suggested three hypotheses regarding the employability of persons certified as defective. They are: (1) these persons would be variable with respect to neuroticism, (2) neuroticism would be more important than intelligence in successful adjustment to work, and (3) neuroticism can be measured in defectives by the same tests used with normals. These hypotheses were all strongly supported by Eysenck's research. For example, in a study with the sample of 104 men certified as mentally defective, Eysenck (1952) employed his usual tests of neuroticism and used a social worker's ratings of work success as the criterion of adjustment to work. The results revealed that "only about one-fourth as much predictive power is given by intelligence tests as by neuroticism tests" (1952, p. 251). He concludes that "Both society and the defectives themselves would benefit from the introduction of routine tests along the lines suggested . . ." (1952, p. 251).

Eysenck's strategy, as we have seen, has been to look for dimensions or types of personality. It has been selected for review because of his prominence as a proponent of this view. In the last major section of this chapter, we shall consider the nature of self-report inventories and their role in the study of the structure of personality. However, before leaving approaches to personality which rely heavily on factor-analytic methods we shall briefly make some cautionary comments with regard to factor analysis.

Factor Analysis: A Word or Two of Caution

The illustrative research of Cattell and Eysenck (as well as considerably more work by other personality psychologists we have not mentioned) pays tribute to the usefulness of factor analysis as a method for summarizing and synthesizing large arrays of data concerning human personality. At the same time, it is probably safe to say that at least some of the appeal of factor analysis stems from its use of involved mathematical computations and the highly scientific aura which usually surrounds these methods. We do not wish to imply that factor-analytic personality research is not scientific. However, complex mathematics alone does not a priori make a line of investigation any more or less scientific than one that does not employ such procedures. In this regard, two notes of caution with respect to the use of factor analysis will be offered, one dealing with the objectivity involved and the other with the validity of its findings.

Since factor analysis is based on exact mathematical formulas and the calculations involved are virtually always performed by computers, it is true that human error is very much reduced, and in this sense, the procedures are objective. However, at various stages of a factor analysis there are decisions which the psychologist must make concerning the appropriate formulas to employ (i.e., the particular method of factor analysis to use) and the level of statistical significance desired. Although there are guidelines for making such decisions, they very definitely involve opinions and are therefore subjective in nature.

It was pointed out in Chapter 2 that a *statistically* significant result, for example a difference between an experimental and control group, does not at all imply that the finding is of practical or social significance. Similarly, a mathematically pure factor which accounts for a large portion of the variance may have little "real" meaning (in the world outside the computer). That is, when the nature of the variables which cluster together to make a factor is examined, the investigator may be unable to comprehend the meaning of the factor and relate it to existing theory. This point is well illustrated by a provocative demonstration analysis[5] which had as its purpose the "discovery" of the primary physical dimensions (factors) of books.

Starting with the conceptually primary dimensions of a book—height, width, and thickness—Overall (1964) devised 12 equations into which the measurements of a book could be entered. Three of these variables (equations) were merely the three primary dimensions, while the remaining nine consisted of various combinations of the three primary dimensions (i.e., differential weights were assigned to the three dimensions). Overall then measured 100 books and computed a score for each book on all 12 variables. The variables were intercorrelated, and the resulting correlation matrix (12×12) was factor-analyzed. Three factors emerged, but rather than being the three primary dimensions, they were meaningful dimensions which could be labeled size, obesity, and squareness! Thus, at least in Overall's study, there were no grounds for the commonly made assumption of factor analysis that the factors which emerge are the "actual" primary factors of the objects or persons under investigation. Overall cautions:

> The important thing to consider is that if factor analysis results sometimes fail to correspond to primary dimensions of the objects being measured such a failure may occur when we attempt to use it as a method for discovering the "real structure of nature" in areas where the structure is unknown (p. 270).
>
> When we do not know beforehand what the primary dimensions are, it is difficult to justify the belief that factor analysis will somehow magically point them out to us (p. 273).

---

[5] Overall (1964) notes that in an effort to demonstrate the veridicality of factor analysis, ". . . a series of demonstration analyses have been undertaken with the objective of showing correspondence between factors and 'real characteristics' or 'primary dimensions' of the things being measured. . . . Demonstration analyses are easily contrived for almost any purpose. Previous analyses have been loaded to yield results corresponding to preconceived primary dimensions. It is just as easy to load examples in such a way that results do not correspond to what we conceive to be primary characteristics of objects. Logically, the demonstration analysis has its proper place as a counter example. A single exception will refute the general argument, but no small number of demonstration analyses can prove its truth" (p. 270).

However, Overall continues:

Does all this mean that factor analysis is a false and worthless methodology? Certainly not. It promises to be one of the most useful research tools in social science and will realize that promise more surely *if we strip it of myths and embellishments* (p. 275, italics added).

Thus, the purpose of the foregoing discussion was to point out some of the limitations of factor analysis and to counter the erroneous though often held notion that factor-analytic personality research is somehow a step above most other personality research on a scientific dimension.

SELF-REPORT PERSONALITY INVENTORIES

Many psychologists who study the structure of personality from a trait approach have relied heavily on *self-report inventories* for their data. Self-report inventories are composed of a large number of statements or questions which the subject is asked to respond to in terms of a limited number of fixed alternatives such as "yes-no," "true-false," and "agree-disagree" (occasionally there is a "cannot say" alternative). Typical items are of the following sort:

I often get mad when things don't turn out as planned.
I enjoy music and dancing.
Are you afraid of high places?
Do you have trouble falling asleep at night?

The items are usually printed in a booklet with separate answer sheets so that the tests can be administered to many subjects at once with little problem. The Minnesota Multiphasic Personality Inventory (MMPI), which we have already had occasion to mention, is one of the most widely known and used self-report inventories, and we shall use it as the basis for our discussion.

The MMPI

The MMPI was developed by Hathaway, a clinical psychologist, and McKinley, a neuropsychiatrist, in 1942 in response to a need for a practical and valid test which could classify patients into the prevailing diagnostic categories of abnormal behavior. Before looking at the manner in which Hathaway and McKinley (1942) set about this task, it may be instructive to consider the alternative method of inventory construction which they rejected.

Each psychiatric diagnostic category is defined by its predominating symptoms. Thus, given a list of the symptoms for each classification, the task becomes one of constructing items which will adequately sample the domain of symptoms. For example, an item which reflects the primary symptom of depression would be: "I am often sad." If the domain of symptoms for each category were adequately sampled, the inventory would have *content validity*. Furthermore, if the items *appeared* to be measuring what they were intended to measure, then the test would also have *face validity*.

The *content validation approach* to inventory construction has a number of difficulties. First, it is important to note that content validity (as well as face validity) does not speak to the issue of whether a test actually works for the purpose for which it was intended. To determine the degree to which the test is successful in classifying patients into diagnostic categories, some means of *external* validation is necessary. For example, the classification obtained by using the test could be compared with that obtained by the independent clinical diagnoses of psychiatrists. It matters little if items on the test adequately reflect the symptomatology of the various diagnostic categories if patients cannot be properly classified by the way they respond to the items. As we shall see shortly, a test with high content validity could fail to work because the subjects are not responding to the content of the items.

Second, an inventory constructed by content validity faces the problem of subtlety of its items. Early test constructors paid little attention to this problem (for example, the Woodworth Personal Data Sheet; Woodworth, 1920), feeling that a test item which was to measure something ought to "look like" it was doing so. More recently, psychologists have tended to gravitate to the other extreme by maintaining that a test item should be constructed so that the respondent is unaware of what it is purported to measure. One of the principal arguments for the use of subtle test items is that obvious items allow the subject to fake his answers, make a good impression, or otherwise distort his "real" personality. At the same time, not a small part of the recent public denunciation of psychological testing as an invasion of privacy (for example, investigations by Congress; cf. American Psychological Association, 1965) is due to the subtlety (lack of face validity) of many of the personality tests in current use.

A recent example of a self-report inventory constructed on the basis of content validity is the Wolpe and Lang (1964) Fear Survey Schedule, which was specifically designed for use in assessing the objects or situations which cause fear or apprehension. The Fear Survey Schedule consists of a list of approximately 75 fears which have been found to be most disturbing to neurotic patients who were treated by Wolpe and his colleagues. Each item is responded to on a five-point scale of fear ranging from "not at all" to "very much." A portion of the Fear Survey Schedule is reproduced in Table 6–8.

TABLE 6–8

Portion of the Fear Survey Schedule

The items in this questionnaire refer to things and experiences that may cause fear or other unpleasant feelings. Write the number of each item in the column that describes how much you are disturbed by it nowadays.

	Not at All	*A Little*	*A Fair Amount*	*Much*	*Very Much*
1. Noise of vacuum cleaners...					
2. Open wounds.............					
3. Being alone...............					
4. Being in a strange place....					
5. Loud voices..............					
6. Dead people..............					
7. Speaking in public.........					
8. Crossing streets...........					
9. People who seem insane....					
10. Falling..................					
11. Automobiles..............					
12. Being teased..............					
13. Dentists..................					

Source: Wolpe and Lazarus, 1966.

Sensitive to the limitations of constructing self-report inventories by content validation, Hathaway and McKinley employed a strategy which makes few theoretical assumptions about the items which make up the test (for example, an item measuring a particular symptom). Initially, item selection proceeded along the same lines that are used in the content validation approach. A pool of 1,000 self-descriptive statements was collected from various psychiatric examination forms and procedures, psychiatric textbooks, and previously used inventories. However, rather than stop there, Hathaway and McKinley administered the 1,000-item inventory to groups of diagnosed psychiatric patients (so classified on the basis of clinical judgments) and groups of normal (nonpatient) subjects. For each of the diagnostic groups and the normal sample, the frequency of endorsement of each item was tabulated. Only those items which clearly differentiated between a diagnostic group and the normal group were retained for the final inventory. For instance, a statement became an item on the Depression scale if, and only if, patients diagnosed as having a depressive disorder endorsed (or did not endorse) the statement significantly more often than normal persons. Thus, it was possible for an item which had little content or face validity to be included on the Depression scale (for example, "I sometimes tease animals"), or any other scale of the MMPI. Constructing a test in this manner is referred to as *empirical* or *criterion keying*.

The MMPI consists of 550 statements which deal with such areas of content as attitudes, educational information, general physical health, sex roles, mood, morale, vocational interests, fears, and preoccupations. There are four validity scales and 10 basic clinical scales for which the MMPI is scored. Their characteristics are summarized in Table 6–9. The function of the validity scales is to provide information concerning the validity of the respondent's answers on the clinical scales. For example, if the Lie (L) scale is elevated, there is an indication that the respondent is attempting to answer the items so as to present himself in a favorable light.

TABLE 6–9

The Validity and Clinical Scales of the MMPI

Scale Name	*Symbol*	*Sample Item*	*Interpretation*
Cannot say	?	No sample. It is merely the number of items marked in the "cannot say" category.	This is one of four validity scales, and a high score indicates evasiveness.
Lie	L	I get angry sometimes. (False)*	This is the second validity scale. Persons trying to present themselves in a favorable light (e.g, good, wholesome, honest) obtain high L Scale elevations.
Frequency	F	Everything tastes the same. (True)	F is the third validity scale. High scores suggest carelessness, confusion, or "fake bad."
Correction	K	I have very few fears compared to my friends. (False)	An elevation on the last validity scale, K, suggests a defensive test-taking attitude. Exceedingly low scores may indicate a lack of ability to deny symptomatology.
Hypochondriasis	Hs	I wake up fresh and rested most mornings. (False)	High scores have been described as cynical, defeatist, and crabbed.
Depression	D	At times I am full of energy. (False)	High scorers usually are shy, despondent, and distressed.
Hysteria	Hy	I have never had a fainting spell. (False)	High scorers tend to complain of multiple symptoms.

* The True or False responses within parentheses indicate the scored direction of each of the items.

TABLE 6–9 (*Continued*)

Psychopathic deviate	Pd	I liked school. (False)	Adjectives used to describe some high scorers are adventurous, courageous, and generous.
Masculinity-femininity	Mf	I like mechanics magazines. (False)	Among males, high scorers have been described as aesthetic and sensitive. High-scoring women have been described as rebellious, unrealistic, and indecisive.
Paranoia	Pa	Someone has it in for me. (True)	High scorers on this scale were characterized as shrewd, guarded, and worrisome.
Psychasthenia	Pt	I am certainly lacking in self-confidence. (True)	Fearful, rigid, anxious and worrisome are some of the adjectives used to describe high Pt scorers.
Schizophrenia	Sc	I believe I am a condemned person. (True)	Adjectives such as withdrawn and unusual describe Sc high scorers.
Hypomania	Ma	At times my thoughts have raced ahead faster than I could speak them. (True)	High scorers are called sociable, energetic, and impulsive.
Social introversion-extroversion	Si	I enjoy social gatherings just to be with people. (False)	High scorers: modest, shy, and self-effacing. Low scorers: sociable, colorful, and ambitious.

Source: Adapted from Kleinmuntz, 1967.

The scoring of the MMPI is a straightforward matter. There are scoring keys which indicate the items which appear on each scale and the scored direction of each item (i.e., true or false). The test can be completely scored by hand in less than five minutes and in considerably less time by a high-speed computer. Interpretation of the scores is not as simple. Rather than merely looking to the scale on which a respondent scored highest to arrive at a clinical diagnosis, the *pattern* of scores on the 10 clinical scales is examined. The pattern of scores is often presented graphically, as in Figure 6–2, in what is called a *psychogram* or *personality profile*. A number of MMPI atlases have been compiled for interpreting profiles (such as Marks and Seeman, 1963). These books contain typical profiles and descriptive information about samples of subjects

FIGURE 6–2

Sample MMPI Profile (Psychogram)

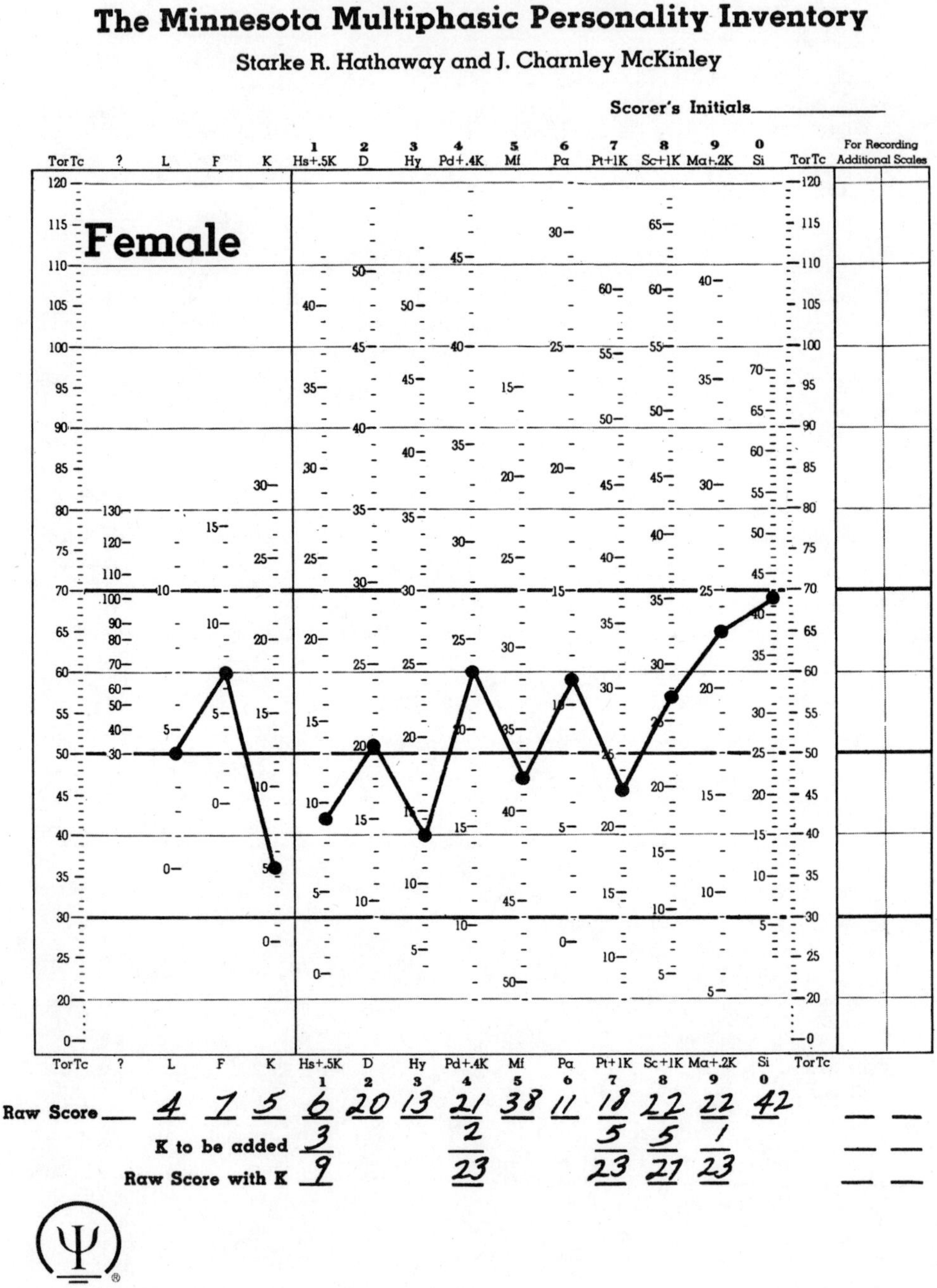

Source: Psychological Corporation. Reproduced by permission.

producing each profile. For example, along with a list of typical and atypical symptoms and behaviors for persons with a given profile, there may be information about the most common diagnostic category of these people, their personal history, course of treatment, and so on. While it is rare to find a perfect match of profiles (i.e., identical scores on all the scales), the examiner is helped in finding the typical profile in the atlas which will be most like that of his respondent by a series of rules or guidelines which must be met for two profiles to be considered similar.

Although the MMPI was originally designed to aid in the diagnosis of psychiatric patients and it still serves this function, it has also been used extensively in personality research. For this latter purpose, several hundred additional experimental scales have been developed (using the basic 550 items). In many cases, the MMPI items which make up an experimental scale are used alone, as is the case, for example, with the Taylor Manifest Anxiety Scale (Taylor, 1953) which has been used widely in basic research on anxiety.

Although people taking tests such as the MMPI have devised various schemes for falsifying (faking) their answers (for example, to make a good impression when applying for a job or to make a bad impression when being tested for eligibility in the army), this is not easy to do and not be detected. In the first place, as we have already pointed out, the MMPI items do not necessarily have face validity. Second, "fakers" are likely to be detected by one or more of the validity scales. There are, however, certain kinds of test-taking attitudes which may distort the personality picture presented by self-report inventories such as the MMPI.

Response Sets

An important assumption often made by psychologists who use self-report personality inventories as part of their clinical work or research is that the individual's response to any given item reflects his disposition toward the *content* of the item. For example, it may be important to assume that a person who responds "true" to the statement "I like parties" attends social functions frequently. Are there sources of distortion which can weaken or invalidate this assumption? The answer appears to be yes, since it has been found that respondents with particular test-taking attitudes may not be answering the items in terms of their manifest content. *Response sets,* as these test-taking attitudes are called, are characteristic and consistent ways of responding to items. *Response acquiescence* is the tendency to agree with items no matter what their content. *Response deviation* is the tendency to answer items in an uncommon or unusual direction. Still another response set which has received much attention in recent years is that of *social desirability,* which is characterized by answering items in the direction which is most socially accepted irrespective of whether that answer is correct for the respondent. For example, an individual who prefers to be alone and dislikes social gatherings might answer "true" to the statement "I like parties" because he felt it was socially desirable to enjoy parties. We shall examine the nature of response sets by looking at social desirability in some detail.

Social Desirability as a Response Set. What evidence is there that social desirability is an important response set? To answer this question, Allen L. Edwards (1953b) performed a straightforward study to assess the relationship between the probability of endorsement of items on a self-report inventory and the social desirability of the items. His hypothesis was: "If the behavior indicated by an inventory item is socially desirable, the subject will tend to attribute it to himself; if it is undesirable, he will not" (1953b, p. 90). In the first part of the study, 140 personality trait items, representing 14 of Murray's needs (see Chapter 8), were written. These items were then given to 152 men and women with instructions to judge the social desirability of each item on a nine-point scale. The instructions presented to subjects are reproduced in Table 6–10. Based on the ratings by the subjects, the position of each personality trait item on a scale of social desirability was calculated.

In the second phase of Edwards' study, the same set of personality trait items was presented to a different sample of subjects, 140 premedical and predental students, as part of a battery of tests. This time the items were administered in the form of a personality inventory with instructions to answer *yes* when an item was characteristic of the respondent and *no* when it was not. The proportion of subjects responding *yes* to each item was computed, and these proportions became the probability of endorsement of a given item. Edwards found that the correlation between the probability of endorsement of each item and the independently determined social desirability scale value of the item was +.87. One statement which had been rated as highly desirable, "I like to be loyal to my friends," was endorsed by 98 percent of the students as an accurate description of themselves. In contrast, the undesirable statement, "I like to avoid responsibilities and obligations," was endorsed by only 6 percent of the respondents when describing themselves.

The finding of a strong positive relationship supported Edwards' contention that by knowing where a statement lies on the social desirability-undesirability dimension ". . . we can then predict, with a high degree of accuracy, the proportion of individuals who will say, in self-description, that the statement does describe them" (1957, p. 3). Using the same basic two-phase design but with different populations of subjects (for example, Norwegian students; Lovaas, 1956, as cited by Edwards, 1957) and of items (for instance, statements from the MMPI; Hanley,

TABLE 6–10

Instructions Used in Obtaining Judgments of Social Desirability for Personality Statements

Below you will find an example of four things that a person says that he likes or would like to do. These likes are called traits. Underneath the list of four traits and opposite the numbers corresponding to each of the traits are nine boxes. These boxes represent different degrees of desirability or undesirability of each trait as it appears in others, as indicated by the adjective at the top. A judge, such as yourself, has made an estimate of the degree of desirability or undesirability of these traits in people by placing an X in the box opposite each trait.

Example: 1. To like to punish your enemies.
2. To like to read psychological novels.
3. To like to make excuses for your friends.
4. To like to go out with your friends.

Trait	*Undesirable*								*Desirable*
	Extreme	Strong	Moderate	Mild	Neutral	Mild	Moderate	Strong	Extreme
1.		X							
2.					X				
3.							X		
4.								X	

The person who judged these traits believes that "to like to punish your enemies" is a definitely undesirable trait in others, "to like to read psychological novels" is neither desirable nor undesirable, "to like to make excuses for your friends" is moderately desirable, and "to like to go out with your friends" is quite a desirable trait in other people.

Indicate your own judgments of the desirability or undesirability of the traits which will be given to you by the examiner in the same manner. *Remember that you are to judge the traits in terms of whether you consider them desirable or undesirable in others.* Be sure to make a judgment about each trait.

Source: Edwards, 1957.

1956), other investigators have also found a high positive correlation between the proportion of people endorsing a statement and its social desirability. Moreover, these relationships do not appear to be reduced even when the respondents are led to believe that their identities will remain anonymous (thereby supposedly eliminating subjects' "need" to present themselves in a favorable or socially desirable light). Thus, it seems safe to assume that the more socially desirable a statement is (as determined by the ratings of others), the more likely it is that the statement will be endorsed as being self-descriptive.

If social desirability is a viable and reliable response set which affects the interpretation of responses on self-report inventories, we must ask about the nature of its influence. At least two possibilities exist. On the one hand, it is possible that subjects taking personality inventories try to make a good impression by describing themselves as possessing more socially desirable traits and fewer socially undesirable traits than they might be found to have if their behavior were evaluated by another method. On the other hand, it may be that behaviors which are judged as desirable in a particular culture are, at the same time, the behaviors which are most common. If this were the case, it would be anticipated that a higher percentage of people would endorse statements which are high on a scale of social desirability than those which are low on social desirability. Thus, subjects would not be misrepresenting themselves. Either of these possibilities or a combination of the two would account for Edwards' findings. It appears then that interpreting the responses of subjects to self-report personality inventories may be complicated due to the effects of social desirability (not to mention other response sets). However, several methods have been devised for controlling the influence of social desirability.

One approach used to control the effects of social desirability is to measure the respondent's tendency to answer items on a self-report inventory in the socially desirable direction and to then adjust his score on the inventory to take the degree of this tendency into account. Another approach involves employing neutral items with respect to social desirability (i.e., statements which are rated in the middle of the social desirability-undesirability scale) as, for example, "I am easily awakened by noise." However, it often proves difficult to find or rewrite items which meet the requirement of neutrality and simultaneously convey the necessary content. For example, it is hard to imagine how one could rewrite the statement, "Most of the time I wish I were dead" (an MMPI item which is rated as extremely undesirable; Hanley, 1956), so as to make it more socially desirable without changing the meaning substantially.

TABLE 6–11

Examples of Items from the Edwards Personal Preference Schedule

Alternatives	*Items*
A B	A: I like to tell amusing stories and jokes at parties. B: I would like to write a great novel or play.
A B	A: I like to have my work organized and planned before beginning it. B: I like to travel and see the country.
A B	A: I feel like blaming others when things go wrong for me. B: I feel that I am inferior to others in most respects.
A B	A: I like to avoid responsibilities and obligations. B: I feel like making fun of people who do things that I regard as stupid.

Source: Edwards (1953a).

A third approach is to use a *forced-choice inventory*. All the statements appearing in the inventory are first scaled for social desirability and then paired according to their scale values. The members of each pair have approximately the same scale value, and the respondent must choose the statement in each pair which is most characteristic of himself. Edwards constructed his Personal Preference Schedule in this way to control for the influence of social desirability. The Personal Preference Schedule is a self-report personality inventory developed for use with nonpsychiatric persons in counseling and research. Examples of items appearing in it are presented in Table 6–11.

Response Styles

While some psychologists have endeavored to rid self-report inventories of the distorting influence of response sets, other psychologists have observed that these characteristic modes of responding might not be sources of error at all. This latter group has suggested that it would be more fruitful to look at test-taking attitudes as *personality traits*. That is, the salient measures of personality in self-report inventories might be *how* an individual responds, rather than *what* he responds to (i.e., the content of the items). Jackson and Messick (1958) have made a useful distinction between response sets, sources of error which are to be avoided or controlled for, and *response styles*, personal modes of responding which may be considered traits. We shall briefly examine the nature of the evidence for social desirability as a response style.

Social Desirability as a Response Style

EDWARDS' APPROACH. In order to measure a person's inclination to respond to self-descriptive statements in the socially desirable direction, Edwards (1953a) developed a Social Desirability (SD) scale. Edwards selected 150 items from the MMPI (from the L, F, and K scales and the Taylor Manifest Anxiety Scale) and asked 10 judges to respond to each of the items in a socially desirable direction. The judges agreed perfectly on 79 of the 150 statements, and these 79 items formed the first SD scale. Later, the SD scale was reduced to 39 items by selecting those items which showed the greatest differentiation between subjects who had high and low total scores.

Edwards hypothesized: "If the SD scale does provide a measure of the tendency of subjects to give socially desirable responses to statements in self-description, then the correlations of scores on this scale with other personality scales, given under standard instructions, should indicate something of the extent to which the social desirability variable is operating at the time" (1957, pp. 31 and 33). A number of studies by Edwards and other investigators (for example, Edwards, 1953a, 1957;

Merrill and Heathers, 1956) have provided evidence in support of this hypothesis. Scales measuring socially desirable traits such as dominance, responsibility, status, cooperativeness, agreeableness, and objectivity have been found to be positively correlated with the SD scale. In contrast, scales measuring socially undesirable traits such as social introversion, neuroticism, hostility, dependency, insecurity, and anxiety have been found to be negatively correlated with the SD scale.

One of the implications of the correlations found between Edwards' SD scale and a number of personality scales is that the traits which these scales are measuring are, despite their names (for example, dominance and social introversion), only different aspects of social desirability. Or, to state the case a bit more conservatively, perhaps it would be more fruitful from the standpoint of predictive and explanatory power and parsimony to view the various traits which have been found to correlate strongly with the SD scale as if they were measures of social desirability. In this regard, two important considerations should be kept in mind. First, correlation does not mean identity. The fact that Drake's Social Introversion Scale (Merrill and Heathers, 1956) and Edwards' SD scale are strongly related (−.90) means only that one can be predicted from the other with a high degree of accuracy. The relationship may be due to social desirability; but it may also be a function of social introversion or a third variable which accounts for both social introversion and social desirability. Second, while a correlation coefficient of −.90 is quite high, it is not perfect (i.e., −1.00), and therefore one variable does not exactly predict the other. In this case, social desirability is said to account for 81 percent of the variance of social introversion ($.90 \times .90 = .81$; see Chapter 2) thereby leaving 19 percent unaccounted for.

Despite these limitations, proponents of different response styles have endeavored to subsume a variety of traits measured by self-report personality inventories under the rubric of a single response style. Edwards, who has championed the cause of social desirability, is no exception. Consider, for example, the persuasive argument he has made for interpreting the trait being measured by the Taylor Manifest Anxiety (MA) Scale as social desirability-undesirability. The MA scale has been found to be negatively correlated with the SD scale,[6] which means that high

---

[6] Edwards (1957) reports a correlation of −.84 between the MA scale and the 39-item SD scale and a correlation of −.60 between the MA scale and the 79-item SD scale. The negative relationship between the MA and SD scales, as well as the substantially higher correlation obtained with the shorter SD scale, could be accounted for by the 22 overlapping items on the 39-item SD scale and the MA scale. On the basis of further statistical analyses, Edwards concludes that the negative correlation between the SD scale and the MA scale cannot be accounted for "merely in terms of the item overlap between the two scales" (1957, p. 88, footnote).

anxiety tends to be associated with low social desirability and low anxiety tends to be associated with high social desirability.

This finding is not surprising when one examines the items that make up the MA scale. Statements like, "I am a very nervous person," "I am certainly lacking in self-confidence," and "I cry easily," which appear on the MA scale, are unquestionably socially undesirable characteristics in our general society. Thus, high scores on the MA scale can be viewed as a function of endorsing these and other socially undesirable statements, whereas low scores on the MA scale would be a function of denying socially undesirable characteristics. (It is interesting to note that in certain subgroups of our culture—as in mental hospitals or homes for the aged—these socially undesirable characteristics are not as undesirable and may even be construed as socially desirable—for example, because they foster attention and care.)

The MA scale has been used in numerous experimental studies investigating the effect of anxiety on performance to select subjects with high and low anxiety. One finding[7] has been that for certain kinds of verbal learning (such as verbal maze, paired-associate, and serial nonsense-syllable learning) low-anxious subjects make fewer errors and reach a criterion of learning faster (in fewer trials) than high-anxious subjects (see, for example, Taylor and Spence, 1952; Ramond, 1953; Montague, 1953). Edwards (1957) attempts to explain these results in terms of social desirability in the following way.

> I believe it possible . . . to describe the low group on the Taylor scale as those who desire to make a good impression on others and the high group as those who are less interested in what others may think of them. I would predict that the group desiring to make a good impression on the Taylor scale, that is to say, those with low scores, might also desire to make a good impression in terms of their performance on the learning task. They are, in other words, perhaps more highly motivated by the desire to "look good," not only in their responses to the Taylor scale, but also in their performance in the learning situation itself. Surely, to be able to learn fast is, in our society, a socially desirable characteristic. If a subject has a strong tendency to give socially desirable responses in self-description, is it unreasonable to believe that he may also reveal this tendency in his behavior in a learning situation where he is aware of what would be considered socially desirable, namely to learn fast, to do his best? The high group, on the other hand, being less interested in making a good impression, showing less of a tendency to give socially desirable responses in self-description, caring less about how others may value them, does not have equal motivation with the low group in the learning situation (p. 89).

---

[7] The relationship between level of anxiety and peformance is rather complex depending, to a large degree, on the nature of the performance task (see Spence and Spence, 1966).

Crowne and Marlowe's Approach. As we have seen, Edwards' basic strategy for validating social desirability as a response style has been to correlate his SD scale with various self-report personality inventories. The same general approach, that of correlating response-style measures with other self-report scales, has been used by most psychologists who have endeavored to substantiate the existence and importance of response styles as personality variables. A notable exception has been the work of Crowne and Marlowe (1964), who have attempted to relate social desirability as measured by a self-report inventory to independently measured behavior in a variety of experimental situations.

Crowne and Marlowe (1960) began by constructing a new scale of social desirability. One of the major problems with Edwards' SD scale is that social desirability is *confounded* with the content of those items having distinct psychopathological implications. Recall that the items comprising the Edwards SD scale are all drawn from the MMPI, which specifically deals with symptoms of psychiatric disorders. When a subject denies that he is very nervous, has little self-confidence, and cries easily, there is no way to tell whether he merely is responding in the socially acceptable direction or actually is free of these symptoms. In short, there is no way to separate the effects of the content of the items and a respondent's tendency to present himself in a favorable (or unfavorable) light. Thus, when Edwards' SD scale is employed with normal subjects, interpretation of scores is ambiguous.

The Marlowe-Crowne Social Desirability scale was designed specifically to avoid the confounding effects of item content (Crowne and Marlowe, 1960). The criterion for item selection was that the behaviors in question be sanctioned and approved by our culture but have a low frequency of occurrence. Additionally, items chosen had to have minimal psychopathological implications. Several examples of items from the final scale (Crowne and Marlowe, 1960) which meet these requirements follow, with the socially desirable response scoring indicated in parentheses.

On a few occasions, I have given up doing something because I thought too little of my ability. (False)
No matter who I am talking to, I'm always a good listener. (True)
There have been occasions when I took advantage of someone. (False) (p. 351)

On the one hand, while never doubting one's own ability, always being a good listener, and never taking advantage of someone else are socially desirable behaviors, they rarely occur. Thus, an individual who responds to items on the Marlowe-Crowne SD scale in the socially desirable direction can be said to be presenting himself in a favorable light (i.e., "faking good"), since it is highly improbable that his behavior actually corresponds to his self-report of it. At the same time, when an individual responds in the socially desirable direction, he is not forced to deny pathological symptoms or culturally unsanctioned behavior (as he is on Edwards' SD scale). On the other hand, in our culture there is nothing "wrong" or "sick" with sometimes having little self-confidence, occasionally being a poor listener, and once in a while taking advantage of another person. Thus, there is no stigma attached to responding to items on the Marlowe-Crowne scale in the socially undesirable direction. In short, the content of the Marlowe-Crowne SD scale represents ideal behavior, meaning that its presence is praised but its absence is not punished.

Crowne and Marlowe initially selected 50 items from existing personality inventories which met their criteria and had 10 psychologists and graduate students in psychology score each item in the socially desirable direction from the viewpoint of a college student. The judges unanimously agreed on 36 items, and all but one judge agreed on 11 other items.

In order to test how free of pathology-relevant content the scale was, this preliminary set of 47 items was then submitted to 10 additional judges who rated the degree of maladjustment implied by each of the socially undesirable responses on a five-point scale, ranging from extremely well-adjusted (1) to extremely maladjusted (5). The mean rating for all the items was found to be 2.8 or just below the midpoint of the scale, thereby indicating that overall the items were indicative of neither maladjustment nor good adjustment. By comparison, when the items on Edwards' SD scale were rated according to the same procedure, the mean rating obtained was 3.9 (which was significantly greater than 2.8, $p < .0001$; see Chapter 2).

Finally, the preliminary scale of 47 items was administered to a group of undergraduate students who were instructed to: "Read each item and decide whether the statement is *true* or *false* as it pertains to you personally." An *item analysis* was performed, and those items (a total of 33) which significantly discriminated between high and low total scores were retained for the final form of the Marlowe-Crowne SD scale. The Marlowe-Crowne and Edwards SD scales are only moderately correlated (+.35) and have no items in common. Further, as would be predicted from the fact that the items on the Marlowe-Crowne scale have substantially less content dealing with psychiatric symptoms than the Edwards scale, the correlations between the Marlowe-Crowne scale and various MMPI scales are generally lower than the parallel correlations for Edwards' SD scale.

Social Desirability and the Approval Motive. Crowne and Marlowe (1964) contended that social desirability is not only a characteristic way of responding on self-report inventories (i.e., a response style), but also is one manifestation of a more general personality construct which they have called the *approval motive*. They reasoned that the tendency of persons to portray themselves in a favorable light reflects a *need for social approval.* To test the utility of this notion in predicting behavior in a variety of situations, Crowne and Marlowe performed a series of experiments in which individuals who were high and low in their need for social approval, as measured by the Marlowe-Crowne SD scale, were compared.

One study (Marlowe and Crowne, 1961) investigated reactions to a long and extremely boring experimental task. The subjects, male undergraduate students, were met individually by the experimenter who introduced himself as a psychologist and acted in an aloof manner to accentuate his importance and authority. After the subject completed several questionnaires (the Marlowe-Crowne and Edwards SD scales and the Barron Independence of Judgment scale), the experimenter, in a very businesslike manner, gave the subject the following instructions: "Now for the experiment itself. The materials are this box and the twelve spools. I want you to take these spools, one at a time, and place them in the box. When you are finished, empty the box and refill it, one spool at a time. Continue to fill and empty the box until I tell you to stop. Use one hand and work at your own preferred speed." While the experimenter pretended to record and time the subject's behavior, the subject packed and repacked the spools for 25 minutes, at the end of which time the subject was asked to fill out a questionnaire containing four questions about his personal reaction to the task.

It was predicted that subjects with a high need for social approval would tend to rate the task more favorably than subjects with a low need for social approval. As can be seen in Table 6–12, this is exactly what happened. For each of the questions concerning their reaction to the spool-packing task, the high-need-for-approval group showed a significantly higher (i.e., more favorable) rating than the low-need-for-approval group. Crowne and Marlowe (1964) account for the findings in the following way.

The experimenters, as a result of their prestige and authoritative manner, reflected in their title, occupation, and behavioral aloofness, were perceived by high-need-for-approval subjects as persons whose favor was worth courting. It seems not unlikely that to many college students professors are viewed as sources of approval gratification as well as dispensers of academic rewards and punishments. In consequence, our high-need-for-approval subjects were strongly motivated to yield to the demands of the situation and to tell the experimenter that his experiment was interesting, important, personally informative, and worth returning to. In contrast subjects less approval dependent were better able to resist stating what seemed socially appropriate and offered, instead, more realistic appraisals of the experiment. Presumably, the less favorable opinions of low-need-for-approval subjects reflect, in part, the greater freedom of this group from social pressures in the formation and expression of their beliefs (p. 46).

While Crowne and Marlowe's explanation in terms of the approval motive certainly accounts for the findings of their experiment in a reasonable and straightforward manner, it is legitimate to ask whether there might not be alternative ways of explaining the data. One such alternative construct is that of *social conformity.* It would be predicted that individuals who tend to yield to social pressure (for example, going along with the majority despite feeling that the minority is correct) would evaluate the spool-packing task more favorably than individuals who tend to resist social pressure. The important and prestigeful experimenter in Marlowe and Crowne's (1961) experiment represented at least

TABLE 6–12

Differences between High- and Low-Need-for-Approval Groups in Expressed Attitudes toward Spool-Packing

Question	*High* ($N = 30$)* *Mean*	*Low* ($N = 27$) *Mean*	*Difference*	*Statistical Significance*
How enjoyable was the task	2.17	−0.70	2.87	$p < .01$
How much was learned from the task	5.37	3.22	2.15	$p < .02$
How important was experiment scientifically	7.37	5.67	1.70	$p < .02$
Desire to participate in similar experiment	3.63	1.67	1.96	$p < .02$

* N = number of subjects.
Source: Adapted from Crowne and Marlowe, 1964.

an implicit form of social pressure in that it is not generally considered socially acceptable to tell a college professor that his "brainchild" is uninteresting, unimportant, and not worth an undergraduate's time and effort.

While it is true that social conformity and the need for social approval are related concepts conceptually, the question arises as to whether they are one and the same. To answer this question in the experiment under discussion, Marlowe and Crowne classified their subjects as high or low in social conformity on the basis of their performance on the Barron Independence of Judgment scale, a paper-and-pencil measure which has been shown to discriminate between conformers and nonconformers. A typical item on the Barron scale is: "It is easy for me to take orders and do what I am told." When high and low conformers were compared on their ratings of the spool-packing task, only the question dealing with how much a subject had learned significantly differentiated between the two groups of subjects (see Table 6–13). Recall that the task was rated as more favorable by the high-need-for-approval subjects than by the low-need-for-approval subjects on all four of the questions (see Table 6–12). Thus, the concept of approval motive is better at predicting the results of the spool-packing experiment than the notion of conformity. Although there is a moderately high correlation between the Independence of Judgment scale and the Marlowe-Crowne SD scale (−.54), the two concepts are not identical.

TABLE 6–13

Differences between High- and Low-Conformity Groups in Expressed Attitudes toward Spool-Packing

Question	*High* (*N* = *31*)* *Mean*	*Low* (*N* = *26*) *Mean*	*Difference*	*Statistical Significance*
How enjoyable was the task	1.31	0.39	0.92	NS†
How much was learned from the task	5.27	3.58	1.69	$p < .05$
How important was experiment scientifically	6.58	6.55	0.03	NS
Desire to participate in similar experiment	3.19	2.29	0.90	NS

* *N* = number of subjects.
† NS = not significant.
Source: Adapted from Crowne and Marlowe, 1964.

It is also interesting to note the difference between Edwards' concept of social desirability and that of Crowne and Marlowe as reflected in the spool-packing experiment. Although the Edwards and Marlowe-Crowne SD scales were correlated significantly with each other in the spool-packing experiment (+.56), the Edwards scale was unrelated to the favorability of the ratings of the task. As can be seen from Table 6–14, subjects[8] high on social desirability as measured by Edwards' scale did not rate the task significantly more favorable than subjects low in social desirability. Further, whereas the Marlowe-Crowne SD scale and the Independence of Judgment scale were correlated significantly, there was no significant relationship found between the Edwards SD scale and the Independence of Judgment scale.

If need for approval is related to a paper-and-pencil measure of social conformity, it is likely to be related to a situation in which there is genuine social pressure and actual consequences for conforming. In one experiment reported by Crowne and Marlowe (1964), co-eds were told that they were going to participate in a study of perceptual discrimina-

[8] Only approximately half of the subjects completed the Edwards SD scale.

TABLE 6–14

Differences between High and Low Edwards SD Groups in Expressed Attitudes toward Spool-Packing

Question	*High (N = 14)* Mean*	*Low (N = 15) Mean*	*Difference*	*Statistical Significance*
How enjoyable was the task	0.36	0.47	−0.11	NS†
How much was learned from the task	3.79	3.93	−0.14	NS
How important was experiment scientifically	6.00	5.87	0.13	NS
Desire to participate in similar experiment	2.07	2.07	0	NS

* *N* = number of subjects.
† NS = not significant.
Source: Adapted from Crowne and Marlowe, 1964.

tion. After completing the Marlowe-Crowne SD scale, the subject and four students (two males and two females), who posed as subjects but were actually confederates of the experimenter, were shown a series of 20 slides, each containing two clusters of dots. Each slide was presented for a one-second interval, and the subject's task was to tell which of the two clusters of dots was larger. In fact, the discrimination of the larger cluster was virtually unambiguous and required no special ability. Sixteen of the twenty trials were critical or conformity trials in which the four confederates each gave the incorrect answer (i.e., chose the smaller cluster). The order of responding was rotated after each trial, so that the subject responded in each of the five possible positions four times.

The results were clear-cut. As predicted, high-need-for-approval subjects yielded to the majority's incorrect judgments on 59 percent of the critical trials, whereas low-need-for-approval subjects yielded to the majority on 34 percent of the critical trials (a statistically significant difference, $p < .02$). The finding supports Crowne and Marlowe's (1964) contention that social conformity constitutes "a means of satisfying a need for approval from others" (p. 73).

Another prediction which would be made from the construct of approval motive is that persons with a high need for approval should be more responsive to rewards of a social nature than persons with low approval motivation. Thus, if the reward for correct responses in a learning task were the approval of the experimenter, it would be expected that learning would be facilitated by a subject's need or desire for social approval. Crowne and Strickland (1961) tested this general hypothesis in a verbal conditioning experiment. The subjects, male and female undergraduates, first spent a few minutes talking to the experimenter about themselves, during which time the experimenter estab-

FIGURE 6–3

Proportions of Plural Nouns Given by High- and Low-Need-for- Approval Groups under Positive Reinforcement and Nonreinforced Control Conditions

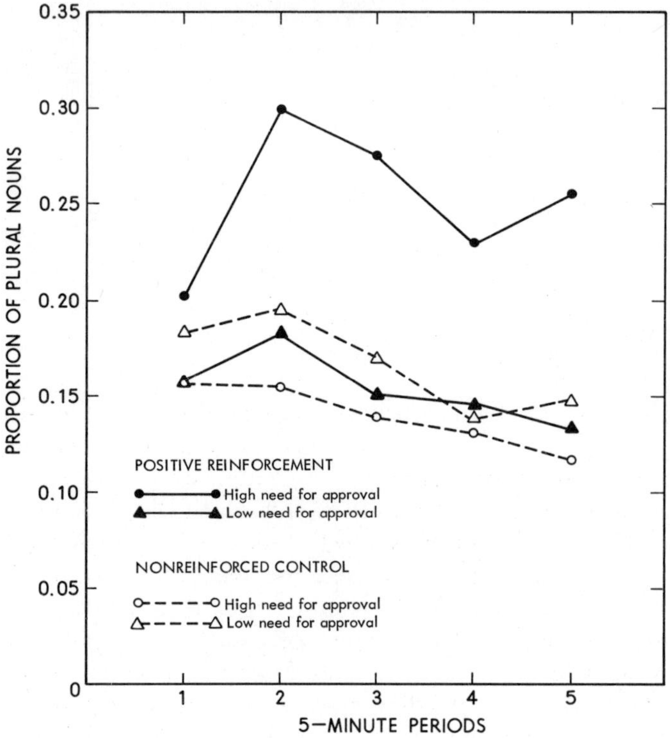

Source: Crowne and Marlowe, 1964.

lished himself as a source of social approval. The subject was then instructed merely to say all the words he could think of one at a time without using them in phrases or sentences and without counting the words. In the *positive reinforcement* condition, the experimenter said "Mm-hmm" and nodded his head affirmatively every time the subject said a plural noun. In the *negative reinforcement* condition, each plural noun was immediately followed by analogous negative feedback (the experimenter's "Uh-uh"). To establish a base rate of plural nouns, subjects in a *nonreinforced control* condition simply said words without any kind of social reward given by the experimenter.

Two experimental hypotheses were tested. First, in the positive reinforcement condition, it was predicted that high-need-for-approval subjects would have a significantly higher rate of plural nouns than low-need-for-approval subjects. Second, under negative reinforcement, it was predicted that high-need-for-approval subjects would show a signifi-

FIGURE 6–4

Proportions of Plural Nouns Given by High- and Low-Need-for- Approval Groups under Negative Reinforcement and Nonreinforced Control Conditions

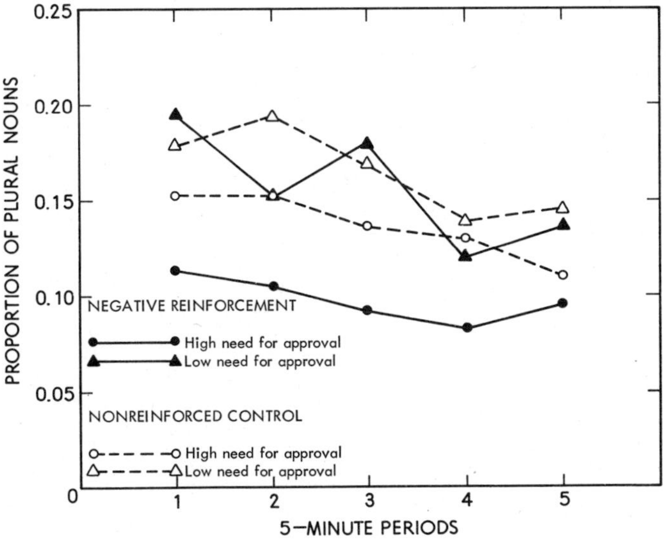

Source: Crowne and Marlowe, 1964.

cantly greater decrease in the proportion of plural nouns elicited than low-need-for-approval subjects. The second hypothesis follows from viewing negative reinforcement in an interpersonal situation as the denial of approval or punishment. Overall, both hypotheses received support, as can be seen from Figures 6–3 and 6–4. Additionally, it should be pointed out that the results reflect the fact that the subjects were "unaware" of the response-reward contingency. Subjects who were able to verbalize what the critical response was (i.e., plural nouns) during a postexperimental interview were not retained for the final analyses.

Crowne and Marlowe's efforts to understand the influence of social desirability on self-report inventories began by postulating a motivational state—the approval motive—which would account for the tendency of some people to present themselves in a favorable light. Their basic strategy has been to find the behavioral correlates of the need for social approval outside the sphere of test-taking behavior. Although the study and explication of the need for social approval is by no means finished, Crowne and Marlowe have made it clear that the construct is useful for predicting a variety of behaviors. In addition to a greater proclivity to evaluate a very dull and boring task favorably, to be more responsive to social reward in verbal conditioning, and to be more conforming—the behavioral correlates which we have already discussed

—persons with a high need for social approval (as compared to persons with low approval motivation) are likely to give popular word associations, to set conservative goals in risk-taking situations, and to be susceptible to persuasion.

Evaluation of Response Sets and Response Styles

Our discussion of response sets and styles has focused on social desirability and has presented the evidence *for* their existence and validity. While the arguments favoring a response-set interpretation of self-report personality inventories are impressive, they have certainly not gone unchallenged. Indeed, the controversy between a response-set and a content interpretation of self-report inventories has been one of the most pronounced in the recent history of psychology and is still quite alive. Formally, the controversy has taken the form of the presentation of an argument for either position, which is followed by a rebuttal from the opposition, which in turn may be followed by a defense and counterargument, and so on. The "battle" is reflected in the titles of important articles which have addressed the issue such as "The Challenge of Response Sets" (Block, 1965) and "The Great Reponse-Style Myth" (Rorer, 1965).

There appears to be little hope for a settlement of the controversy in the near future. As we pointed out in Chapter 1, as long as some positive evidence for a theory or construct exists, scientists are slow to give up their ideas even in the face of considerable negative evidence. Furthermore, although there is free and open confrontation in the psychological literature between proponents of the two camps, there is at times little *communication* between investigators with opposing views. Due to the complex nature of the problem of interpreting self-report inventories, research methodology and theoretical conceptualization have become highly technical and specialized, with the result that there tends to be little understanding of the "other" point of view. Until proponents of both camps can agree on common methods and terminology, differences in results can always be attributed to differences in procedures and to semantic impasses. However, despite the lack of definitive statements regarding interpretation of existing self-report inventories, there appears to be little diminution in their use in research and applied personality assessment.

REFERENCES

American Psychological Association. Special issue: Testing and public policy. *American Psychologist,* 1965, **20,** 857–993.

Block, J. *The challenge of response sets.* New York: Appleton-Century-Crofts, 1965.

Cattell, R. B. *Personality.* New York: McGraw-Hill, 1950.

Cattell, R. B. *The scientific analysis of personality.* Baltimore: Penguin Books, 1965.

Crowne, D. P., and Marlowe, D. A new scale of social desirability independent of psychopathology. *Journal of Consulting Psychology,* 1960, **24,** 349–54.

Crowne, D. P., and Marlowe, D. *The approval motive: Studies in evaluative dependence.* New York: Wiley, 1964.

Crowne, D. P., and Strickland, B. R. The conditioning of verbal behavior as a function of the need for social approval. *Journal of Abnormal and Social Psychology,* 1961, **63,** 395–401.

Edwards, A. L. *Manual for Edwards Personal Preference Schedule.* New York: Psychological Corporation, 1953. (a)

Edwards, A. L. The relationship between the judged desirability of a trait and the probability that the trait will be endorsed. *Journal of Applied Psychology,* 1953, **37,** 90–93. (b)

Edwards, A. L. *The social desirability variable in personality research.* New York: Dryden, 1957.

Eysenck, H. J. *Dimensions of personality.* London: Routledge & Kegan Paul, 1948.

Eysenck, H. J. *The scientific study of personality.* London: Routledge & Kegan Paul, 1952.

Gough, H. G. An additional study of food aversions. *Journal of Abnormal and Social Psychology,* 1946, **41,** 86–88.

Hanley, C. Social desirability and responses to items from three MMPI scales: D, Sc, and K. *Journal of Applied Psychology,* 1956, **40,** 324–28.

Hathaway, S. R., and McKinley, J. C. *Minnesota Multiphasic Personality Inventory.* Minneapolis: University of Minnesota Press, 1942.

Jackson, D. N., and Messick, S. Content and style in personality assessment. *Psychological Bulletin,* 1958, **55,** 243–52.

Kleinmuntz, B. *Personality measurement: An introduction.* Homewood, Ill.: Dorsey Press, 1967.

Marks, P. A., and Seeman, W. *An atlas for use with the MMPI: Actuarial description of abnormal personality.* Baltimore: Williams & Wilkins, 1963.

Marlowe, D., and Crowne, D. P. Social desirability and response to perceived situational demands. *Journal of Consulting Psychology,* 1961, **25,** 109–15.

Merrill, R. M., and Heathers, L. B. The relation of the MMPI to the Edwards Personal Preference Schedule on a college counseling center sample. *Journal of Consulting Psychology,* 1956, **20,** 310–14.

Montague, E. K. The role of anxiety in serial rote learning. *Journal of Experimental Psychology,* 1953, **45,** 91–96.

Overall, J. E. Note on the scientific status of factors. *Psychological Bulletin,* 1964, **61,** 270–76.

Ramond, C. K. Anxiety and task as determiners of verbal performance. *Journal of Experimental Psychology,* 1953, **46**, 120–24.

Rorer, L. G. The great response-style myth. *Psychological Bulletin,* 1965, **63**, 129–56.

Spence, J. T., and Spence, K. W. The motivational components of manifest anxiety: Drive and drive stimuli. In C. D. Spielberger (Ed.), *Anxiety and behavior.* New York: Academic Press, 1966. Pp. 291–326.

Taylor, J. A. A personality scale of manifest anxiety. *Journal of Abnormal and Social Psychology,* 1953, **48**, 285–90.

Taylor, J. A., and Spence, K. W. The relationship of anxiety level to performance in serial learning. *Journal of Experimental Psychology,* 1952, **44**, 61–64.

Wolpe, J., and Lang, P. J. A fear survey schedule for use in behaviour therapy. *Behaviour Research and Therapy,* 1964, **2**, 27–30.

Wolpe, J., and Lazarus, A. A. *Behavior therapy techniques: A guide to the treatment of neurosis.* New York: Pergamon Press, 1966.

Woodworth, R. S. *Personal data sheet.* Chicago: Stoelting, 1920.

chapter 7

Cognitive Approaches to Personality

The approaches to personality which we have examined thus far have placed relatively little stress on the thinking or *cognitive* underpinnings of behavior. However, some theorists have stressed the role of the intellect in personality, and it is to these cognitive approaches that the present chapter is devoted.

The kind of observation from which a cognitive approach begins is exemplified by Festinger's introduction to *A Theory of Cognitive Dissonance* (1957):

> A person who *believes* a college education is a good thing will very likely encourage his children to go to college; a child who *knows* he will be severely punished for some misdemeanor will not commit it or at least will try not to be caught doing it. This is not surprising, of course; it is so much the rule that we take it for granted. . . . [However] a person may *know* that smoking is bad for him and yet continue to smoke; many persons commit crimes even though they *know* the high probability of being caught and the punishment that awaits them (pp. 1–2, italics added).

The positions which we shall examine in this chapter deal with the relationship between beliefs, cognitions, or types of knowledge of the kind referred to above and behavior. The first theory, that of George A. Kelly, examines the manner in which cognition and behavior may become consistent with one another, while the second, that of Leon Festinger, emphasizes the nature and consequences of inconsistencies between thought and action.

KELLY'S PSYCHOLOGY OF PERSONAL CONSTRUCTS

In Chapter 1 we suggested that a definition or theory of personality is very much dependent upon a model of man. That is, the way a theorist views the subject of his study, the human being, will, in large part, determine his theory of personality. But how does one develop a conception of the nature of man? Although we are not generally aware of the ongoing process, each of us develops such conceptions as we view others in our environment and observe our own behavior. For example, both a man who takes advantage of people and a man who has been swindled will probably feel that most persons are opportunists and that such behavior is the norm. George A. Kelly has argued that the personality theorist should view *man in general* in similar terms to the way *man individually* views or *construes* his own behavior.

Kelly was a psychologist and therefore was in the business of attempting to predict and control human behavior. In the midst of this endeavor, Kelly found something paradoxical about the way personality psychologists studied man. It was as if the psychologist stood in another world looking down on alien beings who were the subject of his investigations. He would examine these foreign specimens systematically, generate hypotheses about their behavior, and then test these hypotheses in experiments. If the hypotheses were confirmed, the theoretical notions which led to the predictions gained some support. The psychologist went about this business in an intellectual, rational fashion. The beings he was studying, however, were supposed to be neither rational nor intellectual; rather they seemed to be impelled by dark, mysterious forces which were entirely irrational. But with a little detached thought it became obvious that the psychologist is no different from the people he studies and certainly has no more claim to intellectual and rational powers than any other man.

Since the psychologist as a scientist goes about his daily endeavors theorizing and testing hypotheses in an effort to gain some power of prediction and control over other human beings, one might hypothesize that all men, in their daily interactions with people and things in their environment, behave in a similar way. The young child who has not received the second helping of ice cream he wants and, in an effort to secure it, cuddles up with tearful eyes to a visiting grandparent can be viewed as a scientist at work. Perhaps the child is acting on the theory, however implicit it may be, that grandparents are likely to be beguiled by affection and also that they tend to be more lenient with second portions of dessert than parents. His hypothesis might be: "I have a better chance of getting that ice cream if I play on grandpa's sympathy." He could then proceed to test this hypothesis or prediction by tearfully snuggling up to his grandfather. If it turns out that grandpa somehow succeeds in securing the ice cream for him, then the hypothesis is confirmed and the theory receives some support. In the future he will be more confident in using this theory. If, however, grandpa is not as soft as his grandson thought him to be or is not capable of convincing the parents that a second helping would do no harm, then the hypothesis is not supported. In this case, the child may very well try a new strategy the next time ice cream is served for dessert. This example illustrates the point that all humans are constantly involved in the prediction and control of events in their environment. Through such observations and interpretations, Kelly came to view man *as if he were a scientist.*

Man-the-scientist has many theories about the nature of events in the real world, and it is through these theories that he deals with his environment. Kelly has assumed, it should be noted, that events in the real world actually have existence. That is, they do not just exist in the minds of men. But at the same time, man's theories or conceptions of these real events also have existence, and thus they can be the subject of scientific investigation.

Kelly (1955) suggested that "man looks at his world through transparent patterns or templets which he creates and then attempts to fit over the realities of which the world is composed" (pp. 8–9). He called these templets *constructs.* A construct is a representation of some event in the person's environment, a way of looking at something which is then tested against the reality of the environment. Examples of constructs include "good vs. bad," "beautiful vs. ugly," "active vs. passive," "black vs. white," and "happy vs. sad."[1] These concepts are ones which many people use to construe events in their lives. It is probably true, however, that each of these constructs has a slightly different meaning for each person, and it is only because of the limitation of our language that they appear common to all people. Thus, every man has his own unique set of *personal constructs.*

A person hypothesizes that a particular construct will adequately fit some event in his environment. He then puts this hypothesis to the test by interacting with the event, be it interpersonal or material in nature, in the manner dictated by the construct. The little boy in our previous example acted in accordance with his construct, "grandparents are benevolent," by first making a specific prediction from this construct (i.e., that he would get a second helping of ice cream by cajoling grandpa) and then acting upon it to test its validity. If a prediction is confirmed, the construct from which it was derived receives support and is therefore maintained as useful. If the construct leads to incorrect predictions, then

[1] According to Kelly, all constructs are bipolar and dichotomous, and when a construct is used to construe an event, only one pole is being used. This point is discussed fully later in the chapter.

it is likely to undergo some revision or may even be discarded altogether. The measure which is used to assess the validity of a construct is its *predictive efficiency.* If a construct helps a person *anticipate events,* it is said to have predictive efficiency, of which there are relative degrees.

Constructive Alternativism

Kelly's personality theory, which he entitled the Psychology of Personal Constructs, is based on the philosophical position of *constructive alternativism,* which Kelly (1955) explains this way:

> . . . there are always some alternative constructions available to choose among in dealing with the world. No one needs to paint himself into a corner; no one needs to be completely hemmed in by circumstances; no one needs to be the victim of his biography (p. 15).

This position, which imparts free will to man, can be seen in striking contrast to the deterministic views of Freud, who saw man as having an unchangeable, partially universal "construct" system. Freudian man is very much the victim of his biological endowment (i.e., the instincts man is born with are universal) and his experiences in the first few years of life. Kellian man, on the other hand, has his own personal, unique system of constructs and always has the option of changing these ways of construing the world. In fact, according to Kelly, our outlooks (constructs) rarely are the same today as they were yesterday. They are constantly being tested in attempts to anticipate future events. The inevitable failure of our constructs from time to time makes their revision a necessity if we are to construe the world in the most (predictively) efficient manner. The constructs that undergo the most frequent modification are those that make predictions concerning immediate events and therefore lead to very quick feedback concerning their ability to anticipate.

In a similar way, a good scientist is perpetually revising his theory according to the results of his experimentation. In this regard, it is interesting to note how a psychologist's model of man and his resulting personality theory influence his own theorizing and scientific outlook. Kelly (1955) considered his Psychology of Personal Constructs wholly ". . . expendable in the light of tomorrow's outlooks and discoveries. At best it is an ad interim theory" (p. 14). Although Freud's theories very definitely underwent change over the 40-odd years that he wrote, Freud was somewhat reluctant to give up old ideas. When revision was necessary, he frequently attributed the new concept to an extension of one he had already expounded, rather than admitting that a change in his thinking had occurred.

Although events have reality in and of themselves, they do not belong to any construct in particular. In line with constructive alternativism, the same event can be viewed from a variety of different perspectives. One interesting example of how different a situation becomes when it is construed from a different construct involved a patient in a psychiatric hospital (Neale, 1968). The patient's behavior was among the most deviant on the ward as evidenced by her unintelligible speech, extremely poor personal habits, ludicrous behavior in the presence of other patients and visitors, and occasional violent outbursts. One day the aides decided to dress up the patient in an attractive outfit, including nylon stockings, high heels, lipstick, and makeup, and take her to the beauty parlor to have her hair styled and set. When she returned to the ward several hours later, the patient no longer showed any of the blatantly "abnormal" symptoms which had become her trademark. Whereas she was still a patient in a psychiatric hospital and in every other way her circumstances remained unchanged, it was obvious that the way she construed herself had definitely changed, if only temporarily.

Properties of Constructs. Each of our constructs has a particular domain of events which may be encompassed by it. This *range of convenience* puts a limit on the usefulness of the construct. The construct "religious vs. not religious" can be used to construe a variety of human behaviors, but it is hardly applicable for talking about the relative merits of American and European sports cars. It is often tempting to generalize beyond the range of convenience of a construct, but a high price of lowered predictive efficiency is usually paid for such generalization.

All constructs have a limited range of convenience, though the breadth of the range may vary substantially from construct to construct. The construct, "good vs. bad," can be used to construe most events in which evaluation is possible and thus has a wide range of convenience. Contrast this with the construct, "brave vs. cowardly," which is considerably narrower in its scope of application.

Constructs also have a *focus of convenience* (or several focuses of convenience), which is a point in the construct's range of convenience where the construct is maximally predictive. For example, the focus of convenience of the construct "religious vs. not religious" might be the customs and ceremonies of the church. Although cheating on an examination could be construed as "not religious," it would be more efficiently construed under the construct "honest vs. dishonest." Whereas cheating on an examination is an event that is within the *range* of convenience of both constructs, it is only the *focus* of convenience of the latter construct. Thus, if our aim is anticipating Fred's future behavior in a variety of situations, it would be more useful to construe his using concealed class notes during the final examination via the construct "honest vs. dishonest" than via the construct "religious vs. not religious." For example, using the construct "religious vs. not religious," it would be difficult to predict the frequency of Fred's church attendance from his behavior during the final examination. However, presumably using the construct "honest vs. dishonest," it would be easier to anticipate whether Fred would use a fraternity brother's old term paper if he needed an "A" in a course.

Constructs also vary on a dimension of *permeability*. A permeable construct is one that is able to admit new elements to its range of convenience. An impermeable construct is one that has already been used to construe all the elements in its range of convenience and therefore is closed to the construction of new experiences and events. One person's construct of "good vs. bad symphonic music" might be sufficiently permeable to account for any new piece of music he hears. That is, on hearing some "electronic music" for the first time, the person could construe it as either "good" or "bad." Such a construct is completely permeable.

There are relative degrees of permeability ranging from a construct which is completely open to new events to a construct which will admit no new events to its domain.[2] It should be emphasized that the notion of permeability is relevant only to the range of convenience of a given construct. By definition, a construct is impermeable to anything outside its range of convenience.

In this section, we have discussed some of the more important and basic characteristics of constructs. In later sections, we shall have occasion to further elucidate the nature of personal constructs.

Motivation: A Rejected Construct. Earliest man construed the physical world in which he lived as one of static objects. Matter was an inert substance which was measured along spatial dimensions (length, width, and depth) and not in terms of temporal dimensions. Later, man became increasingly aware of movement in the universe, but the movement was viewed as being applied to or superimposed upon the inert objects. Thus, in an effort to account for motion (something which early man did not need to do since his world was construed as static) the notion of *energy* came to be employed by physicists.

Modern psychology, which is barely a century old, has borrowed much from the physical sciences (particularly physics) with regard to both its view of the world and its methodology. If the physical world was naturally inert and had to be set into motion by some form of energy, it seemed reasonable to psychologists to construe man in the same way. If man is by nature a static being, yet he is rarely inactive, what makes or motivates human behavior? To answer this question psychologists have

[2] Kelly implies that, in practice, few constructs are likely to be completely impermeable. Thus, he noted: "An utterly concrete construct, if there were such a thing, would not be permeable at all, for it would be made up of certain specified events—those and no others" (1955, p. 79).

postulated "special enlivening forces" such as motives, drives, needs, instincts, and incentives. Kelly (1960) summarizes the state of motivational theory today in the following way:

> Motivational theories can be divided into two types, push theories and pull theories. Under push theories we find such terms as drive, motive, or even stimulus. Pull theories use such constructs as purpose, value, or need. In terms of a well-known metaphor, there are the pitchfork theories on the one hand and the carrot theories on the other [respectively] (p. 50).

The earliest motivational theories were push theories which posited forces within the individual that impel him to action. Freud's personality theory, in which man is energized by biological instincts (most particularly the sexual drive), is clearly of this type. Murray, a personality psychologist whom we shall discuss in a later chapter, has incorporated both push and pull forces within his personality theory in the form of needs (internal motives) and press (external motives). Behavioristic approaches, which we shall also discuss more fully later, attributes man's behavior to external, social cues and therefore would be classified as pull theories.

But whether we view man as being pushed by forces within him or pulled by forces in the external world (or a combination of the two), to construe man in these ways is to relegate him to the realm of purely *reactive* organisms. Indeed, as Kelly and others have found, most people view their fellow human beings (whose behavior they are attempting to predict or control) in just this way, though they probably would be extremely reticent to construe themselves similarly. When a mother wants her child to pick up his toys and wash for dinner, she "knows" that she must somehow *motivate* him. She may do this by means of positive incentives (as, "We're having chocolate ice cream for dessert") or negative incentives (as, "Do what I asked you this minute or your father will spank you").

Early in Kelly's career he traveled through Kansas to provide psychological services to the schools in the state. Most of the referrals came from teachers who were having problems with some student. A frequent complaint these teachers made was that a particular student was lazy. Laziness, as we commonly use the word, means a lack or minimal amount of action. Thus, if a lazy child is viewed in traditional motivational terms, the problem the teacher faces is one of finding suitable motivation. Here we are talking exclusively of external forms of motivation which the teacher can apply (to a naturally inactive being). What would happen if the teacher simply did not attempt to motivate the student? When Kelly and his associates proposed such a course of action to teachers, they frequently replied that the child would do absolutely nothing—he would just sit there. However, when the teachers tried this, more often than not they were surprised to find that their "laziest pupils were those who could produce the most novel ideas . . . that the term 'laziness' had been applied to activities they had simply been unable to understand or appreciate" (Kelly, 1960, pp. 46–47).

It was experiences such as helping teachers reconstrue their pupils' behavior which led Kelly to the conclusion that the concept of motivation is redundant. *Man is neither inactive nor reactive by nature.* The child who was suddenly not being motivated by his teacher did not turn into an inert substance. It appeared, then, that the basic assumption concerning man's essential inertness and the inevitable corollary that the study of human behavior is synonymous with a search for the energetic forces which motivate man, must be called into question. The logical alternative to the now traditional motivational position which psychology acquired from physics, is that man is:

> . . . motivated for no other reason than that he is alive. . . . Life itself could be defined as a form of process or movement. Thus, in designating man as our object of psychological inquiry, we should be taking it for granted that movement is an essential property of his being, not something that has to be accounted for separately. We should be talking about a form of movement—man—not something that has to be motivated (Kelly, 1960, pp. 49–50).
>
> . . . . Thus, the whole controversy as to what prods an inert organism into action becomes a dead issue. Instead, the organism is delivered fresh into the psychological world alive and struggling (Kelly, 1955, p. 37).

The concept of motivation has been used in psychology to explain two aspects of behavior: (1) why man behaves (is active) at all and, when man is active, (2) why he chooses to move in one direction rather than another. If we accept Kelly's basic notion that man is "already in motion simply by virtue of . . . being alive," it is still incumbent upon Kelly to account for the second aspect of behavior—its directionality.

Kelly envisions man as existing primarily in the dimensions of time and only secondarily in the dimensions of space. Thus:

> If we want to know why man does what he does, then the terms of our whys should extend themselves in time rather than in space; they should be events rather than things; they should be mileposts rather than destinations. Clearly, man lives in the present. He stands firmly astride the chasm that separates the past from the future. He is the only connecting link between these two universes. . . . To be sure, there are other forms of existence that have belonged to the past and, presumably, will also belong to the future. A rock that has rested firmly for ages may well exist in the future also, but it does not link the past with the future. . . . It does not anticipate; it does not reach out both ways to snatch handfuls from each of the two worlds in order to bring them together and subject them to the same stern laws. Only man does that (1960, p. 56).

Following this reasoning, any principle of the directionality of behavior must take into account this "conjunctive vision of man"—man who lives partly in the past, wholly in the present, and partly in the future. Kelly (1955) said it this way: *"A person's processes are psychologically channelized by the ways in which he anticipates events"* (p. 46). This is the basic assumption, the *Fundamental Postulate,* from which Kelly's Psychology of Personal Constructs departs.

The Fundamental Postulate and its Corollaries

Fundamental Postulate. In examining Kelly's *fundamental postulate,* stated above, we notice at the outset that Kelly focuses on *processes* rather than inert substances. His system is *psychological* and therefore limits its range of convenience to the investigation of human behavior. The word *channelized* denotes the stability of behavior; behavior remains relatively stable across time and situations because it is channelized by means of the constructs (*ways*) a person uses to predict (*anticipate*) actual happenings (*events*) in the future. Although Kelly has rejected the traditional psychological view of motivation (i.e., push and pull notions), it appears that his Fundamental Postulate is actually a motivational statement. Thus, as Kelly construes man's behavior, the "motive" to predict future events is what directs his activities.

The Nature of a Construct System. Kelly's first four corollaries specify the nature of a person's construct system. The *Construction Corollary* says: "A person anticipates events by construing their replications" (1955, p. 50). To construe an event means to place an interpretation on it, and it is through these interpretations that man is able to predict events that have not yet occurred. The process of construing involves perceiving not only the similar features which an event has over time but also those features which are *not* characteristic of it. That is, a construct must specify both similarities and contrasts. If the reader will think of some of his own personal constructs, he may not immediately see that differences are implied along with similarities. Constructs such as "good people," "pretty girl," "happy occasion," and "funny movie" appear at the outset to be referring only to similarities among events. However, the contrasts (i.e., "bad people," "homely girl," "sad occasion," and "serious movie") are implicitly there, and must be there, for the construct to be at all useful in anticipating events. Thus, in the example of the little boy wanting more ice cream, his construct was actually, "grandpa is benevolent vs. grandpa is not benevolent," although the opposite pole ("grandpa is not benevolent") was left implicit.

Although the *contrast* is often implicitly present when we employ a construct, it is a *sine qua non* and therefore must be capable of being made explicit. Consider the constructs "happy vs. sad" and "good vs.

bad," in contrast to "happy vs. euphoric" and "good vs. non-Christian." Here it can be seen that to state only one of the construct's poles is insufficient since, in the present examples, the second set of constructs are as legitimate as the first set. Thus, the opposite of a concept often differs with the way a person construes things.

The verbal label one puts on a construct and the construct itself should not be confused. The former is generally necessary when a person needs to communicate his construct to others. But all of us have many constructs to which labels in the form of communicable language cannot be applied. Although this may be because the construct is not well specified (its range of convenience may not be known), more often than not it is due to the limitations of our language. The old "commonsense" maxim which says that if a person cannot express a thought, he really does not have the thought, needs to be called into question. Furthermore, as we shall see when we discuss the assessment of personal constructs, the fact that two constructs have the same label does not mean that they are equivalent, nor does the fact that two constructs are given different labels necessarily mean that the constructs are different.

Finally, to fully understand the meaning of the Construction Corollary a word must be said about *replications*. Kelly (1955) explains it this way:

> Only when man attunes his ear to recurrent themes . . . does his universe begin to make sense to him. Like a musician, he must phrase his experience in order to make sense out of it. The phrases are distinguished events. The separation of events is what man produces for himself when he decides to chop up time into manageable lengths. Within these limited segments, which are based on recurrent themes, man begins to discover the bases for likenesses and differences (p. 52).

No two events are ever identical. Today is different from yesterday or tomorrow, and each of us has changed somewhat from yesterday to today and will be different from the way we are today, and were yesterday, tomorrow. Although events never duplicate themselves, in order to predict future events they must bear at least some similarity to their predecessors. Our task must therefore be to search for those themes or characteristics which remain relatively stable over time. Thus, man anticipates events by construing those aspects of the events which do recur consistently.

In the *Individuality Corollary,* which states that "persons differ from each other in their construction of events" (1955, p. 55), Kelly emphasizes that each person has a set of unique personal constructs. No two people observing the same event will have exactly the same interpretation of it. The difference between people, therefore, lies in their construing events from different vantage points. Thus, like Allport, Kelly is keenly aware of the uniqueness of each individual, but in contrast to Allport, Kelly believes that it is possible to ferret out nomothetic laws about human behavior. Events are never exact duplicates of each other, but there are recurrent themes among them. Similarly, Kelly argues, there are characteristics of personal construct systems that repeat themselves across individuals, and it is the psychologist's task to search for these.

The *Dichotomy Corollary,* which says, "A person's construct system is composed of a finite number of dichotomous constructs" (p. 59), emphasizes the *bipolar* and *dichotomous* nature of personal constructs. A construct must specify both similarity and difference in order to be able to construe the replication of events. Kelly (1955) explains:

> Having chosen an aspect with respect to which two events are replications of each other, we find that, by the same token, another event is definitely not a replication of the first two. The person's choice of an aspect determines both what shall be considered similar and what shall be considered contrasting. . . . If we choose an aspect in which A and B are similar, but in contrast to C, it is important to note that it is the same aspect of all three, A, B, *and* C, that forms the basis of the construct (p. 59).

Thus, if A and B are men and C is a woman and the aspect which we abstract is sex, we can classify all three in terms of the same aspect. With respect to sex, A and B are alike and C is different. If we introduce still a fourth element, D, a lamp for example, it is apparent that the aspect *sex* is not applicable to construing D. That is, D is outside the range of convenience of the construct, "male vs. female."

The idea of dichotomous constructs is perhaps one of the most controversial issues in the Psychology of Personal Constructs. Kelly contends that all human thinking is essentially dichotomous, and this conception is at variance with most contemporary theories of the nature of human thought. If a construct is relevant to a particular event, the event must be placed at *either* one pole of the construct *or* the other. The pole of a construct that is being used at any given moment to construe an event is called the *emergent pole,* while the contrasting pole is called the *implicit pole.*

No problem arises with employing a dichotomy in the case of a construct in which the difference between the poles is unequivocal (as with "male vs. female"). But although things may be either black or white, they are most often a shade of gray (i.e., neither black nor white). Kelly (1955) was aware of this problem and explained how constructs, which are composed of mutually exclusive alternatives, can be used relativistically.

> . . . dichotomous constructs can be built into scales, the scales representing superordinate constructs [see discussion of the Organization Corollary to follow]

which are further abstractions of the separate scalar values. Thus, *more grayness vs. less grayness* is a further abstraction of the construct *black vs. white* (p. 66).

Another important departure from classical logic is the fact that Kelly's dichotomous constructs do not include both contrasting and irrelevant events. In classical logic, everything that is either the opposite of a concept or simply unrelated to it is lumped together. In that sense, with reference to the concept "automobile," motorcycles, ships, and airplanes *as well as* pickles, pianos, and porcupines are treated as equivalent. In Kelly's system, however, the former objects would be construed at the implicit pole of the construct (i.e., "nonautomobiles"), but the latter objects could not be construed by the construct "automobiles vs. nonautomobiles" because they are out of its range of convenience (modes of transportation).

It should be noted that the implicit pole—"nonautomobiles"—is merely a shorthand designation for the opposite of "automobiles." Whereas concepts such as "male," "good," and "living" have contrasts with specific referents in our language, many concepts do not. Therefore, it is often necessary to specify merely the negation of the emergent pole, realizing that it does not include irrelevant elements.

For Kelly the units of personality are personal constructs. The structure or organization of the personality is determined by the relationship of the constructs to one another. This point is presented in the *Organization Corollary:* "Each person characteristically evolves, for his convenience in anticipating events, a construct system embracing ordinal relationships between constructs" (1955, p. 56). People not only differ in the constructs they use to view the world, but, perhaps even more importantly, they differ in the way they organize their constructs. It is therefore possible for two people to have similar personal constructs yet have extremely different personalities because their constructs are ordered differently.

Constructs are organized in a hierarchical structure so that most are superordinate to some constructs and subordinate to others. (Occasionally, a construct is independent of all others in the person's construct system.) A construct can subsume another as one of its elements in one of two ways. First, one construct can be superordinate to another by virtue of each pole of the subordinate construct being an element of one of the two poles of the superordinate. As illustrated in Figure 7–1 (*a*), the construct "good vs. bad" can subsume under its two poles, respectively, the two poles of the construct "moral vs. immoral." "Good" includes all events that are "moral" as well as events that fall outside the range of convenience of the construct "moral vs. immoral" (for example, "living") but are within the superordinate's range of convenience. Simi-

FIGURE 7–1

Two Ways for Constructs to Be Superordinate and Subordinate

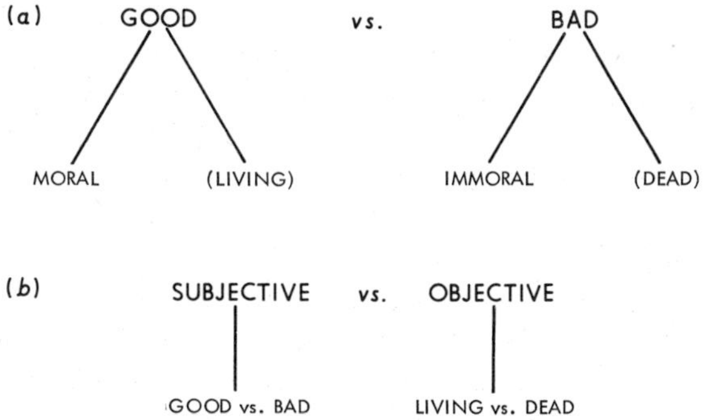

larly, "bad" subsumes all things that are "immoral" plus a number of other things that are neither "moral" nor "immoral" (for example, "dead").

A second way in which one construct can subsume another is for the entire subordinate construct to be an element of one of the poles of the superordinate construct. As illustrated in Figure 7–1 (*b*), the construct "good vs. bad" is subordinate to the "*subjective*" end of the superordinate construct "subjective vs. objective." "Living vs. dead" falls under the "*objective*" end of the construct "subjective vs. objective." That "good vs. bad" can be both superordinate and subordinate is indicative of the complex hierarchical nature of a construct system.

Although a construct system (i.e., the ordinal relationships between constructs) is somewhat more permanent than individual constructs, it can change. Sometimes there is a reversal of superordinate and subordinate constructs. Thus, "moral" could embrace all things that are "good," and "immoral" all things which are "bad." Since a person's construct system develops "for his convenience in anticipating events," predictive efficiency is the criterion for deciding the relative merit of one hierarchical order of constructs over another.

How a Construct System Works: Choice Corollary. To predict a person's behavior, it is necessary to know not only what construct the person will use to construe the relevant events but also which of the two poles of the dichotomous construct he will employ. Kelly (1955) deals with this latter problem in his *Choice Corollary:* "A person chooses for himself that alternative in a dichotomized construct through which he anticipates the greater possibility for extension and definition of his system" (p. 64).

The meaning of *definition* and *extension* of a construct system can be understood in terms of two different kinds of wagers with respect to the anticipation of events. Definition involves a relatively safe wager with a modest payoff, while extension involves a more risky bet but with a more substantial payoff. In the case of definition, the person chooses the alternative (the pole of the construct) that has in the past led to the more accurate prediction of events similar to the present one and therefore has the higher probability of predicting the present event. If the prediction is accurate, the construct becomes more explicit and clear-cut by virtue of its having successfully made an additional prediction. In contrast, extension involves choosing the alternative which has the greater probability of expanding the construct so as to include new events (i.e., increasing its range of convenience). In extension the construct is being used to either anticipate a new event or a familiar event in a new way, and therefore the probability (certainty) of success is less than when definition is the goal. However, if the prediction proves to be correct, then the construct becomes more comprehensive.

Kelly speaks of the difference between definition and extension as one between security and adventure. We often must decide between these two modes of elaborating our construct systems. For example, a student must decide whether to take a course which is similar to one he has already taken, and thus be certain of getting a good grade, or to take a course which he knows little about and may do poorly in, but which will broaden his outlook and knowledge. Or, consider a person who goes to a Chinese restaurant for the first time. He must make a choice between a sirloin steak, which he has eaten before and is sure to enjoy, and Moo Goo Guy Pan, which he has not eaten before and can barely pronounce. In each case, if the person chooses immediate prediction, there is a high probability that his already tested construct will serve him well. thereby providing further definition or clarity for the construct. If he chooses to extend his construct, he faces a greater risk of not being able to predict the immediate situation, but at the same time, the probability that he will gain greater understanding which will aid him in future predictions increases substantially.

Although there is little empirical evidence concerning the decision to define or to extend one's construct system, it is probably the case that a person becomes more likely to choose extension of his constructs as his success in anticipation increases. The poorer his constructs are at predicting future events, the more likely he will be to choose definition. Sechrest (1963) gives an interesting example of this principle.

> A young man is more likely to consider asking the new girl in town for a date when he has been relatively successful in his experiences with the old ones, and he is more likely to ask her when the proposed date is for a relatively familiar function. Thus, he may prefer a girl he knows well if he is about to attend his first formal, country club ball (p. 221).

Both extension and definition (or a combination of the two) serve to elaborate a construct, with the result that its predictive efficiency is enhanced. Accordingly, the choice of which pole of a construct will be used to construe an event (i.e., which will be the emergent pole) has been called the *elaborative choice.*

Changing a Construct System. A construct system's *raison d'être* is to anticipate events as well as possible. It follows, then, that there would be no reason for making alterations in one's already existing system of constructs if there were no problems in effective prediction. But problems do arise, particularly when new events must be construed. If the novel events show some similarity to those with which the person has had previous experience, then there should be less difficulty in construing them by means of already existing constructs. The more novel an event, the less likely that it can easily (with only minor changes) be subsumed into the existing construct system.

Persons who tend to have little variation in their daily lives have relatively stable construct systems. Thus, an elderly woman who lives alone, stays in the house most of the time, and follows the same schedule of limited activities (for example, rise at 10:00, knit 'til 2:30, tea at 3:00, dinner at 6:30, read until 9:30, and then retire) day after day would be expected to have an extremely stable construct system. Is it any wonder, then, that such a woman would have difficulty finding appropriate constructs to construe such new events as men traveling to the moon and human organs being transplanted?

Kelly (1955) deals with the change of a construct system in his *Experience Corollary:* "A person's construct system varies as he successively construes the replications of events" (p. 72). As a succession of new events present themselves to be construed in order to be anticipated, a construct system changes. The constructs are tentative hypotheses which are tested against reality. The feedback as to how well these working hypotheses have predicted future events leads to an alteration of constructs. The altered constructs now are used as new hypotheses and, again on the basis of their adequacy, there is progressive change in the system of constructs.

For Kelly (1955), *experience* involves "successive construing of events. It is not constituted merely by the succession of events themselves" (p. 73). Again pointing to the active nature of man, Kelly says that a person gains little or no experience as a passive observer of events occurring in his environment. If after having witnessed a succession of events we still construe the events in the same way, then we have gained no experience. The professor who delivers the same lectures for eight years cannot, according to Kelly's notion of experience, claim that he has had eight years of teaching experience!

The *Modulation Corollary* specifies the conditions under which change in a construct system can take place: "The variation in a person's construction system is limited by the permeability of the constructs within whose range of convenience the variants lie" (1955, p. 77). The concept of permeability has been discussed in an earlier section and therefore need only be mentioned briefly here. Permeability refers to the degree to which a construct is open to the interpretation of new events. The more permeable a person's constructs are, the greater is the variation (change) which can potentially occur within the system. The Modulation Corollary specifically addresses itself to an even more basic idea: not only must the person construe the new event but he must also be able to construe the *change* itself. That is, the alteration of a construct or group of constructs is an event, and thus for the change to have any influence on the person's behavior, he must already possess a superordinate construct which is capable of construing the change. Kelly (1955) makes this point clear with the following illustration:

> Suppose a person starts out with a construct of *fear vs. domination* and shifts to a construct of *respect vs. contempt.* Whereas once he divided his acquaintances between those he was afraid of and those whom he could dominate, he may, as he grows more mature, divide his acquaintances between those whom he respects and those whom he holds in contempt. But, in order for him to make this shift, he needs another construct, within whose range of convenience the *fear vs. domination* construct lies and which is sufficiently permeable to admit the new idea of *respect vs. contempt.* . . . The permeable construct within whose range of convenience the variants lie may be such a notion as that of *maturity vs. childishness* (pp. 81–82).

Interpersonal Relationships and the Construct System. If, as was indicated by the Individuality Corollary, differences between people are due to differences in the way they construe events, it follows that similarity between people is a function of similarity in construing events. Thus, the *Commonality Corollary,* the Individuality Corollary's counterpart, states: "To the extent that one person employs a construction of experience which is similar to that employed by another, his psychological processes are similar to those of the other person" (1955, p. 90). For two people to exhibit the same behavior (psychological processes), they must not only observe the same events but they must also construe the events in the same way.

An interesting implication of the Commonality Corollary concerns the nature of culture. As the term is generally used, it refers to a group of people who exhibit similar behavior. Typically the common behavior is thought to be the result of similarities in their upbringing and their environment. Kelly (1955) goes several steps further when he says, "People belong to the same cultural group, not merely because they behave alike, nor because they expect the same things of others, but especially because they construe their experience in the same way" (p. 94).

The *Sociality Corollary*[3] sets forth the basic requirement for an interpersonal relationship: "To the extent that one person construes the construction processes of another, he may play a role in a social process involving the other person" (1955, p. 95). In other words, in order for a person to have a social relationship with another, he must have some understanding of how the other person thinks (i.e., he must be able to construe the construct system of the other person). This means that he must be able to anticipate the ways the other person will anticipate events. Thus, the expression "getting into the other fellow's shoes," could be translated as "getting into the other fellow's constructs."

For Kelly (1955), a *role* is a "pattern of behavior that follows from a person's understanding of how the others who are associated with him in his task think" (pp. 97–98). According to this definition of a role, the mere fact that two or more people are together, are conversing with one another, or are working on a mutual task does not mean that there is an interpersonal relationship (i.e., that one or more persons are playing a role in relation to another person in the situation). The basic requirement for playing a role in social situations is that at least one of the individuals present has some understanding of one or more of the other person's ways of seeing things. In this regard, it is important to note that there need not be mutual understanding (i.e., the person playing the role need not be understood by the person(s) toward whom the role is being played). Indeed, many of our role relationships are one-sided. An optimal relationship, of course, involves a mutual understanding of one another's views of the world. This understanding may be limited in scope, as in the case of a student-professor relationship which deals primarily with some academic subject matter; or it may be extremely broad, covering most of each person's construct system, as in a good relationship between husband and wife.

Finally, it should be emphasized that people need not have the same constructs in order to be able to subsume the other's constructs under their own system. As the Commonality Corollary suggests, it is no doubt easier to understand the way another person thinks if one shares similar outlooks, but it is certainly not a requirement for effective role playing.

Consider the differences in the characteristic approaches to life of men and women. None of us would claim, we believe, that men and women construe

[3] In our discussion of Kelly's corollaries to his Fundamental Postulate, two have been omitted, and they are given here for the sake of completeness. *Range Corollary:* "A construct is convenient for the anticipation of a finite range of events only" (1955, p. 68). *Fragmentation Corollary:* "A person may successively employ a variety of construction subsystems which are inferentially incompatible with each other" (1955, p. 83).

all aspects of life in the same way. And yet nature has provided us with no finer example of role relationships and constructive social interaction than in the sexes. If we look at the testimony of nature, we shall have to admit that it often takes a man to understand a woman and a woman to understand a man and there is no greater tragedy than the failure to arrive at those understandings which permit this kind of role interrelationship (Kelly, 1955, p. 100).

The Sociality Corollary has important implications for social psychology. Indeed, Kelly's notion that a true interpersonal relationship does not exist until at least one person begins to understand another's point of view may go a long way in explaining the difficulties we have in communicating with each other in interpersonal situations ranging from everyday interaction (with relatives, friends, and colleagues) to international relations.

The Assessment of Personal Constructs—Role Construct Repertory Test

If we accept the fact that each individual has his own set of personal constructs, the question arises as to how we can assess a person's views of the world. The simplest and most direct way would be to ask the person, and, given that he is able to verbalize his constructs, he can tell us. Unfortunately, this may be more difficult than it seems because, among other reasons, we are not accustomed to thinking about (construing) our own constructs.[4] Thus, the question "What are your constructs?" may prove to have little value. To make the task of assessing one's constructs easier, Kelly devised the *Role Construct Repertory Test* (Rep Test). The Rep Test's domain of applicability is the constructs a person uses to construe significant people in his life. Before discussing the assessment of personal constructs by means of the Rep Test, the reader is invited to examine some of his own constructs and the nature of the Rep Test in the following demonstration.

DEMONSTRATION 7–1: THE ROLE CONSTRUCT REPERTORY TEST

Table 7–1 lists 15 role definitions. Read each definition carefully. On a form which you make, similar to the sample form given in Figure 7–2 (page 184), write the first name of the person who best fits the role in your life in the spaces on the form corresponding to those provided at the top of Figure 7–2 (i.e., after the brief role description). It is essential to use the role definitions *as given* in Table 7–1. If you cannot remember the

[4] The reader may wish to ascertain the difficulty for himself by attempting to make a list of his personal constructs. It should be noted that the reader is in a substantially better position to do this than most people, since he has already had an introduction to the nature of personal constructs which included numerous examples of common constructs.

name of the person, put down a word or brief phrase that will bring the person to mind. Do *not* repeat any names; if some person has already been listed, simply make a second choice. Thus, next to the word "Self" write your own name. Then next to the word "Mother" put your mother's name (or the person who has played the part of a mother in your life; see Table 7–1) and so on until all 15 roles have been designated with a specific individual.

TABLE 7–1

Definition of Roles for Demonstration 7–1

1. *Self:* Yourself.
2. *Mother:* Your mother or the person who has played the part of a mother in your life.
3. *Father:* Your father or the person who has played the part of a father in your life.
4. *Brother:* Your brother who is nearest your own age, or if you do not have a brother, a boy near your own age who has been most like a brother to you.
5. *Sister:* Your sister who is nearest your own age or, if you do not have a sister, a girl near your own age who has been most like a sister to you.
6. *Spouse:* Your wife (or husband) or, if you are not married, your closest present girl (boy) friend.
7. *Pal:* Your closest present friend of the same sex as yourself.
8. *Ex-pal:* A person of the same sex as yourself whom you once thought was a close friend but in whom you were badly disappointed later.
9. *Rejecting Person:* A person with whom you have been associated, who, for some unexplained reason, appeared to dislike you.
10. *Pitied Person:* The person whom you would most like to help or for whom you feel most sorry.
11. *Threatening Person:* The person who threatens you the most or the person who makes you feel the most uncomfortable.
12. *Attractive Person:* A person whom you have recently met whom you would like to know better.
13. *Accepted Teacher:* The teacher who influenced you most.
14. *Rejected Teacher:* The teacher whose point of view you have found most objectionable.
15. *Happy Person:* The happiest person whom you know personally.

Source: Kelly, 1955.

Now look at the first *row* of the matrix in Figure 7–2. Note that there are circles in the squares under *columns* 9, 10, and 12. These circles designate the three people whom you are to consider in the Sort No. 1 (i.e., Rejecting Person, Pitied Person, and Attractive Person). Think about these three people. In particular, how are *two of them alike* in some important way *that differentiates them from the third person?* When you have decided the most important way that two of them are alike but different from the third person, again using your form similar to Figure 7–2, put an "X" in the two circles which correspond to the two persons who are alike. Do *not* write anything in the third circle; leave it blank. Next, write the word or short phrase that tells how the two people are alike in the column marked "Emergent Pole." Then, in the column marked "Implicit Pole,"

FIGURE 7–2

Sample Grid Form of the Rep Test for Demonstration 7–1

SORT NO.	1 Self	2 Mother	3 Father	4 Brother	5 Sister	6 Spouse	7 Pal	8 Ex-pal	9 Rejecting Person	10 Pitied Person	11 Threatening Person	12 Attractive Person	13 Accepted Teacher	14 Rejected Teacher	15 Happy Person	EMERGENT POLE	IMPLICIT POLE
1									O	O		O					
2		O	O	O													
3					O								O		O		
4		O						O					O				
5	O									O		O					
6					O				O					O			
7				O				O			O						
8						O					O				O		
9							O	O				O					
10	O			O	O												
11		O	O								O						
12							O	O				O					
13	O					O	O										
14	O	O	O														
15				O					O					O			

write a word or short phrase that explains the way the third person is different from the other two. Finally, consider each of the remaining 12 persons and think about which of these, in addition to the ones you have already marked with an "X," also have the characteristic you have designated under the "Emergent Pole." Place an "X" in the square corresponding to the name of each of the other persons who has this characteristic. When you have finished this procedure for the first row (Sort No. 1), go to the second row (Sort No. 2). The process should be repeated until the procedure has been carried out for each of the rows. In summary, the steps to be followed for each row (Sort) are:

1. Consider the three people who are designated by circles under their names. Decide how two of them are alike, in an important way, and different from the third.
2. Put an "X" in the circles corresponding to the two people who are alike and leave the remaining circle blank.
3. In the "Emergent Pole" column, write a brief description of the way the two people are *alike.*
4. In the "Implicit Pole" column, write a brief description of the way the third person is *different* from the two who are alike.
5. Consider the remaining 12 persons and place an "X" in the squares

corresponding to those who can also be characterized by the description in the "Emergent Pole" column.

6. Repeat steps 1 through 5 for each row of the matrix.

By the time you have completed the demonstration Rep Test a number of its characteristics should be apparent. Think about how the Rep Test has elicited your constructs. What is the range of convenience of the constructs? Which constructs are relatively permeable and which relatively impermeable? What relation do these constructs have with one another? Do the sorts compare people randomly or is there a rationale behind each sort? Finally, you might ask yourself whether the Rep Test has given you any insights into the way you construe your interpersonal world.

The procedure of the Rep Test is similar to a concept formation task. However, instead of sorting objects, the respondent sorts persons (called figures) who play important roles in his life. The particular sorts which the examiner asks the subject to make will depend upon the purpose of the assessment procedure. The following are examples of sorts used in Demonstration 7–1 with a brief explanation of each (Kelly, 1955, pp. 275–76).

Sort No. 1: *Valency Sort.* The client is asked to compare and contrast a person whose rejection of him he cannot quite understand, a person whom he thinks needs him, and a person whom he does not really know well but whom he thinks he would like to know better. All three of these are somewhat phantom figures, and one may expect that in interpreting them the client relies heavily upon projected attitudes.

Sort No. 3: *Sister Sort.* This is an invitation to construe a Sister figure. It provides an opportunity to see the Sister as like the Accepted Teacher.

Sort No. 5: *Need Sort.* The Self is compared and contrasted with the Pitied Person and the Attractive Person. This gives the clinician an opportunity to study the relative subjective and objective reference which the client gives to his personal needs.

Sort No. 7: *Threat Sort.* The client has an opportunity to construe threat in the context of the Brother, Ex-pal, and Threatening person.

Sort No. 11: *Parental Preference Sort.* The Mother and Father are placed in context with the Threatening person.

The Rep Test can be administered in a variety of ways. Typically, when the Rep Test is used in conjunction with psychotherapy for the purpose of establishing working hypotheses about the person's behavior, it is administered individually. After the person completes the list of role titles either on separate cards or on a sheet of paper, the examiner will present each sort verbally to him. When the Rep Test is given in this manner, the examiner is free to clarify any vague verbal labels the subject may apply to his constructs or to follow up constructs that cannot easily be dealt with systematically. He also has the option of introducing unplanned sorts which suggest themselves as being important as the testing progresses. This form of the test is called the *List Form*.

The results of the List Form of the Rep Test are generally subjected to a clinical analysis in which the constructs are examined for their tone and content as well as for characteristics such as permeability and communicability. In this way, the examiner can become acquainted with the ways the person views significant figures in his life and with the difficulties he has in construing some of these people. This type of analysis is primarily subjective in nature.

In the *Grid Form* of the Rep Test (for example, Demonstration 7–1), a grid or matrix is constructed with significant people in the subject's life on one axis and the constructs he uses to construe them on the other axis. At the intersection of each row and column (of each construct and role title) the subject indicates whether the emergent pole of the construct applies to that person by placing a check mark or "X" there if it does. The absence of a check mark at a particular intersection indicates that the implicit pole is applicable. Each intersect then becomes either an *incident* (i.e., a check mark indicates the emergent pole applies) or a *void* (i.e., a blank indicates the implicit pole applies). Because one of the basic assumptions of the Rep Test is that every construct applies to every figure, the subject examines the remaining figures (those not considered in the sort which elicited the construct) and indicates (by a check mark) if the emergent pole can be used to construe each of them.

Although the Grid Form can be clinically analyzed, it has the advantage of being applicable to a more sophisticated type of analysis. Capitalizing on the linkage among particular constructs due to their being applied to the same persons, Kelly has devised a "nonparametric factor analysis" to reduce the grid to a few basic dimensions. The basic strategy is similar to factor analysis as it was discussed in Chapter 6. When constructs have approximately the same pattern of incidents and voids, they are said to be *functionally similar* and are represented by a *construct factor*. Whether or not constructs have similar verbal labels applied to them, if they are used to construe most of the same people in the same way, they are equivalent for the function they serve, namely, anticipating future behavior. For constructs to be considered functionally equivalent and represented by a common factor, the check patterns need not be identical, only approximately the same, and Kelly presents a mathematical test for determining the closeness of fit. A similar analysis can be made over the columns of the grid to reduce the information concerning the significant figures in the person's life to more manageable units, with the result being one or more representative *figure factors*.

The Role Construct Repertory Test has been widely used in both clinical and research settings and can be considered one of Kelly's most important and ingenious contributions to the study of personality. In fact, more research has been directed toward the Rep Test than the Psychology of Personal Constructs itself. In addition, a number of studies which have little relevance to Kelly's theory have employed the Rep Test.

In considering the utility of the Rep Test there are several important cautionary notes which must be made with regard to the interpretation of the results. First, the Rep Test may often be an effective device for assessing the way a person sees important people in his life. Such information is often extremely helpful in the psychotherapeutic setting, since most human problems concern relationships with other people, particularly those close to us. However, the constructs elicited by the Rep Test are those which the person uses to construe the behavior of others. If the examiner's goal is to predict the behavior of the person himself, then it is necessary to ascertain whether the constructs he applies to others apply to his own behavior as well (Sechrest, 1963). Second, though the Rep Test requires that constructs be set down in words, constructs need not be verbalizable. Therefore, it cannot be assumed that the constructs elicited by the test represent all or even the most important of the person's constructs used to construe the figures in the test. Third, even when the person makes his constructs more or less explicitly known by means of verbal labels which appear to have generally accepted meanings, one cannot be sure that the labels do, in fact, have common referents. For example, constructs such as "successful vs. unsuccessful," "attractive vs. unattractive," and "difficult vs. easy" have highly personalized meanings.

Evidence for the Psychology of Personal Constructs

In this section, we shall examine the nature of the empirical evidence for the theoretical assumptions which underlie the Psychology of Personal Constructs. Unfortunately, as Bonarius (1965) points out in his comprehensive review of research dealing with Kelly's theory, there has been no systematic attempt to test the theory. For our purposes it will be sufficient to look at several representative studies in an effort to illustrate the kinds of investigations and the general research strategy which have arisen from Kelly's position.

Individuality Corollary. Kelly asserted in his Individuality Corollary that people differ from one another because, besides having had experience with different events, they construe (interpret) events differently. Each person, then, has a set of *personal* constructs. It is legitimate to ask how stable or permanent persons' construct systems tend to be. To answer this question, Fjeld and Landfield (1961) asked subjects to take the Rep Test twice. The second time the test was administered, the subjects were instructed not to use the same figures they employed in the first Rep Test, and the trio of role titles which they compared also differed between the two administrations. When the constructs elicited by the two Rep Tests were compared, they were shown to agree substantially, as evidenced by high test-retest reliability (correlation coefficient of +.79). Thus, for a given individual, there is some evidence that his constructs are not only stable across time but they are also relatively independent of the particular events (in this case, people) being construed.

If each person has a unique set of constructs, then it follows that the optimal way to predict his behavior would be to understand his personal constructs as opposed to the constructs which other people use to describe him. To test this hypothesis, Payne (1956) had subjects, in groups of three, predict how the other two people in the triad had completed a social behavior questionnaire. Each subject was given a list of 15 personal constructs of one of his partners and 15 constructs *about* the other partner which his peers had employed in describing him. Payne found that subjects were significantly more accurate at predicting how another person had responded to the questionnaire when they had access to the individual's own personal constructs.

Experience Corollary. Like the Individuality Corollary, the Experience Corollary, which in essence states that man's views of the world change as he construes events over time, makes sense intuitively, and few psychologists (including those skeptical about the Psychology of Personal Constructs) would doubt its validity. (This does mean, however, that these obvious statements do not need to be tested empirically.) The real value of the Experience Corollary (and the Individuality Corollary) is that it has stimulated research which has led to findings which are important extensions of the corollary. We shall discuss three investigations which elucidate some of the conditions for construct change and the nature of that change.

In a study of interpersonal perception, Bieri (1953) showed that social interaction between people will produce a change in the way they construe each other. Following the standard design of studies of interpersonal perception, the subjects first filled out a questionnaire describing an aspect of their behavior. Then subjects were asked to predict another person's answers to the questionnaire both before and after the experimental treatment, which involved a discussion between the two people who predicted each other's questionnaire responses. As predicted, the subjects viewed the other person somewhat differently after their short social interaction. Specifically, subjects came to view the other person as more like themselves.

Lundy (1952) provided an interesting explanation and extension of Bieri's findings in an investigation of the effect of increased social interaction on the perception of others. The subjects were six patients who were participating in group therapy over a period of four weeks. Each patient predicted the responses of the other five individuals on a questionnaire administered before and after the first session and once a week for the remaining three weeks. Lundy reasoned that before any social interaction, the subjects could only guess how the others would answer the questionnaire. After a minimal amount of interaction, subjects would assume that the other persons were similar to themselves (Bieri's finding) in an effort to gain some structure. Only after the subjects had gotten to know one another better (i.e., had more social contact) would they attempt to construe the others differently than themselves. The results supported these hypotheses.

In a field study of changes during individual psychotherapy, Tippett (1959) used as subjects patients who had been in therapy at least three months between two administrations of the Rep Test. Her results are particularly enlightening with regard to the predominant topics of discussion during therapy. When the therapist concentrated on the patient's past, the constructs which underwent the most change were those which were predominantly used to construe figures who are generally associated with a person's early life (for example, parents). When the emphasis was on the present, constructs which dealt with figures who are usually important to a person later in life (for example, spouse) underwent alteration. The change in constructs was evidenced both by the rewording of the verbal labels applied to the constructs and in the pattern of application of the constructs to the figures.

Traditional Personality Constructs as Construed by Kelly's Theory

By now it should be apparent that the Psychology of Personal Constructs is in many respects quite different from most traditional theories of personality. Kelly introduces a number of new terms which are unique to his theory; and, at the same time, terminology which is common to most other theories of personality, such as anxiety, guilt, and aggression, has been conspicuously absent in our discussion. Lest the erroneous impression be given that the Psychology of Personal Constructs considers these and other topics traditionally dealt with by personality theory out of its "range of convenience," we shall briefly look at the way in which Kelly construes several of these personality concepts.

Anxiety. Kelly (1955) defines anxiety as "recognition that the events with which one is confronted lie outside the range of convenience of one's construct system" (p. 495). Thus, the vague feeling of helplessness which we commonly denote as anxiety is, for Kelly, a result of being unable to anticipate an event because one's available constructs do not apply. When a person has no constructs to interpret an event, he cannot fully comprehend what is happening because, in effect, if a person cannot construe an event, the event does not exist for him. Hence, although the anxious individual feels apprehensive or afraid (about his incapacity to anticipate), he is unable to "put his finger" on why he feels this way.

One very prevalent view of mental illness, and most particularly of the so-called neuroses, holds that anxiety plays a major role in the etiology and maintenance of the disorder. If we accept this view as valid, it is interesting to see how the notion is translated into the Psychology of Personal Constructs. The anxious person, rather than being the victim of inner conflicts and dammed-up energy (the psychoanalytic interpretation of neurosis), is one who is having difficulty in construing his environment in general or certain aspects of it in particular. Rather than being overwhelmed by instincts which are seeking expression, he is overwhelmed by happenings in his life which he cannot understand (anticipate). Looked at in this latter manner, psychotherapy then becomes a process in which the patient acquires new concepts which will successfully predict the troublesome events or makes already existing constructs more permeable so as to admit the new events to their range of convenience.

Guilt. Kelly treats guilt as the awareness of having deviated from some important role one plays with respect to other persons. Consider a college student who perceives his major role to be that of a "scholar." Because he is spending too much time at the fraternity house and with his girl friend, it becomes evident to him that he is somewhat alienated from a basic aspect of his role as a scholar, namely studying, and, as a consequence, he feels guilty. Another college student might consider his role to be that of a "playboy," and thus when he found himself studying, he would, according to Kelly's definition, feel guilty. Viewing guilt as Kelly does has utility for several reasons.

> The conventional notion of guilt as man's awareness of the evil within him is not antithetical to this formulation; nor is the psychoanalytic notion of guilt as a kind of spanking administered by the superego. Our proposed formulation is designed to free the research-minded psychologist from the absolutism of "evil" on the one hand, and from the anthropomorphism of the Freudian superego on the other (Kelly, 1955, p. 502).

Aggression. Kelly construes aggressive behavior as the active extension (as opposed to definition) of one's construct system. Aggressiveness need not be hostile or antisocial in nature. For example:

> In the business world aggressiveness is often labeled "a good thing." It is the mark of the "coming" or the "successful" man. Sometimes account is taken of the area of one's aggression. If it occurs in the area of interpersonal relations, the man is fitted out with a white collar and put to work in "sales" or in

"personnel." If it occurs in the area of inanimate things, he is put to work in "the plant," or perhaps in "engineering" or "production," and he is asked to use a different washroom (Kelly, 1955, p. 509).

Sometimes aggressive behavior may indeed be threatening to other people, but this is a function of the consequences to the other's construct system and not necessarily a result of the person's behavior or his intent to do harm. In the Psychology of Personal Constructs, *threat* is defined as the awareness that a major change in one's construct system is imminent. Kelly (1955) gives the following illustration:

The aggressive person—for example the "social pusher"—keeps plunging himself and his associates into ventures which unduly complicate their well-ordered lives. The very fact that he insists on construing himself as belonging to the social group is threatening to those who are already identified with the group. They see, in their impending reciprocal identification with him, a major shift coming up in their own core structures (pp. 509–10).

Hostility. Hostility, in contrast to aggression, is defined by Kelly (1955) as "the continued effort to extort validational evidence in favor of a type of social prediction which has already proved itself a failure" (p. 510). At the outset, this definition seems far afield from the ordinary conceptualization of hostility which emphasizes the person's intent to do harm. Kelly (1955) attempts to understand hostility "from the point of view of the person who feels it and what it is that he is actually seeking to accomplish . . . [and to view] the injury he may imagine that he would like to inflict upon another person, not as a primary goal in itself, but as an incidental outcome of something more vital that he is trying to accomplish" (p. 510).

It will be recalled that constructs are validated by making predictions from them and then putting these predictions to an actual empirical test. When a prediction proves to be accurate, the construct which led to it will remain unchanged and, at least for the moment, no further experimentation need be carried out. If, however, the prediction turns out to be a rather poor prognosticator of the future, three courses of action are available to the individual. He can resign himself to the fact that his prediction was indeed false and therefore that he is in need of a new or revised construct. Or, he can question the validity of his test or the meaning of the results and repeat the test. Finally, he can attempt to change the events, rather than his way of looking at them, so that they will conform to his views of them. Hostility is the use of this third alternative to cope with invalidating evidence for one's constructs.

When a person's expectations about the material world prove unrealistic, attempting to alter physical objects to meet his expectations is costly, but only to the object and perhaps the person himself. For example, if a man expects that his key will open a particular door but finds that the key does not work, he can obtain another key, insert the key once more, or engage in a variety of behaviors to prove that the key does fit the door. If he chooses the last alternative, the most dire consequences that can occur are that upon attempting to force the key to work, it will break off in the lock, and the man will suffer a few cuts and bruises in the course of his attack on the door.

When predictions are made of another person's behavior, the consequences of choosing to change the events—the other person—becomes considerably more significant. Kelly (1955) explains the situation as follows:

> The individual construes another person; he makes a prediction about him; when he turns up contrary evidence, he senses a twinge of anxiety as it appears that the other person may not fall within the range of convenience of his role constructs (or, perhaps, he is threatened by the major revision of his system which the experience indicates may be necessary); then, in order to protect himself either from the anxiety or the threat, he sets out to make the other person into the kind of creature he predicted he was in the first place. This is hostility. The other person is the victim, not so much of the hostile person's fiendishly destructive impulses, as of his frantic and unrealistic efforts to collect on a wager he has already lost (p. 511).

In our daily experiences, we find that hostility is frequently evoked when a person "does not get his own way." Consider the example we have used several times in this chapter of the little boy who wanted a second helping of ice cream. If his grandfather did not help him get the extra dessert, the boy might "throw a temper tantrum" and hit his grandfather. One way to view this situation would be that the boy wanted to "get back" at his grandfather, to retaliate. This would be the most frequently given explanation of the boy's behavior. Another interpretation would hold that the boy's behavior was aimed at changing his grandfather's mind. Since the boy's grandfather, like most grandparents, rarely denied his grandson anything he wanted, it is somewhat unreasonable to conclude that the boy would want to hurt him after just one nonindulgent act on his part.

In this, and many similar circumstances of behavior which we commonly term hostile, it is more reasonable, on the basis of the facts at hand, to conclude that the hostility is motivated by a desire to have one's prediction validated than to conclude that the person is merely being vindictive. Often, however, when we ask the person why he acted hostilely toward another individual, he will reply with some statement to the effect that he wanted to get back at the person who wronged him in some way (as, "Johnny took my bicycle and I wanted to punish him").

That such statements, which come from children and adults alike, are often made is undoubtedly true, but we need not assume that such comments are a product of innate tendencies. A reasonable alternative hypothesis is that we are taught to think in these terms. When, as a child, we act in a hostile manner toward someone else, we are typically told that it is not right to hurt other people and, of even greater significance, that it is wrong to want to do harm to others. If, on the other hand, we were consistently told in childhood that it is not right to try to change others to suit our own wants and desires, the commonly held conception of hostility might be closer to Kelly's notion. It is interesting to speculate about the potential consequences of altering childrearing practices with regard to dealing with hostility. For example, if from an early age we were to be taught to deal with invalidated predictions by either abandoning our less efficient constructs or by replicating the tests of the constructs rather than with hostility, then we might see a general reduction in tensions between people in future generations.

Further, it should be pointed out that hostile behavior, as Kelly construes it, is not a priori undesirable. There are instances where the best way to deal with invalidation of constructs is to attempt to change the events to meet our expectations rather than to abandon our view of things to conform to the events. Civil rights workers who believe that blacks and other minority groups in the United States should be treated equally in all walks of life would be ill advised to change their views when predictions based on them prove to be invalid (as they so often have). Thus, for example, when it became clear in the recent past that blacks were being kept from registering to vote in state elections, an expectation counter to civil rights workers' views of how things should be, they did not give up their views concerning equal voting rights. Instead they attempted to see that anyone wishing to vote had an opportunity to do so, thereby manipulating the events to conform to their constructs.

It may be difficult to accept Kelly's definitions of the common personality constructs just discussed because we are so accustomed to the more traditional definitions. In this regard, it should be kept in mind that the behavior is the same whether it is viewed from the vantage point of the Psychology of Personal Constructs or another theory of personality. The only thing that differs is the *interpretation* we place on the behavior. Relevant to this point is the important distinction between observation and inference. Two personality theorists whose theoretical biases differ considerably (for example, Freud and Kelly) would no doubt make the same observation concerning the little boy's hostile behavior toward his grandfather which was discussed previously, but the inferences they drew from the common observation would prove to have little in common. Indeed, after listening to Freudian and Kellian *explanations* of the boy's behavior, we might very well question whether the two men had observed the same event.

One of the reasons that Kelly's definitions of common personality concepts appear unique is that they are conspicuously independent of value judgments. As we have already made clear, the concepts of aggression and hostility are neither "good" nor "bad" per se. The issue of evaluation is taken out of the domain of psychology, and this gives Kelly's definitions the distinct advantage of being more objective. This absence of evaluation, in combination with Kelly's insistence on understanding a person's behavior by construing his constructs (a point of view Kelly shares with other personality psychologists, such as Carl Rogers), leads to objectivity in the scientific investigation of human behavior and tolerance in everyday interpersonal relations.

Kelly's approach to the study of personality stresses the individual's rational use of cognitions to anticipate events but pays relatively little attention to the manner in which discrepancies in cognitions, constructs, and perceptions are resolved. The next position we shall discuss, Festinger's Theory of Cognitive Dissonance, speaks primarily to these latter issues.

FESTINGER'S THEORY OF COGNITIVE DISSONANCE

Most of us would argue that our attitudes and behavior are rationally consistent. Leon Festinger introduced his Theory of Cognitive Dissonance in 1957 by conceding the general value of this assumption. He noted, however, that inconsistencies sometimes do appear and that he was interested in their effects upon thought and action. After replacing the word *inconsistency* with his own term, *dissonance,* he stated two basic hypotheses (1957, p. 3):

1. The existence of dissonance, being psychologically uncomfortable, will motivate the person to try to reduce the dissonance and achieve consonance.
2. When dissonance is present, in addition to trying to reduce it, the person will likely avoid situations and information which would likely increase the dissonance.

Since 1957, an enormous amount of theorizing and research has been centered around these two propositions. This work has emphasized the psychological (cognitive) processes occurring within individuals, and thus it can be construed as a portion of the study of personality.[5] We shall therefore examine some of this work in the present chapter. Our discussion begins with a consideration of the concept of cognitive balance and a more precise definition of dissonance.

[5] We make this point explicitly because Festinger's work is usually identified with the study of social psychology, rather than being considered a personality theory.

The Concepts of Balance and Dissonance

Balance exists between two cognitive elements that are both valued in the same direction, either positively or negatively, and are "associatively" related to each other. For example, one way of describing the relationship between the three cognitions "I have chosen this one and rejected those," "The one I have chosen is imperfect," and "Those I have rejected are very desirable," is to say that the cognitions are in a state of imbalance.[6] In Festinger's terminology, the three cognitions are *dissonant:* the first one ruled out the possibility of having the other two. Such a relationship exemplifies the term *cognitive dissonance,* since cognitive dissonance is described by Festinger (1957) as "nonfitting relations among cognitions." Festinger (1957) goes on to note that *"these two elements are in a dissonant relation if, considering these two alone, the obverse of one element would follow from the other"* (p. 13). Thus, "I want that car" and "I have chosen this car and rejected that car" are in a dissonant relationship.

The Experience of Dissonance

Perhaps the most important characteristic of dissonance is that it is "psychologically uncomfortable." Just as harmonic dissonance is aesthetically displeasing, just as structural dissonance creates strain in the framework, just as dissonance in interpersonal relationship creates friction, dissonance in the network of beliefs, opinions, or perceptions of reality is difficult to tolerate. Moreover, cognitive dissonance can occur in many types of situations other than the decision-making process as in the example of choosing a car which has been used above. Having principles and living in violation of them creates dissonance between cognitions about standards and those about one's behavior. Holding the belief that cigarette smoking causes cancer and being a smoker brings cognitions about life and pleasure into dissonance. Being 5 years old and wanting to fly airplanes, or being 25 years old and wanting to crawl up into some lovely young mother's lap, or being penniless and wanting to rip into a $7.50 sirloin steak, or being wealthy and wanting to go barefoot to town on a hot summer day, all produce cognitions that are dissonant with each other.

Cognitive dissonance, being psychologically uncomfortable, becomes a reason or motive for *dissonance reduction*—the process of bringing

[6] The cognitive theories of Heider (1944; 1946; 1958), Abelson and Rosenberg (1958), and Osgood, Suci, and Tannenbaum (1957) also use the principle of balance-imbalance. We have chosen to discuss only Festinger's position, since it exemplifies most of the issues and has generated by far the greatest amount of research.

cognitions into a balanced or *consonant* relationship. The strength of this motive is a direct function of the magnitude of dissonance—the greater the dissonance, the greater is the motive to reduce it. The magnitude of dissonance depends upon such things as (1) the importance of the decision, (2) the importance of the alternatives, and (3) the relative attractiveness of the unchosen alternative(s). The more important the decision and the alternatives and the greater the attractiveness of the unchosen alternative relative to the chosen alternative, the greater will be the cognitive dissonance. Figure 7–3 shows, in simplified form, the

FIGURE 7–3

Anticipated (Postdecision) Dissonance as a Function of the Attractiveness and Importance of the Unchosen Alternative

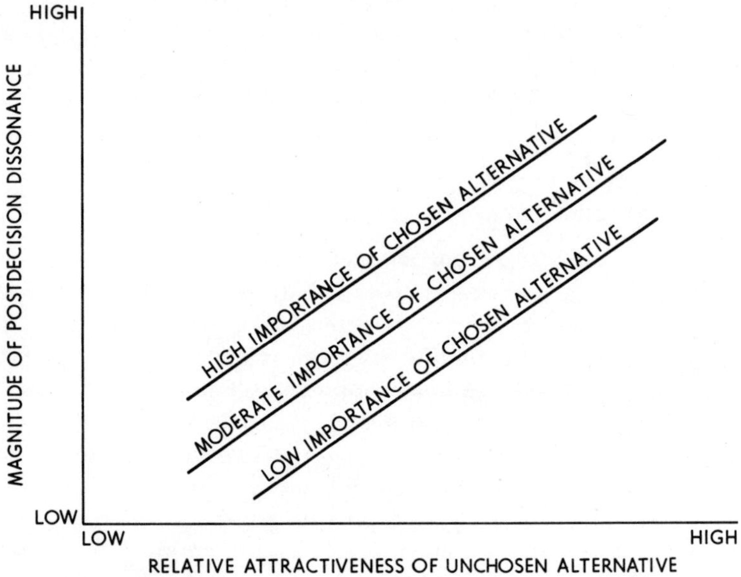

Source: Festinger, 1957.

relationship expected between the relative attractiveness of the unchosen alternative and the magnitude of dissonance when the importance and attractiveness of the chosen alternative are held constant.

As we noted earlier, dissonance may be produced by many situations. One circumstance which is particularly likely to do so is decision-making. Thus, we shall turn our discussion to this topic.

Decision-Making and Dissonance

How do people make decisions? How do they maintain a decision once they make it? How and why do they change one decision in favor of another one? These are three of the questions to which Festinger's theory is addressed.

By "decisions," we are referring to cognitive resolution of alternatives such as: to be or not to be (i.e., a doctor), to buy or not to buy (i.e., a foreign car), and more importantly, to be *and* not to be (i.e., an anaesthesiologist . . . a psychiatrist), to buy *and* not to buy (i.e., a Karmann Ghia . . . a Volvo). Though there is little evidence as to what constitutes the process of decision-making itself, Festinger has some interesting and well-established hypotheses about the predecision process that leads up to it, and the postdecision process in which it is maintained or changed.

Creation and Reduction of Dissonance in Decision-Making. Two experiments reported by Festinger (1964) serve to illustrate the manner in which dissonance is manifested and reduced as a consequence of making a decision.

In one study by Festinger and Walster (1964), Stanford University co-eds participated in what they believed was market research for "Duart-Clairol, Inc." All subjects were given 12 photographs of different hair styles and asked to rate the attractiveness of each on a 13-point scale. Then, while the girls were temporarily engaged in another task, the experimenter selected two photographs which were rated as desirable and as one or two points apart in attractiveness. All subjects were then asked to *rank* the 12 styles which they had previously rated. First, however, half of the subjects were told that they would get their hair done free, but would have to choose between the two styles which the experimenter had selected (*prior-decision* condition). The remaining half of the subjects were not given this information until after they had completed their rankings (*no-prior-decision* condition). All subjects then made their actual choices and were finally asked to rate the photographs again.

The investigators argue that if dissonance occurs after making a choice between alternatives nearly equal in attractiveness, then subjects should feel "regret" immediately after making such a decision. This regret should be reflected in a tendency to reverse one's decision immediately after it is made. Thus, with regard to their experiment, the following prediction is made:

> Subjects in the prior-decision condition, at the time they were asked to state their choice, should be experiencing . . . [the presence of] post-decision dissonance, since, in essence, they have just expressed their decision in the ranking. Consequently, one would expect that there would be a higher incidence of decision reversal in this condition than in the no-prior-decision condition. A decision reversal would be an instance in which the subject, when asked finally which style she wanted, chose the hair style that she had initially rated as less attractive. In short, post-decision regret, if it existed, should lead to tendencies toward decision reversal (Festinger and Walster, 1964, p. 105).

The data clearly support this reasoning. Only 28 percent of the girls in the no-prior-decision group chose the less attractive alternative, whereas 62 percent of the subjects in the prior-decision group showed this form of presumably dissonance-produced regret.

The second experiment (Walster, 1964), investigating postdecision regret, tested the joint propositions that (1) immediately following the decision, the feeling of dissonance makes the rejected alternative seem more attractive than the chosen one, and (2) this regret period will be followed by the process of dissonance reduction. The subjects were army inductees who were asked to choose the job that they would occupy for the duration of their two-year service obligation. Obviously, the participants felt that the decision was an important one. After making their decision from among a number of jobs, they were asked to again rate the jobs—in some cases four minutes after the decision, in others 15 minutes afterward, and for still others 90 minutes following their decision. The data provided strong evidence for regret 4 minutes after the decision and indicated that dissonance reduction was under way by 15 minutes after the decision. Surprisingly, there was no dissonance reduction reported after 90 minutes, possibly due to "boredom" or methodological problems with the experiment.

The two experiments described above provide some evidence that decisions produce dissonance which, in turn, gives way to dissonance reduction. However, it is central to Festinger's position that these processes do not occur before a decision is made. We will now turn our attention to the predecision period.

Predecision Processes. The predecision period—the time prior to the actual *choice* when the alternatives are known and being considered—is characterized by conflict. The individual is faced with two alternatives which are mutually exclusive ("One can't have one's pie and eat it too") and very nearly equal in their initial appeal. By definition, this is the period in which a decision is reached. The question is: How?

Probably most people would agree that the predecision period is characterized by careful examination of the alternatives and by an effort to evaluate them. Elaboration of this process might take many forms, one of which appears particularly popular and reasonable.

> It is possible to maintain . . . that the evaluation of the alternatives in the pre-decision period is a very systematic affair in the course of which the alternatives are reinterpreted so as to produce greater and greater divergence in attractiveness. When the divergence becomes great enough, the person is finally able to make a decision. The *presumed partiality of the information gathering and evaluation is, thus, instrumental in allowing the person to reach a decision* (Festinger, 1964, pp. 3–4; italics added).

This phenomenon, which has a good deal of commonsense appeal, also paves the way for a straightforward theoretical description of decision making. As Festinger (1964) observes:

These theoretical positions would claim that the [biased] spreading apart [of the attractiveness of the alternatives] begins during the pre-decision period in order to make the decision possible. The decision itself does nothing but involve the person in a commitment to a given course of action, and does not sharply alter the psychological processes that go on. After the decision there is still residual conflict, and the spreading apart process continues, since conflict is unpleasant. . . . If the same cognitive processes occur both before and after a decision, we can have a relatively simple theoretical framework capable of dealing with the entire process. In addition, such findings would imply that the "act of decision" is in no way critical from the point of view of the psychological process (p. 6).

The position described above is of interest to Festinger because it is *contrary* to the Theory of Cognitive Dissonance. In other words, Festinger is prepared to argue (and to demonstrate) that this simple account is not an accurate description of the decision-making process. To support his view, Festinger (1964) reports experimental evidence that prior to the actual making of a decision, people do not ordinarily engage in *spreading apart the attractiveness of the alternatives* (*spreading the alternatives,* for short). They do find themselves in a situation of "conflict" between two or more mutually exclusive possibilities, but aside from predisposed preferences, the decision, says Festinger, is made on the basis of something other than an increase in attractiveness of one of the alternatives.

In an experiment by Jecker (1964), high school girls were used as subjects, and the task was to "participate in market research" by rating 15 phonograph records. The ratings were made on a seven-point scale ranging from "don't care" to "would rather have this record than any I can think of right now." After the ratings were made, the instructions used were varied in order to produce different degrees of conflict. All subjects were told that the experimenter intended to give them each one gift record for their participation. Girls in the *low-conflict* condition were also told that 19 out of 20 girls would get two records instead of one, whereas those in the *high-conflict* condition were told that only 1 girl out of 20 would receive more than one record. The experimenter then showed each girl two records that she had initially rated almost identically (i.e., one step apart) and that were both moderately attractive to her. Each subject was told that these would be the two records she might receive and asked to indicate her preference in case she could only have one of them. The time required to make this decision was recorded.

Although the girls now drew slips of paper to supposedly determine whether they received one record or two, the drawing was "fixed." Half of the girls in each conflict condition received both records (the *no dissonance* group), while the other half received only the one they had chosen (*dissonance* group). All subjects were then asked to rate each of the 15 records again.

Before examining the results of the experiment, it would be best to emphasize the important distinction Festinger (1957) makes between conflict and dissonance:

The person is in a conflict situation before making the decision. After having made the decision he no longer is in conflict; he has made his choice; he has, so to speak, resolved the conflict. He is no longer being pushed in two or more directions simultaneously. He is now committed to the chosen course of action. It is only here that dissonance exists, and the pressure to reduce this dissonance is *not* pushing the person in two directions simultaneously (p. 39).

Results of the experiment were first examined in terms of decision time, a widely accepted measure of degree of conflict. The data confirmed the effectiveness of the conflict manipulation, since high-conflict girls took significantly longer to make their decisions than those in the low-conflict group. In order to examine the spreading apart of alternatives, changes in attractiveness on the two ratings were computed for all four groups. These results are presented in Table 7–2.

TABLE 7–2

Mean Change in Attractiveness Ratings Favoring the Chosen Alternative
(increase for chosen plus decrease for rejected alternative)

	High Conflict	*Low Conflict*
Dissonance	+1.0*	+.6†
No dissonance	+ .2	+.3

* Significantly different from zero (i.e., from no change), $p < .01$.
† Significantly different from zero, $p < .05$.
Source: Adapted from Festinger, 1964.

Jecker (1964) argues that the outcome would be predicted from dissonance theory:

The interpretation of the data seems to be reasonably clear. If there is no dissonance created after the decision, then, irrespective of the degree of conflict during the decision, there is little or no systematic re-evaluation of the alternatives. . . . On the other hand, when dissonance is created after the decision, there is a significant re-evaluation of the alternatives for both high and low conflict conditions. Clearly, the suggested interpretation is that such systematic re-evaluation of alternatives to favor the chosen one occurs only after the decision has been made in order to reduce dissonance, and does *not* occur in the pre-decision period in order to enable the person to make the decision (pp. 26–27).

Despite this compelling argument, Jecker realized that an alternative explanation is possible. Suppose that, while making a decision, high-conflict subjects do spread the alternatives. When they then receive both records (no dissonance), the spreading process might be reversed so that the records are again seen as nearly equal. If this process occurred, predecision spreading of alternatives might be masked, leading to the false conclusion that it had not occurred. To exclude this possibility, a second experiment was conducted in which three groups were used. Two of the groups received the high- and low-conflict treatments described previously, except that they made their second evaluation of the records *before* finding out whether they would receive one or both records. Thus, for these girls, conflict varied, but ratings were made before any dissonant information (or postdecision reevaluation) could occur. In the third group, the treatment differed only in that each girl knew she would get only one record. However, in contrast to the other two groups, dissonance would occur immediately after the choice, at which time these girls made their second rating.

The results of this second experiment exclude the conflict-resolution account and provide clear support for the dissonance prediction. As shown in Table 7–3, girls who were subjected to cognitive dissonance showed a significant increase in spread between the selected and rejected alternatives (+.6), while the subjects who did not experience dissonance did not change significantly from one rating to another. Thus, ratings of attractiveness did not diverge or spread until the postdecision period.

TABLE 7–3

Mean Change in Attractiveness Ratings before Knowing Whether One or Both Records Will Be Obtained

Condition	*Mean Change*
Low conflict—no dissonance	−.1
High conflict—no dissonance	−.3
Ordinary decision	+.6*

* Significantly different from zero (i.e., from no change), $p < .02$.
Source: Adapted from Festinger, 1964.

Although Festinger argues that cognitive dissonance is not involved in making a decision, he clearly acknowledges that other cognitive processes are involved in this process. Rather ingeniously, he has identified two of them. Both can be understood with regard to an example. Suppose Sam Smith is a prospective car buyer. If Sam has thoroughly examined all the cars he might buy and is now at home pacing the patio trying to make up his mind, he is probably thinking about more than the cars that he has recently seen. One of the things that Sam is very likely to be thinking about is the car just bought by John Jones, with whom he wants to keep up, a car that is clearly preferable to his present car and that is regrettably preferable to any of the cars his modest budget will allow him to consider. He is remembering that the only one of his alternatives that even approaches the Jones's new car in styling would have to be standard shift, six-cylinder, and radioless to be in his financial range. He is remembering also how each of the other cars falls woefully shy of the Jones's in its own sadly unique way.

This rather common process of thinking about attractive, yet, for all practical purposes, unavailable, alternatives has been demonstrated empirically in an experiment by Walster and Festinger (1964). One group of children was shown an "ideal" toy car (a large red one with a gasoline engine) and several good, but slightly damaged toy cars. A second group of children was shown a "mediocre" toy car (a small sedan with no motor at all) and the slightly damaged cars. The children were asked to choose one car from the collection of slightly damaged ones, either to keep or as a preference. Half the children were given tests to determine what they remembered about all the cars before they made their choice (*predecision* condition) and half after they made their choice (*postdecision* condition).

For subjects who had an "ideal" car with which to compare the several slightly damaged cars, those in the predecision condition remembered more about the "ideal" car than those in the postdecision condition. It appears that in the presence of an ideal, defects show up more and that in decision making, *defects are more significant determinants of the alternative chosen than are positive features.*

There is also another thing that Sam, the prospective car buyer in our example, is likely to be thinking about. He remembers that the last time he bought a car he had a difficult time convincing himself that he had done the right thing. He remembers that at the time he told his wife that he would have been better off keeping the old car and not having to worry about it. It has been shown that the anticipation of this kind of experience (i.e., of dissonance) is a factor in the predecision process that makes it necessary for a person first, before he can decide, to *decide to decide.*

Braden and Walster (1964) conducted an experiment in which high school girls were shown two records and told that they would be given one of them. Half the girls were told that they would be required to read a favorable review of the record they had chosen (*no anticipation of dissonance* condition) and half were told that they would have to read a favorable review of the record they rejected (*anticipation of dissonance* condition). All subjects were then given an opportunity either to choose their record or to have a coin flipped to determine which record they would receive. The results showed that 81 percent of the girls who had no reason to anticipate dissonance decided to choose their own record rather than leave the decision to chance. By comparison, only 29 percent of the girls who anticipated dissonance made their own choice. That is, the majority (71 percent) of these latter girls *avoided* the anticipated dissonance, which would have resulted from reading a review favoring their rejected alternative, by leaving the decision to chance and thereby eliminating any personal responsibility for a wrong choice.

Techniques of Dissonance Reduction

Spreading the Alternatives. We have already mentioned one method of reducing the uncomfortable state of cognitive dissonance, that of spreading apart the attractiveness of the alternatives. Cognitive dissonance is created by a decision to accept one alternative over another which, after the decision has been made, seems almost as attractive or even more attractive than the chosen one. If the chosen alternative can be made to appear more attractive, either by increasing its appeal or decreasing the appeal of the rejected alternative, then dissonance will be reduced (i.e., the chosen alternative will be viewed as more attractive and the choice as the correct one).

However, spreading the alternatives cannot work unless at least one of the alternatives can be changed (i.e., made more or less attractive), and there are several factors that can make such a cognitive element resistant to change. The most obvious is its responsiveness to reality. If the girl you decided to marry just *is* less attractive, more cranky, and besieged with a greater number of intolerable relatives than six other available girls of your acquaintance, you will just have to reconcile yourself to this. Another factor that supports resistance to change is the dependence of other cognitions on the one in question. This is the situation, for example, when the political party you, and perhaps your family before you, have worked hard for nominates a candidate whose position sets him squarely against your political principles. To vote for him would upset your whole network of political ideas. But to vote for his opponent would not set well with your party loyalty and your experience as to which party can best exercise political power.

When dissonant cognitions are resistant to change, dissonance may be reduced by techniques which do not require a change in the cognitions. Two such possibilities are *cognitive overlap* and *selective exposure*.

Cognitive Overlap. The most economical procedure for reducing dissonance is the establishing of *cognitive overlap*. Cognitive overlap leads to the conviction that two dissonant elements are really the same, really lead to the same end, or really serve the same purpose. Thus, after your school has lost the basketball championship to the school that you rejected in making your present college choice, all you have to do to reduce the cognitive dissonance which has resulted from your choice of schools is to remember that your college is much better in football ("Wait'll fall!"), or that your school's basketball team does not in any way reflect the academic excellence of the institution ("Who cares about basketball anyway!").

Selective Exposure. If all else fails, as at least to some degree it will, dissonance reduction may take the form of arranging and controlling one's environment so that what is seen, heard, and read will not upset the delicately, and perhaps somewhat artificially, balanced structure of one's opinions and attitudes. Festinger calls this technique *selective exposure*, and the concept is central to the concerns of all industries and agencies that have to do with the management of public attitudes and choice preferences. The advertising industry is interested in knowing what kind of advertising people will expose themselves to and what kind will have the desired effects. Religious, educational, and political organizations need to know how to effectively communicate with people about their attitudes, beliefs, and ideas. The theory of selective exposure to information has had a powerful impact in all of these areas.

When a person is confronted with information dissonant to his cognitions—with an advertisement praising a product that was not bought, with an article that challenges a deeply felt attitude, with an item that resounds to the glory of a rival—he can either attend to it or not. If he does not or cannot ignore the dissonant information, he can still possibly avoid dissonance by attending to the information selectively. For instance, while reading an article which contains facts which are at variance with some of his ideas and beliefs, he can skip over that which he would rather not see. He can remember selectively, conveniently forgetting what is disconcerting to remember. He can misinterpret the information, reading into it his own ideas and preset nuances of meaning. He can dissociate his situation from that referred to in the dissonant information, maintaining that it does not really apply. And, finally, he can derogate the source of the information, rendering it powerless by association. These processes are not merely sinister and "dishonest." They are tools with which our culture has outfitted us to defend ourselves against unwarranted inconsistency, in an atmosphere that places heavy demands in the direction of "rationality" and "logical coherence."

Festinger has revised and refined his theory of selective exposure to information until it now reads: "When dissonance does exist and when there is an active dissonance reduction process occurring, then there does seem to be evidence for selective exposure to new information so as to help in the dissonance-reduction process" (1964, p. 96). The significance of this position must be understood in light of its history. In its original formulation, the principle of selective exposure consisted of the simple formula that consonant information would be sought and dissonant information would be avoided. Subsequent studies have shown this not to be invaryingly the case, as dissonance-producing information is in fact frequently consulted in many instances.[7]

Festinger and his associates have presented two cases where dissonant information *is* likely to be consulted. First, information that is likely to be useful, either in maintaining one's own position, or in other contexts, may well be consulted in spite of the fact that it is dissonance-producing—the concept of *information utility*. Thus, for example, a member of a minority party may keep up with the political position of the leading candidate, not because he agrees or wants to agree with him, but because he expects him to win and will find it useful to know how he stands on the issues.

The second instance in which dissonant information is likely to be consulted has to do with "subjective confidence," with the ability the person feels himself to have in confronting and overcoming dissonant information. It has been pointed out that when a person is offered the chance to read or hear evidence that will disconfirm his choice or opinion, he is already in a dissonance-producing situation. There is dissonance in the very fact that disconfirmatory evidence exists. It would be hypothesized, therefore, that if this person has a history of success in overcoming contradictory positions, he will be anxious to "engage in battle" the alleged disconfirmation in the confidence that he can subdue it. For example, recall (Chapter 2) that correlational studies do not demonstrate causal relationships. Thus, an inveterate smoker who is also knowledgeable about research methods might expose himself to reports of the (correlational) relationship between smoking and lung cancer because he believes that such data do not demonstrate that smoking actually produces cancer in humans. He could even note the possibility that some hereditary characteristic leads to both susceptibility to cancer and a liking for nicotine and point out that, if this were true, reduced smoking could not protect him from the disease.

Festinger (1957) has reported an experiment that reveals in an interesting manner some of the dynamics involved in maintaining a decision, and how, finally, that decision can come to be changed. Male undergraduate students played a card game with an experimenter. In this gambling situation, the two-person card game was arranged, according to a set of rules, so that the two sides were decidedly uneven. This was explained to the subject, and he was given the opportunity to choose whichever side he wanted to play on. He was told that he would be given $2.50 with which to gamble as his payment for participation and that he could keep

---

[7] Freedman and Sears (1965) have provided an excellent and comprehensive review of this issue.

the money he had at the end of 30 trials. The subject was told that, because the game was uneven, he would be given the opportunity to change his decision, that is, to change sides, one time during the game. But because most decisions, once made, are difficult to change, an element of resistance to change was introduced. The subjects were instructed that if they decided to change sides during the game, the decision would cost them $1. Hence the importance of making the correct decision the first time was stressed.

Then the game began. After 12 trials, the experimenter showed the subject a graph that he said indicated the cumulative probabilities of all possible scores, from which he said the subject could calculate the exact

FIGURE 7–4

Mean Time of Exposure to New Information as a Function of Degree of Dissonance

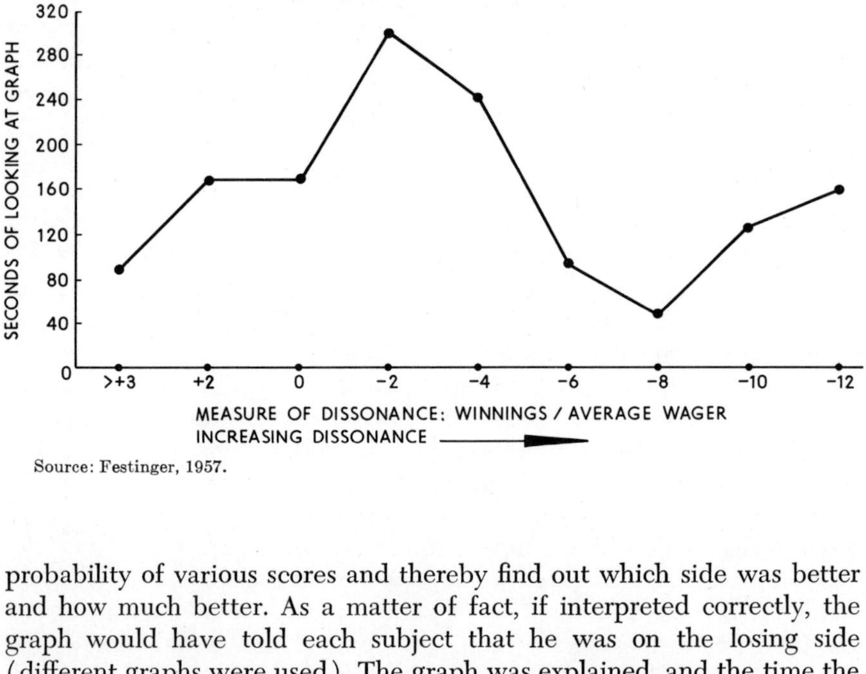

Source: Festinger, 1957.

probability of various scores and thereby find out which side was better and how much better. As a matter of fact, if interpreted correctly, the graph would have told each subject that he was on the losing side (different graphs were used). The graph was explained, and the time the subject spent looking at the graph was recorded. When the subject indicated that he was through, the experiment was concluded.

The results of the experiment, which are presented on Figure 7–4 and Table 7–4, fit predictions from dissonance theory in the following ways.

1. Dissonance theory predicts that if the decision made is seen as the correct one, there will be little or no motivation to acquire information by looking at the graph. This was partially confirmed, as those subjects on the positive end of the dissonance scale (+3.00 to −1.00) spent only

a moderate amount of time looking at the graph. The confirmation was only partial, however, because these subjects did spend an average of about 175 seconds looking at the graph, which is somewhat high. One possible explanation of this is that for those subjects who were winning, the graph itself produced dissonance—a case of involuntary exposure to information—and was then read more carefully to see if it was correctly perceived.

2. It was predicted that subjects whose cognitions were dissonant with their decisions would spend more time on the graph if there was hope for information to reduce the dissonance. This hope would be likely to be present among subjects whose losses had not been alarming. The results revealed that those subjects whose losses were moderate (i.e.,

TABLE 7–4

Relationship between Amount of Dissonance Experienced and Amount of Time Spent Looking at Informative Graph

Intervals on Dissonance Scale (Winnings per Average Wager)	*Number of Subjects in Interval*	*Average Time Spent on Graph (In Seconds)*
+ 3.00 and greater	7	90.7
+ 2.99 to + 1.00	15	178.3
+ 0.99 to − 1.00	9	173.3
− 1.01 to − 3.00	14	308.5
− 3.01 to − 5.00	18	239.9
− 5.01 to − 7.00	7	94.1
− 7.01 to − 9.00	3	43.0
− 9.01 to −11.00	4	122.5
−11.01 to −13.00	6	155.5

Source: Festinger, 1957.

−1.01 to −5.00) spent the most time looking at the graph, as they apparently searched the graph for information that they were actually on the correct side.

3. It was predicted that those whose cognitions were dissonant with their decisions would actively avoid the graph if it was expected that the graph would yield information that would increase the dissonance. This prediction was clearly confirmed, since those subjects who were rather extreme on the scale of dissonance (−5.01 to −9.00) and had therefore had enough experience to convince them that they had chosen the wrong side, spent only a minimum amount of time with the graph.

4. Finally, it was predicted that if cognitions became so dissonant with the decision as to be close to the limit of dissonance tolerability, then the easiest way to eliminate the dissonance would be to increase it to a point where it was greater than the resistance to change. Then

changing sides would eliminate the dissonance. The results showed that time spent on the graph does increase again at the extreme limit of dissonance (−9.01 to −13.00).

Festinger has also presented experimental evidence for his contention that when people expose themselves to information that they believe to be consonant with or irrelevant to their own position, they are unusually vulnerable to the impact of that information. In order to avoid this state of affairs, we read book reviews, ask our friends what things are "about," and try to find out what new acquaintances will be "like" so that dissonant information will not take us by surprise.

Often, however, we have no chance to "check up" on information that we become exposed to. This happens when we come upon something accidentally, as in a newspaper account of political activities, in which we find a policy statement from the other party's candidate that is really quite endearing, and more in line with our own ideas than are those of our party's candidate. It happens when a "fact" becomes generally "known," so that there is no escaping it. And it happens in conversations with friends and associates, who "might say anything." As in voluntary exposure, we have defenses: discrediting of the source, allowing for exceptions, challenging of the facts, and misperception.

Forced Compliance. A special instance of involuntary exposure is the case of *forced compliance*. Educators have discovered the value of role playing in changing old ideas and teaching new ones. Studies about brainwashing as it has been carried out with certain prisoners of war show how forced compliance to patterns of action that are closely identified with an alien ideology has in certain cases led to the adoption of that ideology. According to dissonance theory, in forced compliance there is dissonance between one's original ideas and one's new pattern of action, between cognitions about belief and those about behavior. Festinger (1957) points out that when a person "does what he has to do," in the face of his ideas about what he "ought to do," the dissonance created is greater as the threat or reward is less and as the notion about what one ought to do is more important. For example, there will be more dissonance for the airline stewardess who adopts a new hair style that she feels to be unflattering because she sees in a fashion magazine that it is in style than there would be if she adopted it because the airline required her to. Festinger further hypothesizes that when a person "sticks to his principles" in the face of "temptation" to do otherwise, the cognitive dissonance becomes greater as the promised reward or threatened punishment increases. If our stewardess keeps her hair long in face of stylistic pressure to cut it off, her dissonance is less than it would be if she does so in the face of a threatened job loss. Festinger points out that the way to change a person's belief is to offer him just enough incentive to change his behavior, and the dissonance thereby created between his behavior and cognition will eventually change his belief. Thus, dissonance theory predicts that the stewardess will eventually come to like her new hair style. This is a subtle process, since the dissonance involved in maintaining one's position despite a great incentive to do otherwise may further confirm that position.

Social Support and Cognitive Dissonance

Festinger's Theory of Cognitive Dissonance also provides some insights concerning the role of social support in the maintenance and change of attitudes. When a person holds an opinion which is at odds with the opinions held by members of a social group to which he belongs, the person experiences dissonance in the same way he would if his opinion were in conflict with another of his own cognitions or were challenged by his perception of reality. The magnitude of this dissonance is affected internally by the number of existing cognitions that are consonant with the one in question—the more consonant cognitions, the less the dissonance. Magnitude is affected externally, that is, socially, by two factors: (1) the more nonsocial, objective consonant cognitions there are, the less effect social disagreement will have, and (2) the more people who are in accord with the person's disagreement, the less dissonance is produced by disagreement. Additionally, the greater the importance of the issue in question, the greater will be the dissonance.

Two features of the social group have a bearing on dissonance. One is the *relevance of the group* to the issue. A lady whose ideas about football are dissonant with a number of members of her mother's sewing club will experience a good bit less dissonance than she would if her ideas about childrearing were dissonant with most of theirs. The other significant feature is the *cohesiveness of the group*. The greater the mutual attractiveness that the members have for each other, and especially the greater the attraction the person feels toward those with whom his opinion is dissonant, the greater the dissonance. Of course, the depth and extent of the disagreement affects all of these factors.

Festinger suggests three methods by which dissonance stemming from social disagreement can be reduced: (1) change one's own opinion, (2) change the opinions of those with whom there is disagreement, and (3) make the people with whom there is disagreement in some way significantly different from, and therefore not comparable, to oneself (for example, the "If you were in my shoes . . ." argument). These methods, however, are fairly well restricted to small-group relations. The evidence suggests that, except in rare instances, only individuals who are usually classified as "deviant" are able to maintain perceptions of "reality" that are substantially different from those shared by the majority of their fellows. The only dissonance that can be acknowledged and still tolerated in a large group is that which is shared by a number of members of that group. Social support is necessary for the maintenance of most attitudes, and with social support, as we shall see shortly, it is sometimes possible to maintain opinions and attitudes that are flatly contradicted by "reality."

One observation reported by Festinger is that persons who had more friends and were members of more groups were able to change their minds more frequently than others because it was easy for such people to find social support for new ideas. A change in opinion leads to conversation about it, and dissonance produces conversation of the "What do you think about . . . ?" variety. Conversation seems to drop off once the dissonance has been reduced. It is common experience that in times of rapid social change, barbershops, beauty parlors, social clubs, and public places of all sorts hum with vigorous discussions about "the issues." People are deeply conscious of dissonance among their attitudes and opinions, and between their own and those of others. They are anxious to know "what is going on," "what are people thinking," or "how can sane people feel . . . ?" So they talk and ask, even with strangers, and make a desperate search for social support for each of their separate cognitive elements, and for all of them together. The importance of conversation and other methods of consensual validation in the construction and maintenance of reality is widely recognized. For example, typically the mass media are more effective in changing attitudes with respect to content about which people do not talk readily and with people who are socially isolated.

A peculiar and subtle kind of social support is that which is offered by rumors. Psychoanalysis addresses itself to the kind of dissonance that is experienced when a person or a group of persons feel a strong affect, such as fear, and yet are not able to attribute it to anything. The fear has to be "located" to be dealt with. It has to be attached to something that thereafter becomes frightening, so that it can be defended against. In intrapsychic dynamics this is expressed in phobias and phantasies and irrational projections. In social situations, it is expressed in, among other things, rumors. Rumors about fearful future events often become widely accepted when people are already afraid but have no visible reasons for their fears. Conversely, rumors are usually not widespread where there is no fear.

There are also examples of how social support facilitates the maintenance of beliefs even when they are clearly disconfirmed by public evidence. One such instance concerns a group of Japanese Americans who, during World War II, requested repatriation to Japan whenever the war was over. This drastic and irrevocable decision was obviously made on the basis of the conviction that Japan would win the war. This conviction was maintained through all the reports of Japanese military defeats during the closing years of the war, including the reports and pictures of the Japanese surrender. This information was no match for the cohesiveness and unanimity of mind in this group, which dismissed all dissonant reports as American propaganda. It is reported that the conviction was maintained throughout the voyage back to Japan and was finally given up only when the firsthand confrontation with the destruction and American occupation of Japan tore away their last vestige of defenses.

In the book, *When Prophecy Fails,* Festinger (1956) and his associates describe the birth, development, and eventual dispersion of a group of people who gathered together in a common commitment to "messages" received from "the Guardians" concerning the end of life on this planet. Initially the group engaged in a small amount of spreading of the word and gathering of social support for their eccentric beliefs, especially the central one about the impending end of the earth. However, after a small and cohesive group of deeply committed believers was formed, there was not only a cessation of proselytizing but also an active avoidance of social contact. Once, when national attention was focused on the group because one of their members had been dismissed from his university position for his beliefs, they went to great lengths to remove themselves and their great secret from the public eye. Not that they were insecure in what they believed. On the contrary, many of the group members had impoverished themselves or otherwise made their commitment irrevocable as a consequence of their unwavering confidence.

The group had prophesied that a flying saucer would be sent to rescue them from the flood which would destroy the earth. Disconfirmation came when the members of the group realized that there was no flood, no flying saucer, and no rescue. At the time of disconfirmation, some of the members were apart from the group and waiting alone. Bereft of social support, almost all of them promptly gave up their belief. However, the group members who were huddled together came to the "revelation" that their faith had saved them. Then they did a most incredible thing. They launched into a massive abandonment of their former secrecy and began to proclaim their message to the world. The ban on new members was removed, and until the group's final dispersion, most of its activities were consumed with proselytizing. The members of the group were subjected to extraordinary cognitive dissonance as the result of their pervasive commitment and the undeniable disconfirmation of their mutually held belief. Their heavy reliance on social support as the only possible source of this belief is underscored by their desperate last-ditch effort to maintain it by widening the supportive social circle.

REFERENCES

Abelson, R. P., and Rosenberg, M. J. Symbolic psycho-logic: A model of attitudinal cognition. *Behavioral Science,* 1958, **3,** 1–13.

Bieri, J. Changes in interpersonal perceptions following social interaction. *Journal of Abnormal and Social Psychology,* 1953, **48,** 61–66.

Bonarius, J. C. Research in the personal construct theory of George A. Kelly: Role Construct Repertory Test and basic theory. In B. A. Maher (Ed.), *Progress in experimental personality research.* New York: Academic Press, 1965.

Braden, M., and Walster, E. The effect of anticipated dissonance on pre-decision behavior. In L. Festinger, *Conflict, decision, and dissonance.* Stanford, Calif.: Stanford University Press, 1964. Pp. 145–51.

Festinger, L. *A theory of cognitive dissonance.* New York: Row Peterson, 1957.

Festinger, L. *Conflict, decision, and dissonance.* Stanford, Calif.: Stanford University Press, 1964.

Festinger, L., Reicken, H. W., and Schachter, S. *When prophecy fails.* Minneapolis: University of Minnesota Press, 1956.

Festinger, L., and Walster, E. Post-decision regret and decision reversal. In L. Festinger, *Conflict, decision, and dissonance.* Stanford, Calif.: Stanford University Press, 1964. Pp. 100–110.

Fjeld, S. P., and Landfield, A. W. Personal construct consistency. *Psychological Reports,* 1961, **8,** 127–29.

Freedman, J. L., and Sears, D. O. Selective exposure. In L. Berkowitz (Ed.), *Advances in experimental social psychology.* New York: Academic Press, 1965.

Heider, F. Social perception and phenomenal causality. *Psychological Review,* 1944, **51,** 358–74.

Heider, F. Attitudes and cognitive organization. *Journal of Psychology,* 1946, **21,** 107–12.

Heider, F. *The psychology of interpersonal relations.* New York: Wiley, 1958.

Jecker, J. D. The cognitive effects of conflict and dissonance. In L. Festinger, *Conflict, decision, and dissonance.* Stanford, Calif.: Stanford University Press, 1964. Pp. 21–30.

Kelly, G. A. Man's construction of his alternatives. In G. Lindzey (Ed.), *Assessment of human motives.* New York: Grove Press, 1960.

Kelly, G. A. *The psychology of personal constructs.* New York: Norton, 1955.

Lundy, R. M. Changes in interpersonal perception associated with group-therapy. Unpublished master's thesis, Ohio State University, 1952.

Neale, J. Personal communication, 1968.

Osgood, C. E., Suci, G. J., and Tannenbaum, P. H. *The measurement of meaning.* Urbana: University of Illinois Press, 1957.

Payne, D. E. Role constructs versus part constructs and interpersonal understanding. Unpublished doctoral dissertation, Ohio State University, 1956.

Sechrest, L. The psychology of personal constructs: George Kelly. In J. M.

Wepman and R. W. Heine (Eds.), *Concepts of personality.* Chicago: Aldine, 1963.

Tippett, J. S. A study of change process during psychotherapy. Unpublished doctoral dissertation, Ohio State University, 1959.

Walster, E. The temporal sequence of post-decision processes. In L. Festinger, *Conflict, decision, and dissonance.* Stanford, Calif.: Stanford University Press, 1964. Pp. 112–27.

chapter 8

Motivational Theories: Needs

All theories of personality must somehow account for the impetus and direction of activity which people take and for the wide difference among persons in the ends or goals which they appear to seek. In this sense, all theories of personality are "motivational." Nonetheless, some theories can be distinguished by the fact that they have focused primarily on the identification or measurement of particular motives or needs as a means to understanding, predicting, and controlling human behavior. In the present chapter, we shall examine two motivational need theories and inspect some of the research which they have generated.

MURRAY'S PERSONOLOGY[1]

In 1938, Henry A. Murray and his colleagues published *Explorations in Personality*,[2] a report of two and a half years of research with 51 male subjects of college age. The volume, however, was far more than a research report. Its 700-plus pages contained a major theory of motivation, an introduction to assessment procedures which were shortly to become among the most widely used in psychology, and several individual experiments which have become "classics" in personality research.

[1] Murray and his co-workers defined their area of interest as *"personology,"* arguing that the phrase "'the psychology of personality' [is] a clumsy and tautological expression" (1962, p. 4).

[2] The volume was reprinted in 1962, and thus all direct quotes cite the later year.

We shall begin our discussion by considering the major propositions and constructs of the theory, calling upon both Murray's original work and a later paper which introduced some additions and modifications (Murray and Kluckhohn, 1953).

The theory constructed by Murray and his associates was broadly described as "a theory of directional forces within the subject, forces which seek out or respond to various objects or total situations in the environment" (1962, p. 24). Positing such forces was not a unique venture. Impelling passions and instincts had been suggested by many earlier writers, and the dynamics of Freud's theory were already well known. But Murray sought to do more than acknowledge these forces. He wished to identify and catalog them, assess them in persons, determine their relationship one to another, and take the bold step of writing a comprehensive theory. Recognizing that they did not have "sufficient" data to justify their stand, Murray and his colleagues noted:

> . . . for the present the destiny of personology is best served by giving scope to speculation, perhaps not so much as psycho-analysts allow themselves, but plenty. Hence, in the present volume we have checked self-criticism, ignored various details, winked a little at statistics, and from first to last have never hesitated to offer interpretative hypotheses. Had we made a ritual of rigorous analysis nothing would have filtered through to write about. Speech is healthier than silence, even though one knows that what one says is vague and inconclusive (1962, p. 22).

Primary Constructs

Murray believes that the individual and his environment must be considered together as a person-environment interaction. However, to begin an analysis of this interaction, forces within the individual and forces from the environment are temporarily separated. The former are referred to as *needs* and the latter as *press*.[3]

Needs. A need (*n*) is a *hypothetical construct*, an imagined or convenient fiction which is useful only insofar as it helps the psychologist to deal with facts. It is "an organic potentiality or readiness to respond in a certain way under given conditions . . . it is a noun which stands for the fact that a certain trend is apt to recur" (1962, p. 61). So defined, needs are identified with particular effects or temporary end-states (for example, the need for sex is identified with orgasm). A need must be distinguished from an *actone*, which is a pattern of action (a behavior) which may serve to satisfy a need. An actone may become associated with a need if it is regularly associated with its end-state. For example, verbal "threats" are actones which may function well in the service of a need for

[3] The plural of "press" is press.

power. A given actone can often be used to satisfy a number of different needs (getting married, for example, may directly or indirectly satisfy a man's need for security, sex, food, and so on). Therefore, it is not always possible to identify a person's active needs by observing his behavior. We shall return to the problem of assessment of needs in a later section.

Since need is a hypothetical construct rather than something which is observable, it is encumbent upon the theorist to suggest evidence for its utility or *heuristic value.* Murray (1962) cites 23 points of evidence to support the value of the concept of need and to substantiate the claim that needs, rather than observable behavior (actones), should be the units for the study of personality. Fifteen of the points, which are based on objective data, are included in the following list.

1. Organisms require certain conditions in order to survive. It is apparent, for example, that we all have a "need" for oxygen.
2. For those effects which are universally required by living creatures, a variety of actones may be used. Food may be acquired by growing it, trapping it, stalking it live, or stealing it from a fellow being.
3. In the life of a single individual, we can observe that certain outcomes are regularly attained, but the instrumental actones change markedly with development. "The embryo assimilates food through the umbilical vessels, the infant sucks it from the tendered breast of the mother, the child eats with a spoon what is put before him, and the adult has . . . to get money to buy food" (1962, p. 57).
4. Actones have no intrinsic value. Only those which reliably produce "satisfying" end-states become established.
5. Novel situations often engender a succession of actones, until one is found which produces a desired effect.
6. Some responses can be produced only by novelty (which, of course, is not directly observable). For example, one rarely laughs heartily at a familiar joke.
7. Necessary end-states may be produced by the actones of another person, as in the case of the sick child whose biological requirements are provided by its mother's actions.
8. *Persistence* would be hard to interpret without positing needs. Humans, for example, often *increase* the intensity of their efforts in the face of opposition.
9. "Complex action is characterized by the occurrence of muscular contractions in widely separated parts of the organism—contractions which manifest synchronous and consecutive coordination. Such organizations of movement must be partially determined by a directional process—which is just what a need, by definition, is" (1962, pp. 61–62).

10. The concept of need is necessary to understand differences in the intensity or duration of goal-directed behavior. Intensity of the actones themselves vary from moment to moment.
11. Actones may be swiftly interrupted by the gratuitous presentation of end-states, as when the attention of a guest stops a child's crying. If the actone itself was critical, it would presumably persist.
12. "That a need is an important determinant of certain kinds of behavior is shown by the fact that when it is neither active nor in a state of readiness, responses to specific stimuli do not occur" (1962, p. 62). For example, directly after a large and filling meal one is not likely to accept an invitation to go out to a local restaurant.
13. If a need is active, then objects or events may be used in novel ways in the service of the need. By way of example, Murray notes that when a boy is quarreling with a playmate and sees an apple, he may well throw it at his antagonist rather than eat it.
14. Organisms sometimes become active *in search of,* as well as *in the presence of,* need related stimuli. Thus, "an animal will *explore* for food, and a man will *search* for a sex object" (1962, p. 63).
15. Biological causes of activation may be discovered, suggesting a palpable source for need-related behavior.[4]

The remaining eight points which Murray makes in favor of the concept of need are avowedly subjective, are based largely on their appeal to the internal or private feelings of the reader, and emphasize the importance of motivational interpretations in the practical commerce of our daily lives. They can be summarized by the following comment: ". . . no therapist or, indeed, anyone who has to deal in a practical way with human beings, can get along without some notion of motivational force (instinct, purpose, aim, intention, need, drive, impulse, urge, attitude, inclination, wish, desire, or what not) . . ." (Murray, 1962, p. 66).

Having considered Murray's arguments for the value of the concept of need, let us turn to the breakdown of "kinds of needs" that were suggested and an inspection of the specific needs that were finally posited. The first major division is between the *primary* or *viscerogenic* needs and the *secondary* or *psychogenic* needs. The viscerogenic needs are best thought of as representing the physical requirements of the organism. There are said to be 12 of them: *n* Air, *n* Water, *n* Food, *n* Sex, *n* Heatavoidance, *n* Lactation, *n* Urination, *n* Defecation, *n* Harmavoidance, *n* Noxavoidance (avoidance of noxious stimuli), *n* Sentience (con-

[4] At the time Murray was writing, it had only recently been shown that hormonal injections could produce various maternal and sexual behaviors in laboratory animals. Today the argument can be bolstered by the discovery of centers in the hypothalamus of the forebrain which appear to control thirst, hunger, and perhaps "pleasure."

sciousness), and *n* Coldavoidance. While Murray uses an occasional novel term, there is general agreement that this list represents universal, biological requirements of the organism. Further, agreement is relatively easy to obtain on the conditions which will engender one of these needs, external conditions (a seductive woman for *n* Sex) or internal conditions (increased carbon dioxide for *n* Air).

Murray (1962) enumerates 27 psychogenic needs, although they are not entirely independent of one another. First, let us consider the broad categories of psychogenic needs. Murray suggests needs which express ambition or desire for prestige, those which involve the defense of status, those which deal with exerting or resisting human power, those which involve affection between people, and those which concern the exchange of information. The actual list and the respective category for each need appears in Table 8–1.

The list of needs described by Murray and his associates is long, occasionally complicated, and certainly replete with neologisms. What is to be done with it? Murray argues that an additional step is necessary before anything can be done.

> The representation of the personality as a hierarchical system of general traits or need complexes leaves out the *nature of the environment*, a serious omission. . . . To say that John Quirk had a focal Affiliation drive is equivalent to the statement that "he maintained a life-long friendship with George Smythe," since we have no information about the attributes of George Smythe. Concrete objects and events constitute the data of science, but they cannot be incorporated in a discipline until they can be described as patterns of general attributes. We must build a conceptual home for our perceptions. . . . The question is, how shall we classify situations *in their own right* (i.e., irrespective of the *response* that they evoke in the organism)? . . . We finally hit upon the notion of representing an object or situation according to its effect (or potential effect) upon the subject, just as we had become accustomed to represent the subject in terms of his effect (or intended effect) upon an object (1962, pp. 116–17).

Note that the term *effect* as used in the above context does not refer to the subject's response, but rather refers to what happens to the subject either before he responds (for example, as when insulted by another person) or in the event that he does not respond (for example, being hit by an oncoming car if he does not get out of the way—quickly!). Thus, Murray (1962) notes the following kinds of questions: "Does the object physically harm the subject, nourish him, excite him, quiet him, exalt him, depreciate him, restrain, guide, aid, or inform him?" (pp. 117–18).

Press. Murray and his associates reasoned that needs were but one half of the interactional process that determines behavior, and selected the term *press* to represent the complementary, and equally important,

TABLE 8–1

Murray's List of Psychogenic Needs

Major Category	*Need*	*Behavioral Example*
Ambition	*n* Achievement	Overcoming obstacles
	n Recognition	Boasting
	n Exhibition	Efforts to shock or thrill others
	n Acquisition	Acquiring things, by work or stealing
	n Conservance	Repairing one's possessions
	n Order	Tidying up
	n Retention	Hoarding
	n Construction	Organizing or building something
Defense of Status	*n* Inviolacy	Maintaining one's psychological "distance"
	n Infavoidance	Concealing a disfigurement
	n Defendance	Offering explanations or excuses
	n Counteraction	Acts of retaliation
Response to Human Power	*n* Dominance	Dictating to or directing others
	n Deference	Cooperating with others
	n Similance	Imitating others
	n Autonomy	Defiance of authority
	n Contrariance	Taking unconventional or oppositional views
	n Aggression	Assaulting or belittling others
	n Abasement	Apologizing, confessing, or surrendering
	n Blamavoidance	Inhibiting unconventional impulses
Affection between People	*n* Affiliation	Joining groups
	n Rejection	Discriminating against or snubbing others
	n Nurturance	"Mothering" a child
	n Succorance	Crying for help
	n Play	Seeking diversion by "having fun"
Exchange of Information	*n* Cognizance	Asking questions
	n Exposition	Lecturing to, or interpreting for, others

Source: Adapted from Murray, 1962.

directional forces provided by objects, situations, or events in the environment. Some common examples of press appear in Table 8–2. Murray distinguished two types of press: *alpha press* and *beta press.* The former represents an objective description of environmental situations (for example, a certain grade-point average is required to be admitted to medical school), while the latter represents significant environmental influences as they are perceived by the individual (for example, if I don't make the required grade-point average for medical school I have been a total failure). For a person to function adequately in an interaction with

TABLE 8–2

Common Examples of Press

Press	*Example*
p Achievement	Others getting good grades
p Order	A messy desk
p Counteraction	Being attacked (verbally or physically)
p Autonomy	Overprotective parents
p Abasement	Doing something wrong
p Affiliation	Friendly comparisons
p Play	Saturday night
p Cognizance	Not understanding a lecture

his environment, there must be reasonable correspondence between his alpha press (objective experience) and his beta press (subjective experience) of the same situation. The case in which alpha press and beta press sharply diverge is called delusion.

We shall next turn our attention to the two constructs which serve to integrate needs and press.

Proceedings. The viewpoint that personality must be understood in terms of both the person and his environment leads clearly to the additional assumption that personality must also be understood in terms of the *past history* of the individual. In fact, in one sense, Murray suggests that the person's history might well be considered his personality. In order to study a person's history, a continuous process, it may be beneficial to divide his past into discrete units which Murray has called *proceedings*. Proceedings may be *external,* involving a stretch of time in which a person is engaged in some sort of overt behavior (for example, fixing one's car or going on a date) or *internal,* involving a period of time in which there is no overt action (for example, thinking about how to repair one's car or daydreaming about last weekend's date). While Murray and Kluckhohn emphasize the importance of both internal and external proceedings for understanding personality, they are quick to point out that psychologists can only study overt behavior. Thus, the external proceeding is "the psychologist's simplest *real entity,* the thing he should observe, analyze, try to reconstruct and represent, if possible, with a model, and thus explain; it is the thing he attempts to predict, and against which he tests the adequacy of his formulations and hypotheses" (Murray and Kluckhohn, 1953, p. 9).

While internal and external proceedings are usually closely integrated, at times they may be separate or even disparate. Clearly, if the important proceedings of an individual's life are solely *internal,* his overt behavior may appear quite unsatisfactory from society's point of view. In fact, Murray and Kluckhohn note that perhaps it is completely inaccurate to say that a psychotic person has "gone out of his mind." Instead we might well say that he is wholly "in his mind" and "out of the external, objective world."

Proceedings usually occupy relatively short periods of time. In addition, Murray and Kluckhohn suggest that it is desirable to construe an individual's life according to relatively long periods of time, each of which might be considered a sequence of proceedings. Thus infancy, childhood, adolescence, and so on, constitute convenient and important ways of dividing up an individual's past history.

Unity-Themas. Murray has argued that the period of early childhood may be singularly important in determining an individual's later reactions to needs and press. Beyond the integration of needs and press into temporal periods in an individual's life (i.e., proceedings), Murray found, as a consequence of the efforts to draw personality portraits of his subjects,[5] that often a particular pattern of related needs and press originating in early childhood comes to be a dominant force in the individual's personality. This "key to his unique nature" is called a *unity-thema.* In Murray's words:

> Experience was to teach us that, though the reasons for many of the subject's responses were mysterious and much of his past entirely out of reach, it was possible to find in most individuals an underlying reaction system, termed by us *unity-thema,* which was the key to his unique nature. I say "key" because if one assumed the activity of this unity-thema many superficially unintelligible actions and expressions became, as it were, psychologically inevitable. A *unity-thema* is a compound of interrelated—collaborating or conflicting—dominant needs that are linked to press to which the individual was exposed on one or more particular occasions, gratifying or traumatic, in early childhood. The thema may stand for a primary infantile experience or a subsequent reaction formation to that experience. But, whatever its nature and genesis, it repeats itself in many forms during later life (1962, pp. 604–5).

Murray's Approach to Personality Assessment

The problem of measuring the constructs of need, press, and unity-thema is an important one for us to examine, for it is only in this way that we can determine whether the theory which has led to these concepts

[5] The details of assessment, which are not essential to an understanding of Murray's theory or our discussion, may be of interest to some readers. The assessments were carried out by a Diagnostic Council of five judges. The council interviewed, tested (with a variety of tests and questionnaires), and independently rated each subject over a perod of two years. Finally, "At the end of all the examinations a five-hour meeting was held on each S [subject] at which all the reports and marks were read and discussed and a final mark for each variable was decided upon by majority vote" (1962, p. 265).

will be fruitful in the vast realm beyond the theorist's armchair. Measurement of psychogenic needs is made particularly difficult because it is probable that each of the psychogenic needs which Murray has enumerated are experienced, on some occasions and to some extent, by everyone. Further, Murray and his colleagues assumed that needs are sometimes *manifest* (embodied in overt behavior), sometimes *latent* (inhibited, covert, or imaginal), and that the strength of a need must be measured in both of its forms.

The Assessment of Manifest Needs. Murray details an elaborate systematic procedure for assessing manifest needs, of which we shall provide only a brief summary. The four major criteria for estimating need strength from overt action are: (1) frequency of action, (2) duration of action, (3) intensity of action, and (4) readiness to act. Frequency and duration are simple parameters to measure, since they require only a calendar and a watch. When we say that a friend "needs a lot of sleep," our inference is usually based on these measures and instruments. The third criterion, intensity, may be measured by a graded scaling of responses to a given situation. For example, Murray (1962) suggests the following gradation for *n* Aggression: "criticism given with a smile, a laugh at the O's [other's] expense, a mild insult, a severe accusation, a violent push, a blow in the face, murder" (p. 254). Finally, readiness to act may be measured by the *latency* of a response (for example, "I was asleep as soon as my head touched the pillow") or the *appropriateness* of the object to which it is directed (for example, it takes a rather hungry man to eat shoe leather).

The Assessment of Latent Needs. Dealing with needs which are not objectified in action requires some less obvious strategies. We must begin by considering the (presumed) nature of latent needs.

> The chief differences between an imaginal need and an overt need is that the former enjoys in reading, or represents in fantasy, in speech or in play what the latter objectifies in serious action. Thus, instead of pushing through a difficult enterprise, an S [subject] will have visions of doing it or read books about others doing it; or instead of injuring an enemy, he will express his dislike of him to others or enjoy playing an aggressive role in a play. . . . The term "imaginal need" is convenient for the expression "the amount of need tension that exhibits itself in thought and make-believe action" (Murray, 1962, p. 257).[6]

From this description, the logic of assessment follows easily. A strong latent need "is apt to perceive and apperceive what it 'wants' . . . an S

---

[6] Apart from interest in imaginal or latent needs as phenomena in their own right, Murray (1962) notes: "Also, what is imaginal to-day may be objectified tomorrow" (p. 257).

[subject] under the influence of a drive has a tendency to 'project' into surrounding objects some of the imagery associated with the drive that is operating" (Murray, 1962, p. 260). This reasoning gave rise to the development of a now widely used projective technique of personality assessment (see Chapter 4), the Thematic Apperception Test (TAT).

The TAT materials consist of a set of 20 pictures, with separate sets for males and females and for children. Most of the pictures show at least one person, thus providing someone with whom the respondent can presumably empathize. The subject is given the following instructions:

> This is a test of your creative imagination. I shall show you a picture and I want you to make up a plot or story for which it might be used as an illustration. What is the relation of the individuals in the picture? What has happened to them? What are their present thoughts and feelings? What will be the outcome? Do your very best. Since I am asking you to indulge your literary imagination you may make your story as long and detailed as you wish (Murray, 1962, p. 532).

One of the TAT pictures appears in Figure 8–1 on page 224. (To better understand the discussion which follows, it may be helpful for the reader to respond to the picture, according to the preceding instructions.) Subjects' responses to the TAT cards, which the examiner usually records verbatim, can be scored for the presence of needs as well as press and unity-themas. Both the use of the test and an example of how other data are used to assess personality in terms of Murray's personology can be seen through a brief examination of one of the cases reported in *Explorations in Personality.*

The Case of Virt. Virt was a Russian immigrant, who came to the United States when he was 11 years old. As a Russian Jew living near the German border during World War I, he had suffered religious persecutions in his childhood. Virt's autobiographical account of his childhood experiences is scored (in parentheses) for various press and needs.

> Recollections of those persecutions . . . still prey on my mind: dead bodies with torn limbs dragged in heaps to the cemetery; my uncle forced to dig his own grave before my eyes; my aunt shot in cold blood at my hand; bombs thrown a few feet before me (p Aggression). . . . Suddenly the door [to a cellar in which he and his mother had been trapped without water (p Lack: Water, Food)] was blown open . . . my mother and I stood quite near. I at once ran out to the next building, intent on procuring food and drink . . . I darted across through the bullets and shrapnel and forced open the door of the next building. Imagine the fright of the inmates. They refused to let me go back (p Dominance: Restraint: Enforced Separation from Mother) (Murray, 1962, p. 535).

FIGURE 8–1

Example of a TAT Picture

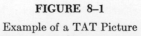

Another persistent recollection which Virt reported concerned the time (when he was eight) that his mother left him alone (*p* Insupport: Separation from Mother) in a Warsaw hotel while she went to get their passports.

"Tired of staying at home, I ventured out," he writes. "I determined in some way or other to go to her" (n Succorance for Mother). He happened to pick up a transfer, took the first car and eventually found his mother. "Lucky for me it was the right car. Otherwise I would have been lost in a strange large city. The surprise of my mother was great when she saw me" (Murray, 1962, p. 535).

Virt was given part of the TAT, and his response to Picture Number 11 (Figure 8–1) follows.

Mother and boy were living happily. She had no husband (Oedipus complex). Her son was her only support (n Nurturance for Mother). Then the boy got into bad company and participated in a gang robbery, playing a minor part. He was found out and sentenced to five years in prison. Picture represents him parting with his mother. Mother is sad, feeling ashamed of him. Boy is very much ashamed. He cares more about the harm he did his mother than about going to prison. He gets out for good behaviour but the mother dies. He repents for what he has done but he finds that his reputation is lost in the city. No one will employ him. He again meets bad companions and in despair he joins them in crime. However, he meets a girl with whom he falls in love. She suggests that he quit the gang. He decides to quit after one more hold-up. He is caught and sent to prison. In the meantime, the girl has met someone else. When he comes out he is quite old and spends the rest of his life repenting in misery (Murray, 1962, pp. 537–39).

The story is scored for *p* Dominance ("bad influences" and the externalization of blame), *n* Acquisition (robbery), *p* Aggression (the punishment of prison), *p* Loss (mother's death), *n* Abasement (the remorse which the boy feels), *p* Rejection (the girl friend's preference for a rival). The complex theme regarding the boy's mother is repeated with his girl friend (i.e., *p* Rejection is substituted for *p* Loss). Murray (1962) argues that the phantasy meaningfully reflects Virt's personality; that is, the boy in the story *is* Virt.

The subject presents the Son-Lover thema followed by the death of the mother, and later the Love thema followed by desertion. In neither case is union between the lovers achieved. We also find a conflict between mother and son over the question of crime and gang robberies. Since the subject's desire for achievement and marriage are much restricted by poverty, and since his much-respected mother was a smuggler in Russia, we may suppose that temptations to rob and cheat have at times occurred to him. (N.B. He cheated repeatedly in the Ethical Standards Test.)

The conflict of the hero with the mother brings to mind some incidents mentioned by the subject when giving his childhood memories. He said that he had occasionally quarrelled with his mother because she nagged him. Once when he was thirteen he ran away and got a job in Pittsburgh. Another time he ran away to Newport News on account of a romantic longing he had for adventure. In regard to the repentance theme in the . . . story the subject said in his introspections: "That's the way I would feel. If I took my car and stayed out all night I would be ashamed for having hurt my mother (n Nurturance for Mother), not for anything I might have done. We are really close to each other. She confides everything to me (p Succorance). She doesn't get on well with my father." The subject's conscience is a personal one. It prohibits him from hurting the woman he loves. He is not guided by an impersonal ethical standard (p. 539).

On the basis of Virt's response to TAT Picture Number 11, his responses to four other TAT pictures, and the autobiographical material,

Murray (1962) finds "a reverbertation of actual experiences and fantasies which occurred in childhood" (p. 544) and suggests that they reflect an underlying unity-thema of "Tragic Love." Thus, even in this brief example, we have seen the identification of needs, press, proceedings (i.e., in the autobiographical passages), and the inference of a fundamental unity-thema.

Murray's Research

The extensive research which Murray and his colleagues carried out was primarily idiographic in nature. That is, rather than study many different individuals, they chose to intensively study a relatively small number of subjects using a large variety of assessment and experimental procedures. A listing of the procedures is given below and serves to illustrate how broad a spectrum of techniques was used.

1. Preliminary Interview.
2. Conference—initial ratings made by the Diagnostic Council (see footnote, page 221).
3. Autobiography.
4. Family Relations and Childhood Memories.
5. Sexual Development.
6. Present Dilemmas.
7. Conversations—informal.
8. Predictions and Sentiments Test—measures the similarity between one's prediction of events and one's hopes regarding the events.
9. Questionnaires.
10. Abilities Test—paper-and-pencil measure of a variety of specific abilities (such as physical, social, observational, art-creative).
11. Aesthetic Appreciation Test.
12. Hypnotic Test—measures susceptibility to hypnotic suggestion.
13. Level of Aspiration Test.
14. Memory for Failures Test.
15. Ethical Standards Test.
16. Observations and Postexperimental Interviews.
17. Sensorimotor Learning.
18. Emotional Conditioning Test—includes Galvanic Skin Response and Tremor Response.
19. Thematic Apperception Test.
20. Imaginal Productivity Test.
21. Musical Reverie Test—used to evoke imaginal processes.
22. Dramatic Productions Test.
23. Rorschach Test.

24. Reactions to Frustration.
25. Social Interaction.

Whereas most of these procedures were specifically designed for an idiographic study of personality, occasionally the techniques of nomothetic investigation were drawn upon and adapted for the study of single individuals. One case in point is the Ethical Standards Test, which was mentioned parenthetically in Murray's summary of the Case of Virt. As we shall see in the ensuing discussion, the major difference between the procedures of the Ethical Standards Test and those of the nomothetic experiment which led to it is that in the former the experimenter's focus of interest is on the performance of a single individual, whereas in the latter the experimenter is primarily interested in the proportion of individuals in a group who exhibit various classes of behavior.

The Ethical Standards Test. The Ethical Standards Test involves solving a series of jigsaw puzzles (containing six to eight pieces), first in the presence of an experimenter and later while alone. Not only is the task timed, but it is also a competitive one, since the subject is told that the three subjects making the highest scores will receive double remuneration[7] for their participation. The correct solution to each puzzle is diagrammed on the underside of the box containing the puzzle pieces, and this is fully revealed to the subject during the portion of the session in which the experimenter is present to check the subject's solutions. Before leaving the room, the experimenter outlines a procedure for the subject to time himself for each puzzle and to record his solutions and comments. Thus, when the experimenter leaves (supposedly to work with another subject but actually to observe the subject through a one-way-vision screen in the next room), the subject has an opportunity to cheat by looking at the correct solutions and by using more than the allotted time.

Personality Differences between Violators and Nonviolators of Prohibitions. The Ethical Standards Test was suggested by a now "classic" experiment by Donald W. MacKinnon entitled, "The Violation of Prohibitions in the Solving of Problems."[8] The subjects, 93 college graduates, were faced with 20 problems, each appearing on a separate sheet of paper. On the table at which they worked were booklets which contained the answers to the problems. After being told that they were permitted to look at certain answers but not at others, the subjects were left, apparently alone, to work on the problems. However, they were in fact surreptitiously observed by the experimenter.

Forty-six percent of the subjects looked at one or more of the prohib-

[7] All of Murray's subjects were paid on an hourly basis for their participation.
[8] Doctoral dissertation, Harvard University, 1933 (reported in Murray, 1962).

ited solutions. However, of even more interest than the frequency of cheating was some of the incidental behavior exhibited by subjects. For example, a striking observation involved the kinds of exclamations made by subjects when a problem proved difficult or impossible to solve. There were four types of such verbalizations: (1) comments indicative of problem solving (rereading the problem aloud); (2) simple emotional outbursts not aimed at any particular object ("'Oh,' 'Gosh,' 'Oh, what the hell'"); (3) emotional outbursts directed toward the frustrating problems themselves ("'You bastard,' 'You crazy bitch,' 'These are the God damnedest things I ever saw'"); (4) emotional outbursts directed toward oneself ("'Jesus Christ, I must be dumb,' 'God, I must be a nitwit'"). There were some major differences between violators and nonviolators with regard to the type of verbalization which they produced. For example, about one third of the violators who spoke to themselves criticized or cursed problems with which they were having difficulty, while not a single nonviolator expressed problem-directed verbal hostility.

Hostility was also greater for the violators when reactions other than speech were examined. More violators than nonviolators "exhibited a destructive, aggressive restlessness manifested in scuffling the feet, stamping on the floor, getting up from the table and stamping back and forth across the room, kicking the leg of the table, pounding the fist, etc." (Murray, 1962, p. 493). In contrast, the restlessness of nonviolators was more likely to be characterized by such self-directed behaviors as "fidgeting, crossing and uncrossing the legs, hunching the shoulders, twisting the head to one side . . . placing finger or thumb to mouth, sucking the thumb, biting finger-nails, licking the back of the hand, placing excreta from the nose or hair to the lips or into the mouth . . . smelling some part of the body, etc." (Murray, 1962, p. 493).

MacKinnon also wished to determine the emotional reactions experienced by violators for having looked at the solutions. Four weeks after being in the test situation, all the subjects were asked whether or not they had looked at any of the prohibited solutions. Nonviolators simply indicated that they had not. The violators, however, exhibited three different types of replies: denying their violations, partially admitting their violations, or completely admitting them. When the 22 subjects who admitted to violations were asked to report their feelings about this transgression, only six stated that they felt any guilt. For the 21 violators who did not admit transgressions, the question had to be put differently. These subjects were asked: "If you had looked at any prohibited solutions how would you have felt about having done so?" Eighty percent of the subjects in this group said they would have had no guilt feelings for violations. In contrast, when the same hypothetical question was put to the nonviolators, 84 percent stated that they would have felt guilt, shame, or "pangs of conscience" if they had looked at the prohibited solutions.

Major Functions of Personality

On the basis of the extensive research program which we have briefly outlined, Murray has come to a number of tentative conclusions with regard to human personality. These conclusions are spelled out by Murray and Kluckhohn in their 1953 paper in the form of six major functions of personality. These functions, which were abstracted from the investigations reported in *Explorations in Personality,* appear to be guidelines for the future rather than a summary of past accomplishments. For this reason, the list has been held for the end of our discussion of Murray's position.

Reducton of Need Tension. Of the six major functions of personality, Murray and Kluckhohn feel that the reduction of need tension is the nearest thing they have to an "all-embracing principle." They argue that needs lead to tension and that tension, in turn, leads to tension reduction. They emphasize that what must be attended to and investigated is the initiating state of tension rather than the end-state in which the person finds himself as a result of the increased tension. This orientation, Murray and Kluckhohn (1953) note, can explain some otherwise peculiar events: ". . . we are provided with an explanation of suicide and of certain other apparently anti-biological effects as so many forms of riddance of intolerable suffering. Suicide does not have *adaptive* (survival) value but it does have *adjustive* value for the organism. Suicide is *functional* because it abolishes painful tension" (p. 36).

Generation of Tension. Whereas Murray's position and that of Freud are in agreement that the reduction of tension is a major function of personality, an important difference between the two theoretical camps becomes evident with a statement of Murray and Kluckhohn's second function of personality, the generation of tension. Murray and Kluckhohn argue that it is not a tensionless state which is satisfying, as psychoanalysis assumes, but rather it is the *process* of reducing tension which creates satisfaction. We are satisfied to the degree that we are able to reduce the tensions which we experience. The thirstier a man is, the more likely he will be to enjoy a cold beer; the more homesick a person is, the more pleasure he will gain from a letter or telephone call from home; and the lower a student's grade-point average, the more an "A" will be appreciated. Thus, Murray and Kluckhohn (1953) conclude that "A tensionless state is sometimes the ideal of those who suffer from chronic anxiety or resentment or a frustrated sex drive; but, as a rule, the absence of positive need-tensions—no appetite, no curiosity, no desire for fellowship, no zest—is very distressing" (p. 36).

Self-Expression. The third major function of personality involves the brief, spontaneous, and free expression of one's most basic nature which all persons experience from time to time. Such self-expression, which may run the gamut from daydreaming to quite intense emotional excitement, is engaged in for no end other than the intrinsic pleasure which it creates.

Scheduling. A fourth personality function concerns decision-making processes similar to those which were considered in our discussion of Festinger's Theory of Cognitive Dissonance (see Chapter 7). Often our decisions involve choices between conflicting goals or aims (for example, Should I study on this beautiful spring afternoon, or should I spend the time outside? If I study, should I read my psychology assignment or write my English theme? If I go outside, should I play tennis or go fishing?). To reduce or resolve such conflicts, we typically schedule our time so that we can satisfy as many of our major needs as possible.

Adjusting of Aspiration Levels. In positing their fifth function of personality, Murray and Kluckhohn observe that very few persons are capable of fully satisfying all of their needs. The frustration which accompanies unsatisfied needs often leads persons to adopt a strategy of lowering their levels of aspiration ("Since my high school grades are poor, I'll be content with going to a junior college") or accepting alternative goals ("Since my high school grades are poor, I'll go into my father's business rather than go to college") in an effort to maximize the satisfaction of needs and the attainment of end-states. Murray and Kluckhohn point to the practice of Yoga, in which all external and social needs are rejected, as an example of the extreme use of this strategy. In contrast, they note that democratic ideologies:

> . . . have encouraged a high level of extrovert aspiration for every individual (e.g., in the United States: a large fortune, leading to privilege and prestige) and, thus, have opposed the natural tendency to reduce the level after repeated failures. The over-all result, in the United States, has been an extraordinary degree of material progress with a high standard of living, on the one hand, and an equally extraordinary degree of discontent (griping about the lack of material "necessities") on the other. The ideology, in other words, prevents many individuals from achieving happiness (1953, p. 40).

Conforming to Social Expectations. Murray and Kluckhohn feel that their final function of personality, the accommodation of the unique individual and his personality to the conventions of society, is the "most difficult and painful" of the six major personality functions. Clearly, for society to function smoothly, each individual member must learn to conform to the social expectations to some degree. A person who refuses to conform to society's rules, standards, or ideals is likely to be ineffective and unhappy. Nevertheless, there are also undesirable consequences if excessive conformity occurs either in a single individual or in a whole culture. Sometimes, for example, so-called "unacceptable" behavior is necessary to uphold one's ideals and principles. In fact, many important and ultimately functional social changes required daring nonconformity from members of society. The American Revolution, the Protestant Revolution, and the Industrial Revolution all began because individuals or groups of individuals acted in opposition to usual cultural and social expectations. It is because conformity is both necessary for some realms of behavior and undesirable in others that the regulation of conformity to social expectations is a critical function of personality.

THE ACHIEVEMENT MOTIVE

Prominent among the lasting accomplishments of Murray's motivational approach to personality is the large amount of research which it has stimulated. A prime example of this is the work of David C. McClelland and his colleagues on the achievement motive. For more than 20 years, McClelland has investigated the need to achieve (i.e., Murray's *n* Achievement) both theoretically and, more recently, from an extremely practical vantage point. While Murray and McClelland share a common bias concerning the nature of human personality, their basic strategies of attacking similar problems differ. Murray, it will be recalled, chose to catalog and study a large number of motivational forces (i.e., needs and press), whereas McClelland has chosen to focus his attention on a single need. McClelland justifies his approach in the following way:

> . . . concentration on a limited research problem is not necessarily narrowing; it may lead ultimately into the whole of psychology. In personality theory there is inevitably a certain impatience—a desire to solve every problem at once so as to get the "whole" personality in focus. We have proceeded the other way. By concentrating on one problem, on *one motive,* we have found in the course of our study that we have learned not only a lot about the achievement motive but other areas of personality as well (McClelland, Atkinson, Clark, and Lowell, 1953, p. vi).

Measuring Achievement Motivation

The first step in studying the achievement motive, or any motive or personality variable for that matter, is to develop a way of measuring it. Initial experimentation in measuring the strength of a primary need, *n* Food, showed that sailors who had been deprived of food for varying lengths of time could be reliably differentiated on the basis of their phantasy responses to Murray's TAT (Atkinson and McClelland, 1948).

On the basis of this success, it was decided to try measuring a psychogenic need, *n* Achievement, by the same technique.

Male students[9] who were exposed to various experimental conditions were asked to write stories about four pictures (two from the TAT and two similar to the TAT pictures). The instructions were very similar to those which Murray used with the TAT, and thus the test was presented to the students as one of creative imagination. The experimental conditions consisted of various achievement-arousing situations (for example, subjects were given success or failure experiences) and nonachievement-arousing situations (the experimental tasks were presented in a casual, relaxed atmosphere). The stories were scored for a number of different categories related to achievement motivation, and those scoring categories which successfully differentiated subjects who had been exposed to varying degrees of achievement arousal were defined as measures of *n* Achievement.

Research on Achievement Motivation

The basic technique of measuring achievement motivation by phantasy has subsequently been used by McClelland and others in a wide variety of investigations. The antecedents and development of achievement motivation have been studied, and it appears the origins of *n* Achievement (abbreviated *n* Ach) are:

> . . . rooted in early training for independence, subsequent harnessing of the dispositions so acquired for socially defined achievement situations, support of the n Ach by warm but demanding parental models, and considerable experience with emotional satisfaction in achievement situations. Certainly such a pattern does suggest that the n Achiever should be experienced in maximizing payoffs, relatively free from anxiety about failure, and therefore, efficient at those tasks he chooses to attempt (Birney, 1968, p. 878).

The modified TAT phantasy measure of the achievement motive has made possible a unique type of psychological investigation. Since the scoring system for TAT stories is applicable to any prose material, McClelland has been able to study *n* Achievement in individuals and groups of individuals who have lived in the past but have left written accounts of their lives. Thus, for example, McClelland and his associates (McClelland *et al.*, 1953) have studied the relationship between independence training and achievement motivation in a number of North American Indian tribes by scoring their folk tales for *n* Achievement.

An even more ambitious task in the same vein has involved McClel-

---

[9] Most of the research on the achievement motive has been done with male subjects. The small number of studies which have investigated *n* Achievement in females points, not surprisingly, to sex differences in the mode of expression of the motive.

land's attempt to explain the economic growth and decline of cultures in terms of the achievement motive. In one aspect of this work, which McClelland (1961) reports in his book entitled *The Achieving Society*, a nation's mean achievement motivation is determined by examining the children's readers of each country for *n* Achievement. By scoring children's stories, which were read during a period from 1920 to 1929 in 23 different countries, McClelland attempted to "predict" the economic growth of the countries between 1929 and 1950. The achievement motive found in the children's stories was correlated +.53 with McClelland's index of economic growth (a measure based on changes in the consumption of electricity as related to the deviation from expected growth). McClelland (1961) concludes from this and other similar studies that the children's stories reflect ". . . the motivational level of the adults at the time they are published, perhaps particularly of the adults responsible for the education of children . . ." (p. 102).

A Program for Developing Achievement Motivation

More recently, McClelland (1965) has devoted his efforts to developing a theory of motive acquisition and a program for increasing human motivation in terms of some very practical problems. Specifically, McClelland has designed a course to increase individuals' (particularly businessmen's) achievement motivation. Realizing that most psychologists have considered the acquisition of motives in adulthood to be difficult or impossible, McClelland says:

> . . . we were encouraged by the successful efforts of two quite different groups of "change agents"—operant conditioners [see Chapter 11] and missionaries. . . . The operant conditioners have not been encumbered by any elaborate theoretical apparatus; they do not believe motives exist anyway, and continue demonstrating vigorously that if you want a person to make a response, all you have to do is elicit it and reward it. . . . Like operant conditioners, the missionaries have gone ahead changing people because they have believed it possible . . . common-sense observation yields dozens of cases of adults whose motivational structure has seemed to be quite radically and permanently altered by the educational efforts of the Communist party, Mormon, or other devout missionaries (1965, p. 322).

The supposition that an individual's motivational structure can change in adulthood has several implications for revising traditional theories of motivation. Perhaps the most important of these, according to McClelland, is the proposition that *all human motives are learned* and even those of biological origin (for example, hunger or sex) cannot be considered to be present until some learning has occurred so that they are associated with cues which can indicate their presence or absence. McClelland (1965) formally defines motives as "'affectively toned associative networks' arranged in a hierarchy of strength or importance within a given individual" (p. 322). Presumably these hierarchies are themselves learned, and defining motives in this way has immediate implications for suggesting how motives might be changed. Specifically, if motives are in fact associative networks arranged in a hierarchical order, then the problem of changing motives in adulthood merely becomes one of introducing new motives or moving up old ones in an individual's existing hierarchy. In short, the problem has now been defined as a problem in learning.

The next step is to determine what kind of learning experiences will increase a particular motive's presence or position in an individual's hierarchy. McClelland's initial efforts drew upon four types of available information. First, experimental work with animals had suggested that the appropriate timing of learning sequences and reward for desired responses would both be essential ingredients of any educational program in motivation change. Second, from experiments in human learning, McClelland borrowed such principles as the careful distribution of practice and the recitation, repetition, and attribution of meaning to what is being learned. Third, McClelland felt that his courses should have those characteristics which are often said to be effective in psychotherapy. Thus, the "teachers" were instructed to be warm, honest, and not overly directive with their "students." Finally, McClelland has drawn from attitude-change research the importance of such things as prestige suggestion and affiliation with new reference groups.

The Research Strategy. In thus borrowing from a wide range of psychological knowledge to find principles for his motive acquisition program, McClelland's initial research strategy can be described as "subtractive" rather than "additive." That is, all possible potent variables are first tried, and later each individual variable is deleted, one at a time, to assess its part in the overall outcome. McClelland explains the scientific and practical advantages of this "shotgun" strategy thusly:

> Despite the fact that many of these variables seem limited in application to the learning situation in which they were studied, we have tried to make use of information from all these sources in designing our "motive acquisition" program and in finding support for the general propositions that have emerged from our studies so far. For our purpose has been above all to produce an effect large enough to be measured. Thus, we have tried to profit by all that is known about how to facilitate learning or produce personality or attitude change. For, if we could not obtain a substantial effect with all factors working to produce it, there would be no point to studying the effects of each factor taken one at a time. Such a strategy also has the practical advantage that we are in the position of doing our best to "deliver the goods" to our course participants since they were giving us their time and attention to take part in a largely untried educational experience (1965, p. 323).

The Program. McClelland's courses for developing *n* Achievement are typically run in groups ranging in size from 9 to 25 businessmen and over a short but highly concentrated period (the optimal period has been found to be somewhere between 6 to 14 days, 12 to 18 hours per day). So far there have been eight such courses in which more than 140 managerial persons in the United States, Mexico, and India have participated. As a result of the experience gained from these initial courses, McClelland (1965) has abstracted 12 theoretical propositions or guidelines for motive change. Although these principles have evolved from a program designed to increase only a single motive, McClelland feels that they should be applicable to the development of motivation in general.

The first thing one must do in any motivational development program is create confidence that the program will work. Thus, Proposition 1 states: "*The more reasons an individual has in advance to believe that he can, will, or should develop a motive, the more educational attempts designed to develop that motive are likely to succeed.*" McClelland has invoked the scientific authority of research, the prestige of Harvard University (where he was chairman of the Department of Social Relations), and all of the suggestive power which experimenter enthusiasm can produce in "selling" the program and setting high expectations for the participants before the actual training begins.[10]

In Proposition 2, the importance of rational arguments in introducing the purpose of the course is stressed: "*The more an individual perceives that developing a motive is consistent with the demands of reality (and reason), the more educational attempts designed to develop that motive are likely to succeed.*"

Proposition 3 provides the first hint of what the training program itself entails. "*The more thoroughly an individual develops and clearly conceptualizes the associative network defining the motive, the more likely he is to develop the motive.*" With this principle in mind, it is easy to understand why McClelland chooses an explanation of the meaning of achievement motivation as one of the first steps in training. All participants are asked to take the phantasy test of *n* Achievement at the outset and are taught to score it for themselves. McClelland (1965) says: ". . . we point out that if they think their score is too low, that can be easily remedied, since we teach them how to code and how to write stories saturated with n Achievement; in fact, that is one of the basic purposes of the course: to teach them to think constantly in n Achievement terms" (p. 325). This aspect of the training involves more than merely teaching a label or the rote use of certain expressions. It is an effort to change personal constructs (cf. Kelly, Chapter 7) by substituting "new con-

---

[10] It is interesting to note that what many experimenters consider "error" and try to exclude, McClelland has purposely built into his program.

structs ('You should become an achiever') for old neurotic or ineffective ones ('rather than being such a slob') . . ." (McClelland, 1965, p. 326).

The next step is to tie changes in thought to changes in action, as seen in Proposition 4: "*The more an individual can link the newly developed network to related actions, the more the change in both thought and action is likely to occur and endure.*" Earlier work by McClelland had shown that persons high in achievement motivation (1) like challenges in their work and prefer moderate risk situations, (2) seek concrete feedback as to how well they are doing, and (3) like to take personal responsibility for achieving work goals. In order to develop these characteristics in the course participants, McClelland makes use of a specially designed business game which allows the participants to learn achievement-oriented actions by both playing the game and observing others play.

> The game is designed to mimic real life: they must order parts to make certain objects (e.g., a Tinker Toy model bridge) after having estimated how many they think they can construct in the time alloted. They have a real chance to take over, plan the whole game, learn from how well they are doing (use of feedback), and show a paper profit or loss at the end. While they are surprised often that they should have to display their real action characteristics this way in public, they usually get emotionally involved in observing how they behave under pressure of a more or less "real" work situation (McClelland, 1965, p. 326).

Behavior developed in the game situation must then be generalized to actual business situations. Accordingly, Proposition 5 states: "*The more an individual can link the newly conceptualized association-action complex (or motive) to events in his everyday life, the more likely the motive complex is to influence his thoughts and actions outside the training experience.*" In this regard, examples of career development are explored by means of actual case studies which the group discusses.

But, however clear it may become to a participant that an achievement orientation is applicable to actual business experience, each participant must be convinced that he, as an individual, is suited to such a way of life. This point is made in Proposition 6: "*The more an individual can perceive and experience the newly conceptualized motive as an improvement in the self-image, the more the motive is likely to influence his future thoughts and actions.*" The importance of candid self-appraisal is emphasized to the participants by telling them of an incident which occurred in one of the courses. A participant decided that he did not wish to become an achievement-oriented person. This honest self-evaluation led the man to leave the course, quit his managerial position, and subsequently retire and become a chicken farmer. (This case is the exception rather than the rule, however, since most participants come to view achievement as desirable.) Participants are aided in their evaluation of the influence of increased achievement motivation on their self-images through such techniques as individual counseling, group dynamics sessions, and silent group meditation.

Just as participants must reconcile increased achievement motivation with their self-concepts, so too must they come to feel that their increased *n* Achievement is in line with, or an improvement on, the existing popular or traditional cultural values of their country. Thus Proposition 7 states: "*The more an individual can perceive and experience the newly conceptualized motive as an improvement on prevailing cultural values, the more the motive is likely to influence his future thoughts and actions.*" Thus, after having examined their own personal values vis-à-vis achievement motivation, the course participants engage in an analysis of the values of their culture with regard to achievement by examining children's stories, myths, popular religion, customs, and so on. For example, in the United States, participants discuss the way in which high achievement motivation can interfere with a person's popularity. Besides rational discussions of such problems, role playing is employed to help the participants understand and accept their new motivational sets in relation to their cultural values.

At the end of the course, each participant writes an essay outlining his aspirations and plans for the next two years. Emphasis is placed on describing one's future realistically and in setting moderate (rather than inordinately high) goals. The essay not only serves to assist participants in making use of the practical implications of the course but it also provides a basis for further evaluation of the candidates and the program. During the two-year follow-up period, questionnaires are sent to the course participants every six months, both to remind them of the goals they have set for themselves and to assess their progress. These procedures have led to the formulation of Propositions 8 and 9: "*The more an individual commits himself to achieving concrete goals in life related to the newly formed motives, the more the motive is likely to influence his future thoughts and actions,*" and "*The more an individual keeps a record of his progress toward achieving goals to which he is committed, the more the newly formed motive is likely to influence his future thoughts and actions.*"

As mentioned previously, McClelland and his associates have found it helpful for teachers in the course (consulting psychologists) to be warm, rewarding, and somewhat nondirective in their dealings with the participants, a result consistent with an earlier study which showed that fathers of high *n* Achievement boys were warmer, more encouraging, and less directive than fathers of boys low on this measure (Rosen and

D'Andrade, 1959). Thus, Proposition 10 states: "*Changes in motives are more likely to occur in an interpersonal atmosphere in which the individual feels warmly but honestly supported and respected by others as a person capable of guiding and directing his own future behavior.*"

One additional feature of McClelland's program, the fact that the course is structured as a retreat for self-study, leads to the two final propositions. Whenever possible, the sessions are conducted in an isolated resort hotel to enhance concentration and exclude outside interference. Furthermore, there is considerable evidence to show that changes in a person's opinions, attitudes, or beliefs are greatly facilitated by joining a new reference group. Thus, in addition to fostering the emergence of a new reference group by having participants study and live together for the duration of the course, there are signs of identification with the group (for example, knowledge of the *n* Achievement coding system and membership certificates). Moreover, McClelland tries to arrange to have all participants in a group come from the same community so that, after leaving the course, the new reference group will physically remain intact and will help maintain the newly acquired motivation. These procedures are reflected in Propositions 11 and 12: "*Changes in motives are more likely to occur the more the setting dramatizes the importance of self-study and lifts it out of the routine of everyday life,*" and "*Changes in motives are more likely to occur and persist if the new motive is a sign of membership in a new reference group.*"

Table 8–3 summarizes McClelland's program for motive development in terms of the procedures used (independent variables), the outcome (dependent variables), and the theoretical processes that are hypothesized to mediate between treatment and results (intervening variables).

The Results of the Program. Having described McClelland's course for increasing the achievement motive and a series of principles which may be applicable to the development of any motive, there remains the all important question, "Does all this work?" While long-term effects have yet to be evaluated, there are some tentative data for two groups of participants, one consisting of 34 businessmen from Bombay and the other of 52 businessmen from Kakinada, a small Indian city. To assess the effects of the course, McClelland (1965) developed what he termed a "crude but objective and reliable" measure of "unusual" entrepreneurial activity, which is defined as "unusual promotion or salary raise or starting a new business venture of some kind" (p. 332). The success of the motive acquisition course was evaluated in terms of the increase in "unusual" entrepreneurial activity from the two-year period immediately preceding the course to the two-year period following the course. The results, which include a control group of businessmen who applied for the course but did not participate, are presented in Table 8–4.

TABLE 8–3

Variables Hypothesized to Affect Motive Change

A *Input or Independent Variables*	*B* *Intervening Variables*	*C* *Output or Dependent Variables*
1. Goal setting for the person (P1, P11)*	Arousal of associative network (salience)	Duration and/or extensiveness of changes in:
2. Acquisition of *n* Achievement associative network (P2, P3, P4, P5)	Experiencing and labeling the associative network	1. *n* Achievement associative network
3. Relating new network to superordinate networks Reality (P2) The self (P6) Cultural values (P7)	Variety of cues to which network is linked Interfering associations assimilated or bypassed by reproductive interference	2. Related actions: use of feedback, moderate risk taking, etc. 3. Innovations (job improvements) 4. Use of time and money
4. Personal goal setting (P8)		5. Entrepreneurial success as defined by nature of job held and its rewards
5. Knowledge of progress (P3, P4, P9)		
6. Personal warmth and support (P10)	Positive affect associated with network	
7. Support of reference group (P11, P12)		

* P1, P11, etc., refer to the numbered propositions in the text.
Source: From McClelland, 1965.

TABLE 8–4

Percentage of Businessmen Engaged in "Unusual" Entrepreneurial Activity during the Two-Year Period before and after Participation in McClelland's Achievement Motivation Course

Sample	*Before Course*	*After Course*	*Increase*	*Statistical Significance*
Bombay	27	67	40	$p < .01$
Kakinada	25	65	40	$p < .01$
Control*	18	27	9	NS†

* Random sample of businessmen from Bombay who had applied for the course but did not participate.
† Not significantly different.
Source: Data from McClelland, 1965.

Additionally, it is interesting to examine a case which illustrates the potential impact of the course:

A short time after participating in one of our courses in India, a 47-year-old businessman rather suddenly and dramatically decided to quit his excellent job and go into the construction business on his own in a big way. A man with some means of his own, he had had a very successful career as employee-relations manager for a large oil firm. His job involved adjusting management-employee difficulties, negotiating union contracts, etc. He was well-to-do, well thought of in his company, and admired in the community, but he was restless because he found his job increasingly boring. At the time of the course his original n Achievement score was not very high and he was thinking of retiring and living in England where his son was studying. In an interview, 8 months later, he said the course had served not so much to "motivate" him but to "crystallize" a lot of ideas he had vaguely or half consciously picked up about work and achievement all through his life. It provided him with a new language (he still talked in terms of standards of excellence, blocks, moderate risk, goal anticipation, etc.), a new construct which served to organize those ideas and explain to him why he was bored with his job, despite his obvious success. He decided he wanted to be an n-Achievement-oriented person, that he would be unhappy in retirement, and that he should take a risk, quit his job, and start in business on his own. He acted on his decision and in 6 months had drawn plans and raised over $1,000,000 to build the tallest building in his large city to be called the "Everest Apartments." He is extremely happy in his new activity because it means selling, promoting, trying to wangle scarce materials, etc. His first building is partway up and he is planning two more (McClelland, 1965, p. 332).

Single cases, of course, do not provide powerful scientific evidence. Nonetheless, the one just cited does lead to enthusiasm about the possibility of changing motives in adulthood.

The Achievement Motive and the TAT—An Assessment Study

In our discussion of both Murray and McClelland, we have made frequent mention of the TAT. Murray felt that the value of this instrument is "its capacity to reveal things that the patient is unwilling to tell or unable to tell because he is unconscious of them" (1951, p. 577). In contrast, McClelland used the TAT to consciously teach people to think and be achievement oriented. A correlational study by Holmes and Tyler (1968) has compared the value of the TAT as an assessment tool with more direct procedures for measuring *n* Achievement, and the results of their study have implications for both the nature of the instrument and the theoretical issue of whether motives are conscious or unconscious.

Using undergraduate males as subjects, Holmes and Tyler selected two types of criterion measures of *n* Achievement: (1) course grades and (2) performance on laboratory tasks (computational and digit symbol tests). Four TAT cards were shown to each subject, and his responses were scored both according to a standard system devised by Atkinson (1958) and by having two judges give their *global* impressions of the subjects' responses on a four-point scale. Additionally, two types of self-report measures were used. For one, the *self-peer ranking* measure, each subject was asked to list the names of 10 male fellow students whom he knew well. He was then given a description of what is meant by *n* Achievement and asked to rate each of the 10 friends as being higher or lower on *n* Achievement than he felt himself to be. Finally, each subject was asked to state whether he would be likely to work harder or less hard than each friend on an academic task. The second self-report was a *self-rating* measure in which subjects were simply asked to compare their own *n* Achievement with "students in general" on a 16-point scale. The correlations between the four assessment measures and the three criteria are presented in Table 8–5. The only correlation that was significantly different from zero was that between self-peer ranking and grades.

TABLE 8–5

Correlations between TAT Scores or Self-Ratings and Criterion Measures of *n* Achievement

	Assessment Method			
	TAT_1 (Atkinson Scoring)	*TAT_2 (Global Scoring)*	*Self-Peer Ranking*	*Self-Rating*
Criterion				
Grades	−.01	−.10	.33*	.17
Computational test	−.08	−.05	†	−.14
Digit symbol test	−.01	−.01	†	.05

* Statistically significant, $p < .005$.
† According to Holmes and Tyler these correlations are not significantly different from zero, but the actual values are not reported.
Source: Prepared from Holmes and Tyler, 1968.

In discussing these results, the investigators make two observations that are particularly relevant to the issues we have been considering. First, they note that the evidence clearly suggests that *n* Achievement is a conscious motive: ". . . when asked properly, Ss [subjects] are able to provide self-assessments which are related to long-term achievement . . . such accurate self-assessments would be impossible in the absence of knowledge about one's achievement motivation, hence it seems clear that Ss are aware of this characteristic" (1968, p. 716). Second, Holmes and Tyler observe that their findings have substantial implications for more general issues in personality assessment. In fact, as we shall see in Chapters 10–12, their conclusions are consistent with other recent arguments for greater reliance on direct assessment (for example, Mischel, 1968). They note:

. . . the fact that the ranking measure was more accurate than the projective measure suggests that the ranking measure deserves more use. Even if the ranking measure were only equally as accurate as the projective measure it would seem preferable to use the ranking measure since it can be administered and scored in only a few minutes by an examiner without any skill or training. This may prove to be a valuable approach for having Ss [subjects] make otherwise difficult abstract self-reports (Holmes and Tyler, 1968, p. 716).

REFERENCES

Atkinson, J. (Ed.) *Motives in fantasy, action, and society.* Princeton, N.J.: Van Nostrand, 1958.

Atkinson, J. W., and McClelland, D. C. The projective expression of needs, II. The effect of different intensities of the hunger drive on thematic apperception. *Journal of Experimental Psychology,* 1948, **38**, 643–58.

Birney, R. C. Research on the achievement motive. In E. F. Borgatta and W. W. Lambert (Eds.), *Handbook of personality theory and research.* Chicago: Rand McNally, 1968. Pp. 857–89.

Holmes, D. S., and Tyler, J. D. Direct versus projective measurement of achievement motivation. *Journal of Consulting and Clinical Psychology,* 1968, **32**, 712–17.

MacKinnon, D. W. The violation of prohibition in the solving of problems. Unpublished doctoral dissertation, Harvard University, 1933.

McClelland, D. C. *The achieving society.* Princeton, N.J.: Van Nostrand, 1961.*

McClelland, D. C. Toward a theory of motive acquisition. *American Psychologist,* 1965, **20**, 321–33.

McClelland, D. C., Atkinson, J. W., Clark, R. A., and Lowell, E. L. *The achievement motive.* New York: Appleton-Century-Crofts, 1953.

Mischel, W. *Personality and assessment.* New York: Wiley, 1968.

Murray, H. A. *Explorations in personality.* New York: Science Editions, 1962.

Murray, H. A. Uses of the Thematic Apperception Test. *American Journal of Psychiatry,* 1951, **107**, 577–81.

Murray, H. A., and Kluckhohn, C. Outline of a conception of personality. In C. Kluckhohn and H. A. Murray with the collaboration of D. M. Schneider (Eds.), *Personality in nature, society, and culture.* New York: Alfred A. Knopf, 1953.

Rosen, B. C., and D'Andrade, R. G. The psychosocial origins of achievement motivation. *Sociometry,* 1959, **22**, 185–218.

chapter 9

Motivational Theories: Self-Actualization

Most theories of personality have been developed, in part, to understand and cope with deviant or "abnormal" behavior. So it was that an interest in the treatment of deviant behavior by Freud led to his development of a theory of personality which included both "normal" and "abnormal" behavior, though the emphasis was placed on the latter. Freud's theory of personality evolved directly from his observations of his patients in psychoanalysis. Although Freud's initial attempts at psychotherapy did precede his formulation of a personality theory, very early in his career the two aspects of his work became inseparably linked. Psychotherapy served as a pregnant source of data about human personality, which, when formulated into theoretical statements, could be tested in therapy. The first of the two theories to be discussed in this chapter, developed by Carl Rogers, also grew out of the study of abnormal behavior.

THE BASIC UNDERPINNINGS OF ROGERS' THEORY

The impact of psychoanalysis, as both psychotherapy and personality theory, has been great; it dominated clinical psychology without rival until at least the early 1940's. The first major opposition to psychoanalytic psychotherapy came in 1942 with the publication of Rogers' book entitled *Counseling and Psychotherapy: Newer Concepts in Practice.* As was the case with Freud, Rogers' *client-centered* psychotherapy and his theory of personality developed almost simultaneously, and most of the empirical evidence for the validity of Rogers' propositions has come indirectly from research in client-centered therapy. It was out of his interactions with persons in psychotherapy that Rogers came to hypothesize that a single, unitary motive, the actualizing tendency, is the basis for all human behavior. Before discussing the details of Rogers' personality theory, two basic concepts which underlie the theory should be briefly mentioned.

First, Rogers' theory of personality takes a *phenomenological* position which, in brief, holds that the reality of phenomena is solely a function of the way in which they are observed. What is real to an individual is that which is in his *internal frame of reference,* his subjective world, which includes everything that he is aware of at a particular point in time. There is nothing intrinsically brown, round, or large about a basketball; one must look to the reacting organism to find out the color, shape, and size of the object. From the standpoint of predicting behavior, phenomenological psychology is a practical psychology in that its basic doctrine says that effective reality is *reality as it is perceived.* For example, if a traffic light turns red but a motorist who is red-green colorblind does not perceive the color of the light to be red, he will not stop at the intersection. Similarly, two people observing the "same" set of circumstances may perceive two very different occurrences, which is so often the case with "eye witnesses" in traffic accidents.

The implication of a phenomenological orientation for a theory of personality is that a person's behavior can only be understood from his own point of view. The important object of study then becomes a person's subjective experiences, for it is these experiences that direct his behavior. Note that subjective experience may or may not coincide with "objective reality," a point which is well illustrated by the case of a young man who had been dreaming about his girl friend. When he was awakened quite abruptly he found himself embracing, rather passionately, not his girl friend but his mother, who had come into his room to wake him. This embarrassing scene was the result of the boy's subjective experience rather than the objective situation.

Second, Rogers' espouses a *holistic* view of personality, the view that behavior must be seen in the framework of the entire person. As we shall see in the ensuing discussion, the holistic view is manifest in a variety of ways in Rogers' theory.

Personality Development

The Actualizing Tendency. Rogers (1959) postulates that all behavior is energized and directed by a single motive which he has called the *actualizing tendency,* "the inherent tendency of the organism to develop all its capacities in ways which serve to maintain or enhance the organism" (p. 196). At a very basic, organic level this inborn t involves the maintenance of the organism by meeting fun needs, such as the need for oxygen, water, and food, and the ment of the organism by providing for development and differentiation of the body's organs and functions and its continual growth and regeneration. But of more importance to human personality is the motivation which the actualizing tendency provides for increased autonomy and self-sufficiency, for expanding one's repertoire of experiences, and for being creative.

The actualizing tendency serves as the criterion by which all experiences[1] are evaluated. Through this *organismic valuing process* those experiences which are perceived as maintaining or enhancing the person are evaluated positively and are sought after. Such positive experiences give the person a feeling of satisfaction. In contrast, experiences which are perceived to be in opposition to the maintenance or enhancement of the person are evaluated negatively and are avoided. (It is interesting to note that although Rogers claims to have no theory of learning, his concept of the organismic valuing process seems very much like reinforcement-based theories of learning and personality discussed in Chapter 11.)

The most important aspect of the actualizing tendency from the standpoint of personality is the tendency toward *self-actualization.* Self-actualization involves all movement of a person in the direction of maintenance or enhancement of the *self,* a key concept in Rogers' theory to which we now turn our attention.

The Development of the Self. In early infancy the child perceives all experience, whether it is produced by sensations in his body or by external agents such as the behavior of his parents, as unitary. The infant makes no distinction between what is "me" and what is "not me." However, as part of the actualizing tendency's process of differentiation, the child soon begins to distinguish between that which is directly part of him and that which is external to him. It is this differentiation which leads to the development of the self. The self or *self-concept* (Rogers uses the terms synonymously) refers to "the organized, consistent conceptual gestalt [whole] composed of perceptions of the characteristics of the 'I' or 'me' and the perceptions of the relationships of the 'I' or 'me' to others and to various aspects of life, together with the values attached to these perceptions" (Rogers, 1959, p. 200). Thus, in line with Rogers' holistic approach, the self is viewed as a consistent organized whole,

[1] "This term is used to include all that is going on within the envelope of the organism at any given moment which is potentially available to awareness. It includes events of which the individual is unaware, as well as all the phenomena which are in consciousness. . . . It is to be noted that experience refers to the given moment, not to some accumulation of past experience" (Rogers, 1959, p. 197).

which implies that all aspects of the self must be in agreement with one another. For example, a person could think of himself as being both dominant and submissive if, and only if, these two contrasting characteristics could be reconciled. One way to do this would be for the person to perceive some situations as being appropriate for domineering behavior and other situations as being appropriate for submissiveness. If a reconciliation were not possible, as would be the case where the individual felt that one or the other type of behavior was always proper, then the self, its wholeness and consistency, would be threatened. The meaning of threat to the self-structure and the defense response which naturally follows will be discussed later.

Additionally, a person's self-concept includes not only his perception of what he is really like but also what he thinks he ought to be and would like to be. This latter aspect of the self is called the *ideal self.*

Operationalizing the Self-Concept via the Q-Sort. While it is true that a person's self-concept can only be fully known by the person himself, it is possible to gain some understanding of the way an individual views himself. Around 1950, William Stephenson (1953) developed the *Q-technique,* a method for making comparative judgments which was particularly suitable for the study of an individual's self-concept, especially as it changed, for example, during the course of psychotherapy. Rogers and his associates were quick to adopt a specific procedure, based on Stephenson's general methodology, called the *Q-sort,* as one of their basic research tools.

Rogers observed that during the course of psychotherapy a client's[2] self-concept generally underwent change. He observed that at the beginning of therapy it was typical for there to be much divergence between the way in which the client actually viewed himself and the way he would like to be (i.e., his ideal self). During psychotherapy these two aspects of the self came closer together. This observation has been amply documented by studies employing the Q-sort. In order to illustrate the Q-sort technique, we shall describe a typical study.

Before entering counseling,[3] clients are given the task of sorting a large number of self-referent statements (for example, "I am lazy"; "I don't like to be with other people"; "I am generally happy"; "I am a domineering person"). These statements are printed on cards and are placed in a series of piles, each corresponding to a point on a continuum ranging from "very characteristic of me" to "not at all characteristic of me." Usually, the client must sort the statements according to some fixed

---

[2] Rogers has come to use the term *client* to refer to the person with whom the therapist is dealing. See the section on client-centered therapy in this chapter for a discussion of the choice of the term.

[3] Rogers uses the words *counseling* and *psychotherapy* almost synonymously when referring to Rogerian therapy.

distribution (i.e., a specific number of statements in each pile), as illustrated in Figure 9–1.

The client first sorts the statements under directions to describe himself as he sees himself at the present moment. After this *self-sort* is completed, the client is asked to sort the same statements again. This time, however, he aims to describe his ideal self, the kind of person he would most like to be. This second sort is called the *ideal sort.* The two Q-sorts are then compared by correlating the ratings. Each statement is assigned two numbers, one representing the pile number for the self-sort and the other the pile number for the ideal sort, and it is these numbers that are correlated. The closer each pair of numbers, the more congruent are the perceived self and the ideal self. Thus, a positive correlation coefficient is indicative of congruence, and a negative correlation is indicative of divergence, of the perceived self and the ideal self; in each case the size of the correlation coefficient is an index of the degree of

FIGURE 9–1

Example of a Forced Q-Sort Distribution of Self-Referent Statements

	Very Characteristic					*Neutral*					*Not Characteristic*
Pile No.	0	1	2	3	4	5	6	7	8	9	10
No. of statements	2	4	6	12	14	20	14	12	6	4	2

congruence or divergence. Correlation coefficients not significantly different from zero indicate a lack of similarity between the perceived self and the ideal self. (See Chapter 2 for a more detailed explanation of correlational analysis.)

The clients are asked to perform self- and ideal sorts again at several intervals during counseling and at the completion of counseling, and each time the correlation between the two sorts is calculated. It thus becomes possible to determine whether there is a change in the relationship between clients' perceived self and ideal self over the course of counseling by comparing the correlations between the two sorts. In order to be sure that any changes found are due to counseling rather than the mere passage of time, experience with the Q-sort, or any other possible extraneous influence, another group of subjects, matched with the client group on such variables as age, sex, education, and socioeconomic level, serve in a control group. The control subjects perform self and ideal Q-sorts at the same intervals as the client subjects. The only difference between the client group and the control group is that the former is exposed to the independent variable, counseling, while the latter is not.[4]

The typical results of studies of changes in congruence between perceived self and ideal self during counseling reveal that, on the average, clients show little congruence before therapy begins but, compared with the control subjects, there is a significant change in the direction of more congruence over the course of counseling. (Rogers feels that it is an incongruence between perceived and ideal self and its resulting psychological maladjustment which brings the majority of people to counseling in the first place.)

The Q-sort is a versatile research tool. A client's single Q-sort of self-referent statements can give a therapist a picture of the client's self-concept. When two Q-sorts under the same or different instructions are performed, the relationship between them can be assessed by correlational analysis. When a large number of Q-sorts are performed, each sort can be compared with every other sort, resulting in a correlation matrix which can then be factor-analyzed (see Chapter 6).

DEMONSTRATION 9–1: THE Q-SORT

To get a better understanding of the Q-sort, the method most frequently used by Rogers and his associates in their research, the reader is invited to perform two Q-sorts of his interests.

1. First, write the name of each of the interests or activities appearing in Table 9–1 along with its number on a separate 3 × 5 index card (or any small piece of paper).

TABLE 9–1

List of Activities for Q-Sort Demonstration 9–1

1. Basketball	14. Sewing or knitting
2. Camping or hiking	15. Shopping
3. Card games	16. Singing
4. Dancing	17. Social drinking
5. Dining out	18. Swimming
6. Drawing or painting	19. Talking with friends
7. Going to movies	20. Tennis
8. Going to parties	21. Travel
9. Hunting or fishing	22. Visiting museums or art galleries
10. Listening to music	23. Walking
11. Playing a musical instrument	24. Watching television
12. Politics	25. Writing letters
13. Reading for pleasure	

[4] The adequacy of a control group consisting of matched, nonclient subjects will be discussed in the section on client-centered therapy in the present chapter. It would be instructive for the reader to think about the problem before reading the authors' remarks.

2. Place each of the activities into one of three piles with respect to your *present* interests. In one pile place those activities which you are *definitely interested* in at the present time; in a second pile place those activities which you are *definitely not interested* in presently; and in a third pile place those activities which you are *ambivalent* about with respect to your present interests.

3. Next, referring to Table 9–2, number nine cards (1–9), enter the description of the corresponding degree of interest, and also write the required number of activities which must be sorted into that pile. The first three columns of Table 9–2 provide the descriptions for the nine cards. On a desk or other flat surface, place these cards in numerical order, thereby forming a 9-point scale. You are now ready to perform the actual Q-sort.

4. You have already sorted the activities into the three gross categories of definitely interested, ambivalent, and definitely not interested. The Q-sort involves sorting the activities on the 9-point scale which you have set up. Start with the "definitely interested" pile and distribute these cards where you feel they belong (i.e., according to how interested you are in the activities *at the present time*). Next, do the same with the "definitely not interested" pile and finally, sort the "ambivalent" pile. (In this way you will be working for the most part from the extremes to the middle of the scale, which is generally the optimal strategy, since more extreme preferences are usually easier to classify than less extreme ones.)

TABLE 9–2

Outline for Q-Sort Demonstration 9–1

Pile No.	*Degree of Interest*	*Required No. in Each Pile*	*Rank*
1	Very strong interest	1	1.0
2	Strong interest	2	2.5
3	Moderate interest	3	5.0
4	Slight interest	4	8.5
5	Ambivalent (neutral)	5	13.0
6	Slight disinterest	4	17.5
7	Moderate disinterest	3	21.0
8	Strong disinterest	2	23.5
9	Very strong disinterest	1	25.0

5. Check each pile to see that the correct number of cards has been placed in each.

6. Check the Q-sort to be sure that each activity is in the pile you think it ought to be.[5]

[5] What you have done through step 6 is the essential procedure of a Q-sort. What follows are procedures for comparing this Q-sort with another one.

7. It is now possible to rank the activities from the one you are most interested in to the one you are least interested in. The ranks for each pile are given in the last column of Table 9–2[6] (page 249). Make a copy of Table 9–3 below on a piece of paper and record the rank of each activity in the column designated "First Sort Rank."

TABLE 9–3

Sample Recording Sheet for Q-Sort Demonstration 9–1

Activity Number	*First Sort Rank*	*Second Sort Rank*	*Difference*	*Difference Squared*
1				
2				
3				
4				
5				
6				
7				
8				
9				
10				
11				
12				
13				
14				
15				
16				
17				
18				
19				
20				
21				
22				
23				
24				
25				
			Sum of difference squared =	

By examining the Q-sort of the activities you have just produced, you can get an idea of what your present interests are, just as a therapist can get some understanding of a client's self-concept by looking at the client's

[6] The activity in pile number 1 will be assigned the rank of "1." The next most preferred activity would receive the rank of "2" except that there are two activities designated in pile number 2. Unless activities are ranked within each of the nine categories (a tedious and time-consuming task which, because of the fine discriminations required, may only be arbitrary at best), we must assume that the activities are equally preferable, within categories. The solution is to assign the average (mean) of the tied ranks. In the case of the two activities in pile number 2, the second and third ranks are tied, which means that each of the activities in this pile will receive the rank of "2.5" (as seen in Table 9–2 on page 249).

Q-sort of self-referent statements. However, usually more than one Q-sort is made and, indeed, one of the most useful features of the Q-sort is that comparisons between sorts are possible.

8. To make such a comparison, repeat steps 2 through 7, except this time sort the activities with respect to your interests some time *in the past,* say, five years ago. (One alternative would be to have a friend perform the Q-sort of his present interests.) Record the rank of each activity in the column designated "Second Sort Rank" on your copy of Table 9–3.

9. You are now prepared to compare the two Q-sorts. Although this can be done by visual inspection alone, correlating the rankings of the activities on the two sorts is a more exact and potentially more meaningful method of comparison. This is easily and quickly done by means of the *rank-order correlation* method which is outlined in simple, step-by-step fashion below.[7]

(*a*) For each pair of ranks (i.e., for each activity), calculate the difference between the ranks. The smaller value can always be subtracted from the larger disregarding algebraic signs (since these values will be squared). Record the differences in the "difference" column on your copy of Table 9–3.

(*b*) Now square each difference and record the squared differences in the last column of your copy of Table 9–3.

(*c*) Add all the squared differences found in step (*b*).

(*d*) Multiply the sum obtained in step (*c*) by *6.*

(*e*) Divide the product obtained in step (*d*) by *9,360.*

(*f*) Subtract the quotient obtained in step (*e*) from *1.00.* This quantity is the rank-order correlation coefficient, which is designated by the Greek letter *rho.*

If *rho* is greater than *.40* disregarding algebraic sign, then the correlation between the two Q-sorts is statistically significant at the .05 level of confidence (see Chapter 2). If *rho* is positive, then there is a close correspondence between the two Q-sorts, meaning that your interests have tended to remain the same. The closer *rho* is to +1.00, the closer are your interests in the two sorts. If *rho* is negative, then your interests now tend to be opposite to those in the past. The closer *rho* is to −1.00, the greater is the divergence.

---

[7] Lest the reader think that the steps in calculating the rank-order correlation coefficient (*rho*) have been magically rather than mathematically determined, the formula is:

$$rho = 1 - \frac{6\Sigma D^2}{N(N^2 - 1)}$$

where D = differences in ranks of each pair and N = number of pairs of ranks (in the present example $N = 25$). *Rho* is approximately equal to the Pearson product-moment correlation coefficient.

The Need for Positive Regard. Rogers postulates that a basic need for all persons is to experience attitudes such as acceptance, respect, sympathy, warmth, and love from significant people in their lives. This *need for positive regard* may be either inborn or learned, and although he tends to favor the latter explanation, Rogers feels that its origin is irrrelevant to his theory. An interesting aspect of positive regard is its reciprocal nature; that is, when a person becomes aware that he is satisfying another's need for positive regard, his own need is also satisfied.

Most often we receive positive regard for specific things we do, and in this sense positive regard is akin to certain types of positive reward such as praise or attention. It is possible, however, to give or receive positive regard irrespective of the worth placed on specific aspects of a person's behavior. This means that the person, as a whole, is accepted and respected. Such *unconditional positive regard* is frequently seen in a parent's love for a child when, regardless of the child's specific behavior, he is loved and accepted. It is similar to what Erich Fromm (1963) has called "motherly love" which, in contrast to "fatherly love," which is conditional, is given to her child "because it is her child, not because the child has fulfilled any specific condition, or lived up to any specific expectation" (p. 35). It is important to note that unconditional positive regard may be given even though all of the person's specific behaviors may not be valued equally.

The concept of unconditional positive regard, like most concepts in Rogers' personality theory, was developed in the context of psychotherapy. Rogers contends that one of the major requisites for successful psychotherapy is that the therapist "prize" the whole person of the client. The therapist must feel and show unconditional positive regard for the experiences of which the client is frightened or ashamed, as well as toward the experiences with which the client is pleased or satisfied. Gradually the client can then feel more acceptant of all of his own experiences, and this makes him more of a whole or congruent person, able to function effectively.

Positive self-regard develops from the positive attitudes shown toward a person by others. Rather than having the positive regard come from other people, the positive regard for one's experiences comes directly from the self. It is as if the self had become a significant other. The development of positive self-regard is another step toward becoming an autonomous person, which is part of the tendency toward self-actualization. When a person perceives his whole self as worthy of positive regard, irrespective of how he evaluates specific aspects of his behavior, he is experiencing *unconditional positive self-regard.*

USE THIS FOR E.

Conditions of Worth. It is difficult for significant others to regard all of a child's behavior equally. *Conditions of worth* thus develop "when the positive regard of a significant other is conditional, when the individual feels that in some respects he is prized and in others not" (Rogers, 1959, p. 209). Conditions of worth are the equivalent of internalized values which form the basis of the superego in psychoanalytic theory (see Chapter 3). It is from this differential consignment of positive regard that the child learns to differentially evaluate his own behavior. The need for positive regard, both from significant others and from one's self, is extremely powerful and consequently can come to supersede the organismic valuing process. Independent of whether an experience itself is in any way maintaining or enhancing the organism, an experience may be valued as positive or negative and subsequently either approached or avoided.

Rogers states, rather categorically, that "a condition of worth, because it disturbs the [organismic] valuing process, prevents the individual from functioning freely and with maximum effectiveness" (1959, p. 210), and thus he considers conditions of worth as being detrimental to the fully functioning person. These points emphasize the primacy of the tendency to actualization in the "normal" development of a person; when conditions of worth become more influential in directing the person's behavior than the organismic valuing process, nature is being tampered with, so to speak.

However, in this regard, Rogers appears to have overlooked the possibility that conditions of worth may coincide with the organismic valuing process. For example, such is the case when a mother tells her child that he must eat his meals. Here the value, and resultant positive regard, the mother places on eating food is very much in keeping with the actualizing tendency. While Rogers apparently has not given much attention to this point, he has anticipated one of the major conflicts between societal values (conditions of worth) and values based on the actualizing tendency by postulating that enhancement of the organism includes moving in the direction of socialization (Rogers, 1965, p. 488).

The Experience of Threat and the Process of Defense

When the self is first formed, it is governed by the organismic valuing process alone, which uses as a criterion of evaluation the principles of self-actualization. However, as the need for positive regard becomes important to the individual and conditions of worth become part of his self, conflicts arise between the self and experience. Where unconditional positive regard exists, all experiences are admitted to the individual's awareness and symbolized accurately; if no experience is more or less worthy of positive regard than any other, then there is no reason to exclude any experience from awareness. However, if conditions of worth are embodied within the self, experiences will vary in the extent to which they are valued (for example, mother says it is better to eat oatmeal than ice cream and cake for breakfast). Those experiences which are consistent with the self and its conditions of worth and thus are valued positively are allowed to enter awareness and are perceived accurately. Experiences which conflict with the self and its conditions of worth and therefore are valued negatively represent a danger to the self-concept and are kept from entering awareness and being accurately perceived.

Suppose a young man has been taught by his parents that each individual has an obligation to be loyal to his country, and he has come to feel that this is how he should behave. While in college he is exposed to points of view which are in opposition to unconditional support of one's country, especially in the case where the individual citizen feels his country's policies are unjust. The young man is about to be drafted into the army to fight in a war which he feels his country is engaged in unjustly, and he decides to leave his country rather than be drafted. This experience is in direct opposition to his self-concept, which places a high degree of positive self-regard on patriotism, and is therefore threatening to him.

For Rogers, *threat* exists when a person perceives[8] that there is an incongruity between some experience and his self-concept. The person experiences threat as vague uneasiness and tension, which is commonly labeled anxiety. Incongruence between self-concept and experience is threatening because the individual's personality is no longer a consistent whole. The young man's behavior is no longer regulated by a unitary force, the actualizing tendency, but is instead governed by several different standards. Rogers (1959) speaks of this division in the following way:

> This, as we see it, is the basic estrangement in man. He has not been true to himself, to his own natural organismic valuing of experience, but for the sake of preserving the positive regard of others has now come to falsify some of the values he experiences and to perceive them only in terms based upon their value to others. Yet this has not been a conscious choice, but a natural—and tragic—development in infancy. The path of development toward psychological maturity, the path of therapy, is the undoing of this estrangement in man's functioning, the dissolving of conditions of worth, the achievement of a self which is congruent with experience, and the restoration of a unified organismic valuing process as the regulator of behavior (pp. 226–7).

It is impossible to conceive of an individual completely devoid of conditions of worth actually existing in the world as we know it. The absence of conditions of worth and the presence of a unified organismic

---

[8] Incongruity between experience and self-concept need not be perceived at a conscious level. Indeed, Rogers postulates that most frequently the individual is able to discriminate an experience as threatening without the threat being symbolized in awareness.

valuing process as the sole regulator of behavior are only goals toward which a person can strive in order to achieve better psychological adjustment. However, to understand how the young man in our example is threatened as a result of the presence of conditions of worth, it would be constructive to consider, hypothetically, how things would have been different had the conditions of worth been absent.

If the young man had been reared in an atmosphere where all his feelings were accepted and prized, he would have come to value all of his experiences equally, and his behavior would be guided by his organismic valuing process. Under these circumstances, his parents' attitude, and subsequently his own, about patriotism might have been of the following sort: "We all have an obligation to be loyal to our country, but we also have an obligation to follow our conscience in matters of right and wrong. Sometimes these two obligations are in conflict, and we must make a choice between the two. But choosing one does not permanently exclude the other as a course of action at a different time and under different circumstances. Nor does such a decision make one mode of behavior any more worthy than the other. Sometimes it is possible to satisfy one urge and sometimes the other." By retaining his own organismic valuing process of experiences, a balance between the two modes of behavior could be achieved, and his whole, consistent self would remain intact.

Our young man was not fortunate enough to grow up in such utopian circumstances (nor is any person), and so we must turn from the completely theoretical situation to the more practical one which confronts him. Having made the choice to leave his country rather than serve in the army, he is potentially vulnerable to disorganization of his personality as a result of the existing state of incongruity between his self-concept and his experience. Anxiety, the emotional response to threat, serves as a signal that the unified self-concept is in danger of being disorganized if the discrepancy between it and the threatening experience is symbolized accurately in consciousness.

The organism defends itself from this impending danger by a process of defense which attempts to maintain the self as it exists at that time. "This goal is achieved by the perceptual distortion of the experience in awareness, in such a way as to reduce the incongruity between the experience and the structure of the self, or by the denial to awareness of an experience, thus denying any threat to the self" (Rogers, 1959, pp. 204–5).

Rogers' two basic defensive behaviors, *perceptual distortion* and *denial,* can be illustrated in the various alternatives the young man could use to defend himself against his threatening experience, namely, leaving the country to avoid serving in the army. Rationalization is a good example of perceptual distortion: "I didn't really leave my country to avoid being drafted. Actually there are many good opportunities for getting ahead in this new country." Phantasy is also a mechanism of defense primarily involving distortion: "I am serving my country by looking after its interests in another country." Reaction formation involves both distortion and denial: "I didn't want to serve my country in the first place. I've always felt that a man owes nothing to his country." Projection also is a composite of the two basic defensive responses to threat: "Look at all those men who have left their country to avoid serving in the army! I'm glad I'm not like them." The ultimate defense would be pure denial that the experience ever occurred: "I've never been called to serve in my country's army." In each case, the defensive behavior serves to keep the young man from becoming fully aware of the actual threatening experience, either by distorting the experience so that it is no longer incongruent with his self-concept or by not allowing any aspect of the experience to enter consciousness.

Rogers views psychological adjustment in terms of the degree of congruence between the self and experience. In other words, a person who is psychologically well-adjusted is one who perceives himself and his relation to people and objects in his environment as they "really" are (i.e., as an objective observer would see them). Such an individual is *open to experience* rather than threatened by it because experience is in agreement with the perception he has of it. When an experience is in conflict with the perceptions of the self, the threatening experience is prevented from being accurately symbolized by perceptual distortion or denial. On the basis of these theoretical notions, Chodorkoff (1954, p. 508) derived the following hypotheses about the relation among self-perception, perceptual defense, and personal adjustment:

1. The greater the agreement between the individual's self-description and an objective description of him, the less perceptual defense he will show.
2. The greater the agreement between the individual's self-description and an objective description of him, the more adequate will be his personal adjustment.
3. The more adequate the personal adjustment of the individual, the less perceptual defense he will show.

To test these hypotheses, Chodorkoff had male undergraduate students serve as subjects. Each student performed a Q-sort of 125 self-descriptive statements under instructions to describe himself. This self-description was compared with another Q-sort of the same statements, made for each subject by two clinically experienced judges. The judges' Q-sort description, which was the objective description of each individual, was based on information about the subject gleaned from projective techniques administered to each subject, consisting of the Rorschach, the TAT, and a word association test, as well as a biographical inventory.

In the word association test, each subject was presented with 50 emotional and 50 neutral words, and his reaction time to each word was recorded. For each subject, the 10 emotional words having the longest reaction time and the 10 neutral words having the shortest reaction time were used in the perceptual defense test. These 20 words were flashed on a screen in random order by means of a tachistoscope, a device for visually presenting material for brief, controlled durations (for example, 1/100 second). The exposure time for each word was increased until it was accurately reported, and this time became the recognition score for each word. Perceptual defense is a hypothetical construct which has been used to denote an unconscious mechanism which resists allowing threatening material to enter consciousness. It was operationally defined in Chodorkoff's study by the difference between the recognition thresholds for charged stimuli (emotional or taboo words such as *whore, bitch, penis*) and the thresholds for neutral stimuli (words such as *house, tree, book*). The higher this difference is, the greater is the degree of perceptual defense.

The third variable of interest in Chodorkoff's study, personal adjustment, was rated, from the projective techniques, by the clinically experienced judges on two rating scales.

The hypotheses were evaluated by performing the appropriate correlations. The first hypothesis compared the accuracy of self-description with recognition thresholds, and it was found that the two variables were negatively correlated—high accuracy of self-description tended to be associated with low recognition thresholds for threatening words. The second hypothesis compared accuracy of self-description and personal adjustment ratings and found them to be positively correlated—high accuracy in self-description was associated with good psychological adjustment. To test the third hypothesis, personal adjustment ratings were compared with recognition thresholds. These variables were negatively correlated—greater psychological adjustment was associated with lower thresholds of recognition. General support for all three experimental hypotheses led Chodorkoff (1954) to conclude:

> In a group of Ss [subjects] who show varying degrees of adjustment and defensiveness, one finds that the more inaccurate and faulty the individual's perception of his environment, the more inaccurate and faulty is his perception of himself; and the more inaccurate and faulty the individual's perceptions of himself and his environment, the more inadequate is his personal adjustment (p. 511).

While Chodorkoff's study has a number of obvious methodological flaws (for example, the objectiveness of the "objective" descriptions is questionable), it does provide some support for Rogers' notions regarding the relationship of psychological adjustment, perceptual defense, and openness to experience. Although Rogers' theory of personality is often abstract, it is very much to the credit of Rogers and his followers that they have endeavored to operationally define their concepts and put them to an empirical test. Chodorkoff's investigation is but one example of this practice.

The Process of Breakdown and Disorganization. So far in our discussion of Rogers' theory of personality we have spoken of events which occur in the course of "normal" personality development. Even the most psychologically well-adjusted individual is occasionally threatened by an experience which is inconsistent with his self-concept and which forces him to distort or deny the experience. Doubtless the majority of people experience anxiety as part of their daily living. But their anxiety is at a moderate, and therefore tolerable, level due to the fact that the inconsistency between self-concept and experience is correspondingly moderate and their defenses are adequate. When experiences become more than moderately incongruent with the self, or when the incongruent experiences occur frequently, the person experiences a level of anxiety that is distinctly unpleasant and may actually interfere with his daily activities. Such individuals are typically called "neurotic" and may seek assistance in reducing their anxiety via psychotherapy. However, the neurotic's defenses are still capable of keeping incongruent experiences out of conscious awareness, thereby allowing the self to remain in a whole, if somewhat tenuous, state.

If the inconsistency between self-concept and experience becomes very great, the individual's defenses may be incapable of distorting or denying the experience. The result is that in the organism's defenseless state the incongruent experience is accurately symbolized in awareness and the consistent, whole self is shattered. A person in such a disorganized state is typically labeled "psychotic," and may exhibit behavior which, to an objective observer, seems odd, irrational, or even bizarre. On closer inspection the behaviors may prove to be congruent with the previously denied experiences. Thus, the behaviors are odd only insofar as they are incongruent with the way in which the person is seen by objective observers. For example, a person who has rigidly controlled his aggressive tendencies, denying that they were part of his self-concept, may openly display hostility toward people with whom he comes in contact.

The Process of Reintegration. While successfully operating defenses are certainly preferable to the consequence of the logical alternative, namely, a disorganized personality, the person always pays a price for having incongruent experiences kept from accurate symbolization in awareness (cf. libido used for defense mechanisms is not available for other ego functions—Chapter 3). An individual who distorts or denies certain experiences must constantly defend himself against these experiences coming accurately into consciousness. The result is that all experiences come to be perceived defensively as potentially threatening rather than as they really are. People who are colloquially described as "always on the defensive" illustrate the consequences of the defensive process. Such people question the meaning and sincerity of even the most innocuous comments made by other people and are quick to respond as if the comments were derogatory toward them. But from their internal frame of reference, the innocent remark by another person *is* derogatory, since it has been perceived in a distorted form.

Furthermore, a person who inaccurately perceives his experiences is not able to function fully. He is not completely open to experience, and thus he misses or must avoid those aspects of life which are potentially threatening to him. Consider, for example, the person who, due to a self-concept which condones only success, is threatened by any experience in which he could potentially fail. By distorting his view of the experience from one which could lead to failure to one which is undesirable or "not worth the time and effort," he successfully avoids the experience. Rather than apply to graduate school, he "decides" that he can do just as well with a bachelor's degree; and, anyhow, he might as well be making money while his friends in graduate school live on meager fellowships. Or he may explain that he didn't try out for the football team because being on the team takes too much time.

When there is incongruity between an individual's self and his experience, and his defenses are active, it is possible to decrease the self-experience discrepancy by a process of reintegration within the personality. This is achieved by reversing the process of defense; that is, the individual becomes clearly aware of hitherto distorted or denied experiences and, *under certain specific conditions,* he is able to make these experiences part of his self-concept. For example, the individual who was threatened by experiences at which he might possibly fail could, in the course of reintegration, come to realize that he might not be admitted to graduate school or that he might be cut from the football team, but these possibilities could become acceptable by integrating them into his self-concept. His self-concept would now contain the construct: "It is not necessary for me to succeed at everything I try," thereby making him less likely to find such experiences threatening.

Rogers maintains that this reintegration process can occur only under conditions in which there is *a reduction in the person's conditions of worth and an increase in his unconditional positive self-regard.* These essential conditions can occur if the individual is exposed to and perceives the unconditional positive regard of a significant other. However, unconditional postive regard can only be communicated if a state of *empathy* exists. The significant other must accurately perceive the internal frame of reference of the individual. In a word, to be empathic, one must step into the other person's skin; he must act and feel *as if* he were the other person, but without losing the "as if" quality. Rogers (1959) explains why empathy is necessary for unconditional positive regard:

> If I know little or nothing of you, and experience an unconditional positive regard for you, this means little because further knowledge of you may reveal aspects which I cannot so regard. But if I know you thoroughly, knowing and empathically understanding a wide variety of your feelings and behaviors, and still experience an unconditional positive regard, this is very meaningful. It comes close to being fully known and fully accepted (p. 231).

Recall that at birth, a person's self-concept is open to all experience. It is only when a person acquires conditions of worth that he begins to value one experience more than another and his self-concept comes to include experiences which he values positively and exclude experiences which he values negatively. Those experiences which have been excluded from the self must be kept from awareness in order to maintain the self as a consistent whole. Thus, the person becomes aware of only the experiences which he regards positively. If, however, all experiences were regarded equally, there could be no conditions of worth. Accordingly, in a state of unconditional positive regard the existing conditions of worth lose their significance and power in directing the person's behavior. The individual becomes open to more experiences, since without conditions of worth all experiences are consistent with the self. For example, a man who values restraint positively and aggression negatively is unable to accurately perceive his need to be aggressive on some occasions. Aggressive behavior is inconsistent with his self-concept: "I am a restrained person," which *ipso facto* makes restraint good. If this condition of worth is dissolved, restraint and aggression have the same unconditional positive value, and they therefore are able to exist harmoniously within a unified self. Sometimes the man behaves with restraint and at other times he behaves aggressively, but there is, in effect, no value placed on either mode of behavior, since neither is valued more or less than the other.

As a consequence of the unconditional positive regard shown by a significant other, the person experiences an increase in his own unconditional positive self-regard which enables him to maintain an openness to experience and lack of defensiveness when the significant other is no longer present. Although increased unconditional positive self-regard and the concommitant decrease in conditions of worth are the prerequisites for the reintegration of one's personality, perceiving the unconditional positive regard of a significant other is not the only way reintegration can be achieved. It is, however, the process by which client-centered psychotherapy is postulated to work.

Before turning to a discussion of client-centered therapy, we should say a word or two about the many minor personality reintegrations which occur in our daily lives. Such reintegration is possible without the unconditional positive regard of a significant other *if there is an absence of threat to the self*. Typically, when we are left alone, we are able to face minor, inconsistent experiences and restructure our self-concept to assimilate these experiences. Rogers (1965) gives the following example:

> . . . the child who feels that he is weak and powerless to do a certain task, to build a tower or repair a bicycle, may find, as he works rather hopelessly at the task, that he is successful. This experience is inconsistent with the concept he holds of himself, and may not be integrated at once; but if the child is left to himself he gradually assimilates, upon his own initiative, a revision of his concept of self, that while he is generally weak and powerless, in this respect he has ability. This is the normal way in which, free from threat, new perceptions are assimilated. But if this same child is repeatedly told by his parents that he is competent to do the task, he is likely to deny it, and to prove by his behavior that he is unable to do it. The more forceful intrusion of the notion of his competence constitutes more of a threat to self and is more forcefully resisted (p. 519).

Rogers (1965) maintains that this process of reintegration which occurs without the help of another person is not effective when the inconsistency between the self and experience is large: "It appears possible for the person to face such [large] inconsistency only while in a relationship with another in which he is sure that he will be accepted" (p. 519). The relationship to which Rogers alludes is that found in client-centered therapy, to which we now turn our attention.

CLIENT-CENTERED PSYCHOTHERAPY

The Meaning of "Client-Centered"

The essence of client-centered therapy[9] is contained in the meaning of its name. Rogers (1965) explains the use of the term "client" in the following way:

> What term shall be used to indicate the person with whom the therapist is dealing? "Patient," "subject," "counselee," "analysand," are terms which have been used. We have increasingly used the term client, to the point where we have absorbed it into the label of "client-centered therapy." It has been chosen because, in spite of its imperfections of dictionary meaning and

[9] Client-centered therapy has alternately been called *nondirective therapy,* since it is the client, not the therapist, who directs the course of treatment.

derivation, it seems to come closest to conveying the picture of this person as we see it. The client, as the term has acquired its meaning, is one who comes actively and voluntarily to gain help on a problem, but without any notion of surrendering his own responsibility for the situation. It is because the term has these connotations that we have chosen it, since it avoids the connotation that he is sick, or the object of an experiment, and so on (p. 7).

In keeping with Rogers' phenomenological position, psychotherapy is *centered* around the client. It is the client's unique problems, feelings, perceptions, attitudes, and goals which are dealt with in therapy. Therapy can only proceed from the vantage point of the client's internal frame of reference. While the therapist can only hope to gain an incomplete knowledge of his client's subjective experiences, he must try to learn as much as possible about the way his client views his experiences and the world in general through empathic understanding.

Minimal Conditions for the Therapeutic Process

Rogers hypothesizes that there are certain necessary, but not always sufficient, conditions which must be met before the therapeutic process can begin. The client must be experiencing some inconsistency between his self-concept and his experiences. The therapist must be experiencing congruency between his self-concept and his experience *with respect to his relationship with the client.* The therapist need not be open to all experiences in his life, but while taking part in the therapeutic relationship he should be relatively free of threatening experiences. Rogers (1959) feels that the therapist can be most effective when he is "completely and fully himself, with his experience of the moment being accurately symbolized and integrated into the picture he holds of himself" (p. 215). Such a fully functioning therapist is capable of experiencing unconditional positive regard for the client as well as empathic understanding of his client's internal frame of reference. These two essential conditions serve to foster a situation which is free of threat and therefore is maximally conducive to reintegration of the client's personality. A final prerequisite for the therapeutic process is that the client perceive, at least to some degree, the therapist's unconditional positive regard for him and empathic understanding of his outlook. This last condition reemphasizes the importance of viewing the client through his internal frame of reference, since it would not matter how much unconditional positive regard or empathic understanding the therapist experienced for the client if the client did not perceive it.

There is some indirect evidence to support most of these hypothesized basic conditions for the therapeutic process. One investigation revealed that less anxious clients have difficulty getting involved in therapy and consequently tend to drop out (Gallagher, 1953), which is relevant to Rogers' contention that the client should be experiencing some inconsistency between his self and his experience.

Seeman's (1954) study of the process and outcome of client-centered therapy showed that both the therapist's liking his client and the client feeling liked tend to be associated with successful therapy. Unfortunately, Seeman used therapist ratings as the sole criterion of success in therapy and, therefore, to the extent that liking or disliking a client influenced judgments of therapeutic success, Seeman's study cannot be considered conclusive.

Fiedler (1950) compared the relationship established between expert and novice therapists and their clients in three different types of psychotherapy: client-centered, traditional psychoanalytic, and Adlerian. Four judges listened to recordings of the therapy sessions, and for each session they sorted 75 statements descriptive of the therapeutic relationship (for example, "Therapist treats patient with much deference"; "Therapist is sympathetic with patient") on a seven-category Q-sort ranging from most characteristic to least characteristic of the session. The results showed that experienced therapists of all three orientations tended to create a relationship in which they demonstrated an understanding of the client's communications, from the client's point of view, thereby lending support to the importance of empathic understanding.

The Process of Client-Centered Therapy

In client-centered therapy, the major responsibility for the therapeutic process falls to the client. Rogers' basic philosophy in this regard is that given the proper circumstances, the client will have the capacity to begin to resolve his problems. This is a position which is directly in keeping with Rogers' view of the development of behavioral disorders. Behavioral disorders are a consequence of conflict between a person's two fundamental evaluative processes, one based on the self-actualization tendency—the organismic valuing process—and the other based on the values of other persons, i.e., conditions of worth. Rogers firmly believes that no behavior disorders would develop if the person were guided solely by the organismic valuing process. It is necessary in client-centered therapy to create a situation in which the client feels free from his conditions of worth, thereby allowing his behavior to be guided by his organismic valuing process. This goal can be achieved in a nonthreatening situation in which the client feels understood (empathic understanding) and accepted as a whole person (unconditional positive regard). Under these conditions the client will be able to accurately examine those experiences which have been inconsistent with his self-concept and of which he was previously unaware because they were either perceived only in a distorted fashion or not at all. How, then, does the therapist create these ideal conditions?

Client-centered therapy proceeds by means of a verbal interchange between the client and the therapist. The therapist shows unconditional positive regard for the client by accepting what the client says without either approval or disapproval. He accepts equally all of the client's feelings and behavior with no evaluation on his part. Typically, this is done by responding to the client's statements with phrases such as "Yes," "I see," and "Mm-hmm."

The therapist communicates his empathic understanding of the client's internal frame of reference primarily on an emotional level and attempts to clarify the client's feelings by synthesizing or reorganizing the feelings which the client has expressed directly or indirectly. Secondarily, on a cognitive or intellectual level, the therapist restates the ideas expressed by the client but without any attempt to reorganize the client's statements so that the feelings involved are clarified. Both types of responses are illustrated in the following excerpt from an actual record of a client-centered therapy session (Snyder, 1947, p. 278). The client is a 20-year-old college girl whose right hand is malformed. See if you can tell which of the therapist's comments involve *clarification of feeling* and which involve *restatement of content.*

Client (C): After I left here last time—that night during dinner the student dean in our house asked to speak to my roommate. My roommate told me about it afterwards—Miss Hansen asked if I would be embarrassed as hostess at the table. She said she didn't want to hurt me! These darn student deans who think that they must guard us! The other student dean I had before never raised the issue. It makes me so mad!

Therapist (T): You feel that this incident helped to accentuate the difficulty.

C: That was the first time with a student dean. Really though, it struck me very funny. She watches us like a hawk. We can't make a move but she knows it.

T: You resent her activity.

C: I just don't like it on general principles. Oh, I suppose that she was trying to save me embarrassment.

T: You can see why she did that.

C: I think that she is really afraid of us—she's queer. I don't know, but so far as I am concerned, I'm pretty indifferent to her.

T: You feel that she doesn't affect you one way or the other.[10]

---

[10] The therapist's first two comments are clarification of feeling, while his last two are restatement of content.

For either type of response to be considered *empathic* understanding, the therapist must experience the cognition or affect from the client's internal frame of reference. This is not easy to do because we are accustomed to viewing others from an *external* frame of reference, as objective, outside observers. Thus, it is necessary for the therapist to actively try to stay within his client's subjective world.

DEMONSTRATION 9–2: PERCEIVING FROM ANOTHER'S INTERNAL FRAME OF REFERENCE

The reader is invited to try perceiving through a client's "eyes." Below are a series of statements made by a 30-year-old man at the beginning of a therapy session.[11] After reading each statement write down in a sentence or two the attitudes or thoughts you have concerning the statement as *you assume the internal frame of reference* of this client.

1. "I thought I'd have something to talk about—then it all goes around in circles. I was trying to think what I was going to say. Then coming here it doesn't work out. . . . I tell you, it seemed that it would be much easier before I came."
2. "I tell you, I just can't make a decision; I don't know what I want. I've tried to reason this thing out logically—tried to figure out which things are important to me."
3. "I thought that there are maybe two things a man might do; he might get married and raise a family. But if he was just a bachelor, just making a living—that isn't very good."
4. "I find myself and my thoughts getting back to the days when I was a kid and I cry very easily. The dam would break through."
5. "I've been in the Army four and a half years. I had no problems then, no hopes, no wishes. My only thought was to get out when peace would come."

Now compare your attitudes and thoughts with those in Table 9–4 (page 266) to see what success you had at adopting the client's internal frame of reference. While your thoughts do not have to be identical to those given in the table, they should be of the general flavor as those in the left-hand column. Rogers (1965) explains why the attitudes in the right-hand column are representative of an external frame of reference by noting that ". . . these are all attitudes which are basically sympathetic. There is nothing 'wrong' with them. They are even attempts to 'understand,' in the sense of 'understanding about,' rather than 'understanding with.' The locus of perceiving is, however, outside of the client" (p. 33).

[11] Statements quoted from Rogers, 1965, pp. 32–33.

TABLE 9–4

Model Therapist's Attitudes and Thoughts Representing External and Internal Frames of Reference*

Internal Frame of Reference	*External Frame of Reference*
1. It's really hard for you to get started.	1. Should I help you get started talking? Is your inability to get under way a type of dependence?
2. Decision-making just seems impossible to you.	2. What is the cause of your indecisiveness?
3. You want marriage, but it doesn't seem to you to be much of a possibility.	3. Why are you focusing on marriage and family? You appear to be a bachelor. I didn't know that.
4. You feel yourself brimming over with childish feelings.	4. The crying, the "dam," sound as though you are repressing a great deal.
5. To you the Army represented stagnation.	5. You're a veteran. Were you a psychiatric patient? I feel sorry for anybody who spent four and one-half years in the service.

* Statements quoted or paraphrased from Rogers, 1965, pp. 33–34.

Is Client-Centered Therapy Effective?

As we have noted previously, Rogers and his co-workers have often attempted to validate their theoretical notions through empirical research. A major compilation of research intended to demonstrate the efficacy of client-centered therapy was published under the title *Psychotherapy and Personality Change* (Rogers and Dymond, 1954). Although an extended description and critique of this body of research is not in keeping with the intended purpose of our discussion of Rogers' motivational theory of personality, we shall briefly look at the general design of the research and make some general points with respect to the assessment of behavioral change.

The research strategy involved assessing variables which were expected to change over the course of therapy (for example, congruence between perceived self and ideal self; self-awareness; TAT protocols) both before and after therapy. The changes on these variables which occurred during psychotherapy were compared to changes which occurred without therapy. The basic experimental design is illustrated in Figure 9–2.

The therapy group consisted of 29 persons who sought therapy at the University of Chicago Counseling Center. It included both students and nonstudents. The *own-control* group was created by asking half of these clients to defer therapy for 60 days. It was thus possible to compare changes during therapy with changes that occurred during the waiting period in the same subjects. This procedure controlled for factors which might influence behavior change, such as motivation for therapy, person-

FIGURE 9–2

Design of Rogers and Dymond Research

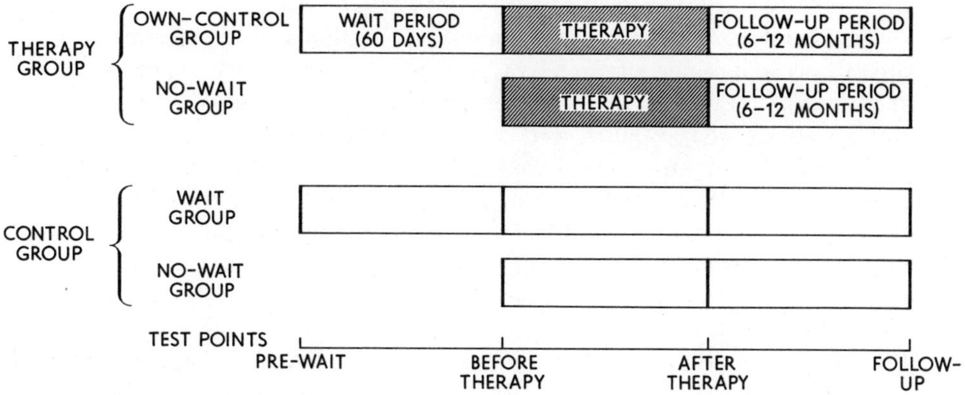

Source: Rogers and Dymond, 1954.

ality characteristics, expectation for therapy, and demographic characteristics (such as age, sex, and socioeconomic level). The 23 subjects in the "*equivalent-control*" group were chosen from persons who volunteered to participate in personality research. Approximately half of these "normal" subjects were matched for age, sex, socioeconomic level, and student-nonstudents status with the *no-wait therapy* group and half with the *own-control therapy* group.

The purpose of the equivalent-control group was to control for the passage of time. Whenever a treatment of some sort is hypothesized to lead to a change in behavior, an alternative hypothesis must also be entertained, namely, that the same behavioral change will come about without the treatment. When we take an aspirin for a headache and the headache goes away, we do not question whether the aspirin was responsible for alleviating the headache. It is possible, however, that the headache would have gone away by itself. In research on the effects of psychotherapy it is necessary to control for the possibility that the patient's problems will be solved or his deviant behavior will change without psychotherapy, a phenomenon which has been called *spontaneous remission.*

The experimental design which Rogers and his associates used for their investigations appears impressive. Nonetheless, Eysenck (1960), who, besides his study of personality, which we discussed in Chapter 6, has devoted considerable effort as a critic of psychotherapy, has shrewdly observed that the design has, in fact, no real control group!

Eysenck criticizes the equivalent-control group by pointing out that there is no reason to believe that "normal" subjects who do not receive psychotherapy should become more psychologically adjusted than they already are. To test the spontaneous remission hypothesis, the control subjects must be equivalent to the therapy subjects on a dimension of psychological adjustment.

The spontaneous remission hypothesis states that such remissions vary directly as a function of time—the greater the time interval, the more spontaneous remissions would be expected to occur. Thus, the own-control group would be considered adequate if, and only if, the waiting period and the therapy period were equated in terms of time. Given this provision, the rate of spontaneous recovery would be expected to be the same during the waiting and therapy periods. Therefore, if the subjects improve significantly more during the therapy period than during the equivalent waiting period, some statement can be made about the efficacy of the therapeutic treatment. If, however, as was the case in Rogers' investigations, the therapy period is substantially longer than the waiting period, then it would be anticipated that more spontaneous remission would occur in the therapy period than in the waiting period regardless of therapy. Under these latter circumstances, greater improvement during the therapy period could not be ascribed to the therapy.

Eysenck's pregnant criticisms of the experimental design which was employed to assess the efficacy of client-centered therapy do not permit any definitive statements about the effectiveness of client-centered procedures possible at this time. However, the problem of an adequate control group is among the most perplexing which besets research on the effects of any psychotherapeutic procedures. Not only are the criteria for a wholly adequate control group far from clear, but there are numerous practical and ethical problems that arise when investigations are performed with actual patients (or clients) in psychotherapy. For example, is it ethical to deliberately have persons who have sought psychotherapy wait for treatment, especially for a period of time equivalent to that which the treatment normally takes? In the light of such considerations, it is once again to the credit of Rogers and his associates that they have attempted such difficult research, since client-centered therapy is among the few therapeutic procedures which have come under the scrutiny of empirical investigation.

THE FULLY FUNCTIONING PERSON: SELF-ACTUALIZATION

In our discussion of Rogers' theory of personality, we have alluded to the *fully functioning person.* Such a person epitomizes psychological health or adjustment in that he is a completely self-actualizing individual. As we have noted, the object of client-centered therapy is to bring a person closer to the ideal goal of self-actualization. What would such a person be like?

In this final section, we turn to a description of the self-actualizing person which has evolved out of the theorizing and research of Abraham H. Maslow. Although Maslow and Rogers hold similar views of the nature of human personality, Maslow has focused more on the "normal" or "healthy" personality. His study of self-actualizing persons relies heavily on the case history method (see Chapter 2) and is based on data from a relatively small and select group of subjects, including both living persons and historical figures such as Thomas Jefferson (cf. McClelland's study of achievement motivation in past societies, page 233). In his report of the research, which was first published in 1950, Maslow justified this approach in the following way:

> . . . I consider the problem of psychological health to be so pressing, that *any* suggestions, *any* bits of data, however moot, are endowed with great heuristic value. This kind of research is in principle so difficult—involving as it does a kind of lifting oneself by one's axiological bootstraps—that if we were to wait for conventionally reliable data, we should have to wait forever. It seems that the only manly thing to do is not to fear mistakes, to plunge in, to do the best that one can, hoping to learn enough from blunders to correct them eventually. At present the only alternative is simply to refuse to work with the problem. Accordingly, for whatever use can be made of it, the following report is presented with due apologies to those who insist on conventional reliability, validity, sampling, etc. (Maslow, 1963, p. 527).

In keeping with this philosophy, Maslow's research has focused primarily on making observations rather than testing hypotheses, and the resulting observations are admittedly subjective in nature. Nonetheless, his description of self-actualized man and the kind of motives which characterize him is among the most interesting essays in psychology.

In the case of qualitative data of the type gathered by Maslow, the ability of the investigator to accurately and graphically summarize his impressions (the basic units of the data) greatly enhances the usefulness of the report. As should become apparent presently, Maslow has a distinct talent in this regard. Accordingly, our explication of Maslow's 15 most salient characteristics of self-actualizing man relies heavily on direct quotations from Maslow's (1963) highly expressive and communicative language.

To begin with, self-actualizing people are characterized by their *efficient perception of reality*. Maslow writes:

> The first form in which this capacity was noticed was an unusual ability to detect the spurious, the fake, and the dishonest in personality, and in general to judge people correctly and efficiently. . . . As the study progressed, it slowly became apparent that this efficiency extended to many other areas of life—indeed *all* areas that were tested. In art and music, in things of the intellect, in scientific matters, in politics and public affairs, they seemed as a group to be able to see concealed or confused realities more swiftly and more

correctly than others. Thus an informal experiment indicated that their predictions of the future from whatever facts were in hand at the time seemed to be more often correct, because less based upon wish, desire, anxiety, fear, or upon generalized, character-determined optimism or pessimism (p. 531).

Maslow observes that self-actualizing persons are characterized by *acceptance* of themselves, of others, and of nature. Thus:

They can accept their own human nature in stoic style, with all its shortcomings, with all its discrepancies from the ideal image without feeling real concern. It would convey the wrong impression to say that they are self-satisfied. What we must say rather is that they can take the frailties and sins, weaknesses, and evils of human nature in the same unquestioning spirit with which one accepts the characteristics of nature. One does not complain about water because it is wet, or about rocks because they are hard, or about trees because they are green. As the child looks out upon the world with wide, uncritical innocent eyes, simply noting and observing what is the case, without either arguing the matter or demanding that it be otherwise, so does the self-actualizing person look upon human nature in himself and in others . . . but resignation too can be observed in our subjects, especially in the face of illness and death (p. 533).

Although self-actualizing people are *spontaneous,* they are not necessarily the most unconventional people in society.

Their behavior is marked by simplicity and naturalness, and by lack of artificiality or straining for effect. This does not necessarily mean consistently unconventional behavior. . . . It is his impulses, thought, consciousness that are so unusually unconventional, spontaneous, and natural. Apparently recognizing that the world of people in which he lives could not understand or accept this, and since he has no wish to hurt them or fight with them over every triviality, he will go through the ceremonies and rituals of convention with a good-humored shrug and with the best possible grace. Thus I have seen a man accept an honor he laughed at and even despised in private, rather than make an issue of it and hurt the people who thought they were pleasing him (p. 535).

Maslow's subjects are *problem-centered* in the sense that they are:

. . . ordinarily concerned with basic issues and eternal questions of the type that we have learned to call philosophical or ethical. Such people live customarily in the widest possible frame of reference. They seem never to get so close to the trees that they fail to see the forest. They work within a framework of values that are broad and not petty, universal and not local, and in terms of a century rather than the moment. In a word, these people are all in one sense or another philosophers, however homely (p. 537).

The subjects appear to have a greater *affinity for solitude and privacy* than the average person and also show a tendency to be *independent from their culture and environment.*

Since they are propelled by growth motivation rather than by deficiency motivation [i.e., motivation stemming from gratification of basic physical and emotional—e.g., love, respect—needs], self-actualizing people are not dependent for their main satisfactions on the real world, or other people or culture or means to ends or, in general, on extrinsic satisfactions. Rather they are dependent for their own development and continued growth on their own potentialities and latent resources. Just as the tree needs sunshine and water and food, so do most people need love, safety, and other basic need gratifications that can come only from without. But once these external satisfiers are obtained, once these inner deficiencies are satiated by outside satisfiers, the true problem of individual development begins . . . self-actualization (p. 539).

Self-actualizing persons exhibit a *continued freshness of appreciation* for even the most ordinary events in their lives. They have:

. . . the wonderful capacity to appreciate again and again, freshly and naïvely, the basic goods of life, with awe, pleasure, wonder, and even ecstasy, however stale these experiences may have become to others . . . any sunset may be as beautiful as the first one. . . . For such people, even the casual workaday, moment-to-moment business of living can be thrilling, exciting and ecstatic. These intense feelings do not come all the time; they come occasionally rather than usually, but at the most unexpected moments (pp. 539–40).

They are also likely to experience what Maslow calls *"the oceanic feeling."* This phrase refers to feelings of "limitless horizons opening up to the vision, the feeling of being simultaneously more powerful and also more helpless than one ever was before, the feeling of great ecstasy and wonder and awe, the loss of placing in time and space with, finally, the conviction that something extremely important and valuable had happened, so that the subject is to some extent transformed and strengthened even in his daily life by such experiences" (p. 541).

Self-actualizing people usually have a *genuine desire to help the human race,* although they tend to have *deep ties with relatively few individuals.* In explaining this latter characteristic of himself, one of Maslow's subjects noted: "I haven't got time for many friends. Nobody has, that is, if they are to be *real* friends" (p. 542).

Maslow describes his subjects as being *democratic* in the deepest sense. Besides their being free of prejudice with regard to superficial characteristics of people such as race, color, political beliefs, and so on, they tend to have some respect for all persons and thus, for example, are willing to learn from anyone who is able to teach them something. At the same time, Maslow says that his subjects do not indiscriminately equalize all human beings. Rather, self-actualizing people "themselves elite, select for their friends elite, but this is an elite of character, capacity, and talent, rather than of birth, race, blood, name, family, age, youth, fame, or power" (p. 544).

Self-actualizing individuals show a keen *ability to discriminate between means and ends.* While they usually focus on ends rather than means, their ends are frequently what most people consider means to ends. That is, they are "somewhat more likely to appreciate for its own sake, and in an absolute way, the doing itself; they can often enjoy for its own sake the getting to some place as well as the arriving. It is occasionally possible for them to make out of the most trivial and routine activity an intrinsically enjoyable game or dance or play" (p. 545).

Maslow's subjects tend to have a *philosophical sense of humor.* Whereas the average man often enjoys humor that pokes fun at some individual's inferiority, that hurts someone, or that is "off-color" (for example, dirty jokes), the self-actualizing man finds humor dealing with the foolishness of man-in-general appealing. Their thoughtful, philosophical humor typically elicits more of a smile than a laugh.

Not surprisingly, Maslow finds that, without exception, his subjects are characterized by *creativeness.* However, the creativeness manifest by self-actualizing persons is different from unusual talent or genius. Rather, Maslow likens it to the

> . . . naïve and universal creativeness of unspoiled children. It seems to be more a fundamental characteristic of common human nature—a potentiality given to all human beings at birth. Most human beings lose this as they become enculturated, but some few individuals seem either to retain this fresh and naïve, direct way of looking at life, or if they have lost it, as most people do, they later in life recover it (p. 546).

Self-actualizing persons tend to *resist enculturation.* While outwardly, in their dress, speech, and manner of doing things, they remain within the limits of convention, they nevertheless "maintain a certain inner detachment from the culture in which they are immersed" (p. 547). Furthermore, although they are not among those in the forefront of social action, they may be committed to social change, as Maslow points out in the following example:

> One of these subjects, who was a hot rebel in his younger days, a union organizer in the days when this was a highly dangerous occupation, has given up in disgust and hopelessness. As he became resigned to the slowness of social change (in this culture and in this era) he turned finally to education of the young. All the others show what might be called a calm, long-time concern with culture improvement that seems to me to imply an acceptance of slowness of change along with the unquestioned desirability and necessity of such change (p. 548).

Finally, Maslow makes it clear that self-actualizing persons are indeed "fully functioning" in the sense that, like all men, they are not perfect:

> They too are equipped with silly, wasteful, or thoughtless habits. They can be boring, stubborn, irritating. They are by no means free from a rather superficial vanity, pride, partiality to their own productions, family, friends, and

children. Temper outbursts are not rare. Our subjects are occasionally capable of an extraordinary and unexpected ruthlessness. It must be remembered that they are very strong people. This makes it possible for them to display a surgical coldness when this is called for, beyond the power of the average man. The man who found that a long-trusted acquaintance was dishonest cut himself off from this friendship sharply and abruptly and without any pangs whatsoever. Another woman who was married to someone she did not love, when she decided on divorce, did it with a decisiveness that looked almost like ruthlessness. Some of them recover so quickly from the death of people close to them as to seem heartless (pp. 550–51).

REFERENCES

Chodorkoff, B. Self-perception, perceptual defense, and adjustment. *Journal of Abnormal and Social Psychology,* 1954, **49,** 508–12.

Eysenck. H. J. The effects of psychotherapy. In H. J. Eysenck (Ed.), *Handbook of abnormal psychology: An experimental approach.* London: Pitman Medical Publishing, 1960. Pp. 697–725.

Fiedler, F. E. A comparison of therapeutic relationships in psychoanalytic, non-directive and Adlerian therapy. *Journal of Consulting Psychology,* 1950, **14,** 436–45.

Fromm, E. *The art of loving.* New York: Bantam Books, 1963.

Gallagher, J. J. The problem of escaping clients in non-directive counseling. In W. U. Snyder (Ed.), *Group report of a program of research in psychotherapy.* Psychotherapy Research Group, Pennsylvania State University, 1953. Pp. 21–38.

Maslow, A. H. Self-actualizing people. In G. B. Levitas (Ed.), *The world of psychology.* Vol. 2. New York: George Braziller, 1963.

Rogers, C. R. A theory of therapy, personality and interpersonal relationships, as developed in the client-centered framework. In S. Koch (Ed.), *Psychology: A study of a science.* Study I. *Conceptual and systematic.* Vol. 3. *Formulations of the person and the social context.* New York: McGraw-Hill, 1959.

Rogers, C. R. *Client-centered therapy.* New York: Houghton Mifflin, 1965.

Rogers, C. R. *Counseling and psychotherapy: Newer concepts in practice.* New York: Houghton Mifflin, 1942.

Rogers, C. R., and Dymond, R. F. (Eds.) *Psychotherapy and personality change.* Chicago: University of Chicago Press, 1954.

Seeman, J. Counselor judgements of therapeutic process and outcome. In C. R. Rogers and R. F. Dymond (Eds.), *Psychotherapy and personality change.* Chicago: University of Chicago Press, 1954. Chap. 11.

Snyder, W. U. (Ed.). *Casebook of non-directive counseling.* Boston: Houghton Mifflin, 1947.

Stephenson, W. *The study of behavior.* Chicago: University of Chicago Press, 1953.

chapter 10

Learning Approaches to Personality: Classical Conditioning and Drive Reduction

Many of the theoretical positions which we have examined thus far might broadly be construed as "learning approaches" to personality in that they pay some heed to the *acquisition* or learning of the individual's behavior. Nonetheless, in a manner parallel to the distinction of a class of "motivational theories" made in Chapters 8 and 9, it can be noted that some positions have focused so sharply on the relationship of learning variables to personality as to be properly singled out as learning approaches. Each of the approaches to be discussed in the final three chapters rely heavily on basic learning principles to account for personality development and the acquisition and maintenance of behavior.

HISTORICAL ANTECEDENTS: PAVLOV AND WATSON

During the early part of the 20th century, the seeds of many strategies for psychological research were being sown. Freud's position was just earning prominence, the Gestalt school of psychology (which may be considered a grandfather of the cognitive theories which were discussed in Chapter 7) was born, and the behavioristic movement in psychology, which became the germ of modern learning theories, was announced with enthusiasm and denounced with vigor. It is this last event toward which we shall direct our attention in the present section.

In America, the predominant psychology of the day in the early 1900's was the science of conscious experience. During this period, research with animals was only on the fringes of the prevailing psychology, since it had been generally accepted (from Descartes on) that consciousness in subhuman species cannot be logically proved to exist. However, one psychologist, John Broadus Watson, inspired in part by the writings of a Russian physiologist named Ivan Pavlov, was conducting experiments with animals and humans which disavowed the importance of consciousness and paved the way for a behavioristic psychology of learning.

One of the major influences on Watson's thinking was Pavlov's concept of the *conditioned reflex* or *conditioned response*. This concept was later to become familiar to all students of psychology. In fact, as one chronicler of modern learning theory rightly points out, Pavlov ". . . discovered most of the relationships which later studies have more fully explored. The translations of his terms have become common in the literature of learning" (Hilgard, 1956, p. 51). Thus, to introduce one of the basic concepts of learning which influenced Watson and to provide a review of some of the terms which will be used throughout this chapter, our discussion of Watson's behaviorism begins with the work of Pavlov.

Pavlov's Experiments and Terminology

During the late 19th century Pavlov was investigating the digestive processes of dogs. He found, however, that the results of his studies of the flow of digestive juices were often disrupted by a then unexpected phenomenon which was to become one of the cornerstones of the psychology of learning. Specifically, the dogs often appeared to anticipate the food (meat powder), which Pavlov used to induce salivation, even *before* the salivary flow had been directly stimulated. Pavlov's initial reactions to these "psychic secretions"[1] were that they were a nuisance which should be eliminated.

However, upon further consideration, Pavlov decided to study the phenomenon on which he had accidentally chanced, rather than simply seeking ways to eliminate it. His first approach was introspective, involving an effort to imagine the situation from the dog's point of view. This strategy proved to lead to blind alleys (his assistants could not agree on what the dog ought to think or feel) rather than to objective results and was subsequently banned from Pavlov's laboratory (Hyman, 1964). Turning next to a more objective and verifiable approach, Pavlov reasoned that since the salivation occurred with some regularity as he began

[1] The term is Pavlov's.

each experiment, the animal's natural or reflexive tendency to respond to the meat powder in its mouth with salivation had somehow also come to be evoked by the mere sight of this food. This latter reaction was not an innate one. It had to be *conditioned* or acquired by environmental events which were potentially under experimental control. Following from this reasoning, Pavlov began to investigate the manner in which such conditioned responses are formed. He successfully taught dogs to salivate to an impressive variety of signals, including a rotating disk, the sound of a metronome, and the presentation of a light. He also discovered a great deal about how such responses are formed, modified, and *extinguished* (became less likely to occur) with the passage of time.

The experiments conducted by Pavlov followed a paradigm now referred to as *classical conditioning.* The order of events in a typical classical conditioning experiment is as follows.[2] First, a *conditioned stimulus* (CS) is presented, which does not initially produce (*elicit*) a reliable response. In many of Pavlov's experiments a light was used for this purpose. Very shortly thereafter (a fraction of a second to no more than a few seconds), a stimulus known to reflexively produce a certain response is introduced. This stimulus is referred to as the *unconditioned stimulus* (UCS), and the response which it produces is the *unconditioned response* (UCR). In many of Pavlov's famous experiments, the meat powder served as the UCS and salivary flow was the UCR. Upon repeated presentations of the CS and UCS (each presentation being referred to as a *trial*), the CS (light) alone began to produce salivary flow even before the UCS was presented. The salivary flow in this latter condition, which is not necessarily identical to the flow produced by the meat powder, is referred to as the *conditioned response* (CR). The entire process appeared to be an extremely simple and objective way to study the process of learning.

Pavlov's research revealed that a CR is not only developed through the association of the CS and the UCS but that it also must be maintained by occasional trials in which this association is again presented. When the CS is paired with the UCS on a particular trial, the arrangement is known as *reinforcement.* Although an established CS will continue to produce the CR for a while, if the UCS is absent for a number of trials (i.e., is not reinforced), the CR is likely to weaken or disappear completely. Both the failure to provide reinforcement and the actual diminution of responding have been referred to as *extinction.*

The form of conditioning described above would have limited meaning for our understanding of either human or nonhuman animal behavior

---

[2] While this order is the most effective one for showing a conditioning effect, others have been the subject of experimentation (for example, *trace conditioning* involves the termination of the CS before the UCS is presented), but discussion of them is generally beyond the intended scope of this book.

if the exact CS used in training were required to produce the CR at a later time. However, both Pavlov's research and a great deal of research which has been subsequently performed clearly show that this restriction usually does not hold. Instead, when a CR to one previously neutral stimulus has been developed, stimuli which are similar to (but not identical with) the original CS may also evoke the response. Additionally, the greater the similarity between the new stimulus and the original stimulus, the greater will be the degree to which the latter can be substituted for the former. This basic phenomenon is known as *generalization,* and the relationship between a stimulus' similarity to the original CS and its ability to elicit the CR is known as the *generalization gradient.* As we shall see, the concept of generalization has often been invoked in an effort to understand and predict complex human behavior in novel situations, in accordance with the situation's similarity to familiar ones.

There is another phenomenon, *discrimination,* which may be thought of as the "other side of the coin" to generalization. That is, if the experimental situation is correctly arranged, the subject will learn to respond only to a particular stimulus and not to others that are similar to it. One of Pavlov's most intriguing experiments illustrates how this may occur. The basic procedure was to always reinforce one CS, a luminous circle, but never to reinforce an ellipse with an axes ratio of 2:1. This discrimination was easily formed, so that the dog salivated when the circle was presented but not when the ellipse was presented. Pavlov then proceeded to make the ellipse increasingly more like a circle (less cigar-shaped and more round), and the dog responded remarkably well, up to a point. Finally, however, the two stimuli appeared to become so similar that the dog could no longer make the discrimination (a ratio of 9:8).

> After three weeks of work upon this differentiation not only did the discrimination fail to improve, but it became considerably worse, and finally disappeared altogether. At the same time the whole behaviour of the animal underwent an abrupt change. The hitherto quiet dog began to squeal in its stand, kept wriggling about, tore off with its teeth the apparatus for mechanical stimulation of the skin, and bit through the tubes connecting the animal's room with the observer, a behaviour which never happened before. On being taken to the experimental room the dog now barked violently, which was also contrary to its usual custom; in short it presented all the symptoms of a condition of acute neurosis. On testing the cruder differentiations they were also found to be destroyed . . . (Pavlov, 1927, p. 291).

In addition to demonstrating how discriminations may be developed, the later phases of the above experiment appear to have numerous implications for human behavior, some of which have been noted or followed up experimentally by contemporary investigators. For example, it has been suggested that over-aspiring parents, who push their children too hard for good grades or other deeds of superlative accomplishment, may produce difficulties analogous to the problem encountered by Pavlov's dog.

In the foregoing discussion, we have described the basic principles of classical conditioning and implied that they may be extended to some aspects of human behavior. John Watson was perhaps the first psychologist to take this possibility seriously. An experiment on the conditioned emotional reactions of a young child, discussed in the next section, is one of Watson's most widely cited studies.

Watson's Strategy

Familiar with Pavlov's work and seeing many of its implications, Watson felt that animal psychologists were not only engaged in scientific research but that they were paving the way for the future of psychology. In contrast to the *structuralist* school of psychology, so named because it sought to discover the structure of the mind or consciousness, Watson founded American *behaviorism,* which declared that psychology was the science of behavior. A few excerpts from Watson's first book (*Behavior* [1914]) will give the flavor of behaviorism as its founder saw it. The arguments clearly reflect Pavlov's influence.

> Psychology as the behaviorist views it is a purely objective experimental branch of natural science. Its theoretical goal is the prediction and control of behavior. . . . The behaviorist attempts to get a unitary scheme of animal response. He recognizes no dividing line between man and brute. The behavior of man, with all of its refinements and complexity, forms only a part of his total field of investigation. . . . It is possible to write a psychology, to define it as . . . the "science of behavior" . . . and never go back upon the definition: never to use the terms consciousness, mental states, mind, content, will, imagery, and the like. . . . Certain stimuli lead . . . organisms to make . . . responses. In a system of psychology completely worked out, given the responses the stimuli can be predicted; given the stimuli the responses can be predicted (pp. 1, 9, 10).

Watson's behaviorism was well received by American psychologists, who elected him by a plurality vote as president of the American Psychological Association for the year 1915.

Most of Watson's experimental work focused on simple motor mechanisms, reflexes, and the influence of controlled environmental stimulation upon relatively simple bits of behavior. He did believe, however, that in the long run similar experimental analyses would be possible for the broader study of personality. Watson (1919) rejected "the muddled writings . . . from the hands of many writers upon self, personality and character," referring to those who found it necessary "to bring into account for self and personality . . . a nucleus, a core, or essence which . . . cannot be expressed in the plain facts of heredity and acquired reactions and their integrations" (p. 396). He eschewed rapid methods of studying personality and stressed the importance of a detailed and thorough analysis of the individual's observable behavior which begins with "discarding of presuppositions." Although he suggested such methods as detailed questioning and systematic naturalistic observation, he favored studying an individual's personality through experimental methods in the laboratory. This last strategy is illustrated by the now famous case of "little Albert," which was published in 1920 by Watson and Rayner.

Albert, an 11-month-old apathetic child, appeared to be afraid of nothing except the loud sound made by striking a steel bar. In order to induce a fear in Albert, Watson and Rayner placed a white rat in front of him and at the same time produced the loud sound he disliked. After a series of seven such presentations, the rat, which had not previously elicited fear in Albert, came to elicit a fear or avoidance reaction (for example, crying, attempts to escape from the situation, and so on). Additionally, the results of presenting Albert with other objects appeared to suggest that the fear generalized on a dimension of similarity to the rat. That is, Albert showed fear of other objects that were similar to the rat in various dimensions of appearance.[3] Watson and Rayner had intended to extinguish the fear which they had produced, but Albert was removed from the laboratory before these efforts could be made.

However, there is, in effect, a sequel to the case of little Albert. Three years later Mary Cover Jones (1924), "with the advice of Dr. John B. Watson," successfully treated a child's fear. Jones's subject, Peter, who "seemed almost to be Albert grown a bit older," came to the laboratory already afraid of white rats and other furry objects. Peter's fear, when

---

[3] Most citations of this report consider the experiment a "classic" demonstration of generalization or spread of a learned fear of an object to other, similar objects (cf. most introductory psychology textbooks), and Watson and Rayner may have perceived the results that way. Nevertheless, generalization to furry inanimate objects was weak, as the following passage from Watson and Rayner's report indicates: "When his hand was laid on the wool he immediately withdrew it but did not show the shock that the animals produced. . . . He finally . . . lost some of the negativism to the wool" (p. 7). His newly acquired fear of hair, which has frequently been taken as evidence of generalization, is difficult to interpret. On the one hand, the following incident is reported: "Just in play W. put his head down to see if Albert would play with his hair. Albert was completely negative" (p. 7). On the other hand, ". . . two other observers did the same thing. He began immediately to play with their hair" (p. 7). Finally, to show that the fear had not transferred to completely unratlike objects in the situation, Albert was retested on *his own blocks*. Not surprisingly, he had not come to fear these. A child's own blocks, though admittedly unratlike, may be presumed to have strong positive associations. Thus, his failure to fear them hardly constitutes convincing proof that the acquired fear had not extended to all previously neutral objects in the situation. (The authors are indebted to Mr. Daniel L. Cowart for observing that the case of little Albert may be "a myth in the making.")

2 years and 10 months of age, was quite severe: "Peter was put in a crib in a play room and immediately became absorbed in his toys. A white rat was introduced into the crib from behind. . . . At sight of the rat, Peter screamed and fell flat on his back in a paroxysm of fear . . ." (p. 309).

Peter was even more afraid of a rabbit, and thus Jones decided to focus on reducing fear of it. Jones's goals for the experiment were (1) to develop procedures for extinguishing the fear and (2) to determine whether such procedures invoked for one feared object would generalize to other feared objects which had not been directly involved in the treatment. The first procedure employed was to expose Peter to fearless, peer models, during a daily play period in the laboratory. During these sessions Peter played with three other children, selected because they had a fearless attitude toward furry rodents and appeared in all other respects to show satisfactory adjustment. A rabbit was merely present during a part of each play period. Peter's progress was regularly assessed by exposing him to the rabbit from time to time in the absence of his playmates. Jones noted impressive improvement "by more or less regular steps from almost complete terror at sight of the rabbit to a completely positive response with no signs of disturbance" (p. 310). Unfortunately, after seven periods of treatment, and before tests of generalization had begun, Peter contracted scarlet fever and was taken to the hospital for two months. When he came back to the laboratory, most of his earlier fear had returned. A nurse reported an incident which may have contributed to the apparent relapse.

> As they were entering a taxi at the door of the hospital, a large dog, running past, jumped at them. Both Peter and the nurse were very much frightened, Peter so much that he lay back in the taxi pale and quiet. . . . This seemed reason enough for his precipitate descent back to the original fear level. Being threatened by a large dog when ill, and in a strange place and being with an adult who also showed fear, was a terrifying situation against which our training could not have fortified him (p. 312).

This setback had one advantage, however. It permitted Jones to examine the efficacy of a more elaborate treatment which involved both exposure to a fearless peer (which now is called modeling and will be discussed more fully in Chapter 12) and counterconditioning. A session of this procedure began with Peter seated in a high chair eating some food which he liked. The caged rabbit was then brought as close as possible to Peter without interfering with his eating. The procedure was completed with the simultaneous exposure to peer models, as indicated from Jones's laboratory notes.

> Lawrence and Peter sitting near together in their high chairs eating candy. Rabbit in cage put down 12 feet away. Peter began to cry. Lawrence said, "Oh, rabbit." Clambered down, ran over and looked in the cage at him. Peter followed close and watched.

Peter with candy in high chair. Experimenter brought rabbit and sat down in front of the tray with it. Peter cried out, "I don't want him," and withdrew. Rabbit was given to another child sitting near to hold. His holding the rabbit served as a powerful suggestion; Peter wanted the rabbit on his lap, and held it for an instant (p. 313).

Recall that one of Jones's interests was to determine whether the experimental treatments would generalize to other furry objects. Her final description of Peter suggests that this goal was met.

He showed in the last interview . . . a genuine fondness for the rabbit. What has happened to the fear of the other objects? The fear of the cotton, the fur coat, feathers, was entirely absent at our last interview. He looked at them, handled them, and immediately turned to something which interested him more. The reaction to the rats and the fur rug with the stuffed head was greatly modified and improved. While he did not show the fondness for these that was apparent with the rabbit, he had made a fair adjustment. For example, Peter would pick up the tin box containing the frogs or rats and carry it around the room. When requested, he picked up the fur rug and carried it to the experimenter.

What would Peter do if confronted by a strange animal? At the last interview the experimenter presented a mouse and a tangled mass of angle-worms. At first sight, Peter showed slight distress reactions and moved away, but before the period was over he was carrying the worms about and watching the mouse with undisturbed interest. By "unconditioning" Peter to the rabbit, he has apparently been helped to overcome many superfluous fears, some completely, some to a less degree. His tolerance of strange animals and unfamiliar situations has apparently increased (p. 314).

It would not be until many years later that procedures (and results) such as those reported by Jones found their way into the mainstream of personality research. However, the experiments of Watson and Rayner (1920) and Jones (1924), and the strategy which underlay them, were destined to have an enormous impact on psychology, and the early behavioristic work which Pavlov and Watson inspired was the forerunner of several of today's behavioristic positions.

One historical account (Woodworth and Sheehan, 1964) has distinguished between Watson and his colleagues and the "later behaviorists," arguing that the division "is justified by the fact that behaviorism had something like a new birth about 1930, with new names coming into view and new forms of behaviorism emerging" (p. 133). It is to three of these later developments that we shall next turn our attention. The first point of research which we shall consider has explored more fully the application of classical conditioning to human behavior. The second has introduced the concept of drive reduction within a behavioristic framework, and the third has focused on the effects of reward on behavior. The following sections discuss, in turn, the nature of these viewpoints, the research they have inspired, and their historical and contemporary relationships to each other.

CLASSICAL CONDITIONING AND COMPLEX BEHAVIOR

Since the time of Pavlov's work and Watson's pioneering experiments, the possibility that a process of classical conditioning is responsible for the development of human social behavior has been explored in a variety of settings. The studies here focused on a number of different aspects of personality. In order to illustrate this research, four examples will be presented. The first concerns the classical conditioning of attitudes; the second concerns conditioning techniques for control of bodily functions; the third involves the possible development of one psychosomatic symptom (asthma attacks) through such conditioning; and the fourth illustrates how a derivative of the classical conditioning paradigm has been employed extensively as a therapeutic tool.

The Classical Conditioning of Attitudes

There are a great variety of social stimuli which elicit evaluative responses from humans. Each of us reacts to the names of certain subgroups, such as Jews, blacks, intellectuals, and many others with an evaluative reaction or *attitude.* We may also show such reactions to proper names. In extreme cases, attitudes may even develop toward articles of clothing, as illustrated by Bandura in the following citation from a metropolitan newspaper.

> Dear Abby:
> My friend fixed me up with a blind date and I should have known the minute he showed up in a bow tie that he couldn't be trusted. I fell for him like a rock. He got me to love him on purpose and then lied to me and cheated on me. Every time I go with a man who wears a bow tie, the same thing happens. I think girls should be warned about men who wear them. (Cited in Bandura, 1968, pp. 306–7.)

Considering anecdotal examples such as the one above, together with the voluminous amount of research that has shown the power of classical conditioning, it is tempting to hypothesize that many attitudes have been produced by a process of association. In fact, research with humans suggests that this may be the case.

A relatively early pair of studies by Razran (1938; 1940) were designed to test the hypothesis that responses which are commonly referred to as attitudes could be modified by association with pleasant or unpleasant stimuli. In one of Razran's studies (1938), 100 judges (whose composition was distributed to correspond to the U.S. adult population in racial and national background, religion, and education) rated photographs of 30 college girls as to their beauty, intelligence, character, entertainingness, ambition, and the degree to which they would be generally liked. Two weeks later the judges were asked to rate the photographs of the girls for a second time but were ostensibly told the names of the girls. Fifteen of the names corresponded to ethnic minorities—five Jewish, five Irish, and five Italian—while the remaining fifteen surnames were chosen from the Social Register and signers of the Declaration of Independence. Liking for the photographs of those with minority group names decreased, as did evaluations of their character and beauty. Among other changes observed, assignment of Jewish names produced an increase in the intelligence and ambition ratings, while the Irish- and Italian-named photographs showed decrements in the intelligence ratings. These biases largely disappeared, however, when the names were presented together with a stimulus which was known to elicit a positive experience. Specifically, Razran employed simple stimulus-pairing which he referred to as the "luncheon technique." The procedure involved representing the items again while the judges were given a free lunch, thereby presumably conditioning the names to the positive experience of eating.

In another study, Razran (1940) had college students and unemployed workers rate a variety of sociopolitical slogans, such as "Workers of the World Unite!" and "No Other Ism but Americanism!" on a scale which measured their personal approval of the slogans and the social effectiveness and literary value of each. The slogans were next divided into two sets. Again employing the luncheon technique, one set was repeated for several sessions while the subjects were enjoying a free lunch. The second set, however, was presented as the subjects were required to inhale a number of putrid odors. Nonexperimental slogans were also presented at various times to make conscious recall of the associations more difficult. When Razran readministered the original test of evaluation of the slogans, he found that those associated with the free lunch clearly showed increases in their favorableness, while those associated with the unpleasant odors showed rating decreases. The evidence also suggested that these findings reflected more than mere conscious recall or an effort to please the experimenter, as disclosed by Razran's report that ". . . the subjects' knowledge of which slogans were combined with pleasant, and which with unpleasant, stimuli was little above chance" (1940, p. 481). The luncheon technique may be applied in a variety of practical settings. It is interesting, for example, that many businessmen favor the practice of finalizing negotiations over a pleasant meal.

More recent studies, which have included sophisticated control procedures, have provided additional support for the contention that conditioning may influence attitudes. An interesting example of this line of investigation is a pair of experiments by Staats and Staats (1958).

These studies were designed to test the hypothesis that attitudes elicited by socially significant stimuli could be changed through classical conditioning when other words are used as the unconditioned stimuli. In their first experiment the CS words were national names. Two of these, *Swedish* and *Dutch,* were paired with UCS words already known to elicit either positive (such as *gift, sacred, happy*) or negative (such as *bitter, ugly, failure*) meaning. As seen in Table 10–1, one group of subjects (Group 1) had *positive* words associated with Dutch and *negative* words with Swedish, whereas for the second group (Group 2) the reverse was true. This procedure is known as *counterbalancing* and provides a control for differences in initial attitudes.

The ostensible purpose of the experiment, as presented to the college students who served as subjects, was to determine how auditory and visual learning take place together. Thus, as each CS word was presented on a slide, the experimenter pronounced one of the words which served as the UCS. The subjects were further instructed that they could learn the CS words by merely looking at them and that they should, at the same time, pronounce the auditorily presented words both aloud and to themselves. In order to avoid associations between the names and particular evaluative words, 108 different UCS words were used, and no pairing occurred more than once. Next, Staats and Staats told the subjects that they were interested in seeing how many of the visually presented words were remembered and how they *felt* about each. The latter rating was on a 7-point scale ranging from pleasant to unpleasant.

In their second experiment, the procedures were identical except that proper male names were used as the CS's with *Tom* and *Bill* being the names for which evaluative associations were conditioned. The findings in both experiments, presented in Table 10–1, clearly indicate that the expected conditioning effect occurred since, *within each group,* the negatively conditioned name was rated as the more unpleasant one.

TABLE 10–1

Mean Conditioned Attitude Scores from the Two Experiments Reported by Staats and Staats

		Names	
Experiment	*Group*	*Dutch*	*Swedish*
I	1	2.67(+)*	3.42(−)†
	2	2.67(−)	1.83(+)
		Tom	*Bill*
II	1	2.71(+)	4.12(−)
	2	3.42(−)	1.79(+)

Note: On the scales, pleasant is 1, unpleasant 7.
* Experimentally conditioned to positive words.
† Experimentally conditioned to negative words.
Source: Adapted from Staats and Staats, 1958.

Use of Classical Conditioning Techniques to Control Bodily Functions

Recall (Chapter 3) that the natural functions of urination and defecation were considered by Freud to have considerable psychological significance. Even if one does not grant that these processes have all the intrapsychic meaning which Freud attributed to them, it is clear that the successful and regular control of the bladder and bowels is necessary for the individual's comfort and health. Moreover, it is sometimes the case that children find it difficult to gain control over both of these functions, and constipation, even in adults, is one of the most widespread functional disorders known to contemporary medicine (Quarti and Renaud, 1964). For these reasons, applied studies of the control of bodily elimination through classical conditioning serve as particularly important examples of the application of the paradigm to human behavior.

Enuresis. An early study (Mowrer and Mowrer, 1938) illustrates the application of classical conditioning to the problem of bed-wetting, technically referred to as *enuresis*, as applied to 30 children between the ages of 3 and 13.[4] The difficulty of the enuretic child, viewed in learning terms, is that the child has not learned to awaken before urination occurs. In other words, for bed-wetting children, the internal stimulation of bladder tension does not produce the necessary response of sleep termination. The strategy adopted by Mowrer and Mowrer to establish the necessary response was to ingeniously pair the bladder stimulation (CS) with the ringing of a bell (UCS), a stimulus which would inevitably awaken the child (UCR) and permit him to reach the toilet in time. The subjects slept on a specially prepared pad, consisting of two pieces of bronze screening separated by heavy cotton fabric. When urination occurred, it seeped through the fabric and closed an electrical circuit which, in turn, sounded a bell. Through such repeated pairings, the bladder tension alone was able to awaken the child before urination occurred. Bed-wetting was eliminated in all 30 cases, with the maximum period of treatment being two months. Although the Mowrers noted that no severly neurotic or psychotic children were included in the experiment, one of their subjects had an IQ of only 65. He, too, responded satisfactorily. Further, they reported that:

> Personality changes, when they occurred as a result of the application of the present method of treating enuresis, have uniformly been in a favorable direction. In no case has there been any evidence of "symptom substitution." Our results, therefore, do not support the assumption, sometimes made, that any attempt to deal directly with the problem of enuresis will necessarily result in the child's developing "something worse" (1938, p. 451).

---

[4] The treatment is specifically *not* recommended for children under three.

Thus, the Mowrers' report may be considered a major demonstration of the potential role of classical conditioning in dealing with a decidedly practical problem.

Constipation. Also employing a conditioning model, a treatment of constipation has been developed by Quarti and Renaud (1964). It is based on the fact that defecation is stimulated by the massage of the pelvi-rectal flecture—the section of the large colon immediately adjacent to the rectal passage. Thus, stimulation constitutes the UCS for defecation, and the treatment depends upon associating it with a convenient CS. For this purpose, Quarti and Renaud devised a special belt, pictured in Figure 10–1, which permits administration of a very mild electric shock to the spinal area. The level of shock used is so mild as to be described by the investigators as "pleasant." The specific treatment, which is self-administered, proceeds as follows:

The subject to be re-educated continues to take his usual laxatives so as to produce one bowel movement per day. As he goes to the toilet he puts on the apparatus, starts operating it prior to defecation and stops the electric stimulation as soon as evacuation is terminated. . . . Gradually the subject should reduce the quantity of laxatives until he will no longer take any. . . . Once conditioning has been established, which generally happens after 20 to 30 applications, the electrical stimulation alone produces defecation according to the individual rhythm of digestion (Quarti and Renaud, 1964, p. 224).

Figure 10–1

Apparatus Used for Treatment of Constipation through Classical Conditioning

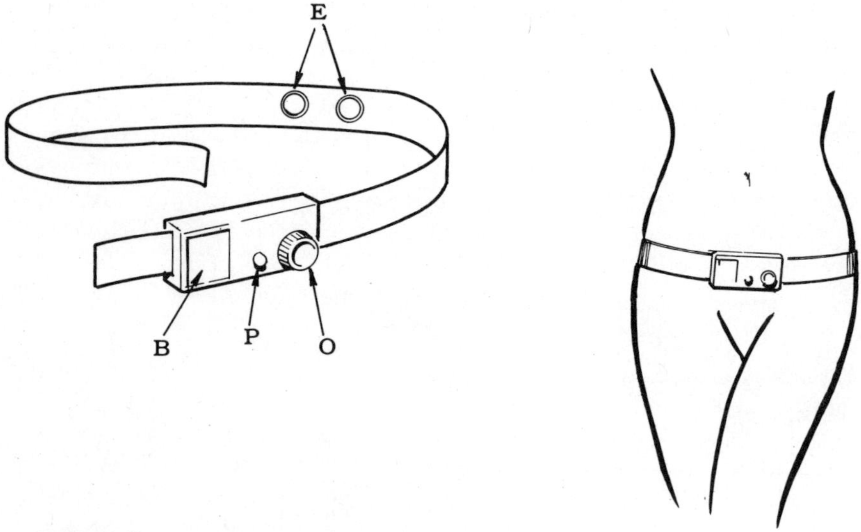

E: Electrodes.
O: On-off switch and intensity control.
P: Pilot.
B: Battery compartment.
Source: Quarti and Renaud, 1964.

As a final step in Quarti and Renaud's procedure, the subject begins to go to the toilet every day at a given hour, usually immediately after breakfast. Thus, according to these investigators, the chosen hour eventually becomes the CS, and the apparatus itself becomes unnecessary. The three cases in which the procedure was reported to have been tried were all successfully treated.

Classical Conditioning and Emotional Reactions

An individual's behavior is often labeled deviant by society when he responds to stimuli which most people find innocuous with an intense emotional reaction. Disorders such as anxiety reactions, insomnia, and a variety of somatic or "nervous" complaints probably fall into this category. Laboratory studies of asthma have suggested, for example, that this disorder may be produced through *aversive classical conditioning* (i.e., the pairing of a neutral stimulus and one that elicits an unpleasant or aversive response). Consider a study by Dekker, Pelser, and Groen (1957), which included two subjects who suffered from severe bronchial asthma. The patients repeatedly inhaled an allergen (UCS) to which they were highly sensitive, and which produced an automatic asthmatic attack (UCR). Whereas the neutral solvent (CS) in which these allergens were dissolved did not initially produce any asthmatic symptoms, after repeated trials it came to elicit attacks of asthma (CR). Moreover, it was later demonstrated that inhaling pure oxygen and even the presence of the inhalation mouthpiece (both of which, of course, could not have initially produced any reaction) were now able to provoke severe attacks of asthma that could not be distinguished from those which were produced by the allergen itself.

Also consistent with a conditioning explanation of asthma, Dekker and Groen (1956) have reported that asthma patients, when encouraged to talk freely about the cause of their attacks, list a variety of causitive factors including the sight of dust, watching someone else swallow an aspirin, knitting, and sunshine. Such stimuli also elicit actual asthma attacks in the laboratory for some patients. For example, Dekker and Groen (1956) report the case of Patient L.

> Patient L had told us that she got an asthmatic attack from looking at a goldfish. After a base line had been obtained, a goldfish in a bowl was brought into the room. . . . Under our eyes she developed a severe asthmatic attack with loud wheezing, followed by a gradual remission after the goldfish had been taken from the room. During the next experiment the goldfish was replaced by a plastic toy which was easily recognized as such . . . but a fierce attack resulted. . . . Upon this she told the investigator the following dream, which she had had after the preceding investigation.
>
> In her home stood a big goldfish bowl. On a shelf high up near the window were her books. In one of them she wanted to read why goldfishes cause

asthma. She climbed on a chair and reached for the book, but it was too high. She lost her balance and fell into the goldfish bowl. She gasped for breath behind the glass. The fishes swam around her. Her neck was caught in a streak of water weed. She awoke with an attack of asthma. She also remembered suddenly how when she was a child her mother threw away her bowl of goldfish, which she loved so much. The patient had saved her pocket-money to buy them. Mother threw the fishes into the water closet and flushed them through (p. 62).

The investigators were largely unsuccessful in their efforts to treat their asthmatic patients with traditional methods of psychotherapy and called for the development of ". . . a more specific deconditioning therapy that makes the conditioning disappear in the same way in which it came" (Dekker *et al.*, 1957, p. 107). Such a therapeutic technique has been developed by Joseph Wolpe.

Systematic Desensitization

Wolpe, a South African born physician and psychologist who is now at Temple University, believes that many forms of maladaptive behavior are nothing more or less than persistent, learned habits. For Wolpe, anxiety is an inappropriate fear response to situations and events that carry no objective threat to the individual, and it plays a central role in the development and maintenance of neurosis (cf. Freud). Wolpe posits that anxiety is learned by classical conditioning. Specifically, a neutral cue (CS), which is present at the same time that another stimulus (UCS) elicits a fear or anxiety response (UCR), comes to elicit a similar response (CR) on future occasions. Wolpe illustrates this learning paradigm with the following prototypic example.

The child places his hand on the big, black, hot coal stove. He quickly withdraws the painful hand, tearful and fearful. His mother comforts him, but later notes that he keeps away from the stove and seems afraid of it. Clearly, the child has developed a beneficial habit of fearing and avoiding an actually harmful object.

But in some cases the experience also had another and less favorable consequence. Suppose in the mother's bedroom there is a large black chest of drawers. The child may have become afraid of this too—purely on the basis of its *physical resemblance* to the stove—a phenomenon known in psychology as generalization. Fear of the chest of drawers is neurotic because there can be no harm in touching it. It can have several undesirable implications. In the first place, the very presence of an unpleasant emotion like fear is objectionable where it is not appropriate. Secondly, the child is now forced to make a detour if the chest of drawers is in his path; and thirdly, he no longer has easy access to any delectable contents of the drawers, such as candy. In these features of this child's case, we have the model of all neurotic fear reactions (Wolpe and Lazarus, 1966, pp. 17–18).

Wolpe (1958) has developed a technique for alleviating anxiety, called *systematic desensitization,* which is based on the *principle of reciprocal inhibition:* "If a response antagonistic to anxiety can be made to occur in the presence of anxiety-evoking stimuli so that it is accompanied by a complete or partial suppression of the anxiety responses, the bond between these stimuli and the anxiety responses will be weakened" (p. 71). Perhaps the first recorded use of the principle of reciprocal inhibition was in Jones's (1924) attempt to eliminate Peter's fear of rabbits, which we had occasion to discuss earlier. Recall that one of the techniques Jones employed began with Peter eating a food which he liked. Then the feared stimulus (a caged rabbit) was gradually brought closer and closer to Peter, without interfering with his eating. In this case, the eating response was antagonistic to the anxiety response.

The technique of systematic desensitization involves three sets of operations, two of which are preliminary steps. First, the anxious individual must be taught a response which is antagonistic to the response of anxiety. Second, specific details of his anxiety must be assessed and an *anxiety hierarchy* must be constructed. Once these preliminary procedures have been completed, the actual systematic desensitization can be implemented. This involves the repeated pairing of the response which is antagonistic to anxiety with anxiety-evoking stimuli. Each of these operations will be illustrated in the following sections.

Deep Muscle Relaxation. Although a variety of responses have been used to oppose the anxiety response (for example, assertive and sexual responses), the response most frequently employed as an antagonist to anxiety is deep muscle relaxation. The physiological concomitants of anxiety (increased heart rate, perspiring, shaking, and so on) are, for the most part, incompatable with a state of deep muscle relaxation. Thus, we never hear someone report that they are both nervous (anxious) and relaxed at the same time.

Relaxation training involves a systematic relaxation of the various skeletal muscle groups (arms, head, neck and shoulders, trunk, hips, and legs). While the specific instructions vary with the particular muscles being relaxed, an excerpt from Wolpe's instructions for relaxation of the arms will serve to illustrate the basic procedure. The subject sits in a comfortable armchair (reclining lounge chairs are often used) with his eyes closed and is given instructions such as the following:

> Settle back as comfortably as you can. Let yourself relax to the best of your ability. . . . Now, as you relax like that, clench your right fist, just clench your fist tighter and tighter, and study the tension as you do so. Keep it clenched and feel the tension in your right fist, hand, forearm . . . and now relax. Let the fingers of your right hand become loose, and observe the contrast in your feelings. . . . Now, let yourself go and try to become more relaxed all over. . . . Once more, clench your right fist really tight . . . hold it, and notice the

tension again. . . . Now let go, relax; your fingers straighten out, and you notice the difference once more. . . . Now repeat that with your left fist. Clench your left fist while the rest of your body relaxes; clench that fist tighter and feel the tension . . . and now relax. Again enjoy the contrast. . . . Repeat that once more, clench the left fist, tight and tense. . . . Now do the opposite of tension—relax and feel the difference. Continue relaxing like that for a while. . . . Clench both fists tighter and tighter, both fists tense, forearms tense, study the sensations . . . and relax; straighten out your fingers and feel that relaxation. Continue relaxing your hands and forearms more and more. . . . Now bend your elbows and tense your biceps, tense them harder and study the tension feelings . . . all right, straighten out your arms, let them relax and feel that difference again. Let the relaxation develop. . . . Once more, tense your biceps; hold the tension and observe it carefully. . . . Straighten the arms and relax; relax to the best of your ability. . . . Each time, pay close attention to your feelings when you tense up and when you relax. Now straighten your arms, straighten them so that you feel most tension in the triceps muscles along the back of your arms; stretch your arms and feel that tension. . . . And now relax. Get your arms back into a comfortable position. Let the relaxation proceed on its own. The arms should feel comfortably heavy as you allow them to relax. . . . Straighten the arms once more so that you feel the tension in the triceps muscles; straighten them. Feel that tension . . . and relax. Now let's concentrate on pure relaxation in the arms without any tension. Get your arms comfortable and let them relax further and further. Even when your arms seem fully relaxed, try to go that extra bit further; try to achieve deeper and deeper levels of relaxation (Wolpe and Lazarus, 1966, p. 177).

The number of sessions needed to teach deep muscle relaxation varies from individual to individual, but on the average less than a half-dozen sessions are required if the subject practices the technique for a short time each day at home.

Construction of Anxiety Hierarchies. In order to treat anxiety by systematic desensitization, a detailed and highly specific accounting must be made of those stimuli which elicit anxiety responses. Sometimes a person will come to a therapist with a well-defined fear of a particular class of stimuli or stimulus situations, such as fear of snakes or of going to the dentist. More often, however, people feel anxious at various times but are not aware of the stimulus conditions which precipitate the feeling. In such cases it is the therapist's task to discover, by detailed questioning, the situations which cause anxiety.

When the stimuli which elicit anxiety have been enumerated, they are categorized in terms of common *themes* (for example, relating to fear of being alone or relating to fear of high places). Within each theme, the stimuli are ordered in terms of the amount of anxiety they evoke in the individual. Examples of such *anxiety hierarchies* are presented in Table 10–2. The ranking of anxiety-evoking situations is a highly individual matter. For example, as is apparent from the "examination hierarchy" in Table 10–2, the same scenes might be ordered differently by another person. Exploration of the nature of the person's anxiety and construction of anxiety hierarchies is usually done concurrently with relaxation training.

TABLE 10–2

Examples of Anxiety Hierarchies

Examination series

1. On the way to the university on the day of an examination.
2. In the process of answering an examination paper.
3. Before the unopened doors of the examination room.
4. Awaiting the distribution of examination papers.
5. The examination paper lies face down before her.
6. The night before an examination.
7. On the day before an examination.
8. Two days before an examination.
9. Three days before an examination.
10. Four days before an examination.
11. Five days before an examination.
12. A week before an examination.
13. Two weeks before an examination.
14. A month before an examination.

Discord between other people

1. Her mother shouts at a servant.
2. Her young sister whines to her mother.
3. Her sister engages in a dispute with her father.
4. Her mother shouts at her sister.
5. She sees two strangers quarrel.

Source: Wolpe and Lazarus, 1966.

Implementation. Relaxation training and construction of appropriate anxiety hierarchies are the prerequisites for the actual procedure of desensitizing the stimuli associated with anxiety. In the desensitization procedure, the subject is instructed to relax his muscles, and he is then asked to *visualize* scenes from his anxiety hierarchy, starting with the least anxiety-provoking situation (i.e., the lowest item on each anxiety hierarchy). After each scene has been imagined for a short time, the subject is instructed to "erase" the scene from his mind and continue just relaxing. He is then asked to signal the therapist if he has felt any anxiety while visualizing the scene. Each scene is repeated, before going on to the next highest scene in the hierarchy, until the subject reports that he experiences no disturbance while visualizing it.

To illustrate the desensitization procedure, a verbatim account of the presentation of scenes during an initial desensitization session is presented below. The subject was a 24-year-old female art student who requested treatment of examination anxiety which had caused her to fail a number of tests. In the course of discussing her anxiety with the therapist, it was discovered that there were also other stimulus situations which made her anxious. Thus, four different anxiety hierarchies were constructed, two of which appear in Table 10–2 (page 291). The first scene that she is asked to visualize is a neutral or control scene (i.e., one that is not expected to elicit anxiety). The next two scenes are the lowest items on their respective anxiety hierarchies (see Table 10–2).[5]

I am now going to ask you to imagine a number of scenes. You will imagine them clearly and they will generally interfere little, if at all, with your state of relaxation. If, however, at any time you feel disturbed or worried and want to attract my attention, you will be able to do so by raising your left index finger. First I want you to imagine that you are standing at a familiar street corner on a pleasant morning watching the traffic go by. You see cars, motorcycles, trucks, bicycles, people and traffic lights; and you can hear the sounds associated with all these things. (*Pause of about 15 sec.*) Now stop imagining that scene and give all your attention once again to relaxing. If the scene you imagined disturbed you even in the slightest degree I want you to raise your left index finger *now*. (*Patient does not raise finger.*) Now imagine that you are at home studying in the evening. It is the 20th of May, exactly a month before your examination. (*Pause of 5 sec.*) Now stop imagining the scene. Go on relaxing. (*Pause of 10 sec.*) Now imagine the same scene again—a month before your examination. (*Pause of 5 sec.*) Stop imagining the scene and just think of your muscles. Let go, and enjoy your state of calm. (*Pause of 15 sec.*) Now again imagine that you are studying at home a month before your examination. (*Pause of 5 sec.*) Stop the scene, and now think of nothing but your own body. (*Pause of 5 sec.*) If you felt any disturbance whatsoever to the last scene raise your left index finger now. (*Patient raises finger.*) If the amount of disturbance decreased from the first presentation to the third do nothing, otherwise again raise your finger. (*Patient does not raise finger.*) Just keep on relaxing. (*Pause of 15 sec.*) Imagine that you are sitting on a bench at a bus stop and across the road are two strange men whose voices are raised in argument. (*Pause of 10 sec.*) Stop imagining the scene and just relax. (*Pause of 10 sec.*) Now again imagine the scene of these two men arguing across the road. (*Pause of 10 sec.*) Stop the scene and relax. Now I am going to count up to 5 and you will open your eyes, feeling very calm and refreshed (Wolpe and Lazarus, 1966, p. 81).

---

[5] The reader may be interested in the outcome of this case. Wolpe and Lazarus (1966) report that a total of 17 desensitization sessions were required for the subject to report no anxiety while visualizing the highest scene on each of her four hierarchies (the two presented in Table 10–2 and two additional ones dealing with being scrutinized and devalued by others). The anxiety reduction transferred from the imagined scenes to the actual situations, and she was able to successfully take and pass her examinations.

The Efficacy of Systematic Desensitization

Systematic desensitization has been used successfully in treating a variety of disorders, including exhibitionism (for example, Bond and Hutchison, 1960), chronic frigidity (Lazarus, 1963), stuttering (Walton and Mather, 1963), adult phobias (Rachman, 1959; Ashem, 1963; Clark, 1963), public speaking (Paul, 1966) and snake (Davison, 1968) phobias in college students, phobic reactions in schizophrenics (Cowden and Ford, 1962), and children's phobias (Lazarus and Abramovitz, 1962).

There is little argument that systematic desensitization has been shown to be a highly efficient and successful treatment method for certain disorders, most particularly phobias or irrational fears. Because of the specific nature of the problems treated, it is possible to measure outcomes *objectively.* Davison (1968), for example, used direct behavioral assessment of snake avoidance in the form of a series of 13 tasks which ranged from somewhat distant interaction with a snake (i.e., touching the glass near a snake while wearing gloves) to intimate contact with a snake (i.e., holding a snake with bare hands for 30 seconds). He also had his subjects indicate their degree of discomfort on a 10-point self-report anxiety scale after each behavioral task was successfully completed. Not only do such pre- and post-therapy measures allow assessment of the "real-life" success of treatment (since desensitization involves the signaling of anxiety while visualizing scenes from the hierarchy) but assessment (albeit subjective) is also made continuously during treatment. Most studies of the effectiveness of systematic desensitization have demonstrated that changes in felt anxiety do transfer from the imagined scenes to the actual situations, which, of course, is essential for the treatment to be considered successful.

There have been a number of direct comparisons of systematic desensitization with traditional insight-oriented psychotherapy (for example, Lazarus, 1961; Paul, 1966; Paul and Shannon, 1966). In each case, desensitization procedures were found to be more efficacious for the specific problems treated than insight therapy, although these studies have been criticized as being unfair comparisons of the two types of therapy (for example, Strupp, 1966).

Paul's (1966) study was concerned with the treatment of interpersonal-performance anxiety as manifested in public speaking. The participants were college students enrolled in public-speaking classes who volunteered to receive help with public-speaking anxiety. The five therapists were highly experienced and were predominantly neo-Freudian and Rogerian in therapeutic orientation. Subjects were assigned to one of three treatment groups: (1) modified systematic desensitization; (2)

insight-oriented psychotherapy; and (3) attention-placebo treatment which consisted of providing the subject with the "attention, warmth, and interest of the therapist" along with a "fast-acting tranquilizer" (actually a 2-gram capsule of sodium bicarbonate). Each therapist worked individually with three of the participants in each treatment group for a total of five one-hour sessions ranging over a six-week period. Additionally, two other groups of subjects served as untreated controls.

Paul's dependent variables included a variety of cognitive, physiological, and behavioral measures of anxiety. Systematic desensitization was found to be the most efficacious treatment (100 percent improvement). The insight-oriented therapy and the attention-placebo treatment did not differ in their effectiveness (47 percent improvement), but they were found to be more effective than the no-treatment controls (17 percent improvement). Paul reports that the improvement was maintained at a six-week follow-up assessment and that there was no evidence of "symptom substitution" (see page 299).

THE CONCEPT OF DRIVE REDUCTION

Clark L. Hull, who also followed in the tradition of Watson, developed an elaborate theory which dominated the psychology of learning for many years. Hull's position, like Watson's and Pavlov's, emphasizes a form of mechanistic behaviorism and avoids all references to consciousness. In fact, Hull's central concept, the habit, was derived from laboratory experiments with conditioned responses (Hilgard, 1956). Although Hull did not address himself to the study of personality, several of his successors have done so. We shall consider two points of view which have grown out of this position.

Dollard and Miller's Social Learning Approach

The "social learning" theory of John Dollard and Neal Miller drew heavily on Hullian concepts[6] and is, to some degree, a simplification of Hull's complex learning theory. The Dollard and Miller position also owes a debt to psychoanalytic theory, and their volume *Personality and Psychotherapy* (Dollard and Miller, 1950) is an attempt to translate psychoanalytic concepts into the language of behaviorism. However, as we shall have occasion to see in the ensuing discussion, Dollard and Miller's position, unlike its psychoanalytic counterpart, has focused on laboratory studies for its support, and in part, for its hypotheses. Many of

[6] Familiarity with Hull's learning theory is not necessary for an understanding of this section. However, the interested reader is referred to Hill (1963) for a short summary of Hull's theory and to Hilgard and Bower (1966) for more comprehensive coverage.

these studies have used infrahuman organisms as subjects, which may seem incongruous since the primary interest of the investigators is human behavior. Dollard and Miller (1950) offer the following justification of their research strategy.

. . . we are working on the hypothesis that people have all the learning capacities of rats so that any general phenomena of learning found in rats will also be found in people, although, of course, people may display additional phenomena not found in rats. Even though the facts must be verified at the human level, it is often easier to notice the operation of principles after they have been studied and isolated in simpler situations so that one knows exactly what to look for. Furthermore, in those cases in which it is impossible to use as rigorous experimental controls at the human level, our faith in what evidence can be gathered at that level will be increased if it is in line with the results of more carefully controlled experiments on other mammals (p. 63).

Four Fundamentals of Learning. Hull's primary formulation revolved around the notion of the *habit*—the tendency for a particular stimulus to evoke a particular response. However, although Dollard and Miller were interested in the learned habits as an account of human behavior, the term *habit* is mentioned only twice, and merely in passing, in their most exhaustive work (1950). Instead, Dollard and Miller base their theory on four fundamental elements of learning—*drive, cue, response,* and *reinforcement*—which they believe are as relevant to the social behavior of humans as to the maze-running behavior of laboratory rats.

DRIVE. Drive is the central construct in Dollard and Miller's theory. *Drive,* which Dollard and Miller define as any strong stimulus which impels action, is the source of energy (cf. libido, Chapter 3) or motivation for learning. Whereas in principle any stimulus may come to serve as a drive, some stimuli innately do so. For example, a strong stimulus of pain, such as a severe headache or touching a hot stove, impels us to action (taking an aspirin or removing our hand from the stove). Such drives are referred to as *primary drives,* and many are said to become stronger with increased deprivation (for example, hunger). In contrast, *learned drives* are those strong stimuli which do not innately energize the organism to act, but which come to serve as motivators of behavior as a result of the individual's learning experiences in his environment. Miller (1951) has succinctly argued for the importance of learned drives for human learning:

People are not born with a tendency to strive for money, for the discovery of scientific truths, or for symbols of social status and security. Such motives are learned during socialization. Many of them (such as jealousy when another man makes love to one's wife) vary greatly in different societies and even among the social classes in our society. . . . Even the primary drives themselves may be modified by learning, so that hunger becomes a desire for a particular type of food appetizingly prepared. Many Frenchmen abhor sweet corn and like snails (p. 435).

The classic laboratory demonstration of a learned drive is a study by Miller (1948). The experiment made use of a specially designed piece of apparatus, illustrated in Figure 10–2, which consisted of two small compartments separated by a vertically sliding door with a wheel above the right hand side of the door. The left compartment was painted white and had a wire grid floor through which an electrical current could be passed, while the right compartment was painted black and had a solid floor. When laboratory rats were tested in both compartments, they showed no preference for either side and no signs of fear (for example, excessive crouching, urination, defecation, or tenseness) in either compartment. The rats were then placed in the white compartment, given a mild shock through the grid floor, and allowed to escape the shock by running to the black compartment through the open door.

Following a number of such trials, the animals were again placed in the white compartment, but this time no electric shock was administered. Nevertheless, they continued to run rapidly through the open door to the black compartment. Moreover, when the door was closed so that the animals could not escape from the white compartment, they displayed signs of fear which were previously absent. While it would appear that fear of the white compartment had been learned, it is also possible that the rats continued to run from the white compartment merely because of a persistent habit which had been established in the preceding trials. To demonstrate conclusively that fear of the white compartment was a learned drive, it was necessary to show that it could lead the rats to the learning of a new response, just as the primary drive, pain from the electric shock, had led to acquisition of the running response. Thus, once more the animals were placed in the white compartment without receiving shock and with the door closed. However, this time the door could be opened by the rat's performing a new response, turning a wheel above the door. An electric clock was automatically started when the animal was placed in the white compartment and stopped when the animal performed the correct response.

At first the rats showed signs of fear and engaged in a variety of behaviors in the compartment. Eventually most of them touched the wheel, which caused the door to open, and ran into the black compartment. After this, the wheel-turning response became more rapid over a series of trials. Thus, it can be concluded that the fear of the white compartment was a *learned drive*. It is considered "learned" because it became associated with a previously neutral stimulus (i.e., the white compartment). It can be called a "drive" because it motivated the learning of a new behavior (i.e., turning the wheel).

FIGURE 10–2

Apparatus for Studying Fear as a Learned Drive

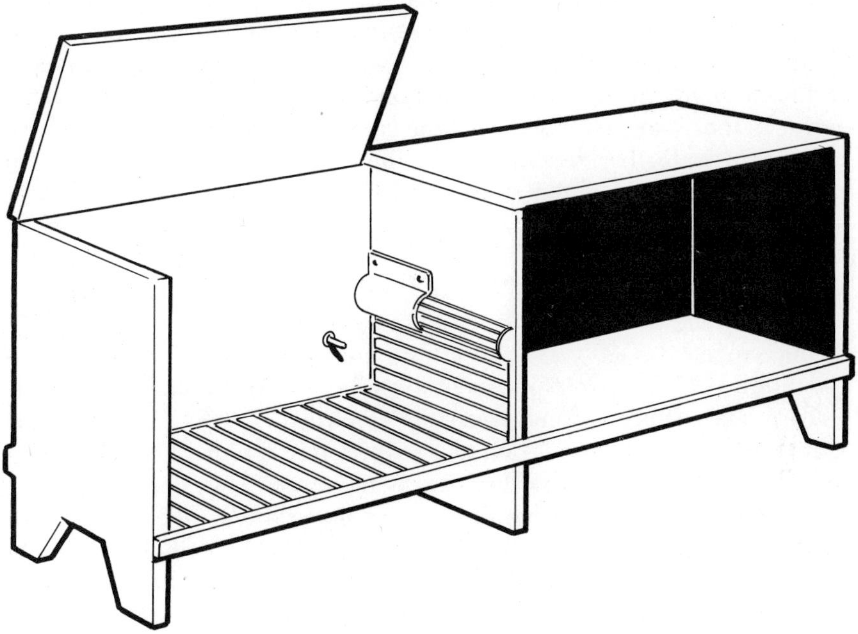

Source: Miller, 1948.

Cue. While drives are said to impel responding, cues serve to determine the nature of the response that will be made. Cues are those stimuli which provide information concerning the most appropriate response. Whereas the crucial dimension of a drive is its strength or *intensity*, the crucial dimension of a cue is its *distinctiveness*. When a heavy smoker has no tobacco and craves a smoke, his behavior will be directed toward establishments brandishing such cues as "Cigarette Machine Inside" or toward people who are smoking. To guide our interactions with them, policemen, physicians, and clergymen display distinctive cues of their offices (uniforms, white coats, robes and collars) when acting in professional capacities. Humans are capable of differentially responding to very subtle and complex patterns of cues, as anyone who has interacted with a sophisticated used-car salesman can readily testify. Further, it should be noted that some stimuli can serve as both drive and cue. A dry throat motivates a person to reduce his thirst by taking something to drink, rather than to eat, from the refrigerator.

Response. The behavior which a drive impels and a cue directs or channelizes is termed a response. Thus, Dollard and Miller's theory has been called an *S-R* (stimulus-response) position, since it involves a causal relationship between stimuli (drives and cues) and responses. It is assumed that a particular combination of drives and cues may elicit any one of a number of responses and that the likelihood or probability of any one response being elicited by the stimulus complex is a function of the strength of the associative bond (represented by the hyphen between the *S* and *R*) between the stimulus (complex) and the response. It is further assumed that the possible responses which an individual may make under a given set of circumstances can be arranged in their order of probability of occurrence, thereby forming a *response hierarchy*.

Reinforcement. For Dollard and Miller (1950) "any specified event . . . that strengthens the tendency for a response to be repeated is called reinforcement" (p. 39). However, they make an additional assumption about the nature of reinforcement beyond this definition. Specifically, Dollard and Miller assume that the empirical outcome which is described in their definition is due to a reduction in the drive that led to the response. For example, in Miller's study of learned fear, discussed above, the response of running from the white compartment to the black compartment was strengthened (reinforced) first by a reduction of pain and later by a reduction of fear (i.e., fear of the stimuli associated with the white compartment). Similarly, eating when hungry is reinforcing because of the resultant reduction in the hunger drive. The parallel between the concept of *drive reduction* and Freud's pleasure principle (see Chapter 3) should be apparent.

A Learning Analysis of a Psychopathological Symptom. In *Personality and Psychotherapy,* Dollard and Miller (1950), have attempted to describe the development and treatment of neurosis in terms of their learning analysis of personality. As an illustration of the use of their principles of learning to explain complex human behavior, we shall briefly examine their analysis of a case of hysterical paralysis. It will be recalled from our discussion of psychoanalytic psychotherapy in Chapter 4 that patients diagnosed as hysterics have some physical complaint for which no organic (physical) cause can be found.

Mrs. C was a 35-year-old married woman who was suffering from paralysis of the legs. Her case history indicated that she had a strong fear of sex. She described her mother as a stern woman whose convictions led her to hit her daughter regularly in order to assure that she would grow up as a "good" girl. Mrs. C resolved in childhood never to marry, but later revoked this decision to escape her punitive home life. She claimed that before her marriage she had no knowledge of sexual intercourse or conception. Thus the marriage immediately precipitated a series of problems. She awoke with nightmares which concerned her being pregnant and developed a particular aversion to sexual intercourse, describing herself as feeling nauseated when her husband touched her.

Despite this apparent excessive anxiety about sex, in the course of 15 years of marriage she conceived four times and had three living children. The last pregnancy, which shortly antedated her paralysis, was particularly painful and led her to more adamant efforts to avoid sexual relations with her husband. The records state that they had intercourse only once or twice a month and then only because of her husband's pleading. After her last pregnancy, Mrs. C suffered from some swelling and weakness in her legs, and a short time later she was admitted to a hospital with her legs in a paralyzed condition. She was unable to walk or stand.

While the exact circumstances which led to Mrs. C's symptoms are not known, Dollard and Miller advanced an educated guess consistent with their social learning position. "It is possible that when she noticed that her legs were not normal, she thought to herself 'this will prevent intercourse,' a thought which would be expected to reduce her anxiety and reinforce the incipient symptom" (Dollard and Miller, 1950, p. 169). According to this analysis, the drive which motivated the learning of the response (the paralysis) was anxiety regarding sexual relations, while the cue which directed Mrs. C to the particular response was the minor problem she was having with her legs. The symptom was learned because it reduced Mrs. C's anxiety (drive reduction), in that sexual intercourse was not possible when her legs were paralyzed. That her symptom was in fact functioning to reduce her sex anxiety is demonstrated by the increase in anxiety (drive) that occurred after the doctors had gotten her to walk again by a combination of physical and verbal pressure. "Mrs. C was angry at her doctors and suffered an attack of rage at one of the nurses on the very night that she was first convinced she could walk" (Dollard and Miller, p. 170).

As would be predicted from Dollard and Miller's theory, due to the increased drive which resulted from the removal of her symptom, Mrs. C was motivated to learn new responses which would reduce the anxiety drive. Thus, after her release from the hospital she first contemplated divorce and then lived with her sister for a time, rationalizing that she was still too weak to tend for her own home and family. It is instructive to note that what Dollard and Miller have presented is a learning theory explanation of *symptom substitution,* the notion that when a symptom is treated without treating what is causing it (for example, an intrapsychic conflict), another symptom will merely replace it. In their words: "This case clearly illustrates the point that the direct removal of a symptom (without treatment of its cause) produces an increase in drive and throws the patient back into a severe learning dilemma [i.e., neurosis]" (Dollard and Miller, 1950, p. 168).

The analysis of an hysterical symptom illustrates the manner in which Dollard and Miller have used a simple learning model to account for fairly complex social behavior. Their approach to personality has focused on the development and maintenance of patterns of behavior (habits) with need and motive-related issues being subsumed by the critical concepts of drive and drive reduction (reinforcement). While their social learning theory appears to have considerable heuristic appeal and utility, it has not been able to stand alone as a contending comprehensive personality theory. However, the concept of drive, which is central to their approach and had, even before Dollard and Miller, played an important role in Hull's learning theory, has led to a considerable body of research dealing with the problem of anxiety.

Manifest Anxiety and Drive

We have already had occasion to introduce the Taylor Manifest Anxiety (MA) Scale in our discussion of social desirability as a response style in Chapter 6. The MA scale was originally developed by Janet Taylor in 1951, to be used in selecting subjects for experimental studies designed to test theoretical assumptions about the nature of the Hull-Spence[7] concept of drive. Anxiety was chosen as the drive on which the research would concentrate, although any other drive (hunger, for example) might have served the purpose of the investigations. Rather than experimentally manipulating drive level, the investigators decided to measure it as it existed, as a more or less permanent characteristic (i.e., trait), in their subjects and then to compare groups of subjects differing in drive (anxiety) level. Thus the MA scale was specifically designed to differentiate high-anxiety and low-anxiety groups of persons.

Construction of the Taylor MA Scale. The MA scale is composed of 50 items from the MMPI (see Chapter 6). The items were selected by expert clinicians on the basis of each item's presumed ability to detect clinical anxiety. Some representative items from the scale are presented in Table 10–3. The items in the table clearly reveal that the scale is interested in tapping a general predisposition as seen, for example, in the use of the terms *frequently, usually,* and *always.* The subject answers "true" or "false" to each item, and his score is the total number of items on which he gives the "anxious" answer (indicated in Table 10–3 by italics). Clinically, the value of the scale is somewhat validated by the fact that it reliably distinguishes between samples of psychiatric patients and "normals" (Levitt, 1967).

In addition to the original 50-item version of the MA scale, a number of modified forms have been developed. Bendig (1956) has suggested a

[7] Kenneth W. Spence was a student of Hull and later a collaborator. After Hull's death, Spence attempted to refine Hull's theory.

TABLE 10–3

Sample MA Scale Items
("anxious" response italicized)

I am usually calm and not easily upset.	TRUE	*FALSE*
I always have enough energy when faced with difficulty.	TRUE	*FALSE*
I have diarrhea once a month or more.	*TRUE*	FALSE
I frequently find myself worrying about something.	*TRUE*	FALSE

short form consisting of the 20 items which have been most successful in predicting a number of clinical criteria of anxiety. Heineman (1953) has constructed a forced-choice version to control for the influence of social desirability. Each of the 50 MA scale items is paired with two other items which are not related to anxiety. One of the additional nonanxiety items is matched with the MA item for social desirability, while the other nonanxiety item differs markedly in social desirability from the MA item. For example (Heineman, 1953, p. 448):

A. I have strong political opinions. [Nonanxiety, unmatched item.]
B. I sometimes tease animals. [Nonanxiety, matched item.]
C. I am a high-strung person. [Anxiety item; same degree of social desirability as Item B.]

The subject is instructed to indicate, for each trio of items, the item which is most characteristic and least characteristic of himself. A children's form of the MA scale has also been developed (Castaneda, McCandless, and Palermo, 1956) and consists of 42 items.

The Relationship between MA Scores and Performance. The Hull-Spence learning position assumes that an increase in drive will increase the strength of *all* the responses which a drive stimulus elicits. For instance, if a man is sexually aroused (i.e., has a high sex drive), the probability that he will seek a sexual partner will be increased. In addition, however, the probability of performing other responses which the individual has in his repertoire for reducing the sex drive will also increase. Thus, he will be more likely to masturbate, receive sexual satisfaction vicariously through reading or movies, and so on. It follows from such a conceptualization that the effect which drive has on the performance of a particular response depends not only on whether the drive elicits that response (which, of course, is a necessary condition) but also on the relationship of *competing responses,* which are also elicited by the drive, to the response in question. If there are no competing responses, or if the response is higher on the individual's response hierarchy (i.e., stronger in the sense of probability of occurrence) than the competing responses, then the Hull-Spence position would predict that the *higher* the drive level, the faster the response will be learned. On the other hand, if the competing responses are of equal or greater strength than the response in question, then the *lower* the drive level, the easier it will be for the response to be learned. The issue of competing responses is most crucial when the response in question is the one and only correct response (or the one that will be reinforced), which is the case in most experimental studies of learning.

EYELID CONDITIONING. The normal reaction to a puff of air to the eye is to blink one's eyelid. Not only does blinking occur frequently, but it is also a response that has virtually no competitors. Thus, eyelid conditioning is particularly suitable for testing the predicted positive relationship between drive and learning in the case in which no competi-

FIGURE 10-3

Schematic Diagram of Classical Conditioning of the Eye-Blink Reflex

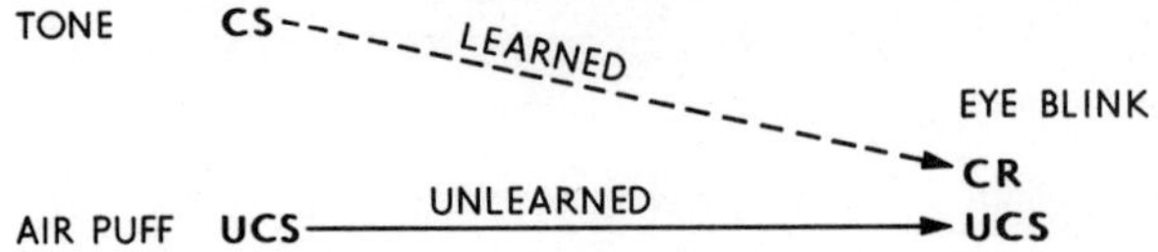

tive responses exist. Eyelid conditioning follows the classical or Pavlovian paradigm, as is illustrated schematically in Figure 10-3. A neutral stimulus (i.e., one that does not naturally elicit the response), such as a tone or light, serves as the CS and is followed closely in time (approximately .5 seconds) by the UCS, namely the puff of air to the eye. The UCS elicits an eye blink, which is the UCR. After a number of pairings of the CS and UCS, the CS comes to elicit an eye-blink response, the CR. The strength of the CR is usually measured as the number of trials (presentations of CS and UCS) in which the eye-blink response occurs after the presentation of the CS but *before the onset of the UCS.* A typical apparatus for eyelid conditioning, which allows for the presentation of the air puff as well as the measurement of an eye blink, is pictured in Figure 10-4.

Spence's (1964) review of studies which have assessed the relationship between eyelid conditioning and anxiety (drive) level revealed that in 21 of 25 independent comparisons the relationship was, as anticipated, positive. The data from two representative experiments are presented graphically in Figure 10-5 (page 304), from which it can be seen that irrespective of the strength of the UCS[8] (each experiment employed two

[8] Classical conditioning performance is usually positively related to the strength of the UCS.

FIGURE 10–4

Equipment Used to Produce and Measure Eye Blinks

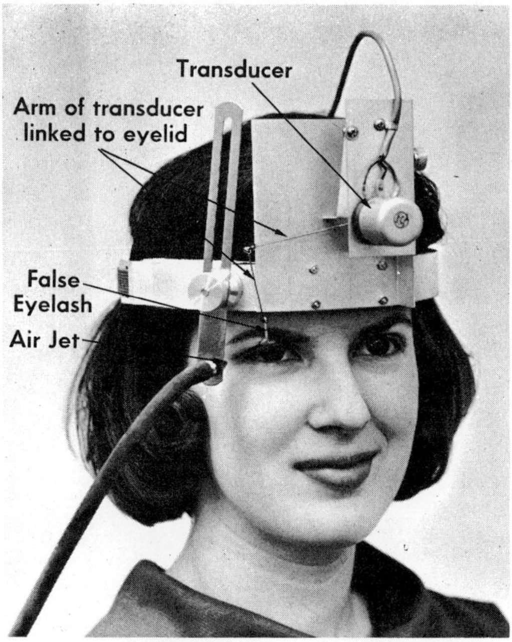

Note: The subject wears a false eyelash which is linked by a thread to the apparatus to measure the blinks. The tube delivers a puff of air which serves as the unconditioned stimulus.
Source: Kimble and Garmezy, 1968.

different levels of air pressure), high-anxiety subjects (defined as those scoring in the top 20 percent on the MA scale) were clearly superior in performance to low-anxiety subjects (lower 20 percent on the MA scale).

Verbal Learning. For the case in which competitive responses may interfere with the learning of a particular response, it would be predicted from the Hull-Spence position that high anxiety would impede, rather than facilitate, learning. This negative relationship between MA scale scores and performance has been substantiated in studies of verbal learning (Spence and Spence, 1966). For example, in an experiment by Montague (1953), high- and low-anxious subjects performed a serial learning task in which they were presented with a list of nonsense syllables and, for each successive item, were required to anticipate the next item on the list. Montague varied two characteristics of the lists of nonsense syllables: the degree of intralist similarity and the association value of the syllables. Presumably, the greater the similarity and the lower the degree of association among the syllables, the greater will be

FIGURE 10–5

Performance in Eyelid Conditioning as a Function of Anxiety (MAS) Level and Intensity of UCS (Air Puff)

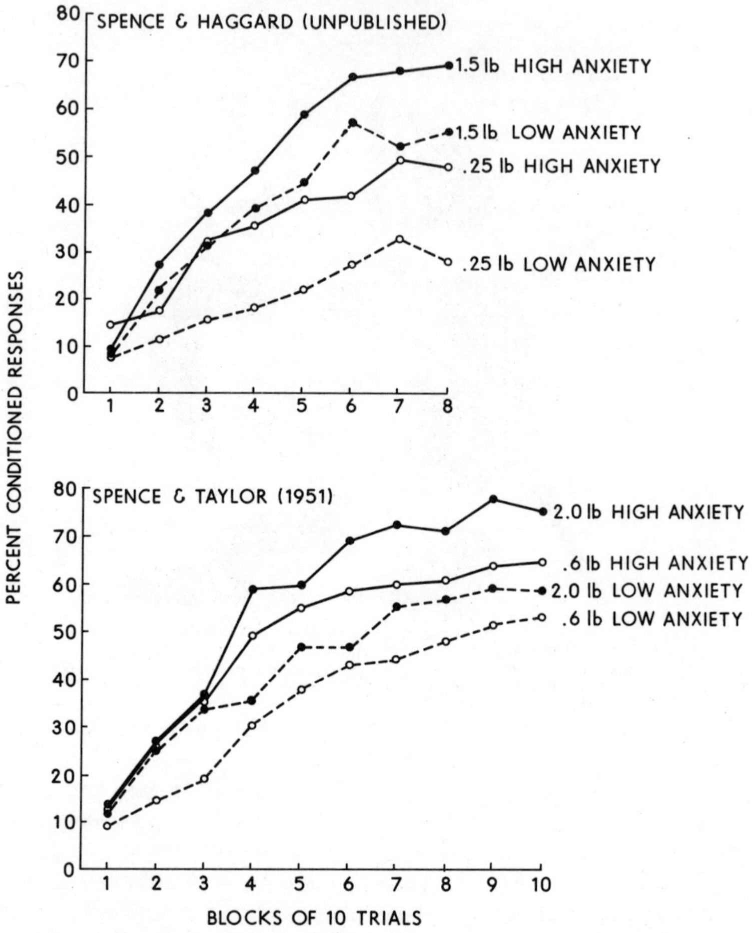

Source: Adapted from Spence and Spence, 1966.

the intralist interference; that is, the more erroneous, competitive responses there will be. As in the eyelid-conditioning studies, when interference from competitive responses was low (i.e., low similarity and high association among syllables), high-anxiety subjects showed superior performance to low-anxiety subjects. In contrast, when the interference of competing responses was high (i.e., high similarity and low association among syllables), high-anxiety subjects were inferior in their performance to low-anxiety subjects. Similarly, Lucas (1952) had subjects recall lists of consonants which were read to them. As the number of duplicated consonants increased (and hence the number of competing responses) the performance of high-anxious subjects decreased, whereas the performance of low-anxious subjects remained the same.

THE RELATIONSHIP OF STRESS, ANXIETY, AND PERFORMANCE. Turning from relatively simple conditioning situations to more complex forms of behavior, a number of investigators have examined the relationships among experimentally manipulated stress, anxiety, and performance. The general hypothesis tested by many of these studies has been well summarized by Spence and Spence (1966):

> Instructions that stress the importance of doing well or state that performance reflects a valued characteristic, such as intelligence for the college-student subject, may be expected to lead most individuals to increased effort and attention and hence to better performance. However, emphasis on doing well may also arouse anxiety (fear of failure) and negative evaluations of performance (failure reports) to intensify it. As anxiety, with its [drive] . . . components, increases in intensity, so do the frequency and intensity of task-irrelevant responses. To the extent that the responses to be acquired can be adversely affected by them, these irrelevant tendencies will lead to performance decrement. Thus, as externally manipulated psychological stress increases, performance might first be expected to increase due to an increase in task-oriented behaviors and then to decrease as irrelevant responses are aroused and begin to be predominant in their influence (p. 313).

As an example of one study which examined this general hypothesis, Siegman (1956) administered the MA scale and the Wechsler Adult Intelligence Scale (WAIS) to 35 male medical and psychiatric patients, all of whom were of at least average intelligence and none of whom were psychotic. The WAIS contains both timed and untimed subtests and therefore allows a test of the hypothesis that one presumed stressor, timing, will be more disruptive for high-anxious than for low-anxious subjects. In Siegman's study, which defined high- and low-anxious subjects as the highest and lowest 10 scorers respectively on the MAS, support for this hypothesis was found. As seen in Table 10–4 (p. 306), high-anxious persons scored better on the untimed tests than the timed tests, whereas for low-anxious subjects the reverse was true.

In the preceding discussion of the effect of anxiety on performance, we have endeavored to present the reader with examples of the characteristic research methods which have been employed, as well as some of the data which support the Hull-Spence position with respect to drive level and learning. During the past two decades, there have been literally hundreds of studies dealing with the influence of anxiety on performance, and it would be erroneous to give the impression that the few experiments discussed above are fully representative of the findings. In fact, the study of anxiety and performance has been plagued with inconsistent findings when predictions are made to classroom or other

TABLE 10–4

The Effects of Manifest Anxiety on Timed and Untimed Measures of Intelligence

	Subtests		
Group	*Timed*	*Untimed*	*Total*
High anxiety	10.1	11.5	10.7
Low anxiety	11.7	10.9	11.4

Source: Data from Siegman, 1956.

life situations. Thus, although it is clearly thought that anxiety as measured by the MAS influences learning, at the present time no unified theory exists which will provide an explanation for all of the extant data.[9]

REFERENCES

Ashem, B. The treatment of a disaster phobia by systematic desensitization. *Behaviour Research and Therapy,* 1963, **1,** 81–84.

Bandura, A. A social learning interpretation of psychological dysfunctions. In P. London and D. Rosenhan (Eds.), *Foundations of abnormal psychology.* New York: Holt, Rinehart & Winston, 1968.

Bendig, A. W. The development of a short form of the manifest anxiety scale. *Journal of Consulting Psychology,* 1956, **20,** 384.

Bond, I. K., and Hutchison, H. C. Application of reciprocal inhibition therapy to exhibitionism. *Canadian Medical Association Journal,* 1960, **83,** 23–25.

Castaneda, A., McCandless, B. R., and Palermo, D. S. The children's form of the manifest anxiety scale. *Child Development,* 1956, **27,** 317–26.

Clark, D. F. The treatment of a monosymptomatic phobia by systematic desensitization. *Behaviour Research and Therapy,* 1963, **1,** 63–68.

Cowden, R. C., and Ford, L. I. Systematic desensitization with phobic schizophrenics. *American Journal of Psychiatry,* 1962, **119,** 241–45.

Davison, G. C. Case report: Elimination of a sadistic fantasy by a client-controlled counter-conditioning technique. *Journal of Abnormal Psychology,* 1968, **73,** 84–90.

Dekker, E., and Groen, J. Reproducible psychogenic attacks of asthma: A laboratory study. *Journal of Psychosomatic Research,* 1956, **1,** 58–67.

Dekker, E., Pelser, H. E., and Groen, J. Conditioning as a cause of asthmatic attacks. *Journal of Psychosomatic Research,* 1957, **2,** 97–108.

Dollard, J., and Miller, N. E. *Personality and psychotherapy.* New York: McGraw-Hill, 1950.

[9] It would be beyond the scope of the present text to discuss this highly controversial area of psychology in detail, but the interested reader should see Spence and Spence (1966).

Hathaway, S. R., and McKinley, J. C. *Minnesota Multiphasic Personality Inventory*. Minneapolis: University of Minnesota Press, 1942.

Heineman, C. E. A forced-choice form of the Taylor anxiety scale. *Journal of Consulting Psychology,* 1953, **17,** 447–54.

Hilgard, E. R. *Theories of learning.* New York: Appleton-Century-Crofts, 1956.

Hilgard, E. R., and Bower, G. H. *Theories of learning.* (3d ed.) New York: Appleton-Century-Crofts, 1966.

Hill, W. F. *Learning: A Survey of psychological interpretations.* San Francisco: Chandler, 1963.

Hyman, R. *The nature of psychological inquiry.* Englewood Cliffs, N.J.: Prentice-Hall, 1964.

Jones, M. C. A laboratory study of fear: The case of Peter. *Pedagogical Seminar,* 1924, **31,** 308–15.

Kimble, G. A., and Garmezy, N. *Principles of general psychology.* New York: Ronald Press, 1968.

Lazarus, A. A. Group therapy of phobic disorders by systematic desensitization. *Journal of Abnormal and Social Psychology,* 1961, **63,** 504.

Lazarus, A. A. The treatment of chronic frigidity by systematic desensitization. *Journal of Nervous and Mental Disease,* 1963, **136,** 272.

Lazarus, A. A., and Abramovitz, A. The use of "emotive imagery" in the treatment of children's phobias. *Journal of Mental Science,* 1962, **108,** 191.

Levitt, E. E. *The psychology of anxiety.* New York: Bobbs-Merrill, 1967.*

Lucas, J. D. The interactive effects of anxiety, failure and intra-serial duplication. *American Journal of Psychology,* 1952, **65,** 59–66.

Miller, N. E. Learnable drives and rewards. In S. S. Stevens (Ed.), *Handbook of experimental psychology.* New York: Wiley, 1951. Pp. 435–72.

Miller, N. E. Studies of fear as an acquired drive. *Journal of Experimental Psychology,* 1948, **38,** 89–101.

Montague, E. K. The role of anxiety in serial rote learning. *Journal of Experimental Psychology,* 1953, **45,** 91–96.

Mowrer, O. H., and Mowrer, W. M. Enuresis—a method for its study and treatment. *American Journal of Orthopsychiatry,* 1938, **8,** 436–59.

Paul, G. L. *Insight versus desensitization in psychotherapy.* Stanford, Calif.: Stanford University Press, 1966.

Paul, G. L., and Shannon, D. T. Treatment of anxiety through systematic desensitization in therapy groups. *Journal of Abnormal Psychology,* 1966, **71,** 124–35.

Pavlov, I. P. *Conditioned reflexes.* New York: Liveright, 1927.

Quarti, C., and Renaud, J. A new treatment of constipation by conditioning: A preliminary report. In C. M. Franks (Ed.), *Conditioning techniques in clinical practice and research.* New York: Springer, 1964.

Rachman, S. The treatment of anxiety and phobic reactions by systematic desensitization psychotherapy. *Journal of Abnormal and Social Psychology,* 1959, **58,** 259–63.

Razran, G. S. Conditioned response changes in rating and appraising socio-political slogans. *Psychological Bulletin,* 1940, **37,** 481.

Razran, G. S. Conditioning away social bias by the luncheon technique. *Psychological Bulletin,* 1938, **35,** 693.

Siegman, A. W. The effect of manifest anxiety on a concept formation task, a nondirected learning task, and on timed and untimed intelligence tests. *Journal of Consulting Psychology,* 1956, **20,** 176–78.

Spence, J. T., and Spence, K. W. The motivational components of manifest anxiety. In C. D. Spielberger (Ed.), *Anxiety and behavior.* New York: Academic Press, 1966.

Spence, K. W. Anxiety (drive) level performance in eyelid conditioning. *Psychological Bulletin,* 1964, **61,** 129–39.

Staats, A. W., and Staats, C. K. Attitudes established by classical conditioning. *Journal of Abnormal and Social Psychology,* 1958, **57,** 37–40.

Strupp, H. H. Who needs intrapsychic factors in clinical psychology? Paper presented at the Albert Einstein College of Medicine, New York, 1966.

Taylor, J. A. The relationship of anxiety to the conditioned eyelid response. *Journal of Experimental Psychology,* 1951, **41,** 81–92.

Walton, D., and Mather, M. D. The relevance of generalized techniques to the treatment of stammering and phobic symptoms. *Behaviour Research and Therapy,* 1963, **1,** 121–25.

Watson, J. B. *Behavior: An introduction to comparative psychology.* New York: Holt, 1914.

Watson, J. B. *Psychology from the standpoint of a behaviorist.* Philadelphia: Lippincott, 1919.

Watson, J. B., and Rayner, R. Conditioned emotional reactions. *Journal of Experimental Psychology,* 1920, **3,** 1.

Wolpe, J. *Psychotherapy by reciprocal inhibition.* Stanford, Calif.: Stanford University Press, 1958.

Wolpe, J., and Lazarus, A. A. *Behavior therapy techniques.* Oxford: Pergamon, 1966.

Woodworth, R. S., and Sheehan, M. R. *Contemporary schools of psychology.* New York: Ronald Press, 1964.

chapter 11

Learning Approaches to Personality: Operant Conditioning

Another branch in the tradition of behaviorism has focused on the manner in which behavior is influenced by the outcomes (rewards and punishments) which have followed it in the past. In the present chapter we shall consider some of the major findings which this perspective has generated, emphasizing possible applications to human behavior in life situations.

THORNDIKE'S LAW OF EFFECT

One of the first psychologists in America to call attention to the importance of consequences for human behavior was Edward L. Thorndike. Although most of Thorndike's theoretical and experimental contributions do not fall within the scope of this book, one of his basic formulations (first suggested in 1898) may be considered the forerunner of the approach to personality described in this section. This formulation, referred to as the *law of effect,* was based on the assumption that one of the most important and characteristic forms of learning, for both animals and men, is trial-and-error learning. When an organism is originally faced with the problem of reaching some goal, whether it is obtaining food or solving an arithmetic problem or successfully influencing other people, the task may be viewed as one of selecting a response to this situation from among a host of possible responses. Responses which do not lead to the goal may be considered errors, and numerous errors are likely to occur when the problem is first presented. Over the course of repeated presentations of the problem, the frequency of errors and the time required to produce a correct response decreases. Ultimately, if learning is successful, the correct response seems to become strongly connected to the problem and performance becomes nearly errorless.

The mechanism which underlies this apparent "stamping in" of the correct response was assumed by Thorndike to depend upon the consequences which the correct and incorrect responses produced, and the law of effect referred to the effects of consequences on the performance of particular responses to a situation or problem. Although the first statement of this law suggested that the strength of the bond or connection between a particular situation and a particular response would be increased if it was followed by a "satisfying state of affairs" (reward) and decreased if it was followed by an "annoying state of affairs" (punishment), Thorndike later reached the conclusion that rewards were far more powerful than punishments. The present section is concerned with exploration and application of this viewpoint by more contemporary psychologists. We shall begin by a discussion of the strategy which has been adopted by those who have followed Thorndike's thinking.

SKINNER'S OPERANT CONDITIONING APPROACH

The tradition of behaviorism which Watson started, fertilized by the tradition of Thorndike, is most often associated today with the name of B. F. Skinner. Although Skinner's research contributions have emphasized the behavior of infrahuman organisms, usually rats or pigeons, he has in his writings (for example, *Science and Human Behavior* [1953]; *Walden Two* [1948]) made numerous suggestions concerning the application of his findings to human behavior. Moreover, as we shall see shortly, those psychologists who have followed in his tradition have made remarkable strides with applications to practical problems.

Skinner and his colleagues form one of the most experimentally productive groups in psychology, and fully detailing all of the sophisticated procedures, findings, and distinctions which they have introduced would require a volume by itself.[1] However, in order to disclose the strategy of research employed by these investigators and introduce its application, some of the major distinctions and developments provided by Skinner's group are briefly discussed.

The Idiographic Approach

Skinner's work has stressed a thorough analysis of an individual subject's behavior. The typical experiment is not concerned with the *average*

---

[1] Reynolds' *A Primer of Operant Conditioning* (1968) is an excellent and succinct treatment of the area.

subject, for the aim of the analysis is to establish experimental control of a particular organism's behavior. Skinner (1956) explains his concentration on the single case as follows:

> In essence, I suddenly found myself face to face with the engineering problem of the animal trainer. When you have the responsibility of making absolutely sure that a given organism will engage in a given sort of behavior at a given time, you quickly grow impatient with theories of learning. Principles, hypotheses, theorems, satisfactory proof at the .05 level of significance . . . nothing could be more irrelevant. No one goes to the circus to see the average dog jump through a hoop significantly oftener than untrained dogs raised under the same circumstances, or to see an elephant demonstrate a principle of behavior (p. 228).

Skinner's neglect of inferential statistics (see Chapter 2), alluded to in the preceding citation, follows from the fact that such statistics deal with averages. That is, from a representative sample of subjects, statistically significant results allow inferences about the population of subjects (i.e., subjects in general). The classic problem of experimentation is reducing variability (error) among subjects who receive the same experimental manipulations. One way to do this is to employ a large number of subjects so that the individual differences among subjects will be "averaged out." Skinner (1956) has chosen an alternative method, that of strict experimental control.

> Faced with practical problems in behavior, you necessarily emphasize the refinement of *experimental* variables. As a result, some of the standard procedures of statistics appear to be circumvented. Let me illustrate. Suppose that measurements have been made on two groups of subjects differing in some detail of experimental treatment. Means and standard deviations for the two groups are determined, and any difference due to the treatment is evaluated. If the difference is in the expected direction but is not statistically significant, the almost universal recommendation would be to study larger groups. But our experience with practical control suggests that we may reduce the troublesome variability by changing the conditions of the experiment. By discovering, elaborating, and fully exploiting every relevant variable, we may eliminate *in advance of measurement* the individual differences which obscure the difference under analysis. This will achieve the same result as increasing the size of groups, and it will almost certainly yield a bonus in the discovery of new variables which would not have been identified in the statistical treatment (pp. 228–29).

If refinement of experimental variables is substituted for large numbers of subjects, there still remains the problem of a control group. In other words, to unequivocally demonstrate that a subject is under experimental control, there must be some base rate to which a comparison can be made. In typical experiments involving groups of subjects, one or more groups of subjects receive the independent variable while another group of subjects is treated exactly alike except that the independent variable is not present. In the *single-subject experimental design* (first discussed on page 33) employed by Skinner and his followers, the independent variable, usually some type of response consequence, is first introduced and the subject's response rate measured under this condition. Then, in a *reversal* phase, the independent variable is withdrawn for a time, which, if the independent variable was controlling the behavior, leads to extinction of the response. Finally, by reintroducing the independent variable, the response is reinstated. Thus, each subject serves as his own control. Whereas in experiments with groups of subjects the statistical significance of results serves as an index of the reliability of the findings, in single-subject experimentation replication of control of the desired behavior serves as the measure of reliability. An example of these procedures is provided in a later section of this chapter.

The Atheoretical Nature of Skinner's Approach

Skinner has contended throughout his career (his first published book, *The Behavior of Organisms,* appeared in 1938) that psychology in general and the study of learning in particular is not yet at the stage where elaborate, formalized theorizing is justifiable. Though in principle he is not "antitheory," Skinner feels that psychology is not ready to establish theories of human nature and behavior. Accordingly, Skinner's own research efforts have been directed toward the complete and detailed description of behavior, which he has called the *functional analysis of behavior.* The aim of such functional analysis is to establish empirical relationships among variables. The Skinnerian approach might be summarized by the following maxim which Skinner (1956) gleaned from Pavlov: "Control your conditions and you will see order."

In keeping with his atheoretical approach, Skinner has eschewed the consideration of all intraorganism variables. He has rejected the explanation of behavior in terms of hypothetical constructs, which, it will be recalled, are merely convenient fictions in a theorist's head which may serve to enhance his conceptualization of observed behavior (see, for example, Chapter 1). He has also avoided explanations which are based on the presumed operation of speculative physiological mechanisms. Skinner feels that such "physiologizing" (as in Hebb, 1966) is not only unnecessary and useless, but that it is often only pseudo-theory.

Thus, in general, Skinnerian psychology has no interest in what is going on within the individual. This is not to say that these things are not important. Rather, Skinner's approach to studying behavior is distinctly *positivistic* in that it deals with operationally defined observables. He employs two main classes—*stimuli,* those observable characteristics of the environment which influence the organism, and *responses,* the overt behavior of the organism. In a sense, Skinnerian psychology deals with an "empty-organism." All variables which come between, or mediate, stimulus and response and cannot be handled in terms of stimulus, response, or some kind of "setting condition" are outside the domain of interest of the Skinnerians. It should be noted, however, that such a position can deal with many of the phenomena which are the basis for positing internal events in other approaches. For example, although Skinner would not speak of "hunger" as an explanation for food-seeking, hours of food deprivation may be used to handle the same behavior.

The Nature of Operant and Respondent Behavior

Skinner (1938) has distinguished between two types of behavior: *operant* and *respondent*.[2] Operant behavior is controlled by the consequences which follow its performance.[3] Examples of operant behavior include driving a car, dressing oneself, taking notes in class, and playing tennis. In each case, successful completion of the behavior results in some consequence, and it is to the consequences of an operant that the psychologist directs his attention. His questions are of the form: "What consequences will maintain a given response?" For example, turning the ignition key makes your car start, depressing the accelerator makes the car move, and turning the wheel allows you to avoid the variety of obstacles which appear in the road from time to time. The behavior is under the control of its consequences in the sense that if the consquences are positive, the behavior is more likely to occur again, whereas if they are negative (for example, if turning the ignition key blows up your car), the behavior is less likely to occur again. Much of our behavior has been learned via *operant* or *instrumental conditioning.*

Respondent behavior is elicited by some identifiable stimulus and thus derives its name from the fact that the subject *responds to* something. The purest examples of respondent behavior are reflexes, such as the pupil of the eye closing down in response to light stimulation, the knee jerk in response to a tap on the patellar tendon, and perspiring in response to heat. Respondents which have been learned (through classical or Pavlovian conditioning) include blushing when someone tells you that you are attractive and feeling "nervous" (hands shaking, perspiring, stomach queasy) right before taking an important final examination or giving a speech. Our earlier discussion of classical conditioning was, of course, a discussion of various forms of respondent behavior.

---

[2] The terms *respondent* and *operant* are used both as adjectives, to refer to a type of behavior or procedure ("operant conditioning"), and as nouns, to refer to a specific response which is a member of the class of respondent or operant behavior ("writing one's name is an operant").

[3] Strictly speaking, it is logically impossible for a given response to be controlled by the consequences which accrue to it, since the consequences occur *after* the response is made. It is possible, however, for consequences which accrued to similar responses in the past to affect a given response.

Finally, it should be noted that there are many behaviors which were originally learned as operants but have since come to function as respondents. These behaviors include those acts which we colloquially call "reflexes" (since they occur almost automatically), such as stopping when a traffic light turns red and paying close attention to a teacher when he begins to talk about an upcoming examination. In each instance, the behavior is controlled by a *discriminative stimulus*,[4] that is, one which preceded the response and which has acquired discriminative properties by virtue of the fact that the behavior under its control has been differentially reinforced in its presence. While a discriminative stimulus appears to control the response, actually it only sets the occasion for the occurrence of the response.

The Measurement of Operant Behavior

Skinner has chosen an elegantly simple dependent measure of operant behavior, the rate of emission of the operant. The subject's responses are typically recorded by a device called a *cumulative recorder*. Each time the subject makes the desired operant, a pen makes a slight move-

FIGURE 11–1

A Facsimile of a Cumulative Recorder

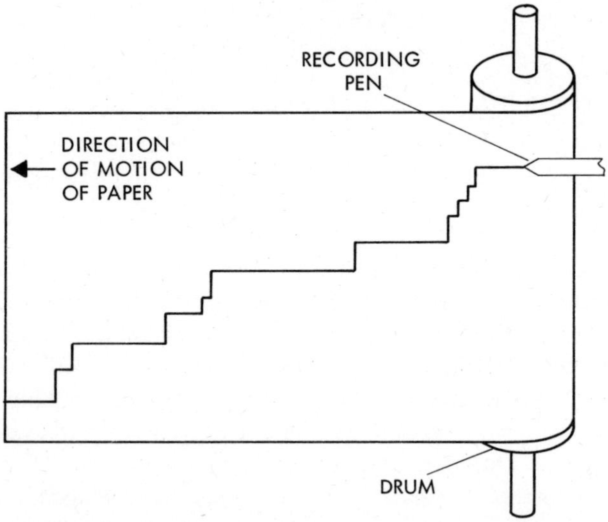

Note: The drum rotates and the recording pen moves upward by a fixed amount each time the subject makes a response. Note that when the responses are made, a straight line is drawn and that the *slope* of the line indicates the response rate. Thus, the more rapidly the animal is responding, the steeper the slope will be.
Source: Hilgard and Atkinson, 1967.

[4] A discriminative stimulus is traditionally abbreviated S^D in the operant conditioning literature.

FIGURE 11–2 (*a*)

Cumulative Record of a Rat's Bar Pressing under Continuous Reinforcement

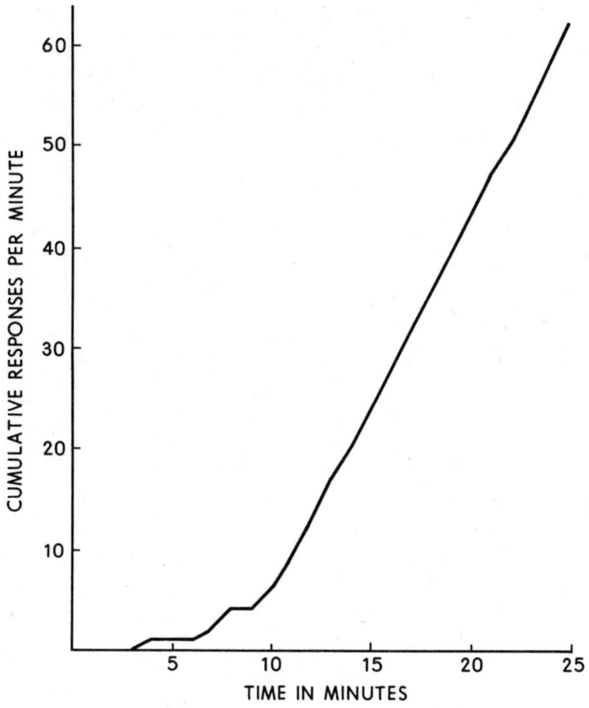

FIGURE 11–2 (*b*)

Noncumulative Record of a Rat's Bar Pressing under Continuous Reinforcement

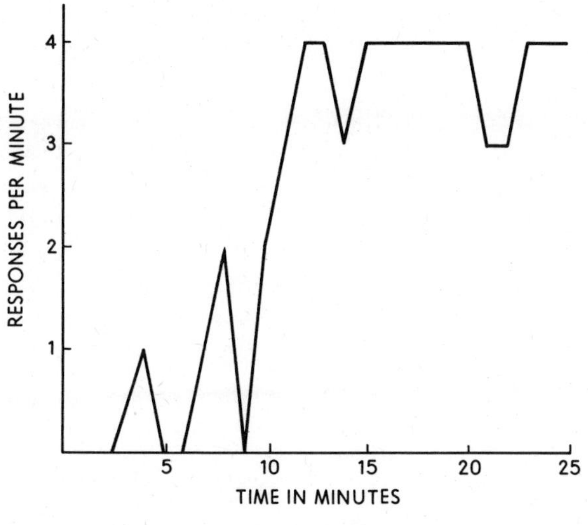

ment on a roll of paper which is moving at a constant speed (see Figure 11–1, page 314). The result is a *cumulative record* of the subject's responses over time. The steeper the slope (angle) of the cumulative curve, the greater is the rate of responding. Thus, a cumulative curve which comes close to being a vertical line represents a very high rate of responding, while a cumulative curve which approaches a horizontal line represents very little responding. *Acquisition curves* usually rise at an angle (the greater the angle, the higher the response rate), whereas *extinction curves* level off. Figure 11–2 (*a*) is a cumulative record of rat's bar pressing performance. Compare it with the conventional record (i.e., noncumulative) in Figure 11–2(*b*) on page 215. Skinnerians, interested primarily in the rate of emission of an operant, have used cumulative records, since they not only reveal the response rate but they also show *changes* in rate. Demonstration 11–1, which follows, will give the reader an opportunity to plot a cumulative record of his own behavior.

DEMONSTRATION 11–1: THE OBSERVATION AND RECORDING OF OPERANT BEHAVIOR

The careful and detailed observation and recording of responses is the first requirement for a functional analysis of behavior. This demonstration will give you some practice in observing some of your own behavior, recording it, and then plotting its frequency as a cumulative curve.

Outline of Procedures. The following steps are involved in this demonstration.

1. *Select a behavior you will observe and record.*
2. *Define the unit of behavior* (number of pages read, cigarettes smoked, and so on).
3. *Define the unit of time* (hours, days, and so on).
4. *Make a convenient recording device* (for example, a 3 × 5 index card marked off in time units). You may also want to keep brief notes of your daily activities.
5. *Observe and record the behavior.*
6. *Make a cumulative record.* Logarithmic graph paper is best for this purpose, but any graph paper will do as long as you plan the scale of the ordinate (vertical axis) carefully. That is, it is necessary to make some estimate of the total (cumulative) number of responses you will make over the entire period of recording, so that you can number the ordinate appropriately and not have your cumulative curve run off the top of the paper.
7. *Plot the cumulative frequency of responses each day.*

Selecting a Behavior. The first step is to choose some response with which you wish to work. Table 11–1 contains a list of behaviors which are

TABLE 11–1

Examples of Behaviors to Observe and Record for Demonstration 11–1

Behavior	*Unit of Behavior*	*Unit of Time*
Reading	Pages	Day or hour
Writing	Pages	Day or hour
Body weight	Pounds lost or gained	Day
Jogging	¼ mile run	Day
Swimming	Laps in a pool	Day
Tardiness	Times late for an appointment	Day
Daydreaming	Minutes spent in	Day or hour
Talking on the telephone	*a*) Minutes spent in *b*) Number of phone calls	Day or hour
Swearing	Curse words	Day or hour
Foreign language vocabulary	Words learned	Day
Studying	Hours spent in	Day
Bull sessions	Hours spent in	Day
Drinking *a*) Coffee *b*) Beer	Number of *a*) Cups *b*) Glasses	Day or hour
Smoking	Number of cigarettes	Day or hour

particularly applicable to the purposes of the demonstration, but you can select another response (perhaps suggested by the examples in the table) as long as it has several features important for this demonstration. The response should be relatively easy to observe and record without disrupting the behavior and without taking very much of your time. It should also occur with reasonable frequency in your life so that it can be observed and recorded. It is obvious that running in the finals of the 100-meter dash in the Olympic Games would not be a sensible choice. Finally, you may find it helpful to select a behavior which you actually wish to increase or decrease, although this is not mandatory for the demonstration. Notice that all the examples in Table 11–1 have this feature.

Working with some behavior you want to modify has the advantage that, directly or indirectly, it may help you make the change you desire. The purpose of this demonstration is not to teach you desirable habits or to get rid of undesirable ones. Nonetheless, it is of interest to note that Lindsley (1966), a student of Skinner and an early pioneer in the clinical application of operant conditioning, has observed that mere recording of deviant behavior (i.e., before any remedial reinforcement contingency is applied), when the subject is aware that a record is being kept of this behavior, is sometimes sufficient to modify it in the desired directon.

Assuredly, the record you make of your behavior will help you to analyze it, which, in turn, may lead you to think of ways of modifying it. For instance, suppose you chose reading as the behavior because you find that you do not read as much as you need to for your work. You may note that on certain days of the week your reading rate is higher than at other times, and thus you may find it helpful to make a concerted effort to read more on these days. In this regard, it will be helpful to keep a brief diary of the events in your life over the course of your recording in order to help you isolate the events which precipitate a change in response rate.

Observation and Recording. After selecting a particular behavior, the next step is to observe it and keep a record of its frequency. This can easily be done by marking off a 3 × 5 index card in time intervals, and then simply making a tally mark each time you perform the behavior, as is shown in Figure 11–3. At the end of each day (or other unit of time you are using), the total number of tally marks is assessed, and this becomes your rate for the day (for example, 26 pages read per day).

FIGURE 11–3

Example of an Index Card Record of Pages Read in a Week for Demonstration 11–1

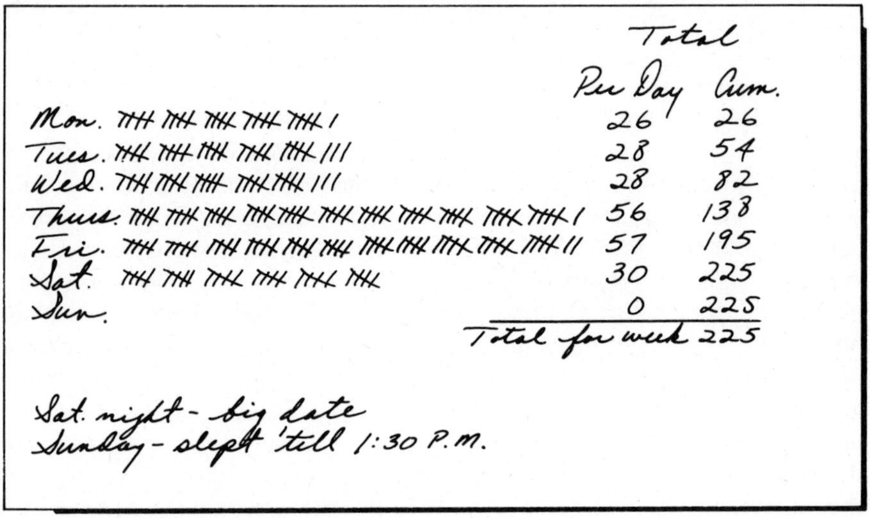

Making a Cumulative Record. Each day's rate should then be plotted on a cumulative record. As is illustrated in Figure 11–4, the *abscissa* or horizontal axis of the graph is marked off in time intervals such as days or hours. The *ordinate* or vertical axis represents the number of cumulative responses per unit of time. Suppose, over a week, a person read 26, 28, 28, 56, 57, 30, and 0 pages per day from Monday through Sunday. Figure 11–4 is a cumulative curve of this data. The first day, a point is placed at 26 responses; the second day, at 54 responses (i.e., 26 + 28); the third day, at 82 (i.e., 54 + 28); and so on. When the points are connected with a ruler, we have a cumulative curve of the person's reading rate for one week.

Figure 11–4

Cumulative Record of a Week's Reading Behavior for Demonstration 11–1

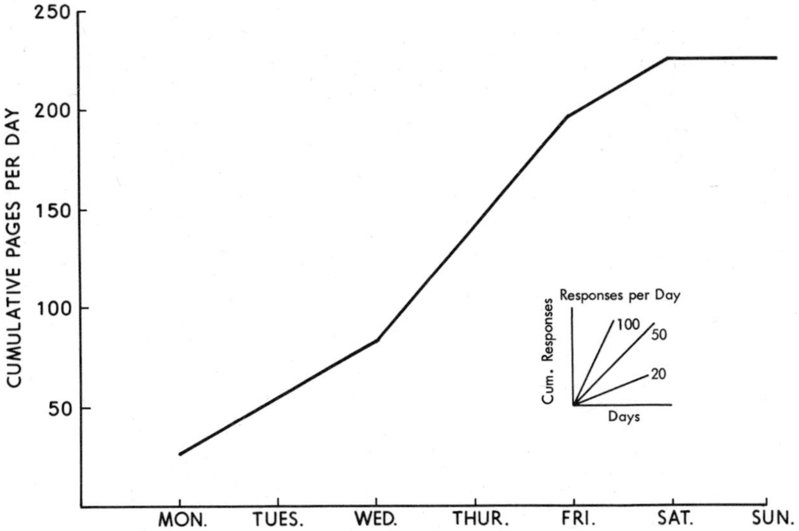

This cumulative record tells us a great deal about the person's reading rate. The nearly straight line connecting the points plotted for the first three days indicates that there was no change in rate over these days. On the fourth day, there was an abrupt change in rate, and this rate was maintained through the fifth day. This change in rate is reflected by the change in slope (angle of ascent) of the curve beginning after the third day. In fact, the slope of the curve has doubled (i.e., is twice as steep), which corresponds to the doubling of the reading rate (i.e., 28 pages per day to 56 pages per day). At the sixth day, the rate dropped off sharply and was approximately the same as that during the first three days, as inspection of the slope of the line shows. Finally, the cumulative curve levels off (i.e., there is no slope) at the seventh day, indicating that no reading was done on that day.

Thus far we have considered the basic strategy of operant conditioning research and the manner in which its basic data are collected. We shall now turn to the major problem which interests operant conditioning investigators, the manner in which behavior may be modified by its consequences.

The Principle of Reinforcement and an Experimental Example

The basic technique of operant conditioning will be described by means of an illustrative experiment. Hall, Lund, and Jackson (1968) were interested in increasing the study behavior of elementary school children. We shall consider the conditioning of study behavior in one of their subjects, Robbie. Robbie was chosen as a subject because he disrupted normal class activities and studied very little. In the first phase of the experiment, Robbie was observed unobtrusively during seven 30-minute periods in which the pupils were supposed to be working in their seats. The purpose of this phase was to obtain a *base line* or normal rate of the subject's study behavior so that the effects of the experimental manipulation (independent variable) could later be assessed. Figure 11–5 presents a record of Robbie's study behavior (which was defined as

FIGURE 11–5

A Record of Study Behavior for Robbie

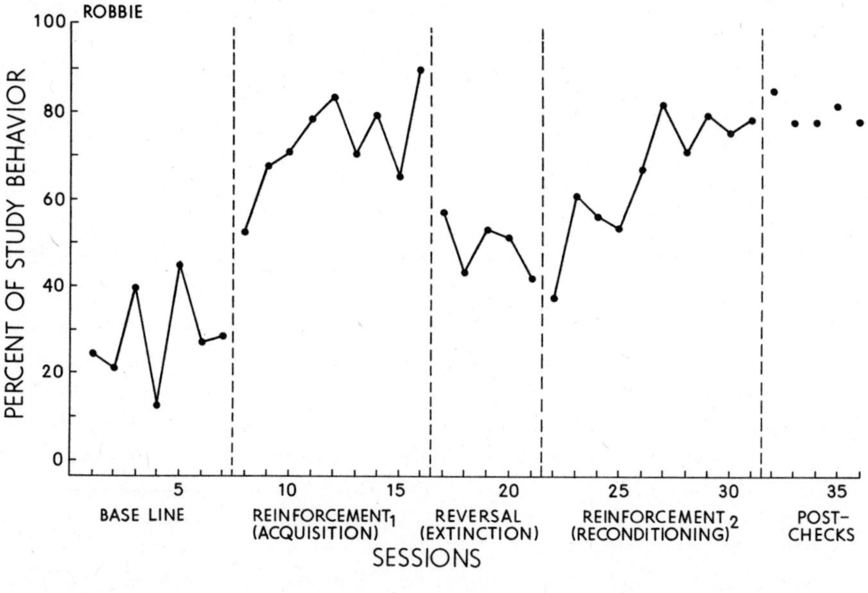

Note: Postcheck observations were made during the 4th, 6th, 7th, 12th, and 14th weeks after the completion of reinforcement conditioning.
Source: Adapted from Hall, Lund, and Jackson, 1968.

his having his pencil on paper for at least half of a 10-second observation interval). As can be seen in the graph, during the base line observation, Robbie engaged in study behavior on the average of 25 percent of the time. The remaining 75 percent of his time was taken up with such behavior as "snapping rubber bands, playing with toys from his pocket, talking and laughing with peers, slowly drinking the half-pint of milk served earlier in the morning, and subsequently playing with the empty carton" (Hall *et al.*, 1968, p. 3). It was also observed during the base line period that for much of his nonstudy behavior Robbie received the attention of his teacher, who urged him to work, put away his playthings, and so on.

Following the base line period, the *acquisition* or learning phase of the experiment was initiated. Now every time Robbie engaged in one minute of continuous study behavior, the observer signaled the teacher, who then promptly rewarded him for the study behavior with her attention. The teacher ignored Robbie at all other times. The results of this procedure were striking, as can be seen in Figure 11–5. When Robbie received attention contingent upon his studying, the amount of studying increased markedly in the first session and continued to rise in subsequent sessions. Robbie spent an average of 71 percent of his time studying during the acquisition phase of the experiment.

The marked change in the amount of Robbie's study behavior can be explained by the *principle of reinforcement:* "If the occurrence of an operant is followed by presentation of a reinforcing stimulus, the strength [of the operant] is increased" (Skinner, 1938, p. 21). A *reinforcer* or *reinforcing stimulus* (teacher's attention in the Hall *et al.* study) is an event which follows a response and increases the probability that the response will occur again. Initial inspection of this definition seems to suggest that it is completely circular and therefore meaningless. That is, if we say that an event served as a reinforcer because we observe that the response which it follows has been strengthened, and if we say that whenever a response is strengthened, reinforcement has occurred, we have, in effect, said nothing. However, as Meehl (1950) has cogently argued, the circularity of the definition is circumvented when the definition is restricted to *transsituational reinforcers,* events which serve to strengthen responses in a variety of situations and with a number of different organisms (for example, food for a hungry animal, social approval or attention for humans). An alternative solution is to make a distinction between the *act* of reinforcement (i.e., the strengthening of a response) and *response consequences,* which are defined as "something given for something done."[5] Thus, it becomes strictly an empirical question as to whether response consequences lead to reinforcement (the strengthening of the response). Although there are problems with the use of the terms *reinforcement, reinforcer,* and *reinforcing stimulus* (to mean response consequences that lead to the strengthening of the response), these terms will be used interchangeably in the present context since they are the terms in current usage by operant conditioners.

At this point, we must also digress for a second distinction which is often employed by operant conditioners. Specifically, it has been noted that while some reinforcers require no particular experience to be effective and can thus be referred to as *innate* or *primary reinforcers* (for

[5] This important distinction was first pointed out to the authors by Dr. Keith N. Clayton.

example, food or water under appropriate circumstances of deprivation), others have become effective because of experiences in which they were associated with reinforcement. These are referred to as *conditioned* or *secondary reinforcers,* and they control much of our social behavior. As Reynolds (1968) has noted:

> A fraternity pin, meaningless at an earlier age, reinforces the behavior of a teenager. The voice of a dog's master, ineffectual at first, comes to reinforce the dog's behavior. Stock market quotations, at first dull lists of numbers, come to reinforce an investor's behavior. Under special circumstances, conditioned reinforcers may be highly individualized, as in the case of idiosyncratic fetishes (p. 51).

Returning to Robbie, our now studious subject, it appears that the introduction of reinforcement in the form of the teacher's attention contingent upon study behavior was responsible for the increased rate of studying. It is important to note that without the base line to which the acquisition rate could be compared, no such statement could be made. In order to be even more certain that Robbie's study behavior is under the control of his teacher's attention, a third phase of the experiment was instituted. In the *reversal* or *extinction*[6] phase, the teacher refrained (as much as was practically possible within the classroom setting) from reinforcing Robbie with attention for his study behavior. If study behavior had been under the stimulus control of the reinforcement, then when the reinforcement was withdrawn it would be expected that the amount of study behavior would drop off (eventually reaching base line level). As Figure 11–5 clearly shows, Robbie's study behavior did decline during the reversal period to a mean of 50 percent.

Had the purpose of the experiment been merely to demonstrate that teacher's attention contingent upon studying could increase amount of study behavior, the first three phases of the experiment—base line (noncontingent reinforcement—i.e., attention not given contingent upon studying), acquisition (contingent reinforcement), and reversal (noncontingent reinforcement again)—would have been sufficient to document this assertion. However, the experiment had the practical purpose of increasing Robbie's study behavior. Thus, in a fourth phase of the experiment, which could be called *reconditioning,* the study behavior–teacher attention contingency was reintroduced with the result being an increase in Robbie's study rate which stabilized at a level between 70 and 80 percent (see Figure 11–5). To check on the effectiveness of the operant-conditioning procedures in maintaining Robbie's study behavior, periodic checks were made after the last reconditioning session for the remainder of the school year, the last check coming in the 14th week.

---

[6] The term *extinction* has been used to refer to both an *experimental operation* (discontinuation of reinforcement) and a *behavioral outcome* (decreased frequency of responding).

These checks indicated that Robbie's studying was being maintained at an average rate of 79 percent (see Figure 11–5). Furthermore, Robbie's teacher reported that the quality of his studying improved along with his increased rate of study behavior. For example, he was now completing written assignments and missing fewer words on spelling tests.

The general procedures just outlined for the operant conditioning of responses will work to establish almost any kind of behavior. Of course, the reinforcing stimulus used must be a strong incentive for the particular subject being conditioned. Additionally, the desired behavior must occur before it can be reinforced. While this is certainly an obvious point, it is nevertheless an extremely important one. In the case of behavior which occurs at least occasionally, as for example Robbie's studying, there is opportunity to reinforce it (although the experimenter may have to wait some time before the behavior is emitted). However, when the base line for a particular behavior which one desires to strengthen is near zero, the standard procedures described above will not work—at least not very efficiently. This is the case with extremely complex behaviors and for such persons as autistic children, mental retardates, and psychotic adults, who often have very limited behavioral repertoires. To help circumvent this problem, the experimenter may *shape* the desired behavior. *Shaping,* which is also called the method of *successive approximation,* involves reinforcing progressively closer and closer approximations of the desired behavior. The procedure of shaping is well illustrated by the following case history of a 40-year-old schizophrenic patient who, for the 19 years of his hospitalization, had been completely mute.

The S [subject] was brought to a group therapy session with other chronic schizophrenics (who were verbal), but he sat in the position in which he was placed and continued the withdrawal behaviors which characterized him. He remained impassive and stared ahead even when cigarettes, which other members accepted, were offered to him and were waved before his face. At one session, when E [experimenter] removed cigarettes from his pocket, a package of chewing gum accidentally fell out. The S's eyes moved toward the gum and then returned to their usual position. This response was chosen by E as one with which he would start to work, using the method of successive approximation. . . .

The S met individually with E three times a week. Group sessions also continued. The following sequence of procedures was introduced in the private sessions. Although the weeks are numbered consecutively, they did not follow at regular intervals since other duties kept E from seeing S every week.

Weeks 1, 2. A stick of gum was held before S's face, and E waited until S's eyes moved toward it. When this response occurred, E as a consequence gave him the gum. By the end of the second week, response probability in the presence of the gum was increased to such an extent that S's eyes moved toward the gum as soon as it was held up.

Weeks 3, 4. The E now held the gum before S, waiting until he noticed movement in S's lips before giving it to him. Toward the end of the first session of the third week, a lip movement spontaneously occurred, which E promptly reinforced. By the end of this week, both lip movement and eye movement occurred when the gum was held up. The E then withheld giving S the gum until S spontaneously made a vocalization, at which time E gave S the gum. By the end of this week, holding up the gum readily occasioned eye movement toward it, lip movement, and a vocalization resembling a croak.

Weeks 5, 6. The E held up the gum, and said, "Say gum, gum," repeating these words each time S vocalized. Giving S the gum was made contingent upon vocalizations increasingly approximating gum. At the sixth session (at the end of Week 6), when E said, "Say gum, gum," S suddenly said, "Gum, please." This response was accompanied by reinstatement of other responses of this class, that is, S answered questions regarding his name and age.

Thereafter, he responded to questions by E both in individual sessions and in group sessions, but answered no one else. Responses to the discriminative stimuli of the room generalized to E on the ward; he greeted E on two occasions in the group room. He read from signs in E's office upon request by E.

Since the response now seemed to be under the strong stimulus control of E, the person, attempt was made to generalize the stimulus to other people. Accordingly, a nurse was brought into the private room; S smiled at her. After a month, he began answering her questions. Later, when he brought his coat to a volunteer worker on the ward, she interpreted the gesture as a desire to go outdoors and conducted him there. Upon informing E of the incident, she was instructed to obey S only as a consequence of explicit verbal requests by him. The S thereafter vocalized requests. These instructions have now been given to other hospital personnel, and S regularly initiates verbal requests when nonverbal requests have no reinforcing consequences. Upon being taken to the commissary, he said, "Ping pong," to the volunteer worker and played a game with her. Other patients, visitors, and members of hospital-society-at-large continue, however, to interpret nonverbal requests and to reinforce them by obeying S (Isaacs, Thomas, and Goldiamond, 1960, pp. 9–10).

In cases such as those we have described, reinforcement was delivered for every desired response. However, in life situations reinforcement is often not given for every response, and one of Skinner's most significant contributions has been his research on *schedules of reinforcement,* which may be considered statements of the contingency on which reinforcement is given.

Schedules of Reinforcement

Schedules of reinforcement have been studied primarily with the rat and pigeon, in a standard situation, although the effects which have been found with these organisms have proved to be broadly generalizable across species (including man) and situations. In a typical experiment, the animal is placed in a specialized experimental chamber which is most commonly referred to as a *Skinner box* (although Skinner disclaims credit for coining the term). The chamber is about the size of the animal's cage and contains a bar which can be depressed in the case of a rat, and a key (a small target) which can be pecked in the case of a pigeon. There is also some sort of apparatus for dispensing reinforcements to the subject (usually food or water). The response which is studied is either the rat's bar pressing or the pigeon's key pecking.

The most obvious schedule of reinforcement is to provide the subject with reinforcement every time he engages in the behavior which the experimenter desires to increase. This procedure, usually referred to as a *continuous reinforcement* (CRF) schedule is, first of all, expensive to the reinforcing agent. Additionally, and of more importance for the study of personality, continuous reinforcement rarely parallels the sort of experience which is found in actual life situations (this is true for subhuman species as well). Thus, investigators have been especially interested in the effects of reinforcement when it is not available on a continuous basis. Such schedules are referred to as *intermittent* or *partial* schedules. Skinner (1956) amusingly relates the circumstances which led to his discovery of the remarkable effectiveness of intermittent reinforcement. Today pellets of rat food come already prepared, but when, in the 1930's, Skinner first began his research, experimenters (or their assistants) had to make their own food pellets using a device which druggists of the day used to make pills.

> The procedure was painstaking and laborious. Eight rats eating a hundred each per day could easily keep up with production [of the pellets]. One pleasant Saturday afternoon I surveyed my supply of dry pellets and, appealing to certain elemental theorems in arithmetic, deduced that unless I spent the rest of that afternoon and evening at the pill machine, the supply would be exhausted by ten-thirty Monday morning. . . . [I asked] myself why *every* press of the lever had to be reinforced. . . . I decided to reinforce a response only once every minute and to allow all other responses to go unreinforced. There were two results: (*a*) my supply of pellets lasted almost indefinitely, and (*b*) each rat stabilized at a fairly constant rate of responding (Skinner, 1956, p. 226).

We shall consider some of the major schedules of partial reinforcement that have been studied with particular emphasis on their application in the control of human behavior. The first schedule we shall discuss is the one which Skinner described in the preceding quotation.

A *fixed-interval* (FI) schedule is one in which the reinforcement is given for the first response made after a prescribed interval of time has elapsed. Numerous life situations appear to operate on fixed-interval schedules, such as the occurrence of college examinations and salaries that are paid in terms of temporal units (by the hour, week, or month).

It has sometimes been recommended that infants be fed on a fixed-interval schedule (for example, every three hours). FI schedules have been widely studied in laboratory experiments with animals. The schedule produces a reliable pattern of responding that appears "scalloped" when cumulatively graphed (see Figure 11–6). Thus, on such a schedule, the animal makes few or no responses immediately after a reinforcement but then begins to respond at an accelerated rate until the time for the next reinforcement. Moreover, it has been argued that the same outcome can be observed in humans.

> . . . we find the principle of increasing rate, prior to reinforcement, to have its application. We are more willing to work harder on pay day; absenteeism is less common; the student who has dawdled along all semester suddenly accelerates his study as examination time approaches in order to secure some slight reinforcement at the end of the term; the business man makes a strong effort to "clean up his desk" in time for vacation; most people increase their efforts to make a reinforcing appointment on time (Lundin, 1961, p. 80).

When compared with a CRF schedule, FI reinforcement, as well as other partial schedules, tends to produce *greater resistance to extinction.*

FIGURE 11–6

Stylized Records of Responding under Basic Schedules of Reinforcement

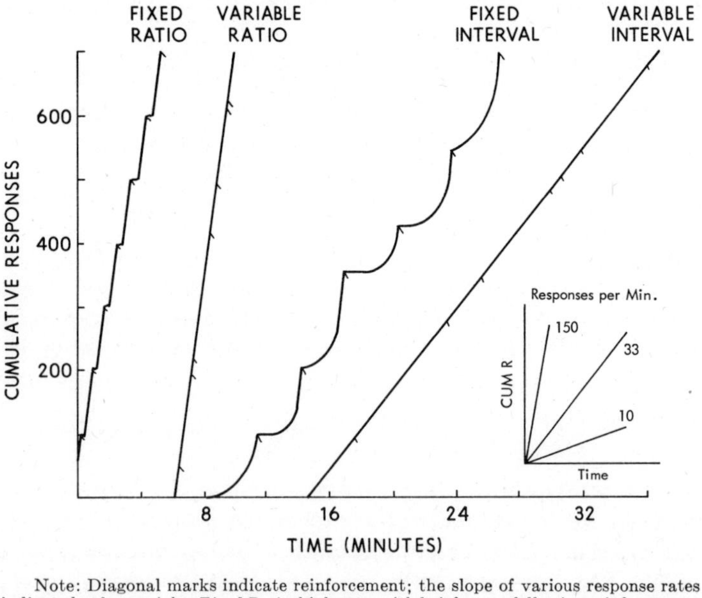

Note: Diagonal marks indicate reinforcement; the slope of various response rates indicated at lower right. *Fixed Ratio:* high rate, with brief pause following reinforcement and abrupt change to terminal rate. *Variable Ratio:* high sustained rate; no pausing after reinforcement. *Fixed Internal:* low overall response rate due to pause following reinforcement; length of pause increases with length of interval; gradual increase to high terminal rate as interval ends. *Variable Interval:* low sustained rate; no pausing after reinforcement.

Source: Adapted from Reese, 1966.

That is, after a behavior has been established by one of these schedules, the experimenter may withhold reinforcement completely but continue to observe the subject making the previously reinforced responses. The extinction phase of a learning experiment thus provides a measure of the strength or durability of the previously established response. When we say that FI schedules produce greater resistance to extinction than CRF schedules, we mean that subjects trained under the former schedules will persist longer after all reinforcement has been terminated.

Fixed-ratio (FR) schedules are those in which a response is reinforced only after it has occurred for a fixed number of times without consequences. Thus, "FR 4" refers to a schedule in which after every three unreinforced responses the fourth response is reinforced. Studies with both animals and humans suggest that FR schedules can be made to produce considerably higher rates of responding than either CRF or FI schedules (see Figure 11–6). Moreover, very high ratios can be built up. That is, an experimenter may begin an organism on an "FR 4" schedule and slowly increase the ratio of unreinforced to reinforced responses until the organism is rewarded as infrequently as one response in every thousand (i.e., FR 1,000). Skinner (1953) has noted both the applicability and the dangers of FR schedules in maintaining human behavior.

> It is a common schedule in education, where the student is reinforced for completing a project or a paper or some other specific amount of work. It is essentially the basis of professional pay and of selling on commission. In industry it is known as piecework pay. It is a system of reinforcement which naturally recommends itself to employers because the cost of labor required to produce a given result can be calculated in advance. . . . A limiting factor, which makes itself felt in industry, is simple fatigue. The high rate of responding and the long hours of work generated by this schedule can be dangerous to health. This is the main reason why piecework pay is usually strenuously opposed by organized labor.
>
> Another objection to this type of schedule is based upon the possibility that as the rate rises, the reinforcing agency will move to a larger ratio. In the laboratory, after first reinforcing every tenth response and then every fiftieth, we may find it possible to reinforce only every hundredth, although we could not have used this ratio in the beginning. In industry, the employee whose productivity has increased as the result of a piecework schedule may receive so large a weekly wage that the employer feels justified in increasing the number of units of work required for a given unit of pay (pp. 102–3).

In everyday life, of course, there is often some (or considerable) variability in the schedules on which humans are rewarded, and such sequences have also been the subject of laboratory investigation. Thus, in the terminology of operant conditioning, a *variable-interval* (VI) schedule is one in which the interval between reinforced trials is randomly varied around a stated time value so that *on the average* the individual is rewarded, say, every two minutes. That is, in "VI 2 minutes," the subject might be reinforced for responses appearing after: 1 minute, 2¼ minutes, 1½ minutes, 4½ minutes, 2½ minutes, ¼ minute. The average of these six intervals is two minutes. Lundin (1961) gives some interesting examples of commonplace human behavior that is controlled by VI schedules.

> The dating behavior of the college coed often operates on this kind of schedule. Unless she is going steady, when her social engagements are guaranteed (regular reinforcement or fixed interval), she does not know precisely when the invitations are going to be forthcoming. If she operates as a strong reinforcer for the behavior of the men in her life, the variable interval may be a low one, and she may be called popular. On the other hand if her VI schedule is a long one (only occasional dates), she waits a long time between invitations, and we may say she is not so popular.
>
> Some kinds of sports activities operate on this schedule, such as hunting and fishing. A fisherman drops in his line, and then he must wait. He does not know precisely when the fish will bite (maybe not at all), nor does he know when the game will fly, even though through past conditioning history he has found certain areas to be situations in which the reinforcements occur. Although these reinforcements of catching the fish or shooting the game are a function of his skill, the aspects of the availability of the reinforcements to him is a function of some undetermined schedule. The enthusiastic sportsman has a regularity of behavior which has had a past history of reinforcement, even though variable (p. 88).

VI schedules tend to produce steady (but relatively low) response rates, rather than the "scalloped" ones of FI schedules (see Figure 11–6, page 326), and are highly resistant to extinction. This latter feature of VI schedules is illustrated by the case of a 21-month-old child whose bedtime temper tantrums were extinguished by his parents (Williams, 1959). By screaming and crying when they tried to leave, the child had been keeping one of his parents or an aunt, who lived with the family, in his bedroom until he fell asleep. Thus, it appeared that the child's behavior was being maintained by the adult's attention (i.e., attention was reinforcing the tantrums). To extinguish this misbehavior, reinforcement was withdrawn. Specifically, the child was placed in his bed as usual, but now the adult left the room immediately despite the child's crying.

As can be seen in Figure 11–7, the child cried for 45 minutes the first time, did not cry at all the second time (it is possible that he was exhausted from the previous crying bout), cried for 10 minutes in the third extinction session, and thereafter decreased gradually to no crying. By the 10th session, the child even smiled when the adult left. However, a week later the child cried when his aunt put him to bed, and she reinforced this behavior by remaining in the room until he went to sleep. This *single* reinforcement, which in effect was dispensed on a VI schedule, was sufficient to increase the rate of crying to the pre-extinction level and to necessitate a second series of extinction sessions. As is shown in Figure 11–7, the rate of crying reached zero by the ninth session of the second extinction series, and no additional bedtime tantrums were reported during the following two-year period.

FIGURE 11–7

Length of Crying in Two Extinction Series as a Function of Successive Occasions of Being Put to Bed

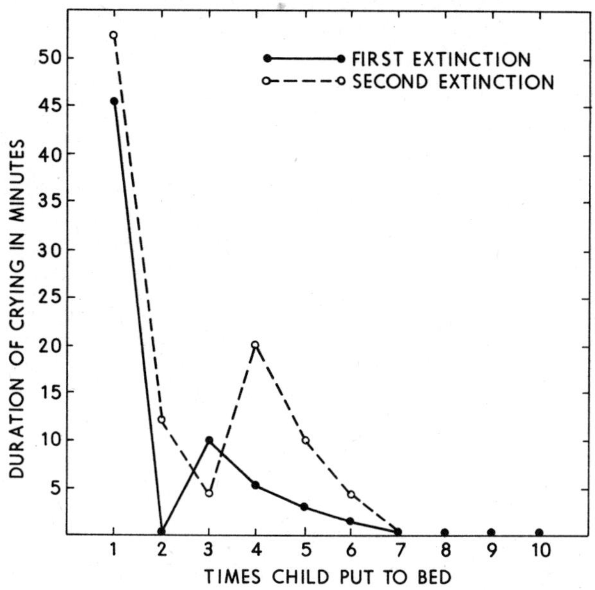

Source: Williams, 1959.

A *variable-ratio* (VR) schedule refers to the situation in which the number of responses required for reinforcement is varied randomly around a stated ratio. For example, a "VR 20" schedule might reinforce a subject after every 19th, 30th, 22nd, 14th, 10th, and 25th response (the average being after every 20th response). The VR schedule is among the most potent for inducing very high, steady rates of responding (see Figure 11–6, page 326) and extreme resistance to extinction. As Lundin (1961) noted:

> The extremely high rates that can be generated by these schedules is illustrated in the behavior of the compulsive gambler. Even though the returns are very slim, he never gives up. Families are ruined and fortunes lost; still the high rates of behavior are maintained, often to the exclusion of all alternate forms of activity. Witness the "all night" crap games in which a single person will remain until all his funds and resources are gone. His behavior is terminated only by his inability to perform operations necessary to

stay in the game. And even on these occasions, if he can muster more funds by borrowing or stealing, he will return to the game. Although gambling may involve other auxiliary reinforcements, social and personal, the basic rate of behavior is maintained by the schedule itself. The degree of control exercised by such a schedule is tremendous. In these cases almost absolute control has been achieved, so that the behavior becomes as certain as that found in respondent conditioning. The degree of control is often unfortunate and dangerous to the individual and his family, and the paradoxical thing about it is that the controlling agency (unless the gambling devices are "fixed") is the simple factor of chance. For this reason one begins to understand why legalized gambling is prohibited in most states. Like Skinner's pigeons, the compulsive gambler is a victim of an unpredictable contingency of reinforcements (p. 91).

The most comprehensive investigation of schedules of reinforcement has been made by Skinner and his associates, the results of which have been presented in a 739-page book (Ferster and Skinner, 1957) containing 921 cumulative records that illustrate the characteristics of the different schedules. The data consist of a quarter of a billion responses made over the course of 70,000 hours of recording. This monumental work has been criticized on the grounds that the book contains no description or summary of the data (just graphs!) and that the overall research strategy is highly uneconomical. At the same time, proponents of the approach, such as Reese (1966), have pointed out that: "This kind of research is one of the things that reaffirms one's belief in the lawfulness of behavior. There are certain characteristics of responding on each basic schedule, whether the schedule is in effect alone or in combination with others, that have been found for many species of animals, including man" (p. 16).

Stimulus Control

Although the principle of reinforcement is indeed a powerful one, it must operate with remarkable precision to be adaptive in real life. For example, even those behaviors whose strength we wish to increase in a wide variety of situations (such as grooming) would be considered socially abnormal if they occurred all the time. It would not be desirable, as a function of reinforcement for hair combing, to induce erstwhile disheveled children or hospital patients to comb their hair continuously through their meals, while studying, and through virtually all of their waking hours. Most behaviors, in fact, are socially approved and desirable only when they occur in *appropriate* situations. Eating is another example of a desirable (indeed, vital) behavior which must be brought under careful control. Thus, while we want to encourage our children to eat vegetables, meat, and occasionally candy, we do not wish them to attempt to eat string, sticks, or the contents of most of the bottles in the medicine cabinet.

In all of these examples, in addition to maintaining or increasing the strength of the operant response, we also wish the behavior to be brought under the control of certain stimuli in the environment. Researchers working within an operant framework are well aware of this necessity. They have noted that much operant behavior is under the control of *discriminative stimuli* or, for short, under *stimulus control.* In other words, for much of human behavior, the behavior occurs at a high frequency only in the presence of certain "setting events." As Reynolds (1968) has noted, relatively few persons attempt to turn off a radio when no sound is coming from it in the first place. In order to understand how certain environmental stimuli may gain control over operant responses, it is most convenient to consider those situations in which behavior seems to occur inappropriately because little or no appropriate discriminative control has been established.

Fox (1966) has suggested that a good example of behavior which is often under inadequate stimulus control is the study habits of college students. He notes:

> The act of studying, regardless of efficiency, is not usually under adequate stimulus control, either by time or by place. The student may study physics at random occasions and at any place he may happen to be on those occasions. Thus, he is subject to all the interfering behaviors conditioned to those occasions. No one occasion becomes uniquely related to study. Even where the student has established regular places and times for study, the immediately preceding occasion is likely to produce behavior competing with that of going to the place of study. He studies physics in the library at ten o'clock if he can resist the reinforcement involved in having coffee with his friends (p. 86).

Fox goes on to report an interesting pilot study in which the study habits of students were brought under effective stimulus control. He sought volunteers of freshmen and sophomore college students, who were told that a method was available which would require them to study only in the daytime and, while leaving their evenings free, would also improve their grades. Five students (two whose initial grades were above average and three whose initial grades were below average) participated in the initial test.

Let us consider how the treatment actually worked with a single student. Suppose, for example, that the student had a 9 o'clock physics class and was then free for an hour at 10 o'clock. The student was instructed by the counselor to go to the library at this time and to begin studying physics. (It was often the case, in fact, that students reported an intention to do just this, but somehow never got around to it.) One of the problems involved in maintaining a schedule, as most readers doubtless know, is that a person is likely to experience some degree of discomfort or perhaps to daydream in such a situation. What does the student do in this instance? The instructions of the counselor were quite specific.

If any of the discomforts of the kind previously described are experienced, the student was instructed to leave his studying immediately and go have coffee with his friends, or engage in any other pleasurable activity of his choosing. There was, however, one small restriction. Specifically, he was told that before leaving he was either to read one page of the text carefully or to solve the easiest problem which has been assigned and then to leave.

On each subsequent day the student was required to read one page more than the previous day before leaving the study room and, thus, gradually learned to spend the entire hour studying physics. After a week, a second course was similarly scheduled in a different room and appropriate hours set. Fox says, "Eventually, every course was so scheduled, and the student was spending the whole of one hour each day on each course" (1966, p. 87).

As Fox notes, each of the steps in this procedure was dictated by a simple principle of behavior (and thus, for our purposes, also serves as a partial review of the preceding sections). First, the counselor assisted the student in making maximal use of available reinforcers. Specifically, since the physics student had expressed anxiety about his ability to stick to his plan to study each day at 10 o'clock (presumably because of the unpleasant nature of studying and the competition of the available social rewards), the strategy minimized the aversive situation (a formal option to leave the studying was introduced), and the student did not initially have to forego entirely the alternative, the positive reward of being with his friends. Second, the principle of successive approximation was used by working up to the full hour of study gradually. Third, a fixed-ratio schedule was employed (so many pages for the reinforcement of leaving the study situation), and this ratio was gradually increased. Finally, the consistent use of a fixed set of stimuli (a particular room and hour of the day) as the occasion for study, is in accord with the principles of stimulus control.

A Note on the Effects of Punishment

Earlier in the chapter, it was noted that although Thorndike's original formulation of the law of effect assumed reward and punishment to work in "equal and opposite ways," he later concluded that punishment was relatively ineffective. Discussion of the research which supports this conclusion (almost all based on infrahuman organisms)[7] is generally beyond the intended scope of this book. Simply summarized, a number of experiments have suggested that punishment produces a temporary

[7] In *Walden Two,* Skinner (1948) observed: "We are now discovering at an untold cost in human suffering—that in the long run punishment doesn't reduce the probability that an act will occur" (p. 260).

suppression of operant responding in rats, but that after punishment is terminated, punished animals require *more* trials to extinction than those who have not been punished. Thus, overall, the number of trials required for complete extinction (cessation of responding) in punished and non-punished animals appears to be the same (cf. Estes, 1944). However, regarding such a generalization, Richard Solomon (1964) has made the following cogent observations: ". . . the attributes of effective punishments vary *across species* and *across stages in maturational development within species.* A toy snake can frighten monkeys. It does not faze a rat. A loud noise terrified Watson's little Albert. To us it is merely a Chinese gong" (p. 241; italics in original).

Because Skinner and many of his followers have agreed that there is sufficient evidence for indicting punishment as ineffective in the control of human behavior,[8] and because punishment is often seriously questioned on ethical grounds, it has been avoided in most applied studies of operant conditioning. However, since some recent work has suggested that punishment may have desirable effects under some circumstances, we will digress briefly from our emphasis on positive reinforcement to consider one situation in which punishment has begun to be accepted as an appropriate therapeutic tool. Specifically, punishment training may claim its greatest importance in the control of human behavior in those situations in which occurrence of a particular response, if not suppressed, would be extremely hazardous for either the individual performing the response or for others in his immediate environment.

For example, Risley (1968) has recently described a case in which punishment proved itself to be an effective and desirable tool in behavior modification, and he includes some interesting findings regarding the hypothesized and obtained side effects of this procedure.

The patient was a six-year-old girl who was diagnosed as having diffuse brain damage, was hyperactive, and whose only vocalizations were howls, moans, and clicking noises. The most predominant behavior she exhibited was climbing in high places, although this was interspersed with sitting and rocking. Risley (1968) presents a vivid description of the potential hazards of this limited repertoire of behavior.

Her climbing was a constant source of concern to her parents due to the threat to her life and limb (her body bore multiple scars from past falls; her front teeth were missing, having been left embedded in a two by four inch molding from which she had fallen while climbing outside the second story of her house), and the attendant destruction of furniture in the house. She had

[8] As we saw in an earlier section, unpleasant stimuli are usually acknowledged to be very powerful stimuli in *classical* conditioning. The question here refers to their effectiveness in modifying the future occurrence of behaviors which they follow (i.e., operant conditioning).

attended several schools for special children but had been dropped from each because of these disruptive behaviors and her lack of progress (p. 22).

Initially, Risley tried a variety of well-established procedures for eliminating the potentially harmful and hazardous climbing behaviors. The first of these was a procedure known as *time out from positive reinforcement,* or, *time out,* for short. Time out involves the removal of some positive reinforcer, contingent upon the occurrence of the response which the experimenter wishes to eliminate. In this case, for example, the patient's physical isolation from social interaction was made a consequence of her climbing behavior. Whenever the little girl climbed, her mother said "No!" sharply, brought her back to the floor, and took her to her bedroom (with no further vocalization and virtually no physical contact) for 10 minutes. Her mother was also asked to interact with the child as much as possible when she was *not* climbing. After 17 days, no visible diminution of this behavior occurred as a function of the time out procedures. Similarly, it did not appear that the climbing was under the control of any of the reinforcers which were supplied by either the experimenter or the mother, after an extensive examination of these possibilities in the laboratory. Thus, because of the clearly hazardous nature of the behaviors being performed, a severe form of punishment was applied.

The punishment was administered by a hand-held shock device, of the type often used for controlling livestock, and was operated by seven 1½-volt flashlight batteries. Despite the seemingly innocuous power supply, such a shocking device has an average voltage output of between 300 and 400 volts, and occasionally spikes to more than 1,000 volts. Subjectively, receiving a shock from such an apparatus is extremely painful. However, there are no immediate side effects of using the device (i.e., there is no redness, swelling, or aching) and, as Risley (1968) noted, "observers of the sessions in which the shocks were applied reported that, on the basis of observable autonomic responses . . . the subject recovered from the shock episodes much faster than the experimenter" (p. 25).

In this study, the contingent application of punishment effectively eliminated the hazardous climbing behavior in a very few sessions. The results are presented as a cumulative record in Figure 11–8. Risley's conclusion appropriately states both the implications and the limitations of the results by noting that his report

. . . should not be interpreted as a blanket endorsement of punishment with children. In the opinion of the author, the punishment procedures were therapeutically justified for this child. Shock punishment was employed only after other procedures to control disruptive and dangerous behaviors had been extensively but unsuccessfully employed. The possibility of deleterious effects and side effects were thoroughly considered before shock was employed in the home. The benefits to the child, in fact, far exceeded the author's expectations. Of course, no statement about the generality of these findings to other children can yet be made. *However, these findings do serve to limit the generality of extrapolations from past research which contraindicates the use of punishment* (p. 34; italics added).

FIGURE 11–8

Cumulative Record of "Climbing on a Bookcase," Showing the Effects of Punishment

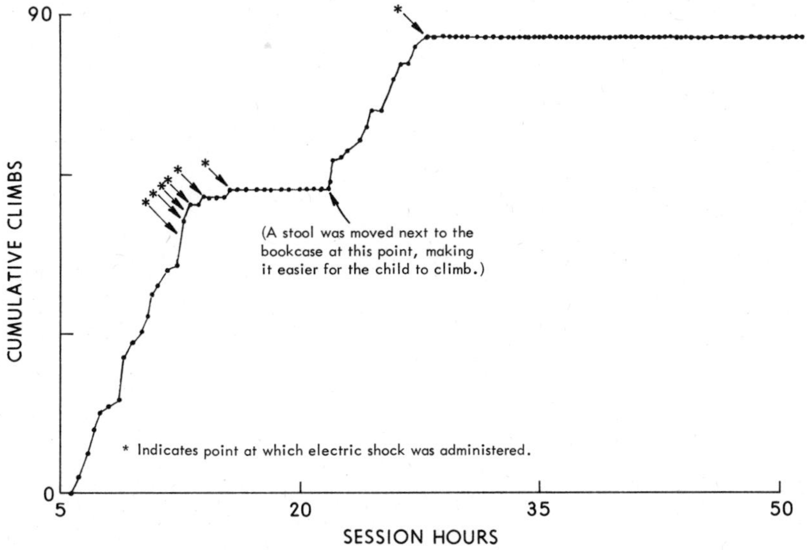

Source: Adapted from Risley, 1968.

DEMONSTRATION 11–2: OPERANT CONDITIONING OF HUMAN BEHAVIOR[9]

The reader may now wish to try his hand at operant conditioning. For this demonstration you will need to enlist the aid of a friend who is willing to participate. Be sure that the friend has about 45 minutes of free time; otherwise he may remember some pressing engagement at particular phases of the conditioning procedures! You will need a watch or clock with a sweep second hand, and pencil and paper.

The Response. The first step is to select the response you will teach your subject. Although the procedures to be outlined will work with complex motor or verbal responses as well as simple ones, it may be best to condition a relatively simple response, at least for your first subject. Some suggested responses are listed in Table 11–2. Other than simplicity, the response you choose to condition should meet two additional require-

---

[9] The procedures used in Demonstration 11–2 are, in part, adapted from Verplanck (1956).

TABLE 11–2

Examples of Responses Suitable for Operant Conditioning in Demonstration 11–2

Motor Responses

- Opening and closing a book (see text for possible components to be used in shaping).
- Taking top off a pen and replacing it.
- Tapping on the table.
- Standing up and sitting down.
- Nodding head.

Verbal Responses

- Criticizing others:
  - Possible comments for shaping:
    - Anything verbal.
    - Any statement.
    - Any negative statement or any statement about others.
    - Negative comment about others.
    - Severe criticism of others.
- Talking about the future.
- Talking about schoolwork.

ments. First, it should terminate fairly quickly so that it can be reinforced. Second, the response should end where it began. That is, when the response is completed, the subject should be able to immediately perform the same response again without either you or the subject having to rearrange the situation. For example, if the response being conditioned is "opening a book," it would be necessary to close the book before the subject made the response again. Such rearrangement naturally would be a salient cue for the subject and thus would bias the operant conditioning.

If the response you select is one your subject makes frequently, then all you have to do is wait until it occurs to reinforce it. If, however, it is an infrequently occurring response, you may have to use shaping procedures. This will necessitate breaking down the total response into logical component parts. For example, suppose you were going to condition "opening and closing a book." You would first reinforce (reinforcement procedures are discussed later) the first movement your subject makes, since this will start the subject moving about. *The first movement the subject makes should be the initial component of any motor response.* Next, you might reinforce *movement of either hand, movement of either hand toward the book,* then *touching the book, opening it partway, opening it fully,* and finally *closing the book.* Of course, if your subject should combine any of the successive steps, that will make the conditioning of the total response more rapid. Shaping is very much an art, and it is only through practice that you will "get a feel" for the procedure. Figure 11–9 illustrates a cumulative record of a response that was initially conditioned by means of shaping.

Reinforcement. Each time the subject makes a correct response (or

FIGURE 11–9

Cumulative Record of "Hand Raising" Shaped by Operant Conditioning

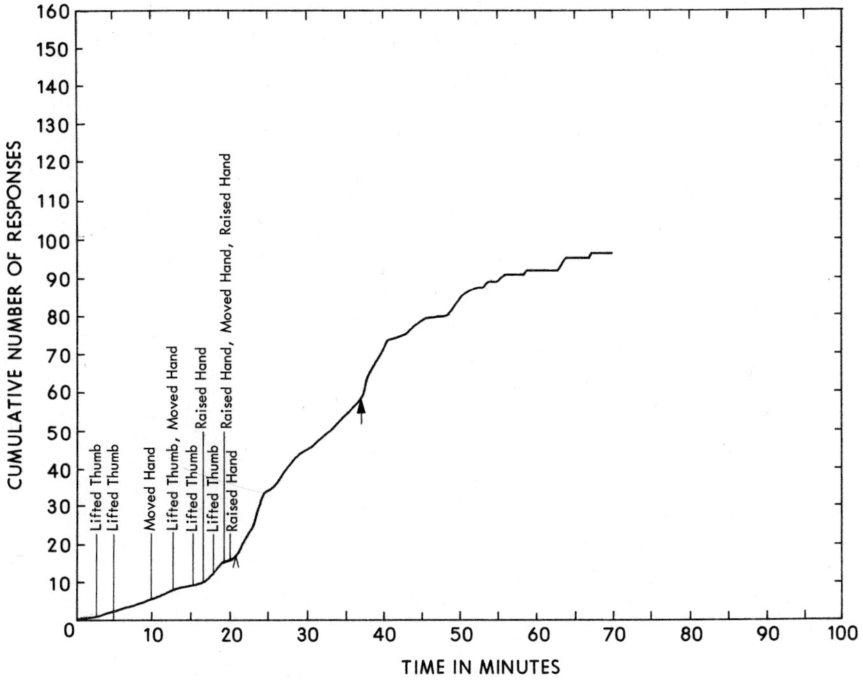

Note: Following the caret (∧) only the complete response was reinforced. Following the arrow (↑) no responses were reinforced (i.e., extinction).
Source: Verplanck, 1956.

an approximation of it if shaping procedures are employed), you will say the word "point." A record of the points the subject earns should be clearly visible to him, and this can be conveniently implemented by instructing the subject to make a tally mark on a sheet of paper each time you give him a point. An alternative procedure, which is preferable only if recording points will interrupt the subject's behavior, is for you to record the responses on a record sheet which is clearly visible to the subject during performance.

The prompt and accurate administration of reinforcement is the *sine qua non* of operant conditioning. The reinforcement should be given immediately after the correct response (or approximation of it) is made, and careful observation of the subject's behavior is necessary to ascertain whether he has made the response as you have defined it.

Procedure. Before your subject arrives for your "experiment," arrange the room so that he will be sitting facing you. Place any equipment needed for the response (for example, a book for the response illustrated above) in close proximity to the subject. If you are using a room with which the subject is familiar, be sure that your placing of equipment necessary for the response does not look out of the ordinary lest this "give away" the correct response. When your subject arrives, explain to him that you are doing an experiment or project for one of your classes. Then the following instructions should be given: *"Your job is to earn points. I will tell you each time you earn a point and you (I) will record it immediately on this sheet of paper* [hand your subject a pencil and paper] *by making a tally mark for each point you receive. Try to get as many points as you can."* Be sure that you do not give any further instructions to the subject. If he asks you a question, merely tell him: *"I'm sorry, but I'm not permitted to answer any questions. Just work for points and earn as many as you can."*

After the instructions are given to the subject, he may very well sit motionless and say nothing for several minutes. Sooner or later, however, the subject will make a response which you will be able to reinforce. Although this initial period of inactivity may be somewhat frustrating for both you and your subject, it will not affect the success of the conditioning. Do *not* try to break the silence or awkward social situation, since this will prejudice the experiment.

Observation and Recording. Once you have given your subject his instructions, your task is simply to observe him very carefully, record the frequency with which he makes the correct response (or approximation of it), and reinforce his responses. Your record sheet should be modeled after the example in Figure 11–10. Do not confuse the subject's record of the points he earns with the record you keep of his behavior and the procedures employed. Your record sheet should *not* be visible to the subject; using a clipboard will take care of this. When a subject makes a correct response, you must note the 30-second time interval in which it occurred by referring to your watch with a sweep second hand. The watch should be kept on the clipboard or in such a position that you do not have to move your eyes very far to see the time. You will also indicate on the record sheet whether a reinforcement was given for a response (by circling the check mark—see Figure 11–10), a procedure which is essential when the subject is shifted to a partial reinforcement schedule.

Finally, you must indicate on the record sheet any change of procedure such as change in reinforcement schedule, additional instructions given, and so on. This can easily be done by making a dark, vertical line at the point of change in procedure. As is illustrated in Figure 11–10, a small, lowercase letter is placed above this line, and it is defined at the bottom of the record sheet in a space provided for comments.

Conditioning. Three phases of conditioning will be used, and the procedures for each are outlined below.

FIGURE 11–10

Model Record Sheet for Demonstration 11–2

✓ = response (✓) = reinforced response

30-Second Time Interval	Total: For Each Interval	Total: Cumulative	30-Second Time Interval	Total: For Each Interval	Total: Cumulative
1.	0	0	25. ✓✓✓	3	66
2.	0	0	26. ✓(✓)✓	3	69
3. (✓) /a	1	1	27. ✓✓✓	3	72
4.	0	1	28. (✓)✓✓✓	4	76
5. (✓) (✓)	2	3	29. ✓(✓)✓✓	4	80
6.	0	3	30. ✓✓(✓)	3	83
7. (✓)(✓)	2	5	31. ✓✓✓✓	4	87
8. (✓)(✓)	2	7	32. (✓)✓✓	3	90
9. (✓)(✓)(✓)	3	10	33. d/ ✓✓✓	3	93
10. (✓)(✓)(✓)(✓)	4	14	34. ✓✓✓✓	4	97
11. (✓)(✓)(✓)	3	17	35. ✓✓✓	3	100
12. (✓)(✓)(✓)(✓)	4	21	36. ✓✓	2	102
13. (✓)(✓)(✓)(✓)	4	25	37. ✓✓	2	104
14. (✓)(✓)(✓)(✓)	4	29	38.	0	104
15. (✓)(✓)(✓)(✓)	4	33	39. ✓✓	2	106
16. b/ ✓✓✓ /c	3	36	40. ✓✓	2	108
17. ✓(✓)	2	38	41. ✓	1	109
18. ✓✓	2	40	42.	0	109
19. ✓✓	2	42	43. ✓	1	110
20. (✓)✓✓✓✓	5	47	44.	0	110
21. (✓)✓✓✓	4	51	45.	0	110
22. ✓(✓)✓✓	4	55	46.	0	110
23. ✓✓(✓)✓	4	59	47.	0	110
24. ✓✓✓(✓)	4	63	48.	0	110

Comments:
a = subject asks what he did to get point
b = start of FR 5
c = subject asks why I stopped giving points
d = start of extinction

1. *Acquisition: Continuous reinforcement.* During this phase, each and every correct response (or approximation of it) is given a point. Continuous reinforcement is the most efficient and effective way to establish a response initially. Continuous reinforcement should continue until the *total* response (i.e., not just a component of it) has been reinforced a minimum of 30 times, although, if you and your subject have the time, you can continue reinforcing each response for a greater number of responses. If, after a number of continuous reinforcements, the subject's rate of responding begins to decrease noticeably, you should simply say: "*Keep earning points.*" This statement usually will restore the previous response

rate. Be sure to indicate on your record sheet the point at which you gave this additional instruction to your subject.

2. *Shift to partial reinforcement.* After the response has been well established (i.e., after a minimum of 30 continuous reinforcements), you will be able to shift your subject to a partial reinforcement schedule with little difficulty. While any of the partial reinforcement schedules discussed earlier in the chapter are applicable, the most convenient for the demonstration is a *fixed-ratio* schedule. Reinforce every fifth response (i.e., FR 5). This means that although you will continue *recording* every response the subject makes, only after each five responses will you give him a point. Note also that you will continue to record the responses in the time interval in which they occur, but the five consecutive responses required for reinforcement to be given need *not* occur in the same time interval. Under the FR 5 schedule you should observe that your subject's rate of responding will increase and that there will be a brief pause after each reinforcement (see Figure 11–6 on page 326). Continue on an FR 5 schedule for a minimum of 10 reinforcements (i.e., 50 responses).

When you shift the subject to a partial reinforcement schedule, you may find that he will begin to emit other responses and make a number of verbal comments (for example, in the case of a fixed-ratio schedule, counting out loud and statements to the effect that he is receiving points for every five responses). Do not let such behavior changes bother you; just continue with the conditioning procedures.

3. *Extinction.* The final phase of the conditioning involves extinction of the response. This is done by withdrawing reinforcement for the given response completely. That is, you will continue to record the number of responses that the subject makes in each 30-second interval, but you will not give him points for any of these responses. Continue the extinction phase until the subject has failed to emit the response during five successive 30-second recording intervals, at which time the subject's task has been completed.

Plotting a Cumulative Record. Once the data for the three phases of conditioning have been collected, the frequency of responding can be plotted on a cumulative record similar to that in Demonstration 11–1. Heavy vertical lines (i.e., parallel to the ordinate) should be drawn to designate that a new phase of conditioning was instituted. Additionally, you should note any special changes in procedure and, in the case of shaping, the response component made, with small vertical lines (see Figure 11–9). Indicate what occurred at these points either by writing directly on the cumulative record or with a small, lowercase letter which refers to a statement written at the bottom of the cumulative record. In short, the cumulative graph should contain all the information on the record sheet and therefore be as complete a record of your subject's learning as possible. Figure 11–11 is a cumulative record of the data presented in Figure 11–10.

FIGURE 11–11

Sample Cumulative Record of Data Presented in Figure 11–10

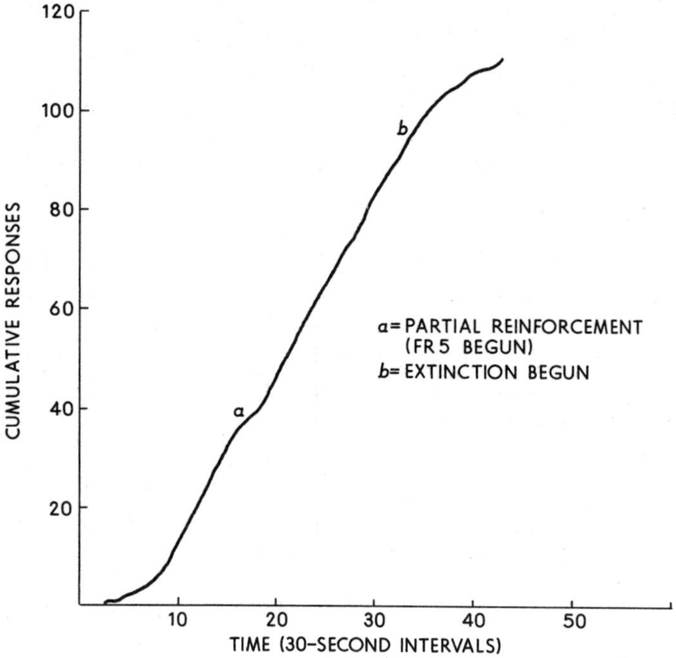

RECENT APPLICATIONS OF OPERANT CONDITIONING

The principles of operant conditioning have many practical applications, and we have endeavored to point out several of them in the foregoing sections. Two relatively recent uses of reinforcement, both of which have major social implications, have been reserved for the conclusion of this chapter.

The Token Economy

The Skinnerian emphasis on the single-subject experimental design for demonstrating principles of behavior and establishing *empirical* laws of learning does not preclude the application of the basic findings to groups of subjects. Indeed, one of the most impressive clinical applications of operant conditioning thus far has been in the simultaneous control and maintenance of the behavior of an entire ward of psychotic patients. The first such program was established at Anna State Hospital (Anna, Illinois) in 1961 and is still operative. Although the details of the operation of an efficient token economy are quite involved (cf. Ayllon and Azrin,

1968),[10] the underlying philosophy upon which its operation is based is quite simple. The patients are asked to "work"[11] for the "good things in life," just as most persons must do. The result is that rather than being cared for by attendants and sitting and staring into space for long periods of time or pacing the floor aimlessly, the characteristic behavior which can be observed on so many psychiatric wards, patients in a token economy care for themselves and are busily involved in various jobs on and off the ward for which they receive rewards of their choice. Functional, "normal" behavior is reinforced, whereas deviant, "sick" behavior is ignored and reaps no desirable consequences.

Each job pays a specified number of tokens or points which are given to patients after they complete a job. Examples of typical jobs for which patients may earn tokens or points are presented in Table 11–3. The tokens are in the form of round metal or plastic chips (similar to coins or poker chips) or small pieces of cardboard with different colors designating different values. If points are given to patients instead of tokens, they are usually marked off on a card, similar to a bank book, which the patient carries with him. The tokens or points are used to bridge the time span between the performance of the job and the actual receipt of the *backup reinforcers*. That is, at a later time, as, for example, at the end of each day, the tokens or points can be exchanged for a variety of incentives. Table 11–4 (page 345) lists examples of reinforcers available in one token economy, along with the number of tokens required for each.

Is the token economy effective? This question may be answered on more than one level. First, it is of interest to ask whether the token economy is successful in maintaining functional behavior on the ward. From all indications the answer to this question is yes. In the most extensive empirical study of a token economy, Ayllon and Azrin (1965) performed a series of six experiments the results of which clearly demonstrated that "the reinforcement procedure was effective in maintaining desired performance. In each experiment, the performance fell to a near-zero level when the established response-reinforcement relation was discontinued [reversal or extinction phase]. On the other hand, reintroduction of the reinforcement procedure restored performance almost immediately and maintained it at a high level for as long as the reinforcement procedure was in effect" (p. 381). The results of one of the experiments, which was designed to evaluate the effect of the token rein-

---

[10] An excellent and complete discussion of Ayllon and Azrin's work with a full report of a number of experiments is found in their book, *The Token Economy: A Motivational System for Therapy and Rehabilitation* (1968).

[11] The terms *work* or *job* are used, in the context of a token economy, to refer to activities which are commonly called work, such as cleaning the ward, serving meals, and acting as librarian, as well as to various adaptive behaviors which the patients should engage in, such as personal care, social interaction, taking responsibility, and so on.

TABLE 11–3

Examples of Jobs on a Token Economy Ward

Types of Jobs	*Duration*	*Tokens Paid*
Dietary Assistant		
Kitchen chores	10 min.	1
Patient assembles necessary supplies on table. Puts one (1) pat of butter between two (2) slices of bread for all patients. Squeezes juice from fruit left over from meals. Puts supplies away. Cleans table used.		
Pots and pans	10 min.	6
Patient runs water into sink, adds soap, washes and rinses all pans used for each meal. Stacks pans and leaves them to be put through automatic dishwasher.		
Secretarial Assistant		
Toothbrushing	30 min.	3
Assists with oral hygiene. Writes names of patients brushing teeth.		
Ward Cleaning Assistant		
Halls and rooms	30 min.	3
Sweep and mop floors, dust furniture and walls in seven rooms and hall.		
Assistant Janitor		
Supplies	10 min.	1
Places ward supplies in supply cabinets and drawers.		
Laundry Assistant		
Hose	15 min.	1
Match and fold clean anklets and stockings.		
Grooming Assistant		
Clothing care	15 min.	1
Patient sets up ironing board and iron. Irons clothing that belongs to patients other than self. Folds clothing neatly. Returns ironed clothing, iron and ironing board to nurses station.		
Recreational Assistant		
Walks	20 min.	3
Assists ward staff when taking group of patients on walks. Walks in front of group.		
Special Services		
Errands.	20 min.	6
Leaves the ward on official errands throughout the hospital grounds, delivering messages and picking up supplies and records pertaining to the ward.		

TABLE 11–3 (*Continued*)

Types of Jobs	*Duration*	*Tokens Paid*
Tour guide Gives visitors a 15-minute tour of the ward explaining about the activities and token system. Answers visitors questions about the ward.	15 min.	10
Self-Care Activities		
Grooming Combs hair, wears: dress, slip, panties, bra, stockings and shoes (three times daily).		1
Bathing Takes a bath at time designated for bath (once weekly)		1
Toothbrushing Brushes teeth or gargles at time designated for toothbrushing (once daily).		1
Exercises Participates in exercises conducted by the exercise assistant (twice daily).		1
Bed making Makes own bed and cleans area around and under bed.		1

Source: Ayllon and Azrin, 1965.

forcement in maintaining the activities of the patients, are depicted in Figure 11–12 (page 346). When tokens were given to patients before they performed their jobs, and were therefore not contingent upon the performance of the job, there was a marked decline in the number of hours which patients worked.

From the standpoint of the *behaviorist,* the token economy has been highly successful in remotivating and rehabilitating so-called psychotic patients. The before-and-after picture of the behavior of patients who participated in a token economy at a large Veterans' Administration hospital attests to this fact.

The program has been quite successful in combating institutional behavior. Prior to the introduction of tokens most patients rarely left the ward. The ward and its surrounding grounds were dominated by sleeping patients. Little interest was shown in ward activities or parties. Before the tokens were introduced, the ward was cleaned and the clothing room operated by patients from "better" wards. During the experimental period the ward was cleaned and the clothing room operated by the patients of this ward themselves. Now, no one stays on the ward without first earning tokens, and, *in comparison to prior standards, the ward could be considered "jumping"* (Atthowe and Krasner, 1968, p. 41; italics added).

TABLE 11–4

List of Reinforcers Available for Tokens

	Tokens
I. Privacy	
Selection of Room 1	0
Selection of Room 2	4
Selection of Room 3	8
Selection of Room 4	15
Selection of Room 5	30
Personal chair	1
Choice of eating group	1
Screen (room divider)	1
Choice of bedspreads	1
Coat rack	1
Personal cabinet	2
Placebo	1–2
II. Leave from the ward	
20-min. walk on hospital grounds (with escort)	2
30-min. grounds pass (3 tokens for each additional 30 min.)	10
Trip to town (with escort)	100
III. Social interaction with staff	
Private audience with chaplain, nurse	5 min. free
Private audience with ward staff, ward physician (for additional time—1 token per min.)	5 min. free
Private audience with ward psychologist	20
Private audience with social worker	100
IV. Devotional opportunities	
Extra religious services on ward	1
Extra religious services off ward	10
V. Recreational opportunities	
Movie on ward	1
Opportunity to listen to a live band	1
Exclusive of radio	1
Television (choice of program)	3
VI. Commissary items	
Consumable items such as candy, milk, cigarettes, coffee, and sandwich	1–5
Toilet articles such as Kleenex, toothpaste, comb, lipstick, and talcum powder	1–10
Clothing and accessories such as gloves, headscarf, house slippers, handbag, and skirt	12–400
Reading and writing materials such as stationery, pen, greeting card, newspaper, and magazine	2–5
Miscellaneous items such as ashtray, throw rug, potted plant, picture holder, and stuffed animal	1–50

Source: Ayllon and Azrin, 1965.

In short, patients who participate in token economy programs, in direct contrast to patients on conventionally run wards, take over the responsibility for caring for themselves, "put in a day's work," spend their earnings on various commodities and activities which we all enjoy, interact more with each other and with members of the hospital staff, and so on. It is behavior exactly opposite to this—being dependent on others for their personal needs, not working at any job, having no interests, withdrawing from social contact—that typically characterizes patients on their admission to psychiatric hospitals. In a very real sense, it is just such deviant, nonfunctional behavior which results in their being hospitalized in the first place. That is, it is this "sick" behavior which prompts relatives to solicit, or the patient himself to seek, treatment in a

FIGURE 11–12

The Total Number of Hours of the On-Ward Performance by a Group of 44 Patients

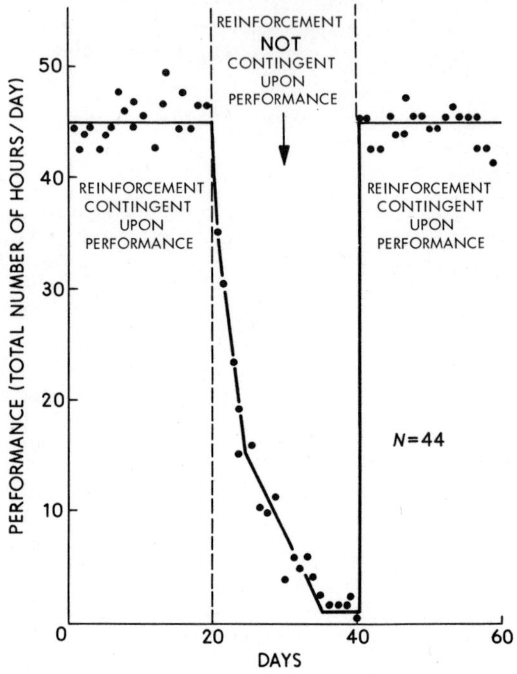

Source: Ayllon and Azrin, 1965.

hospital, and it is often on the basis of observing such behavior that the hospital staff decides to admit the patient. Thus, when the behavior which necessitated hospitalization has decreased or been eliminated, the therapy employed may be considered successful (i.e., if there is a sufficient control for a spontaneous recovery explanation—see Chapter 9).

Clinical applications of operant conditioning procedures such as the token economy would have value even if the changes produced were limited to the hospital wards where the specially contrived contingencies are employed. In many instances, however, the desirable response patterns endure after termination of stay in a token economy or other reinforcement programs. In large measure, these changes are probably due to what Bandura (1969) has called a "change in the locus of reinforcement." For example, in a token economy program, patients learn (or relearn) many behaviors which may produce either money or social rewards in the world outside the hospital. When this is accomplished, the environment can take over the behavior maintenance role for the former patient's behavior in a manner that is fully "natural."

There are, however, psychologists who would argue with the interpretation of even durable behavior changes. As we have seen in previous chapters, more traditional theories of personality, such as those of Freud and Rogers, hold that overt behavior itself cannot be the primary unit of study. Rather, overt behavior serves as an indication or symptom of a more basic (intrapsychic) process. In the case of abnormal behavior, the person's acts serve to guide the therapist to the "underlying" cause or problem (for example, a conflict between the id and ego or discrepancies between the self-concept and experience). It follows that if only the symptoms are treated without dealing with the underlying cause, then another kind of symptom will take the place of the one which was eliminated. While there is evidence to suggest that such symptom substitution does not, in fact, occur when the behavior itself is dealt with, the controversy and debate in the psychological literature regarding symptom substitution is far from settled.[12]

Putting the issue of symptom substitution aside, we can ask whether changes are observed in patients who participate in a token economy on variables which more traditional personality theories consider salient. Although there are less data available concerning this question and the data that are available are more subjective in nature (but so are the phenomena themselves), a general change in patients' self-esteem, self-respect, pride, and sense of worth has been observed. Thus, Atthowe and Krasner (1968) conclude that: "The program's most notable contribution to patient life is the lessening of staff control and putting the burden of responsibility, and thus *more self-respect,* on the patient himself" (p. 41; italics added). While the present authors were visiting a token economy ward, a patient came over to them and with an obvious sense of pride declared, "I earned 50 tokens today."[13] Although there is nothing extraordinary about this remark, it sounds very much like a car salesman telling his wife, "I sold three cars today and earned a $50 bonus" or a college student telling a fraternity brother, "I got an 'A' on that paper I worked so hard on last week." In short, the patient's remark is certainly an example of "healthy" behavior.

The Operant Conditioning of Autonomic Responses

The nervous system (of man and other species) can be divided into a *somatic* and an *autonomic* nervous system. The former is concerned with

---

[12] The interested reader should see Ullmann and Krasner (1965, pp. 13–15) for a concise statement of the concept of symptom substitution and Cahoon (1968) for a recent appraisal of the controversy.

[13] The authors are grateful to Dr. Nathan Azrin and Mr. Floyd O'Brien for the opportunity to visit the Anna State Hospital token economy ward.

the sense organs, higher mental processes, and movement of the striated skeletal muscles; the latter controls the smooth muscles of the visceral organs and blood vessels, the heart muscles, and the endocrine glands. Traditionally, the somatic nervous system has been viewed as under voluntary control of the organism and its functions as being modifiable by operant conditioning techniques. In contrast, the autonomic nervous system has been considered involuntary and subject to modification only through classical conditioning techniques. However, recently accumulated evidence appears to negate the notion that autonomic functions cannot be instrumentally conditioned.

Specifically, a fast-growing body of investigations have shown that man is capable of learning to control such autonomic responses as the galvanic skin response, heart rate, vasomotor responses (constriction and dilation of blood vessels), penile erection, and brain waves. In subhuman species (for example, rat, dog, and cat), other autonomic responses have been conditioned, including salivation, kidney function, gastric responses, and blood pressure.

Galvanic Skin Response. Kimmel and his associates (Fowler and Kimmel, 1962; Kimmel and Kimmel, 1963) have instrumentally conditioned the galvanic skin response (GSR), the change in the electrical conductivity of the skin which is a frequently used measure of emotion. In one experimental group, human subjects were seated in a totally dark room and were reinforced for emitting spontaneous GSR's by the brief onset of a light. Each subject in a control group was yoked (matched) with a contingently rewarded subject in terms of the number of reinforcements he received. The only difference between the two groups of subjects was that the yoked controls received the reinforcement at times when they were not emitting spontaneous GSR's (i.e., noncontingently). After an initial period in which both groups of subjects declined in their rate of responding, the experimental group began to increase the frequency of emitted GSR's, while the control group continued to decrease the frequency of GSR's emitted.

Sexual Response. Sexual deviation in men has been diagnosed (for example, Freund, 1963, 1965, 1967) and treated (for example, Marks and Gelder, 1967) with the aid of measuring penile erection, the male's most obvious response to erotic stimulation. In the diagnosis of sexual deviance, a subject may be shown pictures of nude women (normal stimuli) and pictures of nude men and children (deviant stimuli) while the volume of the penis is being monitored by a transducer. Erection to the normal, but not to the deviant, stimuli leads to a diagnosis of normal sexual interests, whereas the reverse leads to a diagnosis of deviant sexual interests. (Interestingly, if the subject responds with an erection to both sets of stimuli, no diagnosis can be made with this technique.) Following diagnosis, treatment may be carried out by punishing subjects with electric shocks for erections produced while viewing deviant stimuli.

Traditionally, it has been assumed that the suppression of penile erection is not under the voluntary control of the individual. Accordingly, it was felt that subjects would be unable to avoid getting an erection when shown stimuli which were erotically stimulating to them, and thus they would not be able to fake a normal response to deviant stimuli. However, a recent study by Laws and Rubin (1969) appears to demonstrate that subjects can voluntarily inhibit penile erection, thereby invalidating the diagnosis of sexual deviation in the manner described above.[14]

Laws and Rubin (1969) had normal male subjects watch erotically

FIGURE 11–13

Amount of Penile Erection Elicited from Two Subjects by Nine Successive Presentations of an Erotic Film

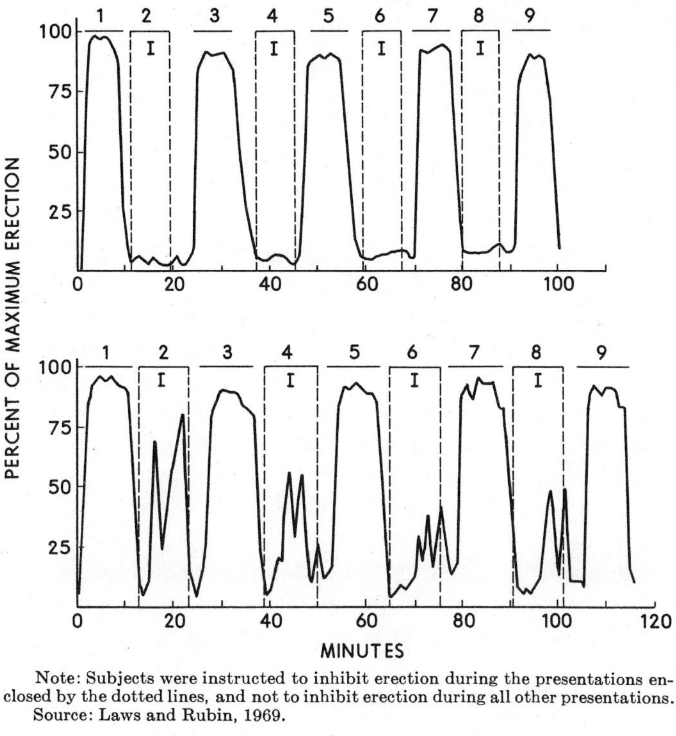

Note: Subjects were instructed to inhibit erection during the presentations enclosed by the dotted lines, and not to inhibit erection during all other presentations.
Source: Laws and Rubin, 1969.

---

[14] This point is not without social implications. In some European countries, the diagnosis of sexual deviance by measuring penile erection to various erotic stimuli is accepted as evidence in a court of law for sex crimes and in determining exemption from military duty on grounds of homosexuality.

stimulating movies while the extent of penile erection was being measured. During successive presentations of the film, subjects were either instructed to attempt to inhibit an erection by any means except not watching the film, or instructed to do nothing to avoid getting an erection. To assure that subjects were indeed observing the film, brief light flashes appeared on the top or bottom of the film intermittently on the average of one every 15 seconds, and the subjects were required to push a button located on the arm of the chair in which they were sitting every time they saw a light flash.

Although the ability to inhibit penile erection varied among individuals, all subjects were able to successfully inhibit the response when instructed to do so. The most impressive results are those of two subjects who were shown the same movie nine times in succession with alternating instructions to either suppress or not suppress penile erection. The data from these two subjects are presented graphically in Figure 11–13 (page 349).

What Is Being Conditioned? Critics (Katkin and Murray, 1968; Kimmel, 1967) of experiments such as the two reported above have pointed out that while the responses being conditioned are autonomic, it is possible that the instrumental conditioning of the responses actually involves the conditioning of some somatic response which, in turn, controls the autonomic response. For example, there is no doubt that somatic mediation was in large measure responsible for the findings of Laws and Rubin. The subjects reported that they were able to inhibit erections by *thinking* (a somatic function) of some detailed, nonsexual material (for example, the multiplication tables, poetry, and so on). The only way to categorically refute the somatic mediation hypothesis is to somehow prevent the somatic nervous system from operation. Toward this end, Neal Miller and his colleagues (Miller, 1969) at Rockefeller University have successfully conditioned autonomic responses in subhuman subjects that were injected with *curare,* a drug which inhibits neural impulses from reaching the skeletal muscles. Although the issue of somatic mediation in instrumental autonomic conditioning is an important one to the psychologist interested in elucidating the basic learning processes involved, psychologists concerned with the practical implications of *control* of autonomic responses need not be concerned with the underlying mechanism.

Implications for Human Personality. The research on autonomic conditioning, particularly with humans, is still at an early stage, and thus few definitive statements can be made regarding it at this time. However, because of the potential importance of the findings thus far for human personality, it is worth briefly discussing some of the possible implications.

Psychosomatic Symptoms. A distinction has been made between hysterical symptoms which primarily involve the somatic nervous system (for example, paralysis of the legs) and psychosomatic symptoms which primarily involve the autonomic nervous system (for example, stomach ulcers). The recent evidence that the functions of the two nervous systems may be modifiable in the same way has led Miller (1969) to speculate on an extension of the interpretation which he and Dollard (Dollard and Miller, 1950; see Chapter 10) had made of hysterical symptoms to psychosomatic symptoms.

For example, suppose a child is terror-stricken at the thought of going to school in the morning because he is completely unprepared for an important examination. The strong fear elicits a variety of fluctuating autonomic symptoms, such as queasy stomach at one time and pallor and faintness at another; at this point his mother, who is particularly concerned about cardiovascular symptoms, says, "You are sick and must stay home." The child feels a great relief from fear, and this reward should reinforce the cardiovascular responses producing pallor and faintness. If such experiences are repeated frequently enough, the child, theoretically, should learn to respond with that kind of symptom. Similarly, another child whose mother ignored the vasomotor responses but was particularly concerned by signs of gastric distress would learn the latter type of symptom (Miller, 1969, p. 444).

Individual and Cultural Differences. It is also possible that less extreme emotional reactions than psychosomatic symptoms can be learned in a similar way. Most individuals have characteristic ways of responding to particular situations. For instance, some people respond to failure with depression and others with anger. It may be that an individual's predominant response to a given situation has been learned because it, rather than some other response, received repeated reinforcement (sympathy, for example). Likewise, persons may learn to respond to the same situations in different ways. A young boy who falls while playing with his father may learn to hold back his tears because his father will be disappointed if his son is a "crybaby" but proud if he is a "big boy." The same child who falls in his mother's presence may burst out crying because he knows that his mother is more concerned about his getting hurt and will reward his tears with sympathy.

The Therapeutic Use of Autonomic Conditioning. Although very little therapeutic use of autonomic conditioning has been made so far, its potential is impressive. Subjects motivated to eliminate autonomic symptoms (for example, high blood pressure) may be taught to do so by giving them feedback concerning the changes in their symptom. Success in creating change in the desired direction would serve as a reward, as it did in the Laws and Rubin (1969) study cited earlier. Miller (1969) reports that he and his associates have had some success in teaching epileptic patients to inhibit abnormal brain waves which are thought to cause their seizures. Miller also suggests the possibility of treating insomnia by reinforcing high-voltage, low-frequency EEG's which characterize sleep (see Chapter 4). Another potential application of instrumental autonomic conditioning is in the control of the dilation and constriction of cranial blood vessels which accompany migraine headaches.

Once again it should be emphasized that the research and speculations concerning instrumental conditioning of autonomic responses must be considered tentative in nature at the present time. Nevertheless, the area of instrumental autonomic conditioning is one of the latest and most exciting advances in psychology, and the implications it seems to hold for the understanding and control of human behavior are by no means trivial.

REFERENCES

Atthowe, J. M., and Krasner, L. Preliminary report on the application of contingent reinforcement procedures (token economy) on a "chronic" psychiatric ward. *Journal of Abnormal Psychology,* 1968, **73,** 37–43.

Ayllon, T., and Azrin, N. H. Reinforcer sampling: A technique for increasing the behavior of mental patients. *Journal of Applied Behavior Analysis,* 1968, **1,** 13–20.

Ayllon, T., and Azrin, N. H. The measurement and reinforcement of behavior of psychotics. *Journal of the Experimental Analysis of Behavior,* 1965, **8,** 357–83.*

Ayllon, T., and Azrin, N. H. *The token economy: A motivational system for therapy and rehabilitation.* New York: Appleton-Century-Crofts, 1968.

Bandura, A. *Principles of behavior modification.* New York: Holt, Rinehart & Winston, 1969.

Cahoon, D. D. Symptom substitution and the behavior therapies: A reappraisal. *Psychological Bulletin,* 1968, **69,** 149–56.

Dollard, J., and Miller, N. E. *Personality and psychotherapy.* New York: McGraw-Hill, 1950.

Estes, W. K. An experimental study of punishment. *Psychological Monographs,* 1944, **57** (Whole No. 263, 3).

Ferster, C. B., and Skinner, B. F. *Schedules of reinforcement.* New York: Appleton-Century-Crofts, 1957.

Fowler, R. L., and Kimmel, H. D. Operant conditioning of the G. S. R. *Journal of Experimental Psychology,* 1962, **63,** 563–67.

Fox, L. Effecting the use of efficient study habits. In R. Ulrich, T. Stachnik, and J. Mabry (Eds.), *Control of human behavior.* Glenview, Ill.: Scott Foresman, 1966.

Freund, K. A. A laboratory method for diagnosing predominance of homo- or hetero-erotic interest in the male. *Behaviour Research and Therapy,* 1963, **1,** 85–93.

Freund, K. A. Diagnosing heterosexual pedophilia by means of a test for sexual interest. *Behaviour Research and Therapy,* 1965, **3,** 229–34.

Freund, K. A. Diagnosing homo- or heterosexuality and erotic age preference by means of a psychophysiological test. *Behavior Research and Therapy,* 1967, **5,** 209–28.

Hall, R. V., Lund, D., and Jackson, D. Effects of teacher attention on study behavior. *Journal of Applied Behavior Analysis,* 1968, **1,** 1–12.

Hathaway, S. R., and McKinley, J. C. *Minnesota Multiphasic Personality Inventory.* Minneapolis: University of Minnesota Press, 1943.

Hebb, D. O. *A textbook of psychology.* (2d ed.) Philadelphia: Saunders, 1966.

Hilgard, E. R., and Atkinson, R. C. *Introduction to psychology.* New York: Harcourt, Brace & World, 1967.

Isaacs, W., Thomas, J., and Goldiamond, I. Application of operant conditioning to reinstate verbal behavior in psychotics. *Journal of Speech and Hearing Disorders,* 1960, **25,** 8–12.

Katkin, E. S., and Murray, E. N. Instrumental conditioning of autonomically mediated behavior: Theoretical and methodological issues. *Psychological Bulletin,* 1968, **70,** 52–68.

Kimmel, E., and Kimmel, H. D. Replication of operant conditioning of the G. S. R. *Journal of Experimental Psychology,* 1963, **65,** 212–13.

Kimmel, H. D. Instrumental conditioning of autonomically mediated behavior. *Psychological Bulletin,* 1967, 337–45.

Laws, D. R., and Rubin, H. B. Instructional control of an autonomic sexual response. *Journal of Applied Behavior Analysis,* 1969, **2,** 93–99.

Lindsley, O. R. An experiment with parents handling behavior at home. *Johnstone Bulletin* (Johnstone Training Center, Bordertown, N.J.), 1966, **9,** 27–36.

Lundin, R. W. *Personality.* New York: Macmillan, 1961.

Marks, I. M., and Gelder, M. G. Transvestism and fetishism: Clinical and psychological changes during faradic aversion. *British Journal of Psychology,* 1967, **113,** 711–29.

Meehl, P. E. On the circularity of the law of effect. *Psychological Bulletin,* 1950, **47,** 52–75.

Miller, N. E. Learning of visceral and glandular responses. *Science,* 1969, **163,** 434–45.

Reese, E. P. The analysis of human operant behavior. In J. A. Vernon (Ed.), *Introduction to psychology: A self-selection textbook.* Dubuque, Iowa: Brown, 1966.

Reynolds, G. S. *A primer of operant conditioning.* Glenview, Ill.: Scott Foresman, 1968.

Risley, T. R. The effects and side effects of punishing the autistic behaviors of a deviant child. *Journal of Applied Behavior Analysis,* 1968, **1,** 21–34.

Skinner, B. F. A case history in scientific method. *American Psychologist,* 1956, **11,** 221–33.

Skinner, B. F. *Science and human behavior*. New York: Macmillan, 1953.

Skinner, B. F. *The behavior of organisms*. New York: Appleton-Century-Crofts, 1938.

Skinner, B. F. *Walden two*. New York: Macmillan, 1948.

Solomon, R. L. Punishment. *American Psychologist,* 1964, **19,** 239–53.

Thorndike, E. L. Animal intelligence: An experimental study of the associative processes in animals. *Psychological Review Monograph Supplement,* 1898, **2** (4, Whole No. 8).

Ullmann, L. P., and Krasner, L. (Eds.) *Case studies in behavior modification.* New York: Holt, Rinehart & Winston, 1965.

Verplanck, W. S. The operant conditioning of human motor behavior. *Psychological Bulletin,* 1956, **53,** 70–83.

Williams, C. D. The elimination of tantrum behavior by extinction procedures: Case report. *Journal of Abnormal and Social Psychology,* 1959, **59,** 269.

chapter 12

Learning Approaches to Personality: Observational Learning

In the preceding chapters, we discussed learning views of personality which were based on the principles of operant and classical conditioning and drive reduction and which grew more or less directly out of traditional theories of learning and basic experiments in the laboratory (often with infrahuman organisms). The present chapter is concerned with another form of learning, learning by observation, and its unique contributions to human personality and social behavior.

The first treatise on observational learning in this century was Gabriel Tarde's *The Laws of Imitation,* published in 1903. In his volume, Tarde argued that ". . . the social being, in the degree that he is social, is essentially imitative, and that imitation plays a role in societies analogous to that of heredity in organic life . . ." (p. 11). Tarde was persuaded that everything of social importance is either inventive or imitative and noted that inventions or innovations have no importance whatsoever if they are not emulated by others. It is doubtful, for example, that the *first* voyage from Europe to America was completed by Christopher Columbus. Columbus is nonetheless most often credited with the "discovery" of this continent because, as a consequence of *his* voyage, subsequent navigators made the trip with ever increasing frequency. Had he not been imitated, his voyage would not be socially important. The final thesis of Tarde's argument is no less than the statement "society *is* imitation."

More recent theorists and investigators would, of course, blush at the sweep of Tarde's argument and, moreover, find his complete deference to "armchair evidence" somewhat embarrassing. Nevertheless, contemporary theorists of diverse persuasions have acknowledged imitative phenomena to be, in some sense, a pervasive influence on social development. The major issue, currently as in Tarde's time, is to elucidate principles which will aid in predicting the influence of social models upon other persons' behavior.

OBSERVATIONAL LEARNING: THE PROBLEM OF DEFINITION

Regardless of the theory of behavior being considered, some attention must be given to the fact that human behavior may in part be determined and modified by the opportunity to observe the behavior of other humans. This phenomenon, variously called *imitation, observational learning, modeling,* and as a special case in psychoanalytic theory, *identification* (see Chapter 3), is a critical aspect of personality development. In addition to theoretical differences as to the processes underlying imitation, there is also considerable confusion regarding the terms used to describe the phenomenon. A series of definitions, provided below, will be followed consistently in the remainder of this chapter and may prove to be helpful in clarifying some theoretical issues.

Modeling will refer to the behavior or alleged behavior of persons in a social context. The behaving individual will be referred to as a *model,* and the specific components of his behavior will be referred to as *modeling cues.* Modeling cues are almost continuously available in real life by directly and personally observing other persons; in these cases we speak of *live modeling.* Often, however, the behavior of others can be observed in movies, television, books, newspapers, and verbal reports. These latter cases may be considered to fall in the general category of *symbolic modeling.*[1]

Persons who receive or are exposed to modeling cues, either live or symbolic, will be referred to as *observers.* The demonstrated consequences of observing a model will be subsumed under the term *observational learning.*

Observational learning, as a consequence of modeling, may take several forms. *Imitation,* one of these forms, refers to the outcome in which,

---

[1] The potential breadth of these definitions is intentional. Modeling cues *are* embodied in virtually all social behavior. However, as the subsequent definitions indicate, modeling, as we have defined it, does not necessarily lead to observational learning, and observational learning does not necessarily lead to imitation.

subsequent to observing a model, an observer's behavior is more like the model's than it otherwise would have been. For example, in many trades, an apprenticeship is used to assure that the novice's performance will become sufficiently like that of the journeyman. On the continuum of this same phenomenon is the possibility that, subsequent to observing a model, the observer's own behavior will be *less* like the model's than it would otherwise have been. A child who sees a peer burned by a hot stove may be less likely to touch this dangerous appliance than he was previously. This outcome, called *counterimitation* by Tarde, *nonimitation* by Miller and Dollard, and *inhibition* by Bandura and Walters, is often overlooked when imitation is thought of as no more than a parroting of what one has seen or heard.

Observational learning can occur, however, without being manifested spontaneously in the future behavior of observers. For example, a person may observe the unique hair style of another, his manner of speech, or his aggressive attitude toward his wife without becoming either more or less like the exemplar than he was previously. Nonetheless, if the observer can recall or reproduce the behavior he has witnessed (for example, when asked to do so), observational learning has occurred. As we shall see, the possibility that behavior can be acquired observationally without being performed has important implications for understanding social learning.

MILLER AND DOLLARD'S THEORY OF IMITATION

Observational learning permits society to transmit and modify behavior in a variety of situations, including those where errors produced by trial-and-error shaping may be extremely costly or even fatal. For instance, a child need not be hit by an automobile while crossing the street when the traffic light is red to learn that such behavior is harmful. It is usually sufficient for a parent to describe to the child what could happen if he did not wait for the light to turn green (i.e., symbolic modeling). Further, the acquisition of language, social values, vocational and professional skills, and all sorts of social practices would be incredibly difficult without the presentation of the exemplary behavior of others. Certainly, the pervasiveness of imitation in human learning was one of the factors which led Miller and Dollard (1941) to use the phenomenon as one of the focal points of their social learning theory, the basic principles of which were outlined in Chapter 10.

Three Types of Imitation

Miller and Dollard have distinguished three types of behavior which might be thought of as "imitation": *same behavior, copying,* and *matched-dependent behavior.* Same behavior, which is only incidently related to imitation as we have defined it above, refers to the situation wherein two (or more) persons are performing in similar or identical ways but are responding *independently* to the available cues. In other words, neither individual has learned or modified his behavior on the basis of the behavior of the other. Two motorists approaching an intersection and stopping because they each see a stop sign (the cue) would be a common example of same behavior.

Copying refers to that situation in which one individual is learning some form of behavior from another person and in which the final goal of the imitation is merely the acceptable reproduction of the model's behavior. Thus, copying is oriented toward reproduction per se, rather than toward using the behavior of another as an aid in the attainment of an additional specifiable goal (reward). It is crucial in copying that the observer have some way of knowing when his own responses are similar enough to the model's to be considered acceptable by some criterion. In learning a foreign language, for example, the teacher will pronounce a word or phrase which the student then tries to mimic. The criterion for sameness is usually the teacher's judgment that the student's pronunciation is a reasonable facsimile of his own.

Matched-dependent behavior can be described in terms of a leader-follower relationship. In the matched-dependent situation, it is assumed that the leader (model) is able to read the critical cues with respect to a particular act but that the follower (observer) is not. The follower is therefore *dependent* on the leader for providing the cues. The concept of matched-dependent behavior assumes that the follower imitates the behavior of the leader in order to gain the end-state (reward) which is reached by the leader. Miller and Dollard considered matched-dependent behavior the most important form of imitation, and consequently they have directed almost all of their research efforts toward it.

An Example of Matched-Dependent Behavior

As an illustration of matched-dependent behavior consider the case of a young couple who had just moved to a new city. During their first night in their new home the wife became ill, and the husband went out to find a drugstore to purchase some medicine. After he drove around for several minutes and found all of the drugstores he passed closed for the night, the husband stopped a passing police car, explained that he was new to the city, and asked for directions to the nearest open drugstore. Rather than give him directions, which would be difficult for a stranger to follow, the policeman suggested that the young man follow him. Thus, the policeman set out with the young man close behind. At each intersection the young man watched the police car in front of him to see if it turned right or left or proceeded straight ahead. After twisting and turning for several minutes, the police car finally pulled to the curb in front of an open drugstore. Although the young husband had left his wife a mere 15 minutes before, it seemed a good deal longer to him (presumably because of the newness of his surroundings). He thanked the policeman for his help, purchased the medicine for his wife, and headed for home. He tried to retrace the route the policeman had taken but soon found himself hopelessly lost. It was only by asking for directions from a series of gas station attendants and fellow motorists that he was eventually able to find his new home and waiting wife, but the return trip took him almost an hour.

The young man's following the policeman to the drugstore is a clear case of matched-dependent behavior. It can easily be analyzed in terms of Miller and Dollard's four fundamental principles of learning (see Chapter 10). The relationship between the behavior of the young man and the policeman is summarized in Table 12–1. The *drive* for both persons was the need to get to a drugstore, although the precipitating factors for this need were different for the young man (his wife's illness) and the policeman (the man's request for help). The *response*, driving a car along a specific route, was the same for both parties (i.e., was *matched*) as was the *reinforcement* they received for their response, reaching the drugstore. However, there is a striking difference between the *cues* that directed the responses of the two men. Since the policeman knew the route to the drugstore, his driving was directed by various landmarks along the way, street signs, and his "cognitive street map" of the area. In contrast, the young man's behavior was *dependent* on the movement of the police car for its direction. He was thus responding to cues provided by the policeman's responses rather than the cues to which the policeman was reacting. That is, since the young man had just arrived in the city and, moreover, was unable to retrace the route he had followed

TABLE 12–1

An Example of Matched-Dependent Behavior Analyzed in Terms of Miller and Dollard's Four Elements of Learning

	Policeman		*Young Man*
DRIVE	Need to get to drugstore		Need to get to drugstore
CUE	Various landmarks such as street signs		Movement of the police car
RESPONSE	Driving along a given route	DEPENDENT (Policeman's driving → Young Man's cue); MATCHED (response ↔ response)	Driving along a given route
REINFORCEMENT	Reaching drugstore		Reaching drugstore

moments before, it is a safe bet that he would have been incapable of finding the drugstore without the policeman's help, except of course by a protracted trial-and-error process.

Miller and Dollard's position states that drive, cue, response, and reinforcement are the *necessary* as well as the sufficient conditions for imitative learning to occur. Thus, if his wife had not become sick, the young man would not have needed to find a drugstore in the middle of the night, and without this drive, the series of events would not have transpired. If for some reason he had been unable to find the policeman or to follow the police car (for example, if he had lost sight of the car), he would have been unable to match the route which the policeman took to the drugstore. Similarly, if circumstances had prevented him from driving behind the police car, as, for example, a flat tire, he could not have reached the drugstore. Finally, if he had not reached the drugstore within some reasonable span of time or if he had not believed that he eventually would arrive at his goal, it is doubtful that he would have continued following the policeman. For instance, had the young man stopped a passing motorist rather than a policeman and had the motorist been unable to find the drugstore he "thought" was open or deliberately taken the young man on a "wild goose chase," presumably the young man would have realized, sooner or later, that his matching behavior was not going to be rewarded and would have ceased to follow the motorist.

An Experimental Demonstration of Matched-Dependent Behavior

In order to validate their analysis of matched-dependent behavior, Miller and Dollard (1941) conducted a series of laboratory studies. In a typical experiment, one child, a "leader" or model, is given a cue informing him in which of two boxes a piece of candy is to be found before a second child, the "follower" or observer, is brought to the experimental room. The physical arrangement of the situation is shown in Figure 12–1. When the observer arrived, he and the model were told to stand at the "start" position and were given the following instructions: "Here are two boxes, there and there. Here is a piece of candy. You are to find the candy. He [the model] gets the first turn, then you get a turn. If you don't find it the first time, you will get another turn" (Miller and Dollard, 1941, p. 125). Since the leader had been shown which box to go to ahead of time and had been instructed to take one piece of candy, he always demonstrated a rewarded response. In one of these experiments, half of the observers, on their turns, found a second piece of candy under the box which the model had chosen, while the remaining observers found their candy under the opposite box. Thus, if the children learned by

FIGURE 12–1

The Experimental Setup Employed by Miller and Dollard in Matched-Dependent Imitation Experiments with Children

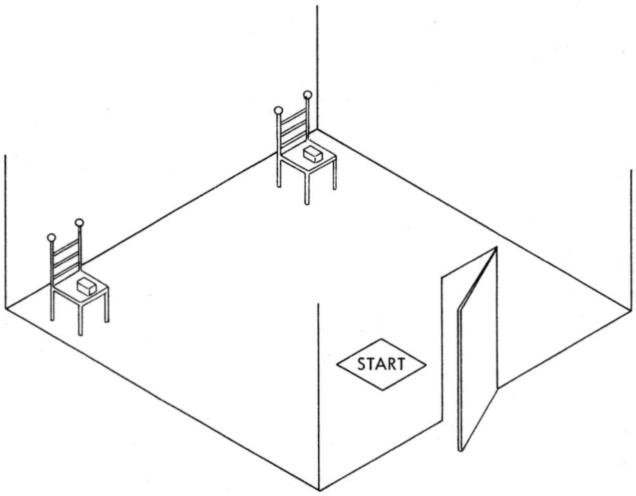

Source: Miller and Dollard, 1941.

observation, the former group would become "imitators" and the latter group "nonimitators."[2] The outcome of the experiment, presented graphically in Figure 12–2 (page 362), shows that this is exactly what occurred. In terms of Miller and Dollard's learning analysis, the observer's drive was hunger, the cue was seeing the model go to a certain box, the response to be learned was either choosing the same box as the model (imitation group) or the opposite box (nonimitation group), and the reward was candy.

Despite the fact that Miller and Dollard's analysis is both clear and workable in laboratory situations and applicable to many real-life instances, it fails to account for a number of situations in which children and adults appear to learn from others observationally. Every day we are exposed to new behavior patterns, through both live and symbolic models, which we do not imitate at the time and hence for which we are not reinforced. Nevertheless, when circumstances are appropriate or conducive for retrieving this information and activating the behavior, we often find that we can do so easily. For example, it is not uncommon for new fathers to leave diaper changing to their wives, although most men have seen their wives perform this chore many times. On that

[2] It may be helpful to think of *avoiding* the behavior of the model as *counterimitation*. However, in the two choice situations employed by Miller and Dollard, counterimitation and nonimitation have very similar meanings.

FIGURE 12–2

Mean Percentage of Imitative Responses of Children Exposed to Imitative and Nonimitative Cues in Miller and Dollard's Experiment

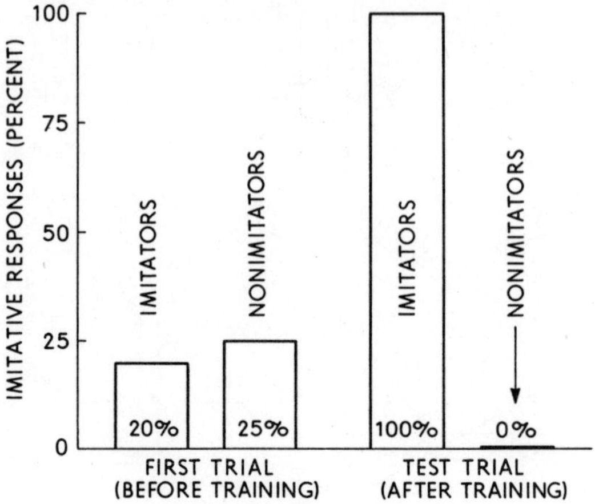

Source: Miller and Dollard, 1941.

fateful and inevitable day that father and infant are left home alone and a diaper requires changing, most fathers are able to rise to the occasion nobly and, often, with remarkable skill. Clearly, the Miller and Dollard paradigm of observational learning cannot account for the father's first success since, despite repeated observations of the response of changing a diaper, the father had never changed a diaper and thus could not have been rewarded for doing so.

The major limitation of the drive-cue-response-reward analysis of observational learning appears to stem from the underlying assumption that imitative behavior has to be performed by the observer and subsequently rewarded for observational learning to occur. Thus, while Miller and Dollard's theory may explain how responses which have been acquired by observing others are *maintained,* it has difficulty dealing with the manner in which at least some imitative responses are originally *learned.* A comprehensive explanation of observational learning must be able to account for the common case in which an individual acquires a response made by a model but does not activate or perform the response. It is more in keeping with actual experience to assume that observation of the behavior of others can lead to effective learning without contingent reward being directly administered to the observer. Such an assumption was first brought to the fore by Albert Bandura and the late Richard H. Walters, whose approach to observational learning makes a crucial distinction between the "acquisition" and the "performance" of observed responses. It is to their position that we turn our attention next.

THE ACQUISITION-PERFORMANCE DISTINCTION OF BANDURA AND WALTERS

The first major statement of Bandura and Walters' *social-behavioristic* approach to personality is contained in their 1963 book entitled *Social Learning and Personality Development.* The emphasis of their position is made clear in the preface to their volume.

> . . . we have outlined a set of social-learning principles that emphasize the role of social variables to a greater extent than existing learning theories and consequently appear more capable of accounting for the development and modification of human behavior. Our social-behavioristic approach represents an attempt to relate these to findings obtained from controlled investigations in a number of areas, including child development and social psychology, as well as traditional experimental psychology (p. vii).

Being a learning position, Bandura and Walters' approach to personality, like Skinner's, eschews traits, types, universal developmental stages, and innate psychological characteristics of the organism. From this vantage point, it is clearly critical to demonstrate how those behaviors which we tend to call personality-related are in fact acquired and maintained. Bandura and Walters generally agree with earlier theorists that the principles of operant and classical conditioning may play a major role in *maintaining* many social behaviors, but argue that these principles are inadequate in explaining the *acquisition* of complex forms of thought and action. Instead, it is suggested that observational learning must play a central role in the acquisition process. It is clear, however, that children and adults do not perform all that they have seen in the behavior of others.

Bandura and Walters have adopted a view of learning by observation consistent with this fact, in which the "*acquisition*" or ability to recall responses is distinguished from the "*performance*" or adoption of these modeled acts. Specifically, acquisition is said to be primarily influenced by stimulus contiguity, an associative learning process, whereas performance is hypothesized to be a function of reward or punishment to the observer or model. The conditions under which performance of imitative responses will occur are relatively straightforward. If an observer anticipates that performing the modeled behavior will lead to positive consequences or if the situation is structured so that imitation is the required or desired behavior, the observer will be more likely to imitate than if he expects negative consequences or if the circumstances are not particularly conducive to imitation. In contrast, the mechanisms underlying the acquisition of modeled acts appear to be exceedingly complex. Bandura's (1969) most recent formulation of the acquisition process involves two representational systems, which he labels "imaginal" and "verbal."

Imagery formation is assumed to occur through a process of sensory conditioning. That is, during the period of exposure, modeling stimuli elicit in observers perceptual responses that become sequentially associated and centrally integrated on the basis of temporal contiguity of stimulation. If perceptual sequences are repeatedly elicited, a constituent stimulus acquires the capacity to evoke images (i.e., centrally aroused perceptions) of the associated stimulus events even though they are no longer physically present. . . . Thus, for example, if a bell is sounded in association with a picture of an automobile the bell alone tends to elicit imagery of the car. Under conditions where stimulus events are highly correlated, as when a name is consistently associated with a given person, it is virtually impossible to hear the name without experiencing imagery of the person's physical characteristics. The findings of studies . . . indicate that, in the course of observation, transitory perceptual phenomena produce relatively enduring, retrievable images of modeled sequences of behavior. Later reinstatement of imaginal mediators serves as a guide for reproduction of matching responses.

The second representational system, which probably accounts for the notable speed of observational learning and long-term retention of modeled contents by humans, involves verbal coding of observed events. Most of the cognitive processes that regulate behavior are primarily verbal rather than visual. To take a simple example, the route traversed by a model can be acquired, retained, and later reproduced more accurately by verbal coding of the visual information into a sequence of right-left turns (e.g., RRLRR) than by reliance upon visual imagery of the itinerary. Observational learning and retention are facilitated by such codes because they can carry a great deal of information in an easily stored form. After modeled sequences of responses have been transformed into readily utilizable verbal symbols, later performances of matching behavior can be effectively controlled by covert verbal self-directions (pp. 133–34).

Since acquisition can only be demonstrated by inducing an observer to perform what he has learned, the actual terms used by Bandura and Walters may be misleading. As we shall see shortly, "performance" is typically assessed experimentally in a more or less free situation in which the observer simply has the *opportunity* to imitate the model's acts. In contrast, when "acquisition" is measured experimentally, although the observer is free to imitate or not to imitate the modeled acts, he is either given incentives for such imitation and/or specifically asked to reproduce the modeled behavior.

Many of the experiments demonstrating the value of the acquisition-performance distinction have involved *vicarious consequences,* outcomes which accrue to the model for his behavior. When these outcomes are positive or desirable in nature, they are called *vicarious reward;* negative or undesirable outcomes are called *vicarious punishment.* In one such study (Bandura, 1965), dealing with aggression, nursery school children were shown a remarkable five-minute film on the screen of a television console.

The film began with a scene in which a model walked up to an adult-size plastic Bobo doll and ordered him to clear the way. After glaring for a moment at the noncompliant antagonist the model exhibited four novel aggressive responses each accompanied by a distinctive verbalization.

First, the model laid the Bobo doll on its side, sat on it, and punched it in the nose while remarking, "Pow, right in the nose, boom, boom." The model then raised the doll and pommeled it on the head with a mallet. Each response was accompanied by the verbalization, "Sockeroo . . . stay down." Following the mallet aggression, the model kicked the doll about the room, and these responses were interspersed with the comment, "Fly away." Finally, the model threw rubber balls at the Bobo doll, each strike punctuated with "Bang." This sequence of physically and verbally aggressive behavior was repeated twice (pp. 590–91).

The major independent variable in Bandura's study concerned the consequences which accrued to the model in the film as a result of his aggressive behavior. One group of children simply watched the film, as it is described above, and thus observed *no consequences* accrue to the model because of his acts. A second group of children saw the same film, but with the addition of a final scene in which the model is rewarded for his aggressive behavior.

For children in the *model-rewarded* condition, a second adult appeared with an abundant supply of candies and soft drinks. He informed the model that he was a "strong champion" and that his superb aggressive performance clearly deserved a generous treat. He then poured him a large glass of 7-Up, and readily supplied additional energy-building nourishment including chocolate bars, Cracker Jack popcorn, and an assortment of candies. While the model was rapidly consuming the delectable treats, his admirer symbolically reinstated the modeled aggressive responses and engaged in considerable positive social reinforcement (p. 591, italics added).

A third group of children also watched the film, but with an added final scene in which the model is punished for his acts.

For children in the *model-punished* condition the reinforcing agent appeared on the scene shaking his finger menacingly and commenting reprovingly, "Hey there, you big bully. You quit picking on that clown. I won't tolerate it." As the model drew back he tripped and fell, the other adult sat on the model and spanked him with a rolled-up magazine while reminding him of his aggressive behavior. As the model ran off cowering, the agent forewarned him, "If I catch you doing that again, you big bully, I'll give you a hard spanking. You quit acting that way" (p. 591, italics added).

After exposure to the film, each child was brought into an experimental room which contained a plastic Bobo doll, three balls, a mallet, a peg board, plastic farm animals, and a dollhouse which was equipped with furniture and a miniature doll family. This wide array of toys permitted the subject to engage either in imitative aggressive responses (i.e., the model's responses) or in alternative nonaggressive and nonimitative forms of behavior. The subject was subsequently left alone with this assortment of equipment for 10 minutes, and his behavior was periodically recorded by judges who observed him from behind a one-way-vision screen. Children's aggressive behaviors in this situation constituted the *performance* measure of the study.

In order to assess the degree to which children could demonstrate or reproduce the modeled behaviors, irrespective of whether they had performed them when alone, the experimenter reentered the room after the performance test well supplied with sticker pictures and an attractive juice dispenser. He gave the child a small treat of fruit juice and informed him that, for each imitative response he could reproduce, an additional juice treat and sticker would be given. The ability to reproduce the model's behavior in this situation constituted the *acquisition* measure.

The results of this study provide direct support for distinguishing between two separate measures of imitation, acquisition and performance. As Bandura had posited, vicarious consequences influenced performance but not acquisition of the model's aggressive responses. Specifically, children who observed a model punished produced significantly less aggression in the free play situation than those children who observed a rewarded model or one who incurred no consequences. In sharp contrast, when incentives were specifically offered for demonstrating acquisition of the model's acts, all of the groups showed the same high level of learning.

A number of subsequent experiments (for example, Grusec and Mischel, 1966; Liebert and Fernandez, 1969; Spiegler and Liebert, 1969), conducted within the theoretical tradition of Bandura and Walters, have further demonstrated the value of distinguishing between the acquisition of a model's behavior and performance of the same behavior. Specifically, they have regularly shown that observers acquire more than they spontaneously perform. However, more recent evidence, while continuing to support the basic conceptualization, also reveals that vicarious consequences may influence *acquisition* under some circumstances.

For example, Liebert and Fernandez (1970) conducted a study to compare the effects of vicarious consequences upon the acquisition and performance of imitative responses in a choice situation. The study was based upon the assumption that vicarious consequences, positive or negative, convey two closely related bits of information to observers. First, they inform the observer that performance of the modeled behavior can engender reactions from others. In turn, to the extent that this information signals the importance of the model's responses and thus the potential usefulness of being able to recall them later, vicarious consequences should enhance the observer's *attention* to the model's performance as it occurs. Second, vicarious consequences provide information as to the direction of reactions of others, that is, whether they will be desirable or undesirable. In this latter capacity, the information provided by vicarious consequences permits the observer to infer the outcomes which he will receive for similar performances.

This informational analysis, which is clearly an outgrowth of the acquisition-performance distinction, suggests that vicarious reward would increase, and vicarious punishment would decrease, an observer's willingness to reproduce the model's behavior relative to an observer who was not exposed to vicarious consequences (i.e., control subjects). In contrast to this "obvious" effect upon performance, the analysis suggests a somewhat more subtle possibility—namely, that the acquisition of imitative responses would be facilitated by *both* vicarious reward and vicarious punishment. Recall that the informational analysis posits that one function of vicarious consequences, positive or negative, is to focus attention on the model's behavior. It follows that the closer one attends to the modeled responses, the better he will recall them.

In order to provide an initial test of this reasoning, Liebert and Fernandez had six- and seven-year-old girls indicate which item in each of 12 different pairs of toys they preferred. Each pair was pictured in a color slide. The commercial value of the items varied widely among the pairs, but within each pair the alternatives did not differ in retail cost. For example, one slide presented a pair of binoculars and a radio, both in black leather cases; another depicted two wooden spools, one red and one blue. Before performing herself, each child had an opportunity to watch an adult female perform the task. This adult was either consistently rewarded, consistently punished, or incurred no consequences as a result of her selections. The subjects were then shown the full series of slides twice. In the first of these showings (Test I), an assessment of performance, the experimenter simply asked each subject to "tell me which toy you like best." In the second showing (Test II), an assessment of acquisition, the experimenter specifically asked the child to reproduce the model's selections, and he offered the child rewards for doing so.

The mean number of matching responses in all groups is presented in Figure 12–3 (page 368). The overall results of the experiment appear to provide support for the reasoning on which the study was based. Specifically, the data suggest that the effects of both vicarious reward and vicarious punishment may be predicted quite precisely by analysis of the information which was presumed to be provided by each. Thus, observation of a rewarded model led to more imitation during Test I than did observation of an exemplar who received no consequences. Moreover, as predicted, vicarious punishment decreased imitation relative to the controls (no vicarious consequences) in this same situation. These outcomes are consistent with the view that in an otherwise ambiguous situation inex-

FIGURE 12–3

Mean Number of Imitative Toy Choices Produced in Liebert and Fernandez's Experiment as a Function of Vicarious Consequences and Incentive Conditions

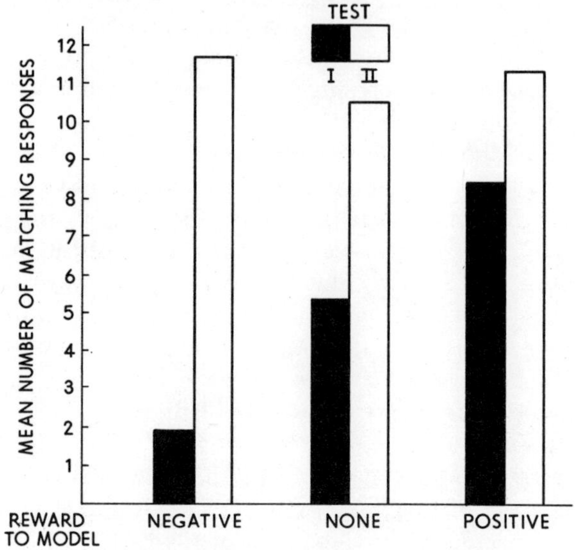

Source: Adapted from Liebert and Fernandez, 1970a.

perienced observers use the consequences of others to infer what their own outcomes are likely to be.

In contrast to the performance test (Test I), comparisons of acquisition (Test II) revealed virtually perfect levels of matching for observers exposed to both rewarded and punished adult performers. Thus, paralleling the study by Bandura (1965) which was cited earlier, an explicit request to reproduce the model's behavior, combined with an incentive for doing so, effectively "wiped out" the differences between these previously (in Test I) divergent groups. However, unlike the data reported by Bandura, observers in the no-consequences control group performed less well than those in the two experimental groups. One possible explanation for the apparent difference of the results of the two investigations is that the effects of vicarious consequences upon acquisition are discernible only for relatively complex or uninteresting tasks, such as the one used in the Liebert and Fernandez study, and not for intrinsically fascinating performances such as the hostilities modeled so vividly in Bandura's experiment.

While it is apparent from this and earlier studies that witnessing punished responses is indeed unlikely to lead to spontaneous imitation, such vicarious punishment may facilitate the acquisition of the modeled responses and hence actually increase the probability that they can be reproduced should the environmental contingencies ever unambiguously favor their occurrence. This finding may have a number of implications for usual socialization practices. For example, parents may be ill-advised to attempt to teach their children *not* to perform behaviors which are potentially injurious to them or are socially inappropriate by pointing out models who are engaging in the undesirable behavior and emphasizing the negative consequences which accrued, or would accrue (in the case of a fortuitous model), to it. While such "lessons" may, for a time, keep a child from playing with fireworks or using proscribed expressions, if the circumstances become conducive for engaging in such behavior (for example, the urging of peers), the child may be better able to do so because of his parents' negative teaching than if these well-intended lessons had not been provided. Similarly, as Bandura has noted often (for example, Bandura, 1963), the argument made by some that the depiction of crime in mass media drama has no harmful effects on young observers because of the inevitable negative outcomes which follow such behavior (as when the villain is caught and jailed) may be questioned in the light of findings which demonstrate that vicarious punishment does not impede acquisition.

THE PERVASIVE ROLE OF IMITATION

Most of the research concerned with observational learning has focused either on elucidating the underlying mechanisms of the phenomenon or on exploring the breadth of behaviors in which imitation does, or may, play an important role. Examples of the former type are the experiments, discussed in the previous section, concerned with documenting the hypothesis that observational learning can occur without reward and with demonstrating the effects of vicarious consequences upon acquisition and performance. In this section, we turn our attention to the latter focus by indicating some of the areas of personality in which learning by observation has been shown to be a potent technique for the development and modification of behavior.

Imitation and Language

The manner in which children learn to understand and successfully communicate through language is among the most important questions studied by psychologists. It has often been noted that the appropriate use of language is central to virtually all aspects of education and social development. Further, successful and appropriate language communication is closely linked to the individual's place in society, whereas the inability to communicate clearly hampers and may virtually eliminate a person's ability to cope with even the simplest educational and social situations.

Traditionally, psychological accounts of language learning have been developed by theorists who have included language learning in their discussions of a general acquisition process (for example, Miller and Dollard, 1941; Mowrer, 1960; Skinner, 1957). Skinner, for example, appears to believe that language is learned, in large measure, by waiting for children to emit approximations of the forms of speech which are ultimately desired and then by gradual shaping (by parents or other socializing agents) until the correct sounds and sentence forms can be reproduced in appropriate situations with a high degree of fidelity.

In contrast to the views espoused by learning theorists, linguists and psycholinguists (for example, Chomsky, 1959; Fodor, 1966) have cogently argued that the extant learning theories cannot adequately account for complex verbal behavior. Chomsky (1959) offers the following pregnant critique of a "conditioning" viewpoint:

> . . . it seems quite beyond question that children acquire a good deal of their verbal and nonverbal behavior by casual observation and imitation of adults and other children. It is simply not true that children can learn language only through "meticulous care" on the part of adults who shape their verbal repertoire through careful differential reinforcement, though it may be that such care is often the custom in academic families. It is a common observation that a young child of immigrant parents may learn a second language in the streets, from other children, with amazing rapidity, and that his speech may be completely fluent and correct to the last allophone, while the subtleties that become second nature to the child may elude his parents despite high motivation and continued practice. A child may pick up a large part of his vocabulary and "feel" for sentence structure from television, from reading, from listening to adults, etc. Even a very young child who has not yet acquired a minimal repertoire from which to form new utterances may imitate a word quite well on an early try, with no attempt on the part of his parents to teach it to him (p. 42).

Within the context of the view of social learning espoused by Bandura and Walters, several recent experiments have suggested that under some circumstances *principles* for generating novel responses can be acquired through the observation of others (for example, Bandura and McDonald, 1963; Bandura and Mischel, 1965; Liebert and Ora, 1968). If principles of language usage, rather than mere words, can be shown to be acquired through imitative learning, then this would seem to provide a plausible account of the process of language learning.

One recent investigation (Bandura and Harris, 1966) examined the effects of observation of a model in conjunction with other variables on children's production of particular language constructions. The general procedure was to ask second-grade children to make up sentences which included a particular word presented by the experimenter, first during a base rate period and then again after some form of intervening training. The results of the study demonstrated that those children exposed to a combination of (1) an adult model's production of sentences with and without the relevant construction (for example, prepositional or passive phrases), (2) reward to both the model and the observer for sentences containing the relevant construction, and (3) attention-focusing instructions showed a greater increment in the production of the relevant construction in their sentences than did a control group.

This study clearly suggests that children's language productions may be modified through modeling in conjunction with other variables. It is likely, however, that the children in the Bandura and Harris experiment had been exposed to the grammatical constructions many times in their lives prior to entering the experimental situation. Therefore, the question still remained as to whether children could actually acquire new or novel language rules as a function of observation.

Odom, Liebert, and Hill (1968) performed an experiment which was designed to test the possibility that children could abstract and use *new* language rules from the observation of models. Second-grade boys and girls were asked to make up sentences using nouns presented to them on large cards. The subjects were told that any sentence was acceptable, that the sentences did not have to be true, and that they could be either statements or questions. All subjects were given a base-rate assessment of their production of prepositional phrases. Children in the two experimental conditions were then exposed to a model who was rewarded for producing particular phrases. In one experimental condition, the children were exposed to modeled prepositional phrases of the usual English form (*preposition-article-noun,* as, "The boy went *to the house.*") and were themselves rewarded for using such phrases in the sentences they made up. In the other experimental condition, subjects were exposed to and subsequently rewarded for the production of sentences containing unfamiliar prepositional constructions of the form *article-noun-preposition* (as, "The man was *the door at.*"). Surprisingly, children exposed to the *new* rule condition, as well as those exposed to the familiar English rule condition, demonstrated an increase in the frequency with which they used the *familiar* constructions (i.e., *preposition-article-noun*) relative to children in a control group who saw no model and received no reward. Apparently, instead of abstracting a new rule from the model's productions, the subjects in these conditions in some way "reordered" the unfamiliar language constructions to make them correspond to language rules with which they were already familiar.

The combined results of the Bandura and Harris and Odom *et al.* experiments suggest that young children's adoption of language rules may involve the use of complex problem-solving strategies. If the chil-

FIGURE 12–4

Mean Number of Relevant Prepositional Constructions in Liebert *et al.'s* Experiment during Base Rate and Training

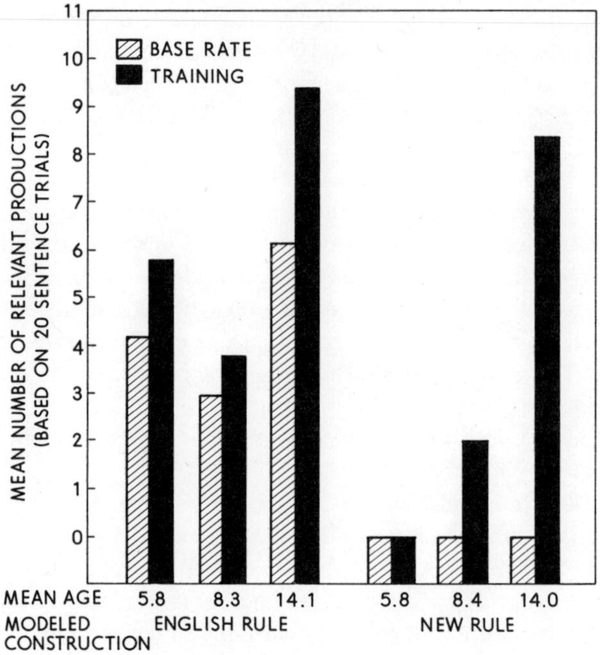

Source: Liebert *et al.*, 1969.

dren did in fact perceive the situation as a problem-solving one, then their reordering of the model's constructions may be viewed as one of several possible strategies. The strategy selected by children in the Odom *et al.* study, which involved using a previously learned language rule, apparently was selected over a host of alternatives, including the one leading to the "correct" solution and subsequent reward. It is plausible, however, that older children might be able to identify and use the rewarded (unfamiliar) rule.

To test this possibility, Liebert, Odom, Hill, and Huff (1969) employed procedures which were similar to those used by Odom *et al.*, except that children of three age groups participated. These groups consisted of preschool children (mean age = 5.8), second-grade children (i.e., those of the age previously used, mean age = 8.3), and young teenagers (mean age = 14.0). After a base rate period wherein the frequency with which the children produced familiar prepositional constructions was assessed, half of the children in each age group were exposed to a model who produced English rule prepositional phrases and the other half to a model who produced parallel new rule phrases. Following this training, the subjects' production of relevant prepositional phrases was assessed.

The results, which are presented in Figure 12–4, provide further support for the hypothesis that children's adoption of language rules can be influenced by modeling and reward procedures and also provide information regarding the relationship of this influence to age. In both rule conditions, the findings lend support to the hypothesis that the ability to abstract a language rule, exemplified in the sentences of a model, is directly related to the age of the children. Thus, as seen in Figure 12–4, the oldest children produced (after training) more rewarded prepositional sentences than the children in either of the two younger groups. Moreover, the oldest children in the new rule group, unlike the younger ones, abstracted and used this novel construction in their own sentences.

It is clear that the modeling procedures outlined above could be adapted for practical application, especially in teaching disadvantaged and retarded children (who are known to have particular difficulty with language learning). The application of modeling to practical human problems is discussed in detail in a later section.

Self-Control and Internalization

Most theories of personality include some discussion of the manner in which persons come to maintain a variety of response patterns in the absence of external constraints. This phenomenon, which we may refer to as the development of self-control, has been a central issue for researchers interested in imitation. For purposes of this discussion, self-control will refer to behavior in situations in which *the individual must monitor his own actions in some way in the absence of any social constraints in the immediate situation.* Moreover, the term generally implies that there is some sort of immediate incentive to behave in one way, but the individual "controls himself" and behaves in an alternative manner that does not provide as much immediate gratification. We shall discuss three aspects of self-control: *resistance to temptation, self-reward and self-imposed standards,* and *delay of gratification.* Each of these aspects of self-control has been shown to be influenced by observational learning.

Resistance to Temptation. Resistance to temptation refers to behavior in those situations in which individuals are presented with an opportunity to behave in a socially prohibited fashion which will provide some reward (such as cheating on an exam, stealing, taking cookies from a forbidden cookie jar, and so on). Although no other persons are present in the situation, the individual may nonetheless "resist the temptation" and not deviate. There is a considerable body of evidence which suggests that resistance to temptation is largely *situation determined.* For example, an early and very extensive study of honesty and deceit (Hartshorne and May, 1928; Hartshorne, May, and Shuttleworth, 1930) placed thousands of children in a variety of situations in which transgressions such as lying, stealing, and cheating were possible without detection. These investigators found substantial *intraindividual inconsistencies* in performance. Thus, if two children are put in a particular situation where they may potentially cheat, and child A cheats but child B does not, one cannot predict with very much accuracy that in a second cheating situation child A will again be more likely to cheat than child B.[3] Resistance to temptation is influenced not only by the situation in which the individual finds himself but also by observation of the consequences which others experience for deviant behavior. This phenomenon is clearly illustrated in an experiment by Walters, Leat, and Mezei (1963). The subjects, five-year-old boys from lower-class homes, were brought into a room containing an assortment of attractive toys and a dictionary. The children were told that they were not to touch the toys but that they were permitted to look at the dictionary. Subsequently, they were divided into three groups. The *model-rewarded* group saw a two-minute film in which a four-year-old boy was playing with the very same toys that were available in the experimental situation. When the boy had played with the toys for a short time, his mother entered the scene and joined in the play activities. She encouraged the lad's play, smiled, and made a number of affectionate gestures as he played. Children in the *model-punished* group also observed a movie in which a young boy exhibited deviant behavior, but in this film the mother shook her head and finger at the boy as she entered the room, whereupon the boy ". . . dropped the toys, jumped onto a chesterfield [sofa], and held a blanket up to his face" (Walters *et al.,* 1963, p. 237). Subjects in the *control* group saw neither of the films.

Boys in all three groups were then left alone with the taboo toys and the uninteresting dictionary for 15 minutes although, in fact, a hidden observer recorded their willingness to deviate during this stringent test period. Looking at Table 12–2, which presents the major results of the study, it is apparent that vicarious reward and punishment had differential effects on resistance to temptation. Subjects exposed to a rewarded

---

[3] There is, of course, some degree of generality to honesty, but it is not very great. Burton (1963), in a reanalysis of Hartshorne and May's data, suggests that this small degree of similarity is based on *physical* and *semantic* generalization. Physical generalization refers to the actual similarity of the materials used in the tests (for example, two tests involving block designs are more similar than a block design test and one which requires hitting a target with bean bags). Semantic generalization is based on the similarity of the labels which are applied to two or more tests (for example, tests of skill, of intelligence, and so on).

model deviated more quickly (lower latency) and spent more time in deviant behavior than subjects who observed either a punished model or no model at all. In fact, most subjects who observed a punished model exhibited no deviant behavior.

TABLE 12–2

Group Medians* of Latency of First Deviation and Time Spent in Deviating (Total Test Time = 900 Sec.) in the Experiment of Walters, Leat, and Mezei

	Model-Rewarded Movie	*Model-Punished Movie*	*Control (No Movie)*
Latency of first deviation (sec.)	85	900	285
Time spent in deviating (sec.)	28	0	7

* The *median*, like the mean, is a measure of the central tendency of a group of scores and is defined as the score above and below which 50 percent of the scores lie (i.e., the middlemost score) when the scores are arranged in numerical order.
Source: Adapted from Walters, Leat, and Mezei, 1963.

The Regulation of Self-Administered Rewards and the Setting of Self-Imposed Standards. The regulation of self-administered rewards and the setting of self-imposed standards commonly refers to the circumstance in which the individual has some sort of material rewards amply available but dispenses them sparingly to himself and only for sufficiently high levels of performance. All people set standards for themselves, which in part determine the amount of effort they will expend. Moreover, it is clear that there are vast individual differences among persons with regard to the stringency of their self-imposed standards. Often one can observe students, of comparable abilities, differing in their evaluation of various course grades. Some students, for example, will severely chastise themselves for failing to get an "A" on a particular examination or in a particular course, whereas others will appear to be pleased and delighted with the minimal pass which a "C−" provides.

Research on self-reward has been relatively slow in beginning, probably because standards of achievement have often been construed as simply reflecting some underlying dispositions or traits of the individual rather than as being important learned responses in their own right. The experimental situation which characterizes the study of self-reward involves four necessary conditions: (1) the individual must perform a task which he believes to be one of achievement or skill; (2) rewards must be available in abundance; (3) no external socializing agent must be present; and (4) the individual must administer rewards to himself *contingently* so that his self-imposed criterion determines the amount and frequency of the rewards which he receives. Given such a situation, an important question is whether self-reward must be learned in a particular situation or whether it comes from some automatic or universal aspect of development. A study by Liebert and Ora (1968) was designed to explore this very question and also to determine the influence of incentives upon self-imposed criteria. The task was a miniature bowling game which consisted of a three-foot runway with score lights on an upright section at the end of the runway. The game, which is pictured in Figure 12–5, is played by rolling a small ball down the alley; after the ball

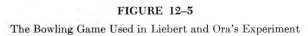

FIGURE 12–5

The Bowling Game Used in Liebert and Ora's Experiment

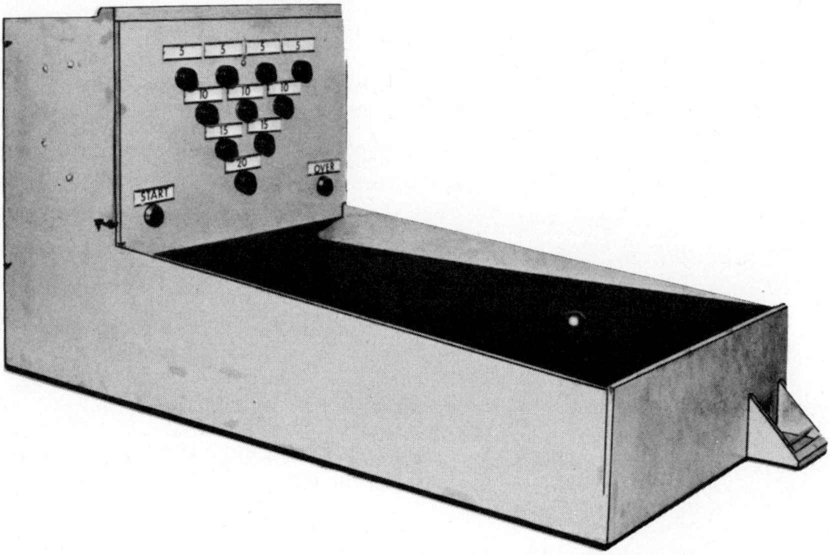

Photo by Thomas M. Hall

disappears at the end of the alley, one of the four score lights ("5," "10," "15," or "20") comes on. It has been regularly found that young children accept the game as one of skill, although, in fact, the apparatus is programmed to produce a fixed pattern of scores.

In the experiment by Liebert and Ora, before playing the game, children were exposed to different incentives in order to determine whether self-imposed criteria depend upon external rewards. It was hypothesized that it is easier to impose a difficult standard on one's self when it is not particularly costly to do so than when upholding a high standard requires forfeiture of something of value. The children in the experiment were first brought into a conference room and, in the *high-incentive* group, were shown a wide variety of toys and school supplies, ranging in value from 10 cents to about $12. Each child was asked whether he liked the items and which ones he liked best. He was then informed that he might win one of these toys in the game he was going to play, but that a very large number of chips (token rewards) would be required. Subjects in the *low-incentive* group were not told about this display of prizes but were, instead, asked to give their reactions to a display of dull-looking textbooks also located in the same room. Children in the experimental groups were then given training in self-control by either observation of another person or direct instructions.

In the *modeling* condition, an adult male experimenter, the training agent, bowled 10 trials in the child's presence, rewarding himself with plastic chips for all scores of 20 but never for lower scores. The intended contingency of this behavior was further communicated through the training agent's enthusiastic utterance for each score of 20 ("Twenty, that's a *good* score. That *deserves* a chip") and his disparaging of all lower scores ("Fifteen, that's *not a very good score*. That *doesn't deserve a chip*"). In the *direct training* condition, the subject bowled 10 trials in the training agent's presence and was encouraged to reward or refrain from rewarding himself in a manner analogous to the procedure used for modeling (Fifteen, that's *not a very good score*. I don't think you deserve a chip for that score"). Children in a *control* condition received no training. All children were then permitted to perform alone.

TABLE 12–3

Mean Number of Deviations from the Standard Provided by the Training Agent in Liebert and Ora's Experiment

Subgroup	*Control*	*Modeling*	*Direct Training*
Low incentive	7.42	0.92	0.08
High incentive	12.75	3.25	2.92

Source: Liebert and Ora, 1968.

The results of the study are presented in Table 12–3. As expected, children in the modeling and direct training groups showed far more self-control than those in the control groups. That is, subjects in the control groups were more likely to reward themselves for scores of less than 20 than were subjects in the experimental groups. Moreover, also as anticipated, the presence of high-magnitude incentives *increased* the likelihood that deviation from the stringent rule would occur. In conclusion, then, it appears that at least under the conditions of this experiment, self-reward was learned in response to the demands of the particular situation.

In the foregoing experiment, children merely had to choose between adhering to the standard which had been provided or deviating from it in order to secure additional rewards. In life situations, however, children are often exposed to standards from more than one source (mother, father, teachers, playmates, and so on), and frequently these standards may be discrepant. For instance, many children in our culture are reared by parents who preach abstinence from tobacco and alcohol but may or may not practice such self-control themselves. Additionally, such children will inevitably be exposed to both peers and adults who engage in these gratifications and encourage them to do so. In this example the socialization process involves the provision of discrepant behavioral alternatives which differ in the degree of self-indulgence that they reflect.

In order to experimentally examine this frequently observed situation, McMains and Liebert (1968) performed an investigation in which children were exposed to *multiple models*. Using the same bowling game employed in the Liebert and Ora study cited previously, fourth-grade boys and girls first played the game with an adult training agent by alternating rolling the ball for a total of 10 trials each. During this training period, the adult imposed a *stringent* criterion (taking chips for scores of 20 only) on the subject. For half the subjects, the training agent modeled the same stringent self-reward criterion when he himself played the game (*consistent training*), while for the other half of the subjects, the training agent displayed a more lenient self-reward criterion (taking chips for scores of 15 as well as 20) during his turns (*discrepant training*). Following this initial training, subjects were permitted to perform alone for 20 trials, and their adherence to the stringent standard was measured (Test 1). During the second phase of the experiment, another social agent (a model) also performed on the bowling game, and the child merely observed this adult's self-imposed standards. The second agent either displayed the same stringent standard which the subject had been taught or modeled the more lenient one. After this, a second measure of the children's own self-imposed standards was obtained (Test 2).

Table 12–4 contains the mean self-leniency scores (i.e., the average number of times subjects rewarded themselves for scores of less than 20) during Test 1. It is apparent from the data that subjects who observed the social agent, who taught them the stringent rule, abide by the same rule were less lenient themselves when they performed than subjects who observed the social agent deviate from the standard he advocated for them.

The results of Test 2 are presented in Figure 12–6. It is clear from these data that children who were trained to a stringent criterion but found that both the person who trained them and a second performer deviated from this standard were least willing to adopt the standard for themselves when performing alone. Not only did these children display,

TABLE 12–4

Mean Self-Leniency Scores for All Subjects during Test 1 in McMains and Liebert's Experiment

Criterion Imposed by 1st Agent	*Criterion Modeled by 1st Agent*	*Mean Self-Leniency Score*
Stringent (20 only)	Stringent (20 only)	1.83 (Boys) 0.25 (Girls) 1.04 (Total)
Stringent (20 only)	Lenient (20 and 15)	4.91 (Boys) 4.04 (Girls) 4.33 (Total)

Source: McMains and Liebert, 1968.

on the average, nearly five deviations from the stringent standard when performing alone, but virtually all of them (92 percent) violated this stringent standard at least once when self-rewards were available without constraint. In marked contrast, when the children were told to adhere to a highly stringent standard *and* observed both the agent who trained them and another person adhere to the same stringent criterion, the standard was adopted very readily. Girls trained under these conditions adopted the stringent standard uniformly and without exception,

FIGURE 12–6

Mean Self-Reward Leniency Scores as a Function of Consistent (Stringent) or Discrepant (Lenient) Multiple Modeling in McMains and Liebert's Experiment

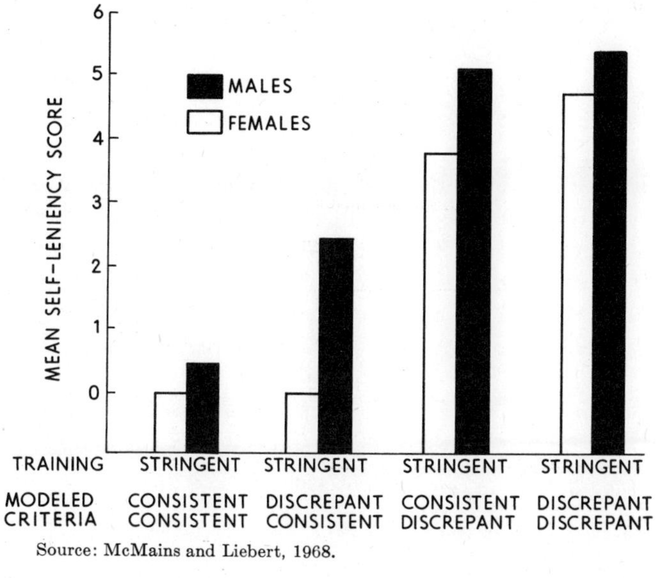

Source: McMains and Liebert, 1968.

and the boys rewarded themselves for substandard scores, on the average, less than once during the 20 trials when they performed alone. Taken together these findings suggest that the appropriate combination of direct training and modeling may serve to "internalize" a standard of behavior even when performers are permitted to govern their own actions. In contrast, it is clear that severe social injunctions which are not supported by example (the familiar "Do as I say, not as I do!" phenomenon) may prove to have little effectiveness as socialization practices.

Delay of Gratification. Delay of gratification refers to the self-imposed postponement of some immediate reward in favor of some potentially more valuable delayed reward. A common life example is an individual's decision not to drop out of school for a moderately good job now, but instead to persist in harsh economic circumstances in order to continue his education (which presumably will provide a superior job after training has been completed). A person's ability to delay some small immediate reward for the sake of a larger outcome for which he must wait is a critical prerequisite for the achievement of success in many human endeavors and, as we noted in Chapter 3, was considered a significant function of the ego by Freud.

It is likely that a willingness to delay gratification can be acquired through observational learning, and this possibility has been demonstrated experimentally by Bandura and Mischel (1965). In the first part of their study, fourth- and fifth-grade children were given a delay-of-reward test which involved confronting them with a series of 14 choices between a small immediate reward and a larger delayed outcome (for example, a small candy bar which they could have immediately or a larger one which required a week of waiting). On the basis of this assessment, children who displayed either predominant preferences for immediate reward or predominant preferences for delayed reward were assigned to one of three conditions. One group observed an actual adult model make a series of choices between a less valuable item and a more valuable item which required delay[4] (*live modeling* condition). For children who, in the initial assessment, preferred delayed reward, the model consistently chose the immediate reward item, whereas for those children who preferred immediate reward, the model selected the delayed reward item in each case. Additionally, the model briefly summarized his philosophy of life, which embodied the attitude toward delay of reward he was modeling, and occasionally commented on his choice. For example, when the choice was between a plastic chess set obtainable

[4] The items between which the adult model chose were appropriate rewards for adults (chess sets, magazines, and so on) and were different from the items between which the subjects subsequently chose. Thus, the subjects were only able to imitate the *principle* exhibited by the model's behavior and could not merely copy his choices.

immediately and a more expensive wooden set which could be obtained in two weeks, the model commented, " 'Chess figures are chess figures. I can get much use out of the plastic ones right away' " (Bandura and Mischel, 1965, p. 701). A second group of subjects was exposed to the same modeling cues except that the model's choices and comments were presented in written form (*symbolic modeling* condition). A third group of children served as controls for the possible effects of mere exposure to rewards on subsequent delay-of-gratification behavior and thus was just shown the series of paired objects (*no-model-present* condition). All children were then given a delay-of-reward test in the model's absence. Finally, to assess the stability of changes in delay-of-reward behavior

FIGURE 12–7

Mean Percentage of Immediate-Reward Choices by High-Delay Children (*a*) and Delayed-Reward Choices of Low-Delay Children (*b*) during the Three Phases of Bandura and Mischel's Experiment

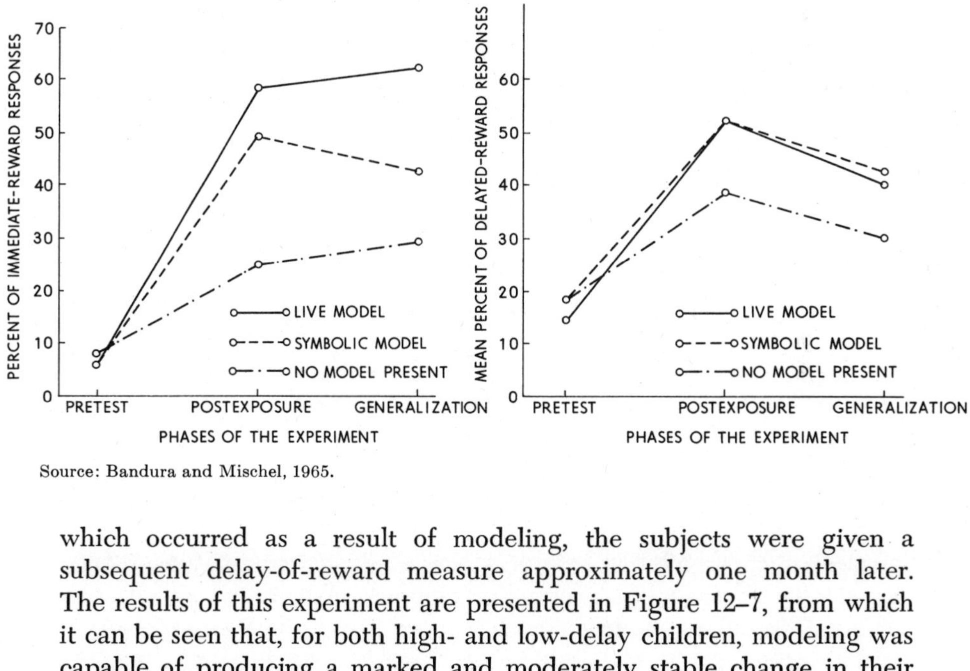

Source: Bandura and Mischel, 1965.

which occurred as a result of modeling, the subjects were given a subsequent delay-of-reward measure approximately one month later. The results of this experiment are presented in Figure 12–7, from which it can be seen that, for both high- and low-delay children, modeling was capable of producing a marked and moderately stable change in their behavior. These data further illustrate the generality of modeling procedures as a potent means of modifying yet another aspect of personality.

Modeling as a Determinant of Helping Behavior

As seen in the foregoing discussion, there is a great deal of research which suggests that observing a model may markedly influence a variety of behaviors. One type of social response which has recently been the focus of many such imitation studies is helping behavior. For example, it has been demonstrated that children will be more likely to contribute some of their earnings (on a bowling game) to a charity if they have seen an adult model do so than if they have not (Rosenhan and White, 1967), that observation of a sharing adult may make children who have previously not shared more likely to do so (Doland and Adelberg, 1967), and that the gift-giving of adults is influenced by the amount of contributions apparently made by their co-workers (Blake, Rosenbaum, and Duryea, 1955).

Two recent experimental reports will serve to illustrate this line of research. Unlike many of the earlier studies, the experiments of Bryan and Test (1967), and Hornstein, Fisch, and Holmes (1968), have used "street-corner" rather than laboratory settings to test their hypotheses, a strategy which puts additional demands on the ingenuity of the investigator but significantly broadens the base of evidence for hypotheses which have been supported in the laboratory.

Bryan and Test (1967) conducted a series of naturalistic studies designed to assess the effect of models on helping behavior. In their first experiment, entitled "Lady in Distress: A Flat Tire Study," an undergraduate female was stationed next to a Ford Mustang with a flat tire on the left-rear wheel and an inflated tire leaning beside it. The purpose of the experiment was to determine whether observation of a helping model by passing drivers would increase the likelihood that they would stop and assist the apparently forlorn lady. During the experimental period, an Oldsmobile was located about a quarter of mile up the road and was clearly visible to motorists driving toward the lady and her disabled Mustang. In this "modeling scene," the Oldsmobile was jacked up, and a young girl was watching while a man changed a flat tire. During the control period, held at a comparable time, the modeling scene was absent. The experiment was conducted in a residential area of Los Angeles, and each treatment condition continued for the time required for 1,000 noncommercial vehicles to pass. Although the total number of vehicles which stopped to help was a small percentage of those which passed (fewer than 3 percent), the presence of a model significantly increased the number of drivers who stopped to offer their assistance.

Bryan and Test's second experiment, which they entitled "Coins in the Kettle," was designed to determine the effects of modeling on donations to a Salvation Army kettle in front of a large department store in Princeton, New Jersey. Once every 60 seconds a man dressed as a white-collar worker (the model) approached the kettle and contributed 5 cents. The 20 seconds thereafter were considered the modeling period. After a lapse of another 20 seconds, the next 20-second segment was designated the no-modeling period. It was found that donations occurred significantly more often in the modeling than in the no-modeling periods.

Shoppers who observed the model donate saw, besides the actual donating behavior, the model thanked for his contribution as well as the pleasant interaction which ensued between donator and solicitor (an instance of vicarious reward). Thus, it is possible that observing a charitable model who received *no* social reward for his behavior might not influence the observer. To test this hypothesis, another experiment, "Coins in the Kettle II," was conducted in which the model was not thanked for his contribution. Nonetheless, shoppers donated significantly more often during the modeling period than during the no-modeling period.

Overall, Bryan and Test's data clearly demonstrate that modeling can influence helping behavior in naturalistic settings, but they do not elucidate any of the mechanisms which underlie this process. An experiment by Hornstein *et al.* (1968) has explored this issue. The study is based on the proposition that "an observer uses the model's experiences as a valid predictor of his own future experiences" (Hornstein *et al.*, 1968, p. 222). This assumption leads to the expectation that when the observer and the model are perceived as *similar,* the observer will see the model's experiences as a valid predictor of what his own experiences would be if he engaged in similar behavior. Thus, in such a case, the observer should be more likely to imitate the model if the model had positive experiences than if he had negative experiences. On the other hand, when the observer and model are seen as very *dissimilar,* the observer will not consider the model's experiences to be a valid predictor of his own. In this instance, the observer should be no more likely to imitate the model if the model had positive experiences than if he had negative experiences.

To test these hypotheses, Hornstein *et al.* inconspicuously deposited addressed but unstamped envelopes containing a man's wallet and a letter on the sidewalk in a midtown Manhattan business district. The wallet's contents, for all subjects, was shrewdly designed to create the impression of an "average" owner, Michael Erwin. It contained $2 in cash, an identification card, postage stamps, membership cards for two fictitious organizations, a receipt for a rented tuxedo, the calling cards of a florist and a podiatrist, and other nondescript contents that contributed to its "legitimacy."

A typewritten letter, which provided the modeling cues, gave the impression that the wallet had been lost twice. When the wallet was lost initially, its finder (the model) put the wallet in an envelope to be mailed to its owner, enclosing a letter describing his feelings about finding and returning it. However, before he could mail it, the well-intentioned finder lost the wallet himself. The pedestrian who found the letter a "second" time, and who thereby became a subject in the experiment, had to decide between returning the wallet (and imitating his predecessor's prosocial behavior) or keeping the wallet and the money for himself.

To manipulate the similarity of observer and model, the letter was either written in familiar English (*similar model* condition) or in an ungrammatical, broken English which created the impression of a foreign writer (*dissimilar model* condition). In each of these conditions, the letter described the writer's feeling of pleasure at returning the wallet (*positive letter* condition), expressed his annoyance at being bothered (*negative letter* condition), or did not reveal his feelings (*neutral letter* condition). The letters used are presented in Table 12–5.

TABLE 12–5

The Letters Used by Hornstein, *et al.* to Manipulate the Feelings of Its Original Finder (Model) and His Similarity to the Second Finder (Subject)

Letter Condition	*Model Condition*	
	Similar	*Dissimilar*
*Neutral**	Dear Mr. Erwin: I found your wallet which I am re-returning. Everything is here just as I found it.	Dear Mr. Erwin: I am visit your country finding your ways not familiar and strange. But I find your wallet which I here return. Everythings is here just as I find it.
Positive†	I must say that it has been a pleasure to be able to help somebody in the small things that make life nicer. It's really been no problem at all and I'm glad to be able to help.	It great pleasure to help somebody with tiny things which make life nicer. It is not problem at all and I glad to be able help.
Negative†	I must say that taking responsibility for the wallet and having to return it has been a great inconvenience. I was quite annoyed at having to bother with the whole problem of returning it. I hope you appreciate the efforts that I have gone through.	To take responsibility for wallet and necessity to return it is great inconvenience. Is annoyance to bother with whole problem of return and hope you appreciate effort I went to.

* The neutral letter said no more than this.
† The positive and negative letters began with the neutral statement.

The percentage of wallets returned in each group is presented in Table 12–6, from which it is clear that the authors' predictions were supported. When the letter was apparently written by a similar model, positive and neutral experiences produced more returns than negative experiences, whereas there were no such differences for the dissimilar model condition. The study further demonstrates the role of modeling in naturalistic situations, and illustrates how two characteristics of the model, his similarity to the observer and his feelings, may mediate such

TABLE 12–6

Percentage of Wallets Returned Intact in the Hornstein, *et al.* Experiment as a Function of the Similarity to and Feelings of the Model

Letter Condition	*Model Condition*	
	Similar	*Dissimilar*
Neutral	60.0	26.7
Positive	70.0	33.3
Negative	10.0	40.0

Source: Adapted from Hornstein, Fisch, and Holmes, 1968.

an effect. In the next section, we shall discuss a related topic, the way in which feelings themselves may be developed through observational learning.

Observational Learning and Vicarious Emotional Responses

In addition to acquiring specific patterns of behavior and even general rules for guiding action, there is another class of outcomes associated with observational learning which plays a central role in the development of personality—the occurrence of *vicarious emotional responses.* Our own everyday experience seems to suggest that one person will often develop an emotional response merely by observing that emotion (or its overt manifestations) exhibited by another person. While this phenomenon was for a long time ignored by experimental researchers, it has recently been the subject of investigation in a number of different laboratories. In the present section, we shall consider some of these recent investigations.

One common situation which appears to induce emotions in observers is the dramatic presentation of a play, movie, or even a novel. A study by Tannenbaum and Gaer (1965) attempted to demonstrate that viewers of a screenplay will (1) vicariously experience the emotions exhibited by the protagonist of the drama, (2) experience mood changes corresponding to those exhibited by the protagonist, and (3) show more emotional responsiveness if they "identify" with the protagonist than if they do not. The observers, undergraduate psychology students, all viewed a 20-minute film clip from the classic movie, *The Ox-Bow Incident.* The segment was described as follows:

The cutting opens with a posse being formed to track down some rustlers who had murdered a local rancher and stolen his cattle. Some conflict is apparent, with several members urging a delay until the sheriff arrives. However, they are not heeded, and the posse subsequently encounters three men—the young protagonist (Donald Martin), his father-in-law, and a Mexican helper —who have the branded cattle in their possession. Martin claims that he bought the cattle from the rancher earlier that day. He is not believed but is adamant in his claim of innocence. The posse prepares to hang the trio, over strong objections from several members who again argue that they should await the sheriff's arrival and have the men stand trial in a proper court of law. As Martin is being dragged to the rope he struggles and pleads (Tannenbaum and Gaer, 1965, p. 613).

By ingenious arrangement of other parts of the original film, Tannenbaum and Gaer produced three different "endings" which were seen (by different groups of subjects) after the scenes described above. In the *happy-ending* condition, observers saw a sequence in which the posse rides back to town, encounters the sheriff, and learns that the rancher was only wounded and that the real culprits have been apprehended. In the *sad-ending* condition, the posse agrees to the protagonist's plea that they wait until morning before hanging him. Nonetheless, the following dawn, with the sheriff still on the way, the majority votes to go ahead with the lynching, and the pleas of the accused are without avail.[5] In the *indeterminate-ending* condition, the film ends after the posse has waited through the night but before the vote about the lynching. A fourth group of subjects, who served as *no-ending* controls, simply observed the initial 20-minute film clip.

All observers were given a set of scales to assess their mood state before they viewed the film (Test 1), after the initial segment of the film but before the ending (Test 2), and after the ending (Test 3). Degree of identification with the protagonist was measured by having the observers rate themselves and the hero on a series of scales; the more similar the two sets of ratings, the greater was the degree of identification.

As predicted, all observers showed an increase in mood stress from Test 1 to Test 2, thereby indicating that the film did induce an emotional response vicariously. Moreover, high-identification observers changed significantly more than low-identification observers. Turning to the effects of the different endings, it can be seen in Table 12–7, which presents the mean change scores from before to after the ending, that direction of mood stress change corresponded to the protagonist's feelings. Specifically, the sad-ending group increased in stress level, whereas the other three groups decreased, the stress reduction being most pronounced in the happy-ending condition. Moreover, the differences be-

[5] The actual ending of the original movie corresponded most closely to the sad ending used by Tannenbaum and Gaer. Subjects were asked whether they knew the outcome of the original movie, and those who could recall the film's plot were not included in the analysis.

tween high and low identifiers in each group were in the theoretically predicted direction.

In addition to eliciting emotional reactions directly, modeling may also play an important role in the acquisition of emotional responses to previously neutral stimuli. It will be recalled that in Chapter 10 we discussed the work of Dekker and Groen which illustrated how direct classical conditioning might constitute one means by which inappropriate stimuli gain control over emotional reactions. There is also reason to believe that such conditioning can occur vicariously, through the mere observation of models. This possibility has been demonstrated by several experiments in which a performer (model) undergoes a classical conditioning procedure whereby an initially neutral stimulus (CS) is paired with an electric shock (for example, Barnett and Benedetti, 1960; Berger, 1962).[6] In such a situation it has been shown that the observer, *who is never shocked,* will come to exhibit emotional responses to the CS alone.

TABLE 12–7

Mean Changes in Mood Stress in Each Group
(from Before to After Viewing Their Respective Endings)
in Tannenbaum and Gaer's Study

	Identification Level		
Film Ending	*High*	*Low*	*Total*
Sad	+4.84	+1.63	+3.24
Happy	−9.45	−3.71	−6.58
Indeterminate	+0.86	−2.40	−0.77
Control	−1.36	−3.42	−2.39

Note: Positive changes indicate an increase, and negative changes a decrease, in mood stress.
Source: Adapted from Tannenbaum and Gaer, 1965.

It is not surprising, however, that these studies have found persons to differ markedly in the degree to which they show such vicarious conditioning. Moreover, the development of conditioned emotional responses necessitates that the observer vicariously experience the aversive consequences which, presumably, produce affective arousal. Thus, it is plausible that the observer's degree of arousal in a vicarious conditioning situation will influence his acquisition of the emotional responses of a model. An experiment by Bandura and Rosenthal (1966) provides a test of this line of reasoning. As in earlier studies, all subjects observed an-

[6] In these studies the model (a confederate of the experimenter) typically does not actually receive the electric shock but instead winces or groans in a convincing manner.

other person perform a simple task. During this performance a buzzer was occasionally sounded, and immediately thereafter the performer reacted as if he had just received a potent electric shock. In this *acquisition phase* of the experiment, the observer received no electric shocks but his *galvanic skin response* (GSR)[7] was recorded. Next, in order to determine whether the buzzer alone could now produce an emotional response in the observer, during the *test trials* phase of the experiment, the buzzer sounded on six occasions without a "shock" response being displayed by the model. Finally, during the *extinction phase* of the experiment, all observers heard 10 presentations of the buzzer alone.

Prior to the acquisition phase, each subject received one of five treatments designed to induce different levels of arousal, both physiologically and psychologically. The treatment conditions were, in the order of decreasing arousal production: (1) injection of a large dose of epinephrine;[8] (2) injection of a small dose of epinephrine; (3) placebo injection plus the threat that, after observing the model, the observer, too, would receive electric shock; (4) placebo injection alone; and (5) control group which received neither injection nor threat.

Figure 12–8 presents the mean percentage of conditioned GSR responses for all subjects during each phase of the experiment. Since, prior to acquisition, the buzzer was a neutral stimulus for the subjects and thus produced no GSR's, the percentage of responses during acquisition provides a direct index of the potency of vicarious training. The data from the test trial period reveal that the GSR came to be elicited by the CS (the buzzer) alone. Finally, in accord with numerous investigations of the role of arousal on performance, a moderate (as opposed to either extreme) degree of affective arousal was optimal for facilitating conditioned emotional reactions.

As illustrated in the experiments described, observation of another person's emotional responses may lead to an emotional response on the part of the observer. It is also likely that these vicariously learned responses will, in turn, influence other aspects of the observer's behavior. Such a phenomenon is clearly illustrated in two experiments conducted by Aronfreed and Paskal (Aronfreed, 1968).

In the first experiment, six- to eight-year-old girls were given the choice of pressing either of two levers on a number of trials, in the presence of an adult experimenter. One of these levers led to a candy reward for the child 60 percent of the time it was pressed; the other turned on a red light 60 percent of the time but never produced a reward. During

---

[7] GSR refers to electrical changes which occur on the skin and are recorded from electrodes to certain parts of the body (for example, the palms of the hands). The measure is considered a sensitive indicator of changes in emotional state.

[8] Epinephrine (adrenalin) is a stimulant of the sympathetic nervous system. Many experiments have shown its arousal-inducing properties for other forms of behavior.

training, in one experimental condition, the adult showed signs of joy whenever the red light went on and displayed warmth and affection toward the child; in a second condition, the adult showed signs of joy at the appearance of the light but no affection toward the child; in the third group, the adult was affectionate whenever the light was on but did not show joy at its appearance. During the test phase of the experiment, the adult was seated a good distance from the child, and the child herself could no longer see the red light, although it was visible to the adult. The child made additional choices between the two levers, and the

FIGURE 12–8

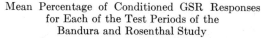

Mean Percentage of Conditioned GSR Responses for Each of the Test Periods of the Bandura and Rosenthal Study

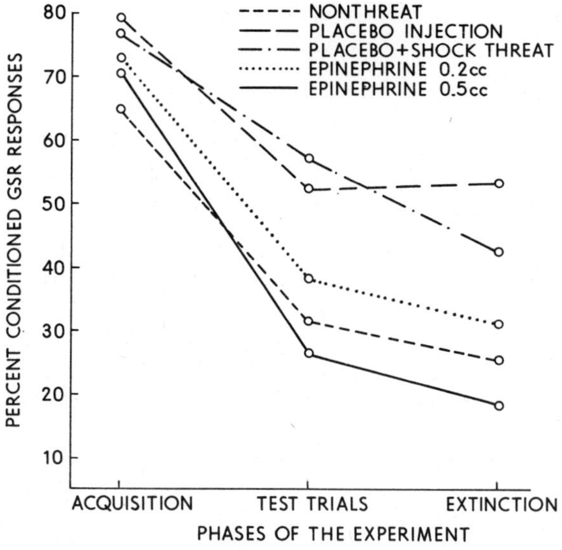

Source: Bandura and Rosenthal, 1966.

adult always displayed joy when the light went on but did not attend to the child at all. Thus, the children were faced with the choice between forsaking candy and giving the adult joy, or getting candy and depriving the adult of pleasure. When the adult had been both affectionate to the child and had shown joy at the appearance of the light, the children pushed the "light" lever during the test more than in either of the other two conditions. Apparently, if another person is warm and affectionate, giving him pleasure may sometimes outweigh the importance of gratifying one's self.

In a second experiment, using girls of the same age, the task was to classify small replicas of real objects in terms of their appropriateness for a house, a dog, or a school. To indicate her classifications, the child depressed one of the three levers of a "choice box," corresponding to the three categories. None of the toys, however, were appropriate for a dog, and consequently the middle lever was rarely used during the initial phases of the experiment. Prior to beginning their initial trials, the children were told that both they and the experimenter were to wear earphones in order to detect occasional noises that might come from the choice box. The primary experimental group then went through a series of experiences designed to produce a sympathetic response based on vicarious experience. Specifically, for 6 of the first 12 trials (which constituted the first phase of the experiment), the child heard a highly aversive loud noise, not contingent upon her choices, which lasted for seven seconds. Moreover, three seconds before the child heard these noises, the experimenter began to show signs of distress by placing her head in her hands (presumably because of the noise in her own earphones). These distress cues persisted until the noise was terminated.

In the second phase of the study, the adult experimenter modeled a sympathetic response for the child. No longer wearing her earphones, the adult used her own choice box to classify each toy just after the child had indicated her classification. She informed the child that she, the experimenter, might be able to terminate the noise which the child would sometimes hear in the earphones. After hesitating for several seconds following the child's classification, for 6 of the 12 trials in this phase of the experiment the adult chose one of the two outer levers on her choice box (recall that the outer levers—representing school and home—were the only correct choices). For the other six trials, the child began to hear a slightly aversive noise in her earphones following her classification response. As in the first phase of the experiment, the noise was not contingent upon the child's previous choice and was not predictable across trials. Each time the noise occurred, the adult quickly pressed the middle (incorrect) lever and indicated to the child that she had specifically chosen this lever in order to turn off the noise. Thus, she clearly modeled a sympathetic reaction (i.e., temporarily foresaking the task) in order to alleviate the child's distress.

During the third and final phase of the experiment, another young girl was introduced as the new subject, and the "primary" subject was now given the role which had just been performed by the experimenter. That is, while the experimenter now sat as a mere observer, the two girls, each with a choice box, made their successive choices. For this phase of the experiment, the new subject wore earphones, but the primary subject did not. On 6 of the 12 trials the new subject, who was in fact an experimental stooge, placed her head in her hands as a distress signal, in a manner identical to the one which the experimenter herself had displayed earlier. If the primary subject made the distress-relieving response (i.e., was sympathetic) by pressing the incorrect middle lever, the stooge immediately raised her head in apparent relief. If, on the other hand, the primary subject made a task-oriented response (i.e., was nonsympathetic), the stooge continued in apparent distress until five seconds after the subject had made her choice. In contrast to the first two phases of the experiment, in which subjects virtually never pushed the middle lever, half of the 26 subjects pushed the middle lever on at least 6 of the 12 trials (recall that only 6 had produced distress cues from the stooge) and almost all of the remaining subjects chose the pain-relieving middle lever on 4 or more trials. Thus, it is quite apparent that, on the basis of observational learning of empathic reactions, children learned to forsake making a correct, task-oriented response in order to relieve the distress of another child.[9]

APPLIED USES OF MODELING

Recent years have seen a tremendous burgeoning of interest in basic imitative phenomena, in terms of both theory and research. Not surprisingly, a major offshoot of these enterprises has been a parallel effort to apply emerging principles and procedures to the solution of practical human problems. In this section, we shall review some of these applied efforts.

The Role of Modeling in Traditional Psychotherapy and Counseling

Traditional psychotherapy, such as psychoanalysis (see Chapter 4) and client-centered therapy (see Chapter 9), involves a process of verbal interchange. Typically there are many sessions over a period of time ranging from a few months to several years or more. Proponents of traditional psychotherapy often stress the importance of establishing good rapport between the therapist and the patient. Under these characteristic circumstances, there would seem to be ample opportunity for the patient to observe and perhaps emulate some of the therapist's behavior. Some evidence exists to support the hypothesis that this process occurs. Rosenthal (1955) found that patients who improved over the course of psychotherapy tended to modify their moral values (especially those dealing with sex, aggression, and authority—common therapy topics) in the direction of their therapists' moral values. On the other hand, the

---

[9] Aronfreed and Paskal also had four control groups which provided further evidence that such sympathetic behaviors only occur with appreciable frequency when (1) the child's own pain has first been associated with that of another, (2) she has learned by observation how to terminate the painful noises, and (3) she subsequently can see the apparent relief of the other child.

moral values of unimproved patients tended to become less like those of their therapists.

That there have been relatively few reports of the role of modeling in traditional psychotherapy is no doubt a joint function of at least two factors. First, traditional psychotherapy theory has no place for such phenomena, and therefore, second, the existence of imitative processes goes unnoticed or underestimated. One notable exception is a report by Alexander (1967) of a fortuitous incident which occurred in the course of traditional play therapy with a nine-year-old boy who had a history of behavioral problems in the home and at school. Alexander reports that although he had succeeded in establishing a "good, warm, accepting and comfortable relationship" with the client and had made a number of interpretations over a period of three and a half months, the client had never verbally expressed his feelings. For example, the lad typically dealt with anger either by physically or emotionally withdrawing from the situation or by temper tantrums.

During the course of one therapy session, Alexander was informed that the room that he and his client were occupying had to be used for another purpose. This had happened once before, and Alexander, accompanied by his young client, "stormed immediately to the main office . . . and firmly declared to the secretary that this was wrong, disruptive, and would have to be straightened out immediately" (pp. 164–65). Moments later, as the pair entered their newly assigned room, the boy said, almost shouting, "That makes me mad too . . ." and went on to describe a parallel incident that had happened to him in school. Alexander goes on to report that this first verbal expression of feeling led to other appropriate expressions of anger at home and at school. While Alexander does not recommend such "acting out" by the therapist in place of a good therapeutic relationship and interpretation, he does suggest that showing, as well as telling, should not be overlooked in traditional psychotherapy.

Modeling procedures are increasingly being employed in counseling (cf. Krumboltz and Thoresen, 1969). For example, a series of well-designed studies by Krumboltz and his associates (Krumboltz and Schroeder, 1965; Krumboltz and Thoresen, 1964; Krumboltz, Varenhorst, and Thoresen, 1967) have shown that it is possible to increase the degree to which high school students seek appropriate occupational and educational information through modeling techniques.

One study (Krumboltz and Thoresen, 1964) compared a combination of modeling and reinforcement with reward alone. Subjects in *model-reinforcement counseling* were initially exposed to a 16-minute tape recording of a counseling interview in which a male student discussed what he planned to do after high school and, in doing so, frequently verbalized information-seeking responses which the model counselor (i.e., in the tape) rewarded. After playing the tape, subjects discussed their own future plans, and the counselor rewarded information-seeking responses both verbally ("mm-hmm," "excellent ideas," and so on) and nonverbally (smiling, head nodding, and the like). This direct conditioning procedure constituted the treatment for the subjects in the *reinforcement-counseling* condition. Subjects in the *control-film discussion* condition watched a film (unrelated to information-seeking behavior) which they then discussed with the counselor. Each of these three conditions was administered in both an individual and a group setting. An inactive control group received no treatment whatsoever. The study is particularly impressive in that rather than assess the subjects' *verbal* information-seeking behavior, the dependent measures consisted of the frequency and variety of *actual* information-seeking behavior (for example, writing for a college catalog) during a three-week period. The model-reinforcement condition proved to be most influential, followed by the reinforcement condition. On the average, individual and group settings were equally effective.

Role Playing and Modeling

This section deals with those modeling procedures, both live and symbolic, which have been used in conjunction with different forms of role playing. Whenever a role is played to demonstrate to an observer how to behave, how to handle certain situations, what to say, and so forth, modeling is involved.

Kelly (1955), whose Psychology of Personal Constructs we discussed in Chapter 7, developed a specialized technique called *fixed-role therapy* which is used to modify or strengthen particular personality characteristics of a client. The client first writes a self-characterization sketch of himself and completes several self-descriptive tests such as incomplete sentences and a Q-sort. On the basis of this information, a panel of therapists writes a fixed-role sketch for the client—a new role he is to play. The aim is to change some of the client's personal constructs (and subsequently his behavior) and thereby make him a more effective person. In constructing the fixed-role sketch, the panel relies as much as possible on the assets which the client already has rather than trying to make him a completely new person. The fixed-role sketch is presented to the client, and the therapist demonstrates the new behaviors for him. The client imitates and practices the new behaviors in the protected environment of therapy before attempting them in his daily life. The therapist's modeling of the new role for the client is important not only in giving the client an idea of how to enact the new characterization but also in convincing him that the role is both "real" and plausible. This point is well illustrated by the following reaction of a client who was presented with a fixed-role sketch which bore the pseudonym, Timothy Ellman:[10] "I was rather nervous about the whole thing and thus was very much inhibited in participation. Dr. Kelly's portrayal of Timothy was of great help in understanding him. I left feeling that Timothy was not spineless, but really very mature. . . ." (Kelly, 1955, p. 442).

Behavioral rehearsal is a specific therapeutic technique, similar to role playing, affording an opportunity to practice a particular behavioral sequence which the person has difficulty coping with in his daily life, but under less anxiety-provoking circumstances and under the direction and supervision of a therapist. The technique has been predominantly used as part of assertive training for persons who find it difficult to express their personal and legitimate rights and feelings (for example, Lazarus, 1965, 1968a, b; Wolpe and Lazarus, 1966). It has also been used to reduce anxiety about and proficiency in performing various specific behaviors such as job interviews, telephoning for a date, starting conversations with strangers, and answering embarrassing questions about one's personal life (Lazarus, 1966). The technique can be employed with children (Gittleman, 1965) as well as adults. In behavioral rehearsal, the therapist will play the role of the person or persons with whom the patient is having difficulty behaving adequately (for example, a domineering spouse), and frequently roles are reversed so that the therapist can model adaptive responses for the patient. When behavioral rehearsal is employed in a group setting, other members of the group (as well as the therapist) are asked to play the role of the patient in the problem situation, which gives the patient an opportunity to observe a variety of possible responses (for example, Gittleman, 1965; Lazarus, 1968b).

An interesting technique which Lazarus (1968a) calls *co-therapeutic modeling* has been used in the treatment of marital discord when the problem results from mutual stubbornness.

> One enlists the aid of a colleague who has two or three private consultations with one of the spouses while the original therapist independently learns the other spouse's point of view. Husband and wife then have a joint interview with the two therapists who argue with each other on behalf of their respective clients. The effect of this procedure has varied from one couple who said they learned how ridiculous they must appear while arguing about inanities, to another couple who maintained that the therapists had given them a blueprint for healthy and constructive marital debates (p. 54).

Sarason and his colleagues at the University of Washington are currently engaged in a series of research projects to modify the behavior of juvenile delinquents via a systematic exposure to role models who dem-

---

[10] Each fixed-role sketch is provided with a given and surname, which presumably makes the character more credible, makes reference to the fixed role (as opposed to client's customary role) clearer and more natural, and makes it easier for the client to identify with the new role.

onstrate relevant socially appropriate behavior (Sarason, 1968). Earlier work concerned with the effect of test anxiety and observation of models on verbal learning had found that learning was facilitated by observing another "subject" (an experimental confederate) perform a similar task prior to one's own performance and that this facilitation was more pronounced for persons with high test anxiety scores than for persons with low test anxiety scores (Sarason, Pederson, and Nyman, 1968). These findings suggested that role modeling might be an efficient and powerful means of teaching young offenders the socially acceptable and adaptive behaviors they lacked. The subjects were all male residents of a reception and diagnostic center for juvenile offenders who ranged in age from 15 to 18 years. Several times a week the boys met in groups of four with two clinical psychology graduate students who served as models. Each session, which lasted about 40 minutes, revolved around a single topic which was highly relevant to the boys' lives, such as applying for a job or resisting group pressure to engage in antisocial behavior.

One study compared the effectiveness of role modeling and traditional role playing with a no-treatment control group. Subjects in all three groups were matched for age, intellectual level, and severity and chronicity of delinquency. In the modeling condition, one of the models first introduced the theme for the session and set the stage for the roles which were to be played. Two models then acted out a previously planned scene, such as a job interview. Next two of the subjetcs acted out the same scene. After an informal discussion of the scene and the manner in which it was portrayed by the pair of subjects, two other boys acted out the same scene. The traditional role-playing condition was similar to the modeling condition except that the roles were verbally described to the boys (actually symbolic modeling) and therefore subjects did not have an opportunity to observe the roles demonstrated before they acted out the scene. A second study simply compared role modeling with a control group.

Sarason (1968) indicates that, in general, the experimental groups exhibited greater behavioral change than did the matched controls. The results were strongest and most positive for the groups in which live models had been observed. Consistent with the previous findings dealing with verbal learning, subjects characterized by high degrees of anxiety and neuroticism received the most benefit from the opportunities to observe the modeling of prosocial behavior.

The Application of Modeling to Problems of the Disadvantaged and Handicapped

An important recent application of modeling techniques has been the use of appropriate role models to enhance the self-esteem and raise the level of occupational aspiration of black students (for example, Henderson, 1967; Smith, 1967). Smith (1967) describes an informal project in which successful adult blacks spoke monthly over the course of the school year to freshman high school students (all blacks except one who was Japanese but was being raised by black foster parents) about their early life and present work. The purpose of the project was both to model achievement by blacks and to illustrate professions to which blacks could aspire. Smith reports that the models (for example, a teacher, an engineer, a lawyer, an anthropologist, a poetess) were for the most part former slum dwellers who had overcome adverse circumstances to reach their present status. At the same time, they were credible models; for example, while aspiring to be a teacher is within the realm of possibility for the average student, being as successful as Willie Mays or Ralph Bunche may not be. Smith reports that he observed an increase in pupils' self-esteem over the course of the project.

Kliebhan (1966; 1967) employed modeling and goal-setting to increase the performance of retarded adolescents in an occupational workshop. The subjects in the modeling group were exposed to a nonretarded model (a college student) who performed the work task, which consisted of attaching samples of tape to pages of a salesman's advertising booklet. The subjects initially were told: "'Terry will show you how to do the task. . . . He's doing a fine job. . . . Watch him . . .'" (1967, p. 222). When compared to control subjects who received only verbal instructions regarding the task, subjects who worked in the presence of the model showed an increase in productivity. The increase was maintained for a short time after the model had left, but then there was a decline in productivity. Goal-setting for the next day's work (after each day's output was counted) resulted in the most productivity, though there was no significant difference between goal-setting and modeling.

It is interesting to note that McClelland's (1965) motive acquisition program, discussed in Chapter 8, employed modeling procedures to advantage in a number of ways. Recall that McClelland's students played a specially devised business game in which they estimated how fast they could construct objects and how much material would be required, and then ordered the material and constructed the objects. McClelland reports that his subjects learn achievement-oriented behavior both by playing the game and by observing others play. Symbolic modeling, in the form of case studies of successful businessmen who exhibit high achievement motivation, is also part of the program. Furthermore, whenever possible McClelland trains subjects from the same company or community together. This has the effect of helping to increase generalization and maintain the attitudes and behaviors gained in the training, since the subjects serve as models for each other.

In a similar vein, as part of an Achievement Motivation Training Program for underachieving high school boys, Kolb (1965) had college students who were outstanding scholars and athletes live with the boys during a summer school program and serve as their counselors. The counselors "behaved in a manner consistent with the behavior of a person with high n Achievement, so that the subjects would have a visible high n Achievement role model to imitate" (p. 785).

Modeling Used in Conjunction with "Reinforcement Therapy"

Modeling procedures have frequently been used in conjunction with operant conditioning techniques (see Chapter 11) in the treatment of various behavioral deficiencies. A major limitation of the operant approach in establishing behavior is that the desired response (or an approximation of it) must occur before it can be rewarded. In the case of such persons as autistic children, mental retardates, and psychotic adults (who often have very limited behavioral repertoires), it is highly uneconomical to wait for a response which has a low probability of occurrence to be emitted (for example, speech in a mute child). Modeling has served a crucial role in this regard when it has been used to elicit the desired response. Ivar Lovaas (1968), a psychologist who pioneered in working with autistic and schizophrenic children to teach them speech and social behaviors, has commented: "In retrospect, it seems virtually impossible to have brought about certain behavioral changes in the schizophrenic children without an imitation approach" (p. 118).

The general procedure for eliciting a response through modeling involves an experimenter demonstrating the desired response for the subject (for example, emitting a word or phrase) and rewarding him (as with food or verbal praise) if the experimenter's response is imitated within a set time interval. An important consequence of this procedure seems to be that imitation itself becomes conditioned. Thus, one technique employed to teach complex behaviors is to first train subjects to imitate a series of simple responses which may have little or no social usefulness (for example, touching one's head). Then the *generalized imitation* is used to teach more complex and useful skills such as speech, brushing one's teeth, and the like (for example, Lovaas, Freitas, Nelson, and Whalen, 1967). The modeling of a response is usually accompanied by a verbal request or question. For example, the experimenter may say: "What is this? This is a *book*." Eventually, it is hoped that the imitative control of the response can be "faded out," so that the response will come under the control of verbal statements alone. Metz (1965) has noted two "side effects" of conditioning generalized imitation in autistic children:

. . . as appropriate learning occurred, "inappropriate" motor and emotional behavior spontaneously disappeared. Not only did the children learn to do what was required by the task, but appropriate emotional responses also seemed to appear. For example, the children expressed joy or delight upon "solving" a problem, an affect rarely seen in these children in other situations. . . . Temper tantrums and "rituals" disappeared even though food and tokens were sometimes withheld for long periods of time . . . (p. 398).

Metz's observations point to important therapeutic benefits besides the acquisition of new responses. The combination of modeling and reward contingent upon imitation appears to be an effective means of giving these children success experiences, which in turn contribute to heightening their self-esteem. Such observations have not been taken into account by critics of behavioristic approaches of this kind when they allege that the results of the treatment are "dehumanizing" (cf. comments on the token economy in Chapter 11).

Lindsley (1966), employing both operant and modeling procedures, has devised a number of techniques for modifying children's behavior in the home. He advises parents to actively participate in the procedures (i.e., to model them) so that the child will come to view them as pertaining to the whole family rather than just as punishment for the child's misbehavior. For example, one interesting method for teaching children to keep things in their proper place involves using a "Sunday Box." Anything which a family member leaves in an improper place is put in the Sunday Box and remains there until the next Sunday, at which time it can be retrieved. Lindsley (1966) advises parents (who are themselves conscientious about keeping things in place) to purposely get something impounded in the Sunday Box in order to demonstrate that the rule holds for the entire family:

For example, one day you are not going to need your briefcase, leave it in some obvious place. Make an uproar when the children see it. Let them put it in the Sunday Box. One day I did this and when my daughters took it, I explained, "My heavens, my briefcase is gone. What will I do? I have tests for the advanced students in it." "No, Daddy, you can't have it; it's in the Sunday Box," I was informed. That day I went to work around the side of the house. From the corner of my eye I saw curtains in the window flutter, and eyes peered out to see if I really did go without it. This kind of strategy is what makes the Sunday Box effective. It is similar to the mayor of the town being seen in traffic court paying his own ten dollar ticket . . . (p. 33).

Vicarious Extinction of Fears

Bandura and his associates recently demonstrated in a series of controlled experimental studies what Jones (1924a, b; see Chapter 10) had reported more than 40 years earlier, namely that children's avoidance behavior can be vicariously extinguished by observing a peer model make approach responses to a feared object without (the model) incurring any adverse consequences. In the first of these studies (Bandura, Grusec, and Menlove, 1967), the strength of nursery school children's fear of dogs was assessed before and after treatment, as well as approximately one month later, by asking the children to perform 14 graded tasks involving progressively more interaction with a dog. One group of children observed a fearless peer make successively more intimate approach responses to a dog in the context of a jovial party (*modeling-positive context*). A second group observed responses by the same model but without the positive party atmosphere (*modeling-neutral context*). To control for the effect of exposure to the dog and the positive atmosphere itself, a third group participated in the parties with the dog, but in the absence of the model (*exposure-positive context*). Finally, to check on the influence of the presence of the dog as well as to control for possible benefits of the positive experiences and interaction with friendly experimenters, a fourth group of children merely participated in the party (*positive-context*). All groups met for eight sessions. Both modeling conditions were found to be more effective than either control group in reducing avoidance behavior, as measured by the number of tasks they completed.

Continuing this line of research, Bandura and Menlove (1968) investigated some of the variables which might be expected to maximize the vicarious extinction effects of modeling. In addition, the modeling sequences were presented by means of films in order to explore the potential therapeutic use of such symbolic modeling. All subjects were shown a series of eight three-minute movies on four alternate days. Children in the *single-model* condition saw movies of a five-year-old, fearless model make successively more intimate contacts with a single dog. The subjects in the *multiple-model* condition saw segments of the same film as well as a number of models (differing in age and sex) interact with a variety of dogs. The size and fearsomeness of the dogs were gradually increased, as was the boldness of approach responses made by the models. A third group of children, who saw movies of amusement parks for an equal amount of time, served as *controls*. The results, which are depicted graphically in Figure 12–9 (page 400), indicated that both the single-model and the multiple-model conditions significantly increased approach responses but only the latter treatment reduced the children's fears to the extent that they were able to perform the most intimate interaction with the dog. Furthermore, whereas the single-model group maintained the level of approach behavior one month after the treatment, the multiple-model children became even bolder over time.

Similar therapeutic modeling effects have also been shown with adults. For example, Spiegler, Liebert, McMains, and Fernandez (1969) produced a 14-minute modeling film to be used in reducing fear of nonpoisonous snakes in adults. The film first presents the meeting of an attractive female undergraduate (Model One) and a noted female herpetologist (Model Two). In successive scenes of the film, Model One

FIGURE 12–9

Median Approach Scores for Children in Each of the Three Conditions and Phases of Bandura and Menlove's Experiment

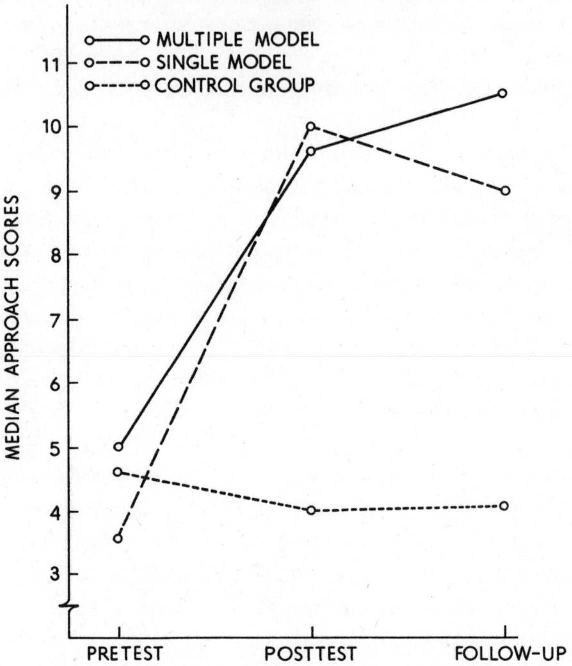

Source: Bandura and Menlove, 1968.

gradually learns to approach and handle several snakes following Model Two's demonstration of each behavior. While wearing gloves, Model One learns to stroke and pick up a small snake and then repeats this procedure with a larger snake. Next, Model One removes the gloves and repeats these successively more difficult tasks bare-handed. Model One is then shown confidently holding the larger snake. Finally, Model Two holds the snake close to her face in an affectionate gesture while it curls itself around her neck. As the film progresses, Model One, who was initially fearful, becomes noticeably more confident in handling the snakes and appears to be increasingly enjoying the procedure. A taped narrative, designed to be equally plausible with or without visual accompaniment, verbally describes what the film depicts and also includes information about snakes and their handling. A series of three experiments has demonstrated the utility of exposure to such a film, even once or twice, in reducing persistent avoidance of harmless snakes.

The first experiment was designed to provide an initial demonstration of the effectiveness of the sound film and to determine the relative contributions of the visual and narrative components of the treatment. A questionnaire dealing with feelings and attitudes toward nonpoisonous snakes was administered to a large number of female undergraduates, and 34 of these co-eds, all of whom reported considerable fear of snakes, were then pretested by means of a graduated behavioral test. In turn, participants were asked to (1) enter a room containing a caged 2-foot water snake, (2) walk to the cage (a distance of about 15 feet), (3) put on a pair of gloves, (4) remove the lid of the cage and look in, (5) reach into the cage and stroke the snake, (6) pick up the snake, (7) remove the gloves, (8) stroke the snake, and finally (9) hold the snake barehanded.

Twenty of the women manifested avoidance behavior judged to be sufficiently stable and severe to warrant treatment. These subjects were assigned to one of four groups, each of which met for a single session. One treatment consisted of viewing the film with narrative, a second employed the film without the narrative, a third presented the narrative without the film, while members of a fourth group served as untreated controls. Behavioral tests were conducted individually one week and one month after treatment by a female experimenter who was "blind" with respect to the treatment to which the subjects had been exposed. Greatest change was produced by the film with the narration condition, the only group which significantly improved relative to the controls; there was no change from one week to one month after treatment.

A second experiment reexamined the principal findings of the first study with another population. Ten undergraduate women from another college were selected in a manner similar to the aforementioned procedures and were assigned to either the film with narrative or the control condition. The treatment again proved to be effective.

The participants in a third experiment were adults from the community-at-large (6 men and 15 women) who had responded to a newspaper advertisement asking for persons who were afraid of snakes and willing to participate in a study of new treatment methods. These subjects were selected by means of the assessment procedures used in the first two experiments and were also briefly interviewed and given comparable expectancies about treatment. They were then matched for level of avoidance behavior (as manifested on the initial behavioral test) and assigned to one of three treatment groups.

Several subjects in the first two experiments had commented that, although the film seemed to help in overcoming their fear, they became somewhat "anxious" while watching *some* of the scenes. It was reasoned that if the participants were relaxed while viewing the film, its effectiveness would be enhanced. Thus, in the third experiment, subjects in the film-with-relaxation group were taught deep muscle relaxation (similar to that used in Wolpe's systematic desensitization; see Chapter 10) by means of a 50-minute prerecorded tape and then shown the modeling film with narrative. A second group was shown the film with narrative only. A third group was given only the relaxation training and, like the film-with-relaxation group, was instructed to practice relaxation and use it in future encounters with snakes. All subjects were treated in groups, and the treatments were administered in two sessions, one week apart.

Posttreatment behavioral tests were individually administered after the first treatment session, before and after the second session, and one week after the second session, with a new and substantially larger snake as a test for generalization. The results of these tests are presented in Figure 12–10. As predicted, the addition of relaxation training to the modeling film substantially enhanced its effectiveness. Subjects in the film-with-relaxation condition performed significantly better after the first treatment and on all subsequent tests than participants in either of the other two conditions. In the first posttreatment behavioral test, subjects in both the film-only and film-with-relaxation conditions significantly increased their approach behavior relative to the pretest. The relaxation-only group did not improve its performance from pretest to immediately after the first treatment, but thereafter showed significant improvement. As in the first two experiments, there was a significant decrease in avoidance behavior after only a single presentation of the

FIGURE 12–10

Mean Number of Behavioral Tests Passed in the Third Experimental Test of Spiegler *et al*'s Film as a Function of Treatment Condition

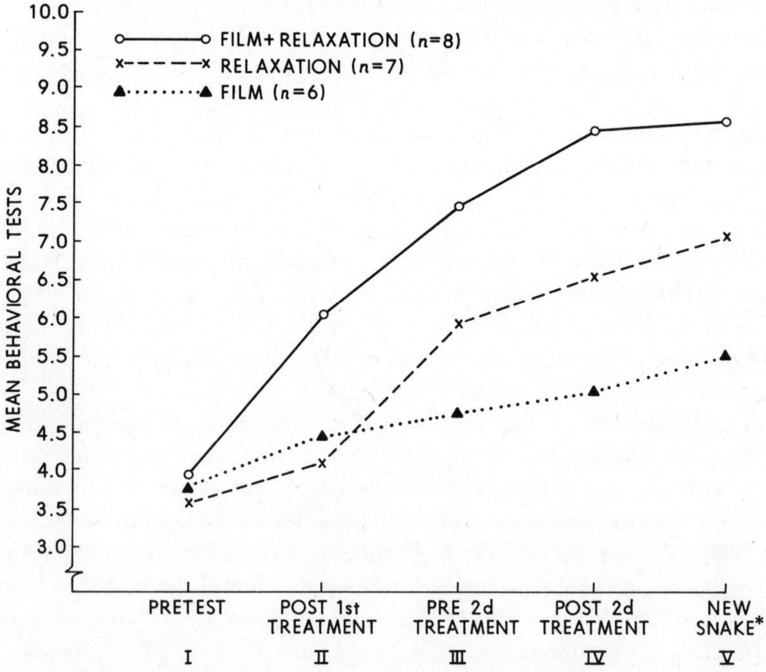

* Two subjects were unable to attend the final assessment (V), thereby reducing the number of subjects in the Film + Relaxation (n = 7) and Film (n = 5) conditions.

modeling film, and a second exposure to the film served to enhance its effectiveness. Finally, it is important to note that no performance loss resulted from introducing the new and larger snake.

Ritter (1968a,b; 1969a,b,c) has recently introduced a promising technique for eliminating abnormal fears. The technique, called *contact desensitization,* involves three steps: (1) modeling desired responses for the client, (2) assisting the client in performing these responses through the use of *behavioral prompts* (for example, having the client place his hand on the therapist's hand as the therapist touches a feared object such as a snake), and (3) gradually withdrawing the therapist's support until the client can independently perform the desired behavior. The efficacy of contact desensitization in treating persons who were unduly afraid of snakes and heights has been demonstrated with a variety of age groups.

As an illustration of the technique, we shall consider the application of contact desensitization with a 49-year-old widow who was profoundly afraid of crossing streets (Ritter, 1969a). The case is particularly interesting because the fear was apparently deep-seated and had proved itself to be extremely durable in the face of other treatment efforts. During the 10-year duration of her phobia, the client had tried both individual and group insight therapy to no avail. Her fear had caused her to withdraw almost completely, and as a consequence of "despair," she had attempted suicide. Ritter's basic procedure is illustrated in the proceedings of the initial session.

> A low traffic location in which a narrow street intersected with a moderately wide street was chosen. The counselor walked across the narrow street for about one minute while Mrs. S. watched. Then the counselor firmly placed her arm around Mrs. S.'s waist and walked across with her. This was repeated a number of times until Mrs. S. reported she was fairly comfortable at performing the task. . . . Street crossing was then continued while physical contact between counselor and Mrs. S. was gradually reduced until the counselor only lightly touched the back of Mrs. S.'s arm as she walked slightly behind her. Contact was then eliminated completely with the counselor first walking along side Mrs. S. as the street was crossed and then slightly behind her. The counselor subsequently followed Mrs. S. approximately three-fourths of the way across the street and allowed her to go the remaining distance alone. Gradually the counselor reduced the distance she accompanied Mrs. S. until eventually Mrs. S. was able to cross the street entirely alone (pp. 170–71).

These procedures were then continued at increasingly wider and more heavily traveled streets. Four specific goals were set by the client, including independently crossing the four streets of a busy intersection. Additionally, the client was made to take additional responsibility for the therapy, including the planning and carrying out of her own practice. All four goals were accomplished within a period of 47 days.

POSTSCRIPT

Interest in observational learning has burgeoned tremendously in recent years. In fact, since 1960, literally hundreds of papers have been published on imitative phenomena. Nonetheless, despite this interest and intensive effort, a comprehensive theory of imitative behavior has not yet emerged. Certain perspectives appear to hold considerable sway (for instance, the one advanced by Bandura and Walters), but many investigations are also being conducted within the context of virtually every one of the vantage points discussed in Chapters 3–11 of this book, and on the level of both basic and applied problems.

This, we feel, is a promising omen. Only when an important phenomenon is explored within the context of many existing theories is the door open to both modifying the theories and maximizing our knowledge of the events studied; and only when problems are simultaneously studied in simple laboratory experiments and in relation to real human problems can a truly broad scope of understanding emerge. These are the ingredients of a strategy which we believe holds the greatest promise for the study of man.

REFERENCES

Alexander, J. F. The therapist as a model—and as himself. *Psychotherapy: Theory, Research and Practice*, 1967, **4**, 164–65.

Aronfreed, J. *Conduct and conscience.* New York: Academic Press, 1968.

Bandura, A. Influence of models' reinforcement contingencies on the acquisition of imitative responses. *Journal of Personality and Social Psychology*, 1965, **1**, 589–95.

Bandura, A. *Principles of behavior modification.* New York: Holt, Rinehart & Winston, 1969.

Bandura, A. What TV violence can do to your child. *Look*, October 22, 1963, 46–52.

Bandura, A., Grusec, J. E., and Menlove, F. L. Vicarious extinction of avoidance behavior through symbolic modeling. *Journal of Personality and Social Psychology*, 1967, **5**, 16–22.

Bandura, A., and Harris, M. B. Modification of syntactic style. *Journal of Experimental Child Psychology*, 1966, **4**, 341–52.

Bandura, A., and McDonald, F. J. The influence of social reinforcement and the behavior of models in shaping children's moral judgments. *Journal of Abnormal and Social Psychology*, 1963, **67**, 274–81.

Bandura, A., and Menlove, F. L. Factors determining vicarious extinction of avoidance behavior through symbolic modeling. *Journal of Personality and Social Psychology*, 1968, **8**, 99–108.

Bandura, A., and Mischel, W. Modification of self-imposed delay of reward through exposure to live and symbolic models. *Journal of Personality and Social Psychology*, 1965, **2**, 698–705.

Bandura, A., and Rosenthal, T. L. Vicarious classical conditioning as a function of arousal level. *Journal of Personality and Social Psychology*, 1966, **3**, 54–62.

Bandura, A., and Walters, R. H. *Social learning and personality development.* New York: Holt, Rinehart & Winston, 1963.

Barnett, P., and Benedetti, D. T. Vicarious conditioning of the GSR to a sound. Paper read at Rocky Mountain Psychological Association, Glenwood Springs, Col., May, 1960.

Berger, S. M. Conditioning through vicarious instigation. *Psychological Review*, 1962, **69**, 450–66.

Blake, R., Rosenbaum, M., and Duryea, R. A. Gift-giving as a function of group standards. *Human Relations*, 1955, **8**, 61–73.

Bryan, J. H., and Test, M. A. Models and helping: Naturalistic studies in aiding behavior. *Journal of Personality and Social Psychology*, 1967, **6**, 400–407.

Burton, R. V. Generality of honesty reconsidered. *Psychological Review,* 1963, **70,** 481–99.

Chomsky, N. Review of B. F. Skinner's *Verbal behavior. Language,* 1959, **35,** 26–58.

Doland, D. J., and Adelberg, K. The learning of sharing behavior. *Child Development,* 1967, **38,** 695–700.

Fodor, J. A. How to learn to talk: Some simple ways. In F. Smith and G. A. Miller (Eds.), *The genesis of language.* Cambridge: MIT Press, 1966. Pp. 105–28.

Gittleman, M. Behavioral rehearsal as a technique in child treatment. *Journal of Child Psychology and Psychiatry,* 1965, **6,** 251–55.

Grusec, J., and Mischel, W. Model's characteristics as determinants of social learning. *Journal of Personality and Social Psychology,* 1966, **4,** 211–15.

Hartshorne, H., and May, M. A. *Studies in the nature of character.* Vol. I. *Studies in deceit.* New York: Macmillan, 1928.

Hartshorne, H., May, M. A., and Shuttleworth, F. K. *Studies in the nature of character.* Vol. III. *Studies in the organization of character.* New York: Macmillan, 1930.

Henderson, G. Role models for lower class Negro boys. *Personnel and Guidance Journal,* 1967, **46,** 6–10.

Hornstein, H. A., Fisch, E., and Holmes, M. Influence of a model's feeling about his behavior and his relevance as a comparison other on observers' helping behavior. *Journal of Personality and Social Psychology,* 1968, **10,** 222–26.

Jones, M. C. The elimination of children's fear. *Journal of Experimental Psychology,* 1924, **7,** 382–90. (a)

Jones, M. C. A laboratory study of fear: The case of Peter. *Pedagogical Seminar,* 1924, **31,** 308–15. (b)

Kelly, G. A. *The psychology of personal constructs.* New York: Norton, 1955. 2 vols.

Kliebhan, J. M. The effects of goal-setting and modeling on the performance of retarded adolescents in an occupational workshop. Doctoral dissertation, University of Illinois. Ann Arbor, Mich., University Microfilms, 1966, No. 66–12, 425. (*Dissertation Abstracts,* 1967, **27,** No. 7.)

Kliebhan, J. M. Effects of goal-setting and modeling on job performance of retarded adolescents. *American Journal of Mental Deficiency,* 1967, **72,** 220–26.

Kolb, D. A. Achievement motivation training for underachieving high-school boys. *Journal of Personality and Social Psychology,* 1965, **2,** 783–92.

Krumboltz, J. D., and Schroeder, W. W. Promoting career planning through reinforcement. *Personnel and Guidance Journal,* 1965, **44,** 19–26.

Krumboltz, J. D., and Thoresen, C. E. (Eds.). *Behavioral counseling: Cases and techniques.* New York: Holt, Rinehart & Winston, 1969.

Krumboltz, J. D., and Thoresen, C. E. The effect of behavioral counseling in group and individual settings on information seeking behavior. *Journal of Counseling Psychology,* 1964, **11,** 324–33.

Krumboltz, J. D., Varenhorst, B. B., and Thoresen, C. E. Nonverbal factors in the effectiveness of models in counseling. *Journal of Counseling Psychology,* 1967, **14,** 412–18.

Lazarus, A. A. Behaviour therapy, incomplete treatment, and symptom substitution. *Journal of Nervous and Mental Disease,* 1965, **140,** 80–86.

Lazarus, A. A. Behaviour rehearsal vs. non-directive therapy vs. advice in effecting behaviour change. *Behaviour Research and Therapy,* 1966, **4,** 209–12.

Lazarus, A. A. Behavior therapy and marriage counseling. *Journal of the American Society of Psychosomatic Dentistry and Medicine,* 1968, **15,** 49–56. (a)

Lazarus, A. A. Behavior therapy in groups. In G. M. Gazda (Ed.), *Basic approaches to group psychotherapy and group counseling.* Springfield, Ill.: Charles C Thomas, 1968. Pp. 149–75. (b)

Liebert, R. M., and Fernandez, L. E. Effects of vicarious consequences on imitative performance. *Child Development,* 1970 (in press).

Liebert, R. M., and Fernandez, L. E. Imitation as a function of vicarious and direct reward. *Developmental Psychology,* 1970 (in press).

Liebert, R. M., Odom, R. D., Hill, J. H., and Huff, R. L. The effects of age and rule familiarity on the production of modeled language constructions. *Developmental Psychology,* 1969, **1,** 108–12.

Liebert, R. M., and Ora, J. P. Children's adoption of self-reward patterns: Incentive level and method of transmission. *Child Development,* 1968, **39,** 537–44.

Lindsley, O. R. An experiment with parents handling behavior at home. *Johnstone Bulletin* (Johnstone Training Center, Bordentown, N.J.), 1966, **9,** 27–36.

Lovaas, O. I. Some studies on the treatment of childhood schizophrenia. In J. Schlein (Ed.), *Research in psychotherapy.* Washington, D.C.: American Psychological Association, 1968.

Lovaas, O. I., Freitas, L., Nelson, K., and Whalen, C. The establishment of imitation and its use for the development of complex behavior in schizophrenic children. *Behaviour Research and Therapy,* 1967, **5,** 171–81.

McClelland, D. C. Toward a theory of motive acquisition. *American Psychologist,* 1965, **20,** 321–33.

McMains, M. J., and Liebert, R. M. The influence of discrepancies between successively modeled self-reward criteria on the adoption of a self-imposed standard. *Journal of Personality and Social Psychology,* 1968, **8,** 166–71.

Metz, J. R. Conditioning generalized imitation in autistic children. *Journal of Experimental Child Psychology,* 1965, **2,** 389–99.

Miller, N. E., and Dollard, J. *Social learning and imitation.* New Haven, Conn.: Yale University Press, 1941.

Mowrer, O. H. *Learning theory and the symbolic processes.* New York: Wiley, 1960.

Odom, R. D., Liebert, R. M., and Hill, J. H. The effects of modeling cues, reward and attentional set on the production of grammatical and ungrammatical syntactic constructions. *Journal of Experimental Child Psychology,* 1968, **6,** 131–40.

Ritter, B. Effect of contact desensitization on avoidance behavior, fear ratings, and self-evaluative statements. *Proceedings of the 76th Annual Convention of the American Psychological Association.* Washington, D.C.: American Psychological Association, 1968. (a)

Ritter, B. The group desensitization of children's snake phobias using vicarious and contact desensitization procedures. *Behaviour Research and Therapy,* 1968, **6,** 1–6. (b)

Ritter, B. Eliminating excessive fears of the environment through contact desensitization. In J. D. Krumboltz and C. E. Thoresen (Eds.), *Behavioral counseling: Cases and techniques.* New York: Holt, Rinehart & Winston, 1969. Pp. 168–78. (a)

Ritter, B. The use of contact desensitization, demonstration-plus-relaxation and demonstration alone in the treatment of acrophobia. *Behaviour Research and Therapy,* 1969, **7,** 157–64. (b)

Ritter, B. Treatment of acrophobia with contact desensitization. *Behaviour Research and Therapy,* 1969, **7,** 41–45. (c)

Rosenhan, D., and White, G. M. Observation and rehearsal as determinants of pro-social behavior. *Journal of Personality and Social Psychology,* 1967, **5,** 424–31.

Rosenthal, D. Changes in some moral values following psychotherapy. *Journal of Consulting Psychology,* 1955, **19,** 431–36.

Sarason, I. G. Verbal learning, modeling, and juvenile delinquency. *American Psychologist,* 1968, **23,** 254–66.

Sarason, I. G., Pederson, A. M., and Nyman, B. Test anxiety and the observation of models. *Journal of Personality,* 1968, **36,** 493–511.

Skinner, B. F. *Verbal behavior.* New York: Appleton, 1957.

Smith, D. H. A speaker's models project to enhance pupils' self-esteem. *Journal of Negro Education,* 1967, **36,** 177–80.

Spiegler, M. D., and Liebert, R. M. Imitation as a function of response commonality and vicarious punishment. Unpublished manuscript, Palo Alto VA Hospital and Fels Research Institute, 1969.

Spiegler, M. D., Liebert, R. M., McMains, M. J., and Fernandez, L. E. Experimental development of a modeling treatment to extinguish persistent avoidance behavior. In R. D. Rubin and C. M. Franks (Eds.), *Advances in behavior therapy, 1968.* New York: Academic Press, 1969. Pp. 45–51.

Tannenbaum, P. H., and Gaer, E. P. Mood change as a function of stress of protagonist and degree of identification in a film-viewing situation. *Journal of Personality and Social Psychology,* 1965, **2**, 612–16.

Tarde, G. *The laws of imitation.* New York: Henry Holt, 1903.

Walters, R. H., Leat, M., and Mezei, L. Inhibition and disinhibition of responses through empathetic learning. *Canadian Journal of Psychology,* 1963, **17**, 235–43.

Wolpe, J., and Lazarus, A. A. *Behavior therapy techniques: A guide to the treatment of neuroses.* Oxford: Pergamon Press, 1966.

Author Index

(Italicized page numbers refer to bibliographic references)

A

Abelson, R. P., 195 n, *211*
Abramovitz, A., 293, *307*
Adelberg, K., 382, *406*
Ahrens, J. B., 78, *93*
Alexander, J. F., 392, *405*
Allport, F. H., 117, *125*
Allport, G. W., 3, 97, 114–25, *125*
Anastasi, A., 93, *93*
Aronfreed, J., 388, 391 n, *405*
Aserinsky, E., 75, *93*
Ashem, B., 293, *306*
Atkinson, J. W., 231, 240, *242*
Atkinson, R. C., 314, *353*
Atthowe, J. M., 344, 347, *352*
Ayllon, T., 28, *33*, 342–46, *352*
Azrin, N. H., 342–46, *352*

B

Baer, D. M., 33, *34*
Bandura, A., 282, *306*, 346, *352*, 357, 362–66, 368–71, 380–81, 387–89, 398–99, 402, *405*
Barnett, P., 387, *405*
Bendig, A. W., 300, *306*
Benedetti, D. T., 387, *405*
Berger, S. M., 387, *405*
Berkowitz, L., *212*
Bieri, J., 188–89, *212*
Birney, R. C., 232, *242*
Blake, R., 382, *405*
Block, J., 162, *162*
Blum, G. S., 59, 61, *66*
Bonarius, J. C., 187, *212*
Bond, I. K., 293, *306*
Borgatta, E. F., *242*
Bower, G. H., 294 n, *307*
Braden, M., 202, *212*
Brill, A. A., 64, *66–67*
Bronfenbrenner, U., 4
Brown, R., 54, *66*
Bryan, J. H., 382–83, *405*
Burton, R. V., 374 n, *406*

C

Cahoon, D. D., 347 n, *352*
Castaneda, A., 301, *306*
Cattell, R. B., 4, 126–27, 129–35, 139, *163*
Chodorkoff, B., 256–58, *273*
Chomsky, N., 370, *406*
Clark, D. F., 293, *306*
Clark, R. A., 231, *242*
Clayton, K. N., 321 n
Cleckley, H., 29, *34*
Cowart, D. L., 279 n
Cowden, R. C., 293, *306*
Crowne, D. P., 154–61, *163*

D

D'Andrade, R. G., 237–38, *242*
Darley, J. M., 13–15, 17–18, *34*, 64
Davidson, H. H., 91, *94*
Davison, G. C., 293, *306*
Dekker, E., 287–88, *306*, 387
Dement, W. C., 37, *66*, 72–78, *93*
Doland, D. J., 382, *406*
Dollard, J., 294–300, *307*, 351, *352*, 357–62, 370, *408*
Duryea, R. A., 382, *405*
Dymond, R. F., 266–67, *273*

E

Edwards, A. L., 18 n, *34,* 148–56, 158, *163*
Engstrom, W. C., 123, *125*
Erikson, E. H., 48–51, *67*
Estes, W. K., 333, *352*
Eysenck, H. J., 4, 129, 135–39, *163,* 267–68, *273*

F

Fernandez, L. E., 366–68, 399, *407–8*
Ferster, C. B., 330, *352*
Festinger, L., 165, 194–211, *212–13,* 230
Fiedler, F. E., 263, *273*
Fisch, E., 382–85, *406*
Fjeld, S. P., 187, *212*
Fodor, J. A., 370, *406*
Fodor, N., 42, *67*
Ford, L. I., 293, *306*
Foulkes, D., 78, *93*
Fowler, R. L., 348, *352*
Fox, L., 331–32, *352*
Franks, C. M., *308, 408*
Freedman, J. L., 205 n, *212*
Freitas, L., 397, *407*
Freud, S., 3, 29, 38–48, 50–52, 54, 56–57, 61–66, *67,* 68–72, 79–87, *93,* 121–22, 127, 168, 171, 193, 215, 243, 285, 298, 347, 380
Freund, K. A., 348, *352–53*
Fromm, E., 252, *273*
Fromm-Reichmann, F., 81

G

Gaer, E. P., 385–87, *409*
Gallagher, J. J., 263, *273*
Garmezy, N., 303
Gazda, G. M., *407*
Gelder, M. G., 348, *353*
Gittleman, M., 394, *406*
Glover, E., 84, *93*
Goldiamond, I., 324, *353*
Gollob, H. F., 64–65, *67*
Gottesman, I. I., 112–14, *125*
Gough, H. G., 136, *163*
Groen, J., 287–88, *306,* 387
Grusec, J. E., 366, 398, *405–6*
Guilford, J. P., 97, *125*

H

Hall, C. S., 62, *67*
Hall, R. V., 319–21, *353*
Hanley, C., 148, 150, *163*
Harris, M. B., 370–71, *405*
Harrower, M. R., 89, *93*
Hartshorne, H., 374, *406*
Hathaway, S. R., 14, 143, 146, *163, 307, 353*
Hays, W. L., 18 n, *34*
Heathers, L. B., 152, *163*
Hebb, D. O., 312, *353*
Heider, F., 195 n, *212*
Heine, R. W., *212–13*
Heineman, C. E., 301, *307*
Henderson, G., 396, *406*
Hilgard, E. R., 4, 275, 294, *307,* 314, *353*
Hill, J. H., 371–72, *407–8*
Hill, W. F., 294 n, *307*
Hire, A. W., 89, *94*
Holmes, D. S., 204–42, *242*
Holmes, M., 382–85, *406*
Hornstein, H. A., 382–85, *406*
Huff, R. L., 372–73, *407*
Hull, C. L., 294, 300–303, 305
Hutchison, H. C., 293, *306*
Hyman, R., 275, *307*

I

Isaacs, W., 324, *353*

J

Jackson, D., 318–21, *353*
Jackson, D. D., 111–12, *125*
Jackson, D. N., 151, *163*
Jecker, J. D., 199–201, *212*
Jones, M. C., 279–81, *307,* 398, *406*
Jouvet, M., 78, *94*
Jung, C. G., 70 n

K

Kallmann, F., 111–12
Katkin, E. S., 350, *353*
Kelly, G. A., 7, *11,* 165–94, *212,* 235, 393–94, *406*
Kimble, G. A., 303, *307*
Kimmel, E., 348, 350, *353*
Kimmel, H. D., 348, 350, *352–53*
Kleinmuntz, B., 90, *94,* 144–45, *163*
Kleitman, N., 75, 77, *93*
Kliebhan, J. M., 396, *406*
Klopfer, B., 91, *94*
Kluckhohn, C., 215, 220, 229–31, *242*
Koch, S., *12, 273*
Kolb, D. A., 396, *406*

Kraepelin, E., 132
Krasner, L., *33*, 344, 347, *352*, *354*
Kretschmer, E., 100–106, *125*, 132
Krumboltz, J. D., 392, *406–8*

L

Lambert, W. W., *242*
Landfield, A. W., 187, *212*
Lang, P. J., 142, *164*
Lanyon, R. L., 25, *34*
Latané, B., 14–15, 17–18, *34*
Laws, D. R., 349–51, *353*
Lazarus, A. A., 143, *164*, 288–93, *307*, 394, *407*, *409*
Leat, M., 374–75, *409*
Levine, J., 64–65, *67*
Levitas, G. B., *273*
Levitt, E. E., 57–58, *67*, 300, *307*
Liebert, R. M., 366–68, 370–73, 376–79, 399, *407–8*
Lindsley, O. R., 317, *353*, 398, *407*
Lindzey, G., *212*
London, P., *306*
Lovaas, O. I., 148, 397, *407*
Lowell, E. L., 231, *242*
Lucas, J. D., 304, *307*
Lund, D., 319–21, *353*
Lundin, R. W., 326, 328–30, *353*
Lundy, R. M., 188–89, *212*

Mc

McCall, R. B., 18 n, *34*
McCandless, B. R., 301, *306*
McClelland, D. C., 231–40, *242*, 269, 396, *407*
McDonald, F. J., 370, *405*
McKinley, J. C., 141, 143, 146, *163*, *307*, *353*
MacKinnon, D. W., 227–28, *242*
McMains, M. J., 378–79, 399, *407–8*

M

Mabry, J., *352*
Maher, B. A., *212*
Manosevitz, M., 25, *34*
Marks, I. M., 348, *353*
Marks, P. A., 145, *163*
Marlowe, D., 154–61, *163*
Maslow, A. H., 269–73, *273*
Mather, M. D., 293, *308*
May, M. A., 374, *406*
Meehl, P. E., 321, *353*
Menlove, F. L., 398–99, 402, *405*
Merrill, R. M., 152, *163*
Messick, S., 151, *163*
Metz, J. R., 397–98, *407*
Mezei, L., 374–75, *409*
Miller, G. A., *406*
Miller, N. E., 294–300, *307*, 350–52, *352–53*, 357–62, 370, *408*
Millon, T., *125*
Mischel, W., 6, 9, *11*, 38, *67*, 97, *125*, 241, *242*, 366, 370, 380–81, *405–6*
Montague, E. K., 153, *163*, 303, *307*
Mowrer, O. H., 112, *125*, 285, *307*, 370, *408*
Mowrer, W. M., 285, *307*
Munroe, R. L., 82, *94*
Murray, E. N., 350, *353*
Murray, H. A., 171, 214–32, *242*

N

Neale, J., 169, *212*
Nelson, K., 397, *407*
Newcomb, T., 3
Norman, W. T., 9, *12*
Nyman, D., 395, *408*

O

O'Brien, F., 347 n
Odom, R. D., 371–73, *407–8*
Ora, J. P., 370, 376–78, *407*
Osgood, C. E., 195 n, *212*
Overall, J. E., 140–41, *163*

P

Palermo, D. S., 301, *306*
Paskal, V., 388, 391 n
Passini, F. T., 9, *12*
Paul, G. L., 293, *307*
Pavlov, I. P., 98–99, 275–78, 282, 294, *307*, 312
Payne, D. E., 188, *212*
Pederson, A. M., 395, *408*
Pelser, H. E., 287–88, *306*
Piaget, J., 33
Pivik, T., 78, *93*
Power, M. E., 123, *125*

Q

Quarti, C., 285–87, *308*

R

Rachman, S., 293, *308*
Ramond, C. K., 153, *164*
Rank, O., 43, *67*
Rapaport, D., 55, *67*
Rayner, R., 279, 281, *308*
Razran, G. S., 282, *308*
Reese, E. P., 326, *353*
Reicken, H. W., *212*
Renaud, J., 285–87, *308*
Reynolds, G. S., 310 n, 322, 331, *353*
Risley, T. R., 333–35, *353*
Ritter, B., 403, *407–8*
Roberts, H. V., 18 n, *34*
Rogers, C., 3, 194, 243–68, *273,* 347
Rorer, L. G., 162, *164*
Rorschach, H., 88
Rosen, B. C., 337–38, *242*
Rosenbaum, M., 382, *405*
Rosenberg, M. J., 195 n, *211*
Rosenhan, D., *306,* 382, *407*
Rosenthal, T. L., 387–89, 391, *405, 407*
Rubin, H. B., 349–51, *353*
Rubin, R. D., *408*

S

Sanford, N., 3, *12*
Sarason, I. G., 394–95, *408*
Schachter, S., *212*
Schneider, D. M., *242*
Schroeder, W. W., 392, *406*
Sears, D. O., 205 n, *212*
Sechrest, L., 178, 187, *212*
Seeman, J., 263, *273*
Seeman, W., 145, *163*
Shannon, D. T., 293, *307*
Sheehan, M. R., 281, *308*
Sheldon, W. H., 100, 104–10, *125*
Shlien, J. M., *34*
Shurcliff, A., 66, *67*
Shuttleworth, F. K., 374, *406*
Siegman, A. W., 305–6
Singer, D. L., 64–65, *67*
Skinner, B. F., 3, 5–6, *12,* 30–31, 33, *34,* 310–19, 321, 324–25, 327, 330, 332 n, 333, *352–54,* 363, 370, *408*
Smith, D. H., 396, *408*
Smith, F., *406*
Smith, G. M., 18 n, *34*
Snyder, W. U., 264, *273*
Solomon, R. L., 333, *354*
Spearman, C., 127
Spence, J. T., 152–53, *164,* 303–5, *308.* *See also* Taylor, J. A.
Spence, K. W., 153, *164,* 300–305, *308*
Spiegler, M. D., 366, 399, *408*
Spielberger, C. D., *164, 308*
Sprott, W. J. H., *125*
Staats, A. W., 283–84, *308*
Staats, C. K., 283–84, *308*
Stachnik, T. J., 10, *12, 352*
Stainton, N. R., 10, *12*
Steiner, M. E., 89, *93*
Stephenson, W., 246, *273*
Stevens, S. S., *307*
Strachey, J., *67, 93*
Stricker, G., 28, *34*
Strickland, B. R., 159, *163*
Strupp, H. H., 44, 60, *67,* 293, *308*
Suci, G. J., 195 n, *212*
Sullivan, H. S., 4, 83
Swanson, E. M., 78, *93*

T

Tannenbaum, P. H., 195 n, *212,* 385–87, *409*
Tarde, G., 355–57, *409*
Taylor, J. A., 153, *164,* 300, *308.* *See also* Spence, J. T.
Test, M. A., 382–83, *405*
Thigpen, C. H., 29, *34*
Thomas, J., 324, *353*
Thoresen, C. E., 392, *406–7*
Thorndike, E. L., 309–10, 332, *354*
Tippett, J. S., 189, *213*
Tyler, J. D., 240–42, *242*

U

Ullmann, L. P., 347 n, *354*
Ulrich, R. E., 10–11, *12, 352*

V

Varenhorst, B. B., 392, *407*
Vernon, J. A., *353*
Verplanck, W. S., 335 n, 337, *354*

W

Wallis, W. A., 18 n, *34*
Walster, E., 197–98, 202, *212–13*
Walters, R. H., 357, 362–66, 370, 374–75, *405, 409*
Walton, D., 293
Watson, J. B., 275, 278–79, 281–82, 294, *308*

Wepman, J. M., *212–13*
Whalen, C., 397, *407*
White, G. M., 382, *408*
Williams, C. D., 328–29, *354*
Williams, R. J., 98–99, *125*
Wolman, B. B., 52, *67*, 81, *94*
Wolpe, J., 142–43, *164*, 288–92, 394, 401, *409*
Wolpert, E., 76, *93*
Woodworth, R. S., 142, *164*, 281, *308*

Z

Zax, M., 28, *34*
Zucker, R. A., 25, *34*

Subject Index

A

Achievement Motivation Training Program, 396
Achievement motive, measurement of, *see* Need for achievement; Thematic Apperception Test
Achieving Society, The (McClelland), 233
Acquisition
  definition of, A. Bandura's, 363
  A. Bandura and R. H. Walters' distinction on, 363–64
  in operant conditioning, 363–69
Acquisition phase, 321, 388
Actones, definition of, 215–16; *see also* Needs
Actualizing tendency, 244–45, 253; *see also* Self-actualization
Adjusting of aspiration levels, 230
Aggression, 63–65, 97–98, 194, 222, 260, 364–66; definition of, G. A. Kelly's, 190
Alpha rhythm, 74–75; *see also* Dreams and dreaming; Sleep
Anaclitic identification, 56; *see also* Defensive identification
Anal aggressive character, 45
Anal retentive character, 46
Anal stage, 45; *see also* Psychosexual development
Anxiety, 20–21, 57–58, 63, 66, 84–85, 135, 147, 152–53, 189–90, 192, 254–55, 258, 288–90, 293, 300–306, 394
  definitions of, G. A. Kelly's, 189; J. Wolpe's 288
  guilt, 58
  moral, 58
  neurotic, 58
  objective, 58
  primary, 57
Anxiety—*Cont.*
  See also Anxiety hierarchy; Castration anxiety; Phobias (fears); Systematic desensitization; Taylor Manifest Anxiety Scale
Anxiety hierarchy, 289–92; examples of, 291; *see also* Anxiety
Approval motive, 155–56, 158–59
Ascendance-submission, 117–18; *see also* Traits and types
Asthma, 287–88
Attitudes, and classical conditioning, 282–84; definition of, 282
Autonomic conditioning, therapeutic use of, 350–52; *see also* Operant conditioning; Vicarious emotional responses
Autonomic nervous system, 347–48, 351
Autonomic responses, 347–48

B

Backup reinforcers, 342; *see also* Reinforcement; Token economy
Balance, 195; *see also* Cognitive dissonance
Barron Independence-of-Judgment scale, 157–58; *see also* Methods of personality assessment
Behavior (Watson), 278
Behavior of Organisms, The (Skinner), 312
Behavioral prompts, 403
Behavioral rehearsal, definition of, 394
Behaviorism, 99, 278, 281, 310, 344
Birth trauma, 43
Body types
  asthenic, 101–2, 104
  athletic, 101–2, 104
  dysplastic, 101, 103–4
  ectomorphic, 105, 108–9

Body types—*Cont.*
endomorphic, 105, 108–9
mesomorphic, 105, 108–9
pyknic, 101, 103–4

C

Cardinal dispositions (traits), definition of, 116
Castration anxiety, 46–47, 87; *see also* Anxiety
Catharsis, definition of, 80
Cathexis, and countercathexis, 58
Central dispositions (traits), 119; definition of, 116
Character disorders, definition of, 82–83
Choice Corollary, G. A. Kelly's, 177–79
Classical conditioning, 276–94, 303, 333 n, 348, 355, 363, 387; aversive, 287
Client-centered therapy, 243, 261–68, 391
Cognitive dissonance, 165, 194–211
and decision-making, 196–203
definition of, 195
and information utility, 205–8
and predecision processes, 198–203
and psychoanalytic theory, 210
See also Social support
Cognitive overlap, 203–4
Commonality Corollary, G. A. Kelly's, 180–81
Common traits, 116–18; *see also* Traits and types
Compulsive behavior, 329–30
Condensation, 69; *see also* Dreams and dreaming
Conditioned reflex, 275–78
Conditioned reinforcers, 322; *see also* Reinforcement; Reinforcers
Conditioned response (CR), 276–77, 287–88, 302
Conditioned stimulus (CS), 276–77, 284–88, 302
Conditions of worth, 252–55, 259–60; *see also* Positive regard
Conflict, 43, 45, 48–51, 83, 198–201, 253, 347
definition of, 59
and cognitive dissonance, 199–201
Conformity, 157–59, 230–31; *see also* Imitation; Modeling
Conscience, 54
Consciousness, levels of, 51, 60, 82
conscious, 41, 51
preconscious, 41, 51
unconscious, 41, 51–52, 87
Constipation, treatment of, 286–87
Constitutional theory, R. J. Williams' position on, 98–99; W. H. Sheldon's position on, 104–10
Construction Corollary, G. A. Kelly's, 173–74
Constructive alternativism, 168–73
Constructs, properties of, 169–70; *see also* Personal constructs
Contact desensitization, 403–4
Continuous reinforcement (CRF), 315, 326–27, 339–40
Control, 15, 311, 350
Conversion reaction, definition of, 79; *see also* Hysteria
Copying, 347
Correlation coefficient, 21–22, 117; *see also* Rank-order correlation
Correlation matrix, 108–9, 127–29
Counseling and Psychotherapy: Newer Concepts in Practice (Rogers), 243
Counterbalancing, 284
Counterconditioning, 280; *see also* Systematic desensitization
Counterimitation, 357, 361 n
Countertransference, definition of, 83
Creativity, 20
Criterion keying, and construction of personality inventories, 143
CRF, *see* Continuous reinforcement
CR, *see* Conditioned response
CS, *see* Conditioned stimulus
Cue, 295–98, 357, 359–60, 362
Cumulative record, 314–16, 318–19, 337, 340–41
Cumulative recorder, 314–15
Curare, 350
Cyclothymia, 132

D

Deep muscle relaxation, 289–90; *see also* Systematic desensitization
Defense mechanisms, 83, 253–58; definition of, 60; *see also* Denial; Displacement; Perceptual distortion; Projection; Rationalization; Reaction formation; Regression; Repression; Sublimation; Undoing
Defensive identification, 46, 56; *see also* Anaclitic identification
Delay of gratification, 52, 59, 373, 380–81
Denial, as defense mechanism, 62–63, 255
Dependence, 44
Dependent variable, 16, 129, 238
Depression, 144, 351

Dichotomy Corollary, G. A. Kelly's, 175–76
Displacement, as defense mechanism, 62, 82
Discrimination, 277; *see also* Generalization
Discriminative stimulus, 331; definition of, 314
Dissonance, *see* Cognitive dissonance
Dissonance reduction
  information utility, 205
  techniques of, 195, 197–98, 203–9
  See also Cognitive dissonance; Cognitive overlap; Forced compliance; Selective exposure; Spreading the alternatives
Distorted displacements, 82
Dizygotic twins, 110
Drake's Social Introversion Scale, 152; *see also* Methods of personality assessment
Draw-a-person test, 88; *see also* Methods of personality assessment
Dreams and dreaming, 62, 68–79, 287–88
  definition of, 68
  interpretation of, 70–72
  principle of condensation, 69
  related to eye movements, 72–77
  stages of sleep, and eye movements, 75
  See also Nonrapid eye movements; Rapid eye movement periods
Dream deprivation, consequences of, 77–79
Dream interpretation, 70–72
Drive, 171, 295–306, 359–60, 362
  learned, 295–97
  primary, 295
Drive reduction, 281, 294–306, 355

E

Edwards Personal Preference Schedule, 150–51; *see also* Methods of personality assessment
Edwards Social Desirability scale, *see* Social desirability
EEG, *see* Electroencephalogram
Ego, 40, 52–54, 56–61, 120–21, 347, 380; *see also* Ego strength
"Ego cathexis," 58
Ego defense mechanisms, 60–63; *see also* Ego
Ego ideal, 54
Ego strength, 133–35; *see also* Ego
Elaborative choice, 179
Electra complex; *see* Oedipus complex
Electroencephalogram (EEG), 72–75, 351
Emergent pole, 175, 186; *see also* Personal constructs
Empathy, 260
Empirical keying, *see* Criterion keying
Enuresis, treatment of, 285–86
"Eight Stages of Man," E. H. Erikson's, 48–51
  autonomy *vs.* shame and doubt, 49–50
  basic trust *vs.* mistrust, 49
  ego integrity *vs.* despair, 51
  generativity *vs.* stagnation, 51
  identity *vs.* role diffusion, 50
  industry *vs.* inferiority, 50
  initiative *vs.* guilt, 50
  intimacy *vs.* isolation, 50
Erogenous zone, 43
Eros, 41 n
Erroneous impressions, demonstration of, 9–11
Ethical Standards Test, 226–27; *see also* Methods of personality assessment
Exhibitionism, treatment of, 293
Experience Corollary, G. A. Kelly's, 179, 188
Explorations in Personality (Murray *et al.*), 214, 223, 229
External proceedings, 220
External validity, 119, 142; definition of, 32
Extinction, 276, 322, 327–30, 333, 337, 340
  as a behavioral outcome, 322 n
  as an experimental operation, 322 n
Extinction phase, *see* Reversal phase
Extraversion, *see* Extroversion
Extrinsic orientation, religious, 124
Extroversion, 135, 145, 230; *see also* Introversion
Eyelid conditioning, 301–4

F

Factor analysis, 119, 125–41, 186
Factor loadings, 132
Fear Survey Schedule, 142–43; *see also* Methods of personality assessment
FI, *see* Fixed-interval schedule
Fixation, 44, 122
Fixed-interval schedule (FI), 325–28
Fixed-ratio schedule (FR), 325–27, 332, 340
Fixed-role therapy, 393
Four fundamentals of learning, N. E. Miller and J. Dollard's, 295–98, 359–62

Forced-choice inventory, 151
Forced compliance, 208–9
Fragmentation Corollary, G. A. Kelly's, 181 n
Free association, 80
"Freudian slips," 39
Frigidity, treatment of, 293
FR, *see* Fixed-ratio schedule
Frustration, 44
Fully functioning person, characteristics of, 268–73; *see also* Self-acutalization
Functional analysis of behavior, 312; *see also* Operant conditioning
Functional autonomy, 122–25; definition of, 122
Fundamental postulate, G. A. Kelly's, 173–82
Fundamental rule (of psychoanalysis), 80

G

Galvanic Skin Response (GSR), 226, 348, 388–89; *see also* Methods of personality assessment
Gambling, *see* Compulsive behavior
Generalization, 169, 277, 279 n, 280–81, 288, 396, 402
  physical, 374 n
  semantic, 374 n
Generalization gradient, 277
Generalized imitation, 397; *see also* Imitation
Genital stage, 48; *see also* Psychosexual development
GSR, *see* Galvanic Skin Response
Guilt, definition of, G. A. Kelly's, 190

H

Habit, 294–95
Helping and modeling, 381–85
"Heritability of Personality," 112
Heuristic realism, 97, 114
High School Personality Questionnaire (HSPQ), 113–14; *see also* Methods of personality assessment
Holistic view of personality, C. Rogers', 244
Homosexuality, treatment of, 109, 349, 349 n
Hostility, 191–94, 228; definition of, G. A. Kelly's, 191
HSPQ, *see* High School Personality Questionnaire
Humor, 63–66, 115, 272
Hypochondriasis, 136, 144
"Hypnocatharsis," 80
Hypnosis, H. A. Murray's research in, 226; and psychoanalytic therapy, 79–80
Hypomania, 145
Hysteria, 79, 145, 298–300, 350–51; *see also* Conversion reaction
Hysterical paralysis, 298, 350–51

I

Id, 40, 52–56, 58–60, 63, 347
Ideal self, 246; *see also* Self, C. Rogers' position on
Ideal sort, 247
Identification, 55–56, 122, 356, 386; *see also* Anaclitic identification; Defensive identification
Idiographic approach, 5, 118–20
  G. W. Allport's, 118–20
  H. A. Murray's, 226
  B. F. Skinner's, 310–12
Imitation, 122
  pervasive role of, 369–72
  types of, 357–58
  See also Copying; Matched-dependent behavior; Modeling; Observational learning
Implicit pole, 175, 186; *see also* Personal constructs
Inconsistency, *see* Cognitive dissonance
Incorporation, 44, 55
Independent variable, 15, 129, 238, 311–12, 320
Individuality Corollary, G. A. Kelly's, 174–75, 187–88
Individual traits, G. W. Allport's, 118
Inhibition, and modeling, 356
Innate reinforcers, *see* Primary reinforcers
Instincts, 41, 171
Instrumental conditioning, *see* Operant conditioning
Intelligence Quotient (IQ), 138, 285
Intermittent schedule, 325
Internal frame of reference, 244; demonstration of, 265
Internalization, 372–81; definition of, 55
Internal proceedings, 220
Interpretation of Dreams (Freud), 69
Intrapsychic conflict, 42, 59, 63, 80, 299
Intrapsychic factors, definition of, 36
Intrinsic orientation, religious, 124
Introjection, 55
Introversion, 135, 145; *see also* Extroversion
Item analysis, 155

L

Language, and imitation, 369–72
Latency period, 48; *see also* Psychosexual development
Latent needs, *see* Needs
Law of effect, E. L. Thorndike's, 309–10, 332
"Law of Parsimony," 7 n
Laws of Imitation, The (Tarde), 355
Letters from Jenny (Allport), 119
L-data, 129–30, 133–34; *see also Q*-data; *T*-data
Level of aspiration, 230
Libido, 40–45, 48, 56; *see also* Psychic energy

M

Manic-depressive psychosis, 100, 104, 132
Manifest anxiety (MA), 300–306; *see also* Anxiety; Taylor Manifest Anxiety Scale
Manifest needs, *see* Needs
Marlowe-Crowne Social Desirability scale, *see* Social desirability
MA scale, *see* Taylor Manifest Anxiety Scale
Matched-dependent behavior, 357–62
Maudsley Medical Questionnaire, 136; *see also* Methods of personality assessment
Methods of personality assessment
  direct and indirect, 37
  H. A. Murray's approach to, 221–27
  projective techniques, 87–93
  See also Barron Independence-of-Judgment scale; Drake's Social Introversion Scale; Draw-a-person test; Edwards Personal Preference Schedule; Ethical Standards Test; Fear Survey Schedule; Galvanic Skin Response; High School Personality Questionnaire; Maudsley Medical Questionnaire; Minnesota Multiphasic Personality Inventory; Picture Arrangement Test; Q-sort; Response acquiescence; Response deviation; Response sets; Role Construct Repertory Test; Rorschach Ink Blots; Scale of Temperament; Scatter diagram; Self-report personality inventories; Social desirability; Szondi test; Taylor Manifest Anxiety Scale; Thematic Apperception Test; Woodworth Personal Data Sheet
Methods of personality research
  case study, 27–33
  and control, 15–18
  correlational, 19–27, 127
  experimental, 13–19
  twin-study, 110–11
  See also Factor analysis; Dependent variable; Independent variable; Scatter diagram; Single-subject design
Minnesota Multiphasic Personality Inventory (MMPI), 113–14, 141, 143–48, 150–51, 300; *see also* Methods of personality assessment
Model, 356
Modeling, 232, 280, 356
  applied uses of, 391
  co-therapeutic, 394
  cues, definition of, 356
  live, 380–81
  multiple, 378–80, 399
  and reinforcement therapy, 397–98
  and role playing, 393–95
  symbolic, 356–57, 380–81, 395–96, 399
Models and similarity of, 384–85; *see also* Copying; Imitation; Matched-dependent behavior; Observational learning
Modulation Corollary, G. A. Kelly's, 179–80
Motives
  definition of, D. C. McClelland's, 233–34
  perseverative, 122–23
  transformation of, 122–23
  See also Achievement motivation; Approval motive; Functional autonomy; Thematic Apperception Test
Multivariate research, 129–34

N

n achievement, *see* Need for achievement
n approval, *see* Need for approval
Need for achievement, 159–62, 231–42, 397; measurement of, 231–33
Need for approval, 159–62
Needs, 148, 171, 214–42
  and actones, 215–16

Needs—*Cont.*
assessment of, 222–23
definition of, H. A. Murray's, 215
manifest, 222
latent, 222–23
primary (viscerogenic), 217
secondary (psychogenic), 217–19, 222, 232
Negative correlation, 22–23
Neoanalysts, *see* Neo-Freudians
Neo-Freudians, 39, 44, 48, 293
Neurosis, 57, 81, 190, 288, 299
Neuroticism, 135–39, 395
Nomothetic approach, 5, 118, 227
G. A. Kelly's, 175
H. A. Murray's, 227
Nondirective therapy, 261 n; *see also* Client-centered therapy
Nonimitation, 356, 361 n
Nonrapid eye movements (NREM), 76–79; *see also* Dreams and dreaming

O

"Object cathexis," 58
Observational learning, 356–57
Oedipus complex, 30, 46–48, 56, 82, 84, 87, 225; *see also* Oedipal conflicts
Oedipal conflicts, 46–47, 54; *see also* Oedipus complex
Oedipal desire, 87
Operant behavior, definition of, 313; recording of (demonstration), 316–19; *see also* Operant conditioning
Operant conditioning, 309–52, 313 n, 355, 363
functional analysis in, 312
reconditioning in, 322
reversal phase in, 312, 322
See also Classical conditioning; Extinction; Single-subject design
Oral eroticism, 44–45
Oral sadism, 45
Oral stage, 44–45; *see also* Psychosexual development
Organismic valuing process, 245, 253
Organization Corollary, G. A. Kelly's, 176–77

P

Paranoia, 145
Partial schedule, *see* Intermittent schedule
Pavlovian conditioning, *see* Classical conditioning
Penile erection, and operant conditioning, 348–49
Penis envy, 47; *see also* Oedipus complex
Perceptual distortion, 255–56
Perceptual defense, 256–57
Performance, 305; A. Bandura and R. H. Walters' distinction, 363–69
Personal constructs, 166–94
definition of, 167
focus of convenience, 169–70
and motivation, 170–73
permeability, 170, 180
properties of, 169–73
range of convenience, 169
Personal dispositions, *see* Individual traits
Personality and Psychotherapy (Dollard and Miller), 294
Personality, definitions of
G. W. Allport's, 3
U. Bronfenbrenner's, 4
R. B. Cattell's, 4
H. J. Eysenck's, 4, 135
J. P. Guilford's, 197
E. R. Hilgard's, 4
H. A. Murray's, 220
T. Newcomb's, 3
H. S. Sullivan's, 4
Personality profile, *see* Psychogram
Personality, types of
affectothymic, 132
cerebrotonic, 107–9
extroverted, 135
introverted, 135
neurotic, 135–37
sizothymic, 132
somatotonic, 107–9
viscerotonic, 107–9
See also Anal aggressive character; Anal retentive character
Personology, H. A. Murray's, 214–31
Phallic stage, 46; *see also* Psychosexual development
Phenomenological position, C. Rogers', 244
Phobias (fears), 84, 210, 403
in psychoanalytic therapy, 83–87
treatment of, 293
See also Anxiety
Physique and Character (Kretschmer), 100
Physique, primary components of, W. H. Sheldon's, 105–6
Pleasure principle, 42, 52

Picture Arrangement Test, 88; *see also* Methods of personality assessment
Positive correlation, 22–23
Positive regard, 252–53
Positive self-regard; *see* Positive regard
Predecision processes; *see* Cognitive dissonance
Press, 215, 218–21, 223, 231
 alpha, 219–20
 beta, 219–20
Primary reinforcers, 321–22; *see also* Reinforcement
Primary process, 52–53; and reflex action, 52
Primer of Operant Conditioning, A (Reynolds), 310 n
Principle of reinforcement, B. F. Skinner's, 321
Problem of Anxiety, The (Freud), 57
Proceedings, 220–21; *see also* Personology, H. A. Murray's
Projection, as defense mechanism, 61, 256
Projective techniques, *see* Methods of personality assessment
Propriate feelings, 121, 123
Proprium, 121, 123
Psychasthenia, 145
Psyche, 3
Psychic energy, 41–42, 55–56; *see also* Libido
Psychoanalysis, 38, 109, 391
Psychodiagnostik (Rorschach), 89
"Psychogenic traumas," 112
Psychogenic needs, *see* Needs, secondary
Psychogram, 145–46
Psychopathic deviate, 145
Psychosexual development, definition of, 43; *see also* Anal stage; "Eight Stages of Man"; Genital stage; Latency period; Oral stage; Phallic stage
Psychosis, definition of, 100
Psychosomatic symptoms, 350–51
Psychotherapy
 client-centered, 261–68
 example of, J. Dollard and N. E. Miller's, 298–99
 insight-oriented, 293–94
 psychoanalytic, 79–83
 See also Systematic desensitization; Token economy; Vicarious extinction of fears
Psychotherapy and Personality Change (Rogers and Dymond), 266
Psychotic, 258
Psychoticism, 135
Punishment, 332–35, 349, 363, 365,
Punishment—*Cont.*
 367; *see also* Classical conditioning, aversive; Reinforcement, negative

Q

Q-data, 129–30, 133–34; *see also* *L*-data; *T*-data
Q-sort, 246–51, 256, 263, 395; *see also* Methods of personality assessment
Q-technique, 246; *see also* Q-sort

R

r, *see* Correlation coefficient
Rank-order correlation (*rho*), 251; *see also* Correlation coefficient
Range Corollary, G. A. Kelly's, 181 n
Rapid eye movement periods (REMP), 75–76, 78–79; *see also* Dreams and dreaming
Rationalization, as defense mechanism, 62, 255–56
Reaction formation, as defense mechanism, 61, 256
Reality principle, 53
Reciprocal inhibition, 289; *see also* Counterconditioning; Systematic desensitization
Reflex action, 52
Reflexes, 313
Regression, as defense mechanism, 62
Regret, 197–98; *see also* Cognitive dissonance
Reinforcement, 276, 295–98, 319–30, 337, 342, 359–60, 392
 negative, 160–61
 positive, 160
 therapy, 397–98
 See also Continuous reinforcement; Fixed-interval schedule; Fixed-ratio schedule; Punishment; Variable-interval schedule; Variable-ratio schedule; Vicarious consequences; Vicarious reward
Reinforcer, definition of, 321; transsituational, 321; *see also* Reinforcement; Reinforcing stimulus
Reliability, internal, 118; test-retest, 117–18, 188
REMP, *see* Rapid eye movement periods
Repression, as defense mechanism, 60–61
Resistance, definition of, 82
Resistance to temptation, 373–75

Respondent behavior (conditioning), definition of, 313, 313 n, 330; *see also* Classical conditioning
Response, 295–98, 359–60, 362; *see also* Four fundamentals of learning
Response acquiescence, 147; *see also* Methods of personality assessment; Response sets; Response styles
Response consequences, *see* Reinforcement
Response deviation, 147; *see also* Methods of personality assessment; Response styles
Response hierarchy, 298, 301
Response sets, 147–48, 162; *see also* Methods of personality assessment
Response styles, 151–62
Reversal phase, 33, 312, 322, 342; *see also* Operant conditioning
Reward, 281, 362–63; *see also* Reinforcement
rho, see Rank-order correlation
Role confusion, 50
Role Construct Repertory Test (Rep test), 182–87, 189; demonstration of, 182; *see also* Methods of personality assessment
Role, definition of, G. A. Kelly's, 181
Rorschach Ink Blots, 88–93, 226, 257; *see also* Methods of personality assessment, projective techniques

S

Same behavior, 357–58
Scale of Temperament, W. H. Sheldon's, 107–8; *see also* Methods of personality assessment
Scatter diagram, 22–23; *see also* Methods of personality assessment
Schedules of reinforcement, 324–30
Schizophrenia, 83, 100, 104, 110–12, 132, 143, 397
  and body types, 404
  treatment of, in operant conditioning, 323–24
Scientific Study of Personality, The (Eysenck), 136
S^D, *see* Discriminative stimulus
Secondary dispositions (traits), definition of, 116
Secondary process, 53
Secondary reinforcers, 322; *see also* Reinforcement; Reinforcing stimulus
Selective exposure, 204–8; *see also* Cognitive dissonance
Self, development of, 245–46
Self—*Cont.*
  G. W. Allport's position on, *see* Proprium
  C. Rogers' position on, 245–48, 260–61
  J. B. Watson's position on, 278–79
Self-actualization, 243–73
Self-concept, 245–48, 254–55, 258–61, 347; *see also* Self
Self-control, 372–81; definition of, 373
Self-expression, 230
Self-imposed standards, 373, 375–80
Self-report personality inventories, 141–62; *see also* Methods of personality assessment
Self-reports, 37–38
Self-reward, 373, 375–80; *see also* Self-imposed standards
"Setting events," 331
Sex typing, 56
Sexual deviation, 348–49
Sexual response, and operant conditioning, 348–50
Shaping, 323, 336, 357, 370; *see also* Successive approximation
Significant difference, in statistical analysis, 18
Single-subject design, 33, 341; *see also* Operant conditioning
Skinner box, 325
Sleep, 75; *see also* Dreams and dreaming
Sleep spindles, 74
Social-behavioristic approach, 363
Sociality Corollary, G. A. Kelly's, 181–82
Social desirability, 147–62; *see also* Methods of personality assessment
Social Learning and Personality Development (Bandura and Walters), 363
Social learning, A. Bandura and R. H. Walters' approach, 363–69; J. Dollard and N. E. Miller's approach, 294–300
Social support, and cognitive dissonance, 209–11
Somatotyping, 106, 109
Source trait, definition of, 133
Spontaneous recovery, *see* Spontaneous remission
Spontaneous remission, 267–68, 346
Spreading the alternatives, and cognitive dissonance, 199–203
Stages of sleep, 75; *see also* Dreams and dreaming; Electroencephalogram
Statistical significance, 18, 140

Stimulus control, 324, 330–32; *see also* Discriminative stimulus
Stimulus-response (S-R) position, 298
Stress, 305
Structuralist school, 278
Structures of personality, relationships between, 40, 56; *see also* Ego; Id; Superego
Studying, treatment of, 321–22
Subconscious, *see* Consciousness, levels of
Sublimation, as defense mechanism, 60
Successive approximation, 323, 332; *see also* Shaping
Superego, 40, 52, 54, 56, 58–59, 63, 190, 253
Surface trait, definition of, 133
Symbolism
  and dreams, 68–72
  examples of, 70
  in psychoanalytic therapy, 70, 85–87
Symptom substitution, 285, 294, 347, 347 n; definition of, 299
Systematic desensitization, 288–94, 402
  compared with insight-oriented psychotherapy, 293–94
Szondi test, 88; *see also* Methods of personality assessment

T

"Talking cure," 80; *see also* Psychotherapy
TAT, *see* Thematic Apperception Text
Taylor Manifest Anxiety Scale (MA), 147, 152–53, 300–306; *see also* Methods of personality assessment
T-data, 129; *see also* *L*-data; *Q*-data
Temperament, primary components of, W. H. Sheldon's, 106–7
Thanatos, 41 n
Thematic Apperception Test (TAT), 87–88, 223–26, 231–32, 240–41, 257, 266; example of, 224; *see also* Methods of personality assessment, projective techniques
Theory of Cognitive Dissonance, A (Festinger), 165
Threat, 191, 253–58
Time out, from positive reinforcement, 334; *see also* Punishment
Token economy, 341–47
  job examples, 343–44
  reinforcers used, 345
Token Economy: A Motivational System for Therapy and Rehabilitation, The (Ayllon and Azrin), 342 n
Trace conditioning, 276 n
Traits, dimensions of, 115–16
Traits and types, definitions of, 97–98, 115; G. W. Allport's theory of, 114–25
Transference, definition of, 82–83
Twin-study, *see* Methods of personality research

U

UCR, *see* Unconditioned response
UCS, *see* Unconditioned stimulus
Unconditional positive regard, 252–53, 259–61, 263; *see also* Positive regard
Unconditional positive self-regard, 252, 259–60; *see also* Positive regard
Unconditioned response (UCR), 276–77, 285–88, 302
Unconditioned stimulus (UCS), 276–77, 284–88, 302–4
Unconditioning, *see* Counterconditioning
Undoing, as defense mechanism, 61–62
Unity-thema, 223; definition of, 221; *see also* Personology, H. A. Murray's
Unconscious, 63–66

V

Validity
  face, 142
  of factor analysis, 139
  content, 142
  external, 119
  internal, 118
  of a personal construct, 168
  scales of the Minnesota Multiphasic Personality Inventory, 144
Variable-interval schedule (VI), 326–29
Variable-ratio schedule (VR), 326–27, 329–30
Varieties of Temperament, The (Sheldon), 104
Verbal learning, 303–5
VI, *see* Variable-interval schedule
Vicarious consequences, and punishment, 364, 367, 369, 375; *see also* Reinforcement
Vicarious emotional responses, 385–91
Vicarious extinction of fears, and modeling, 398–404; *see also* Anxiety; Phobias (fears)
Vicarious punishment, 364, 367; *see also* Punishment

Vicarious reward, 383; *see also* Reinforcement; Vicarious consequences
Viscerogenic needs, 217–18; *see also* Needs
VR, *see* Variable-ratio schedule

W

WAIS, *see* Wechler Adult Intelligence Scale
Walden Two (Skinner), 310, 332 n
Wechler Adult Intelligence Scale (WAIS) 305–6; *see also* Intelligence Quotient
When Prophecy Fails (Festinger), 211
Wish fulfillment, 53
Woodworth Personal Data Sheet, 142; *see also* Methods of personality assessment

370